BIOGRAPHICAL DICTIONARY OF NEO-MARXISM

BIOGRAPHICAL DICTIONARY OF NEO-MARXISM

Edited by

ROBERT A. GORMAN

Greenwood Press
Westport, Connecticut

Library of Congress Cataloging in Publication Data

Main entry under title:

Biographical dictionary of neo-Marxism.

  Bibliography: p.
  Includes index.
  1. Communism—Biography—Dictionaries.   2. Socialism
—Biography—Dictionaries.   3. Communism—Dictionaries.
4. Socialism—Dictionaries.   I. Gorman, Robert A.
HX23.B57   1985   335.43'092'2 [B]   84-27968
ISBN 0-313-23513-9 (lib. bdg.)

Library of Congress Catalog Card Number: 84-27968
ISBN: 0-313-23513-9

First published in 1985

Greenwood Press
A division of Congressional Information Service, Inc.
88 Post Road West
Westport, Connecticut 06881

Printed in the United States of America

10 9 8 7 6 5 4 3 2 1

For my parents,
whose love, guidance, and support light the way

Contents

Preface

The list of names included in this volume emerged from a complicated and lengthy process involving Marxist scholars from every region of the world. The problem is self-evident: depending on where the line is drawn the number of entrants could easily double or triple. As it is, the final list from each nation or region is a product of the collective wisdom of at least three well-known, usually indigenous experts and does, I think, comprise a fair and representative sampling of each area's significant neo-Marxian theory and practice. The essays were then written by scholars with an intimate interest in and knowledge of a particular entrant. Unanticipated difficulties have nonetheless cropped up, further complicating the selection and writing processes. Several distinguished radicals—most, but not all, East Europeans—have for personal and political reasons asked me to omit their names. Moreover, some entrants have asked me to omit relevant biographical information. While each case was dealt with individually, in almost every instance I have acceded to the request. The notation "n.a." indicates that relevant information is either unavailable or is being purposefully withheld.

Many important Marxists who are omitted from this book can be found in the *Biographical Dictionary of Marxism* (also published by Greenwood Press), which surveys Marxian thinkers who qualify as materialists, whereas this volume deals with nonmaterialist Marxists. The terms *orthodox* and *nonorthodox* might be pertinent were it not that many Third World Marxists—who are included in the *Biographical Dictionary of Marxism*—consider themselves "unorthodox" with regard to revolutionary tactics and strategies even though unquestioningly accepting the "orthodox" science of historical materialism. In any case, relevant terms are defined and analyzed in the introductions of each book. Where a materialist's impact on neo-Marxism is noteworthy I have listed his or her name herein with the notation, "See the *Biographical Dictionary of Marxism*." An asterisk in the text indicates that a separate entry is listed in this book for the preceding name; a dagger, that an entry can be found in the *Biographical Dictionary of Marxism*.

In addition to the over 205 biographical entries, ten group, movement, or journal entries are listed as well: *Arguments*, Austro-Marxism, empiriocriticism, legal Marxism, liberation theology, the Prague Spring, *Praxis*, Situationist International, *Socialisme ou Barbarie*, and structural Marxism. (The Frankfurt School is examined in the Introduction.) Although their most important representatives are usually allotted separate entries, these ten headings have been judged as crucial to understanding the evolution of neo-Marxism in their respective nations or in the West generally.

Each essay is followed by a two-part bibliography consisting of significant primary works (paragraph A) and useful secondary material (paragraph B). It is intended as a friendly guide to further relevant reading, not as a complete listing of either primary or secondary sources. There are, happily, many essays published herein that are the first systematic summaries and analyses of their subjects now available. In these cases, of course, paragraph B has been omitted. Where politics rather than theory has distinguished an entrant, paragraph A became superfluous. Wherever possible, English translations of original works are listed.

There are several potentially useful ways to use this biographical dictionary. It is, of course, designed primarily as an accessible tool for researching individual neo-Marxist theorists. Organized alphabetically, the essays on major twentieth-century nonmaterialist radicals—with bibliographies—are quickly and easily located. The index, in which key terms are matched with their appropriate author(s), permits readers to track down the source and meaning of technical words and phrases that have turned many radical journals into lexical nightmares. The list of Entrants by Nationality (Appendix I) encourages area specialists to relate radical theorizing to the diversity of national and regional cultures, facilitating cross-cultural comparison and analysis. Finally, the Introduction highlights Marx's own contributions to the subsequent proliferation of Marxian theories by emphasizing the potentially incompatible theoretical premises he embraced. Readers can thus easily link both neo-Marxist schools and specific neo-Marxists back to their source in Marx, evaluate their faithfulness, and speculate on the subtle distinctions between useful innovation and apostasy.

I want to applaud enthusiastically each and every contributor for the consistently high quality of their work, for their support and, when it was necessary, sympathy, and their willingness to spend valuable time and energy on a collective project they believed in. Greenwood Press's Cynthia Harris remained helpful, informative, and efficacious during the entire duration of this project, and I thank her. I ruefully admit that the pressures and frustrations of working constantly for almost three years with over one hundred busy scholars from six continents, as well as with numerous translators, typists, and aides, have occasionally overwhelmed my ability to cope gracefully. Those closest to me have probably suffered most. Yet, remarkably, their understanding and patience never dimmed. To Elaine, Jesse, and Colin I again pledge my love and appreciation, and promise to try harder next time.

BIOGRAPHICAL
DICTIONARY
OF
NEO-MARXISM

Introduction: The Mosaic of Marxism

Marxism today is a mosaic of dissimilar, often conflicting theories decorating a shared evaluation of past and present and a hopeful reading of the future. This is not as surprising as it might at first appear to be. Every enduring philosophy bends and twists in history in response to changing conditions. Living philosophies will adapt, or die. Marxism, however, is exceedingly vulnerable to the demands of a philosophically diverse group of believers who have emerged in cultures, and are responding to social conditions, that are significantly different from those found in nineteenth-century Europe. It is, in brief, a system of philosophy and a praxis created by an individual who perceived systematic philosophy to be, at best, trivial, and possibly a hindrance to progressive action.

Marx maintained this hostile attitude toward philosophy because he felt that life's fundamental questions were already answered.[1] Moreover, the goals of nineteenth-century European bourgeois philosophy were cynical and self-serving. Capitalism generates the urge for business success, which Marx argued was necessarily based on exploiting and dehumanizing workers. Bourgeois philosophy flaunted abstractions in order to mystify and placate individuals whose prime need was merely to alter their ways of living together. It actually buttressed elite hegemony, and its rhetorical commitment to truth was as hollow as the empty ideas it constantly recycled. Science, for Marx, must pierce this rhetoric with concrete, verifiable hypotheses, even if these "little . . . conform to the interested prejudices of the ruling classes."[2] As a scientist, Marx therefore wanted to "settle accounts with our former philosophical conscience."[3] This meant he would work hard for revolution and socialist equality and research those economic, social, and political issues which could be concretely measured and which could facilitate society's transformation. "The philosophers have only interpreted the world, in various ways; the point is to change it."[4]

By rejecting philosophy, however, Marx neglected important questions relevant to both his radicalism and the validity of his social science. What, for example, is the mind's relationship to matter? Is it passively determined, or does it actively create its material environment? Questions like these, with which his followers have endlessly struggled, Marx considered "purely scholastic": a consequence of ideological confusion. They interest only "the philosophical mind, puzzling over the origin and nature of its supposed detachment from real life."[5] Marx's own nonphilosophical mind was concerned with more concrete issues. People, he felt, must satisfy basic needs, and how they do so shapes their relationships to nature and society. In a world filled only with their practical activities they are not concerned with abstract logical dilemmas. Valid knowledge facilitates human understanding, which generates more efficient need-satisfying activities. It is, for most of us, unrelated to transcendent truths, nor does its "epistemological" worth concern us. A thought is incorrect if it confirms and perpetuates human servility, hindering satisfaction of real needs. In any case, however, thoughts—true or false—are internally connected to our surroundings. Truth and falsity are thus appended to social systems. Societies that oppress humanity, that hinder the satisfaction of real needs, generate false ideas (which Marx called philosophy); those liberating humanity yield true ideas (i.e. science).

An important issue now begs to be clarified. Marx forcefully and accurately perceived the link connecting capitalism and bourgeois philosophy. As a fervent believer in the desirability and necessity of socialist justice, Marx quickly, and logically, rejected bourgeois theorizing and advocated revolutionary action. But Marx never proffered the oppressed a theoretical justification for their political actions. It appears that the mature Marx expected workers to respond automatically, nonreflectively, to certain material conditions in a revolutionary manner. This presumption is justified only if we define human actors either as nonreflective homunculi naively reacting to external social stimuli that predictably evolve in history, or as helpless beings unthinkingly realizing a human essence. Yet these harsh interpretations of men and women being manipulated by uncontrollable forces are what Marx found to be the essence of capitalism—in response to which he advocated revolution as a release of liberating human energy. The apparent confusion results from the lack of a systematic social theory that makes cognitive sense, prompts reflective citizens to rebel, and justifies egalitarian institutions. While rejecting bourgeois theory makes perfect sense given Marx's own anticapitalist bias, rejecting theory itself is tantamount to discarding the proverbial baby with the bath water. In brief, by denying both the validity of contemporary theorizing and the need to provide a philosophical anchor for his revolutionary critique, Marx did not escape the need to justify his own denial philosophically. Marx's theoretical ambiguity caused his followers, beginning with Engels, to compose their own philosophical answers to supplement Marx's critique. Although Marx ignored important philosophical issues, henceforth Marxist social theory would focus on little else.

In order to compete effectively with bourgeois alternatives, neo-Marxists have formulated coherent philosophies consistent with Marx's own writings. This project, however, is further complicated by the fact that, while overtly rejecting philosophy altogether, Marx also provided several inchoate philosophical perspectives. Taken together, these are mutually exclusive and contradictory. But Marx avoided such a logical conclusion by denigrating philosophy and avoiding systematic theorizing. Hence neo-Marxists are forced to select from Marx one theoretical thread and weave a convincing revolutionary social theory. Then they use this woven blanket to cover from view Marx's own inconsistencies, which are scattered throughout his copious writings, and invoke the elixir known as dialectics to turn blatantly contradictory evidence into positive proof. In this manner dissimilar versions of Marxism are rationalized by the same book or phenomenon, and everyone believes his or her own theory accurately depicts the master's. While dialectics *is* an invaluable analytical method, it too can be philosophically justified in different ways and can generate antithetical political strategies. What dialectics means, in other words, depends on foundational meta-dialectical principles. A wide variety of these are found in Marx's work, despite Marx's conscious effort to spurn such decadent philosophizing. Each neo-Marxist school adopts one such perspective and uses it to justify its own dialectical social theory. Ironically, Marx's decision to reject philosophy has generated a lively theoretical debate among modern Marxists and a profusion of Marxist schools offering alternative visions of valid social inquiry and meaningful revolutionary action.

Although analytical categories can be used to distort texts, confuse readers, and produce self-serving apologias, they are also necessary for an accurate understanding of the influence of Marx's large and multifaceted corpus of writings. In this case, the categories we now adopt seem pertinent for two reasons. First, they are useful and accurate tools for measuring the profusion of twentieth-century Marxist theories. Each theorist listed in this volume rather snugly fits into one of the proffered categories. Those who do not are likely not first-rate theorists and have been included primarily because their practical contributions have tangibly influenced the subsequent evolution of Marxist theory. Second, the categories encompass the mélange of disparate and contradictory ideas found in Marx's work. The underlying presupposition here is that meaningful social theory is a unity of theory and praxis, that is, it is composed of theoretical principles (ontology, epistemology, methodology, ethics), which generate a guide to action (politics). Marx, we have seen, rejected systematic theorizing and hence opened the back door to philosophy in the form of mutually irreconcilable principles justifying economic, historical, or political assertions. The categories now used to explain neo-Marxism are thus the unintended residue of Marx's own antitheoretical bias. They depict simultaneously Marx's ambiguous legacy and the vitality of current Marxian theorizing.

When reading Marx and examining the evolution of Marxism, one detects at least six distinct philosophical perspectives, each justifying potentially unique answers to the theoretical and practical questions good social theory asks. Contemporary Marxism encompasses a range of philosophies that includes materialism, idealism, empiricism, and experientialism, as well as those either rejecting the notion of objectivity altogether or inextricably attaching it to history. Each Marxian school adopts one philosophy, traces it in Marx, and plumbs its theoretical and practical consequences. Modern Marxism, therefore, hermeneutically rectifies Marx's inconsistencies without muting his critique of capitalism or his revolutionary politics. It includes not only orthodox Marxism-Leninism but also various nonmaterialist theories as well.

This volume examines only nonmaterialist versions of Marxism and labels these "neo-Marxist." *The Biographical Dictionary of Marxism*, a companion book also published by Greenwood Press, surveys the entire spectrum of Marxian materialism: beginning with a materialist reading of Marx, it encompasses seminal materialists from Engels to orthodox Marxist-Leninists to the many Third World radicals who devise new revolutionary strategies for non-Western material conditions.

The remainder of this Introduction will illustrate that neo-Marxism is a heterogeneous movement hiding chasms as wide as those separating schools of non-Marxist philosophy. While Marxists are obviously aware of these internal fissures (witness their vicious denunciations of former comrades), non-Marxist Westerners usually are not. All too often they naively box and dispose of everyone and everything labeled "Marxist," ignoring what could be a fruitful convergence of ideas. Many neo-Marxists are philosophically closer to traditional Western values than to Soviet-style Marxism. One desired consequence of this project will be to legitimate Marxian radicalism as a viable alternative to liberalism for nonpropertied Westerners.

IDEALISM

Materialism sees nature and society shaped by the impersonal patterns of matter in motion. By establishing first the material foundation of human needs and then the economic prerequisites of human fulfillment, it effectively explodes the myth that capitalism actually protects individual freedom. Westerners are, nevertheless, wary of it. Even oppressed individualists bridle at a theory that defines subjectivity and freedom passively, as molded by uncontrollable matter. Materialist Marxism thus had the unintended consequence of propelling many critical thinkers back into liberalism, where they reform an imperfect system rather than embrace a potential Stalin. The materialist obliteration of subjectivity has, ironically, minimized its appeal in the capitalist West while enhancing its fate in economically undeveloped lands lacking a bourgeois tradition. Many Western Marxists have responded by reformulating Marxism. If truth can be defined as an abstract quality—not concrete matter—experienced by thoughtful subjects in propitious material conditions, then Marxism may be a social theory Westerners can live with, asserting the primacy of the dialectic's subjective moment. Idealist Marxism reintegrates active subjects into historical progress.

Idealism finds valid knowledge in abstract, nonmaterial objectivity. Truth exists as an a priori reality that, although subjectively cognized, is not a product of subjectivity. Idealism has taken various forms in history depending on criteria of valid inquiry, ranging from rationalism to spiritualism and instinctualism.

Idealist Marxism normally takes two forms. The first, Hegelian idealist Marxism, bears the imprint of Hegel's metaphysical philosophy of history. Hegel distrusted sense perceptions, which he felt revealed only the appearance of things, not their truth. The mind's logical concepts epistemologically precede empirical experience. However, each reflective subject is a messenger for a transpersonal, universal force—what Hegel calls "Spirit" or "Mind"—that exists independent of empirical subjectivity as the sum of absolute truth. This objective nonmaterial "subject" governs the world's development, including human history. Hegel's idealism thus posits an a priori truth that will be cognitively perceived as Spirit dynamically materializes in cultural values and institutions. Moreover, Spirit's passage through history is energized by a precognitive logic that governs all movement. Each particular thing in the universe, as well as the universal totality that generates all concrete particulars, negates itself and then synthesizes the contradiction in new, more progressive unities, from which the process will reoccur. The entire process, for Hegel, constitutes Reason. History's goal is the unification of subject and object, that is, humanity's reflective cognition of Spirit. This will occur when Spirit materializes in concrete values and institutions. At this stage of history, which Hegel felt would coincide with the rise of nation-states, culture will unify subjective freedom and objective necessity. Humanity, in other words, will consciously depict Spirit in its culture and state. Good citizens will crystallize necessity and truth, reflectively willing freedom by obeying reasonable law.

Marx's debt to both Hegel and the so-called left Hegelians[6] is enormous. Hegelian idealist Marxists see it as crucial to a proper understanding of Marx's entire written corpus. Marx's early articles in *Rheinische Zeitung* (1842–43) as well as his doctoral dissertation (1841) are blatantly Hegelian in both substance and style. Even at this early stage, Hegelian Marxists argue, Marx's strategy is clear: he will modify Hegel to the extent of reestablishing the link between Spirit and the concrete world, which Hegel often ignored. Reason, in other words, congeals in human activities. In the *1844 Manuscripts* Marx defined praxis as the primary receptacle for Reason, Spirit's outlet in the everyday world. Dissatisfied with Hegel's overly abstract theory, Marx used praxis to pull Spirit into individual subjects, obliterating Hegel's separation of thought and action, knowledge of history and history itself. Without rejecting idealism, argue Hegelian Marxists, Marx transformed Hegel's Spirit into a quality consciously perceived and expressed by people living in real economic and social conditions. Marx argued that these facts of everyday life must be rationalized to coincide with the liberated consciousness of enlightened human agents. Praxis is therefore rational in reflecting both the empirical life-world and universal truth.

The project of concretizing Hegelianism is depicted in Marx's *Introduction to a Critique of Hegel's Philosophy of Right* (1843) and *On the Jewish Question* (1843). Human emancipation, for Marx, is conditioned by economic, social, and political realities and can thrive only when the latter are Reasonable. Praxis—i.e. rational, progressive, free individual activity—will emerge only in rationalized social conditions. In this coming unity of subjectivity and objectivity our true or essential natures, our "species-essence," will be realized. Marx did not yet, in 1843, advocate explicitly the abolition of private property, believing instead that free, reflective citizens living in reasonable institutions would spontaneously establish equitable living arrangements.

In the *1844 Manuscripts* Marx redefined Hegel's theory of labor from an abstract cognitive activity to a process linking an active, need-satisfying subject to the real world. Alienation occurs when actual social conditions inhibit praxis, blocking our potentially creative and fulfilling interaction with nature. Alienation, in other words, occurs in historical and social settings that hinder Reasonable actions, eliminating labor as praxis. It is a social condition generated by real people and terminated by rational activity. For both Hegel and Marx, therefore, humanity dialectically perfects itself in history through labor, culminating in the achievement of species-essence,[7] which is a particular manifestation of history's universal Idea. Although cognized only in rational conditions, species-essence transcends and defines these conditions. It is an a priori category that materializes and is subjectively realized when history's rational evolution is completed. Marx then argued that the misery of capitalist life triggers reflective, rational thought and actions among its most exploited economic group. Workers therefore represent the interests of both social justice and universal truth. Human essence materializes in authentic proletarian self-consciousness.

Marx's scholarly work, from this Hegelian perspective, focuses on the process by which capitalism engenders authentic proletarian self-consciousness. Until 1846 Marx emphasized capitalism's alienating qualities, its submersion of human authenticity in commodity fetishism and the injustices of the market. After 1846 he stressed the empirical relationships by which workers are first exploited and then radicalized. While Marx was progressively more atuned to the concrete material factors of capitalist oppression, he also suggested that both alienation and exploitation are more than their material components. The negation of human potential under capitalism is conceptually measured against an idealized species-being. Hegelian Marxists point out that Marx believed alienation preceded capitalism and helped cause it, and humanity's essential state is open to nature and society.[8] The former implies that self-perceptions mature in history and cause new social and economic forms. The latter interprets capitalism as blocking self-realization and fulfillment. Together, they express the Hegelian notion of Reason historically realizing itself in reflective self-consciousness. Marx's post-1846 preoccupation with concrete particulars represents a change in emphasis, not substance.[9] Materialists have naively ignored the subtlety of Marx's Hegelian dialectic, focusing entirely on the one-dimensional, nonspeculative terminology from the later work. Predictably, Hegelians contend, materialist Marxism eventually lost its reflective revolutionary spark, descending first into Kautskyite reformism and then Stalinist totalitarianism.

Hegelian Marxists believe that in appropriate, historically conditioned material conditions—which Marx described in detail after 1846—humanity will reflectively perceive the interpenetration of subject and object, particular and universal, and then rebel against capitalism's institutionalized inhumanity. History is therefore evolving toward human freedom, realized in the revolutionary praxis of reasonable actors. Its current tool is the working class, for their tragic suffering is the impetus to correct thinking and apt revolutionary action. Freedom and necessity coalesce in an essential truth cognitively experienced by reasonable workers at a mature stage of capitalist development.

Hegelian idealist Marxism flourished in the 1920s among European Marxists rejecting what they perceived as the dogmatic, antihuman determinism of the Second International. Unlike the Second International, it proffered a revolutionary alternative that resurrected the subjective component of Marx's dialectic. Hegelians were also concerned about Marxism's dwindling appeal among European workers. By emphasizing human spirit and subjective cognition, Hegelians aspired to winning workers' allegiance and strengthening the revolutionary movement throughout industrialized Europe. Marxism, they argued, could no longer simultaneously emancipate and dehumanize its potential constituency.

The Hegelian version of Marxism, amply represented in this volume, gestates with Labriola, Luxemburg, Pannekoek, Gorter, Brzozowski, Jaurès, and several others. It finally emerges full-blossomed in the work of Lukács, Korsch, Gramsci, and later Kojève, Hyppolite, Marcuse, and Kolakowski. Readers will also note the influence of Hegelianism on certain feminist Marxists and many less popular theorists who reemphasize the subject's role in history's objective dialectic.

Now we turn to the second form of idealist Marxism: non-Hegelian or classical idealist Marxism. Hegelians view humanity historically and define freedom as a merging of subjectivity and universality that occurs only at a certain stage of society's material development. Human nature is inconceivable apart from the global movement of history. Classical idealists, on the other hand, define truth as an objective, ahistorical quality that transcends temporality. Human nature is static, never changing even as humanity lives through various historical stages of ignorance regarding its real dimensions. There is a clear sense in which humanity's essential, objective nature conditions human evolution in history. Classical idealists therefore evaluate the truth, falsity, and desirability of cultures on their approximating a timeless ideal. This differs somewhat from the Hegelian position, which recognizes the "truth" of all cultures and putative views of human nature as partial manifestations of an increasingly self-evident universal process. Both forms of idealism, Hegelian and classical, define truth as an a priori abstraction subjectively realized in thought, conditioned by matter but not its epiphenomenon. The post–World War II evolution of idealist Marxism exhibits both tendencies, but moves steadily in a non-Hegelian direction.

Hegelian and materialist Marxisms define bourgeois ideas as transitory developmental stages in a global movement leading to socialism. Dehistoricized idealist Marxism, on the other hand, can accommodate the entire range of bourgeois philosophies. Non-Hegelian idealists can "radicalize" a bourgeois view of human nature by demonstrating first its resemblance to Marx's early ideas concerning species-essence, and then capitalism's negative impact on its realization. The ensuing possibilities for Marxist theory are vast and are represented in this volume by numerous exponents of radicalized humanism, structuralism, Freudianism, theology (Christianity, Judaism, Islam, Hinduism, Buddhism, etc.), even mysticism. The direct link to ideas popular among middle-class intellectuals assures this kind of idealist Marxism a potentially broad-based constituency of knowledgeable, sympathetic activists. Not surprisingly, many non-Hegelian idealist Marxists become cultlike symbols for legions of affluent but alienated young people. Commercial publishers quickly acknowledge the silver lining in these brewing clouds of protest.

EMPIRICISM

A priori Marxists—materialist and idealist—do not ignore empirical data but instead situate it within a greater reality whose meaning is more than a mere sum of verifiable parts. They are, therefore, backed into an awkward position in this age of advanced technology. The most distinctive feature of modern civilization, its extraordinary productive and technological achievements, springs from a scientific method based on the priority of specific empirical facts. The popular Marxist argument that proletarian science is superior to empirical science in terms of satisfying workers' needs comes dangerously close to rejecting the spirit of empirical inquiry and with it dreams of additional miraculous accomplishments in industrial, medical, and space technology. Since these will surely improve workers' lives, nonempirical Marxists are in effect asking workers to sacrifice practical interests to realize a workers' utopia. Consequently, motivated by a desire to improve proletarian living conditions as well as meet international political and economic commitments, orthodox Marxist states today avidly pursue a program of empirical scientific research and development. They thus subsidize two distinct kinds of science: bourgeois empiricism, which, although reified and antihuman, is invaluable for survival; and dialectical materialism, with its universal concepts that define empirical particulars. The former harnesses measurable physical laws governing organic matter; the latter protects socialism and ensures history's inherent potential for proletarian rebellion.

In response, Marxism has generated a movement aiming to synthesize dialectical materialism and empirical science and arguing that Marx himself was an empirical social scientist whose dialectical hypotheses were based squarely on concrete, measurable evidence. The scientific laws of historical materialism, from this view, are manifest in actual empirical conditions. Since empiricism focuses solely on experienced reality it is potentially exact and demystifying, exploding bourgeois myths and establishing scientifically the necessity of proletarian rebellion and socialist equality.

Empirical science claims that all wordly things are conditioned in their existence or occurrence by causal factors within a grand system of nature. These causal factors constitute a net of determining relationships that provide a basis for accurate pre- and postdiction. Scientific method consists of rules generating systematic observation, description, and measurement based on universally acknowledged, impersonal criteria of verification. Empirical scientists generalize from collected data and postulate theories explaining the real world as a determined product of repeating patterns of events. From one general theory is deduced the behavior of a whole species of identical objects. Human perception, for example, is conditioned by received and interpreted external stimuli that are verifiable. Empirically valid generalizations regarding human attitudes and behavior are deductively applicable to all identically situated human beings. Empirical or behavioral social science, therefore, explains reflective behavior by including as research variables subjective factors—feelings, moods, desires, etc.—operationalized and verified according to accepted principles of empirical method.

The philosophical source of empirical science lies in bourgeois preconceptions regarding the natural and social worlds, particularly Descartes's dichotomy of mind and matter: his belief that human reality is qualitatively different from nonreflective matter. The logical corollary, which became the linchpin of bourgeois philosophy, is that the universe consists of "subjective" (human) and "objective" (material) components. Only the latter, factual reality, is explained by empirical scientific method. Science is limited to this objective, factual world; it explains what "is," not what "ought" to be.

These seminal thoughts—man as an autonomous, nonsocial animal, the separation of fact and value, and the nonpolitical quality of science—philosophically justify empirical social science but are themselves not empirically verifiable. The self-proclaimed "neutrality" and "impartiality" of empirical scientists is thus built on this naively accepted commitment to nonverifiable bourgeois values, which, moreover, embody the material interests of entrepreneurs and rationalize bourgeois institutions. Empirical science, therefore, is the methodological reflection of liberal-democratic-capitalist culture. Its unquestioned bourgeois assumptions determine what questions scientists will ask and what variables they will find relevant. Their supposedly value-free data unknowingly express foundational values that divide social reality into isolated, empirically verifiable phenomena.

Marxism replaces these bourgeois principles with reflective, critical assertions regarding the social character of individuality, the indissoluble unity of fact and value, and the desirability of proletarian revolution. Empirical Marxism, however, in contrast to a priori and experiential Marxist alternatives, bases these critical normative assertions solely on empirical evidence and undertakes social inquiry guided by universally acknowledged principles of empirical scientific verification. Empiricism, in other words, can negate the class interests it now represents if the unquestioned myths regarding individuality, science, and politics are shattered by empirical evidence. The method of bourgeois empirical science must, in brief, demythologize capitalism's unspoken rules, interests, and values. Marx's critical theories and hypotheses are valid only to the extent they explain the actual empirical world and only to the degree that they are verified by modern empirical methods. Empiricism, then, is not necessarily a tool of bourgeois interests, although it is today and has been historically.

Materialism, too, concerns itself with concrete empirical phenomena. But materialism is also valid prior to empirical verification. Each empirical "fact" artificially abstracts a small quantity of matter from a social and natural context that is perceived as complex and irreducible. For materialists, matter evolves dialectically. What we sensually experience as isolated elements are actually defined by the entire material totality. Hence the interpenetration of all aspects of this reality invalidates a method that seeks only cause–effect relationships among a limited number of artificially extracted variables. Materialists deny the validity of an empirical datum that is uncritically cut from its total surroundings. They seek, then, empirical illustrations of an a priori world view, not empirical verification. They interpret the universal in the particular, theoretically combining facts to comprehend a priori social and natural laws. Although all matter must be sensually perceived, it is not accurately explained by a method that ignores underlying, pre-empirical truth.[10]

Materialists argue that empirical science, whose logic occludes the dialectical totality, is doomed like capitalism to annihilation. Just as socialism will succeed capitalism, and workers capitalists, the real science of dialectical materialism will methodologically surpass empiricism. It is this "real" (that is, a priori) quality of dialectical materialism that empirical Marxism denies. Marx's theories of matter, history, and revolution emerge from his extensive empirical research and are valid only when explaining a constantly increasing corpus of empirical data. A Marxism that is true "in itself," prior to empirical evidence, is useless to serious social scientists and dangerous to the unenlightened.

Marx devoted several early writings to criticizing Hegel's abstractionism, what Marx called his double inversion of concrete being and abstract thought.[11] *On the Jewish Question* extends the anti-abstractionist critique to religion, stressing the practical empirical forms and consequences of religious expression. Even the *1844 Manuscripts* tries to demystify bourgeois culture, interpreting alienation as an empirically based and verified process of dehumanization. *The German Ideology* substitutes "real knowledge" and "positive science" for bourgeois idealism's "empty phrases about consciousness." Marx's early thoughts regarding historical materialism in *The German Ideology* and *The Poverty of Philosophy* are neither "arbitrary" nor "dogmatic," but, instead, based on real evidence that is verified "in a purely empirical way."[12]

After 1847, Marx's project of explaining and transforming the real world generated historical and economic studies that are fiercely loyal to empirical reality. These include *The Class Struggles in France* (1850), *The Eighteenth Brumaire of Louis Bonaparte* (1852), a series of articles published in the *New York Daily Tribune* and the *New American Encyclopedia* (1853–59), *Wage-Labour and Capital* (1849), *Grundrisse* (1857), *Capital* (1867), and *Theories of Surplus Value* (1862–63). The first three works describe and analyze events primarily in nineteenth-century France and proffer apt strategies for revolutionary action. *Wage-Labour and Capital* demonstrates "empirically, on the already existing historical data which were emerging everyday anew,"[13] the economic stages of capitalist development, beginning with the emergence of exchange value and culminating in the lowering of wages and the worsening of living and working conditions. *Grundrisse* analyzes capitalism in terms of two interrelated phenomena: "money" and "capital." The former signified not merely paper or metal but an entire system of relationships, including the social, political, legal, psychological, and artistic. Marx described different functions of money and exposed the contradictions between and within them. He placed the entire scope of these social relations in historical perspective, describing their empirical origins and intimating their final destination. The latter, capital, is also a system of social relations but one based on incessant accumulation and exploitation and heading toward its own negation. Money, in brief, is a process by which economic values are socially exchanged fairly and equally (the "law of equivalence"), whereas capital works to extract an extra, or surplus, value from workers. Capitalism embodies an inner tension between its major components. *Grundrisse* outlines how these inherent contradictions become manifest empirically in the economy as well as in the gamut of capitalist social relationships.

In *Theories of Surplus Value* and *Capital*, Marx condemned utopian socialists for naively reducing a specific form of labor performed in capitalism (i.e. wage labor) to labor "in general," a purified, universal concept. Both bourgeois and utopian socialist political economy thus naively reverse the proper relation of abstract and concrete, carrying Hegel's error into the realm of economics.[14]

Capital seeks answers to the perennial questions regarding the nature of commodities, price, and value that plagued Adam Smith and David Ricardo, without, however, abandoning the actual dynamics of capitalism (i.e. the verifiable human relationships that signify a market economy). In particular, Marx utilized the labor theory of value, which he adopted and modified, to subvert the idealistic myths of classical political economy, marshaling factual evidence to prove that capitalism is inherently exploitative.

Commodities, according to Marx's revised labor theory of value, embody two distinct values: a utility in satisfying human needs (i.e. "use value"); and one derived from their crystallized labor time. When products are exchanged in capitalism they are evaluated solely on the basis of the latter, what Marx called "exchange value." General labor time, that is, the average time needed by a skilled worker to produce a specific product at a specific stage in the development of the productive apparatus, determines exchange value. Exchange value is thus based on the social processes of circulation and exchange, not a commodity's intrinsic nature, and occurs when individuals are private owners of products and wish to exchange them with each other; that is, in capitalism.

Although Marx, like Adam Smith, believed labor produces value, he also distinguished between concrete, specific activity that produces a socially useful product and abstract, generalized, homogeneous activity that produces a commodity with exchange value. Wage labor is geared to produce only commodities, hence capitalism subordinates use value to exchange value, real human needs to the market's exigencies and private profit.

Notwithstanding a cursory perusal of factors influencing the practical imbalance between price and value, *Capital* aims primarily at explaining why real value is generated by socially necessary labor time. In a bourgeois culture that was nearly fixated on commodity prices, Marx upbraided classical economics for once again reversing the proper roles of abstract and concrete by assuming that commodities are the source of value and then equating them to success and virtue. By selling our time and activities to employers we are, in turn, transformed into commodities ourselves. We then ignore the real source of value, which lies in our own concrete labors. This reversal, where commodities, not people, become autonomous and controlling, is the source of fetishized interpersonal relationships. *Capital*'s "fetishism of commodities"—what Marx earlier called "alienation"—is a specific behavioral pattern of men and women in capitalism that hides empirical economic reality and, in addition, is the source of capitalist profit.

Labor, according to Marx, creates value but does not itself possess value. The worker, therefore, becomes a commodity by selling labor power, not labor. Labor power is thus a commodity whose value is determined by the socially necessary labor time required to keep it alive and productive. This will vary with time, place, and culture;[15] however, the physiological minimum that is necessary to keep workers alive always marks the lowest limit of wages. What makes labor power unique, for Marx, is its propensity to create exchange values greater than the values necessary to maintain it. The excess of value created by labor power over the value workers are paid is "surplus value." In equivalent exchange (when value equals price), capitalists receive more exchange value from workers than it costs to maintain them. The surplus is realized through the circulation of these commodities in the marketplace[16] and constitutes the source of capitalist profit. Other forms of capital (e.g. money, land, machines, fuel, natural resources) can, when used, acquire surplus value but not create it. Capitalists, aware of this, squeeze every last bit of labor power from each employee while ignoring the dehumanizing consequences of this process, except when the latter becomes a potential limit on working capacity. The imbalance in capitalism's productive relationships—the fact that workers do not receive the full value they create, which accrues to those who do not labor—is what Marx called exploitation. The social forms of capitalist exploitation, that is, the alienated ideas and institutions of bourgeois culture, rationalize the actual pattern of interaction commodity production requires.

The rate of profit for capitalists is the ratio of surplus value gained in production to the entire capital expended, including "constant capital" (value of rent, raw materials, equipment, technology, etc.) plus "variable capital" (workers' wages). The "organic composition" of capital is the ratio of variable to constant capital. Although constant capital is required for production, only variable capital creates surplus value. Consequently, exploitation is measured not by rates of profit but by "relative surplus value," that is, the ratio between surplus value and the amount expended on wages. The most profitable industries are therefore not necessarily the most exploitative. Capitalism is defined by human exploitation regardless of the relative success, wealth, or attitude of particular entrepreneurs. Merely capping allowable rates of profit, as suggested by reformers and utopians, might economically hurt certain capitalists but could not eliminate the exploitative character of capitalism.

Capitalists strive to maximize rates of surplus value and profit. Capitalism, therefore, has an inherent, empirically verifiable tendency toward the accumulation of wealth and unlimited growth. The positive consequences are obvious: reinvestment in research and capital expansion, technological development, job and productivity increases. However, the unsubstantiated myths of bourgeois political economy occlude what are equally obvious—and empirically verifiable—symptoms of trouble. The rise in capital accumulation and technological efficiency generates labor-saving devices that streamline factory production, meaning that less human labor is required to produce the same volume of goods. In *Capital*'s terminology, the rate of variable to constant capital decreases. Since surplus value is realized only from variable capital, the evolution of capitalism is stained by a gradual but persistent decrease in average rates of surplus value and profit. This, for Marx, is an empirically verifiable law of capitalist development, with devastating implications. Capitalism, in effect, negates its own raison d'être by hindering the creation of surplus value. Entrepreneurs react predictably by intensifying worker exploitation (e.g. lowering wages, lengthening the work day, neglecting work place conditions—all tolerated because there exists a "reserve army" of unemployed labor willing to supplant the dissatisfied) and increasing foreign contacts (e.g. grasping inexpensive resources and reliable markets for manufactured goods). However, Marx's data indicated that these measures would not stem declining profits, nor would they prevent the gradual impoverishment of small industry and the concentration of productive capacity in a dwindling number of large corporations. Successful entrepreneurs defray financial losses by increasing production to the point that it exceeds the purchasing capacity of workers, thus precipitating further plant closings and new mergers. Each new point of economic equilibrium regenerates the entire cycle.

These incessant economic crises indicate a contradiction between capitalist forces of production and the social conditions they engender. The polarization of workers and entrepreneurs generates a worsening in the quality of life for the former, while the latter dwindle in numbers. The surviving entrepreneurs hire professional managers, who mobilize workers into more efficient, cohesive, and productive work units. Ironically, this increasingly social character of the capitalist work place only hastens capitalist disintegration, as workers begin sensing their united power and abilities. The private appropriation of surplus value turns increasingly anachronistic. "Centralization of the means of production and socialization of labour at last reach a point where they become incompatible with their capitalist integument. Thus integument is burst asunder. The knell of capitalist private property sounds. The expropriators are expropriated.''[17] Although capitalism promotes technological progress and labor organization, and hence performs a vital economic and social function, it simultaneously establishes the conditions for its own abolition.

Marx's ''laws'' of capitalist accumulation, the falling rate of profit, and the polarization of classes are, for empirical Marxists, valid only when verified by the observed facts of capitalist development. From this view, Marx never postulated an absolute, a priori principle defining capitalism as inherently unfeasible and revolution as one moment of a transcendent material or ideal totality. Furthermore, the utility of Marx's theories must now be measured against new variables which Marx could not have foreseen (e.g. imperialism, inflation, advertising, unionization, government economic intervention). If, as empirical Marxists anticipate, Marxism can effectively explain this behavior of real people in specified, verifiable circumstances, then its utility has not diminished and its long-run predictions are statistically valid.

Empirical Marxism, as a systematic alternative to orthodoxy, encompasses such thinkers as the Russian empiriocritics, Eduard Bernstein, Max Adler and the Austro-Marxists, the Italians Galvano Della Volpe and Lucio Colletti, Georges Gurvitch, John Desmond Bernal, the so-called dependency or world systems theorists (e.g. Immanuel Wallerstein, Andre Gunder Frank, Samir Amin, Theotonia Dos Santos) and E. P. Thompson. There are, to be sure, practical and philosophical disagreements among members of this group, particularly regarding the abstract principles that will replace Cartesianism and justify empirical verification. But the unifying belief in the epistemological priority of empirical data, the practical commitment to formulating revolutionary strategy in response to concrete conditions, and the professional impulse to apply Marxist theory to all empirically verifiable domains—even those heretofore ignored by orthodoxy—distinguishes empirical Marxism and makes it an attractive alternative for nontraditional empirical scientists.

EXPERIENTIALISM

Both idealism and materialism presume that an a priori truth guides the free behavior of authentic human actors. Although empirical Marxism counters a priorism with verifiable evidence, it nevertheless merely shifts scientific criteria from one impersonal reality to another. Empirical social science, bourgeois or Marxist, depicts causal, verifiable relationships that are valid, in specific circumstances, for any human actor. Self-determining action is therefore impossible. Moreover, empirical social science is philosophically justified only via a priorism, either Cartesian or dialectical. Hence it too presupposes there is an objective reality that mediates the activities of free actors and potentially justifies the authority of a technocratic elite. The bleak historical consequences of a priorism and empiricism have pushed some Marxists to expound their emancipatory Marxist rhetoric while simultaneously redesigning Marxist theory to eliminate its "objective," potentially dictatorial components. Marx's socialist utopia, from this experiential Marxist point of view, is manifest only in the reflective experiences of its beneficiaries. As scientific theory and revolutionary praxis, Marxism is justifiable only through the radical self-consciousness of capitalism's dispossessed.

Experiential philosophy, based on the epistemological primacy of consciousness and the commitment to self-determining freedom, has roots in the ancient and medieval worlds but did not fully blossom until the Enlightenment. With the onset of liberalism, particularly Hobbes's bleak vision of a warring world of purely self-interested subjects, medieval a priorism was decisively shattered by the radical notion of human autonomy. Ironically, however, the bourgeois class sponsoring this revolution had concrete economic, social, and political needs that made some form of a priorism indispensable. Self-interest had somehow to be fused with objectivity in order better to protect bourgeois property, prestige, and liberty. The synthesis—manufactured by John Locke and perfected by reform liberals like J. S. Mill, T. H. Green, Dewey, and Hobhouse—conjures a natural truth based on self-evident "reason," which guides egotistical actors to peaceful, cooperative interaction while simultaneously protecting liberal political and economic rights. Liberals unhappy with this strained synthesis of experiential knowledge and absolute truth embraced empiricism, which impersonally, factually described the objective world while leaving liberal institutions untouched. By the second decade of this century experientialism—except for purists like Kierkegaard and Nietzsche—was known only in the mutilated forms of liberalism and empiricism.

Edmund Husserl strove to rescue subjectivity from a priori and empirical captors and to milk existentialism for that universality it flagrantly snubbed. Husserlian phenomenology firmly anchors scientific truth in reflective consciousness and then formulates a body of rules or procedures facilitating an observer's ascent into successively purified states of reflective subjectivity. These "reductions," when properly instituted, culminate in an observer's reflective experience of the "transcendental ego," the purest possible state of reflective awareness, a transcendental merging of subjectivity and objectivity. The transcendental ego encompasses universal consciousness, from which observers constitute absolute knowledge—the source of contingent empirical facts. Such knowledge takes the form of *eidé*, or essences: apodictic, pre-empirical truths manifested in, and giving meaning to, particular facts perceived in the everyday world. Knowledge of these essences, what Husserl calls eidetic science, is the only means of attaining the universality traditionally associated with scientific inquiry. *Eidé*, however, exist prior to subjective constituting acts, somehow determining or guiding intersubjectively valid perceptions. Husserlian phenomenology thus exhibits an inherent tendency toward an a priori idealism, notwithstanding its experiential intentions.

The task of creating a nonsolipsistic, nonidealistic experientialism has turned Husserl's transcendental phenomenology back toward existentialism. Whereas

Husserlian phenomenology focuses solely on conscious experiences, existential phenomenology describes human existence: the reality within which consciousness occurs, the objective being that philosophically accounts for free subjectivity and makes reflection itself possible. It then transforms Husserl's notion of intentional consciousness reaching toward its object into a theory of existence, not merely mind. Being, in other words, is intentionally positioned toward space and time; it is temporally and spatially "open" to the world. This key existential phenomenological thesis provides experientialism an objective foundation (i.e. the spatial and temporal openness of being) for reflective thought and action.

Experientialists argue that Marxism, particularly its theory of alienation, can provide theoretical tools for creating radical social theory that also preserves the integrity of free subjects. Although Marx, of course, was neither a phenomenologist nor a philosopher intent on stretching the limits of subjectivity, he did, argue experientialists, believe in humanity's irreducible freedom and autonomy. Marx's life work, even the later economic writings, was devoted to justifying and realizing a society of self-determined citizens, unencumbered by oppressive capitalist institutions. Human beings, for Marx, have freely created the conditions that now enslave them and can, potentially, change them. Marxism explains how and when this occurs. The putative contradiction between free humanity enslaved by its own products is nullified by Marx's concept of alienation.

Rejecting Hegel's idealist sublation of nature, Marx argued that external nature comprises an "inorganic body" that sustains human life. Actors relate to nature through their labors, which creatively alter nature to produce needed goods. Within nature's objective constraints, therefore, human actors intentionally transform the world when satisfying their species-needs. Humanity, though conditioned by nature, nonetheless creatively directs energies into fruitful activities. Labor, as creative praxis, is a quintessential human attribute that distinguishes us from nonhumans. It turns alienated only when dehumanized, that is, when drained of creative freedom and directed toward fulfilling artificial needs. This occurs when humanity unintentionally creates an oppressive, dehumanizing world in which fallacious images are naively internalized by actors who have freely forfeited their freedom. Labor, in brief, is naturally intentional and self-determined, but alienated by conditions humanity itself creates. Marx's alienation is neither inevitable nor irreversible.

Experientialists apply this framework to understanding Marx. They argue that while his strategy and mode of discourse changed, all Marx's writings presumed humanity's irreducible freedom. The early work, including the *Critique of Hegel's Doctrine of the State*, *On the Jewish Question*, and especially the *1844 Manuscripts*,[18] describe humanity's innate, natural freedom and capitalism's inhibiting, alienating influence. Later, in *The German Ideology* and particularly *Grundrisse* and *Capital*, alienation became the unadvertised background for a more empirical examination of capitalist economics. Prior to 1846, Marx philosophically measured everyday experiences in capitalism, finding them deformed and inauthentic. Afterward, he translated philosophical critique into a science that factually substantiated humanity's fall into inauthenticity. Here, economic phenomena were seen as crystallized forms of human praxis that eliminated the very possibility of praxis. The later scientific works thus demystify reified, fetishized activities with empirical analysis. They do to classical political economy precisely what Marx had earlier done to Hegel: purge it of abstractions that obscure the human origins of society and emasculate humanity's free potential. In brief, the early philosophical anthropology is implicit in the later scientific critique. The latter's objective, factual, nonphilosophical style must not hide this basic truth.

Experiential interpreters of Marx heartily concur that only man, among all forms of life, "starts, regulates, and controls the material reactions between himself and Nature," appropriating nature "in a form adapted to his own wants. . . . [W]hat distinguishes the worst architect from the best of bees is this, that the architect raises his structure in imagination before he erects it in reality."[19] History, in other words, is made first in the reflective minds of human actors and then in self-determining praxis. A priori and empirical Marxisms, experientialists believe, have perverted this, Marx's central, truly revolutionary insight.

Although it is possible to stretch Husserl's transcendental ego into both a purified proletarian vision and a tool for dialectical analysis (e.g. Enzo Paci), readers of this volume will discover that most experiential Marxists opt instead to work with some variation of existential phenomenology. In the hands of people like the early Marcuse, Sartre, Merleau-Ponty, and legions of lesser known, predominantly French radicals clustered around journals like *Arguments*, being-in-the-world throws humanity into history as well as the entire scope of society's sanctioned values, behavior, and institutions. Societies, like their citizens, are open to time and space, living as the dynamic interactions of history; current events and behavior; physical resources, institutions, structures, and processes; ideals, values, expectations, and goals for the future; and a world environment where all these take shape. What results is a multidimensional view of social life, where individuals are conditioned by material economic relationships as well as by a common history. Experiential Marxism is thus dialectical not in the orthodox sense but by revealing life's spatial and temporal multidimensionality, the ways in which economic, social, and political phenomena intersect with each other and with temporality. However, the phenomenologically derived social and historical dialectic can live only in and through the reflective self-consciousness of aware subjects. Instead of dogmatic blueprints, experiential Marxism proffers only a perception of history that is useful for explaining reflective social experiences but guarantees nothing. Experiential Marxism, therefore, is contingent in a very human sense: its dialectical analysis is verified, and its revolutionary politics realized, only in the thoughtful beliefs and actions of capitalism's exploited masses.

CRITICAL THEORY AND NEW LEFTISM

A priori, empirical, and experiential schools of Marxism all presume that objective knowledge is both real and knowable. For some Marxists, however, history has gruesomely illustrated that objective truths invariably deteriorate into reigns of "justifiable" terror, transforming potentially emancipatory social theory and praxis into a human hell where physical survival is its own reward. Real emancipation, for these "nonbelievers," will only survive where the air is clear of positive philosophical systems that menacingly promise absolute fulfillment.

Marxist nonbelievers take seriously Marx's warnings against abstract philosophizing and his emphasis on concrete social processes. Social theory, by this reading of Marx, effectively blocks meaningful social change and mystifies nonspecialists. Truth is inexpressible in abstract thought-systems. As Marx implied, particularly in the early writings, ideas that satisfy needs of dominant social groups are "true"; those inhibiting human satisfaction, "false." Since both needs and dominant groups change in history, so will criteria of valid knowledge. At any particular time, needs and dominant groups are conditioned by society's productive capacity, which determines how we labor, what is produced, and who rules. Oppressive societies fulfill an elite's interests rather than general human needs and hence generate "false," nonscientific ideas. Genuine democracy will elevate all human kind to dominance and satisfy their needs with true, "scientific" knowledge. The Marxist commitment to epistemological absolutes—a priori, empirical, or experiential—is simultaneously nondialectical (absolutizing a partial aspect of society's dynamic totality) and dangerous (potentially justifying a dictatorship of scientists).

The Frankfurt School of Critical Theory combines a deep suspicion of all positive thought-systems with an admission that truth may nevertheless exist and progressive social change is indeed justifiable. The problem, wrenchingly experienced by critical theorists during a time when Europe was lurching between Nazism and Stalinism, is that philosophical systems invariably ossify into dogmatic dictatorships that reduce reality to absolute theory. Marxian dialectics, as interpreted by critical theorists, catches the hidden social interconnections that, when perceived, sublate oppressive values and institutions—bourgeois, bureaucratic socialist, or fascistic. Authentic Marxism is therefore critique rather than pure doctrine and aims at realizing human emancipation by piercing the ideological rhetoric of left and right. In this sense, it resembles Marx's own efforts at deflating capitalism by exposing the exploitation of everyday life.

The relativism and passivity associated with critical theory is vividly illustrated in the work of its two most famous theorists, Max Horkheimer and Theodore Adorno. Critical theory's fear of positive systems—even egalitarian ones—and potentially exploitative actions makes it a revolutionary theory that, for critics, is neither revolutionary nor theoretical. For Marcuse, Fromm, Habermas, and others the price of critical, nonpolitical relativism is too high: each abandoned the Frankfurt School in search of seminal principles that could justify nonexploitative political action. On the other hand, Adorno, Marcuse, Franz Neumann, Leo Lowenthal, Claus Offe, Karl Wittfogel, and others have translated the Frankfurt School's nondogmatic spirit into useful critical studies of social systems ranging from fascism to bureaucratic socialism.

New leftism, at least to the extent one can generalize about such an antitheoretical movement, argues that since knowledge is manufactured only to serve the material needs of hegemonic interests, it is itself meaningless. History, as Marx saw, is an incessant battle of conflicting classes, where thought is merely one more weapon for achieving power. If strategically effective, a theory is valuable; if not, it is worthless and expendable. From this perspective, the "old" left's philosophy of dialectical materialism is "true" only when preserving and expanding the power of Communist Party officials—and then only for them. Its reductionist materialism purposely immobilizes workers and reinforces the Party's privileged social, economic, and political positions. For new leftists, Marxism must be emancipatory in the sense of mobilizing the exploited masses for revolutionary action. Words or ideas encouraging revolution are justified regardless of content. Action, not reflection, is what matters. The revolution will be intellectually justified after it is won, with an as yet unknown set of ideas that propagate proletarian hegemony.

For obvious reasons, a volume like this one is probably not the best forum for new leftism. Nevertheless, readers can taste samples of this most opportunistic of Marxian theories, ranging from the tactical commitment to violence (e.g. Sorel, Ulrike Meinhof, Rudi Dutschke, the Johnson-Forest Tendency) to squeezing the revolutionary potential from bourgeois laws and institutions (e.g. Stoughton Lynd). Critics of new leftism balance its focus on practical political successes against its utter disdain for philosophizing and conclude by questioning whether new left leaders, in power, could be trusted any more than other power-hungry, Machiavellian despots.

CONCLUSION

Neo-Marxism was born in Marx's ambiguous legacy and nurtured by practical exigencies, which generated new Marxian theories when circumstances judged old ones lacking. It now encompasses a broad spectrum of theories ranging from opportunism to idealism, empiricism, experientialism, and pure critique, each of which can justify unique political tactics. Marxism's children have indeed gone their separate ways. However there are several blood traits that are the irreplaceable core of Marxism, the minimum required of any individual calling himself or herself a Marxist. Although each Marxist school philosophically justifies these principles according to its own logic, they nevertheless unite an otherwise heterogeneous Marxist family.

First, Marxism is dialectical. Whereas non-Marxian theory fragments reality into distinct levels and components and then emphasizes merely one, Marxism's universe is a multidimensional, interpenetrating totality. Real natural, social, or personal knowledge encompasses the net of dynamic connections binding particulars to each other and to the totality. Marxian social inquiry acknowledges this multidimensionality by linking temporally and spatially isolated phenomena, generating explanations that reflect life's irreducible complexity.

Second, Marxism evaluates capitalism as an alienating, exploitative system that denatures humanity and subordinates human welfare to the pecuniary interests of a hegemonic elite. Capitalist oppression is manifest economically in workers being denied the full value of their labors and culturally via institutions and values that inhibit the full development of human potential.

Third, Marxism believes that of all forms of human organization only socialism (i.e. public ownership of the productive apparatus and control of distribution) can guarantee that workers are fairly treated in the work place while simultaneously reaping the full benefits of advanced industrial culture. Socialist economies maximize use rather than exchange value, thereby producing only what society as a classless, organic unity of citizens requires. Hence socialism substitutes rationality for capitalism's irrational market and brings our productive capacity under human control.

Finally, Marxism originates in Marx. Neo-Marxists use the words he spoke and wrote to legitimate their social theories. Of course, competing schools of Marxism are inspired by Marx because he does, indeed, inspire competing Marxisms. Perceptive radical scholars and activists can easily find relevant textual justification for a priorism, empiricism, experientialism, reflective critique, and revolutionary activism—rationalizing each significant meaning of contemporary neo-Marxism.

Marxism, therefore, is dialectical, indicts capitalism, advocates socialism, and knows relevant texts. This comprises its unity and generates an anticapitalist alliance of all radicals seeking progressive change and socialist justice. However the diversity of neo-Marxist theories impels each member of this alliance to make difficult and complex theoretical decisions having significant practical consequences. Since critical inquiry and radical action necessarily presuppose a set of theoretical principles, these choices can be ignored but not avoided.

This book illustrates both the unity and diversity of Marxism. Each entrant, to one degree or another, is a Marxist, and hence a willing participant in a worldwide movement advocating critical research and human emancipation. Each entrant also exhibits the unique theoretical and practical biases of a relevant neo-Marxist school. Finally, each entrant embodies a unique perspective conditioned by specific biographical, regional, national, and international factors. The choices faced by serious readers regarding the validity and usefulness of neo-Marxism, the particular school that best encapsulates radical theory and practice, and the unique contours of specific historically and spatially conditioned perspectives are all set forth herein. Final decisions, of course, are not.

NOTES

1. Marx examined philosophical questions primarily in the *1844 Manuscripts*, *The German Ideology*, the 1857 Introduction to *Grundrisse*, and the 1859 preface to *A Contribution to the Critique of Political Economy*. Even in these works, however, philosophical positions are suggested but not systematically defined.

2. Karl Marx, "Preface," *A Contribution to the Critique of Political Economy* (1859), in *Early Writings* (New York: Vintage Books, 1975), p. 427. Hereafter cited as *KMEW*.

3. Ibid.

4. Karl Marx, *Theses on Feuerbach* (no. 11), *KMEW*, p. 423.

5. Ibid.

6. Including David Straus, Bruno Bauer, Arnold Ruge, and Moses Hess. The Hegelian left emphasized Hegel's logic and hence believed in the desirability and necessity of progressive change. With the exception of Hess, the left Hegelians were not socialists, advocating instead liberal and secular reforms. The "right Hegelians" emphasized Hegel's nationalism and interpreted the status quo as Spirit's legacy to nineteenth-century Europe.

7. Species-essence, as described in the *1844 Manuscripts*, comprises two aspects: first, humans are essentially conscious, cognitive creatures, reflectively perceiving and creatively modifying nature; and second, humans are essentially "open" to nature and society. Consequently, by satiating real "personal" needs we also meet the needs of all humanity and realize nature's splendor and promise.

8. See Karl Marx, *Economic and Philosophical Manuscripts*, in *KMEW*, p. 352.

9. The new idiom includes phrases such as "labor theory of value," "labor power," "surplus value," "abstract and concrete labor," "wage labor as a commodity," "social being," "fetishism," "exchange value," and "use value." From a Hegelian perspective, these terms refine and extend—but do not negate—his earlier concepts of "praxis," "species-being," "essence," and "alienated labor."

10. Cf. "Narrow empiricism . . . confines itself to collecting laws of motion and interconnection manifested in those facts, and is skeptical about all bold generalizations and theories. Like dogmatism, empiricism cannot see beyond the limited experience of the present moment." See Maurice Cornforth, *The Theory of Knowledge* (New York: International, 1963), p. 146. Susan Stebbing, *Philosophy and the Physicists* (New York: Pelican Books, 1944), p. 7, makes this same point from a non-Marxist perspective.

11. See Karl Marx, *Critique of Hegel's Doctrine of the State*, in *KMEW*, pp. 80, 98.

12. Marx and Engels, *The German Ideology*, pp. 36–49.

13. Karl Marx, *Wage Labour and Capital*, in *KMEW*, p. 248.

14. See especially the first chapter of Karl Marx, *Capital*, 3 vols. (New York: International, 1975), vol. 1. *Theories of Surplus Value*, 3 vols., (Moscow: Progress, 1969–72) is a critique of classical and socialist economic theory, focusing on Adam Smith (vol. 1), Ricardo (vol. 2), and the British socialist followers of Ricardo (vol. 3).

15. Marx equivocated regarding the exact meaning of the physiological minimum, probably because of the changing nature of available evidence. *Wage Labour and Capital* and *The Communist Manifesto* surmised that capitalist accumulation drives wages to the physiological minimum in the sense of providing only enough to keep a supply of workers alive and active. Workers are absolutely impoverished as they grow in size but receive a shrinking sum of total social value. *Grundrisse*, *Capital*, and *Value, Price and Profit* contended that the absolute needs of labor (i.e. the physiological minimum) are conditioned by cultural factors. Rising wages coexist with a progressive deterioration of social conditions. Capitalism thus causes the relative impoverishment of workers, who receive a decreasing proportionate share of socially created values—even as wages rise on an absolute scale.

16. Volume 2 of *Capital* examines in some detail how the circulation of commodities affects an entrepreneur's rate of profit.

17. Marx, *Capital*, vol. 1, p. 763.

18. See especially Marx, *Economic and Philosophical Manuscripts*, in *KMEW*, pp. 327–78.

19. Marx, *Capital*, vol. 1, p. 177.

Biographies of
Neo-Marxists

A

ABRAMOWSKI, JOSEF EDWARD (1868–1918). Born on 17 August 1868 in Stefanin (the Ukraine), Abramowski was a noted Polish philosopher, sociologist, and psychologist. After completing high school in Warsaw he studied natural science, philosophy, and sociology in Krakow, Geneva, and Paris. He wrote his first published article at the age of fifteen and began to take part in workers' movements a year later. As a theorist and agent in the socialist movement in Poland, Abramowski participated in the founding meeting of the Polish Socialist Party (PPS) in Paris and was elected to the Society of Polish Socialists Abroad. In the years 1891–93 he began to study the social and economic history of early Europe. *Feudalism*, the resulting published work, considers not only the factors of economic growth but also the cultural conditions and moral turning points in Europe's historical process. After 1893 he relinquished his membership in socialist political movements and began speaking in favor of new, cooperative socialist institutions known as "ethical circles" and "societies of friendship." Abramowski is thus acknowledged as the founder of Polish utopian cooperative communities. During the wave of revolution in 1905–7 he initiated a boycott of czarist countries and published the monograph *Universal Conspiracy Against the State* in 1905. After 1907 he discontinued his social activities and turned to research in the area of psychology. In 1915 he accepted the chair in psychology at the University of Warsaw.

Inspired by Marxist philosophy, Abramowski became interested in social growth. At the same time, under the influence of Bergson's intuitionism and early twentieth-century neo-Kantianism, he began studying the role of individuals in the social process. For Abramowski, the contact of a person with worldly phenomena begins with the irreducible notion of intuition. However, although perceiving subjects as free, intuitive actors, what they communicate, after perception, is conditioned by social institutions, mores, and language. Hence social phenomena have both subjective and objective sides. Social progress thus requires psychological as well as institutional changes.

Abramowski's concept of "ethical socialism" was formulated in the context of Eduard Bernstein's* revisionism and the beginnings of reformist opposition

tendencies in Europe's workers' movements. Abramowski criticized both orthodoxy and Bernsteinian reformism. He noted, presciently anticipating the future,
that small, elitist, dogmatic revolutionary parties would ultimately generate bureaucratization and terror. Social democratic reformism, however, sacrifices the
working class to the bourgeois state. For Abramowski, authentic socialism required institutions that maximized the inherent freedom of the individual by
creating conditions for productive activity limited only by necessary legal re-
straints on antisocial behavior. Political revolution therefore had to be preceded
by moral revolution. The final source of revolution could only be the revolu-
tionized consciences of the people, who, torn from their passive acceptance of
the state, would eventually create a spontaneous, cooperative, stateless socialist
society.

Abramowski thus postulated an anarchistic socialism, what he called a "republic of cooperation," and what Oskar Lange† later termed "constructive
anarchism." Abramowski favored universal education and social programs to
develop the potentials of Polish citizens, taking into account the irreducible
uniqueness of each person. He formulated the motto "Freedom for Poland and
freedom for every person in Poland" and advocated the creation of cooperative
community associations. Abramowski had a strong influence on later educational
and social battles that took place in pre–World War I Poland.
BIBLIOGRAPHY:

A. "Problems of Socialism," "Ethics and Revolution," and "Socialism and the State:
Contributions to the Critique of Contemporary Socialism," all in *Filozofia spoleczna:
Wybór pism* (Warsaw: Państwowe Wydawn, 1965).

B. Oskar Lange, *Socjalizm; zarys bibliograticzny i metodologiczny* (Krakow: T.U.R.,
1928); B. Cywiński, "The Political Thought of E. Abramowski," in *Founders of Polish
Political Thought* (Wroclaw: Państwowy Zaklad Wydawn, 1978).

PIOTR OGRODZIŃSKI

ADLER, MAX (1873–1937). Adler was born in Vienna on 15 January 1873
into a Jewish commercial family and died on 28 June 1937 in the same city.
After completing his legal studies in 1896, he practiced law in Vienna. Before
long he became deeply involved in the work of the Austrian Social Democratic
Party, helping in 1903 to establish a workers' study circle and in 1904 founding,
with Rudolf Hilferding,† the highly regarded series *Marx-Studien*. Although he
served in the Austrian parliament during 1920–23, he clearly preferred to function
primarily as a teacher and theoretician. He was appointed extraordinary professor
of sociology at the University of Vienna in 1920 and retained the post until his
death. He was arrested and held for a brief period after the civil war of 1934,
but was subsequently permitted to return to his teaching.

Adler was the most philosophically inclined among the influential group of
Marxist† theoreticians who emerged in Vienna shortly after the turn of the
century. Responding to the vigorous current of neo-Kantian thought that flowed
from a number of Central European universities at the time, he endeavored to

develop a firm philosophical basis for modern sociology by interpreting Marx from a Kantian perspective. Refusing to accept the widely held view that Marx was a metaphysical materialist, he argued that Marxism presupposed the existence of a series of a priori categories that alone permit the human mind to obtain and organize knowledge concerning man's social existence. Fundamental to Adler's interpretation was his conviction that Marx had posited implicitly the existence of a transcendental consciousness that links each individual to the whole of humanity. Thus, mankind's social relationships are not simply the result of historical responses to utilitarian needs but are rather rooted in the very nature of the human species. From this point of view, Marxism appears to be based upon a Kantian critique of social reality, and the basic principles of socialism are granted the status of rationally determinable ethical postulates.

Adler's enthusiasm for Kant did not, however, lead him in the direction of reformism, as might have been expected. Indeed, during the 1920s he moved still further to the left, criticizing fellow Austro-Marxist* Otto Bauer* for his relative moderation and fatalistic tendency toward passivity in the face of the mounting crises that confronted Europe at the time. He warned of the "illusions" of parliamentary democracy, which he considered, in classical Marxist terms, to represent merely a veiled dictatorship of the bourgeoisie. Moreover, he did not hesitate to call for the establishment of a dictatorship of the proletariat, although he believed that this might be done legally and with a minimum of violence.

During the formative period of the First Austrian Republic he advocated the creation of a governmental structure that would combine traditional parliamentary institutions with revolutionary workers' councils, arguing that such an arrangement would provide at least some representation for the nonsocialist elements in the population and thus facilitate peaceful progress toward social democracy. Despite his radicalism, Adler did not urge Austria to follow in the path of the Bolsheviks, whom he accused of having established a dictatorship of a minority over both the majority of the proletariat and the rest of the Russian population. A legitimate dictatorship of the proletariat, he maintained, would be characterized by the rule of the majority. True democracy, however, would only be achieved with the coming of socialism in the sense that only then would a system be established that would be in keeping with the objective reality of human nature.

BIBLIOGRAPHY:

A. "Kausalität und Teleologie im Streite um die Wissenschaft," *Marx-Studien*, 1 (1904), pp. 195–433; *Marx als Denker* (Berlin: Buchhandlung Vorwärts, 1908); *Marxistische Probleme* (Stuttgart: Dietz, 1913); *Demokratie und Rätesystem* (Vienna: Brand, 1919); *Engels als Denker* (Berlin: Verlagsgenossenschaft "Freiheit", 1920); *Die Staatsauffassung des Marxismus* (Vienna: Verlag Wiener Volksbuchhandlung, 1922); *Neue Menschen* (Berlin: Laub, 1924); *Das Soziologische in Kants Erkenntniskritik* (Vienna: Verlag der Wiener Volksbuchhandlung, 1924); *Kant und der Marxismus* (Berlin: Laub, 1925); *Politische oder soziale Demokratie* (Berlin: Laub, 1926); *Lehrbuch der materialistischen Geschichtsauffassung* (Berlin: Laub, 1930); *Das Ratsel der Gesellschaft* (Vienna: Saturn-Verlag, 1936).

B. Norbert Leser, *Zwischen Reformismus und Bolschewismus* (Vienna: Europa, 1968); Alfred Pfabigan, *Max Adler: Eine politische Biographie* (Frankfurt: Campus, 1982); Robert A. Gorman, *Neo-Marxism: The Meanings of Modern Radicalism* (Westport, Conn.: Greenwood Press, 1982).

KENNETH CALKINS

ADORNO, THEODORE (1903–1969). Adorno was born in Frankfurt am Main, Germany, on 11 September 1903 of a German-Jewish father and an Italian-Catholic mother. He studied philosophy, psychology, and musicology at the University of Frankfurt and received his Ph.D. in 1924. The following year, his musical interests led him to Vienna to study composition under Alban Berg, a master of modern music, for two years. His love of music sustained him throughout his lifetime. From 1928 to 1932, he was the editor of a Viennese musical journal, *Anbruch*. He finished his *Habilitationschrift* on Kierkegaard in 1931 and started teaching at the University of Frankfurt, where he became closely associated with the Institute for Social Research. After Hitler came to power, Adorno left for England and joined the Institute for Social Research in New York City in 1938. During the years 1941–49 he lived in California, where he coauthored the *Dialectic of Enlightenment* with Max Horkheimer.* From his close collaboration with American social scientists in the investigation of the problem of prejudice, begun in 1944, emerged the study, *The Authoritarian Personality* (1950). Together with his friend Horkheimer, he returned to West Germany after World War II and took part in the reconstruction of the institute at the University of Frankfurt in 1949. He became its director in 1959 and a professor of sociology and philosophy at the University of Frankfurt. He died while vacationing in Switzerland on 6 August 1969.

Adorno's life work may be characterized as a one-man multidisciplinary enterprise, as he was equally at home in several fields, including philosophy, sociology, social psychology, aesthetics, and music. An extremely prolific writer, his oeuvre amounts to over twenty volumes published in German. His notorious German style served to polarize his readership; often it was ridiculed as ''Adorno-Deutsch,'' but many admirers and followers tried to imitate his opaque language. His major achievements consist of many philosophical treatises, such as his exposition on Kierkegaard and a critique of Husserl and Heidegger. Throughout his life, Adorno insisted on blending philosophy, sociology, and aesthetics, the three areas of scholarship in which he was most at home both by training and inclination.

In the middle phase of his scholarly career, Adorno is mainly known as coauthor of the *Dialectic of Enlightenment* and *The Authoritarian Personality*. During the war years, he composed a series of aphorisms that were later published under the title, *Minima Moralia*. The volume is indeed ''reflections from a damaged life,'' as the subtitle indicates. The problems of an intellectual existence in exile is the theme, and Adorno pleads for a new moral philosophy. His message is summed up in the closing sentences:

> The only philosophy which can be practiced responsibly in the face of despair is
> the attempt to contemplate all things as they would present themselves from the
> standpoint of redemption. . . . Perspectives must be fashioned that displease and
> estrange the world, reveal it to be, with its rifts and crevices, as indigent and
> distorted as it will appear one day in the messianic light. To gain such perspectives
> without velleity or violence, entirely from felt contact with its objects—this alone
> is the task of thought. (p. 247)

After his return to Germany, Adorno's theoretical interests and attitude were determined by three major historical events: (1) the Auschwitz experience, summed up in his famous dictum, "No poetry after Auschwitz"; (2) the continued stabilization of Western capitalist-industrial societies; and (3) the bureaucratization and rigidification of Eastern (Soviet-type) societies under Stalinist† regimes.

Adorno's sociology, which he often called "critical theory of society," was first of all a critique of the positivist-empirical and compartmentalized academic social sciences, which he characterized as the handmaiden of dominant social-political forces in the service of the manipulation of the masses. The main features of modern empirical science were a schism of theory, method, and substantive areas; the loss of totality; a drive for quantification at the expense of the loss of meaning of societal phenomena. In contradistinction, he advocated the inseparability of philosophy and sociology, a fusion of scientific and artistic cognition, and speculation as a source of invaluable insight into the societal mechanism. He opted for a selected use of Marxian† categories, such as the dominance in capitalism of exchange value and reification. Adorno's theory of society is, indeed, an amalgamation of the theories of Marx, Hegel, and Freud. Adorno's critical theory of society measures societal reality against what it pretends to be and explores its contradictions and formulates problems from within a perspective of a just and true society. Freud is hailed because he aimed at demolishing the phenomenal world and inquired into the essential problem of the "history of civilization as a history of repression." The Hegelian distinction between essence and appearance is adhered to. In opposition to empirical sociology that registers and measures only surface phenomena of societal reality, Adorno's sociology sets the task of penetrating the surface in order to illuminate essences and find the objective laws of societal movements.

The summary of Adorno's life work and his views on the possibilities of philosophy and praxis can be found in his *Negative Dialectics*. In that book he pleads for the transcending of a self-imposed methodological restraint in the social sciences and of the division between science and art. In opposition to generally accepted canons of traditional social science, such as objectivity and democratism, Adorno insists on subjectivity and elitism, stating that "the objectivity of dialectical cognition needs not less subjectivity, but more." In opposition to Marx, Adorno holds that philosophy cannot be realized in revolutionary praxis, and his final conclusions therefore speak of despair and, indeed, border on nihilism. Many critics have pointed out that Adorno's philosophy is but "an expression of helplessness and despair" (Leszek Kolakowski*) and adds up to "an assortment of ideas borrowed uncritically from Marx, Hegel, Nietzsche, Lukács,* Bergson and Block.*" George Lukács dismissed Adorno's philosophy together with that of the whole Frankfurt group as "bourgeois conformism masked as nonconformism."

Within the Frankfurt School, problems of culture and aesthetics have been largely Adorno's (and also Walter Benjamin's*) special province. In publications as early as the *Dialectic of Enlightenment*, followed by numerous essays, the theory of the "culture industry" has been advanced. In doing so, Adorno (and Horkheimer, too) was more in line with the orthodox Marxist position: late capitalist society is characterized by commodity production, and works of art and culture are subject to the same rules that apply to any other commodity. In consequence, a concentration of the means of (cultural) production results in a "culture industry," in which exchange value and profit motives are the determinant factors. With the "culture industry" (equivalent to mass culture and mass media), the dialectic of enlightenment enters the phase of mass deception. Relying on the basic Marxian premise that "the class that has the means of material production at its disposal has control at the same time over the means of mental production," the idea of the pacifying and stupefying role of the media is discussed more on a reflective than an analytical level. The final effect of the "culture industry" will be anti-enlightenment. Thus, "culture industry" becomes the means for "fettering consciousness"; it also impedes the development of autonomous individuals who judge and make conscious decisions for themselves.

It is often pointed out that Adorno's position regarding socioliterary investigations is exactly the opposite of Georg Lukác's. However, Adorno's sociology of music, developed mainly in his monographs on Wagner, Mahler, Stravinsky, Schonberg, and Berg, makes use of several Marxist philosophical-sociological categories such as commodity production and reification: their concern is with the social meaning and function of music. On the other hand, Adorno's posthumous *Aesthetische Theorie* (1970), which is his major statement on the philosophy of art, contains a denunciation of praxis, thus coming close to what his colleague Max Horkheimer thirty years earlier had termed a "traditional" position. Eagerly awaited because it was assumed to be the legacy of critical theory, the work instead became highly controversial. Adorno's theory of art amounts to a theory of modernism or of the avant-garde. It was unfavorably compared with that of Walter Benjamin, who provided the "true alternative" with his "materialist theory of art." Rejecting materialism's reflection theory, the concept of the organic work of art, Adorno embraced the historical approach of Hegel. He insisted on the autonomy of artistic works and developed a theory of the correlation between the aesthetic and social sphere that corresponds to a conception of history as a unified process (*Universalgeschichte*) with its various constituent spheres (social, political, economic, and aesthetic). Hence the dialectic between art and society does not exist in terms of an infrastructure–superstructure dichotomy with the aesthetic sphere as mere reflection. In defense of writers like Kafka and Joyce, Adorno thought that modern writers try to manifest the dialectic of social change and artistic innovation. Thus, they attain authenticity through the negation of the affirmative tradition. The correlation between art and society is not in terms of class relations; authentic works of art represent the *whole*. The task of aesthetics is defined as grasping and theoretically working out the dialectic of the social and aesthetic sphere. The text is the starting point in this "structuralist-hermeneutics"; the explication of the text or work of art can offer insight into societal conditions. Its aim is to decipher objective meanings with the help of a theoretical framework. Adorno assigns to the authentic work of art the task of defending truth, of being oppositional and emancipatory in this age of "culture industry." Thus, in the final analysis, *Aesthetische Theorie* contains a truly utopian proposition.

BIBLIOGRAPHY:

A. *Prisms* (London: Neville Spearman, 1967); *The Authoritarian Personality* (New York: Norton, 1969); *Negative Dialectics* (New York: Seabury, 1973); *Minima Moralia* (London: New Left Books, 1974); *The Positivist Dispute in German Sociology* (London: Heinemann, 1976).

B. Susan Buck-Morss, *The Origin of Negative Dialectics* (New York: Free Press, 1977); Zoltan Tar, *The Frankfurt School* (New York: Wiley, 1977); Judith Marcus and Zoltan Tar, eds., *Foundations of the Frankfurt School of Social Research* (New Brunswick, N.J.: Transaction Books, 1984); Martin Jay, *Theodore Adorno* (Cambridge, Mass.: Harvard University Press, 1985).

ZOLTÁN TAR

ALTHUSSER, LOUIS (b. 1918). Born on 16 October 1918 in Birmandreïs, Algeria, Althusser was educated in Algeria, Marseille, and Lyon in France, and received a degree in philosophy in 1948 at the Ecole Normale Supérieure in Paris. His thesis, "The Notion of Content in Hegel's Philosophy," was prepared under the supervision of philosopher Gaston Bachelard.* After completing his degree, Althusser began teaching at the Ecole Normale Supérieure and was for a time *secrétaire* of the school. In his youth, Althusser was active in the Catholic youth movement, joining the Jeunes Etudiants Catholiques in 1937. In 1948 he joined the French Communist Party (PCF).

Althusser's work is complex, highly controversial, and often ambiguous; but at the same time it has been tremendously influential in shaping the issues addressed by contemporary Marxists.† Althusser's texts consist of a philosophical investigation of the science and philosophy founded by Marx. They are also interventions in a particular historical conjuncture. The context for the development of Althusser's project is the period of de-Stalinization following the Twentieth Congress of the Communist Party of the Soviet Union (CPSU). Althusser rejects the economism and dogmatism of Stalinism† and at the same time rejects the left's attempt to purge itself of Stalinism by drawing on a Hegelian Marxist humanism, which, relying on Marx's early works, evokes themes of freedom, alienation, reification, and the placement of "man" at the center of history. Althusser locates the basis for his criticisms and for his reformulation of Marxism in a rereading of Marx. The project is thus reflexive (or circular) in that Althusser rereads Marx to trace the development of a scientific Marxism, but he also utilizes that scientific Marxism as the method guiding the rereading of Marx and the social whole.

In place of economism, the position that all change (including the transition to socialism and communism) can be explained as being determined by the economic infrastructure alone, Althusser proposes a special role for ideology in explaining the reproduction of conditions of production. Ideology is neither false ideas nor false consciousness, but neither is it scientific. It is a system of representations within which individuals "express, not the relation between them and their conditions of existence, but *the way* they live the relation between them and their conditions of existence." Ideology is a lived relation that expresses a "unity of the real relation and the imaginary relation between [individuals] and the real conditions of existence" (*For Marx*, pp. 233–34). Ideologies exist in apparatuses (for example in ideological state apparatuses such as the school, the church, the family, trade unions) and their practices. In these material practices, "governed by material rituals which are themselves defined by the material ideological apparatus" (*Lenin and Philosophy*, p. 169), ideology positions (a term borrowed from Lacan) individuals as centered, unified subjects in a particular relation to their conditions of existence. Althusser characterizes this process as a hailing or interpellation (a term borrowed from Freud) of the subject. Subjects, in this ideological subjection, live out their relation to existence, so structured, thereby reproducing their conditions of existence.

Because Marxism is, for Althusser, not an ideology but a science, it allows us to appreciate the role of ideology in every society, as well as to appreciate the way in which particular ideologies are constituted within a complex, structured, concrete social whole. This whole is constituted in and among four levels: the economic, the political, the ideological, and the theoretical. In contrast to the conception of society as a dialectic of base and superstructure with the superstructure an epiphenomenon of the base, or the conception of society as a homogeneous, expressive totality, Althusser conceives of a decentered, structured whole, within which each of the levels has a certain relative autonomy and independence. The levels develop unevenly, generated by and thereby generating contradiction. The levels articulate upon one another in a hierarchy of effectivity, their relative autonomy and independence based on a dependence to the whole: "The structure of the whole and therefore the 'difference' of the essential contradictions and their structure in dominance, is the very existence of the whole" (*For Marx*, p. 205). The interplay of difference is regulated by the economic, which is determinant "in the last instance," in that it "determines which of the instances of the social structure occupies the determinant place" (*Reading Capital*, p. 224)) within a particular mode of production. Although determination by the economic is "never active in the pure state" (*For Marx*, p. 113), it does determine the hierarchy of effectivity of the various levels of the social whole.

The motor of history is, then, contradiction, not the subject, as in Marxist humanism and in the early Marx as Althusser reads him. History is, for Althusser, a process without a subject within which all phenomena (including subjectivity) are overdetermined in the articulation of the semi-autonomous levels in concrete historical conjunctures. Causality is depicted as structural (as opposed to mechanistic or expressive) in that effectivity is exercised in and through overdetermined contradictions within a complex structure in dominance. Structural causality displaces the humanist problematic that places the subject at the center of history ("man makes his own history") and replaces it with the affirmation of the primacy of contradiction over the subject as well as over process and structure as the motor of history.

Because ideology is "an organic part of every social totality" (ibid., p. 232), and because the totality is an "ever pre-given complex whole" (ibid., p. 207), this presents a problem for Marxism's ability to separate ideological consciousness (which takes itself for its essence) from the real problems to which it exists in relation. In one of the most controversial and ambiguous moments in his work, Althusser attempts to escape this dilemma by implying a kind of privileged position for the science of Marxism (historical materialism or the science of history). This new science enables us to "know the world outlooks which philosophy represents in theory; it enables us to know philosophy." It revolutionizes philosophy, which becomes dialectical materialism, the theory of theoretical practice. Philosophy ceases to be idealist, the goal of which is to "interpret the world," and "becomes a weapon with which 'to change it': revolution" (*Lenin and Philosophy*, p. 19).

The support for the distinction between Marxism as a science and ideology derives from Althusser's particular rereading of Marx. Althusser reads Marx symptomatically. This entails a search for each text's theoretical problematic (a term borrowed from Jacques Martin), defined by Althusser as the underlying unity and starting point for reflection of the objects of thought in a particular theoretical formation. Althusser locates several periods in the evolution of Marx's problematic from a humanistic to a scientific one: 1840–44, the early works, based on a Kantian–Fichtean problematic; 1845, works of the break, based on Feuerbach's anthropological problematic; 1845–57, transitional works; and 1857–83, mature works, based on a scientific, Marxist problematic.

Althusser's symptomatic reading of Marx relies on an anti-empiricist, Marxist epistemology. Empiricism holds to the radical separation of subject and object, and the scientificity of theory resides in its ability to provide the subject with knowledge of the "real" object through observation. In contrast, Althusser asserts that there can be no identity of essence between objective reality and our knowledge of it. Rather, a science operates on and transforms already ideological raw materials (concepts or facts) into the concrete-in-thought (knowledge). This abolishes a distinction between theory and practice in that theory is a particular kind of practice, where by practice is meant "any process of transformation of a determinate given raw material into a determinate product, a transformation effected by a determinate human labour, using determinate means (of 'production')'' (*For Marx*, p. 166). The scientificity of Marxism resides then in that it is not ideological (it does not guarantee a unity of subject and object) and in that by utilizing a Marxist epistemology it can account for itself ''by taking itself as its own object'' (ibid., p. 39). In reading Marx symptomatically, Althusser considers the project a ''question of producing, in the precise sense of the word, which seems to signify making manifest what is latent, but which really means transforming (in order to give a pre-existing raw material the form of an object adapted to an end), something which in a sense already exists'' (*Reading Capital*, p. 34). In the transition from the early to late Marx, Althusser reads just this same transition from idealism, humanism, and an idealist epistemology to a Marxist science and epistemology:

> The Young Marx of the *1844 Manuscripts* read the human essence at sight, immediately, in the transparency of its alienation. *Capital*, on the contrary, exactly measures a distance and an internal dislocation (*décalage*) in the real, inscribed in its structure, a distance and a dislocation such as to make their own effects themselves illegible, and the illusion of an immediate reading of them the ultimate apex of their effects: fetishism.'' (Ibid., p. 17)

Althusser has been severely criticized, both by those who have been completely unsympathetic to his project and by those who have been largely sympathetic. Most significantly, he has been criticized for his theoretical antihumanism, which he has continued to defend; for being a structuralist, which he has denied; for suggesting the autonomy of science, which he attempts to deny; for being functionalist, particularly by implying that the sole function of ideological state apparatuses is to reproduce the conditions of production; for taking a theoreticist position that is divorced from political practice, which he attempts to correct by asserting that ''philosophy is, in the last instance, class struggle in theory'' (*Essays in Self-Criticism*, p. 150). Althusser's significance, however, resides much less in the articulation of any particular theoretical or political formulation than in the effectivity of his interventions in reshaping the terrain within which contemporary Marxist theory and practice continues to develop. In particular, we should recognize Althusser's role in bringing to the forefront the appreciation of the relative autonomy of practices within the social whole, the role of contradiction in the development of the social whole, the lack of guarantees in the development of a revolutionary politics, the conception of ideology as a lived relation embodied in apparatuses and practices, and finally the interpellation of subjects at the center of ideological discourse.

BIBLIOGRAPHY:

A. *For Marx*, trans. Ben Brewster (New York: Random House, 1969); with Etienne Balibar, *Reading Capital*, trans. Ben Brewster (London: New Left Books, 1970); *Lenin and Philosophy and Other Essays*, trans. Ben Brewster (London: New Left Books, 1971); *Politics and History* (London: New Left Books, 1972); *Essays in Self-Criticism* (London: New Left Books, 1976).

B. Saul Karsz, *Théorie et politique: Louis Althusser* (Paris: Gallimard, 1974); Alex

Callinicos, *Althusser's Marxism* (London: Pluto, 1976); Simon Clarke et al., *One Dimensional Marxism: Althusser and the Politics of Culture* (London: Allison & Busby, 1980); Robert A. Gorman, *Neo-Marxism: The Meanings of Modern Radicalism* (Westport, Conn.: Greenwood Press, 1982).

JENNIFER DARYL SLACK

ALTVATER, ELMAR (b. 1938). Elmar Altvater is a German Marxist social scientist and activist who studied economics at the University of Munich and received the Ph.D. in 1968. Since 1970 Altvater has been a professor in the Department of Political Science at the Free University of West Berlin, where he teaches political science, political economy, and sociology. Altvater is a member of the editorial board of *PROKLA* (Problems of the Class Struggle), which represents a "left-wing pluralism" and emphasizes radical theory formation as the basis of a strategy for social change. Altvater was a founding member of the Freiheit for Rudolf Bahro* Committee in 1979 and has been actively involved in the struggle for human rights, particularly those of political prisoners.

Altvater's theory of the crisis, for which he has gained an international reputation, can be summed up as follows: The economic crisis is not an isolated phenomenon but signals simultaneous political and social crises. The crisis must be looked at in a broad historical context as the necessary result of the accelerated accumulation of capital and encompasses the inner dynamics of capital: production, circulation, consumption, as well as the state and the relations on the world market. The crisis is a necessary destructive process that enables yet further accumulation; it is a corrective that Altvater refers to as the "cleansing function." It manifests itself in the devaluation and destruction of capital, the obverse side of which is structural unemployment. Strategies to overcome the crisis cannot be successful as long as they remain within the structural boundaries of capitalism. Since the hegemony of the ruling class is not exclusively economically mediated, all aspects of the social reproduction process must form an integral part of an alternative reconstruction movement, which must especially address the everyday experiences of the wage-dependent workers who are the producers of social wealth. The struggle in the Federal Republic is further complicated by the failure of liberalism and the great difficulties in organizing the German workers against authoritarian tendencies. Hence it is in the student, youth, ecology, peace, *Burgerinitiativen* (citizens coalitions), and women's movements that Altvater sees the beginning of such radical alternatives that will eventually generate the necessary transition from private to social consumption.

Since the beginning of the 1980s, Altvater has concentrated on the crisis tendencies of the international credit system. He has lectured worldwide on this topic and has attended as well as organized numerous international conferences. Altvater is particularly interested in developing a theory that deals with the Amazon, the fast-expanding region of Brazil that, in terms of the involvement of multinationals, Brazil's stupendous foreign debts, price development, markets for raw materials, etc., now significantly influences the world economy.

BIBLIOGRAPHY:

A. *Gesellschaftliche Produktion und ökonomische Rationalitat* (Frankfurt: EVA, 1969); *Die Weltwährungskrise* (Frankfurt: EVA, 1969); *Zur Kritik der Politischen Ökonomie des Ausbildungssektors* (Berlin: Erlangen, 1971); *Inflation, Akkumulation, Krise*, 2 vols. (Frankfurt: EVA, 1976); *Vom Wirtschaftswunder zur Wirtschaftskrise* (Berlin: Olle und Wolter, 1979); *Erneuerung der Politik* (Hamburg: VSA, 1982); *Alternative Wirtschaftspolitik jenseits des Kapitalismus* (Wiesbaden: Westdeutscher, 1983).

                                                          MAGDALENE MUELLER

AMIN, SAMIR (b. 1931). Samir Amin was born on 4 September 1931 in Cairo, Egypt. He received degrees from the Institute of Political Studies and the Institute of Statistics at the University of Paris and, in 1957, a Ph.D. in economics from the University of Paris. After completing his doctoral work, Amin returned to Cairo to work for the Economic Development Organization as a senior economist. In 1960 he left Egypt to work as a technical planning advisor to the government of Mali. Since then he has lived and worked outside of Egypt as a professor at the universities of Poitiers, Paris, and Dakar and as the director of the United Nations African Institute for Economic Development and Planning in Dakar.

Amin's work was known to only a small circle of academics in the United States until the 1970s. Since then his theoretical work has become relatively widely distributed among those interested in the historical development of capitalism. However, the bulk of his empirical studies, which test his theoretical notions about development, have yet to circulate in the United States. Amin was one of the earliest social thinkers to construct a model of world capitalist accumulation and development. His doctoral thesis (1957) contains the outlines of the theory that over the years he has refined but never fundamentally altered. Amin's model is similar to most models of a capitalist world-system insofar as capitalist accumulation is assumed to take place through a global division of labor where unequal exchange and exploitation characterize the nature of the relations throughout the system's hierarchy. The principal ways in which his theory diverges from many others are related to his interpretation of history's universal tendencies. He argues that although there are universal historical tendencies there is not a linear evolutionary law of development. Similarly, there are universal economic tendencies within any mode of production, but these tendencies do not have a fixed, predetermined course. Thus, although he presents a case for the proposition that all societies go through three stages (primitive communism, tributary mode of production, and capitalism), he equivocates about the necessity of a transition to a specific type of stage in the future. He is certain there will be a transition; however, depending upon the dialectics of the future class struggle, the next stage might be characterized as either a communist or as a statist (or state collective) mode of production. What is important about this equivocation is not an unwillingness to make predictions but rather a conviction that the dialectics of the class struggle will determine the outcome. Similarly, because of the perceived dialectic between the forces and relations of production,

Amin can argue that regions (not states, but a combination of states with some basis for a common bond) within the periphery potentially can break from the capitalist world-system and construct their own new social formations. Regional rather than state delinking seems to be emphasized because most states do not have the resources to generate their own world. Amin thus conceptualizes the possibility of a complete separation, not merely a revolution that leads to a so-called socialist government whose actions continue to be affected by its relations in the capitalist world-system.

BIBLIOGRAPHY:

A. "Les Effets structurels de l'intégration internationale des économies précapitalistes: Une étude théorique du mécanisme qui a engendré les économies dites sous-développées" (Doctorat d'état en sciences économiques, University of Paris, 1957); *The Maghreb in the Modern World* (Harmondsworth: Penguin, 1970); *Accumulation on a World Scale*, 2 vols. (New York: Monthly Review Press, 1974); *Unequal Development* (New York: Monthly Review Press, 1976); *The Arab Nation* (London: Zed Press, 1978); *Class and Nation* (New York: Monthly Review Press, 1979); *The Contemporary Arab Economy* (London: Zed Press, 1982).

KATHLEEN RITTER

AMPUERO DÍAZ, RAÚL (b. 1917). Raúl Ampuero Díaz was born in Ancud, Chile, on 19 December 1917. He finished a law degree at the University of Chile in 1944, but his career was devoted to internal management of the Socialist Party of Chile. One year after its founding, Raúl Ampuero joined the party in 1934. He helped create and became secretary general of the Socialist Youth thereafter in the 1930s. Disillusioned with participation in the moderate Popular Front (1938–41), he backed Salvador Allende's† split with the Old Party leadership in 1943 and began serving on the Central Committee. Since the Party continued splintering and declining, Ampuero, supported by Allende, took over as secretary general in 1946 to rebuild the organization; he held that top position subsequently during the years 1946–48, 1950–53, 1955–57, and 1961–65. In 1952 the Party divided once more, when Ampuero enlisted behind independent presidential candidate Carlos Ibáñez while Allende ran on his own with Communist assistance. Again discontented with supporting a moderate reformer, Ampuero soon turned against President Ibáñez and launched the Workers' Front thesis in 1955. That strategy spurned coalitions with centrist groups and called for alliances only with working-class parties, especially the rival Communists. Under that banner, Ampuero's Popular Socialist Party reunited with Allende's Socialist Party in 1957. They forged with the Communist Party of Chile an enduring electoral partnership known as the Popular Action Front (FRAP). Partly based on his stronghold among copper miners, Ampuero was elected to the national Senate from 1953 to 1969. After leading the Socialist Party for two decades, Ampuero was expelled in 1967. That split stemmed from his quarrels with other party chiefs and with their attempt to broaden the FRAP to revive Popular Front–style coalitions with reformist parties. He formed the tiny dissident

Popular Socialist Union, which abstained from Allende's victorious Popular Unity coalition in the 1970 presidential contest. Thereafter Ampuero faded from the political scene.

Throughout his career, this unorthodox Marxist urged the Socialist Party to establish greater internal discipline and greater external independence from centrist reformers and the Communists. Ampuero also implored his comrades to define more clearly their Marxian ideology and proletarian orientation. Trying to carve out a nationalistic position independent from the social democrats and the communists, he found faults with Maoism† and Castroism† as well as Stalinism.† Instead, Ampuero saw Titoism† as the most attractive foreign model.
BIBLIOGRAPHY:

A. *La izquierda en punto muerto* (Santiago: Orbe, 1969).

B. Ernst Halperin, *Nationalism and Communism in Chile* (Cambridge: MIT Center for International Studies, 1965); Julio César Jobet, *El Partido Socialista de Chile*, 2 vols. (Santiago: Editiones Prensa Latìnamericana, 1971); Paul W. Drake, *Socialism and Populism in Chile, 1932–52* (Urbana: University of Illinois Press, 1978).

PAUL DRAKE

ANDERSON, PERRY (b. 1938). Born in London in 1938, Perry Anderson has been a member of the editorial committee of *New Left Review* (*NLR*) since 1962. Perry Anderson's principal activity has been his vigorous editing of the magazine *New Left Review*, the major and longest-surviving journal of the British new left. After assuming the editorship in 1962, Anderson elaborated a new and more specialized project for the journal, largely derived from his analysis of British society and culture, (see "Origins of the Present Crisis" [*NLR*, 23]). Beyond or aside from its political coverage, *NLR* took as its main cultural aim to raise the level of Marxist† theory in Britain, where it was not traditionally strong, principally by translating and introducing into Britain works of continental Marxists.

In addition to his frequent contributions to the journal, Anderson's editorial work led more or less directly to three books: *Considerations on Western Marxism* (1976), a work largely of intellectual history on the development of Marxism in Germany, France, and Italy between 1918 and 1968; *In the Tracks of Historical Materialism* (1983), an essay on Marxist thought and its vicissitudes since the mid-1970s, particularly vis-à-vis French structuralism; and *Arguments Within English Marxism* (1980), a work principally devoted to the English historian Edward Thompson,* assessing his contributions to historical materialism.

Anderson has also published two out of a projected series of four volumes on the history of Europe: *Passages from Antiquity to Feudalism* (1974) and *Lineages of the Absolutist State* (1974). The promised third and fourth volumes will deal respectively with "the chain of the great bourgeois revolutions from the Revolt of the Netherlands to the Unification of Germany" and with the structure of contemporary capitalist states; the project as a whole centers on the development of the state as a central problem for historical materialism.

BIBLIOGRAPHY:

A. *Lineages of the Absolutist State* (London: New Left Books, 1974); *Passages from Antiquity to Feudalism* (Atlantic Highlands, N.J.: Humanities Press, 1974); *Considerations on Western Marxism* (London: New Left Books, 1976); *Arguments Within English Marxism* (London: New Left Books, 1980); *In the Tracks of Historical Materialism* (London: Verso, 1983).

MICHAEL DONNELLY

ARGUMENTS GROUP. To understand the importance of the *Arguments* group as an example of the reaction within the French intelligentsia during the 1950s to the Stalinist† Marxism† of the French Communist Party, one must recall that a renewal of Marxist studies occurred after World War II due to two specific developments. First, the return to Hegel, sparked by the teachings of Alexandre Kojève* in the 1930s and the translation and commentaries by Jean Hyppolite* of the *Phenomenology of Spirit* in 1941, resulted in the valorization of the dialectic of reason and history and, for many Marxists who rejected the dogmatism of the current line of Marxist inquiry, resulted as well in a return to Marx's critical method. Second, the rediscovery of the *1844 Manuscripts* (available since 1932 in the translation of the incomplete Landshut and Mayer edition, but little studied until 1945) revealed Marx's acceptance of Hegel's dialectic of negativity and the development of a concretized concept of alienation, which the French retained as the focal point of the subsequent critique of orthodox Marxism. At the turning point in 1956, with the Hungarian invasion and the Polish revolt, several French intellectuals (Colette Audry, Roland Barthes,* Jean Duvignaud,* and Edgar Morin*), inspired by the nonsectarian Italian journal *Ragionamenti*, founded a journal in France on the same model, *Arguments*, inviting articles from all political camps and thereby providing a vital forum for intellectual exchange about Marxist issues outside the Communist Party.

The initial statement of purpose in *Arguments* was both broad and clear:

> To revise with no limit whatsoever the clichés [*idées reçues*] and the current ideologies; to exercise a radical critique, with neither dogma nor forbidden terrain, concerning dominant or supposedly revolutionary reality and thought; to place in question all aspects—social, political, human, literary and artistic, scientific and philosophical—of the contemporary world so that the problems and crises of these aspects might emerge. (*Arguments*, 1)

There were three phases of the *Arguments* project. First, until 1959, the activity consisted of an interrogation and investigation both of problems posed by the revolution and Marxism, and of the French left's problems, which emerged with de Gaulle's rise to power. Second, until the journal's "scuttling" by the group itself in 1962, "the research of *Arguments*," wrote Morin in the final issue, "has been both horizontal and vertical. Horizontally, we try to conceive of the planetary politics, and vertically, we attack the foundations of politics; we proceed, by zigzag and clumsily, to situate and to raise the problematic of man in the twentieth century" (*Arguments*, 27–28), an attempt to develop a new, "planetary'' way of thinking, which linked philosophical reflection to knowledge provided by the social sciences. Third, established in 1960, the Arguments collection of books (edited by Editions de Minuit) extended their project beyond the quarterly journal. The purpose of this collection, in Morin's words, was to ''exhume from the ashcan of history . . . the heterodox Marxist thinkers like Lukács,* Marcuse,* Adorno,* the leftist critics of Marxism like Karl Korsch* . . . and also the philosophers rejected from dialogue by political taboo, like Martin Heidegger'' (*Arguments*, 27–28). This collection also presented major works of several members of the *Arguments* group itself—Kostas Axelos,* François Châtelet,* Pierre Fougeyrollas,* Georges Lapassade, Henri Lefebvre,* and Edgar Morin. Most of these intellectuals shared several steps of their political and personal development: resistance fighting against the Nazi occupation as members of the Communist Party; subsequent disillusionment with and expulsion from the Party in the 1950s; activity in the Parisian corps of academicians. In an essay entitled ''Is There a Marxist Philosophy?'' published in the final issue of *Arguments* (then in *Vers une pensée planetaire*, 1964), Kostas Axelos best sums up the six years of their ''adventure'' and the breadth of their enterprise:

> We tried to scan the horizon—with failure inscribed on that horizon. We confronted problems of *thought* and of *language*: problems of *ideology* (nos. 2, 3, 4, 5), of the *dialectic* (no. 7), of *anticipatory thought* (no. 9), of the *contemporary novel* (no. 6), of *poetry* (no. 19), of *literary criticism* (nos. 12–13), of *revisionist thought* (nos. 14, 16), of *intellectuals* (no. 20), of *language* and of *silence* (no. 27–28). We devoted an issue to the *cosmological problem* (no. 24). We questioned the *problem of man* (no. 18) and the *problem of love* (no. 21). We asked questions about *workers' councils* and the *Hungarian revolution* (no. 4), about *contemporary capitalism and communism* (no. 6), about the *French crisis* (nos. 8, 10) and about the *French working class* (nos. 12–13), about the *global problem* and the *planetary era* (nos. 15, 16), about *bureaucracy* (no. 17), about *difficulties of well-being* (no. 22), about *China* (no. 23), about *technical civilization* (no. 27–28) and about *politics* itself (nos. 25–26, 27–28). (p. 191)

Within their enterprise from the beginning existed a profound ambiguity, which would result in the journal's demise in 1962: on the one hand, free of Party constraints, the group undertook an explicit extension and revision of Marxist thought; on the other hand, given the nonsectarian orientation that they chose, a virulent anti-Stalinism emerged, often resulting in total iconoclasm. Despite the heterogeneity of the *Arguments* contributors' perspectives, their thought posed questions that had been repressed by Party discipline, about the Marxism of Soviet socialism, about the nature of the superstructure and its relation to the base, about the weaknesses of Marxist theory of knowledge, about class struggle in advanced capitalism and the proletariat's failure to triumph in Western society. Finally, returning not only to the Marx of the *1844 Manuscripts* but also to his *Doctoral Thesis*, the *Arguments* group attempted to resolve problems both in Marx's view of alienation and in the transcendence of philosophy. Central to their concern was to what extent Marx originated a new type of thought that avoided the traps of the Western philosophical tradition. In general, the group members agreed that Marx did found a new form of knowledge, yet one that was ambiguous insofar as it remained grounded in old traditions. In Marx's *Doctoral Thesis*, the group located what appeared to be Marx's desire to abolish philosophy as one goal of communism; since Marx seemed to consider philosophy as an alienated mode of thought, did he have a new thought to offer that would avoid philosophy's traps? If so, what was this thought's nature and its relation to alienation? This line of inquiry led the *Arguments* theorists to question the goal of philosophy in the new technological age, in the age of global unification and global alienation. Edgar Morin has stated (in *Science avec conscience*, 1982) that while his initial work in *Arguments* was an anthropological investigation, it evolved toward an "anthropo-cosmological" reflection in 1962–63, the need to revise the general conceptions not only of Marxism but also of the world and of thought structures. Thus, the *Arguments* theorists emphasized the "crisis of totality," the "necessity of a questioning, multidimensional, inevitably fragmentary way of thinking, but without ever necessarily abandoning fundamental and global questions" (p. 10). As Jean Duvignaud concludes in *France: The Neo-Marxists* (1962), "The best service and the sincerest homage that we can render to the memory of Marx, is to deal with Marxism as he dealt with the systems of his age. That is, to challenge the social organization set up in his name, realizing that new dreams must be invented for a new world" (p. 323).

The answers to *Arguments* inquiries became diverse and sometimes opposed, depending on the individual theorist in question. For example, Axelos and Fougeyrollas proposed a Heideggerian critique of Marx, while others, like Châtelet and Lefebvre, relied on Jean-Paul Sartre's* *Being and Nothingness* and the critical project of *Materialism and Revolution*. Furthermore, as the journal continued into the 1960s, the group members became increasingly dispersed, both geographically and in terms of orientation to solutions of their inquiry. Nonetheless, their original project did unfold in a common, if quite heterogeneous direction: based on the initial belief that society had entered a "planetary" era and that Soviet politics and particular national economic struggles no longer constituted the center of concern, the *Arguments* group members were drawn to existentialism to ground their critique of Marxism and to found their "thought for the new age."

BIBLIOGRAPHY:

A. The complete text of all twenty-eight issues has been edited by Privat (Toulouse) in two volumes: *Arguments*, vol. 1, issues 1–17 (1956–1960); vol. 2, issues 18–28 (1960–1962). Edgar Morin has edited a four-volume collection of articles from *Arguments*, all published by the Union Générale d'Editions, Paris (10/18 Collection): *Arguments/1: La Bureaucratie* (1976); *Arguments/2: Marxisme, révisionnisme, meta-marxisme* (1976); *Arguments/3: Les Intellectuels/La Pensée anticipatrice* (1978); *Arguments/4: Révolution/classe/parti* (1978). See also the individual biographical sketches.

B. The abovementioned chapter by Jean Duvignaud, published in *Revisionism: Essays on the History of Marxist Ideas*, ed. L. Labedz, (New York: Praeger, 1962), situates succinctly the *Arguments* group in terms of the general critique of Marxism in postwar France. Yves Bourdet, "Le Néo-révisionnisme," in *Communisme et marxisme* (Paris: Brient, 1963), a severe critique of the *Arguments* project; Louis Soubise, *Le Marxisme après Marx (1956–1965): Quatre marxistes dissidents français* (Paris: Montaigne, 1967), a study of the positions of Axelos, Châtelet, Fougeyrollas, and Lefebvre; Mark Poster, *Existential Marxism: From Sartre to Althusser in Postwar France* (Princeton: Princeton University Press, 1977), pp. 36–71, 209–63, gives a precise overview of the positions of several *Arguments* theorists; as does Arthur Hirsch, *The French New Left: An Intellectual History from Sartre to Gorz* (Boston: South End Press, 1981), pp. 84–107, particularly highlighting the works of Henri Lefebvre.

CHARLES J. STIVALE

ARONOWITZ, STANLEY (b. 1933). Born in New York City in 1933, Stanley Aronowitz is best known as an independent radical activist and intellectual who draws theoretical strength from critical theory as well as Marxist† categories. In the 1950s he worked as a steel, auto, and electrical worker. By 1960 he was serving as an organizer for the Amalgamated Clothing Workers of America, and from 1964 to 1967 he held the position of international representative for the Oil, Chemical, and Atomic Workers. In the late 1960s he worked as a community organizer in New York and an antiwar and socialist activist. He coedited *Studies in the Left*, a major American new left journal of the period, and he contributed articles to numerous progressive publications. He cofounded the New American Movement (NAM), a 1970s socialist and democratic organization, and later he helped merge NAM into the Democratic Socialists of America (DSA). He coedits *Social Text, a Journal of Political and Cultural Theory*. He has completed a Ph.D. at the Union Graduate School and served on the faculties of the New School, the University of California at Irvine, Columbia University, and the City University of New York, Graduate Center.

While significant as an activist, Aronowitz gained appreciable attention with his first book, *False Promises: The Shaping of American Working Class Consciousness* (1973). Drawing heavily from George Lukács* and Herbert Marcuse,* he outlined the cultural politics that critically define everyday working-class reality in the United States. He specifically emphasized institutional socialization toward deference to authority, analyzing the specific roles of media, gender, race, and leisure in American society. He heavily criticized the bureaucratic character of American unions, and he pointed to the limited explanatory value of orthodox Marxist analysis.

Aronowitz wrote numerous academic and political articles after *False Promises*, but his next major work, *The Crisis in Historical Materialism* (1981), fundamentally challenged the traditional Marxist reliance on political economy and historical materialism. Again, relying on the critical theory of the Frankfurt School, Aronowitz challenged the primacy of class within an American milieu marked by fundamental racial and sexual divisions. He calls for a concept of "material culture," elevating race, sex, and class to equal theoretical standing, thus establishing a principle of the "multiplicity of determinations." Modern theory needs to discover the historically disguised unity of these three elements, according to Aronowitz. His later work builds on his initial Freudian–Marxian synthesis, extending it considerably through a more complete attack on historical materialism.

BIBLIOGRAPHY:

A. *False Promises, The Shaping of American Working Class Consciousness* (New York: McGraw-Hill, 1973); *Food, Shelter, and the American Dream* (New York: Seabury Press, 1974); *The Crisis in Historical Materialism: Class, Politics and Culture in Marxist Theory* (New York: Praeger, 1981); with Cary Goodman, *Urban Suicide or Urban Renewal* (New York: Universe Books, 1981).

RICHARD GUARASCI

AUSTRO-MARXISM. Emerging amid the frenetic and conflict-ridden atmosphere of *fin-de-siècle* Vienna, the Austro-Marxists engaged in some of the most original attempts to adapt Marx's† ideas to the circumstances of the twentieth century. Among those most frequently identified with this group were Max Adler,* Friedrich Adler, Otto Bauer,* Rudolf Hilferding,† and Karl Renner. Although they did not develop a consistent and unified school of thought, their efforts to draw general lessons from the specific problems they confronted led the Austro-Marxists to focus their attention upon a series of common themes and to approach these themes from a common perspective.

In view of the chronic instability of life in Vienna just before and after World War I, it is hardly surprising that the optimistic reformism of the German revisionists was greeted with considerable skepticism by the Austro-Marxists and that they tended to approach the world from the orthodox perspective of the former Austrian Karl Kautsky.† They were generally, however, unwilling to accept without qualification what appeared to them to be the oversimplified materialism of the dominant German school. They therefore endeavored to create a firm philosophical basis for socialist scholarship by linking the ethical and epistemological teachings of Kant to the revolutionary dynamism of Marxism. This neo-Kantian effort to bridge the gap between the left and right wings of socialism before the war set the stage for later attempts by the Austro-Marxists to discover a viable middle road between bolshevism and social democracy. It also generated among Austro-Marxists an active interest in the empirical life-world, which dogmatic orthodox historical materialists often ignored.

It is understandable that the Austro-Marxists also devoted a great deal of attention to the issues raised by the growth of nationalism and that they tended to discover in the national differences decried by many socialists positive cultural values that should not simply be consigned to the "rubbish heap of history." More surprising is the fact that they made major contributions to the analysis of imperialism. Otto Bauer and Rudolf Hilferding, for instance, were among the first to posit the idea that the exploitation of the less developed areas of the world by the industrialized West was the major reason why capitalism had managed thus far to avoid the fate Marx had so confidently predicted for it.

The situation facing the Austro-Marxists after World War I led them to engage in lively speculation about the basic character of political power as well as about the legitimate use of force to bring about change. Having achieved a dominant position in Vienna, without, however, being able to gain the support of a majority in Austria as a whole, they tended to place great emphasis upon the apparent imminence of the triumph of socialism but were unable to devise a strategy that could overcome the intransigent opposition of the Catholic Church, the proto-fascist Heimwehr, and the vast mass of the population in rural areas and small towns. It was in this context that Otto Bauer proposed that when the power of the major contending classes reaches an equilibrium the state can temporarily assume a neutral character, and it was under these circumstances that the Austro-Marxists incorporated into the Social Democratic Party's Linz Program of 1926 the doctrine that the establishment of a dictatorship of the proletariat through violent means is acceptable, but only as a defensive measure in response to attacks by the agents of capitalism upon the rights of the majority.

The Austro-Marxists have often been criticized for placing undue reliance upon the impersonal forces of history to bring about the "inevitable" victory of socialism. Nevertheless, it can hardly be denied that their fate was in large measure sealed by the failures of democratic forces in other countries rather than by their own theoretical rigidity. Moreover, it should be remembered that when they were confronted by the ultimate challenge in 1934, they did fight back, however ineffectively, against the overwhelming repressive forces that were by that time arrayed against them.

BIBLIOGRAPHY:

B. Norbert Leser, "Austro-Marxism: A Reappraisal," pp. 117–33, in *The Left Wing Radicals Between the Wars*, ed. Walter Laqueur and George L. Mosse (New York: Harper & Row, 1966); Norbert Leser, *Zwischen Reformismus und Bolschewismus. Der Austromarxismus als Theorie und Praxis* (Vienna: Europa, 1968); Hans-Jörg Sandkühler and Rafael de la Vega, eds., *Austromarxismus* (Vienna: Europa, 1970); Peter Kulemann, *Am Beispiel des Austromarxismus* (Hamburg: Junius, 1979).

KENNETH CALKINS

AXELOS, KOSTAS (b. 1924). Born in Athens, Greece in 1924, Axelos studied concurrently at a local high school, in the French Institute, and in the German School and then entered law school. During World War II he participated in the Resistance and joined the Communist Party. When he was excluded from the Party in 1945 and condemned to death by the conservative government, Axelos left Greece for Paris. He there began studies in philosophy at the Sorbonne and in October 1951 entered the Centre National de la Recherche Scientifique (CNRS), where he remained until 1957. After two years as research attaché in the Ecole Practique des Hautes Etudes, Axelos began study in philosophy at the University of Paris I. In February 1958, Axelos became the editor of the leftist political journal *Arguments*,* and even after the *Arguments* group's dissolution in 1962, he edited the Arguments series, begun in 1960, for the Editions de Minuit. At the time of his involvement with the *Arguments* project, Axelos defended at the Sorbonne, then published in the Editions de Minuit, two sections of his doctoral thesis, *Heraclite et la philosophie* (1962) and *Marx, penseur de la technique* (1961; see bibliography for reference to the English translation), finally completing this initial trilogy in 1964 with *Vers une pensée planetaire*.

Between his contributions to *Arguments* and the aforementioned philosophical enterprise, the works of Kostas Axelos constituted one of the most extensive sources of the critique of Marxism† in the late 1950s and early 1960s. We can begin an overview of Axelos' initial project through the works' subtitles: the study of Heraclitus; *La Première Saisie de l'être en devenir de la totalité*; the critique of Marx; *Penseur de la technique: De l'aliénation de l'homme à la connquête du monde*; and the proposal for "planetary thinking," *Le Devenir-pensée du monde et le devenir-monde de la pensée*. In the first two works of the trilogy, Axelos sought to discover a truly dialectical mode of thinking, examining Western thought's critical stages, from the pre-Socratics (the genuine totality of Heraclitus's concept of becoming) to the culmination in Marx. On the one hand, Axelos answered the charge of "economic determinism" leveled against Marx's *1844 Manuscripts* by Jean-Yves Calvez (*La Pensée de Karl Marx*, 1956) and other Catholic writers, by maintaining that Marx founded "economic" alienation on "human" alienation. On the other hand, Axelos acknowledged the problems of the primacy of the economy in Marx's concept of alienation. In particular, Axelos felt that Marx's concept failed both to ground an open totality and to invent a truly revolutionary theory of knowledge, since his concept of alienation also failed to allow sufficient autonomy to political and philosophical alienation. Reducing human reality to work and to satisfaction of material needs, from Axelos's perspective, Marx did not emphasize the necessity for human reality to create itself, to attain the full satisfaction of desire. Furthermore, Axelos maintained, in the second book, that the result of the capture of human thought and action in work was to reintroduce metaphysics and dualism, still thinking in terms of the distinction of man-nature. Thus, this first phase of Axelos's work constituted a critique of Marx but not a rejection, since Axelos hoped to complete the development of thought which had been impossible for Marx in the mid- to late nineteenth century.

In the essays constituting *Toward Planetary Thinking* (most of which originally appeared in *Arguments*), Axelos proposed a transcendent passage toward a new mode of thought: with the conquest of nature practically complete in the twentieth century, Axelos argued for a way of thinking similar to Jean-Paul Sartre's* proposal in *Being and Nothingness*, thought that would ground man's poetic self-creation on the same plane as his relation with nature, avoiding metaphysics. This approach to reality is best characterized as *play*, an open, concrete, and actual process based on unity while still foregrounding multiplicity and change. And the global title of this trilogy, *Le Déploiement de l'errance* reflects the dominant role of play in Axelos's project through the influence of Martin Heidegger on the *Arguments* theorists. For the term *errance* translates Heidegger's notion of *die Irre*, the simultaneous sense of mistakenness in Western thinking (English: error) and of wanderings (English: errant) on a path toward truth. Thus, Axelos's use of *errance*, this copenetration of truth and error in Western thought, maintained the necessity of a new way of thinking, "planetary thinking," to conceive of reality not in terms of unequivocal basic elements or principles but in terms of the perpetual *play* of aspects, elements, and powers, inaccessible to reason-stating assertions. In his "Introduction to Planetary Thinking," Axelos argues that in *errance* "there is no longer any reference to an absolute . . . but only to the play of 'That' ['*Cela*'], . . . constituting an approach to 'That,' to the ungraspable, neither an idea, nor a person, nor a thing" (p. 47), *cela* defined as "being-in-becoming of the fragmentary and fragmented totality of the multidimensional and open world" (Axelos, *Entretiens*, p. 63; cf. Bibliography). Echoing Edgar Morin's* concern "Que faire?" (What is there to do?) with "Que penser?" (What is there to think?), Axelos answers, "Play the game. By allowing ourselves to be carried away by the play of time, which is —at the same time?— movement and rest, concentration and dispersion, gathering and shattering" ("Introduction," p. 48). And to this change in thought would correspond a change in action, in using the technique as play: "It is thus by means of—and through—the deployment of technique that the power of thinking does and will arise" ("Introduction," p. 18).

BIBLIOGRAPHY:

A. The specific references to Kostas Axelos's political thought are the works in the abovementioned trilogy and his articles in *Arguments*, some collected in *Vers une pensée planetaire* and in the four-volume edition of *Arguments*, ed. Edgar Morin (Paris: U.G.E., 10/18, 1976–78). Axelos develops the proposals of the initial "historico-systematic trilogy" in two more trilogies, the second, "methodological and systematic" in nature, entitled "The Deployment of the Game" (*Contribution to Logic*, 1977; *The Game of the World*, 1969; *For a Problematic Ethics*, 1972); the third entitled "The Deployment of an Investigation" (*Arguments of a Research*, 1969; *Horizons of the World*, 1974; *Problems at Stake*, 1979). See *Entretiens "réels" imaginaires et avec "soi-même"* (Montpellier: Fata Morgana, 1973); and *Alienation, Praxis and Techné in the Thought of Karl Marx* (Austin: University of Texas Press, 1976). Excerpts from the introductory and concluding chapters of *Vers une pensée planetaire* are translated as "Planetary Interlude" in Jacques Ehrmann, ed., "Games, Play, Literature," *Yale French Studies* (Boston: Beacon Press, 1971). Excerpts from *Horizons du monde* are translated as "Play as the System of Systems," in *Sub-Stance*, 25 (1980), pp. 20–24.

B. Louis Soubise, *Le Marxisme après Marx* (Paris: Montaigne, 1967); Gilles Deleuze, "Faille et feux locaux," *Critique*, 275 (April 1970); Henri Lefebvre and Pierre Fougeyrollas, *Le Jeu de Kostas Axelos* (Montpellier: Fata Morgana, 1973); Ronald Bruzina, "Translator's Introduction" in Kostas Axelos *Alienation, Praxis and Techné in the Thought of Karl Marx* (Austin: University of Texas Press, 1976); Mark Poster, *Existential Marxism in Postwar France* (Princeton: Princeton University Press, 1977).

CHARLES J. STIVALE

B

BACHELARD, GASTON (1884–1962). Gaston Bachelard was born in Bar-sur-Aube, France. After attending the Collège de Sézanne, he left school for the postal department. While working for this department in Paris (1907–13), he obtained his *license* in mathematics (1912) at the Faculté des Sciences. Mobilized in 1913, he spent six years in the army. In 1919, after the war, he taught physics and chemistry at the Collège de Bar-sur-Aube while preparing for his *license* in philosophy, which he received in 1920. In 1922 he achieved *agregé* in philosophy, and in 1927 he received his *doctorat en lettres* with his two remarkable theses, *Essai sur la connaissance approchée*, and *Etude sur l'évolution d'un problème de physique*, which were very well received and were published by J. Vrin the following year (1928). At the age of forty-three, Bachelard came to the center of the complex intellectual, artistic, and political ferment of interwar Paris. In 1930 he was appointed to the Faculty of Letters at Dijon, and in 1940 he was called to the Sorbonne, where he taught history and philosophy of science until his retirement in 1954. Throughout the latter half of his life he was a prolific writer, publishing twenty-four books and many articles and reviews. He was a popular and highly influential teacher and, except for the Occupation years, an active participant in the philosophical and artistic life of Europe.

Although Bachelard was never politically active and belonged to no party, he was an unremitting advocate of everything progressive in the culture of his time. Generations of students have been moved by his language of radical creativity and conceptual/cultural revolution. It would be difficult to find a significant current work in the human sciences and philosophy that does not work with, if not within, Bachelard's language and problematic. Along with Jean Cavaillès* and Georges Canguilhem,* Bachelard initiated one of the two major trends in contemporary French thought, that of "savoir, rationality and the concept," as Michel Foucault* has characterized it.

In terms of Marxian† political theory, Bachelard's most important contributions were, first, to call attention to the dynamic and complex scientific revolutions of the early twentieth century. He understood the beginnings of relativity theory and quantum mechanics as at once falsifying the static absolutism of the

Kantian-Newtonian world view that was and still is so important for the ideological self-justifications of capital and, simultaneously, the antitheoretical and anti-intellectual movement of positivism. Bachelard was among the first—with A. Koyré—to stress the practical and concrete significance of theoretical formulations, of theoretical labor. This deep concern with the relation of theory to practice is the second and, perhaps, the most important contribution Bachelard has made to the left. Again and again he returned to this theme, characterizing it throughout his authorship as dialectical and fundamentally revolutionary. (See on this particularly *La Formation de l'esprit scientifique*, 1938; *Le Rationalisme appliqué*, 1949; and *Le Matérialisme rationnel*, 1953.)

Third, Bachelard understood scientific and technical labor as the rational activity of the human species in pursuit of self-development and self-improvement. We are, he believed, nothing independently of this historical process of self-creation. In this belief he echoed the themes of the writings of the early Marx, which had just become available in France during the 1920s.

Fourth, in his historical studies (see, for example, *Le Pluralisme cohérent de la chimie moderne*, 1932) and elsewhere, Bachelard both practiced and demonstrated the sort of cultural critique that has come to be known as deconstruction. To him, our conceptual formations, theories, world views, however necessary they are as the results of our historical-economic activity, either serve actively and directly to further the development of the species or retard this development in specific and determinable ways.

Finally, much of the foregoing might lead one to take Bachelard for an Hegelianizer or another follower of the liberatory humanism of the Enlightenment. Yet Bachelard can be so characterized only in a very limited sense. Few writers have explored the significance of the notion of revolution with greater thoroughness. Since our actions, perceptions, and self-conceptions are determined by (and determinative of) the complex systems of knowledge and institutions, if such systems are deformed or overthrown, every aspect of human being will be changed, perhaps beyond recognition. This notion of discontinuity—in history, and in the sciences—has had profound consequences in most of current theorizing on the left.

BIBLIOGRAPHY:

A. *Le Pluralisme cohérent de la chimie moderne* (Paris: Vrin, 1932); *La Formation de l'esprit scientifique* (Paris: Vrin, 1938); *Le rationalisme appliqué* (Paris: P.U.F., 1949); *La Dialectique de la durée* (Paris: P.U.F., 1950); *Le Matérialisme rationnel* (Paris: P.U.F., 1953).

B. Miriam Glucksmann, *Structuralist Analysis in Contemporary Social Thought* (London: Routledge & Kegan Paul, 1974); Rosalind Coward and John Ellis, *Language and Materialism* (London: Routledge & Kegan Paul, 1977); Edith Kurzweil, *The Age of Structuralism* (New York: Columbia University Press, 1980).

LAURENCE E. WINTERS

BADALONI, NICOLA (b. 1924). Nicola Badaloni, born in Livorno in 1924, is currently professor of the history of philosophy at the University of Pisa and member of the Central Committee of the Italian Communist Party (PCI). In the 1960s he was involved in the theoretical debate triggered by Dellavolpism, taking positions in the party reviews *Rinascita*, *Il Contemporaneo*, and *Società*, together with other influential intellectuals such as Cesare Luporini* and Valentino Gerratana,* against Galvano Della Volpe's* approach and in defense of a historicist perspective, a reevaluation of the continuity between Hegel and Marx,† and the importance of dialectics. Besides these studies he carried out important research on Giordano Bruno, G. B. Vico, Tommaso Campanella, and the diffusion of Newtonianism in Italy. In the 1970s and the early 1980s these two research directions continued and developed. He has produced studies of the history of modern philosophy and participated in theoretical and political debates on questions dealing with Marxism† and with contemporary life and actual political problems.

Badaloni's historicist interpretation of Marxism is tied to the tradition of Italian Marxism, above all to the philosophy of praxis and to Antonio Gramsci,* a tradition also adopted by the official leadership of the PCI. In the name of this tradition Badaloni first criticizes Della Volpe, who is accused of gnosiology, and then claims a continuity between Hegel and Marx above all in the recognition of the "real objectivity of contradiction." "The result of the Marxian method," asserts Badaloni (in *Marxismo come storicismo*, 1962), "is therefore not a *defined abstraction*, but the discovery of a *real contradiction* within the system, a system well developed qualitatively, which is made the object of study." The historicist perspective is, however, closely examined, always on the basis of Gramsci's thought and also in relation to the genesis of the new Italian Communist social formation. In fact, on the one hand the theoretical and historical specificity of Marxism consists in its being tightly connected to the very emergence of the working class and of seizing in this genesis the perspective of a "new Communist civilization"; on the other hand this genesis is not a sudden and automatic explosion, but covers an entire historical epoch, which is referred to as a "transition." Badaloni views the transformation of the "productive forces" as the principal driving element of this fundamental contradiction. In general, history, for Badaloni, is a bridge between theory and politics. On the concrete historical level he uses the concepts of supremacy and self-government rather than those of domination and dictatorship of the proletariat. His vision of the historical process leading to communism sees the rise of workers as closely bound to changes in both the general historical context as well as in specific political rules that have generated worker participation in society and government.

BIBLIOGRAPHY:

A. *Marxismo come storicismo* (Milan: Feltrinelli, 1962); *Per il comunismo. Questioni di teoria* (Turin: Einaudi, 1972); *Il marxismo di Gramsci* (Turin: Einaudi, 1975); *Forme della politica e teoria del cambiamento. Scritti e polemiche 1962–1981* (Pisa: ETS, 1983); *Introduzione a Vico* (Bari: Laterza, 1984).

B. F. Cassano, *Marxismo e filosofia in Italia 1958–1971* (Bari: De Donato, 1973); G. Bedeschi, *La parabola del marxismo in Italia 1945–1983* (Bari: Laterza, 1983).

                                                                    VITTORIO DINI

BADZIO, YURIJ (b. 1936). Born in 1936 in a village in the Trans-Carpathian region of the Ukraine, Yurij Badzio is a Ukrainian literary critic and social theorist. In 1958 he received his degree in philology from the University of Uzhhorod. In 1961 he began his graduate studies at the Institute of Literature of the Ukrainian Academy of Sciences in Kiev. In the early 1960s Badzio became actively involved in the "Sixties Group," a circle of young Kievan intellectuals devoted to producing literary works in the Ukrainian language, countering the dictates of the prevailing Russification policy. At this time, Badzio joined the Communist Party (CPSU) and published widely in Soviet Ukrainian literary journals. In 1965 he took part in a public protest against the politically motivated arrest of several leading Ukrainian intellectuals, after which he was dismissed from the staff of the Institute of Literature and expelled from the Communist Party. Following the wave of political arrests in the Ukraine in 1972, Badzio began a large-scale socio-historical and theoretical analysis of the problem of nationality under socialism. The completed book of 400 pages was confiscated by the authorities, and Badzio was arrested in 1979. He was sentenced, on charges of anti-Soviet agitation and propaganda, to a twelve-year term, the first seven years to be carried out in a strict-regime camp, followed by five years of internal exile. He is presently serving the first part of his term in Mordovia.

Some of the key ideas that Badzio developed in his book were summarized in an essay-length letter sent to the Central Committee of the CPSU. A copy of this letter is the only document of Badzio's work available in the West. The value of the letter is highlighted by the fact that it is one of the very few social theoretical analyses to find its way out of the Ukraine, a region of the Soviet Union that is less accessible to Western journalists and tourists than the major cities in the Russian Republic. In the letter, Badzio discusses the treatment of the nationality question in Marxist†-Leninist† theorizing. He traces the evolution of contemporary Soviet nationality policies to Lenin's idea of the fusion of nations into one socialist state. Badzio concludes that such "internationalization" of Soviet society was conceived strategically to centralize political power in a single Soviet state rather than to implement any principles of Marxism. Badzio argues that the Soviet nationality policy has led to the current situation, where Russian culture and language dominate political, scientific, cultural-artistic, and educational institutions in the Ukrainian Republic. He further contends that this policy is continuous with a tradition of Great Russian chauvinism and is progressively driving non-Russian nationalities into extinction. Badzio feels that the confounding of "bourgeois nationalism" with national culture and identity has been used to oppress national minorities in the Soviet Union by systematically distorting their history and denying them full rights to livelihood in the present. The ideal form of socialism that Badzio proposes aims to preserve the bases of a nationality's culture, permitting full symbolic-creative expression of its social being.

BIBLIOGRAPHY:

A. "The Right to Life," *The Ukrainian Review*, 26, no. 4 (Winter 1979), pp. 13–20; *An Open Letter* (New York: The Representation in Exile of the Ukrainian Public Group to Promote Implementation of the Helsinki Accords [the representation is shared by General Petro Grigorenko and Leonid Pliushch], 1980).

MARTA ZAHAKEVICH

BAHRO, RUDOLF (b. 1935). Bahro was born in Bad Flinsberg/Isergeb, in the People's Republic of Poland. He is the author of *The Alternative*, which was published in the West in 1977. Bahro lived in East Berlin until his arrest in 1977 on charges of treason. In August 1978 Bahro was tried as a spy, convicted, and sentenced to eight years in prison. In 1979, after widespread international protest, he was released and deported to the Federal Republic under the auspices of a general amnesty. Bahro now lives in West Germany, where he is a professor at the University of Hannover. Nearly overnight Bahro became the leading socialist theoretician and propagandist for the "Greens," a West German political party. Bahro studied philosophy at Humboldt University in East Berlin from 1954 to 1959. In 1975 his dissertation, which deals with the chances for upward mobility for educated Party cadres in nationalized factories, was rejected on grounds of "insufficient scientific substance"—despite its being approved by his three professors. From 1952 until his arrest Bahro had been a member in good standing of the East German Communist Party. In 1959–60 he participated as a Party agitator in an agricultural collectivization project. Bahro was editor of the Greifswald University newspaper from 1960 to 1962, at which time he became a consultant at the headquarters of the Union for Science in East Berlin. From 1965 to 1967 he was associate editor-in-chief of the important journal *Forum*, published by the youth organization of the Communist Party. After 1967 Bahro was involved with state-financed projects in engineering and economic planning. His last leadership position in the GDR was as division manager for industrial labor organizing at the VEB Gummikombinat in East Berlin.

The Alternative, which Ernest Mandel† referred to as "one of the most important contributions to the debate on socialism since the second World War" (*Die Zeit*, 11 April 1977, p. 47), immediately became a best seller, particularly among the West European left. Supported by extensive quotes from the works of Marx,† Engels,† and Lenin,† Bahro launches a relentless attack on bureaucratic socialism and Soviet hegemony. Bahro can, therefore, be placed in a critical Marxist tradition that includes Rosa Luxemburg,† Antonio Gramsci,* the Frankfurt School, and Robert Havemann*—whose *Dialectics Without Dogma* deals with similar issues and generated similar excitement in the GDR. Bahro wrote his book under the direct influence of the Czech reformist movement known as the Prague Spring,* the so-called Harich group in Germany, Ernst Bloch,* and the Eurocommunist movement. He accuses the Soviet Union and other Warsaw Pact societies of creating an "industrialization-despotism," the bureaucracy of which is stultified and incapable of reform. *The Alternative* is thus counted, especially by Westerners, among the most important and provocative critical works to have appeared on the relation between socialism and democracy.

The Alternative consists of three parts. In part one, "The Phenomenon of the Noncapitalist Road to the Industrial Society," Bahro critically analyzes the historical development of the Russian Revolution that culminated in "real existing socialism." Forced industrialization on the basis of the old division of labor, according to Bahro, meant the surrender of the "subjective factor" and led to a stratified society in which alienation and the Communist Party's domination over workers persisted. Part two, "The Anatomy of Real Existing Socialism," shows that existing socialism is a far cry from what Marx had envisioned, a society where "the free development of the individual is the condition for the free development of all." In real existing socialism, Bahro argues, the socialist breakthrough into humanized social relations did not and could not take place. Instead, Eastern European countries are caught in a demoralizing international power struggle that generates ever higher military spending, while the promise for peace that is so integral to socialism remains suspended within the politics of deterrence. Real existing socialism, Bahro asserts, lacks a relevant political theory for today's workers. The official orthodox theory, based on the writings of Engels and Lenin, is perceived as obsolete. This theoretical deficit causes practical problems both at home (e.g. legitimizing Party domination) and abroad (e.g. legitimizing Marxism-Leninism to the hungry and powerless masses in the third world). International communism thus finds itself in a state of crisis because its center, the "quasi-theocratic" Soviet state, has become ideologically bankrupt.

> The monopolistic power that the [Soviet] state holds over the production apparatus, over the reproductive process, over distribution and over consumption has led to a mechanism that has a propensity to kill or privatize all subjective initiatives. The obsolete political organization of the new society, which cuts deeply into the economic process, puts an immediate end to emancipatory social forces" (*The Alternative*, p. 10).

In part three, "A Strategy for a Communist Alternative," Bahro stipulates that the formation of an international federation of Communists is the necessary precondition for the concrete realization of the alternative. This alternative, which is already incubating in real existing socialism as well as in the industrially developed countries, involves an all-encompassing cultural revolution based on the radical transformation of the division of labor and above all on a redefinition of needs. The alternative is a "new direction" society must follow and requires that families be defunctionalized and the opposition between "labor time" and "leisure time" overcome. Ultimately, Bahro sees the alternative realized in a society that consists of a free "association of communes."

With Rosa Luxemburg's dictum "Freedom for the dissenter" as his motto, Bahro seeks both a coming together of "green" and "red" political forces and an alliance between them and all other groups that seek social change. Although a committed socialist, Bahro nevertheless argues that the working class can no longer (indeed Bahro questions if it every really could) achieve human emancipation for all. Bahro's plea is for a broad mass coalition comprised of the Greens, the women's movement, the ecological movement, and all progressive but nonviolent social groups. Human survival, according to Bahro, depends on our ending monopoly capitalism and the structural violence generated by patriarchy. To attain these sweeping social changes progressive forces must motivate precisely those sections of the population that are predisposed to authoritarian-type solutions in times of crisis, to change their living habits and overcome their compulsive consumerism. Bahro, therefore, not only echoes Herbert Marcuse's* Great Refusal but also calls for a change of personal and social priorities that will eliminate the false needs that now inhibit authentic social change.

Bahro has been an instrumental force at the many socialist conferences that have been taking place in the Federal Republic of Germany since 1980. One point he often argues is that the subjective forces of production are becoming more and more intellectualized, that is, increasingly self-conscious of its problematic position in capitalism. Whereas orthodoxy views the aggravation of the antagonistic relations of distribution as the causal factor of the current world economic crisis, Bahro sees a continually contracting supply of resources artificially limiting consumption in capitalist society, generating confusion, frustration, and—potentially—discontent among middle-income workers and intellectuals. Their unfulfilled needs, according to Bahro, are dictated by the market, not by the appropriation of unpaid labor and the laws that govern production. Hence the call to change priorities aims at redirecting modern aspirations into progressive channels, offering socialism as the true fulfillment of modern life. Bahro's more orthodox Marxist critics emphasize, instead, the economic contradictions of capitalism, that is, its rising unemployment and declining wages. The availability of adequate food, shelter, and health care is in jeopardy for more than 7 million unemployed workers in the countries of the European Common Market. These needs, they argue, can hardly be deemed "false." Bahro's middle-class intellectual audience, according to his radical critics, is comprised largely of people who are not immediately at the point of production.

Since the inception of the recent European peace movement, Bahro has repeatedly called for the political integration of the Eastern and Western European blocs into a new European community of nations. In his own eloquent words:

> The fracture of Europe along the frontier between the blocs is no longer historically productive. On the contrary, the two systems—both in their different ways non-socialist—mutually obstruct each other's chances of internal development. Because they have the same industrial foundations, and ultimately face the same—i.e., ecological—challenge, they should both aim to evolve toward an identical goal. Ecological humanism and democratic socialism provides its governing coordinates.
> ("The Russians Aren't Coming," p. 128)

BIBLIOGRAPHY:

A. *The Alternative in Eastern Europe* (London: New Left Books, 1978); "The Russians Aren't Coming," in *Dynamics of European Nuclear Disarmament* (Nottingham: Spokesman, 1981); "A New Approach for the Peace Movement in Germany," in *Exterminism and Cold War* (London: New Left Books, 1982).

TINEKE RITMEESTER

BANFI, ANTONIO (1866–1957). Born in Vimercate, Milan, on 30 September 1866, Banfi received a baccalaureate under the neo-Kantian Pietro Martirietti at the University of Milan in 1905. He later studied in Germany, where he encountered the thought of Riehl, Larson, Spranger, and particularly Simmel. An enthusiastic follower of Simmel's philosophy, Banfi introduced his works into Italy. Banfi also studied the neo-Kantianism of the Marburg School, Husserl, and Scheler. After his return to Italy he taught first in the *"liceo"* and afterward at the University of Milan. In 1925 Banfi signed Croce's antifascist manifesto. In 1932 he became professor of the history of philosophy at the University of Milan, and in 1941, having come into contact with the clandestine center of the Italian Communist Party (PCI), he actively participated in the struggle for national liberation. His home became a coordinating center for Italian radicals and a refuge for militants and those who were politically persecuted. In 1943, jointly with Eugenio Curiel, he established the Youth Front for National Independence and Freedom, an educational and organizational youth center for the struggle against fascism and Nazism. After the liberation he established in Milan a Center for Culture (Casa della Cultura). Continuing his political militancy as a member of the PCI, Banfi was elected senator in the postwar government. From 1940 to 1949 he directed the *Giornale di studi filosofici*, surrounded by a group of faithful students. In his last years he turned toward the history of Chinese civilization and modern Chinese Marxism, leaving studies on these subjects that were published posthumously in 1971. Banfi died in Milan on 22 July 1957.

From its beginning, Banfi's philosophical search focused on the theme of the crisis of civilization. The main stimulus was provided by Banfi's contact with European philosophy from Nietzsche to Husserl, and from Spengler to Tillich. Banfi saw the need for a synthesis that would avoid dogmaticism and remain open and problematic. Such a synthesis must include both the real life-world as well as the "irrational," i.e., those unsystematic, nonrational factors that manifest themselves as an essential part of reality. The perspective that emerges was one of critical rationalism. Following Kant, Banfi became more attentive to the conditions of "possibility and thinkability" than to the precise structure of reason. Knowledge and meaning, for Banfi, were generated by a process based on the confrontation of existing forms of rationality.

On the philosophical plane, the rational perspective is expressed in humanism and in a concrete ethics. Banfi saw in these factors an avenue of crisis resolution: historical humanism as a construction enlightened by reason. On such a ground there is a meeting of critical rationalism and Marxism. Banfi's theory of Marxism† was therefore on the one hand a humanist ethics and a social praxis and on the other an active political militancy. It was not conceived as a general and comprehensive world vision or a totalitarian philosophy. Furthermore, it was this particular perspective on Marxism that caused Banfi to be considered by many a non-Marxist, in spite of his militancy. At one point the PCI threatened to close down *Philosophical Studies*, which was perceived as nonorthodox and eclectic. Through this conception of Marxism as a concrete historical ethics that simultaneously affirms the universal human purpose of the working class Banfi felt he had updated and completed the image of the true modern "Copernican man."

By counterposing to a closed and dogmatic metaphysics an open and constructive morality that generates a process of human liberation, Banfi eventually shifted his attention to the cultural sphere. During his frequent travels to China he encountered Chinese civilization and Marxism, in which he saw the dimensions of a humanism not religious but ethical, not idealistic but naturalist, not individualistic but social.

BIBLIOGRAPHY:

A. *L'uomo copernicano* (Milan: Mondadori, 1950); *La ricerca della realtà* (Florence: Sansoni, 1959); *Europa e Cina* (Florence: La Nuova Italia, 1971); *Bibliografia Banfiana*, ed. Roselina Salemi (Parma: Pratiche Editrice, 1982).

B. Fulvio Papi, *Il pensiero di Antonio Banfi* (Florence: Parenti, 1961); Evandro Botto, *Il neo-marxismo* (Rome: Studium, 1976), pp. 178–94.

VITTORIO DINI

BARAKA, IMAMU AMIRI (JONES, LEROI) (b. 1934). Born Everett LeRoi Jones in Newark, New Jersey, on 7 October 1934, Amiri Baraka is a poet, dramatist, essayist, novelist, critic, and cultural revolutionary; he is the author of hundreds of literary works that carry an unambiguously political message. He is best known as an architect of militant black nationalism, although he has turned increasingly toward Marxism† in recent years. He graduated from Howard University with a baccalaureate in English in 1954. During the 1950s and 1960s, LeRoi Jones developed a growing reputation as a poet, editor, and social critic. From 1961 to 1967 he accepted several visiting teaching appointments at universities throughout the country, including the New School for Social Research, the University of Buffalo, Columbia University, and San Francisco State University. Throughout this period he maintained a close tie with the beat movement; he founded the Totem Press and the magazine *Yugen* in 1958 and published two volumes of poetry by 1964. His conventional literary achievements were marked by such emblems of success as Whitney and Guggenheim fellowships and an Obie Award for the best American play. Jones visited Cuba in 1960 in support of Fidel Castro† and was subsequently arrested. Becoming frustrated with the white American legal, economic, and cultural structure, Jones turned his artistic attention increasingly to political and racial issues and especially to expressing his disgust for white values. He also began to employ drama as his medium of expression; in 1964 four of his plays were produced within a few months of each other: *The Baptism*, *The Toilet*, *Dutchman*, and *The Slave*. After a brief attempt to establish a black arts theater school in Harlem (which was closed because of political pressure), Jones returned to his native Newark and devoted himself to militant black nationalism and to avowedly communal and political art. In Newark he founded the Spirit House and the Spirit House Movers theatrical company. By 1967 Jones had offended much of the literary establishment, which had begun to assimilate him only a few years before; his preference for savagery, murder, raw language, and destruction of white by black and his refusal of logic created a new audience for his work. In July 1967 Jones was arrested for possession of firearms during the riots, or insurrection, of Newark. Having denied the charges, Jones underwent a trial marked by its overt political and racial character. He was convicted more for having written poetry (especially a poem titled ''Black People!'' published in the December 1967 *Evergreen Review*) than for possessing firearms; his sentence was far more stringent than those of others convicted of similar formal charges. In 1968 Jones became involved in the formation of the Black Community Development program. In a total break with white cultural traditions he became a minister of the Muslim Kawaida faith and took the name Imamu Amiri Baraka.

Although he speaks in all genres, Baraka's increasingly polemical, revolutionary writing has found its most evocative voice in drama. He has said,

> The Revolutionary Theatre should force change. . . . And what we show must cause the blood to rush, so that pre-revolutionary temperaments will be bathed in this blood, and it will cause their deepest souls to move. . . . We will scream and cry, murder, run through the streets in agony, if it means some soul will be moved, moved to actual life understanding of what the world is, and what it ought to be. (''The Revolutionary Theatre,'' in *Home: Social Essays*, pp. 210–15)

With an aesthetic based seemingly on chaos, juxtaposition, and chance, Baraka has created a theater that defies traditional analysis and classification. In making a revolutionary theater, he has sought an art that he sees as ''mystical sociology and abstract politics.'' Since the mid-1970s Baraka has made the transition, in his own terms, to ''Marxism, Leninism,† Mao Zedong† thought, scientific socialism.'' It remains to be seen precisely how Marxism will inform his aesthetic, move his vision of the future beyond a black nationalist utopia, and lead to a literature that will change the social structure he has denied. Thus far, his own adaptation of Marxism has remained largely personal.

BIBLIOGRAPHY:

A. *Home: Social Essays* (New York: Morrow, 1966); *The Motion of History and Other Plays* (New York: Morrow, 1978); *Selected Poetry of Amiri Baraka–LeRoi Jones* (New York: Morrow, 1979); *The Autobiography of LeRoi Jones* (New York: Freundlich, 1983).

WILLIAM PLATER

BARTHES, ROLAND (1915–1980). Roland Barthes was born in Cherbourg, France, in 1915. He received his baccalaureate in philosophy in 1933–1934.

Between 1935 and 1939 he studied classics at the Sorbonne, teaching then, and during the Occupation, at various *lycées*. After the war he taught in Bucharest and Alexandria. Concerning himself with sociology and lexicology, he worked at the Centre National de la Recherche Scientifique (CNRS), and in 1960 he joined the Ecole Practique des Hautes Etudes. During this time he became involved in the *Arguments** group of dissident Marxist academics, while publishing critical articles in popular journals and newspapers. In 1962 he was appointed director of studies of the Ecole Practique, joined the editorial board of *tel quel*, and helped to found the journal *Théâtre populaire*. In 1975 he became a professor of literature and semiotics at the Collège de France, where he taught until his death in 1980.

It is to his early work that we must turn to examine Barthes's contributions to the development of neo-Marxism. In his first published book, *Writing Degree Zero* (1953), which grew from articles published in the journal *Combat* (1947), literature and literary criticism are presented as a form of political action. In this study he is still working within the language and the presuppositions of Jean-Paul Sartre's* *What Is Literature?* (1947), while going beyond Sartre both in his notion of writing literature as praxis and in his protostructuralist presentation of the nature and role of bourgeois literature. Barthes pursued these themes in a series of essays and fragments during the next ten years, adding to his interest in the politics of writing and criticism a concern with the nature and function of popular culture (see *Mythologies*, 1957, and *Critical Essays*, 1964). Although he became involved in the structuralist movement of the 1960s and added psychoanalytic theory to his literary reflections, the political significance of literary art and popular culture—and their revolutionary potential—were never far from his mind (see *The Eiffel Tower*, 1979).

In his major works of the 1970s, the traditional Marxist† categories and the then familiar structuralist linguistics were replaced by an analytics of desire as it expresses itself in cultural forms and discovers itself there in its moments of rapture—of breaking with Law, and seeking to be Other. In this theoretical confluence, such diverse phenomena as the May 1968 upheavals, sexual orgasm, and artistic and scientific innovation are all united as manifestations of the revolutionary force of that Desire. Barthes never formalized or systematized this theory and seemed to confine himself to testing "methods" of writing and criticism that he believed could be drawn from it. However, he remained fascinated with the specificity of experiences and art works, even speaking about writing a novel shortly before his untimely death. This focus on particularity and concretion was something Roland Barthes shared with Gaston Bachelard,* Michel Foucault,* and Georges Canguilhem,* on the one hand; and on the other, with an entire generation of existentialists. Among Barthes's most important contributions to neo-Marxism is this refusal to gloss over particularity. Such glosses, as we now realize, are one of the most characteristic features of dogmatisms of every stripe.

BIBLIOGRAPHY:
A. *Critical Essays* (Evanston: Northwestern University Press, 1972); *Mythologies* (New York: Hill & Wang, 1972); *Elements of Semiology* (New York: Hill & Wang, 1977); *Writing Degree Zero* (New York: Hill & Wang, 1977); *The Eiffel Tower* (New York: Hill & Wang, 1979).

B. Miriam Glucksmann, *Structuralist Analysis in Contemporary Social Thought* (London: Routledge & Kegan Paul, 1974); Rosalind Coward and John Ellis, *Language and Materialism* (London: Routledge & Kegan Paul, 1977); John Sturrock (ed.), *Structuralism and Since* (New York: Oxford University Press, 1979).

LAURENCE E. WINTERS

BASSO, LELIO (1903–1978). Lelio Basso was born in Varazze (Savona) on 25 December 1903, and died 16 December, 1978. He came to socialism on the Italian wave of enthusiasm for the Russian Revolution which generated the social upheavals of 1919. He was also influenced by the political theory of U. G. Mondolfo and then of Rodolfo Mondolfo,* which defended the humanistic character of socialism and of Marxism.† Even in those early years, the years of the arrival of fascism, Basso did not accept reformist and legalistic positions. He carried out organizational and intellectual activities opposing fascism, and in 1928 he was arrested and interned for three years. Arrested again in July 1939 and in March 1940, he succeeded in renewing his ties to underground socialist groups, and in 1943 he formed the Movimento di Unità Proletaria (Movement of Proletarian Unity), which was to become one of the constituents of the Partito Socialista di Unità Proletaria (PSIUP), founded the day after liberation from fascism. He participated in the debate on and the drafting of the Constitution of the Republic. He opposed both the reformist position of Nenni and the hegemony of the Communist Party. At the beginning of the Center-Left government (1964) he helped to reestablish the PSIUP, together with the left of the Socialist Party, which did not accept a coalition with the Christian Democratic Party. He was elected deputy continuously until 1972, when he was elected senator. In 1958 he founded the review *Problemi del socialismo*, which he directed until his death. He founded the Lelio and Lisli Basso-Issoco Foundation, which operates out of Rome. He was a member and spokesman for the International Bertrand Russell Tribunal for American crimes in Vietnam and president of the Second Russell Tribunal on repression in Latin America.

The thought of Lelio Basso can be characterized as a rereading and reformulation of the Marxist concept of transition to socialism, and as original research on the connection between socialism and democracy in advanced capitalistic societies. Inspired by his and others' rigorous research on the concrete historical experiences of revolutionary processes (from the Great Revolution of 1789 to the Commune of Paris, the Russian Revolution of 1917 and the council experiments) and above all by theoretical reflections not only of Marx but of Rosa Luxemburg,† Basso advocated the necessity of a revolutionary break with every hypothesis and process that is reformist and involves compromise.

"The problem in essence," says Basso in an article from 1958, is to conceive of the conquest of power by one class not as an instantaneous fact which happens overnight, but as a process which develops over time. . . . If we imagine it to be an instantaneous event, then it is difficult to admit that it can take place in a peaceful way, because a class which still holds all the power cannot be induced to renounce it all of a sudden without offering resistance. But if we conceive of the conquest of power as a process of continuous development . . . then it is possible to imagine that the rising class can conquer an ever-growing portion of power in a peaceful manner, without it being necessary for each new conquest to rely on a recourse to violence. This has happened, we have seen, through the bourgeoisie in some countries, and could also happen through the proletariat. ("Marxismo e democrazia," republished in *Problemi del socialismo*, 19, 4th series [January–March 1978], p. 25)

The necessary reforms from a socialist perspective are structural reforms, which are not compatible with capitalistic development, even in the more advanced phase of neocapitalism. Basso believed that an expanded mass democracy would overcome the abstract formalism of bourgeois democracy as well as avoid the reduction of the theories of revolution and of socialism to the totalitarian theory of the party that is peculiar to Stalinism. Law itself, for Basso, must be directed toward the institutionalization of socialism. Basso's own contribution to the development of the Republican Constitution is directed at this objective, in particular Article 3, Section 2: "It is the task of the Republic to remove the obstacles of economic and social order which, by in fact limiting the liberty and equality of the citizens, impede the full development of the human personality and the effective participation by all workers in the political, economic, and social organization of the country."

BIBLIOGRAPHY:

A. *Il principe senza scettro* (Milan: Feltrinelli, 1951); *Neocapitalismo e sinistra europea* (Bari: Laterza, 1969); "Introduction" to Rosa Luxemburg, *Scritti politici* (Rome: Riuniti, 1970); *Scritti sul cristianesimo* (Turin: Marietta, 1983).

B. Stefano Merli, *La "scelta socialista" di Lelio Basso* (Padua: Marsilio, 1981).

VITTORIO DINI

BAUER, OTTO (1881–1938). Otto Bauer was born in Vienna on 5 September 1881 and died in Paris on 4 July 1938. The son of a wealthy Jewish textile manufacturer, he studied law at the University of Vienna, earning a doctorate in 1906. Even before he finished his studies he began publishing articles on Marxist† theory in the leading German socialist journal of the day, *Die Neue Zeit*. In 1907 he was appointed secretary of the Social Democratic delegation in the Austrian Reichsrat. In the same year he became a founding editor of the Austrian socialist theoretical journal *Der Kampf*. Mobilized in 1914, he was captured by Russian forces in November and spent much of the war in a camp in Siberia. Freed after the February Revolution, he traveled for a time in Russia before returning to Vienna in September 1917. After the fall of the Hapsburg monarchy, Bauer served as foreign secretary of the Austrian Republic from November 1918 until July 1919, when he resigned as a result of the failure of efforts to unite Austria with Germany. He was elected to the Constituent Assembly in 1919 and served during the period 1920–34 in the Austrian parliament as the most prominent spokesman of the Social Democratic delegation. Forced to flee into exile in Czechoslovakia during the fighting between Social Democratic parliamentary forces and the government in February 1934, he became a leading figure in the newly established Revolutionary Socialists of Austria, who tried to carry on the struggle from abroad. He left Czechoslovakia in April 1938, after the Nazi seizure of Austria, moving in May to Paris.

Bauer's first major work, *Die Nationalitätenfrage und die Sozialdemokratie*, which he published in 1907, catapulted him into the forefront of Marxist scholarship in Austria. In it he challenged the widely held view that socialism would lead inevitably to the decline of national differences. He considered modern nationalism to be closely tied to the success of capitalism, with its radical improvement in communications and expansion of educational opportunities. The class character of capitalism, however, prevented peasants and workers from participating actively in the dominant national cultures. Only with the coming of socialism would the masses become fully immersed in cultural life and thus have an opportunity to absorb and modify the national character of their own community. The result would be a strengthening and deepening of national differences. Without the distorting impact of class conflict, however, national hatreds would be overcome by a general recognition of the positive contributions to be made by each nation to the cultural wealth of mankind as a whole. It was also in this work that Bauer proposed a number of ideas about imperialism that would later be developed fruitfully by fellow Austro-Marxist* Rudolf Hilferding.† He explained the tendency of the economically advanced states to expand into less developed areas as a product of the natural desire of capitalists to counter cyclical depressions by securing spheres of influence in which profits would be both larger and more stable. Stressing the connection between monopoly capitalism and imperialism, he argued that the emergence of cartels and the revival of protectionism facilitated this process. As a result surplus value was drained out of the less developed areas into the industrialized areas of the world, helping to postpone the impending crisis of capitalism.

Bauer shared the concern of a number of other Austro-Marxists about the place of ethical considerations in Marxist philosophy. Rather than accept the orthodox point of view that ethics should be founded essentially upon utilitarian considerations, he argued in a number of his early works that Marxists could profitably combine Kantian philosophy with Marxist science. Kant's categorical imperative provided, according to Bauer, a universal principle that was fully compatible with the goals of socialism. Far from tending to obscure class differences, Bauer maintained, Kantian ethics demonstrated that the objectives of the proletariat not only were destined by the scientifically ascertainable forces of history to be realized but also were morally superior to those of any other class. In the course of his effort to provide a theoretical rationale for the role played by the Austrian Social Democrats after the fall of the Hapsburg monarchy,

Bauer argued that when an "equilibrium of class forces" develops the state can at least temporarily lose its oppressive character and achieve a certain degree of autonomy as an institution. Under such circumstances it is permissible for Marxist parties to join coalitions with bourgeois parties and become directly involved in governmental activities. In the long run, however, a social revolution would be both necessary and inevitable. He was hopeful that this could be achieved by peaceful means, but he believed that at some point the bourgeoisie might well resort to violence, and he insisted that at such a moment socialists must be prepared to establish a proletarian dictatorship and meet force with force. This concept of defensive revolutionary violence was incorporated in the Austrian party's Linz Program of 1926.

Although Bauer at first endorsed the view of many Western Marxists that the Bolsheviks' attempt to impose socialism upon a socially and economically backward society would lead necessarily to the despotism of a minority, by the 1930s he had concluded that the modernizing impact of the five-year plans was inherently progressive and that the Soviet regime would eventually evolve in the direction of political as well as social democracy.

BIBLIOGRAPHY:

A. *Die Nationalitätenfrage und die Sozialdemokratie* (Vienna: Brand, 1907); *Der Weg zum Sozialismus* (Vienna: Brand, 1919); *Die österreichische Revolution* (Vienna: Wiener Volksbuchhandlung, 1923), abridged English translation, *The Austrian Revolution* (New York: Burt Franklin, 1970); *Kapitalismus und Sozialismus nach dem Weltkrieg* (Vienna: Wiener Volksbuchhandlung, 1931); *Zwischen zwei Weltkriegen? Die Krise der Weltwirtschaft, der Demokratie und des Sozialismus* (Bratislava: Prager, 1936); *Werkausgabe* (Vienna: Europa, 1975–79).

B. Norbert Leser, *Zwischen Reformismus und Bolschewismus. Der Austromarxismus als Theorie und Praxis* (Vienna: Europa, 1968); Otto Leichter, *Otto Bauer: Tragödie oder Triumph?* (Vienna: Europa, 1970).

KENNETH CALKINS

BAX, ERNEST BELFORT (1854–1926). Philosopher, historian, and essayist, Bax was an early member of the pioneering Marxist† organization in Great Britain, the Social Democratic Federation, founded by Henry M. Hyndman.† In 1885 he joined William Morris* in the schismatic Socialist League and for a time worked closely with Morris in propaganda activity. When the League took an anarchist turn, Bax rejoined the Federation and henceforth remained loyal to Hyndman and his attempt to apply Marxist ideas to British developments.

Bax's Marxism was highly idiosyncratic. He blended the ideas of Marx with late Victorian ethical and religious concerns and attempted, in the tradition of nineteenth-century German philosophical speculation, to construct a new metaphysical framework. Bax denied Marx's claim that fundamental philosophical questions had been superseded by the dialectical understanding of history. His Marxist philosophy, developed in a series of essays and books between 1880 and 1910, was grounded in the notion of the "alogical." Viewed as an elemental force, presupposed by consciousness and the phenomenal world, the "alogical" enabled Bax to explain the moral experiences that, he believed, were neglected by contemporary Marxists. He defended his position through correspondence and a public polemic with Karl Kautsky† and in private conversations with his friend, Friedrich Engels.†

Apart from his philosophy, which seemed to one colleague the "fag end of a pre-socialist way of thinking," Bax contributed to Marxist historiography and social criticism. His three studies of Germany during the Reformation remain valuable. But his fierce attacks on Victorian institutions and mores, written for the socialist press, were often little more than mechanical applications of his Marxist beliefs. Bax's strong hostility to contemporary efforts toward the emancipation of women also limited his effectiveness as a socialist speaker and writer.

BIBLIOGRAPHY:

A. *The Religion of Socialism* (London: Sonnenschein, 1885); *The Ethics of Socialism* (London: Sonnenschein, 1887); *The Problem of Reality* (London: Sonnenschein, 1892).

B. Stanley Pierson, "Ernest Belfort Bax: 1854–1926: The Encounter of Marxism and Late Victorian Culture," *Journal of British Studies*, 12, no. 1 (November 1972), pp. 39–60.

STANLEY PIERSON

BENJAMIN, WALTER (1892–1940). Walter Benjamin was born in Berlin in 1892 and received his earliest education there in the Friedrich Wilhelm Gymnasium and in the Thuringian Landerziehungsheim in Haubinda. It was in the latter that he first encountered the educational principles of Gustav Wyneken. Benjamin was apparently attracted to the antiauthoritarian aspect of these ideas, but later broke with Wyneken when the latter urged his followers to join the war effort. In 1912 Benjamin enrolled as a philosophy student in Freiberg and made his first trip to Paris, important for his later work as an interpreter of French culture. In Freiberg and later back in Berlin, Benjamin moved in a circle that included people interested in such diverse topics as educational liberation, Zionism, literature, philosophy, and leftist politics. Leaving Berlin, his informal studies continued in Munich, and his formal ones in Bern. In Munich he pursued the study of language, partly under the influence of Martin Buber, and at Bern he wrote his doctoral dissertation on Romantic art criticism. Already by 1919 he had also met and been influenced by Ernst Bloch.* Before finishing what was to have been his *Habilitationschrift* on the origin of German tragic drama, which was finally published in 1928, Benjamin worked on his essay on ethics ("Fate and Character"), Goethe, and political violence. In the 1930s Benjamin traveled extensively, partly a condition of his exile from Germany, and worked as a literary journalist and literary critic first in the Weimar Republic and later in Paris. It was during this time that he also became associated with the Frankfurt School, although his connection to it was never as formal as the other leading members. Most of his later writings centered on his *Das Passagen-Werk*, his study of modernity, and reflected his increasing commitment to Marxism and antifascist activity. His suicide in 1940, while trying to get into Spain and away from the Nazi invasion of Paris, occurred in the context of ill health and the refusal of Spanish guards to let him enter Spain.

Even though Benjamin wrote a number of important works before he became a Marxist,† it is doubtless true that most of his writing has great relevance for Marxist thought, since the original part of his Marxist work draws so heavily upon his earlier work. Like Herbert Marcuse,* Lucien Goldmann,* George Lukács,* and Theodore Adorno,* other German-speaking aestheticians who became Marxists in the period between the wars, Walter Benjamin approached Marxism using the categories of nineteenth- and twentieth-century German philosophy, his understanding of twentieth-century art and culture, for example, surrealism and expressionism, and his own direct experience of capitalism and fascism. In the aesthetic, antiquarian, and religious concerns of the young Benjamin can be seen traces of his later emphasis on history, human action, and liberation, even though these early writings differ from overly reductive forms of Marxism in their stress on the aesthetic and the realm of experience. Thus in Benjamin's doctoral dissertation his description of how the German romantics elevated the aesthetic over all other forms of experience is counterbalanced by his realization that this aesthetics ran parallel in many ways to Fichte's philosophy, where action, not art, occupies center stage. Again in *The Origin of German Tragic Drama*, Benjamin was clearly aware of the tradition in German art criticism, beginning with Worringer, that interpreted baroque drama as an early version of the expressionists' depiction of the alienation of contemporary life. Finally, in Benjamin's early writings on language and Jewish mysticism, it is clear that he is concerned with the same themes of ethics and emancipation that are expressed later in his Marxist *Theses on the Philosophy of History*. This does not mean, of course, that there exists a perfect unity in all of Benjamin's work. Doubtless Jürgen Habermas's* comment that Benjamin sometimes did not even introduce his friends to each other, thus keeping the different aspects of his thought compartmentalized, is important to keep in mind.

Benjamin sought to become Germany' greatest literary critic. He insisted during his last fifteen years that his goal as a literary critic was to write a study of modernity using the Parisian arcades as the primary symbol (*Das Passagen-Werk*). The editor of the scrupulous edition of *Das Passagen-Werk* that finally appeared has argued that its notes and fragments must also be understood in the light of the finished pieces, published or unpublished, that surfaced before *Das Passagen-Werk* was finally published: the studies of Baudelaire; "The Work of Art in the Age of Mechanical Reproduction"; and the "Theses on the Philosophy of History." His early writings on Marcel Proust, Franz Kafka, and Bertolt Brecht† probably should also be included.

The striking thing about Benjamin's project is that he was usually analyzing and defending authors who did not have an immediate connection with historical reality. Thus the centerpiece of Benjamin's study of modernity was to be Baudelaire, not a twentieth-century avant-garde writer at all, but one who, certainly on conventional interpretations, did not directly confront historical reality. Benjamin asked why it was so difficult to connect many of the greatest modern authors to historical reality and answered that modern experience is essentially fragmented. Fetishism, a state of consciousness in which we do not see the whole for the parts, was described by Marx in the nineteenth century as characteristic of economic human beings. In *Passagen-Werk* Benjamin sees it as characteristic of the ordinary everyday experience of modern human beings. Baudelaire's poetry is interpreted as an indirect description of the fragmented reality.

Benjamin describes the Paris World's Fair as a microcosm of the entire world of commodities. One would think that to exhibit all these commodities together would end their fragmentation, but this is not the case. Fragmentation is exacerbated because world's fairs emphasized the individualistic acts of buying and selling rather than the more social act of meeting human needs. Starting from the general standpoint of capitalist fetishism, Benjamin analyzed its exacerbation in nineteenth-century culture. Benjamin's standpoint is closer to Marx's than is sometimes assumed. For Marx's theory of fetishism postulated modern society as an organic whole that nevertheless was bound up with increasingly fragmented individuals. Benjamin's analysis of fetishism is a concretization of this idea. However, Benjamin had a greater sensitivity to the actual growth of fragmentation in modernity. He suggests that in modern society human beings are estranged from their own experience. For Benjamin, experience is a holistic concept that integrates past and present and in this sense is obliterated by the fragmented world of the market, a world that worships the particularity of things and ignores the temporal whole. Experience is similarly destroyed by the atomization generated by such noneconomic phenomena as crowds, urban life styles, and bureaucratization. Since fragmentation destroys the integral nature of human experience, Benjamin argues that great modern authors such as Proust and Baudelaire attempt to restore that integrity.

Although not all will agree that Benjamin's oeuvre is unified and consistent, most readers of Benjamin would, I think, recognize that his greatest contribution was to take literary images that seemed isolated and fragmented and show their relation to the history of the modern world. Both Benjamin's conception of the task and his execution of it have helped set new standards for Marxist criticism.

BIBLIOGRAPHY:

A. *Illuminations* (New York: Schocken, 1969); *Charles Baudelaire: A Lyric Poet in the Era of High Capitalism* (London: New Left Books, 1973); *The Origin of German Tragic Drama* (London: New Left Books, 1977); *Reflections* (New York: Harcourt Brace Jovanovich, 1979); *Das Passagen-Werk*, in *Gesammelte Schriften* (Frankfurt: Suhrkampf, 1982).

B. Susan Buck-Morss, *The Origin of Negative Dialectic* (New York: Seabury, 1977); Jürgen Habermas, "Consciousness Raising or Redemptive Criticism," *New German Critique*, 17 (Spring 1979), special Walter Benjamin issue; Werner Fuld, *Walter Benjamin Zwichen den Stuhlen: Ein Biographie* (Munich: Hanser, 1979).

NORMAN FISCHER

BERGER, JOHN (b. 1926). Born in London in 1926, Berger was trained as a painter at the Central and Chelsea schools of art. He worked as a painting and drawing teacher and exhibited at important London galleries. During the early 1950s he helped organize the Communist Party–influenced Artists for Peace exhibitions. He wrote art criticism for the left Labour Party paper *Tribune* and for ten years, starting in 1951, for the *New Statesman*. His critical essays appeared also in the *Daily Worker*, the *Observer*, and other British newspapers, and in the American Communist magazine *Mainstream* in 1958 and 1959. As these dates demonstrate, Berger stayed close to the Communist Party (CP) at a time when the many artists and intellectuals who had earlier been attracted to the Party and its associated organizations (such as the Artists International Association) had left following the British Party's refusal to condemn the Soviet invasion of Hungary. He published art books in East Germany on the Communist artists Guttuso and Leger, in 1957 and 1966, respectively. At the same time he was never a strict party-liner, and was an early supporter of the post-1956 new left. In 1968 he attacked the Soviet invasion of Czechoslovakia and since then has moved steadily away from orthodox left politics, while remaining a Marxist† and a revolutionary in his writing on art and his political orientation generally.

With the rapid decline of the previously significant influence of the British CP on artists, at a time when the continuing cold war had put an end to any public leftism among the denizens of the American art world, John Berger emerged and remained almost alone as a Marxist writer on art working outside the confines of Party hackdom, and with a large British and then international readership. This alone would make his career of great importance; although he is no longer a working critic and has never been an art historian, he is certainly the spiritual father, or uncle at least, of today's flourishing crop of Marxist art writers and historians. (His own work was influenced by three Marxist historians, German and Austrian emigrés to Britain Arnold Hauser, Francis Klingender, and especially Frederick Antal.) Berger's earliest work, represented by the collection *Permanent Red*, focused on the work of individual artists, primarily of our time, with an eye to the social influences on and meaning of their work. The basic question guiding his criticism was, Berger said in the Introduction to this book, "Does this work help or encourage men to know and claim their social rights?" By this he meant not that art should be propaganda but that expanding our capacity for visual experience "increases our awareness of our own potentiality." Good art is revolutionary in that it draws our attention to the limits set by today's society to our various potentialities; thus "Goya's way of looking at a massacre amounts to the contention that we ought to be able to do without massacres."

An important theme of Berger's criticism was what he called "the difficulty of being an artist," not just financially but also in terms of satisfying creativity, which Berger ascribed to the lack of a sense of hope in a decadent society in which the only source of regeneration, an active socialist movement, is lacking. This theme is pursued most completely in the book, *Success and Failure of Picasso* (1965), which was Berger's first real publishing success. Four years later Berger published a sort of Eastern bloc counterpart, *Art and Revolution*, a study of the Russian dissident artist Ernst Neizvestny, in which the qualities the critic finds in Neizvestny's work are explained as a response to "the contradiction between the original spirit of the October Revolution and the grave compromises imposed by Stalin" (p. 72).

In 1972 Berger reached a wide audience with the television series *Ways of Seeing*, the basis for a widely read book. In this effort, which functioned more or less as a Marxist response to Sir Kenneth Clark's wholly conventional art historical series *Civilization*, Berger used images and (relatively few) words to explore the function of art in present-day capitalism, both in the form of museum exhibitions and in its avatar of advertising imagery, and to propose an understanding of the central place of oil painting in art history from the Renaissance on as referring to the experience of the possession of commodities. The first essay in *Ways of Seeing* stresses the ways in which photography and motion pictures have altered our experience of painting. In Berger's view modern means for the mass reproduction of images bears the potential for "a new kind of power" over the use and exploration of personal and social experience—a potential blocked today by the artificially maintained cult of art, whose real root is the vast money-value of art works. Since the early 1970s, Berger himself has moved steadily away from his earlier focus on painting. At the same time his work has increasingly taken the form of autonomous creation, rather than that of criticism. He has published novels, poetry, and literary translations and has collaborated with the photographer Jean Mohr on books exploring such varied themes as a doctor's life, immigrant workers, and the nature of photography. He wrote the screenplays for three films by the Swiss director Alain Tanner: *The Center of the World*, *The Salamander*, and *Jonah Who Will be Twenty-five in the Year 2000*. His current writing centers on the experience of peasants in the Haute Savoie community in which Berger has been living for some time and the destruction of their form of life by capitalist development. Despite the difference in the material studied, the theme is essentially the same as in Berger's earlier writing about art: the necessity of appropriating the achievements of the past, whether embodied in painting or in peasant culture, as a part of a general appropriation of the power to shape and transform personal and social life itself.

BIBLIOGRAPHY:

A. *A Painter of Our Time* (novel) (London: Secker& Warburg, 1958); new ed., (London: Writers and Readers, 1976); *Permanent Red* (London: Methuen, 1960); *Corker's Freedom* (novel) (London: 1964); *Success and Failure of Picasso* (Harmondsworth: Penguin, 1965); with Jean Mohr, *A Fortunate Man: The Story of a Country Doctor* (New York: Holt, 1967); *Art and Revolution* (New York: Pantheon, 1969); *G* (novel) (New York: Viking, 1972); *Ways of Seeing* (Harmondsworth: Penguin, 1972); *The Look of Things* (New York: Viking, 1974); with Jean Mohr, *A Seventh Man* (New York: Viking, 1975); *Pig Earth* (New York: Pantheon, 1979); with Jean Mohr, *Another Way of Telling* (New York: Pantheon, 1982).

PAUL MATTICK, JR.

BERKMAN, ALEXANDER (1870–1936). Berkman was born in 1870, in Vilner, Russia, to middle-class parents. In 1888 he emigrated to the United States, where he met his lifelong companion, Emma Goldman.* After he failed in an assassination attempt during the 1892 Homestead Steel Strike, Berkman was sentenced to prison. It was while in prison that Berkman read and studied philosophy, and became an anarcho-communist. In 1905, Berkman was released and became the editor of Goldman's *Mother Earth*, and from 1916 to 1917 he wrote and edited his own anarchist paper, *The Blast*. After being arrested for protesting against military conscription, Berkman was deported to Russia in 1919. By 1920, he had disavowed the Bolsheviks and the revolution in Russia, arguing that the Bolsheviks were a new tyranny ruling in the name of the people. Berkman went to France, where in 1929 he wrote *The ABC's of Anarcho-Communism*. Alexander Berkman committed suicide in 1936.

Berkman believed that Marx's† working-class revolution was merely a necessary prelude to anarchism. He accepted Marx's critique of capitalism. Humanity was indeed being exploited and enslaved by capitalism, with the permission and support of liberal democratic government and laws. Whereas capitalism stands for violence and disorder, anarchism means freedom, liberty, and harmony. Workers must withdraw their support from capitalist governments in order to abolish evil. Berkman argued that working-class power needs to be realized and centralized through a true workers' union, which could work toward abolishing capitalism. Anarchism, in Berkman's opinion, is in full agreement with Marxism (*ABC's of Anarcho-Communism*, p. 110). Both theories postulate the inevitable exploitation of workers in capitalism, and both advocate capitalism's abolition. Economic and social equality are the goals of each theory. Berkman believed that socialists participating in government are betraying the workers they claim to represent. These socialists have been politically corrupted, have lost their original radicalism, and are thus unable and unwilling to fight capitalism. In anarchism, humanity can live peacefully, without exploitation and in total freedom. Socialism, on the other hand, creates a potentially powerful government that can easily usurp its limited mandate. Berkman's anarcho-communism presupposes workers voluntarily choosing to live and work in a cooperative union. All exchanges of goods, as Marx anticipated, would be based on need. Anarcho-communism can be achieved only through a working-class revolution that is "merely the boiling point of evolution" (*ABC's of Anarcho-Communism*, p. 226). The purpose of the revolution is to reorganize society, not to destroy it. Berkman perceived the new society as a federation of independent, self-supporting, free communities.

BIBLIOGRAPHY:

A. *The Kronstadt Rebellion* (Berlin: Der Syndikalist, 1922); *The Bolshevik Myth: Diary 1920–1922* (London: Hutchinson, 1925); *Now and After: The ABC's of Anarcho-Communism* (New York: Vanguard Press, 1927); *The Blast* (New York: Greenwood Press, 1968); *Prison Memoirs of an Anarchist* (Pittsburgh: Frontier Press, 1970).

B. Leonard I. Krimerman and Lewis Perry, eds., *Patterns of Anarchy* (New York: Anchor Books, 1966); Henry J. Silverman, ed., *American Radical Thought* (Lexington, Mass.: Heath, 1970).

JOSEPH M. HAZLETT

BERLINGUER, ENRICO (1922–1984). Born in Sassari, Sardinia, in 1922 to a well-to-do landowning family, Enrico Berlinguer joined the Resistance and the Italian Communist Party (PCI) in 1943. After serving as head of the PCI's youth organization from 1950 to 1956, Berlinguer was elected to parliament in 1968. He became secretary-general of the party in March 1972 and served in that capacity until his death. The strategic innovation for which he is best known, the "historic compromise" with the Christian Democratic Party, was first proposed in September 1973. Berlinguer suffered a stroke while delivering a speech in Padua on 7 June 1984 and died four days later.

Berlinguer's leadership of the PCI since 1972 brought an extension and elaboration of the strategic formulations of Antonio Gramsci* and Palmiro Togliatti,* particularly regarding the notion of a "national-popular strategy." What was implicit in Gramsci and explicit in Togliatti was developed by Berlinguer into a fully articulated consensus strategy, designed to attenuate the sociopolitical tensions accompanying major changes in the social order.

In 1973 Berlinguer announced a major shift in the Party's alliance strategy. The Party had long pursued under Togliatti a policy of enlarging the social base of the party to encompass the "middle strata." Now Berlinguer called for an analogous unity of political forces, i.e., an alliance with Italy's other great mass party, the Christian Democrats (DC). He termed the shift the "historic compromise" because it represented an attempt to come to terms with the historical fact that a large body of Italy's popular and working classes have looked to a Catholic party for political representation. By forming an alliance with the DC, the Party would establish a unified bloc of "democratic forces" broad enough to withstand the tensions generated by the coming to power of a Communist Party (after the 1976 election the PCI's support in parliament had become indispensable to Italian governments). Thus, Italy would be spared the kind of lacerating divisions that had split Chile into two opposing socio-economic camps and brought on the military coup.

To induce the Christian Democrats to accept the PCI as a governmental partner, Berlinguer attempted to certify the Party's democratic and Western credentials. He declared that a pluralist, parliamentary democracy was not just the most fertile "terrain" for the advancement of working-class politics but also an end in itself, a universal good transcending capitalism. At the same time, Berlinguer supported Italy's continued membership in NATO; Italy's withdrawal from NATO would only undermine détente and reinstate the logic of opposing power blocs. An attenuation of that logic was seen as a precondition for greater autonomy of each country within the blocs and for an international climate of opinion tolerant of socio-economic innovation. A further distancing from the Soviet Union came in 1981 with Berlinguer's declaration that the forward impetus given to working-class movements worldwide by the 1917 Revolution had been "exhausted"; "stagnation" and "involution" had set in in the East, whereas the motor force for revolutionary socialism had shifted to the Third World and Western Europe. In the most politically advanced countries of Western Europe a creative effort was underway to clear a "third path" to socialism, distinct from Soviet and reformist Social-Democratic models.

After the 1979 elections, the PCI's prospects for entering the government receded greatly. Following the debacle of governmental relief to the victims of the 1980 earthquake, the PCI abandoned calls for a "historic compromise" and insisted on a "democratic alternative" to rule by the DC. While stressing the importance of putting the Christian Democrats into the opposition, Berlinguer justified this shift largely in terms of a need to halt the "degradation" of public power and to "moralize" Italian public administration—i.e., not in terms of a class analysis, but with an eye to formation of a broad democratic consensus.

BIBLIOGRAPHY:

A. "Reflections After the Events in Chile," *Foreign Bulletin of the PCI*, no. 5 (1973), originally in *Rinascita*, no. 38 (1973); *The Italian Communists Speak for Themselves* (Nottingham: Spokesman, 1978), includes translations of most of Berlinguer's important speeches and essays during the phase of the "historic compromise."

B. Vittorio Garresio, *Berlinguer* (Milan: Feltrinelli, 1976); Tomaso Giglio, *Berlinguer o il potere solitario* (Milan: Sperling & Kupper, 1982).

LAWRENCE GARNER

BERNAL, JOHN DESMOND (1901–1971). Born in Nenagh County, Tipperary, Ireland, John Desmond Bernal was an important influence on orthodox Marxism's† attitude toward empirical science. He did significant research in X-ray crystallography, which helped establish the study of molecular biology. Bernal was a professor at Birkbeck College in London and received both the Lenin Prize and the U.S. Medal of Freedom with Palm. He focused his scientific expertise on planning for D-Day during his stint with the Allied Combined Operations organization during World War II. Bernal became a Communist while at Cambridge in the early 1920s and lectured to other scientists on its merits. He was active in the British Association and the Pugwash Conferences, actively promoted trade unionism among natural scientists, and helped found the British Society for Social Responsibility in Science. By the late 1950s and 1960s Bernal's influence had declined as a result of cold war tensions and the growing public awareness of Stalin's atrocities. Bernal died in London on 15 September 1971.

Bernal taught that science expands along with economic development, and hence Marxian social theory will generate not only a just and classless society but one in which science matures and assumes its proper place as a guide to public policy. "Bernalism" was thus based on the assumption that the elimination of capitalist irrationality and exploitation would generate a socialist society run efficiently and effectively by empirical scientific rationality. While Bernal argued that this ideal was being institutionalized by Stalin, his loyalty to the Soviet Union was eventually strained by the Lysenko controversy and the Soviet Union's apparent willingness to sacrifice science at the altar of ideology. Bernal's major accomplishments—despite the influence of his two books in social theory, *The Social Function of Science* (1939) and *Science in History* (1954)—were in his chosen profession of biology. However, he complements the more theoretical efforts of that group of empirically oriented Marxists that includes Max Adler,*

Eduard Bernstein,* Galvano Della Volpe,* Lucio Colletti,* Georges Gurvitch,* and others, all of whom tried philosophically to reconcile dialectics and empirical science.

BIBLIOGRAPHY:

A. *The Social Function of Science* (Cambridge: MIT Press, 1967); *Science in History* (Cambridge: MIT Press, 1969).

B. Maurice Goldsmith and A. L. McKay, *The Science of Science* (New York: Simon & Schuster, 1966); Gary Wersky, *The Visible College* (New York: Holt, Rinehart and Winston, 1978); Maurice Goldsmith, *Sage: A Life of J. D. Bernal* (London: Hutchinson, 1980).

ROBERT A. GORMAN

BERNSTEIN, EDUARD (1850–1932). Born in Berlin on 6 January 1850 into a middle-class Jewish family, Bernstein's formal education was limited. At the age of sixteen he began an apprenticeship in a bank, eventually becoming a bank clerk. In 1872 he joined the Eisenacher socialist group, which in 1875 merged with the Lassallean socialist group to form the German Social Democratic Party. In 1878 he left for Switzerland to escape Bismark's anti-Socialist laws, and there he edited the official party newspaper, *Der Sozialdemokrat*, which was distributed clandestinely in Germany, and studied the works of Karl Marx† and Friedrich Engels.† In 1888 the Swiss government, pressured by Bismarck, closed and banished party offices from Switzerland. Bernstein and *Der Sozialdemokrat* moved to London, where he worked closely with Engels and became acquainted with Fabian socialism. After Engels's death, Bernstein was named executor of his estate and, with Karl Kautsky,† his literary executor. In 1901 Bernstein returned to Germany, where he published articles in *Die Neue Zeit* and, in 1899, completed *Die Voraussetzungen des Sozialismus* (Evolutionary Socialism), which became the major early work of Marxian revisionism. Although orthodox Marxists condemned this critique—which Bernstein always argued preserved the essential core of Marxist theory—Bernstein nevertheless managed to represent German Social Democracy in the Reichstag for eighteen years during the 1902–28 period. Bernstein opposed World War I, and in 1915 voted against war credits. In 1917 he left the Social Democratic Party and joined the more left-wing Independent Socialist Party (USPD), but rejoined the former after the war. Bernstein died in Berlin on 18 December 1932.

Bernstein always remained a Marxist in believing that Marx's theories correctly explained the broad tendencies of human history. Each historical mode of production has produced opposing classes whose conflicts push history toward the present, where the dominant class of owners economically exploits workers while rationalizing oppression in bourgeois institutions and values. When historical materialism effectively explains actual history, it embodies the scientific spirit that ennobles Marx's best work. Unfortunately, for Bernstein, Marx was irreconcilably torn between science and Hegelian a priorism, the belief in objective forces impersonally generating revolutionary violence as the preordained path to socialism. Although Marx never entirely abandoned science, his mature work was, ultimately, "a slave to a doctrine" (*Evolutionary Socialism*, p. 210), that is, empirically nonconfirmable. Hence, Marxism is flawed and contradictory, "proving a theory laid down before its drafting; a formula lies at the basis of it in which the result to which the exposition should lead is fixed beforehand" (ibid., p. 209). Since the utopian, metaphysical Marx inspired Europe's orthodox workers' parties, Marxism had, Bernstein argued, lost all touch with reality. Bernstein therefore abandoned abstract orthodoxy, adopting a method that did not force facts into preconceived categories.

Bernstein empirically refuted orthodoxy's material laws of history. For instance, although industrial mergers, which increase the economic role of giant companies, take place, the actual distribution of wealth is expanding, not contracting. The apparent discrepancy is explained by the growth of joint stock systems, where ownership is dispersed among thousands of investors, dramatically increasing the number of property owners. Maturing capitalism, in fact, disperses wealth and encourages the emergence of small capitalists. Moreover, as capitalist technology matures and efficiency spreads, there is an enormous increase in the number of technical, bureaucratic, and service-oriented jobs, whereas traditional blue collar factory work comprises a falling percentage of the total labor force. When combined with the putative growth in small-scale rural landowners, this evidence disproves Marx's theory of the inevitability of class polarization. A rising middle class, neither proletarian nor capitalist, is muting the social effects of worker–capitalist antagonism, decreasing the likelihood of violent proletarian rebellion. Furthermore, an elaborate system of credit, cartels, protective duties, and military conquest, as well as growth in international trade, now guarantees to capitalism inexpensive resources and ready markets. The indicators of proletarian rebellion are rapidly disappearing.

Bernstein believed that other events also invalidated Marx's reductive hypotheses. Worker socialization of the productive process was not occurring, as social functions became increasingly differentiated and autonomous. Capitalist exploitation of workers was declining as wages rose and conditions improved. Marx's ominous warning in the *Manifesto* that in capitalism workers have no nation, family, property, or freedom entirely misconstrued the actual character of a mature working class: families prosper; the number of property owners grows; workers are increasingly integrated into public decision-making processes through political reforms; and as World War I would disarmingly illustrate, workers willingly die for their country even in an imperialist-inspired conflict. In sum, workers are not about to erupt in one violent revolutionary conflagration, and it is plainly "utopian to imagine that the community could jump into an organization and manner of living diametrically opposed to those of the present day" (ibid., p. 125).

Bernstein also questioned the utility of Marx's theory of value, which is unmeasurable and abstract, a mystification of economic reality. Since no reliable means exists to measure the intensity and quality of human labor, a commodity's price is more effectively explained by empirically verifiable factors. But Marx's economics is incapable of explaining real, empirically defined concepts. Moreover, Marx's theory that exploitation is positively correlated to the rate of surplus value is not factually justifiable, there being verifiable instances when the former declines even while the latter increases. Using surplus value as a measure of exploitation was, for Bernstein, misleading and factually incorrect.

Bernstein's political strategy was tailored to the real-life situation of workers in mature capitalism, not an a priori *Weltanschauung*. While believing in the desirability of socialist equality, he argued that it is self-defeating for Marxist parties to impose, from above, a deterministic metaphysics. Marxists, therefore, must accept the world as it is, not as they wish it to be. Orthodox tactics promoting violent revolution, dictatorship of the proletariat, total nationalization, working-class purity, and so on are neither supported by the character and beliefs of modern workers nor warranted by the actual quality of bourgeois institutions. "The question is not whether certain institutions 'ought' to exist, but rather, the reality dictates that it 'is,' whether Marxists want it or not" (ibid., p. 186).

The quickest path to socialism in contemporary Europe, given these realities, is from within established political institutions. By extending and perfecting liberal freedoms with piecemeal parliamentary reforms, workers can reconstruct and eventually take over the economy. The power of unions will grow, as will the number of workers in secure, well-paying jobs. Over an extended period of gradually accumulating needed political reforms, workers will become socialized by degrees, working cooperatively while enjoying the possessions and freedoms of their steadily improving social positions. The actual transfer of ownership will be procedural, without the violent disruptions that Marx anticipated. Although social change is evolutionary, spontaneous revolutionary insurrections might occur and should be supported. Bernstein opposed abstractionism from either left or right. Marxist parties must be committed to the real needs of workers. In contemporary Europe this translated to political and economic reforms as well as pursuing parliamentary alliances with groups heretofore spurned, including peasants and petit bourgeoisie.

Bernstein performed the miraculous feat of integrating Marxism and liberal democracy, providing a safe and undefiled haven for nonviolent Marxists seeking a peaceful road to socialism. His revisionism attracted many German workers who were recipients of steadily increasing wages, welfare benefits, and improved working conditions and were already organized into powerful and effective political organizations. The plight of these workers was not hopeless, nor did revolution seem inevitable. Revisionist Marxism legitimized their comforts without sacrificing Marxist principles. British workers, with their traditions of peaceful reformism and Fabian socialism, were also highly receptive. As capitalists raised wages and improved working conditions throughout France and Central Europe, Bernstein's Marxism became a lightning rod for workers' changing aspirations. Bernstein's legacy, in addition to the historical and scholarly works published in these years, is the reformist mentality adopted by all of Europe's Social Democratic parties.

Explaining Bernstein's reformism solely in terms of his "Kantianism" misses the point. Bernstein admired Kant's critique of intellectual orthodoxy and used it in combatting materialist "cant," that is, its unacceptable ethics and mystical longing for a socialist utopia. But Kantianism is a consequence of Bernstein's empirical critique, not its source. If empirical facts had confirmed Marx's determinist hypotheses, then Bernstein would not have questioned orthodoxy in the first place, and Kant would be superfluous.

Bernstein is not entirely convincing even on his own terms, for many assertions are not empirically substantiated. A growing corpus of data, today, indicates that mature capitalism was, as Marx forecasted, increasing the concentration of wealth, diminishing competition, and aggravating endemic business cycles. On the other hand, some of Bernstein's points, although empirically correct, were theoretically shortsighted. For example, the number of middle-size businesses has indeed remained constant. But Marx's theory concerning the concentration of capital is not thereby disproved, for evidence also indicates that successful middle-size firms are regularly swallowed by large ones and replaced by others. The constant number of middle-size firms does not negate the growing percentage of wealth and productive capacity concentrated in the giant industrial conglomerates. Similarly, wages, in an absolute sense at least, are rising. But Marx was probably also aware of this tendency. In *Grundrisse*, and again in *Capital*, he clearly implied that exploitation is not measured solely by a relative decline in wages but also by capitalism's appropriation of humanity's physical, intellectual, and emotional well-being. Even as wages rise, Marxists measure the growing exploitation of workers in the deteriorating quality of social and personal relationships. In this sense, Marx's theory is still empirically valid.

Bernstein's immediate reception by European Marxists was mixed. Predictably, he was excoriated by the orthodox movement, particularly Russian Bolsheviks. Lenin† claimed he represented an elite corp of workers, whose rapidly rising wages and standards of living obscured the hideousness of bourgeois society. The long-run tendencies of capitalism, Bernstein notwithstanding, would cleanse the working class of this small group of sycophants. Reformist Marxism, therefore, represented a reactionary elite whose numbers and influence would soon dissipate. Orthodoxy dismissed Bernstein as a reactionary in scientist's garb. Nonorthodox Marxists, however, were not as severe. They admired his project of demystifying orthodox materialism, even while shuddering at his quietistic political strategy. For them Marxism had indeed become an obscure metaphysics, requiring a strong dose of empirical critique. Bernstein had taken the first step in a long overdue expurgation.

BIBLIOGRAPHY:

A. *Evolutionary Socialism* (New York: Schocken, 1965).

B. Peter Gay, *The Dilemma of Democratic Socialism* (New York: Columbia University Press, 1952); G.D.H. Cole, *A History of Socialist Thought*, vol. 3 (London: Macmillan,

1956); Lucio Colletti, "Bernstein and the Marxism of the Second International," in *From Rousseau to Lenin* (London: New Left Books, 1972).

ROBERT A. GORMAN

BLOCH, ERNST (1885–1977). Born in the German city of Ludwigshafen in 1885 into an assimilated Jewish family, Ernst Bloch was an intellectually pre-cocious child who by the age of seventeen had already written books on theology and physics. He began his university studies at Munich in 1905 under the psychologist Theodore Lipps. In 1907 he studied philosophy, physics, and music at Würzburg under Oswald Kulpe, and from 1908 to 1911 he studied in Berlin under the world famous philosopher and sociologist Georg Simmel. By 1919 Bloch had emerged in Germany as a major political and cultural essayist, publishing in Germany's leading journals and magazines. Forced to flee the Nazis in 1933, Bloch moved to Zurich, where he met Karola Piotrkowski,* who would become Bloch's third wife as well as a radical architect whose writings and designs became well known throughout Europe. Bloch eventually arrived in the United States, where he wrote philosophy as well as antifascist tracts while living in New York City, Marlborough, New Hampshire, and Cambridge, Massachusetts. He accepted his first academic appointment in 1949 at the University of Leipzig. Bemusedly tolerated by the East German government in the early 1950s, by 1957 he had become the subject of a sustained and cruel state-sponsored campaign to discredit his professional standing—including, at one point, having all his students arrested. Bloch sought and gained, in 1961, political asylum in West Berlin, where he received a guest professorship at Tübingen. His last years were spent lecturing, teaching, writing, and receiving the West's acclaim as an independent and creative Marxist.† Bloch died at the age of ninety-two in the city of Tübingen.

Ernst Bloch carried the project of idealist Marxism to what most Marxists agree is an inexcusable extreme, creating a revolutionary theory Alfred Schmidt* once called a "mystical, teleological cosmology." Bloch postulated a neo-Platonic essence, or perfection, toward which humanity and the universe are reaching. This perfect state will appear in the future, when humanity cognizes—and the universe empirically expresses—what is now a hidden truth. But no objective, autonomous laws will guide us. Each intentional actor must surmount the barriers of ignorance, despair, and a seemingly inhospitable environment to achieve perfection. A necessary precondition for this enormous task is a positive attitude toward the future, or what Bloch called "hope": a kind of knowledge revealing the world as it can be. Philosophy provides this hope, realizing the latent possibilities in humanity and the universe by teaching actors to fulfill, in free actions, cosmic destiny. Philosophy, in other words, should be utopian. It either reaches into the future for absolute truth or stagnates in the past or present, assuring civilization's absolute destruction. Western philosophy has traditionally emphasized perfection or salvation as a return to a lost reality, or a reality repeating in history. Hence, it unknowingly rallies forces of human destruction and death.

We either go forward toward truth or we perish. There is no middle ground. Bloch's personal experiences with Nazism inject an urgency into what complacent young Westerners might consider an overly apocalyptic inspiration.

Bourgeois philosophy's obsession with "facts" and reified attitudes renders it incapable of grasping truth as a not-yet-realized utopia. Marxism, in contrast, is future-oriented, a theory of utopia and a praxis to bring it about. It satisfies Bloch's criterion for philosophy: offering knowledge of a classless, liberated, nonalienated, "perfect" reality of the future and also the will to create it. Marxism is, therefore, an act of hope. Almost as an afterthought, Bloch paid his dues to orthodoxy by affirming the materiality of the universe and declaring that matter evolves, through an inner dynamic, toward perfection. The historical path is strewn with outmoded and surpassed modes of production, each destroyed by the revolutionary will of those seeking a better future. Capitalism's oppressed workers are harbingers of the socialist utopia. The very survival of humanity depends on their success in seizing the productive apparatus and realizing humanity's essence in societies based on cooperation and equality. Anything less (such as reformism), according to Bloch, compromises the future and eventually destroys everyone.

The Marxist utopian must actively lead workers toward history's truth, but there is no inevitability to social progress. The Party must decisively create apposite conditions for the task at hand. Bloch's abstract, mystical metaphysics at first directed him to support Leninist† parties and Stalin's† "future-oriented" trials, purges, and mobilizations. During this period he was tolerated by East Germany's orthodox hierarchy, despite a vast theoretical gap separating them. Finally convinced that communism—East Germany–style—was not the utopia he had anticipated, Bloch eventually crossed the Western border and lived his remaining years as a philosopher of utopian Marxism, more comfortable with the Romantic traditions of classical German thought than the sharp-edged materialism of Eastern Europe.

BIBLIOGRAPHY:

A. *Das Prinzip Hoffnung*, 3 vols. (Frankfurt: Suhrkamp, 1954–59); *Gesamtausgabe*, 16 vols. (Frankfurt: Suhrkamp, 1959); *Man on His Own* (New York: Herder & Herder, 1970).

B. Leszek Kolakowski, *Main Currents of Marxism*, vol. 3 (London: Oxford University Press, 1978); Wayne Hudson, *The Marxist Philosophy of Ernst Bloch* (New York: St. Martin's Press, 1982).

ROBERT A. GORMAN

BLOCH-PIOTRKOWSKI, KAROLA (b. 1905). Karola Bloch-Piotrkowski was born 22 January 1905 in Lodz, Poland. She lived in Moscow from 1914 to 1918. A political activist, feminist, and architect, Bloch-Piotrkowski studied in Berlin, Zurich, and Vienna. She joined the German Communist Party (KPD) in 1932 and was expelled (because her husband was Ernst Bloch*) in 1956. She fled the Nazi regime as a Jewish Communist activist in 1933, stopping in Zurich,

Vienna, Paris, Prague, and finally the United States, where she arrived in 1938. Bloch-Piotrkowski presently lives in Tübingen in the Federal Republic of Germany.

Karola Bloch-Piotrkowski is a socialist whose contributions to the socialist cause are mostly of a practical nature. In her political activism she had been profoundly influenced by her compatriot Rosa Luxemburg.† In a broader sense she is dedicated to the philosophy of Ernst Bloch, which seeks to strike a balance between theoretical knowledge and political activism. In 1931 Bloch-Piotrkowski belonged to Der Rote Student in Berlin, which tried to counteract the Nazi influence on students by organizing discussions, workshops, etc. The rapid growth of the Nazi Party influenced her decision to join the KPD. Bloch-Piotrkowski lived on the so-called red block in Berlin until her escape and worked for the organization Rote Hilfe, which organized aid for the unemployed and for Communist prisoners. In 1934 Bloch-Piotrkowski took part in the Student Congress Against Fascism in Switzerland. In 1936 she began working for the Emigration Committee in Prague. In her fight against fascism she was also active as a spy for the KPD, partaking in several dangerous missions across Nazi Germany. During her exile in the United States (1938–49) she continued to work for the KPD and was also a member of the American Communist Party. Professionally, Bloch-Piotrkowski worked as an architect and was able to provide for her unemployed husband and her young son during the difficult years of American exile. After Ernst Bloch was invited to enter the German Democratic Republic in 1949, Bloch-Piotrkowski joined him. Working in the GDR as a certified engineer, Bloch-Piotrkowski was responsible for the design and construction of the socialist kindergarten. In the GDR encyclopedia *Die Frau*, Bloch-Piotrkowski wrote on the concept of architectural design from a socialist point of view. She produced a television series about "planning a sensible layout of the home," and began work on a socialist history of the kitchen, a work that would draw the social and economic consequences of residential architecture. In 1961 Karola and Ernst Bloch were on a lecture tour in the Federal Republic when the Berlin Wall was built, whereupon both decided to remain in the West. In West Germany they settled in Tübingen and immediately aligned themselves with the radical left. Bloch-Piotrkowski's unfinished research was left, irretrievable, in East Germany. Bloch-Piotrkowski was the founding member and principal fund-raiser for Hilfe zur Selbsthilfe (Help to Self-Help), which has organized halfway houses for young exconvicts. In 1980 she also helped organize and fund a feminist shelter for battered women and children.

Inspired by her husband's political radicalism and philosophy of hope, Karola Bloch-Piotrkowski has become a leader and role model for the German left. She is a popular featured speaker at mass rallies of the left and at political meetings held by the Green Party. She often holds public readings from her autobiography and gives interviews to the German television and film media. She has become one of today's most popular German radical activists.

BIBLIOGRAPHY:

A. "Zeitgemäzte Haushaltsgeräte," in *Form und Zweck* (Berlin: Jahrbuch, 1957–58), pp. 17–26; "Vom Bauen" and "Zweckmatzige Kuche," in *Kleine Enzyklopädie. Die*

Frau, ed. Irene Uhlmann (Leipzig: VEB Bibliographisches Institut, 1964), pp. 246–65, and 316–28; *Aus meinem Leben* (Pfullingen: Neske-Verlag, 1981).

B. *Karola Bloch*, a film documentary by Helga Reidemeister (West Berlin, 1981).

MAGDALENE MUELLER

BLUM, LEON (1872–1950). Blum was born in Paris in 1872, the son of a Jewish silk and ribbon manufacturer, and was educated at the Lycée Charlemagne and Lycée Henri IV, where he studied philosophy under Bergson. In 1890 he entered the Ecole Normale Supérieure, where like many of his contemporaries he came under the influence of the socialist librarian Lucien Herr. After failing his first-year exams, he entered the Sorbonne Law School, took his degree in 1894, and joined the Conseil d'Etat, rising eventually to solicitor general. Herr introduced Blum to Jaurès* in 1896 and convinced both of them that Dreyfus was innocent. Blum joined the intellectual left-wing Groupe de l'Unité Socialiste in 1899 and Jaurès's Parti Socialiste Français in 1902. He helped Jaurès to edit *La Petite républicaine*, and wrote for *Le Matin* and *L'Humanité*, but in the period before World War I he was better known for his theatrical and literary criticism in *La Revue blanche* and his very liberal study on marriage, *Du mariage* (1907). In 1914 he became *chef de cabinet* for the socialist minister of public works, Marcel Sembat, and in 1918 wrote *Lettres sur la reforme gouvernmentale* in *La Revue de Paris*, which attacked the ossified and conservative workings of government. He left the Conseil d'Etat in 1919 on becoming a deputy, member of the Socialist Party executive, and chairman of their parliamentary group. He took over Jaurès's role at the center of the party and opposed joining the Third International, a stand that culminated in his famous speech at the Socialist Party congress at Tours in 1920. Such ideas were so unpopular, however, that his motion to remain in the Second International† was withdrawn before the vote. He became the leading figure of the rump Socialist Party after 1920, founded its new journal *Le Populaire* in 1921, and as its "political director" wrote many of its editorials during the interwar years. Deputy for Narbonne from 1929, he led the Socialist Party toward a pacifist, but staunchly antifascist position and eventually took them into the Popular Front with the Communists and Radicals. After the Popular Front victory at the polls in 1936, he became prime minister and secured many reforms of pay and conditions for industrial workers against a background of strikes and factory occupations. He was unable to control the flight of capital and inflation and took a noninterventionist position on the Spanish Civil War, which was unpopular with the Communists and the left of his party. He resigned in June 1937, having failed to gain the full economic powers he needed from the Radical-dominated Senate. Prime minister again briefly in 1938, he was one of the few deputies who voted against Pétain in 1940 and was arrested by the Vichy authorities, who "tried" him at Riom for causing the French defeat, but he turned the hearing into a vindication of his position and a condemnation of Pétain. In 1942 he was handed over to the Germans and remained their prisoner until 1945, when he returned to France and published his prison manuscripts under the title *A l'échelle humaine*. He resumed his seat in the Chamber and his place in the Socialist Party and was very briefly prime minister again in 1946–47. After this he retired from active politics and died in 1950.

Blum's political writings concentrated on the idea that a social revolution was the only true transformation of society and that while economic justice was important, revolution had to achieve freedom and dignity for the individual over and above material equality. He followed the Jaurèsian synthesis of philosophic and political materialism, but maintained that while the change of ownership of the means of production was vital, it was instrumental to revolution rather than an end in itself. This humanist view of freedom and social justice as the goals of socialism was sustained by his strong neo-Kantian idealism. Blum opposed joining the Third International† because he rejected the Leninist† conception of the Party and the Bolshevik style of revolution, characterizing the first as intolerant, the second as inapplicable to France, and both as being outside Marxist† orthodoxy. He insisted on a socialist party that recruited widely and had freedom of thought and expression. He said that the socialist movement would have to await the evolution of a genuinely revolutionary consciousness before it could act. In *Pour être socialiste* (1919) he firmly declared that socialism was founded on values that were practical expressions of a moral ideal. While in the 1920s Blum still recognized the possibility of the revolutionary seizure of power, he now proposed that the Socialist Party take any opportunity it had to exercise power, during which time some amelioration of the distribution of wealth could be attempted. Participation in a nonsocialist government was still anathema to Blum, but in 1933 he proposed that the Socialist Party be prepared simply to occupy power as a means of preventing it from falling into the hands of the fascists. Although such an occupation of power would not provide opportunities for socialist reform, Blum used Jaurès's arguments against Karl Kautsky† in defense of bourgeois republican democracy to justify his idea. With the publication after World War II of his prison writings, Blum returned to many of his earliest ideas about oppression, freedom, and justice. He insisted that the object of the revolution was not only to liberate man from economic and social domination and all its attendant forms of servitude but to ensure him all his personal rights and freedoms within the collective society. This reaffirmation of humanist socialism led many in the post war Socialist Party to claim that he had abandoned Marxism, and there was a rally behind Mollet against him and his protégé, Hans Mayer.*

Blum was not a dramatically original Marxist thinker, but he did faithfully continue and develop the Jaurèsian theses in the socialist movement. He was influential for the generation between the wars and relaunched humanist socialism after 1945, a concept that is still present in French socialism.

BIBLIOGRAPHY:

A. *Nouvelle Conversations de Goethe avec Eckermann* (Paris: Editions de la Revue Blanche, 1901); *Du Mariage* (Paris: Ollendorf, 1907); *Lettres sur la reforme gouvernmentale* (Paris: Grasset, 1918); *Pour être socialiste* (Paris: Editions Socialistes, 1919);

L'Exercise du pouvoir (Paris: Gallimard, 1937); *A l'échelle humaine* (Paris: Gallimard, 1945); *For All Mankind* (London: Victor Gollancz, 1946); *Oeuvres*, 9 vols. (Paris: Albin Michel, 1954–63).

B. C. Audry, *Leon Blum ou la politique du juste* (Paris: Julliard, 1955); J. Joll, *Three Intellectuals in Politics* (New York: Pantheon, 1960); L. E. Dalby, *Leon Blum: Evolution of a Socialist* (New York: Yoseloff, 1963); J. Colton, *Leon Blum: Humanist in Politics* (New York: Knopf, 1966); G. Ziebura, *Leon Blum et le Parti Socialiste* (Paris: Colin, 1967); W. Logue, *Leon Blum: The Formative Years* (Dekalb: Northern Illinois University Press, 1973); J. Lacouture, *Leon Blum* (Paris: Seuil, 1979).

JOHN C. SIMMONDS

BOROKHOV, BER (1881–1917). Born in 1881 in the Ukraine, Borokhov was a leading figure in the left wing of the Zionist movement and attempted to develop a Marxist† analysis of nationalism in general and the Jewish question in particular. After growing up in the town of Poltava, an early center of Zionist activity and a place of exile for Russian radicals, Borokhov moved to Ekaterinoslav. There he was briefly an activist in the Russian Social Democratic Party but was expelled, probably for his Zionism. He then formed a small socialist Zionist group and worked with Menahem Ussishkin, the leader of Russian Zionism. Borokhov began writing numerous essays on Jewish affairs and was influenced by empiriocriticism,* a philosophical-psychological school associated with the writings of Richard Avenarius and Ernst Mach, and by empiriomonism, a Marxist version of it propounded by A. A. Bogdanov. In 1905 Borokhov wrote "The National Question and the Class Struggle," in which he developed the key elements of his theory, further developed the following year in "Our Platform," written for the newly created socialist Zionist party, the Poale Zion (Workers of Zion), which he was central in founding. Arrested by the tsarist police in June 1906, Borokhov spent a period in prison and then fled to Central Europe, where he continued writing, working for his party, and pursuing research to develop a foundation for Yiddish philology. With the advent of World War I, he was forced to leave for New York, where he led a left-wing opposition to the mainstream of the Poale Zion there. He returned to Russia in late summer 1917 and died in Kiev of pneumonia in December.

In the period 1904–5 Borokhov's writings shifted from an empiriocritical to a more concrete Marxist terminology and analysis. Underlying all of his theories, however, was the assertion that the Jews composed a marginal and hence perpetually vulnerable national minority with an abnormal social and economic structure. His "Economic Development of the Jewish People" (1916) attempted to demonstrate this through an analysis of Russian Jewish class structure, utilizing census statistics. He developed his theoretical premises, however, in "The National Question and the Class Struggle," in which he sought to explain nationalism by supplementing Marx's notion of "relations of production" with his own of "conditions of production." In his preface to the *Contribution to the Critique of Political Economy* (1859), Marx argued that in "the social production of their lives,'' all human beings enter into "relations of production" (property relations) independent of their wills, which constitute the economic base of society. One's place in the relations of production defined one's class.

Borokhov argued that production is dependent on different conditions in different times and places, hence the necessity of speaking of the varying geographic, anthropological, and historical conditions of production that led to the formation of nations. He saw land as the most important of such conditions and defined nationalism as the "feeling of kinship created as a result of the visioned common historic past and rooted in the common conditions of production" (*Class Struggle and the Jewish Nation*, p. 15).

Whereas class struggle originates in the conflict between developing forces of production and existing relations of production, Borokhov argued that national struggles emerge when the development of a nation's forces of production conflicts with its existing conditions of production, compelling it to seek better conditions. Borokhov argued in "Our Platform" that the Jews, lacking a homeland, were subject to highly abnormal conditions of production and were therefore always in jeopardy. The Jewish proletariat was marginal in its host countries and tied to Jewish capital, which was concentrated in consumer goods, not basic industries. Moreover, Jews were continually compelled to migrate. Unlike normal nations, the Jews did not occupy all places in the processes of production. In short, having abnormal conditions of production, the Jews were forced perpetually to migrate and faced mounting insecurity in a world of intense national competition. As such, a radical solution was needed to resolve the Jewish problem: national liberation. In their own homeland, argued Borokhov, occupying all levels of production and not living as a marginal minority, the Jews would have a normal national existence. The Jewish proletariat would be able to wage a class war on its own grounds and in solidarity with international socialism. "Proletarian Zionism," he wrote, "is possible only if its aims can be achieved through the class struggle; Zionism can be realized only if proletarian Zionism can be realized" (ibid., p. 17). Borokhov even argued that historical necessity would bring the Jews to Palestine through a spontaneous, almost natural migratory process. (He later rejected this notion.) He asserted that given Russian realities and the development of modern capitalism, the Jewish situation had become untenable and the only plausible response was a revolutionary reconstitution of Jewish life in the form of political independence in Palestine.

BIBLIOGRAPHY:

A. *Ktavim*, 3 vols. (Tel Aviv: Hakibbutz Hameuhad and Sifriat Poalim, 1955, 1958, 1966); *Class Struggle and the Jewish Nation: Selected Essays in Marxist Zionism by Ber Borochov*, ed. Mitchell Cohen (New Brunswick, N.J.: Transaction Books, 1984).

B. Mattityahu Mintz, *Ber Borokhov: Hamaagal harishon 1900–1906* (Tel Aviv: Hakibbutz Hameuhad, 1976); Jonathan Frankel, *Prophecy and Politics: Socialism, Nationalism and the Russian Jews, 1862–1917* (Cambridge: Cambridge University Press, 1981); Mattityahu Mintz, "Ber Borokhov," *Studies in Zionism*, no. 5 (April 1982).

MITCHELL COHEN

BRÜCKNER, PETER (1922–1982). Peter Brückner was born on 13 May 1922 in Dresden and died on 10 April 1982 in Nizza. In 1933 Brückner's Jewish mother, who was from England, was able to escape from Nazi Germany, leaving behind Peter and his father. The latter refused to work for the Nazis and thus remained an unemployed engineer. Brückner was sent to boarding school in Zwickau. After his graduation in 1940 he was forced by the Nazis to register in the so-called Department for Jews. Nevertheless, due to a mistake Brückner was drafted into the army and sent to Vienna, where he escaped the certain death that was his birthright in his homeland. Brückner first came into contact with the Communists in 1940 while still in West Saxony. In 1942 he joined the Austrian Communist Party (KPO) and in 1945 the German Communist Party (KPD). From 1945 to 1948 Brückner studied psychology and medicine in Leipzig. In late 1948 he left the eastern sector of Germany and also gave up his Party membership, being unwilling to follow the Party line unquestioningly. He continued his psychology studies in Munster, while also studying philosophy and psychopathology. He received his Ph.D. in 1957. At this time Brückner got involved in left-wing politics again and felt intellectually drawn to the Frankfurt School as well as to the representatives of Marxist† psychoanalysis. Brückner became head of the counseling department at an orphanage and later head of a private institute for market psychology in Mannheim. In 1962 he received a lectureship in advertising and market psychology at the School of Economics in Mannheim, where he became chairman in 1963. During the year 1963–64 Brückner advised the Students for a Democratic Society (SDS) movement and became a member of the Republikanischen Club in 1967. That same year he was appointed a full professor of psychology and subsequently promoted to chairman of the Department of Psychology at the Technical University in Hanover. In 1968 Heidelberg University had an injunction issued against Brückner, whereupon he was suspended from his teaching duties at the University of Hannover in 1972. Grounds for the suspension included Brückner's alleged support of a "criminal" organization. He was reinstated and again, in 1977, suspended for alleged subversive remarks. Brückner was eventually acquitted in the ensuing legal proceedings but died before reassuming his professional position.

In his writings Brückner deals with the contemporary phenomenon of alienation, which is studied as a development of thought that reflects the dialectical unity of theory and praxis. His early work focused on problems of methodology and techniques and questions of clinical psychology. *Zur Psychologie des Mitläufers* (1964) contains the first elements of what would later be called his political psychology. In *Zur Pathologie des Gehorsams* (1965) Brückner investigates the psychological origins of civil obedience and disobedience, a theme further developed in *Freiheit, Gleichheit, Sicherheit* (1966). At this point in his professional development Bruckner is not yet able to differentiate between classes, and only refers to *Volk* (the people in a general sense). After the killing of Benno Ohnsorg (a student who participated in the demonstrations against the Shah held in Berlin in 1967) by a German policeman, Brückner began to realize that much of his idealized early thought was contradicted by the oppressive nature of German political reality. Together with the radical political scientist Johannes Agnoli, Brückner published *Die Transformation der Demokratie* (1967), in which he argues that scientific inquiry is itself a problem of praxis and that political psychology must examine its own social and historical context. In *Provokation als organisierte Selbstfreigabe* (1970) Brückner begins outlining a radical political strategy based on principles of Marxism. In *Zur Sozialpsychologie des Kapitalismus* (1972), despite what Hans Mayer* sees as remnants of a Jacobinian idealistic heritage, Brückner recognizes the limitations of political psychology, which can only interpret individual phenomena, and he moves toward outlining a social psychology that will simultaneously explain alienated life and help liberate its victims.

During his last years Brückner became well known as a radical leader of the German left. Although no longer able to teach, Brückner gave public lectures throughout the FRG, drawing large and sympathetic crowds. He died after suffering from a long and agonizing heart disease, which likely was related to his harassment by German authorities.

BIBLIOGRAPHY:

A. *Zum Beispiel Peter Brückner. Treue zum Staat und kritische Wissenschaft*, ed. A. Krovoza, A. R. Oestmann, and K. Ottomeyer (Frankfurt: EVA, 1981). This work contains important excerpts from, and a complete bibliography of, Brückner's works.

MAGDALENE MUELLER

BRZOZOWSKI, STANISLAW (1878–1911). The Polish philosopher, novelist, playwright, and literary critic Stanislaw Brzozowski (pseudonym: Adam Czepiel) was born in the city of Maziarnia, near Celm. He studied natural history at Warsaw University until his radical political activities prompted Russian authorities to expel him. His short life was marked by poverty, illness, and the unfounded rumor that he was a Russian spy. Brzozowski's professional career began in 1901, when he started writing literary and philosophical articles and books such as *The Contemporary Polish Novel* (1906), *Contemporary Literary Criticism in Poland* (1907), and *The Legend of Young Poland* (1909). His most famous essays are included in *An Introduction to Philosophy* (1906), *Culture and Life* (1907), *Ideas* (1910), *Voices in the Night* (1912), and *The Philosophy of Polish Romanticism* (1924). Brzozowski's early writings related literature to the whole of cultural and social life. He matured—under the influence of philosophers and poets such as August Cieszkowski, Adam Mickiewicz, Cyprian Norwid, Nietzsche, Avenarius, Fichte, Sorel,* and Marx†—into a romantic radical. In his last years he turned toward Catholicism, particularly the works of Cardinal John Newman. Brzozowski died of tuberculosis in Florence, Italy, in 1911.

Brzozowski's major work of theory, *Ideas*, posits a metaphysics of absolute freedom and creativity based on a "philosophy of labor." Reality is a function of humanity's practical connections to the world, epitomized in our inherent ability to labor. This creative action that produces needed goods is praxis in the true Hegelian sense: more than subjectivism or voluntarism, it embraces objective tendencies of economic and social development. It is, in other words, an essential unity of subject and object expressed as human creativity. Truth is manifest in authentic freedom, which always takes the form of praxis. History is produced by human action rather than preexisting laws (for example, materialism) and therefore is not predetermined. Yet truly free action fulfills history's objective tendencies.

Brzozowski's philosophy of labor metaphysically rationalized socialism. Since praxis is the essence of authenticity for everyone, a just society is realized through the collective labors of authentic workers. Free labor, not arbitrarily guided by bureaucrats or dictators, generates dignity. Brzozowski's Marxism demands the proletariat's spiritual rejuvenation, which means worker self-government and labor as praxis. This will accompany their seizing a capitalist productive apparatus that is objectively decaying anyway; hence, an undetermined act of praxis culminates capitalism's historical tendency toward dissolution. Socialism is thus a human adventure in which workers confront and conquer nature and actualize an essential, idealized humanity. When Brzozowksi, in his last years, added strong doses of Polish nationalism and Catholicism, he was less a Marxist than a speculative, idealist metaphysician calling forth a spiritual or emotional worker's revival.

BIBLIOGRAPHY:

A. *Idee* (Lemberg, Poland: B. Poloniecki, 1910).

B. C. Milosz, "A Controversial Polish Writer Stanislaw Brzozowski," *California Slavic Studies*, 2 (1963), pp. 53–95; A. Werner, "Stanislaw Brzozowski," *Obraz literatury polskiej, XIX i XX wieku. Literatura okresu Mlodej Polski*, 4 (1977), pp. 549–617; Leszek Kolakowski, *Main Currents of Marxism* (London: Oxford University Press, 1978).

ROBERT A. GORMAN

BÜRGER, PETER (b. 1936). Born in 1936, Peter Bürger teaches literature and romance literature at the University of Bremen. The renewed interest in Marxist† aesthetics in the West German student movement quickly led to a confrontation of the classical positions of George Lukács* and Theodore Adorno.* In his *Theory of the Avant-Garde* (1974), Bürger attempts to overcome this antinomy by placing the two positions within a larger history of the "institution of art." In contrast to Walter Benjamin's* binary model of auratic and postauratic art, Bürger elaborates several historic models with varying modes of aesthetic production and reception: medieval, courtly-absolutist, bourgeois, and avant-garde. In bourgeois art, characterized by individual production and reception, the work is designated as autonomous because of its separation from everyday life-practice and as organic because, imitating nature, its constructed character is purposefully hidden. Bürger argues that, although the aesthetics of autonomy are elaborated theoretically in the period of German idealism, the model of autonomous literature is not completed until the aestheticism of the late nineteenth century. The subsequent exhaustion of the model, however, evokes a radical attack from the historical avant-garde movements—dadaism, surrealism, and futurism—which are understood as strategic efforts to overcome the bourgeois separation of life and art and to institute an alternative model based on concepts of montage and allegory borrowed from Brecht and Benjamin. Although this attack further destabilizes the bourgeois institution of art, it cannot successfully merge beauty and everyday practice. Therefore neither Lukács's aesthetics, indebted to classical bourgeois theory, nor Adorno's aesthetics, derived from the avant-garde movements, can claim priority in a historical situation where no normative position is any longer credible. In the place of normative aesthetics, Bürger argues for analyses of the respective social functions of literature.

BIBLIOGRAPHY:

A. *Aktualität und Geschichtlichkeit. Studien zum gesellschaftlichen Funktionswandel der Literatur* (Frankfurt: Suhrkamp, 1977); *Vermittlung—Rezeption—Funktion: Asthetische Theorie und Methodologie der Literaturwissenschaft* (Frankfurt: Suhrkamp, 1979); *Theory of the Avant-Garde* (Minneapolis: University of Minnesota Press, 1983).

B. W. Martin Lüdtke, ed., *Theorie der Avantgarde: Antworten auf Peter Bürgers Bestimmung von Kunst und bürgerlicher Gesellschaft* (Frankfurt: Suhrkamp, 1976).

RUSSELL BERMAN

C

CANGUILHEM, GEORGES (b. 1904). Canguilhem received his doctor of medicine degree in 1943 with his thesis, *Le Normal et le pathologique*. In 1954 he succeeded Gaston Bachelard* as head of the Institut d'Histoire des Sciences of the University of Paris. His studies of the history of the life sciences show four characteristics that will be familiar to those who have read Michel Foucault,* Bachelard, or Louis Althusser.* Canguilhem is unremitting in his criticism of any and all assertions concerning a "teleology of reason." What are called "stages in the development of reason" are, for Canguilhem as for Bachelard, hard-won achievements of the species, always subject to the contingencies of history. Second, he develops his historiography of science in systematic opposition to other precursors in the field. This approach has done much to confer significance to this field of historical research—establishing a quasi-scientific status to the history of the sciences that integrates this history with its object of study. Third, the actual texts of the object of investigation are taken as signs— or perhaps fragments—of an effective but hidden conceptual system that informed their authors and generated their assertions and denials. This too will remind the reader of the historical work of Bachelard and Foucault. Finally, the advancement of science is understood as a product of conceptual, practical, and socio-political conflicts and conjunctures—a dialectic of scientific thought and technological realizations.

Canguilhem proposes a nonreactionary vitalism; rejecting on the one hand the organicist sociology of order of Durkheim and others and, on the other hand, the now fashionable neo-Darwinist metaphysics of inequalities and territorial imperialism. He understands life as essentially normative, in the sense of being institutive of norms. Life is much more than just normal, more than just conforming to norms; the very fact of being alive is characterized by the instituting of, and the pursuit of, ever new norms. On the socio-historical plane, this normativity fits nicely with Foucault's idea of the application of the strategies of power to the "species-being," or body of humanity, controlling and directing—and most importantly, rendering possible—the creative investment of living desire. Most orthodox Marxists,† although generally concerned with rendering their thought "scientific," have ignored biology and medicine since the Lysenko affair. Canguilhem has aided neo-Marxists in the development of a philosophy of life to complement their accounts of history and culture.

BIBLIOGRAPHY:

A. *Besoins et tendances* (Paris: Classiques Hachette, 1962); *Idéologie et rationalité dans l'histoire des sciences de la vie* (Paris: Vrin, 1977).

B. Miriam Glucksmann, *Structuralist Analysis in Contemporary Social Thought* (London: Routledge & Kegan Paul, 1974).

LAURENCE E. WINTERS

CANTIMORI, DELIO (1904–1966). Delio Cantimori was born in Russi (Ravenna) on 30 August 1904 and died in Florence in September 1966. Having been educated in the period of the hegemony of idealism, he was an admirer of the actualism of Giovanni Gentile and also an adherent of fascism. As early as 1934, after his first stay in Basel, where he did research on Italian heretics, he began his study of Marx† and Lenin† and abandoned the illusion that fascism was the true Italian revolution. In the years between 1930 and 1940 and afterward his historical interests included humanism and the Protestant Reformation, Italian heretics, Weimar Germany, the National Socialist movement (in 1935 he edited and wrote the introduction to the first large collection published in Italy of the writings of Carl Schmitt, *Principii politici del Nazionalsocialismo*), Marxism, and communism. In 1935 he married Emma Mezzomonti, who was already a collaborator in the journal *Soccorso rosso*; in 1939 they secretly had as a guest in their home the Communist leader Velio Spano, a sign of contact and collaboration with the party even before the fall of fascism. In 1939 he became a full professor at the University of Florence. Beginning with the academic year 1940–41 he held a chair at the Scuola Normale Superiore in Pisa. In 1942 he began his collaboration with the publishing house Einaudi. From 1942 to 1952 he was part of the editorial board of the theoretical review of the Italian Communist Party (PCI), *Società*. In 1951 his Italian translation of the first volume of *Das Kapital* appeared. In 1948 he joined the PCI, which he would leave in 1956, although silently and not necessarily as a result of the events in Hungary. Moreover, he continued to offer support to the PCI even afterward, until his death as the result of a fall from a ladder in his library at home.

Having received his intellectual training in the school of idealism and historicism, Cantimori became more and more involved over the years with authors such as Febvre, De Sanctis, Marx, Warburg, Max Weber, and Jacob Burckhardt. He viewed Marx's thought as a "method of interpreting history and social and political life and also social and political action that serves the function of overcoming capitalistic society" (*Studi di storia*, p. 274). He mistrusted any vision of Marxism as a general, abstract ideology, presupposed for concrete and historical research. Instead Cantimori asserts in his important essay "Interpretazioni tedesche di Marx nel periodo 1929–1945" that "Marx's thought is *historical, qualifying, specific, not abstracting* or *generalizing*" (ibid., p. 154). It is not a doctrine "which Marx and Engels worked out at their desks and which then was superimposed and inserted into a scheme of first universal history, then economics, and finally nature." It is necessary again to propose historical materialism as a method, following the suggestion of Antonio Labriola,† and in opposition to Croce's polemic against Marxism as an historiographic canon and the German positivistic and social democratic distortions.

But it is also necessary to refuse to put Marxism to a directly political and partisan use, thereby resisting any actual temptation of Zhdanovism, a use that is in fact propagandistic and not scientific. Here Cantimori takes up a Weberian entreaty for science "free of assumptions," while also affirming on the other hand the omnipresence of the interest in politics. The task of history is to carry out particular, specific, rigorous research with materials and tools that are rigorously controlled, without abstract prejudices that are uncontrolled and uncontrollable.

BIBLIOGRAPHY:

A. *Studi di storia* (Turin: Einaudi, 1959); *Storici e storia* (Turin: Einaudi, 1971).

B. Giovanni Miccoli, *Delio Cantimori* (Turin: Einaudi, 1970); Michele Ciliberto, *Intellettuali e fascismo. Saggio su Delio Cantimori* (Bari: De Donato, 1977).

VITTORIO DINI

CARDOSO, FERNANDO HENRIQUE (b. 1931). A prominent sociologist and economist from São Paulo, Brazil, Cardoso studied under sociologist Florestán Fernándes at the University of São Paulo, where he wrote a doctoral dissertation on the question of slavery in the states of Paraná, Santa Catarina, and Rio Grande do Sul. Cardoso once was a professor of the university until his teaching rights were removed by government decree after the coup of 1964. He published studies on capitalism and slavery in Rio Grande do Sul, the industrial entrepreneur and economic development in Brazil, and dependency and development. During the 1970s he returned to Brazil from exile and settled in São Paulo, where he headed a research institute, Centro Brasileiro de Análise e Planejamento. Later he entered politics, becoming a federal senator from São Paulo.

Cardoso was influenced by the dialectical method and thought of Marx,† but he also followed mainstream sociological writing in the tradition of Max Weber; thus his writing is mixed with concepts drawn from both tendencies. His early work attacked bourgeois economists who emphasized comparative advantages whereby some countries were producers of raw materials and others were producers of industrial goods. He emphasized a dialectical approach to the study of structures and history. He saw the international political economy as divided into centers and peripheries, and he wrote about "situations" of dependency rather than a theory of dependency. He stressed a structural dependency of external and internal forces. The external forces included multinational firms, foreign technology, and international financial systems in the name of imperialism, whereas the internal forces operated through the practice of local classes and groups whose interests and values coincided with those of foreign interests. Cardoso believed that underdevelopment evolves from the relationship of peripheral to central societies. Underdevelopment is the consequence of commercial and later industrial capitalism, which expanded and linked the world market to nonindustrial economies. Imperialism is not distinguishable sharply from dependency, but he argued that a new stage of imperialism had appeared after World War II. Therefore Lenin's† conception of imperialism in the form of finance capital needed to be updated in terms of multinational capital, which today accounts for accumulation in the periphery.

Cardoso identified new forms of economic dependency in some countries. He felt that in Brazil, for example, the economy experienced internal structural fragmentation so that the advanced sectors of the economy were tied to the international capitalist system. Imperialism in the contemporary stage permitted some local participation and an international division of labor so that some parts of the dependent economy could be included in the investment plans of big corporations. Cardoso called this "associated dependent development." Thus, international capital could penetrate peripheral economies, especially in the manufacturing of products to be consumed by the domestic bourgeoisie, so as to stimulate development in some parts of the economy of a dependent country. Given the weakness of the national bourgeoisie and its inability to carry out a bourgeois capitalist revolution, it could only tie itself to dependent capitalism by associating with international capital as a dependent and minor partner.

BIBLIOGRAPHY:

A. *Capitalismo e escravidão no Brasil meridional* (São Paulo: Difusão Européia do Livro, 1962); *Empresario industrial e desenvolvimento económico no Brasil* (São Paulo: Difusão Européia do Livro, 1964); *Politíca de desenvolviemento em sociedades dependentes* (Rio: Zahar, 1971); "Dependency and Development in Latin America," *New Left Review*, 4 (July–August 1972), pp. 83–95; "Associated-Dependent Development: Theoretical and Practical Implications," pp. 142–76, in *Authoritarian Brazil*, ed. Alfred Stepan (New Haven: Yale University Press, 1973); with Enzo Faletto, *Dependency and Development* (Berkeley: University of California Press, 1979); *As idéias e seu lugar* (Petropolis: Vozes, 1981).

RONALD H. CHILCOTE

CARRILLO, SANTIAGO (b. 1915). Born on 18 January 1915 at Gijón in Spain, Santiago Carrillo is one of the major European postwar Communist leaders. By his own admission, Carrillo is better understood as a pragmatic political activist rather than a Marxist† theoretician. It is thus ironic that he is best known outside Spain as one of the leading theorists of Eurocommunism, mainly on the strength of his 1977 publication *'Eurocomunismo' y estado*. His development of the themes of Eurocommunism, however, must be seen against the background of his role within the Communist Party of Spain (PCE). Involved in politics from a very early age, Carrillo became secretary of the Juventud Socialista (JS) when he was nineteen. He was imprisoned in Madrid between 1934 and 1936 after the Asturian and Catalan revolts and was involved on his release in the unification of the JS and the Juventud Comunista, becoming secretary-general of the Juventud Socialista Unificada in 1936. That year he joined the PCE and was immediately co-opted as a supplementary member of the Buró Político (later the Comité Ejecutivo). In 1939 he became secretary of the Communist Youth International.

Forced into exile after the Spanish Civil War, Carrillo moved between the Soviet Union and South America, assuming responsibility in 1942 for the organization of the PCE in Spain. Having arrived in France in 1944, he became heavily involved in the PCE's period of mimesis of the Communist Party of the Soviet Union (CPSU), and over the next twelve years he consolidated his position within the leadership of the Party. The Fifth Congress of the PCE in Prague in 1954 marked the advent of Carrillo's personal imprint upon the functioning of the Party, and his criticisms of the "old guard" led by Dolores Ibárruri,† Vicente Uribe, and Ignacio Gallego reached a crisis point in the following year in arguments over the admission of Spain to the United Nations. The rigidly Stalinist† Moscow-based faction made moves to oust Carrillo, but these were abandoned in the light of Nikita Khrushchev's† "secret speech." After the 1956 plenum of the PCE, in which he proposed a policy of "national reconciliation" with other anti-Francoist forces in Spain, Carrillo became de facto leader of the Party, a position formalized in 1960, when he became its fourth secretary-general.

It was Carrillo's initiative that led to moves toward greater democratization within the PCE, although his role in this respect is ambivalent. A formidable political manipulator with an enormous capacity for work, much of his activity in the 1960s and 1970s was centered around considerations of his own position as leader of the Party. Carrillo never lost his belief in the general strike as the most effective means to overthrow Franco's dictatorship, and in 1964 he engineered the expulsion from the PCE of two of its leading intellectuals, Fernando Claudín* and Jorge Semprún, after they had argued that the Party remained undemocratic in its functioning and was committed to a "subjectivist" vision of events in Spain out of touch with reality. Two years later he cautiously criticized the Soviet Union over the Sinyavsky and Daniel trials, and when he subsequently condemned the 1968 Soviet invasion of Czechoslovakia was himself subjected to charges of anti-Sovietism by the Moscow-backed group led by Eduardo García and Agustín Gómez. These two were expelled from the Party in 1969, whereupon Enrique Líster became the spearhead of opposition to the secretary-general, but by co-opting twenty-nine new members to the Central Committee, Carrillo was able to expel his rival from the PCE in 1970. Thereafter Carrillo was to forge close links with the Italian Communist Party (PCI) as the rift between the PCE and CPSU grew. This culminated in the famous joint declaration by the PCE and PCI issued at Livorno on 12 July 1975, which was a blueprint for the "Eurocommunist" positions later espoused formally by Carrillo.

Between 1974 and 1976 Carrillo was involved in attempts to set up united opposition groups to Franco, but when the dictator died in late 1975 the PCE leader turned his efforts to bringing about the legalization of his party in Spain.

Having returned to that country illegally in February 1976 and taken part in a series of clandestine meetings with other political leaders, Carrillo gave a dramatic press conference on 10 December 1976, in which he pledged the PCE's respect for constitutional propriety, stressed the need for accords between capitalists and the working class, and announced that as a 'Eurocommunist' party it was fully independent of Moscow. Arrested a few days later, he was released by the end of the year, and in April 1977 the PCE was legalized. The general election results of July that year, in which the PCE gained only 9.2 percent of the vote, were a disappointment. Carrillo's position as secretary-general came under renewed challenge, and the disaffection of some sectors of the Party was fueled by the signing of the Pacta Moncloa in 1977, whereby the PCE promised cooperation with a Suárez-led centrist government. The March 1979 election, in which there was only a marginal improvement in support for the PCE, marked the onset of bitter struggles between the PCE and the Partit Socialista Unificat de Catalunya (PSUC) over the dropping of the label *Leninist* in the Party statutes. Rifts developed between Carrillo-backing ''Eurocommunists,'' orthodox Marxist-Leninists (known as ''Afghans'' in view of their support of the Soviet invasion of Afghanistan), and ''renovatory Eurocommunists,'' who believed that Carrillo's professed positions were insincere. After the disaster of the 1982 general election, in which the Communists received only 3.2 percent of the vote, Carrillo resigned as secretary-general of the PCE, although he remained its spokesman in the Cortes. In April 1985 Carrillo was formally expelled from the PCE's Central and Executive Committees and replaced as parliamentary leader by a former protegé, Gerardo Iglesias. The current PCE leadership favors a ''convergence'' strategy, which seeks party alliances with socialists and single-issue groups such as feminists, pacificists, and ecologists. Ironically, given his Eurocommunist background, Carrillo endorsed a more confrontationist and ideological role for the Party. Fernando Claudín has commented in his biography of the PCE leader, published in 1983, that ''in the course of his prolonged activity in leadership, between the ages of nineteen and sixty-eight, Santiago Carrillo played an ever more relevant role in the turbulent history of Spain in the last fifty years.''

In *''Eurocomunismo'' y estado*, often regarded as a bible of Eurocommunism, Carrillo developed themes that had been foreshadowed in the 1975 Livorno declaration, and the work might be seen as representing the theoretical expression of the political process he first initiated in Spain in 1956. His actions as secretary-general, however, bear many of the hallmarks of the Stalinism† to which he was attracted in his youth, and caution should be exercised in evaluating the authenticity of Carrillo's commitment to the positions that have come to be known as Eurocommunist.

It is important to be clear that Eurocommunism has never been a precisely elaborated strategic, tactical approach expressing the aims and methods of the Western European Communist parties. The term is more usefully seen as a rubric that covers the response of a number of leading figures in these parties to what was increasingly perceived as the bankruptcy of classical Marxist-Leninist revolutionary tactics in advanced Western capitalist societies. This response was formed around three central themes: the assertion that democracy and socialism are consubstantial; the claim that the Communist parties in question are fully independent of Moscow; and the belief that the transition to socialism can be achieved peacefully. Thus, the main characteristics of Eurocommunism have been outlined by Carrillo as follows:

> The parties included in the "Eurocommunist" trend are agreed on the need to advance to socialism with democracy, a multi-party system, parliaments and representative institutions, sovereignty of the people regularly exercised through universal suffrage, trade unions independent of the State and of the parties, freedom for the opposition, human rights, religious freedom, freedom for cultural, scientific and artistic creation, and the development of the broadest forms of popular participation at all levels and in all branches of social activity. Side by side with this, in one form or another, the parties claim their total independence in relation to any possible international leading centre and to the socialist states, without ceasing on that account to be internationalist. (*"Eurocommunism" and the State*, p. 110)

Although this conception is often said to owe much to the formulations of Karl Kautsky† and Palmiro Togliatti,* it raises many problems concerning its relationship to classically understood Marxist theory. Carrillo's view of the state in modern capitalist society is derived from Antonio Gramsci's* conception of hegemonic blocs consolidating their power through the use of ideological and repressive state apparatuses, although he notes that the range and extent of the state's activity has increased enormously since World War II. However, the view of the state as essentially antithetical to noncapitalist interests is tied to an implicit suggestion that the abolition of capitalist private property is equivalent to the abolition of capitalist productive relations and that a whole gamut of productive forces—science, technology, the organization of labor, etc.—are neutral, ready to be utilized by whatever power bloc exercises hegemony. Carrillo also holds to the orthodox thesis of state monopoly capitalism derived from Lenin,† which emphasizes the moribund character of imperialism and the ripeness of the highly socialized productive forces of capitalism for the transition to socialism. In the same work, however, he argues that the transition will be a two-stage affair, having first to arrive at the phase of "advanced democracy." Carrillo explicitly rejects the desirability of working toward the "dictatorship of the proletariat," arguing that such a goal is counterproductive because of the negative connotations that have come to be associated with the term. While the conception of the Communist Party as democratic centralist is retained, the question is never confronted of how such a party is to enter into alliances and whether these are to be with other parties, or classes, or both.

Two major drawbacks to Carrillo's conception of Eurocommunism are that its emphasis on the parliamentary road gives such emphasis to the electoral struggle that popular initiatives at grass-roots level are marginalized and that his refusal to call Eastern Bloc countries nonsocialist suggests an inconsistent and insincere vision of what socialism entails.

BIBLIOGRAPHY:

A. *Problems of Socialism Today* (London: Lawrence and Wishart, 1970); *Dialogue on Spain* (London: Lawrence and Wishart, 1976); *"Eurocommunism" and the State* (London: Lawrence and Wishart, 1977).

B. María Eugenia Yagüe, *Santiago Carrillo, perfil humano y político* (Madrid: Cambio 16, 1977); Fernando Claudín, *Santiago Carrillo, crónica de un secretario general* (Barcelona: Planeta, 1983).

PAUL HEYWOOD

CASTORIADIS, CORNELIUS. See *SOCIALISME OU BARBARIE.**

CAVAILLÈS, JEAN (1903–1944). Jean Cavaillès was born in Saint Maixent, France, in 1903, and attended the Ecole Normale Superieur. He studied in Germany with Edmund Husserl and other German mathematical philosophers and taught philosophy at the *lycée* in Amiens. He received his *doctorat* in 1938 with his two theses, *Méthode axiomatique et formalisme, essai sur le problème du fondement des mathématiques* and *Remarques sur la formation de la théorie abstraite des ensembles*. The themes of the foundation of mathematics and set theory were to concern Cavaillès throughout his brief career. He was appointed to the University of Strasbourg just as war was declared. He was mobilized and captured and escaped shortly thereafter to resume teaching with the faculty of Strasbourg, which had then been moved to Clermont-Ferrand. During this time he helped to found, and became an active member in, the Resistance. He continued these activities after having been called to teach at the Sorbonne. He was captured again by the Germans in September 1941. He escaped again in 1942 and returned to active struggle. Captured still again in August 1943, he was shot by the Nazis early in 1944.

It is difficult to assess in general terms the technical contributions of Cavaillès. However, Gaston Bachelard,* Michel Foucault,* and Georges Canguilhem* have all written of their appreciation of Cavaillès's contributions to the development of the "philosophy of rationality." Cavaillès understood the formal systems of mathematics and science as at once the finest creations of human intellectual labor and, at the same time, entities with a significant degree of autonomy—with a life of their own insofar as they fulfill the rules that have been followed/created in their production and serve our needs as tools; and finally, insofar as they are able to appear to be independent of our individual wishes, and even to be exercising control over our actions and thoughts. Much of Foucault's characterization of "*épistème*" is recognizable here; and Bachelard was demonstrably influenced by these considerations.

Beyond his contributions to a progressive philosophy of science and mathematics, many Marxists† and post-Marxist theorists have generalized these insights into formal systems and applied them to the analysis of social formations, so struck have they been by the life and death of Cavaillès and by the resonances in his work of Marx's *Eighteenth Brumaire*.

BIBLIOGRAPHY:

A. *Méthode axiomatique et formalisme* (Paris: Hermannelo, 1937); *Remarques sur la formation de la théorie abstraite des ensembles* (Paris: Hermann, 1937); *Sur la logique et la théorie de la science* (Paris: P.U.F., 1947); *Transfini et continu* (Paris: Hermann, 1947).

B. G. Ferriers, *Jean Cavaillès, philosophe et combattant* (Paris: P.U.F., 1950).

LAURENCE E. WINTERS

CHÂTELET, FRANÇOIS (b. 1925). The intellectual itinerary of this French Marxist† philosopher differs considerably from the profiles of the *Arguments** group theorists (Kostas Axelos,* Jean Duvignaud,* Pierre Fougeyrollas,* Henri Lefebvre,* Edgar Morin*), with whom he was briefly associated. First, Châtelet was not a member of the French Resistance during World War II as were the others, but rather began his studies in philosophy at the Sorbonne in 1943, finishing them in 1948, after which he taught for several years in Oran and Tunis. Second, despite continuous study of Marx's works in preparation of his doctoral thesis, directed by Jean Hyppolite,* Châtelet resisted active political participation, joining the Communist Party at a time (1955–59) when most leftist intellectuals were mounting a severe critique of its rigid dogmatism. Finally, Châtelet contributed essays only in two issues of *Arguments* (no. 21, 1961; no. 27–28, 1962, the final issue), and despite his relationship with these "existentialized Marxists" (cf. Poster, *Existential Marxism from Sartre to Althusser*, 1977), his association with the *Arguments* group was too brief to include him as a full-fledged "member." Although he does share their experience of teaching in French *lycées* and universities, his subsequent direction differed radically from those followed by the *Arguments* theorists: whereas each one developed his individual conception of the "planetary thinking" proposed during their collaboration, Châtelet moved beyond existentialism, embracing Althusser's* structuralist* Marxism, a commitment reflected by his communication presented at the centenary of *Capital's* publication in 1967 (reprinted in the collection of Châtelet's essays, *Questions objections*). During the last twenty years, Châtelet's activity has been that of a philosopher (studies of Plato, Hegel, contemporary philosophy, and *Capital*), editor of numerous collective works on philosophy and ideology, and professor of philosophy at the University of Paris-VIII.

In the preface to Louis Soubise's study of "Four Marxist Dissidents," Châtelet defined what his reflections on Marxism shared with the *Arguments* theorists:

> We tried to define ourselves in relation to Marx, but because philosophy had taught us [a theoretical attitude] which nothing in Marx's works condemned (quite the contrary), we also thought that we had to *legitimate* our discourse and our stance,

that we had to recognize the meaning and the scope of the word *science*. . . . At that time, [we were] among the first fighters of scientific Marxism in France. (*Le Marxisme après Marx*, pp. 8–9)

In Châtelet's critical struggle the origin and the end of philosophy, and the signification of these concepts, were examined in *La Naissance de l'histoire: La Formation de la pensée historienne en Grèce* and in *Logos et praxis: Recherches sur la signification théorique du marxisme*, both developed during the late 1950s, i.e., while Châtelet was still a member of the Communist Party. In the first book, Châtelet attempted, on the one hand, to show that if the Greeks lacked a correct concept of temporality and were thus unable to develop an historical perspective of society, they nonetheless laid the groundwork for the subsequent elaboration of this perspective. On the other hand, Châtelet's goal was much broader, to emphasize the extent to which an historicist perspective depended on the development of man's political consciousness and knowledge of real liberty. He extended this analysis in *Logos et praxis*: since philosophy originated in the attempt to resolve the class conflicts arising from contradictory ideas held by different groups within Greek society, philosophical resolution of such conflicts necessitated linking logos with praxis. But for Châtelet, it was not until Hegel and Marx that such a philosophical resolution was achieved: prior to them, logos was presented as general and universal truth, but had lost its connection with praxis. The breakthrough occurred in Hegel's *Phenomenology*, where the concept of satisfaction, the dialectic of human becoming, resolved the conflict between the ideal and the real. Then, by reaffirming the link between logos and praxis, Marx brought philosophy into the realm of action, grounding universal satisfaction in alienation. Thus, Châtelet emphasized the existentialist conception of Marxism, especially by concluding his study with the notion of death as an ultimate form of alienation and by calling for a reflection reminiscent of the thought (*pensée*) extolled by other *Arguments* theorists: "It is not at all a question of denying finitude, nor of ignoring its importance . . . ; but [finitude] as such, is in no way the determining element of the actual human problematic; it will become so only when free man will be able to *think* his destiny and not, like today, to force himself to make his history" (*Logos et praxis*, pp. 191–92). Châtelet hesitated to conceive of the possibility of such a "planetary thought," but in affirming that "Marxism is not the only mode of *dépassement* ("going beyond") that has been proposed," he veers away from orthodoxy and toward a conception of existentialist Marxism, which, as Mark Poster maintains, was incomplete since Châtelet "could not define those structures of consciousness and action which made the revolution probable, beyond the simple acceptance of Marx's concepts by the masses in an act of rational self-consciousness" (Poster, *Existential Marxism in Postwar France*, p. 237).

Châtelet described his participation in the *Arguments* project as belonging to his interventions into "controversies, direct or indirect": it was "a way for the Marxist that I pretended 'to try to be,' to liberate himself from 'determination in the final instance,' from explication by reduction; an effort . . . to establish communication in a manner other than by the conceptual hierarchy of different realities'' (*Questions objections*, p. 246). And in the 1960s, Châtelet likewise warmly greeted Althusser's *Pour Marx* and *Lire le Capital* for his analysis of "historical materialism as an anti-philosophy of history, Althusser having opened a perspective that I had lacked in *Logos et praxis*'' (ibid., p. 247). Châtelet's subsequent disenchantment came from what he perceived as Althusser's reiteration of the great classical and doctrinal structures, thereby relegating to a secondary status Marx's efforts to define and practice something more than a merely speculative relation between theory and action.

BIBLIOGRAPHY:

A. *La Naissance de l'histoire* (Paris: Editions de Minuit, 1962); *Logos et praxis* (Paris: SEDES, 1962); *Platon* (Paris: N.R.F., 1965); *Hegel* (Paris: Le Seuil, 1968); *La Philosophie des professeurs* (Paris: Grasset, 1970); in collaboration with G. Lapouge and O. Revault d'Allonnes, *La Révolution sans modèle* (Paris: Mouton, 1974); with E. Pisier-Kouchner and J. M. Vincent, *Les Marxistes et la politique* (Paris: P.U.F., 1975); *Profil d'une oeuvre: Le Capital I* (Paris: Hatier, 1975); and *Questions objections* (Paris: Denoël-Gonthier, 1979), a collection of essays dating from the mid-1950s to the early 1970s, including his two articles published in *Arguments*.

B. Louis Soubise, *Le Marxisme après Marx (1956–1965)* (Paris: Montaigne, 1967), with a preface by Châtelet; and Mark Poster, *Existential Marxism in Postwar France* (Princeton: Princeton University Press, 1977).

CHARLES J. STIVALE

CLAUDÍN, FERNANDO (b. 1913). Born in 1913 at Saragossa, in Spain, Claudín is principally known for his magnum opus, *La crisis del movimiento comunista* (1970), which critically analyzed the history of the Communist movement from a nonstructural Marxist† perspective. He has also, however, been an important political activist in his own right within the Spanish Communist Party (PCE). In his youth he was on the Central Committee of the Juventud Comunista (JC) and formed a close relationship with Santiago Carrillo,* who was head of the socialist youth movement that merged with the JC in 1936. Little is known of Claudín's role in the Spanish Civil War, 1936–39. Exiled to the Soviet Union in 1939, he later worked alongside Carrillo in both Mexico and France, returning to the Soviet Union in 1947 as a leader of the PCE delegation in Moscow. As a leading member of the PCE hierarchy he played a full part in the Party's total subordination to Stalin's† directives, but following the latter's death in 1953 he began to question both the nature of the Soviet system and the internal functioning of his own party. His differences with Carrillo over these issues culminated in a report being presented by Claudín in 1964 to the Executive Committee of the PCE in which he severely criticized the Party leadership for its ''subjectivist'' interpretation of events in Spain and its deliberately misleading presentation of issues to Party militants. He was subsequently expelled from the PCE in 1965 for ''fractional activity,'' along with Jorge Semprún, his chief supporter. It has often been pointed out that Claudín's 1964 interventions anticipated the ''Eurocommunist" positions later adopted by the PCE secretary-general, Carrillo, who indeed remarked some years later that Claudín had been "right too soon."

Following his expulsion, Claudín concentrated on historical and theoretical research, publishing in 1970 his major analysis of the Communist movement, *La crisis del movimiento comunista*. In it he located the roots of an irreversible crisis of the movement in its complete subjugation to Stalin's interpretations of Soviet *raisons d'état*, arguing that the monolithicity of the Comintern was in contradiction to all basic tenets of Marxism. Claudín condemned Stalinism as a dogmatization and perversion of Marxism that had resulted in the betrayal of revolution in other countries in order to secure for the Soviet Union a division of the world with capitalist powers. Despite this, he retained belief in the vitality and relevance of a genuine Marxist vanguard opening the way to new forms of the revolutionary movement.

After the publication in 1975 of his historical study *Marx, Engels y la revolución de 1848*, Claudín took up the themes of the emergent "Eurocommunist" trend, and his *Eurocomunismo y socialismo* (1977) secured his status as a leading theorist of "left" or "critical" Eurocommunism. Identifying the essential twin features of Eurocommunism as the effort to adopt to the specific conditions of advanced capitalism a conception and strategy for the transition to socialism and the diremption between this and the "communism" of Moscow, Claudín exposed a number of shortcomings in the positions adopted by the PCE and the Communist parties of Italy (PCI) and France (PCF). He criticized these parties for holding to a vision of monopoly capitalism that saw it as antithetical to all nonmonopoly factions of the bourgeoisie, arguing that this perspective failed to acknowledge the "relative autonomy" of the state. By this he meant that the state could fulfill its essential task of ensuring the functioning reproduction of the capitalist system as a whole only through exercising a certain autonomy with respect to any class or fraction of a class among the ruling bloc, a thesis originally adumbrated in Marx's analysis of Bonapartism and systematically elaborated in the 1970s by Nicos Poulantzas.* Claudín further suggested that the "two-stage" strategy for transition proposed by the Eurocommunist parties, in which a distinction was drawn between "advanced democracy" and socialism, gave primacy to the political struggle in the form of elections and underplayed the more important social struggle and working-class self-organization. Claiming that Antonio Gramsci's* notion of the "war of position" had been unacceptably constrained into an unconvincing gradualist mold, Claudín argued for the necessity of facing up to the inevitability of a power struggle during a "period of uncertainty," which would follow a "series of ruptures." He rejected the notion of a single party of the working class, calling instead for the struggle within parliaments and other representative bodies to be backed up by mass struggle in every sphere of social and political life. A further criticism of the Eurocommunist parties was that they refused to consider the Eastern Bloc countries nonsocialist. Claudín expanded upon this theme in his next work, *La oposición en el 'socialismo real'* (1981), in which he investigated the repression of opposition groups in these countries.

He argued that the refusal of Eurocommunist leaders to place on trial the anti-democratic and dictatorial nature of these regimes, whose very existence brought the socialist idea into disrepute, served the interests of capitalism.

Currently head of the Spanish Socialist Party's research center, the Fundación Pablo Iglesias, Claudín's most recent publication, in 1983, was a biographical study of the figure most commonly associated with Eurocommunism, Santiago Carrillo, secretary-general of the PCE from 1960 to 1982.

BIBLIOGRAPHY:

A. *The Communist Movement* (New York: Monthly Review Press, 1975); *Documentos de una divergencia comunista* (Barcelona: El Viejo Topo, 1978); *Eurocommunism and Socialism* (London: New Left Books, 1978); *La oposición en el 'socialismo real'* (Madrid: Siglo XXI, 1981); *Santiago Carrillo, crónica de un secretario general* (Barcelona: Planeta, 1983).

PAUL HEYWOOD

COLLETTI, LUCIO (b. 1924). Born in Rome in 1924, Colletti is a professor of theoretical philosophy at the University of Rome. A student of Galvano Della Volpe,* Colletti has been for nearly a decade one of the major exponents of the so-called Dellavolpiana School. From 1957 to 1962 he was editor of the well-known theoretical review *Società*, an organ of the Italian Communist Party (PCI). Having abandoned the Communist Party, he has functioned, since 1964, as an important reference point in the rebirth of theoretical Marxism† in Italy and as an influence on French and English leftists. From October 1966 to December 1967 Colletti directed the review *La sinistra*, and helped author the first part of *Il manifesto* (1969). Through both of these efforts, he attempted to explicate the dissension within the PCI. With the publication of his politico-philosophical *Intervista* (1974), his distancing from Marxism becomes apparent, and it is explictly stated. In his later work it increases in intensity and polemical vigor.

Colletti's work follows the general outline of Della Volpe's in interpreting Marxism as an empirical science that inductively validates Marx's formal theories. Colletti, however, was more concerned with resuscitating the revolutionary aspect of Marxism. He therefore supplied a theoretical dimension noticeably lacking in Della Volpe: the interpenetration of science and action, the revolutionary implications of Marxist social science. Whereas Della Volpe could hide in an isolated world of Marxist theory while Party officials dictated courses of action, Colletti saw an indissoluble linkage between theory and action. Like Della Volpe, and for the same reasons, Colletti felt that Hegel's influence on Marx has been exaggerated. Colletti traced Marx's philosophical heritage to Kant. Without really being aware of it, Marx was significantly influenced by Kant's insistence on both the independent reality of objective phenomena and science as the only intersubjectively valid form of knowledge. These two aspects of Kantianism—an autonomous objective world and a science to cognize it—are pivotal to the bourgeois systematization of natural science, which Colletti admired. They are also the inchoate origins of Marx's science of historical materialism. Hegel, on the other hand, connected the domains of science and morality and dismissed empirical science as inaccurate. Kant, then, was closer to materialism than Hegel. If, philosophically, Marx's roots go to Kant, in terms of political theory Colletti traced Marxism to Rousseau. The major political themes that occupied Marx in his *Critique of Hegel's Doctrine of the State*, the basis of Marxist political theory to this day, are from Rousseau's critique of representative government. These include the state's dependence on society, a critique of parliamentarism, a counter-theory of popular sovereignty, and a general critique of the capitalist state. Marxist political theory has never surpassed these, although of course Marx's innovative economic and historical discoveries introduced the missing factor of scientific credibility.

For Colletti, Marx's critique of Hegel's inversion of subject and predicate inspired a life-long project of making social theory concrete. All of Marx's assertions—from the theory of alienation to the analysis of commodity production—explain real, empirically verifiable phenomena and therefore are predicated on the epistemological priority of facts. Marx studied not society "in general," but one particular society: capitalism. And he did it scientifically, spurning ideal or material abstractions. Echoing Della Volpe, Colletti felt that science requires theories relevant to the phenomena they explain. Orthodoxy absurdly formulates reality as simultaneously "being" and "not-being." Contradictions can exist only between propositions. Real phenomena, on the other hand, are defined by an empirically verifiable existence. Verified contradictions are contradictions in reality, and for that very reason particular or historically determinate ones, anchored in objective historical facts rather than a priori rationality. Colletti's methodology reflects and extends his mentor's. Knowledge takes two forms: a process occurring in nature, and one born in logical mental activity. The first places real limiting conditions on thought. The second "cancels out" empirical reality in the interests of logical purity, transforming it into thought's consequence or effect. Colletti, like Della Volpe, explicitly recognized materialism as the philosophical point of departure for scientific inquiry. Either reality exists in a concrete material sense or intersubjectively verifiable science is impossible. But even though matter is a condition for the existence of thought—thought's "cause"—we cognize reality only by thinking about it. Although objective matter makes science possible, knowledge is also the product of a subjective thought process that categorizes perceived matter, defining "fact" and "fiction." Thought is, in this sense, the "cause of its cause" (*Marxism and Hegel*, p. 119).

Colletti perceived two types of extant Marxist theory, neither scientifically adequate. First, there is metaphysical materialism, based solely on the heterogeneity of thought and being, and the latter's priority. Impersonal laws characterize matter and shape all human phenomena, including thought. Second, idealist Marxism ignores the heterogeneity of being and thought, emphasizing a dialectical thought process that determines history by successively negating matter. Materialist Marxism artificially separates knowledge and reason; idealist

Marxism isolates knowledge from the concrete factual world. Both distort society's subtle and complex blending of objectivity and subjectivity by cutting the (objective) material means of production from the (subjective) experienced relations of production. The unity of matter and thought, structure and ideology, is obliterated.

Colletti's method is factually accurate but simultaneously explains facts in terms of the logical categories by which they are experienced. Like Della Volpe's method it combines the deductive application of general hypotheses and the inductive compilation of empirical data: facts verify hypotheses. Scientists extract from a specific, concrete world a series of meaningful explanatory concepts that are verified empirically. However, Colletti rejected the Cartesian foundations of modern social science, substituting a materialism based on the interpenetration of subject and object. These foundational ideas justify Marx's historical and economic theories, just as Cartesianism justifies bourgeois formal theories. For Colletti, matter places limits on subjectivity, but only through consciousness can we identify both the limits and the reality itself. Consciousness thus ''causes'' us to understand the objective ''cause'' of consciousness. ''The subject is *part* of the object, a moment within the object, and hence is itself *objective*. Both subject and object are part of an *objective* object-subject process'' (*From Rousseau to Lenin*, p. 10). Conscious subjectivity is a reflective moment of objective social being. Consciousness, therefore, is the only aspect of social life capable of reflecting on, and cognizing, the objective totality. Colletti established two points: (1) objective matter exists; but (2) it consists of a dynamic synthesis of disparate elements, a unity of heterogeneous parts. Although his materialism confirms the fundamental priority of being over thought, being itself is a dynamic totality of matter *and* creative thought.

Since society's superstructure reflects the base and is part of it, Colletti defended the unity of sociology and economics and rejected economism. By dichotomizing matter into autonomous, impenetrable categories of production (objectivity) and ideology (subjectivity), orthodox Marxism smothers the real world with impersonal abstractions. Authentic deductive theory, echoing subjectively meaningful perceptions, is an integral part of objectivity. It is hypothetically drawn from reality and empirically verified with real evidence. Hence, it is as real as the explained social phenomena, expressing concepts actually experienced by cognitive actors. Stripped of this hypothesized meaning, facts are random, unfocused, and confusing. Just as ideas are an irreducible moment of material reality, theory is a necessary component of scientific inquiry. Social actors are objective entities whose unique trait is their subjective, reflective thought processes. Scientifically valid hypotheses outline objective patterns of behavior actors reflectively experience. No mechanistic pattern exists in history leading automatically to revolution, independent of conscious decisions. Each valid theory expresses, potentially, the subjective beliefs of observed actors. Marx's deductive hypotheses are, therefore, calls to revolutionary action, factual truths that actually express workers' growing discontent. Their scientificity is confirmed by empirical (objective) evidence and the actual (subjective) commitment of those studied. Empirical science is therefore subjective and objective. In the case of bourgeois social science, the former is represented by Cartesianism and the liberal values flowing therefrom. Scientific inquiry in capitalism implicitly expresses this subjective world view and explicitly supports liberal principles and institutions. On the other hand, Marxist social science takes off from Marx's revolutionary deductive theories. It presumes a multifaceted, multidimensional, interpenetrating totality and explicitly advocates proletarian revolution. Science and values are forever inextricably connected. Orthodox Marxist materialism and bourgeois empiricism radically separate objectivity and subjectivity, hence ignore their own abstract, unrealistic philosophical and political values. The issue is *which* values shall support scientific inquiry, determining the scope of relevant phenomena and the significance of empirical data. Empirical science alone, divorced from revolutionary theory, generates a Bernstein-style acquiescence to the status quo. Revolutionary theory, isolated from empirical verification, is both unrealistic and dogmatic, a real danger to freedom and human (subjective) integrity. Authentic Marxism is empirical and revolutionary, a social science that explains and alters reality.

Marx's mature work, particularly *Capital*, illustrates, for Colletti, the subtle blending of science and revolution. As a scientist, he discovered objective relationships, laws governing the development and demise of capitalist production. In this role he makes only judgments of fact that are empirically verified and universally valid. But Marx also acknowledges matter as a dialectical unity of opposites, an objective totality nurturing creative subjects. The determinate whole, a unity of heterogeneous parts, consists of empirically valid economic laws, explaining intentional acts. Objectivity and subjectivity join in economic class, the objective consequence of the productive apparatus but also the subjective political agent for realizing history's laws. Marx's science embodies "objective factors of production . . . simultaneously presented as subjective agents or social classes" (ibid., p. 16). When empirical laws are manifest in working-class consciousness, then reality will be transformed in a manner consistent with scientific evidence. This, however, is not an automatic process; Marx was not a determinist. Workers congeal as a revolutionary class because of determinate economic factors *and* authentic political consciousness. Without a revolutionary working-class ideology, factual data indicating capitalism's demise remain unfulfilled. Empirical science is simply not enough. The scientist's social role involves an active commitment to empirical facts and the working-class revolutionary movement. Marxist empirical scientists must actively oppose the phenomena they study.

Colletti believes bourgeois empirical science to be elitist and reactionary. However, the main alternative, orthodox Marxism, "is in crisis today, and it can only surmount this crisis by acknowledging it. But precisely this acknowledgement is consciously avoided by virtually every Marxist, great or small" ("A Political and Philosophical Interview," p. 21).

BIBLIOGRAPHY:

A. With C. Napoleoni, *Il futuro del capitalismo* (Bari: Laterza, 1970); *From Rousseau to Lenin* (London: New Left Books, 1972); *Marxism and Hegel* (London: New Left Books, 1973); "A Political and Philosophical Interview," *New Left Review*, 86 (July–August 1974); pp. 3–28; *Tra marxismo e no* (Bari: Laterza, 1979); *Tramonto dell'idologia* (Bari: Laterza, 1980).

B. Perry Anderson, *Considerations on Western Marxism* (London: New Left Books, 1976); Giuseppe Bedeschi, *La parabola del marxismo in Italia* (Bari: Laterza, 1983).

VITTORIO DINI and ROBERT A. GORMAN

COREY, LEWIS (FRAINA, LOUIS) (1892–1953). Born in Italy in 1892, Louis Fraina came to America as a young child. He was active in several radical groups in the early 1900s, serving as editor of *The New International* and *Revolutionary Age*, the first organs of the pro-Bolshevik left in the United States. An organizer of the Communist Party, he served as a Comintern representative in Mexico in 1921 and 1922 but broke with Communism and soon began writing under a new name, Lewis Corey. He won prominence as a Marxist† economist in the 1930s and briefly flirted with the Communists, Trotskyists,† and Lovestonites. Corey abandoned Marxism after the Nazi–Soviet Pact. He became a professor at Antioch College in 1942 and educational director of the AFL's Meat Cutters Union in 1951. A founder of the Union for Democratic Action (forerunner of the Americans for Democratic Action), Corey had to fight a government effort in 1952 to deport him for his old activities. He died on 16 September 1953.

In his pre-Bolshevik period Corey popularized the concept of "mass action," or extraparliamentary activities aimed at the seizure of power. Developed in Europe as a syndicalist weapon to be used against socialists who advocated a peaceful, electoral path to the transfer of power, in America it was used to urge industrial unionism as the primary path to revolution. Corey's reevaluation of Marxism in 1940 concluded that it was a response to European, not American, development. Unlike Europe, America had not needed help from socialists to complete its bourgeois democratic revolution. Since a majority of the population was nonproletarian, democracy and Marxism were incompatible. Stripped of Marxism, socialists would have to appeal to all "useful functional groups within society."

BIBLIOGRAPHY:

A. *The Unfinished Task* (New York: Viking Press, 1942).

B. Esther Corey, "Lewis Corey (Louis C. Fraina), 1892–1953: A Bibliography with Autobiographical Notes," *Labor History*, 4 (1963), pp. 103–31.

RICHARD KLEHR

D

DE BEAUVOIR, SIMONE LUCIE ERNESTINE MARIE BETRAND (b. 1908). A French novelist, philosopher, essayist, and political activist, Simone de Beauvoir was born in Paris, France, on 9 January 1908. She describes her earliest years in *Memoirs of a Dutiful Daughter* (1959). De Beauvoir earned a degree in philosophy from the University of Paris. In 1929, while still a student, she met Jean-Paul Sartre,* the future Nobel prize-winning novelist and philosopher, who was to be her intellectual and personal companion until his death in 1980 (see *Adieux: A Farewell to Sartre*, 1984). From 1931 to 1944 de Beauvoir taught in various *lycées*; intellectually she concentrated upon literature rather than on politics or social issues. Her first novel, *L'Invitée* (*She Came to Stay*, English ed., 1954) was published in 1943. She lost her teaching position during the Occupation; henceforth she and Sartre earned their living solely by their pens. De Beauvoir herself has stated: ''My essays reflect my practical choices and my intellectual certitudes; my novels the astonishment into which I am thrown by the whole and by the details of the human condition. They correspond to two different orders of experience which cannot be communicated in the same manner'' (*Force of Circumstance*, p. 319). To date de Beauvoir has published six novels, one book of short stories, her four-volume autobiography, a play (untranslated), two philosophical works, two books on social questions, accounts of her travels in the United States and China, and other literary and personal essays. She won the Prix Goncourt in 1954 for her novel, *Les Mandarins* (American ed., 1956), which describes the post–World War II milieu of the French intelligentsia. *Le Deuxieme Sexe* (*The Second Sex*, American ed., 1952) was first published in 1949.

De Beauvoir's political activities are also linked with Sartre's. As she has explained, ''Philosophically and politically the initiative has always come from him'' (*Force of Circumstance*, p. 645). Nonetheless de Beauvoir claims that she did not enter into any of their joint projects ''without first having analyzed it and accepted it on my own account'' (ibid., p. 644). Sartre definitively committed himself to a life of political activism in 1940, as France faced defeat at the hands of Nazi Germany. He attempted to influence the postwar European order by editing the review, *Les Temps modernes*, and by organizing the Rassemblement Democratique et Révolutionnaire (RDR), which, according to de Beauvoir, was intended to be a mediating influence between the advanced wing of the reformist petit bourgeoisie and the revolutionary proletariat. Its initial goal was the creation of a socialist Europe independent of the two blocs. When the cold war made neutralism impossible Sartre and de Beauvoir sympathized with the Soviet Union in order to express their identification with the oppressed. Following the invasion of Czechoslovakia by the Warsaw Pact armies of 1968, however, they broke ties with the Soviet Union and made no further visits there. Both became increasingly involved with anticolonialist Third World "liberation movements"; they opposed French (Gaullist and non-Gaullist) policy toward Algeria, and signed the "Manifesto of the 121," in which the right of civil disobedience was recognized. Sartre publicized the work of the late Frantz Fanon,* author of *The Wretched of the Earth*, who identified violence as a means by which colonialized people could free themselves from internalized feelings of inferiority; de Beauvoir wrote the preface for Gisele Halimi's *Djamila Boupacha* (1962), an account of a young Arab woman's imprisonment and torture at the hands of the French army in Algeria. To demonstrate their opposition to the war in Vietnam, both participated in the Bertrand Russell War Crimes Tribunal held in Copenhagen in 1967, which found the U.S. government guilty of genocide. Following the French student revolt of 1968, de Beauvoir and Sartre assisted *gauchistes* sympathetic to the politics of Mao Zedong;† according to de Beauvoir, the events of May 1968 "proved that the struggle for control by the workers was possible and that the creative initiative of the masses was a necessity" (*All Is Said and Done*, p. 444). Although neither she nor Sartre ever formally joined any political party, de Beauvoir has stressed "the indispensable necessity for creating a vanguard capable of carrying a revolution in the developed capitalist countries through to a successful conclusion" (ibid., p. 444).

De Beauvoir has paid particular attention to problems affecting women and the aged after writing books on these subjects (*The Second Sex; La Vieillesse*, 1970; *The Coming of Age*, English ed., 1972). *The Second Sex*, however, was not conceived as a feminist manifesto. Although de Beauvoir claims that her own femaleness "had never been a burden" (*Force of Circumstances*, p. 108), she began her study as grounding for her autobiography. At the time of writing she did not consider herself to be a feminist, if a feminist was defined as a person "struggling for specifically feminist claims"; for de Beauvoir there were "many more problems . . . more important . . . than those which affect us (women) specifically" (*All Is Said and Done*, p. 469). However by the early 1970s she had identified herself with feminism and regarded women's problems as "essential" (ibid., p. 468).

De Beauvoir, like Sartre, sought to join existentialism to the Marxist† dialectic and historical materialism. They both saw similarities between the two philosophies. Marxism, like existentialism, de Beauvoir states, also places the individual within a "situation" in the "historical and economic world" (*The Ethics of Ambiguity*, p. 19); the act of revolt implies the rejection of a given (class) situation, and the positing of a new state of being and set of values that acquire meaning through the making of that choice. However, for de Beauvoir human will is not merely a reflection of objective conditions; regardless of his or her personal, class, or social situation, an individual who revolts makes a decision "whose source is only in himself" (ibid., p. 20). In her later books (*The Long March*, 1958; and *All Is Said and Done*) de Beauvoir places a greater emphasis upon socio-economic structures and in personal childhood experiences as determinants of choice and behavior. Nonetheless, men and women remain free to choose freely either to transcend or to betray themselves and others.

De Beauvoir also posits freedom as a goal and a good to be chosen for itself. True freedom, however, cannot be found in merely personal whim. Since, for de Beauvoir, each person is defined only by his relationship to the world and other individuals and thus depends upon others to open up the future for him, and to assist (or thwart) his projects, the freedom of one is ineluctably linked to the freedom of all. Oppositely, "oppression" must be opposed by one and all because it reduces persons to things. Political activity should aim at opening the oppressed to their own freedom so that freedom may be freely chosen; hence the only moral political choice is to side with the oppressed. Yet, in any given situation, attention must be paid to the means by which oppression is fought lest the revolutionary, in his or her seriousness or through his or her passion, turn politics against individuals rather than to their service.

In *The Second Sex*, de Beauvoir explores women's generic situation as the Other, a potentially sovereign subject who, in order to realize her femininity, sexuality, and survival, must renounce her freely chosen projects and turn herself into an object and prey for men in a world defined by men. "The drama of woman," she writes, "lies in this conflict between the fundamental aspirations of every subject (ego) who always regards the self as the essential, and the compulsions of a situation in which she is the inessential" (p. xxviii), condemned, like all oppressed people, to immanence rather than transcendence. According to de Beauvoir, "femininity" is a social creation. Biology does not determine the female destiny or require the assumption of a subordinate position. Moreover, women often view themselves as they are defined by men, rather than in accordance with their own true nature. Nonetheless women's generic situation is rooted in the human condition as it has historically evolved. Men have been able to transcend their species/animal existence in pursuit of projects through which they shape the future and put their lives at risk, whereas women have remained linked to repetitive animality. Women have joined men in (justly) celebrating masculine values as superior. Without values or a history of their own they have remained confined in a domain defined by men. According to de Beauvoir, all ideologies are male, and all male ideologies are directed at justifying the oppression of women. Through socialization processes beginning in earliest childhood, women are taught to accept and internalize these ideologies and thus to consent to their oppression.

So that she can fulfill her vocation as a female, a young woman is taught to be "weak, futile, docile" (*The Second Sex*, p. 314), to cultivate her appearance in order to become a sexual object for a man, and thus to acquire a secure social and economic status through marriage. Caught between her desire for erotic satisfaction and affection and her distaste for becoming prey, the young woman is often too divided against herself to resist this social pressure. In marriage, however, sexual intercourse, no longer freely chosen, becomes an institution. The wife loses her identity in the world and the home becomes her only space. If a mother is herself unhappy, she will often seek compensation through her children, oppressing them as well. Only when rid of her domestic duties in middle age can a woman regain her freedom, but this occurs at "the very time when she can make no use of it" (ibid., p. 550). Not permitted by society to accomplish anything, many women vainly seek their true being "through narcissism, love, or religion" (ibid., p. 639). Independent women refuse to confine themselves to being female, yet are also loath to renounce their sexuality. Thus they remain doubtful as to both their professional and sexual future.

De Beauvoir denies that there is any such thing as a specifically "feminine" nature or character. If women are to become emancipated they must become full-scale human beings who develop relationships with men and work in freedom and "take over the tools of men and use them for their interests" (*All Is Said and Done*, p. 473). Socialism has promised sexual equality but has not achieved it. Thus although a socialist revolution is necessary it is not sufficient in itself. "In short," de Beauvoir writes in the final volume of her autobiography, "I used to think that the class war should take precedence over the struggle between the sexes. Now I think that they should both be carried on together" (ibid., p. 470).

BIBLIOGRAPHY:

A. *The Ethics of Ambiguity* (New York: Philosophical Library, 1948); *America Day by Day* (New York: Grove Press, 1953); *The Second Sex* (New York: Knopf, 1953); *The Long March* (New York: World, 1958); *Memoirs of a Dutiful Daughter* (New York: World, 1959); *The Marquis de Sade: An Essay* (London: John Calder, 1962); *The Prime of Life* (New York: World, 1962); with Gisele Halimi, *Djamila Boupacha* (New York: Macmillan, 1962); *Force of Circumstance* (New York: Putnam, 1964); *A Very Easy Death* (New York: Putnam, 1965); *Brigitte Bardot and the Lolita Syndrome* (New York: Arno Press, 1972); *The Coming of Age* (New York: Putnam, 1972); *All Is Said and Done* (New York: Putnam, 1974); *Adieux: A Farewell to Sartre* (New York: Pantheon, 1984).

B. Robert D. Cottrell, *Simone de Beauvoir* (New York: Frederick Unger, 1975); Jean Leighton, *Simone de Beauvoir on Woman* (Cranbury, N.J.: Associated University Presses, 1975); Carol Ascher, *Simone de Beauvoir: A Life of Freedom* (Boston: Beacon Press, 1981).

KAREN ROSENBLUM-CALE

DEBRAY, RÉGIS (b. 1940). Born in Paris on 2 September 1940 into an upper middle-class household, Jules Régis Debray received the philosophy prize in the annual Concours Général when he was sixteen. In 1959 he graduated first in his class from the prestigious Lycée Louis-le-Grand and received the highest score on the entrance exam to the Ecole Normale Supérieure. That same year, after vacationing in the United States, Debray unexpectedly returned by way of a Cuba in the blush of Fidel Castro's† successful revolution. Debray was infected by the optimism and energy of Fidel's revolutionary Cuba. At the Ecole Normale Supérieure Debray studied with Louis Althusser,* who encouraged his prize student to join the French Communist Party (PCF). Debray revisited Cuba in 1961. After receiving his degree in philosophy in 1963, Debray traveled to Latin America, where he remained until the end of 1964. He visited every Latin American country but Paraguay, contacted numerous revolutionary organizations, and interviewed the Venezuelan rebel leader Douglas Bravo. Debray began to study seriously the tactics of Cuban-style guerrilla movements and to assume that theory would take care of itself after a successful guerrilla campaign. This denigration of theory, like the Cuban Revolution itself, contradicted orthodox Communist policy. Debray resigned his membership in the PCF in 1963. In 1965 he earned his *agrégé* in philosophy and taught at the University of Nancy. In January 1966 he returned to Cuba as professor of the history of philosophy at the University of Havana, where he remained for six months. After a preliminary trip in 1966, in late 1967 Debray again arrived in Bolivia to accompany Che Guevara† in his fateful guerrilla struggle among Bolivian peasants. He was taken prisoner in 1967 and sentenced to thirty years in prison. After three years of sometimes brutal incarceration, Debray was pardoned and returned to France. In 1981 François Mitterrand appointed Debray a special advisor on Latin American affairs. Debray is the author of numerous scholarly works, polemics, short stories, and novels.

Like Che, Frantz Fanon,* and other Third World guerrilla leaders, Debray distrusted national bourgeoisies and opposed the orthodox Communist strategy of working peacefully—via electoral coalitions—with their progressive elements. Debray was an early advocate and admirer of "Fidelism," which he defined as a form of revolutionary nationalism based on a protracted war against oligarchies allied with US imperialism and an insurrectional, rural-based guerrilla struggle (or *foco*; hence the tactical term *foquism*) to overthrow existing regimes. Debray also believed a national revolutionary organization, needed to coordinate the guerrilla struggle, could grow from within the guerrilla movement itself, apart from orthodox Communist Party bureaucracies. As the Cuban experience proved, the vanguard Marxist†-Leninist† party (which tends to be locked into tired formulas that inhibit successful people's wars) is therefore unnecessary and undesirable in guerrilla insurrections. These tactical considerations are outlined in Debray's "Castroism: The Long March in Latin America" (1964), "Problems of Revolutionary Strategy in Latin America" (1965), and *Revolution in the Revolution?* (1967). These works are anchored firmly in the actual empirical environment of Latin American revolutionary struggles, ignoring abstract theoretical speculation.

After his incarceration in Bolivia Debray recanted somewhat, attributing Che's failure to his not recognizing the importance of urban proletariat support, his lack of systematic research and theory about class composition, his failure to prepare carefully the guerrilla's zone of operations, and his ignorance of Bolivia's national historical process. In brief, Debray moved back from Che's voluntaristic, peasant-based "foquismo" strategy and toward more Leninist strategies (see "Time and Politics," 1969, *A Critique of Arms*, 1974, *Trials by Fire*, 1974, and *Che's Guerrilla War*, 1974). He even delved into theoretical issues related to the nexus of diamat and Althusserian dialectics, something he had previously rejected out of hand. In *The Chilean Revolution: Conversations with Allende* (1971), Debray opined that revolutionaries in certain areas (e.g. Chile, Western Europe) should cooperate with reformists via electoral and political alliances in order to transform the capitalist system from within. Nonetheless, Debray insisted that conditions for armed insurrections throughout much of Latin America are improving and require on the part of revolutionaries patience and energetic work to radicalize workers and peasants. To the consternation of orthodox Marxists, however, Debray still argued that the revolutionary party must emerge from within the revolutionary masses and react solely to their needs.

Debray has spent the past decade in France writing short stories, novels, journalistic pieces, and the caustic and popular *Teachers, Writers, Celebrities: Intellectuals of Modern France* (1979). His most recent work on theory, *Critique of Political Reason* (1984), emphasizes the political importance of myth, religion, and irrationality, the irrelevance of "scientific" Marxism in the battle for political hegemony, and the necessity for a revitalized Marxism to attach itself to people's emotions, hopes, and fears. Although the style rings sentimental and pious, the substance is eclectic, combining aspects of Georges Sorel,* Antonio Gramsci,* Marx, Lenin, Jean-Paul Sartre,* and his own "foquismo." It is safe to say that Debray's remarkable influence in France, Latin America, and elsewhere in the Third World is a result of his romantic image and his tactical advice to guerrilla leaders rather than any creative contribution to Marxian theory.

BIBLIOGRAPHY:

A. *Revolution in the Revolution?* (New York: Monthly Review Press, 1967); *Defensor en Camiri* (Montevideo: Siglo Ilustrado, 1968); *On Trial: Fidel Castro and Régis Debray* (London: Lorrimer, 1968); *Ensayos sobre America latina* (Mexico: Era, 1969); *Strategy for Revolution* (New York: Monthly Review Press, 1970); *The Chilean Revolution: Conversations with Allende* (New York: Pantheon, 1971); *Prison Writings* (London: Allen Lance, 1973); *Che's Guerilla War* (Baltimore: Penguin, 1975); *Dialogue on Spain* (London: Lawrence & Wishart, 1976); *A Critique of Arms* (New York: Penguin, 1977); *Teachers, Writers, Celebrities: Intellectuals of Modern France* (London: New Left Books, 1981); *Critique of Political Reason* (New York: Schocken, 1984).

B. Leo Huberman and Paul M. Sweezy, eds., *Régis Debray and the Latin American Revolution* (New York: Monthly Review Press, 1968); Jack Woddis, *New Theories of Revolution* (New York: International, 1972); Hartmut Ramm, *The Marxism of Regis Debray* (Lawrence: Regents Press of Kansas, 1978).

ROBERT A. GORMAN

DEBS, EUGENE VICTOR (1855–1926). Debs was born in Terre Haute, Indiana, on 5 November 1855. His first involvement with a labor union took place in 1875, when he joined and became the secretary of the Local Brotherhood of Locomotive Firemen. In 1885 he was elected to the state legislature on the Democratic ticket. He served only one term. In 1894 Debs formed the American Railway Union and became involved in the Pullman Strike, for which he was arrested and convicted of conspiracy. While in prison, Debs read and was inspired by socialist writings. In 1896 Debs officially announced his conversion to socialism and became a member of a socialist organization called the Brotherhood of Cooperative Commonwealths. In 1897 the Social Democratic Party was formed, and Debs ran for president as its candidate in 1900, 1904, 1908, and 1912, capturing over 900,000 votes in the 1912 election. In 1918, at Canton, Ohio, Debs gave a speech condemning the United States and its involvement in World War I. He was arrested, tried, and sentenced to ten years for violation of the Espionage Act. While in prison, Debs once again ran for president. President Harding pardoned Debs in 1921, and Debs spent the next few years lecturing and promoting the Socialist Party. Eugene Victor Debs died on 20 October 1926.

Debs's socialism was more communitarian than the type advocated by his Marxist† contemporaries. He was, in other words, concerned with concrete problems related to establishing a socialist commonwealth, not just overthrowing capitalism. This socialist commonwealth, Debs believed, was the next stage, following capitalism, in the evolution of humanity. Debs argued that workers have the moral right to use any weapon necessary to defeat capitalism, which must be overthrown, not merely reformed. The power to accomplish this is inherent within workers themselves and can be cultivated through sound organization and education. Workers must be educated because ignorance is an enemy of socialism. Debs believed capitalism divided and exploited its workers and agreed with Marx's assertion that capitalism alienated workers from their own labors. He believed the profit system to be the main cause of social evils such as inequality, competition, poverty, unemployment, crime, and overcrowded prisons. Government and law support capitalism because capitalists control the government.

Debs wanted a single, united federation of labor unions. Through this organization he believed workers could exert their political and social power to alter the system radically. Worker solidarity and union organization would liberate enslaved humanity. Debs believed the Socialist Party was the revolutionary party of the workers and could, through education and organization, precipitate the socialist revolution. In his speeches, he claimed a vote for the capitalist parties was a vote for poverty and wage slavery, while a vote for the Socialist Party was a vote for human emancipation. Debs believed that Marx discovered the social and historical laws that make socialism both inevitable and desirable, but failed to describe adequately socialist social, economic, and political institutions. Marx's central message—that capitalism will be replaced by socialism, which will evolve into communism—must now be translated into a plausible, alternative socialist life style.

Debs wanted to reorganize society based on mutualism and cooperation. He believed that the mechanics of socialism had to be explicitly demonstrated before workers would willingly establish a universal commonwealth based on its principles. Consequently he argued that a workers' state should be established in the western United States to show that socialism is possible. Only those people who accepted and comprehended the goals of socialism would be permitted into the commonwealth. Property would be owned by all, and members provided for according to their needs. Money would have no use in this society because all workers would own the means of production and distribution. Debs believed that socialism would generate world peace and a new beginning for humanity.

BIBLIOGRAPHY:

A. *Debs: His Life, Writings, and Speeches* (Girard, Kans.: The Appeal to Reason, 1908); *Debs and the War: His Canton Speech and His Trial in the Federal Court at Cleveland, 1918* (Chicago: National Office Socialist Party, 1923).

B. Ray Ginger, *The Bending Cross: A Biography of Eugene V. Debs* (New Brunswick, N.J.: Rutgers University Press, 1949); Howard W. Morgan, *Eugene V. Debs: Socialist for President* (Syracuse: Syracuse University Press, 1962); Ronald Radosh, *Debs* (Englewood Cliffs, N.J.: Prentice-Hall, 1971); Harold W. Currie, *Eugene V. Debs* (Boston: Twayne, 1976).

JOSEPH M. HAZLETT

DE GIOVANNI, BIAGIO (b. 1931). Biagio De Giovanni, born in Naples 21 December 1931, is professor of political philosophy at the University of Naples. Having received his training in the study of philosophy of law, he did research on strictly legal topics such as objectivation, Vico, and Neopolitan Vicoism. In 1968 he joined the Italian Communist Party (PCI) and undertook militant activities in Bari and in Naples that eventually led to national posts in the organizational structure of the party. Since 1979 he has been a member of the Central Committee. But his presence has been felt most significantly in theoretical debate, with contributions to all Party organs, from the daily *L'unità* to the weekly *Rinascita* and the theoretical review *Critica marxista*. In 1981, in order to conduct research of a freer and more open but also very specific nature, he founded and still edits (together with Cacciari, Bodei, and others) the review of political philosophy and theory entitled *Il centauro*.

De Giovanni's reading of Marx† is very close to that of the tradition of Italian Marxism centered around Antonio Gramsci*; in particular, reference is often made to the contributions of Cesare Luporini* and Nicola Badaloni.* The central theme of his interpretation is the relationship between economy and politics and the possibility of also utilizing that relationship in our epoch, which is one characterized by an ever deepening crisis of the state as the central organism of control and supremacy. According to De Giovanni, the relationship between economics and politics in Marx cannot be reduced to the poles of a dualism between civil society and the state, but rather it is legitimate—and even indispensable—to find a political theory of class in *Das Kapital* itself, through the entire line of dialectical exposition from the first to the second and even third volumes, from production to circulation to distribution. From Marx's critique of political economy there also emerges a critique of what De Giovanni calls the "invariance" of the bourgeois form of politics, that is, the continual attempt to reunify the process that acts as a stimulus for the separation of economy and politics. Gramsci is for this reason the most authentic successor of Marx in that he understood the necessity of grasping theoretically the complexity of the capitalistic process of crisis-transformation and of mastering it with political means, of actively transforming the economic crisis into a crisis of political supremacy.

During the profound crisis of capitalism after the 1960s—with its transformation of the relationship between state, production, and market—the "social" and the "political," i.e., society and the state, have become more and more intertwined. This has brought about contemporaneous developments toward a socialization of politics and a politicization of the social realm. De Giovanni therefore views favorably the strategy of the labor movement to work from *within* the state *for* a new state.

BIBLIOGRAPHY:

A. *Hegel e il tempo storico della società borghese* (Bari: De Donato, 1970); *La teoria politica delle classi nel "capitale" di Marx* (Bari: De Donato, 1976).

B. R. Esposito, "Ragione e mutamento: ipotesi a confronto," *Critica marxista*, 20, no. 3 (May–June 1982), pp. 149–68.

VITTORIO DINI

DELEUZE, GILLES (n.a.). It would be difficult if not impossible to summarize or to assess the work of such a philosopher as Gilles Deleuze, who in collaboration with Félix Guattari* has written two of the most significant and remarkable texts of the past decade. In 1972 together they published *Anti-Oedipus: Capitalism and Schizophrenia*, which is widely regarded as the most important philosophical text arising from the events of May 1968. This volume was followed in 1975 by *Kafka; pour une littérature mineure*; and *Mille plateaux* in 1980. These collaborative texts are only the most recent in a long publishing career of Deleuze, who has written on Nietzsche, Spinoza, Hume, Kant, and Bergson, as well as on such literary figures as Proust and Sacher-Masoch. What was for Deleuze in his studies of historical figures a unique mode of reading texts and commenting on them becomes in his more recent collaborative work a profound concern for doing philosophy—understood as creativity in the realm of ideas, of concepts.

Few if any of the traditional philosophical concepts remain in the *Anti-Oedipus*; even those language games still operative in his influential studies of Nietzsche and Spinoza are gone in the works he has authored with Guattari. In *Anti-Oedipus* and *Mille plateaux* a whole new language (or perhaps several new languages) is eleborated—a language very much generative of/generated by the counterculture of the 1970s and 1980s of resistance to bureaucratic and militaristic domination. In this context the best that can be done is to point out several particularly important features of this language, a language that moved Michel

Foucault* to say that "the future is Deleuzian." One of the things that will strike the reader of *Anti-Oedipus* and *Mille plateaux* is that works of art and literature, socio-historical formations, scientific theories, and technology all are afforded an equal ontological status. Each is discussed as an autonomous "form of life" in possession of its own desire, internal politics, and effective relations with other "life forms," called "assemblages" or "machines." What is revealed is a virtual Spinozist notion of the "univocity of being"—things are all on the same plane or, to put this in better terms, there are many planes but none has priority over another. This points to another aspect of Deleuze's thought. It is radically antitranscendental while not falling simply into one or another textbook alternative. He rejects any and all reference to conditions for possibility "in general," insisting that specific conditions exist immediately alongside of their conditioned effectuations as a part of their actuality—but only one part among others. This theme is developed in his studies of Kant and Spinoza and guides his reading of Nietzsche; but in *Anti-Oedipus* even the making of such claims has become part of those claims—part of the discourse itself.

There are three notions in the works of Deleuze and Guattari that have become particularly important in the development of left thought in the 1970s. The first, and probably the most provocative, is that of "machine"—or "machinic assemblage" in the language of *Mille plateaux*. Briefly, a machine is a group of disparate elements, some discursive and some nondiscursive, that cofunction and subsist. This notion is the forerunner of Foucault's idea of investments of power (*déspositifs*) and has played a role in numerous institutional analyses such as those by Jacques Donzelot,* Pasquino, and Castel. It has aided the understanding of how the daily practices, self-justifications, knowledges sought and acquired, and physical structures of institutions cofunction to reach their self-given ends and to maintain themselves internally and in relation to other machinic-assemblages. The institutional analyses based on the work of Deleuze and Guattari have managed to avoid the oversimplifying excesses of the orthodox Marxist† left.

The actual energetic functioning of these "social machines" is driven by the degree of differential investment of desire at points in the system—driven, that is to say, by intensities, ebbing and flowing through the channels and pathways of the assemblage. The idea of an intensity in general, first drawn from Nietzsche, has become central to the philosophy of libidinal economics and the politics of the body and, as well, is present throughout "New Wave" culture of the 1980s. Just as energetic intensities flow over the surface of social institutions—machines—and psychological desiring intensities over the surface of the body of the individual, so people wander or are driven from place to place, country to country, job to job, over the body of capital. This notion we owe to Deleuze and Guattari; and it has allowed the neo-Marxist left to see in small, localized refusals and rebellions, significant features of the strains upon, and weaknesses in, the world-system.

BIBLIOGRAPHY:

A. With Félix Guattari, *Kafka; pour une littérature mineure* (Paris: Editions de Minuit, 1975); with Félix Guattari, *Anti-Oedipus: Capitalism and Schizophrenia* (New York: Viking Press, 1977); with Félix Guattari, *Mille plateaux* (Paris: Editions de Minuit, 1980).

B. Miriam Glucksmann, *Structuralist Analysis in Contemporary Social Thought* (London: Routledge & Kegan Paul, 1974); Rosalind Coward and John Ellis, *Language and Materialism* (London: Routledge & Kegan Paul, 1977).

LAURENCE E. WINTERS

DELLA VOLPE, GALVANO (1895–1968). Born in the Italian city of Imola on 24 September 1895, Della Volpe studied with Rodolfo Mondolfo* at the University of Bologna, where he received a degree in philosophy. He taught history and philosophy at the Bolognese Liceo Galvani until 1938, when he won the competition to teach the history of philosophy in the education faculty at the University of Messina. Della Volpe isolated himself in academe, remaining a full-time university professor until 1965. His early thought focused on critically reconciling Giovanni Gentile's idealism and actualism with Benedetto Croce's historicism. His early published thoughts on Hegel and Hume indicate the intense opposition to idealism that would later influence his Marxist† theorizing. His writings on aesthetics, which culminated in the *Critique of Taste*—a book many philosophers consider Della Volpe's most sophisticated theoretical work—emphasize both the technical and discursive aspects of art objects. Della Volpe joined the Italian Communist Party (PCI) in 1944 and made a significant contribution to Marxist theory during the years 1947–60. His relationship to the Party was inconsistent: at times he was the obedient scholar, parroting the current line; at other times he energetically criticized Soviet diamat and Soviet legalism in radical theoretical journals such as *Società*. Orthodox PCI spokesmen termed Della Volpe's ideas nondialectical ''scientism'' and accused him of organizational factionalism, despite the fact that Della Volpe never openly broke with the PCI or its leadership. The so-called Dellavolpian school—which was merely several individuals focusing on and developing Della Volpe's ideas, rather than an organized group—consisted of Giulio Pietranera (political economy), Raniero Panzieri* (a PCI militant who wrote about worker self-government), Lucio Colletti* (philosophy and methodology), Umberto Cerroni (philosophy of law), Mario Rossi (history of philosophy), Nicolao Merker (history of philosophy), Alessandro Mazzone (history of philosophy), Carlo Violi (editor of a bibliography of Della Volpe's work), Ignazio Ambrogio (aesthetics), and Rocco Musolino (aesthetics).

Logica come scienza positiva (1950), Della Volpe's major work, traces Marx's philosophical heritage through the critical, empirical work of Aristotle, Galileo, and Hume. Della Volpe interpreted Hegel as an idealist who justified both Christianity and the German nation-state. The Hegelian connection to Marx, which people like George Lukács* and Antonio Gramsci* traced through the mediating work of the left Hegelians, is dismissed outright. Hegelianism, for

Della Volpe, is an idealist metaphysics that Marx categorically rejected. Hegel's reversal of priorities, the use of abstraction to explain particulars, cannot be scientifically justified. Marxism, as scientific critique, reverses Hegel's reversal. It is nondogmatic, nonmetaphysical, and fact-oriented—a total critique of bourgeois myth.

When empirical science is cleansed of Cartesianism, however, it is merely an unfocused, static compilation of data, with no criteria for theory formation and no basis for limiting the scope of relevant data. Empirical scientists, in this situation, are helplessly bombarded by an entire universe of disparate, meaningless social facts that must be theoretically arranged and categorized. Della Volpe found the answer to this question of meaning in "deterministic abstractions." Granted, empirical phenomena are explained by means of conceptual abstractions or theories. The choice, for Della Volpe, is between generic, a priori theories, which squeeze reality into abstract categories, and historically determinate theories that accept things as they are. In other words, the theories that we use to organize and explain empirical reality must be part of that reality. This is what Marx meant by historical materialism: each historical era marked by unique ideas, values, and institutions from which social scientists draw the hypotheses required to begin empirical inquiry. Marx's theories regarding the tendencies of capital, the nature of labor power, class polarization, revolution, and so forth are drawn from his experiences in capitalism. Their utility for collecting data is based on their historical concreteness: they recognize things for what they are, rather than for what they are not. The same hypotheses are scientifically irrelevant and superfluous when lifted from the historical era of capitalism.

Della Volpe's theory of deterministic abstractions is materialist and historicist. Within any historical period, the quality of life and thought is conditioned by matter in motion. Each society satiates material needs through a unique productive apparatus marked by particular relationships of production. Because these are the tools for meeting basic irrepressible material wants, they mediate citizens and cultural institutions, molding the latter's form and content. The economic base, therefore, has a determining influence on social ideas. For Della Volpe, the alternative to materialism is idealism, and as the critique of Hegel illustrates, this deforms reality by imposing unverifiable subjective abstractions on objective, concrete phenomena.

Notwithstanding the theoretical primacy of matter over thought, however, Della Volpe is equally critical (in his writings) of mainstream orthodox materialism. Engels† erred by adding to Marx's materialism a metaphysical dialectic, an objective view of the universe that is ahistorically valid. Marxism heuristically explains capitalism but is not an objective a priori truth. It is historically determinate, emerging from and reflecting capitalist society and facilitating empirical inquiry. It is verified only by supporting facts, not by abstract reasoning. If verified, Marx's theories are scientifically valid only for the historical era from which they are originally drawn. They are not pat formulas valid universally and transhistorically. Orthodox Marxism, like idealism, forfeits scientificity when it abstractly interprets concrete factual reality, in effect denying reality's concreteness. Stalinism,† by implication, epitomizes an irrational dictatorship of abstractions, a belief that truth must triumph even if, in the process, it mercilessly destroys reality. In sum, after stripping empirical science of bourgeois preconceptions, Della Volpe substitutes a philosophy of "historicist materialism," which rationalizes Marx's major hypotheses and then guides empirical inquiry.

Because Marxism is historically determinate and data-oriented, there is a methodological unity to natural and social science. Both modes of experimental inquiry require induction (the recognition of matter as something outside thought and the accumulation of relevant material facts) and deduction (positing reasonable theories as the framework within which facts are gathered and interpreted). Deduction (reason) must prove itself inductively. Facts are inextricably connected to what Della Volpe calls an "hypothesis-idea," or are insignificant. Orthodox materialism is guilty of overemphasizing reason, assuming its utility and truth independent of factual verification. Bourgeois empirical science, on the other hand, loses its philosophical raison d'être (which in any case cannot, today, be factually supported) and aimlessly flounders in an endless flow of data. As Marx and Galileo recognized, science needs both theory and facts. The logic of natural and human science is therefore identical. In utilizing thought to explain the interrelationships of things, that is, formulating hypotheses, the logical "principle of tauto-etherology" as the unity of opposites (the "same" and "other" united into one) is involved. On the other hand, when inductively measuring theories against actual facts, the latter are recognized as independent phenomena. Here, the logical "principle of identity" is needed. Scientific logic, therefore, is a composite of both principles, which Della Volpe painfully called the "principle of tauto-etherological identity." It expresses simultaneously the significance of empirical facts as well as unifying ideas, both necessary aspects of reality.

Marx's unique contribution to scientific theory, for Della Volpe, is recognizing that, within a historically determinate locale, material phenomena that appear isolated are actually dynamically linked in a grand social totality that is, in the last resort, shaped by the economic base. Moreover, the observed pattern is one of negation and progressive sublation, that is, capitalism shapes a culture that annuls and surpasses its own determining productive apparatus. Marxism thus fits neatly into the logic of science. It is a series of theoretical hypotheses regarding the interpenetration of matter (the principle of tauto-etherology) drawn from a specific historical milieu whose concrete facts inductively confirm the original theory (the principle of identity). Empirical social scientists, accumulating evidence according to universally accepted methods of empirical inquiry, will substantiate Marx's portentous suggestions concerning capitalism's demise and simultaneously provide explosive fuel for the simmering class struggle. Della Volpe believed that sociology will become an empirical science that is also materialist and revolutionary.

BIBLIOGRAPHY:

A. *Opere*, ed. Ignazio Ambrogio (Rome: Riuniti, 1972–73); *Logic as a Positive Science* (London: New Left Books, 1980); *Critique of Taste* (London: New Left Books, 1982).

B. Franco Cassano, *Marxismo e filosofia in Italia 1958–1971* (Bari: Dedalo, 1973); Mario Alcaro, *Dellavolpismo e nuova sinistra* (Bari: Dedalo, 1977); John Fraser, *An Introduction to the Thought of Galvano Della Volpe* (London: Lawrence & Wishart, 1977); Giuseppe Colombo, *Della Volpe premarxista* (Rome: Studium, 1979); Giuseppe Bedeschi, *La parabola del marxismo in Italia 1945–1983* (Bari: Laterza, 1983).

VITTORIO DINI and ROBERT A. GORMAN

DE MAN, HENDRIK (HENRI) (1885–1953). Hendrik De Man was born in 1885 at Anvers in Belgium, where he became a leader of the Socialist youth. He studied in Germany, Austria, and Britain, making a living as a journalist at the same time. In Leipzig he joined the Marxist† left and before World War I became director of the Ecole Ouvrière Supérieure in Brussels. He was conscripted during the war, worked in the United States from 1920 to 1922, and returned to become a professor at the Institute of Labor in Frankfurt. From his studies on the activity of work he published *Zur Psychologie des Socialismus* in 1926, translated into French as *Au-delà du marxisme*. The book had a considerable impact because it was a thoroughgoing critique of Marxism in the contemporary world of the 1920s. De Man claimed that Marxism was out of date because it was based on nineteenth-century philosophical ideas and took no account of modern conditions of work and psychological studies of work. He said that the first theoreticians of socialism emerged before the existence of the working class, were mainly bourgeois, and explained exploitation in a utilitarian mode. The workers' movement was initiated by intellectuals, whose socialism was based on moral distress rather than economic deprivation, and was taken up by artisanal workers who wanted to protect their established position against change. The exploitation and oppression felt by the workers in the 1920s was not a mechanical result of their pauperization but was caused by the fact that their expectations and needs had outstripped their ability to satisfy them, producing tension and a feeling of exploitation. Fear of unemployment and increasing alienation from the productive process angered workers who believed in the traditional European norms of work equality and personal responsibility. Socialism for de Man was the establishment of all those rights that would allow man the development of his "integral personality," but Marxism had limited itself to man's material needs and made the workers as acquisitive as the bourgeoisie.

Disillusioned by the failures of socialism and the rise of Hitler in the 1930s, de Man persuaded the Belgian Socialist Party to make a coalition with middle-class parties, with the intention of nationalizing credit as a means of securing full employment. Vice-president of the Belgian Socialist Party, he was a minister in the Zeeland government and remained after the German invasion, declaring in 1942 that he would take no more political action. Condemned for collaborationist attitudes in 1946, he fled to Switzerland and died in 1953.

BIBLIOGRAPHY:

A. *Au-delà du marxisme* (Brussels: Eglantine, 1927); *Psychology of Socialism* (London: Allen & Unwin, 1927); *Le Socialisme constructif* (Paris: Alcan, 1933); *Die Socialistische Idee* (Jena: Diederich, 1935).

B. A. Philip, *Henri de Man et la crise doctrinale du socialisme* (Paris: Gambier, 1938); P. Dodge, *Beyond Marxism: The Faith and Works of Hendrik de Man* (The Hague: Martinus Nijhoff, 1966).

JOHN C. SIMMONDS

DERRIDA, JACQUES (b. 1930). Jacques Derrida was born in Algeria in 1930. He presently teaches history of philosophy at the Ecole Normale Supérieure and at Yale University. Never a Marxist† and often criticized from the left, Derrida came to prominence in 1967 with the publication of three remarkable books: *Speech and Phenomena*, *Writing and Difference*, and *On Grammatology*. Since then his philosophical acumen and his experimental writing style have kept him at the center of controversy in both France and the English-speaking world. It is ironic perhaps that Derrida has had far more influence on philosophy and criticism in this country than in France. There are, however, several important ideas that French neo-Marxism owes to Jacques Derrida.

In his *Speech and Phenomena*, as in his earlier and largely unnoticed "introduction" to his translation into French of Husserl's *Origin of Geometry* (1962), Derrida attacks what he perceives as the implicit essentialistic metaphysics of phenomenology. Consciousness itself, he argues, is thoroughly and necessarily mediated by language and thus by other cultural codes—and also by the very temporal flux that Husserl thought constitutive of consciousness on its most fundamental level. This critique, too technical for a context such as this, helped break the domination of phenomenology and existentialism over French universities and has revived the critique of metaphysics initiated in the last century by Hegel and Marx.

Although we probably owe the notion and practice of deconstruction to Gaston Bachelard,* it was Derrida who brought it to the attention of the wider intellectual community. A radically antinaturalist method, deconstruction seeks to reveal the implicit assumptions and processes that underly and constitute the basic concepts that, in their turn, structure our world and ourselves. It is a laying bare not of a personal unconscious as in psychoanalysis or of a historical unconscious as in the critique of political economy, but rather of a sort of epistemic unconscious—of the latent intellectual content that maintains the world as it appears. Deconstruction has proven a powerful tool for cultural and ideological critique. In neo-Marxism, which has generally rejected the orthodox "base–superstructure" analysis of cultural objects, deconstruction has become part of the theoretical life of the West. Derrida's "grammatology," in a narrower sense, utilizes deconstruction to break texts into their own impersonal, determining, but always elusive language structures.

BIBLIOGRAPHY:

A. *Speech and Phenomena* (Evanston, Ill.: Northwestern University Press, 1973); *On Grammatology* (Baltimore: Johns Hopkins University Press, 1977); *Writing and Difference* (Chicago: University of Chicago Press, 1978).

B. Miriam Glucksmann, *Structuralist Analysis in Contemporary Social Thought* (London: Routledge & Kegan Paul, 1974); Rosalind Coward and John Ellis, *Language and Materialism* (London: Routledge & Kegan Paul, 1977).

LAURENCE E. WINTERS

DJILAS, MILOVAN (b. 1911). Milovan Djilas was born on 12 June 1911 of peasant parents in Pobišće, Montenegro, along the Albanian frontier. His childhood was that of a peasant—a peasant growing up on a battlefield during the Balkan War and World War I. His first career was writing, and he went to Belgrade University to study literature in 1929. At the university he became a Communist agitator and was arrested, tortured, and imprisoned for his activities under the royal dictatorship of King Alexander in 1932–36. In prison Djilas first met influential Communists like Moša Pijade† and Alexander Ranković; his belief in communism was crystallized during long periods of solitary confinement, and he became one of the most dedicated Stalinists† in the Yugoslav Communist leadership. Djilas sided with Tito† in the intraparty struggles of the late 1930s and was appointed to the Central Committee of the reorganized Yugoslav Communist Party in 1938 and to its Politburo a year later. During World War II Djilas became along with Tito, Pijade, Ranković, and Edvard Kardelj one of the top leaders of the Yugoslav Revolution. Djilas was in charge of the Montenegrin theater of the war for the partisans, holding the rank of lieutenant-general, and he also served as editor of the party newspapers *Borba* and *Nova Jugoslavija* and as head of a diplomatic mission to Moscow to negotiate aid with Stalin in 1944. After the war he was minister for Montenegro and minister without portfolio in the Communist government. Between 1948 and 1953 he along with Kardelj and Boris Kidrić was an architect of "self-management," a cornerstone of "Titoism." In 1953 he became vice-president of Yugoslavia and president of its Federal Assembly. He also oversaw the deemphasis and decentralization of the Yugoslav Communist Party during its Sixth Congress into the League of Yugoslav Communists (SKJ). For his continued critique of communism he was stripped of all power and posts by the extraordinary Third Plenum of the SKJ in 1953–54 and subsequently was imprisoned in the years 1956–61 and 1962–66. Currently, he resides in Belgrade with his second wife, and he continues to produce provocative political and literary writings only allowed for publication abroad.

Djilas's attempts to democratize Yugoslav communism stemmed from a growing disillusionment with Stalin† and Soviet Communism which began during World War II. After the rupture in relations between the Soviet Union and Yugoslavia in 1948 he became a principal ideologist of Titoism and eventually was disillusioned with all forms of communism. Finally, he went from disillusionment to dissent and to proposing alternatives.

In 1953–54, as part of a continuing effort to humanize Yugoslav communism, Djilas published a series of highly critical articles in *Borba* and *Nova Misao*. They were published in book form in the West under the title *Anatomy of a Moral* in 1959. In them he warned that abusive bureaucratization was an "internal contradiction" of the revolution, and he pleaded for ideological toleration that would allow the development of a diversity of opinion free from the threats of persecution to assure future democratic progress. The ideas presented in these essays were more fully developed in Djilas's classic, *The New Class*, which appeared in 1957. In *The New Class* Djilas had chosen the Soviet Union as his principal model, but it was clear that his critique was directed at all Communist (Stalinist) societies, including his own. Those aspects of his seminal work that were applauded as its major strengths by Western reviewers in 1957—the delineation of the new class and the recognition of national communism—still prove to be of enduring value today to its readers and its author.

Djilas pointed out that Soviet society was generally viewed wrongly as being statically monolithic, with all of its energies theoretically channeled toward one goal—the creation of a classless society. Actually, Soviet society was very dynamic, but with a rigid class structure. Bureaucrats formed an elite; Communist Party members formed an elite; and Party member-bureaucrats formed a super-elite—the new class—whose power lay not as with traditional elites in the ownership of the means of production but in the administration of these facilities for its own benefit. The manipulation of this power by the members of the new class generated corruption, waste, and alienation in Soviet society because popular criticism of their activities was not tolerated under Stalinism. To Djilas this defined them as a class according to classical Marxist criteria.

The second concept of significance advanced by Djilas in *The New Class* was national communism, and it had a direct relationship to the rise of the new class. He began by explaining, "Communism is only one thing, but it is realized in different degrees and manners in every country. Therefore, it is possible to speak of Communist systems, i.e., various forms of the same manifestation" (p. 173). He argued that for Communists to bring about successful revolutions, to establish their oligarchical authority, and to maintain their power, international communism must be adapted to national conditions. Thus, Marxism†-Leninism†-Stalinism was viewed correctly as Russian national communism.

But Soviet Communism was international communism as long as the Soviet Union could force its ideology on its satellites and other Communist parties around the world. Consequently, Djilas said that the concept of national communism had no real meaning until after World War II, when other national Communist regimes began developing, partly in response to Soviet-Russian imperialism. The new ruling classes in other Communist states also came to reflect their national interests. He observed that "in reality, national communism is communism in decline" (p. 190).

The New Class reflected Djilas's disillusionment with the reality of contemporary communism in all of its national forms, but his break with Marxism was not clearly enunciated until twelve years later with the publication of *The Unperfect Society*. It followed naturally from political works like *The New Class* and *Conversations with Stalin*, a memoir of his wartime and postwar encounters with the Soviet dictator published in 1962, to carry out a theoretical critique of Marxism and firmly establish Djilas's new world view of democratic socialism. The power-political realities of communism in the post–World War II world (e.g. the Soviet invasion of Hungary in 1956 and Czechoslovakia in 1968) and his own experiences finally convinced Djilas of even the theoretical impossibility of Marxism: "Every human community is a community of diverse aspirations. This confirms that no system ever can be good for, and acceptable to all men" (*The Unperfect Society*, p. 198). Marxism as a global ideology in the form of communism was crumbling, demonstrating that Marx's ideas were "unrealizable." Communism had reached its peak under Stalin, but it was disintegrating into national forms, which became more conservative and, unlike the international variety, were capable of coexistence and détente. Djilas stated that although a valuable "rational core" of Marx's ideas—the classless society and the economic dependence of man—remained, communism and capitalism were now corrupted by each other and their local environments. For the long run, native types of democratic socialism and social democracy seemed to him to be the best compromises.

In Djilas's alternative society human rights and freedom would be guaranteed, and totalitarianism, especially that of bureaucratic absolutism and/or a cult of personality, would not be tolerated. Inherent too in this vision is complete pluralism, breaking up the ideological stagnation of communism with a society predicated on constant and consistent critical evaluation from diverse quarters based on valid criteria with the transcendence, not the destruction, of the old by the new.

BIBLIOGRAPHY:

A. *The New Class* (New York: Praeger, 1957); *Anatomy of a Moral* (New York: Praeger, 1959); *Conversations with Stalin* (New York: Harcourt Brace & World, 1962); *The Unperfect Society: Beyond the New Class* (New York: Harcourt Brace & World, 1969); *Tito* (New York: Harcourt Brace Jovanovich, 1980).

B. Dennis Reinhartz, *Milovan Djilas: A Revolutionary as a Writer* (New York: Columbia University Press, 1981).

DENNIS REINHARTZ

DONZELOT, JACQUES (n.a.). The work of Jacques Donzelot, like that of Michel Foucault,* has developed in reaction to the events of the late 1960s in France and throughout the Western world. Reflection on these events led many intellectuals of the left to return with fresh eyes to issues of institutionalized politics, repressive beliefs, and the forces of personal and group desire. Donzelot's principal concern has been, first, with the structures and relations that govern political culture and, second, with developing a notion of political culture as the practice that organizes the world in such a way as to allow political calculation and practice. Finally, Donzelot deals with the history—or "archae-ology"—of the "production and circulation" of socio-political discourses. In these interests, Donzelot takes up and furthers one aspect of the work of his friend and mentor, Foucault.

Donzelot is known in English for his *Policing of Families* (1980), a study of the ways in which the family has been comprehended and manipulated in nine-teenth- and twentieth-century capitalist societies. He understands this study as a corrective to the orthodox Marxist failure on the one hand to concern itself directly with the functioning of political power and, on the other, to focus on the personal dimension of the development of the social subject. Again, following Foucault, we see in this intention of Donzelot the notion of bio-politics, which is to say, the application of power directly to the human body.

In the *Policing of Families*, the Marxist functionalist approach of seeking to determine what role such and such a phenomenon plays in the reproduction of the relations of production is rejected in favor of a search for what interventions or strategies have been inflicted on the family to keep it to some degree part of the larger machine—capital. He finds these strategies to have been primarily various sorts of applications of power to the body—of the children, of the parents, of the family unit as a whole. Social "policy" concerning the family has tra-ditionally been focused on such spheres as nutrition, health, and sexuality, in short, on the control, limitation, and canalization of desiring energies for the "good" of the family, and for society in general.

BIBLIOGRAPHY:

A. *Policing of Families* (New York: Pantheon, 1980).

LAURENCE E. WINTERS

DOS SANTOS, THEOTONIO (n.a.). A prominent social scientist from Minas Gerais, Brazil, Dos Santos was associated with the University of Brasília during the early 1960s. After the 1964 coup, he went into exile and associated with the Centro de Estudios Socioeconómicos (CESO) of the University of Chile, where he brought together a number of Chilean and Brazilian social scientists to study imperialism and its impact on dependent societies. After the Chilean military coup of 1973, he sought refuge in Mexico, where he continued his research and writing at the Universidad Nacional Autónoma de México (UNAM). Granted amnesty, in 1980 he returned to Brazil where he taught briefly at the Catholic University of Minas Gerais and the Federal University of Minas Gerais and unsuccessfully ran for governor of the state of Minas Gerais in 1982.

Dos Santos is known for his conceptualization of the new dependency, which denotes the period of multinational dominance after World War II. In contrast, he associated colonial dependence with trade monopolies established over land, mines, and labor of colonial societies and financial-industrial dependency with the period of imperialism at the end of the nineteenth century. He focused on the widely accepted relationship in which a dominant country expands as the result of dependence of another country. He accepted the premise of imperialism that understands the expansion of advanced capitalist centers through their expansion over the world economy, but he also insisted that such expansion is determined partially by laws of internal development. He emphasized the unequal and combined nature of development, as suggested in the writing of Leon Trotsky,† and he also was influenced by Paul Baran,† who insisted that unequal trade relations based on monopolistic control at the center result in transfers of surplus from dependent to dominant countries.

He analyzed relations of dependency through an examination of the international commodity and capital markets. He also looked at productivity as affected by these international relations, and in particular, he studied the structure of agrarian and mining exports. He was concerned to what extent the unequal and combined capitalist development at the international level is reproduced at the internal national level. He focused on the structure of industry and technology as related to the interests of the multinational corporations. He concluded that the system of dependent reproduction is part of the system of world economic relations based on monopolistic control of capital and that a system of dependent production and reproduction leads to backwardness and misery. Dos Santos attempted to elaborate on the concept of dependency by examining theory in Marx,† Lenin,† and others. He argued for the study of dependency within a Marxist approach, and he showed the compatability of concepts and theories around dependency and imperialism. Ultimately, he suggested a way out of dependency through a revolutionary approach to socialism.

At present he is working on the effects of scientific and technological revolution on contemporary capitalism in an attempt to show the evolving contradictions between the needs of scientific development and the conservation of capitalistic relations of production.

BIBLIOGRAPHY:

A. "The Concept of Social Classes," *Science and Society*, 34 (Summer 1970), pp. 166–93; *Dependencia y cambio social* (Santiago: Cuadernos de Estudios Socioeconómicos, 1970); "The Structure of Dependence," *American Economic Review*, 60 (May 1970), pp. 231–36; "The Crisis of Development Theory and the Problem of Dependence in Latin America," pp. 57–80, in *Underdevelopment and Development*, ed. Henry Bernstein (Harmondsworth: Penguin Books, 1973); "Brazil: The Origins of a Crisis," in *Latin America: The Struggle with Dependency and Beyond*, ed. Ronald H. Chilcote and Joel C. Edelstein (Cambridge, Mass.: Schenkman, 1974); *Imperialismo y dependencia* (Mexico City: Era, 1978).

RONALD H. CHILCOTE

DU BOIS, WILLIAM EDWARD BURGHARDT (1868–1962). W.E.B. Du Bois was one of the preeminent black American scholars and civil rights leaders of the twentieth century. He was born in Great Barrington, Massachusetts, in 1868 and educated at Fisk and Harvard universities. He also attended the University of Berlin. He received a Ph.D. in history from Harvard in 1895. Du Bois taught at Wilberforce College, the University of Pennsylvania, and finally at Atlanta University, where he became professor of sociology. He was founder and general secretary of the civil rights group known as the Niagara Movement from 1905 to 1909. He was also one of the founders of the National Association for the Advancement of Colored People (NAACP) in 1910. As director of publicity and research for the NAACP, Du Bois served from 1910 to 1934 as editor of *The Crisis*, the official journal of the NAACP.

In contrast to the accommodationist beliefs of Booker T. Washington, Du Bois urged black Americans and liberal whites to wage a legal battle against racial discrimination. He also urged that young blacks be educated in the liberal arts rather than concentrating on technical and vocational education. A "talented tenth," a black educated elite, could lead the rest of the black people to progress. As a scholar, Du Bois used the social sciences to raise the consciousness of both blacks and whites by trying to show that racism was the chief cause of the oppressed condition of blacks and colored peoples throughout the world. Du Bois was also a longtime leader of the pan-African movement, linking the struggle of black Americans for freedom with the struggle of black Africans to throw off the yoke of European colonialism. In 1919 he organized the first of several pan-African conferences he would organize or attend throughout his life.

In the 1920s Du Bois became increasingly critical of integration as a means of achieving black liberation. According to Du Bois, integration was not working. Du Bois became more of a separatist. Blacks had to help themselves. He called for the creation of black institutions, such as black cooperatives, to help blacks gain economic self-sufficiency. He expounded on the virtues of racial separation. This brought him into conflict with the integrationist NAACP. In 1934 Du Bois resigned as editor of *The Crisis* and broke with the NAACP, largely due to this ideological dispute. He returned to Atlanta University, where he served as chairman of the Sociology Department from 1934 to 1944.

The last years of Du Bois's life were spent in the quest for world peace, the continuing fight for black liberation, and the struggle against imperialism. In 1951 Du Bois fell victim to the wave of McCarthyism sweeping the country. In February of that year he was indicted by a federal grand jury for being an unregistered agent for a foreign power. This indictment apparently stemmed from his circulation of the Stockholm Peace Appeal, a petition that advocated the prohibition of nuclear weapons. After a five-day trial, Du Bois was found not guilty in November of 1951, but the experience had a profound effect on him. It accelerated his disillusionment with America and pushed him further toward the left. In 1961 he became a member of the Communist Party of the United States and became a resident of Ghana, at the invitation of President Kwame Nkrumah. He eventually became a citizen of Ghana. Du Bois was a prolific writer. His major works include *The Suppression of the African Slave Trade to the United States of America, 1638–1870* (1896), *The Souls of Black Folk* (1903), *Black Reconstruction in America, 1860–1880* (1935), and many others.

Although he was never an orthodox Marxist,† Du Bois was very interested in socialism for most of his intellectual life. In 1911 he briefly joined the Socialist

Party. As early as 1907 he described himself as a "Socialist-of-the-Path" meaning that, although he did not believe in the complete socialization of the means of production, he did believe that progress was dependent upon greater government ownership of the means of production. The path to progress inevitably led to socialism. It was a view he always held, that socialism was the progressive wave of the future. Du Bois increasingly came to view the oppression of blacks in America and Africa, and the oppression of colored people all over the world, as inextricably linked with the domination of capitalism. Hence he believed American racism was very closely tied to capitalist domination. Capitalists, he argued, used racism to push a wedge between white and black workers so that both could be exploited. Thus Du Bois was encouraged by the spread of socialism after World War I. He was initially skeptical of the Russian Revolution, but after a trip to the Soviet Union in 1926 he was much encouraged by the Soviet experiment. For him, it too was the wave of the future.

Du Bois, however, became increasingly disillusioned with American socialism. Rather than joining hands with black workers against racism, white American workers were racists themselves. For example, many of them fought to keep blacks out of trade unions. Du Bois began to doubt whether white workers could overcome their racism. Moreover, he felt that American Socialists did not adequately speak to the problem of racism in America. Otherwise eloquent Socialists like Norman Thomas were tongue-tied on the question of racism. For Du Bois, racism was a blind spot for the American radical left. Blacks could not join hands with American Socialists to achieve their liberation, they had to work for that liberation themselves.

In his later years, Du Bois began to put the problems of racism and capitalism in a more international context. This was in connection with his mounting concerns about imperialism and world peace. In the age of the cold war, Du Bois praised the Soviet Union and China and criticized the United States as a menace to world peace. He believed, as he did early in his life, that the road to progress lay through socialism and communism. He saw the Soviet and Chinese experiments as successful and believed that they were evolving toward the Marxist goal of communism. In China, for example, human nature was being transformed, said Du Bois. Self-seeking, capitalistic individuals were being transformed into cooperative citizens. Socialism and communism were ideological models for the future.

Capitalism, on the other hand, was crumbling. In the age of McCarthyism, free discussion, the essence of democratic capitalism, was being stifled. Elections were being subverted by outright bribery, according to Du Bois. The hope for socialism in the West was not bright because white workers had been co-opted with higher wages, wages gained not through capitalist concessions but through the exploited labor of colored peoples in the colonial and developing world. Also, the black bourgeoisie had sold out the mass of black people and were acquiring the capitalistic attitudes of the white bourgeoisie. Du Bois continued to urge blacks to fight racism through the legal process. He also urged them to fight for world peace and justice through the United Nations, where "friendly" nations like the Soviet Union and India would help.

Finally, in his last years, Du Bois reconciled somewhat with the American left, although he remained cautious. He joined the Communist Party of the United States in 1961. Later, disillusioned with America, he moved to Ghana, where he died on 27 August 1963.

Du Bois, then, was one of the first black leaders to make the linkage between capitalist domination and American racism. Moreover, he placed racism in the wider context of imperialism and worldwide capitalist domination, linking the plight of America's blacks to the plight of oppressed colored peoples throughout the globe. However, he was also critical of the American left and what he saw as its ambivalence on the question of racism. He was no less critical of the black bourgeoisie, that talented tenth for whom he had held such hope. They were becoming absorbed into the capitalist system. Du Bois was a profound influence not only on American radicals but also on generations of black moderates, militants, and nationalists.

BIBLIOGRAPHY:

A. *The Suppression of the African Slave Trade to the United States of America, 1638– 1870* (New York: Longmans, Green, 1896); *Black Reconstruction in America, 1860– 1880* (New York: Harcourt Brace, 1935); *Color and Democracy* (New York: Harcourt Brace, 1945); *The World and Africa* (New York: Viking Press, 1947); *In Battle for Peace* (New York: Masses and Mainstream, 1951); *Africa in Battle Against Colonialism, Racialism, Imperialism* (Chicago: Afro-American Books, 1960); *An ABC of Color* (Berlin: Seven Seas, 1964); *Socialism Today* (Chicago: Afro-American Books, 1964); *Autobiography* (New York: International, 1968); *W.E.B. Du Bois Speaks* (New York: Pathfinder, 1970); *The Seventh Son* (New York: Random House, 1971); *The Emerging Thought of W.E.B. Du Bois* (New York: Simon and Schuster, 1972).

B. Francis L. Broderick, *W.E.B. Du Bois: Negro Leader in a Time of Crises* (Stanford: Stanford University Press, 1959); Elliott M. Rudwick, *W.E.B. Du Bois: A Study in Minority Group Leadership* (Philadelphia: University of Pennsylvania, 1960); Leslie Lacy, *Cheer the Lonesome Traveler* (New York: Dell, 1970).

EARL SHERIDAN

DUTSCHKE, RUDI (1940–1979). Born in 1940, Dutschke grew up in Luckenwalde in the German Democratic Republic. Due to conflicts with the bureaucracy over the course of his education, he moved to West Berlin in August 1961, two days before the erection of the Berlin Wall and the closing of the border. Studying sociology at the Free University, Dutschke played a central role in the rise of the student movement. Together with Bernd Rabehl he founded the Berlin section of the Subversive Aktion in 1962–63, a splinter group of the Situationist International,* which in 1964 merged with the Sozialistischer deutscher Studentenbund (SDS). In West Berlin, the Subversive Aktion soon became the majority faction within the SDS, leading to increasingly militant demonstrations against Western imperialism in the Third World (e.g. demonstrations against

Tshombe on 18 December 1964 and against the Shah of Iran on 2 June 1967) and against the right-wing West German tabloid press of Axel Springer. In the course of this political activity and his own research on the history of the Socialist movement, Dutschke came into contact with figures such as George Lukács,* Herbert Marcuse,* Leo Löwenthal,* and Ernst Bloch,* either in private meetings or in public discussions. Dutschke spoke at many demonstrations and was repeatedly arrested. On 11 April 1968, Josef Bachmann attempted to assassinate Dutschke, who, despite his recovery, suffered permanent mental and physical damages. After entering England in December 1968, he was expelled in 1969 and moved to Ireland; a second attempt to settle in England in order to study with Joan Robinson led to another expulsion. After teaching at the University of Aarhus in Denmark in 1971, he returned to the Federal Republic and in January 1973 once again addressed a Vietnam demonstration (in Bonn). His dissertation on Lenin,† Lukács, and the Comintern was completed in 1974 for Urs Jaeggi.* Dutschke's political concerns during the late 1970s included opposition to the West German practice of *Berufsverbot*, i.e., the exclusion of leftists from civil service employment; human rights in Eastern Europe and the Soviet Union; ecology; and especially, opposition to nuclear power. In September 1979 he became a member of the Greens in Bremen. He died on 24 December 1979 from consequences of the 1968 attack.

Dutschke's extensive studies of Marxist† theory and the history of the Communist movement culminated in his one major theoretical work, *Versuch, Lenin auf die Füsse zu stellen* (1974). Anxious to articulate a criticism of the ossification of socialism in Soviet-style societies but committed to the development of a contemporary socialist practice in the West, Dutschke returns to the period of the Russian Revolution of 1917 and, paying special attention to the positions of Lenin and Lukács, reconstructs the Marxist discussion concerning the possibility of socialist revolution in backward societies. He reviews the problem of a Marxist periodization of "production epochs" with particular reference to "oriental despotism," an "Asiatic mode of production," and especially, the specific character of Russian capitalism in the early twentieth century. Dutschke argues that, in the wake of Marx's declaration of the superiority of a "scientific socialism" over the various pre-1848 utopian tendencies, Second International† socialists, including Lenin and the Bolsheviks, could conceive of progress in Russia only in terms of a Western European model of capitalist modernization. Yet, "our thesis is that the Russian development is caught in a half-Asiatic structural complex, as inseparable from the Tartarization as from the Turkish occupation which led to the emergence of an Asiatic system of landed property" (*Geschichte ist Machbar*, p. 135). However, in the specific context of Asiatic backwardness, capitalist modernization could only be carried out by a party apparatus as an avant-garde elite, which engenders the bureaucratic character of contemporary Soviet socialism and which, Dutschke insists, cannot serve as a model for Western movements, which must find a fundamentally different path to socialism.

BIBLIOGRAPHY:
   A. *Versuch, Lenin auf die Füsse zu stellen. Uber den halbasiatischen und den wes-
teuropäischen Weg zum Sozialismus. Lenin, Lukács und die dritte Internationale* (Berlin:
Klaus Wagenbach, 1974); *Die Sowjetunion, Solshenizyn und die westliche Linke*, ed.
Rudi Dutschke and Manfred Wilke (Reinbek bei Hamburg: Rowohlt, 1975); *Geschichte
ist Machbar. Texte über das herrschende Falsche und die Radikalität des Friedens*, ed.
Jürgen Miermeister (Berlin: Klaus Wagenbach, 1980); *Mein langer Marsch. Reden,
Schriften und Tagebücher aus zwanzig Jahren*, ed. Gretchen Dutschke-Klotz, Helmut
Gollwitzer, and Jürgen Miermeister (Reinbek bei Hamburg: Rowohlt, 1980).

RUSSELL BERMAN

DUVIGNAUD, JEAN (b. 1921). The intellectual itinerary of the French sociologist Jean Duvignaud resembles that of many French leftists born in the
1920s: having begun studies in philosophy in the late 1930s, Duvignaud joined
the French Resistance and the Communist Party to fight the Nazi Occupation
during World War II. Following the Liberation, Duvignaud completed his studies
in philosophy, teaching at the University of Paris during the 1950s. He also
remained a member of the French Communist Party until the early 1950s, when
his disagreements with the Stalinist† line caused his exclusion. With Colette
Audry, Roland Barthes,* and Edgar Morin,* Duvignaud founded the review
*Arguments** in 1956 and contributed to this group's critique of Marxism and
development of leftist thought until the review's dissolution in 1962. At that
time, Duvignaud was directing the Centre d'Etudes des Sciences Sociales at the
University of Tunis, where he remained until the late 1960s, when he accepted
his present position as professor of social sciences at the University of Tours.

   The essential elements of Jean Duvignaud's contribution to the *Arguments*
project are found in his article, "Peut-on sortir du ghetto?" which constitutes,
in revised form, the fourth chapter of his essay *Pour entrer dans le XXe siècle*
(1960). In explicitly associating his essay with the works of Kostas Axelos* and
Edgar Morin, to envisage "planetary thinking," Duvignaud sought to leave
behind the "swamp of rotten ideas" that the twentieth-century thinker has in-
appropriately adapted to present circumstances. The "ghetto" to which Duvignaud refers is both the political sects of party politics and the literary cliques of
intellectual discourse. After tracing the "ghettoization" of the European intelligentsia, primarily Socialist and Communist, Duvignaud confronted the essential
problem of how to leave the "ghetto."

   First, Duvignaud undermined the canonic postulates of fundamental belief of
the Marxist† French intelligentsia: the postulate of the absolute existence of a
universal, germinal history for mankind; the postulate that one can and should
"modify society by direct action and by the collective violence of a group of
initiates" (*Pour entrer dans le XXe siècle*, p. 125); the postulate that man is a
slave, or that he is "alienated." Duvignaud argued that it is no longer sufficient
to theorize about an eventual new revolution of the proletariat, that it is now
essential "to operate the mental conversion which can make [new perspectives]

emerge'' (ibid., p. 131), a conversion which will remain impossible "for those who persist in constructing the 'ideal type' of socialism" (ibid., p. 132). Then, Duvignaud conceived of a "micro-socialism": " 'politics' that would be defined as a function of partial aggregates rather than politics aiming to change the entire world by unifying it" (ibid., p. 135). The goal of this "micro-socialism" is to "enliven the dynamism of small groups and to constitute limited communities" (ibid., p. 136), a project whose possibility was augmented, argued Duvignaud, by the accrued adherence to "peaceful coexistence." This admittedly utopian ideal would be achieved by creating "organic communities," on local or even on a limited national scale, "which break the actual structures of society and reanimate the social mobility frozen in dead institutions and ideologies." These organic groups would be supported solely by "collective creativity" (ibid., p. 137). And this collective freedom, for Duvignaud, constituted "a permanent revolution modifying developmental structures of diverse human histories" (ibid., p. 139), dating not merely from 1917 but back from the medieval communes. It is a permanent revolution transcending both capitalism and socialism, "the great collective power which makes man what he had become, without valorizing the internal logic of this becoming" (ibid., p. 140).

BIBLIOGRAPHY:

A. *Pour entrer dans le XXe siècle* (Paris: Grasset, 1960); articles in volumes 2 and 3 of *Arguments*, ed. Edgar Morin (Paris: U.G.E., 10/18, 1976–78).

B. L. Labedz, ed., *Revisionism: Essays on the History of Marxist Ideas* (New York: Praeger, 1962).

CHARLES J. STIVALE

DZYUBA, IVAN MYKHAILOVICH (b. 1931). Dzyuba, a well-known Soviet literary critic and writer, was the leading Ukrainian dissident of the 1960s. Born in 1931 in a village in the Donetsk region of the Ukraine, Dzyuba was the son of a peasant. He graduated from the Donetsk Pedagogical Institute and did postgraduate work at the Ukrainian Academy of Sciences' Institute of Literature. Dzyuba authored some 100 articles in Soviet periodicals and was a member of the Ukrainian Writers' Union. He was an outspoken supporter of the younger generation of liberal and nationally conscious Ukrainian literati known as the Sixties Group. Dzyuba played a prominent role in mobilizing the Ukrainian public to protest the arrests and trials in the Ukraine in 1965–66. In response to the crackdown on Ukrainian dissidents, Dzyuba wrote the influential treatise *Internationalism or Russification?* in late 1965. In 1966 Dzyuba gave an important speech at a large, unofficial gathering at the Babyn (Babi) Yar ravine, commemorating the twenty-fifth anniversary of Nazi executions of Jews and Ukrainians at that site, in which he called for mutual respect and understanding between Ukrainians and Jews.

In *Internationalism or Russification?* Dzyuba severely criticized Soviet nationality policy for departing from Leninist norms and practices and for its unbridled Russian chauvinism. He argued for a genuine internationalism that respects and promotes the culture, development, and self-esteem of minority nationalities, such as the Ukrainians and other non-Russians in the Soviet Union. Dzyuba's book was officially circulated among top Ukrainian officials and was also the leading *samizdat* (underground) publication in Ukraine. The publication of *Internationalism or Russification?* in the West in 1968 led Soviet authorities to castigate Dzyuba in a 1969 pamphlet entitled *What I. Dzyuba Stands for and How He Does It*. Dzyuba was reportedly protected from arrest for several years by Petro Shelest, first secretary of the Ukrainian Communist Party from 1963 to 1972, who apparently sympathized with some of Dzyuba's criticisms. Dzyuba was finally arrested in April 1972 and subsequently sentenced to five years' imprisonment. Demoralized and suffering from tuberculosis, he was pressured to recant his dissident views, which led to his release from imprisonment in November 1973. In *Facets of a Crystal* (Kiev, 1976) the ''broken'' Dzyuba provided a self-critical analysis of his earlier treatise.

BIBLIOGRAPHY:

A. *Internationalism or Russification?* 3rd ed. (New York: Monad Press, 1974).

JAROSLAW BILOCERKOWYCZ

E

EMMANUEL, ARGHIRI (b. 1911). Arghiri Emmanuel was born in Patras, Greece, in 1911. He joined the Greek liberation forces in 1942 and took part in the movement against the Greek government in exile in Cairo. For his part in the movement he was condemned to death, then granted amnesty and finally released from prison in 1946. He moved to Paris, where he studied at the Sorbonne, earning a doctorate in sociology. He has worked as the director of economic studies at the University of Paris-VII.

Emmanuel is best known for his seminal work, *Unequal Exchange*, in which he convincingly argues that one of the central and most accepted economic propositions, a proposition formulated by Ricardo in his theory of comparative costs, is patently wrong. Specifically, he proves the error of the proposition that the exchange of specialized goods made possible by a geographic division of labor yields each partner in the exchange comparable gains. Emmanuel demonstrates that unequal gains normally follow from such exchanges, particularly when wages for the exchange product of one area are high and wages for the exchange product of the other area are low. From this notion of unequal exchange he forms an explanation of underdevelopment in the capitalist world.

BIBLIOGRAPHY:

A. *Unequal Exchange: A Study of the Imperialism of Trade* (New York: Monthly Review Press, 1972).

KATHLEEN RITTER

EMPIRIOCRITICISM. The Western school of empiriocriticism of Ernst Mach and Richard Avenarius gave rise to a revisionistic movement within early twentieth-century Russian Marxism.† Among those deeply influenced by Mach, one finds N. Valentinov (born N. V. Vol'sky in 1878), V. Bazarov (born V. A. Rudnev in 1874), and A. Bogdanov (born A. Malinovsky in 1873). Bogdanov clearly was the best known of this group, maintaining that his philosophy had transcended the dualism found in Mach's writings, a claim he symbolized by calling his own philosophy empiriomonism. A doctor by profession, Bogdanov became active in the Russian worker's movement shortly prior to the turn of the century. Following the 1903 split of the Russian Marxist movement into Bolsheviks and Mensheviks, Bogdanov became a close friend of Lenin,† until his continuing philosophical speculations produced antagonisms and, in part, gave rise to Lenin's book *Materialism and Empiriocriticism*. Although Bogdanov took no part in the 1917 revolutions, he returned to Russia to lead a movement for development of a proletarian culture. He died in 1928 as the result of an unsuccessful experiment he had conducted upon himself.

Alexander Bogdanov's main philosophical writings unfortunately remain untranslated (*Empiriomonism: Essays in Philosophy*, 1906; *The Philosophy of Living Experience*, 1913; *Tectology*, 1922). They focus upon the interaction of man with nature as the basis of both understanding and knowledge. Two forms of cognitive organization result from such interaction or praxis: the objective that constitutes the cognitive rules of the group, and the subjective or organizational rules of the individual. The dualism that appears to separate group (objective) and individual (subjective) knowledge derives not from diverse perceptions of some hypothetical thing-in-itself but from the system of organization itself within which it is evaluated. To Bogdanov, what a group of physicians "see" when examining my brain is identical with what I perceive as mind. The apparent difference arises from the system of organization used, which in turn is shaped by observers' physical needs. Building upon this emphasis on organization of knowledge, Bogdanov—and empiriocritics generally—maintained that the superiority of the twentieth-century working class lay in this group's unmatched ability to organize group experience around their collective needs, thus creating a fuller picture of reality adequate to fulfill Marx's demand to change the world.
BIBLIOGRAPHY:

A. *Empiriomonizm: Stat'i po filosofii*, 3 vols. (St. Petersburg: no publisher listed, 1906); *Autobiography*, in *Makers of the Russian Revolution*, ed. H. Georges and M. Jean-Jacques (Ithaca: Cornell University Press, 1974), pp. 286–89.

B. Michael M. Boll, "From Empiriocriticism to Empiriomonism: The Marxist Phenomenology of Aleksandr Bodganov," *Slavonic and East European Review* (January 1981): Robert A. Gorman, *Neo-Marxism—The Meanings of Modern Radicalism* (Westport, Conn.: Greenwood Press, 1982): pp. 181–83.

MICHAEL M. BOLL

ENZENSBERGER, CHRISTIAN (b. 1931). Born in Nürnberg in 1931, Enzensberger teaches English literature at the University of Munich. In addition to his contributions to neo-Marxist literary theory, his oeuvre includes a study of Victorian poetry (Tennyson and Swinburne) and translations of Lewis Carroll, Edward Bond, and Giorgos Sefeiris.

The politicization of West German intellectual life during the 1960s was linked particularly to a paradigmatic change in the character of literary scholarship, which, during the first two postwar decades, had generally ignored socio-historical questions, relying instead on a conservative and antimodernist aesthetics of form. In the context of the student movement, a methodology debate commenced that initially recovered and then reexamined the competing positions within the Marxist† tradition, articulated by George Lukács,* Walter Benjamin,* Bertolt Brecht,† and Theodore Adorno.* This historical reappropriation engendered several neo-Marxist literary theories in the 1970s, including Enzensberger's *Literatur und Interesse* (1977). Enzensberger differentiates between interest (self-interest and class interest) and sense; every society organized around class differences suffers from a legitimation crisis (sense deficit), which literature obscures by presenting fictional models of meaningful life. The content of literary works therefore necessarily plays an affirmative role in the stabilization of ruling interests. Paradoxically, Enzensberger joins this denunciation of literary ideology to an idealization of structure as the locus of a utopian reconciliation of competing interests, as he demonstrates with reference to *The Merchant of Venice* and *Oliver Twist*. The treatment of literature as simultaneously ideological and utopian apparently represents an effort to synthesize the politicized aesthetics of the student movement, after its collapse, with key themes from the Frankfurt School in the context of the neoconservative turn in West German culture in the mid-1970s.

BIBLIOGRAPHY:

A. *Viktorianische Lyrik: Tennyson und Swinburne in der Geschichte der Entfremdung* (Munich: Hanser, 1969); *Smut: An Anatomy of Dirt* (New York: Seabury Press, 1974); *Literatur und Interesse: eine politische Ästhetik mit zwei Beispielen aus der englischen Literatur* (Munich: Hanser, 1977).

B. Peter Uwe Hohendahl, ''Literatur und Interesse: Eine politische Ästhetik von Christian Enzensberger,'' pp. 178–93, in *Basis. Jahrbuch für deutsche Gegenwartsliteratur*, vol. 10 (1980).

RUSSELL BERMAN

ENZENSBERGER, HANS MAGNUS (b. 1929). Born in 1929 in Kaufbeuren in Bavaria, Enzensberger spent his childhood in Nürnberg. Because of Allied bombings after 1942, he was evacuated to the Franconian countryside. After the war he studied literature and philosophy in Erlangen, Freiburg, Hamburg, and Paris, completing a dissertation on the poetics of Clemens Brentano in 1955. Subsequently he worked for German radio and in the publishing industry; he also held teaching positions in Ulm and Frankfurt. His first volume of poetry, *Verteidigung der wölfe*, appeared in 1957. Extensive travels included visits to the United States (1957 and 1967–68), Cuba (1968–69), and the Soviet Union (1963). In 1965 he founded the journal *Kursbuch*, which he edited until 1975 and which became one of the most influential organs of the West German new left. Since 1980 he has edited the journal *Transatlantik* in Munich.

Enzensberger profoundly influenced the development of left-wing culture in West Germany during the 1960s and 1970s. In an exemplary manner, his own poetry and novels reflect the changing character of oppositional politics: from an initial melancholy criticism of the postwar status quo through the radicalization and engagement of an expressly Marxist† phase commencing in the mid-1960s

(*Das Verhör von Habana*, 1970) to the pessimism and skepticism of the 1970s (*Mausoleum*, 1975). The transformation of his understanding of literature was reflected in *Kursbuch*, most notably in 1967–68, when an "end of literature" and a turn to direct politics was proclaimed. As a brilliant essayist Enzensberger repeatedly intervened in West German cultural and political life, for instance, with attacks on the news magazine *Der Spiegel* in 1957, a polemic with the playright Peter Weiss in 1966, and in an exchange of letters on politics and Auschwitz with Hannah Arendt (*Merkur*, 1965). Aside from the theoretical ramifications of these various episodes, his central and explicitly theoretical essays concern the function of culture and the role of manipulation in modern society. With his notion of a "consciousness industry," he claims to go beyond the Frankfurt School's complaint that a "culture industry" trivializes literature and art ("The Industrialization of the Mind," 1962). Enzensberger focuses instead on the mechanisms of domination and their penetration into everyday life. Following Brecht's theory of radio, Enzensberger envisions a "socialist strategy" to transform the function of the electronic media through self-organization in order to develop their subversive potentials ("Constituents of a Theory of the Media," in *The Consciousness Industry*).

BIBLIOGRAPHY:

A. *The Consciousness Industry: On Literature, Politics and the Media* (New York: Seabury Press, 1974); *Politics and Crime* (New York: Seabury Press, 1974); *Mausoleum: Thirty-Seven Ballads from the History of Progress* (New York: Urizen Books, 1976); *Raids and Reconstructions: Essays on Politics, Crime and Culture* (London: Pluto Press, 1976); *Critical Essays* (New York: Continuum, 1982).

B. Joachim Schickel, *Uber Hans Magnus Enzensberger* (Frankfurt: Suhrkamp, 1970); Ingrid Eggers, *Veränderungen des Literaturbegriffs im Werk von Hans Magnus Enzensberger* (Frankfurt: Lang, 1981).

RUSSELL BERMAN

F

FALS BORDA, ORLANDO (b. 1925). Colombian sociologist and philosopher, Orlando Fals Borda was born in Barranqiulla on 11 July 1925. Fals Borda received a bachelor of arts in 1947 from the University of Dubuque (Iowa), master of arts in 1952 from the University of Minnesota, and a Ph.D. in 1955 from the University of Florida (Gainesville). In 1959, Fals Borda, together with several other sociologists, including Camilo Torres Restrepo,* founded Colombia's first faculty of sociology, now a department of the Faculty of Human Sciences of the National University. Fals Borda has held various research, educational, consulting, and governmental posts. Now a professor of sociology at the National University, he has also held positions as the director of the Sociology Department at the National University, head of the Division of Social Anthropology at the University of Colombia, and general director of the Ministry of Agriculture. Fals Borda has also served as an investigator with the Colombian Institute of Anthropology, technical advisor to the Colombian delegation to the First Inter-American Center of Housing and Planning, and counsel on rural affairs and housing from the United Nations to the government of Brazil.

Fals believes that the social sciences have a social and political function, that research serves as a methodological catalyst that will hasten the processes of structural and revolutionary change. He stresses that no philosophy, not even Marxism, should be accepted in a dogmatic fashion. Rather, each constitutes a "tool" that must be appraised to determine how it can best be utilized in a society in transition, such as Colombia. If the "tool" does not correspond empirically to a country's reality, it should be made more pertinent ("The Negation of Sociology and Its Promise," pp. 164–65).

Fals Borda's major contribution to contemporary thought is his reformulation of the dialectic to fit Colombian reality. He contends that scholars tend to jump from one stage of historical development to another without providing systematic information about the acute periods of transition between stages. He bases his analysis on the concepts of social telesis (Lester Ward), social disequilibrium and conflict (Karl Mannheim, Gustav Landauer, and others), as well as the inherent dialectic. Fals has employed the concepts of utopia, topia, and subversion. As society moves in time along the dialectic, it experiences rhythms that lead from relative stability to intense change to relative stability and so forth. Utopian ideas (missional, liberal, socialist, pluralist) signal the beginning of each of the great periods of transition. The introduction of utopia results in conflicts among elements of society (thesis, antithesis). Following the resolution of these conflicts only a residue of the utopia remains. A new relatively stable social order (topia), with implicit tensions and incongruities reappears (synthesis).

Fals divides Colombian history into five periods or orders: ayllic, seigniorial, bourgeois, liberal-bourgeois, and order 5 (the present). He also demarcates four transitional stages: Christian, liberal, socialist, and neosocialist. These he calls "subversions," or "condition[s] reflecting the internal incongruities of a social order . . . [lasting] from the articulations of a prevailing order (after the impact of utopian thought) to the emergence of a new social order" (*Subversion and Social Change in Colombia*, pp. 13–14). Subversion implies "contradictions of significant enough nature to bring about complete transformation of the social order" (ibid., p. 14). When subversion reaches a certain point, "organisms, techniques and attitudes conducive to change develop, producing acute perplexity, anomie or insecurity in the patterns of social interaction" (ibid.). This occurs through the employment of mechanisms of control (political hegemony, leadership ability, and social diffusion). "These mechanisms impose direction on social change" (ibid.). Following this, there exists a period of conflict between values and counter values and between norms and counter norms. This process leads to a period of reconciliation and co-optation, a time of adjustment between the old order and the subversion. During the adjustment the new topia emerges, with residues left from the confrontation. The new order is formed. This order, soon transformed into the new tradition, carries within it the contradictory residues that lead to emergence of another subversion, and the process continues.

BIBLIOGRAPHY:

A. *Peasant Society in the Colombian Andes: A Sociological Study of Saucío* (Gainesville: University of Florida Press, 1955); *Subversion and Social Change in Colombia* (New York: Columbia University Press, 1970); "The Negation of Sociology and Its Promise: Perspectives of Social Sciences in Latin America Today," *Latin American Research Review*, 15, no. 1 (1980), pp. 161–66.

DAWN FOGLE DEATON

FANON, FRANTZ (1925–1961). Born in the French Antilles and raised in Martinique, Frantz Fanon has exerted an enormous influence among oppressed nonwhites in America and throughout the Third World through his writings. Fanon studied medicine and psychiatry at the University of Lyons, France, and while there edited the black student journal *Tom-Tom*. After receiving his medical degree in 1951, he was appointed head of the Psychiatric Department at Blida-Joinville Hospital in Algeria. He became an energetic supporter of the Algerian Revolution, overtly and covertly aiding rebels during the 1954–56 period. He resigned his hospital position in 1956, devoting himself to writing and actively working to promote anti-imperialist revolutions in the Third World. In 1956 he attended the First Congress of Black Writers and Artists in Paris and became editor of the Algerian National Liberation Front's (FLN) newspaper *El Moud-jahid*, in Tunis. In 1957–58 Fanon attended inter-African congresses at Bamako and Cotonou and in 1959 was seriously injured by a mine at the Algerian–Moroccan border. In 1960 Fanon was appointed ambassador of the Algerian Provisional Government to Ghana. At this time Fanon contracted leukemia. Shortly thereafter he went to the Soviet Union for treatment and, in 1961, died of this disease while undergoing treatment in a Washington, D.C., hospital.

In *Black Skin, White Masks* (1952), Fanon's first published work, he used his own personal experiences as a black man living in Martinique and France to describe the conscious and semiconscious psychological techniques by which black men and women are persuaded to feel and live racial guilt. Fanon condemned colonialism for fostering racism, but at this early date still advocated integration based on racial equality. Nor was Fanon as yet explicitly socialist. The years 1954–56 were transitional ones for Fanon, as he evolved from a humanitarian idealist to a more pragmatic, Marxist-oriented revolutionary who perceived oppression in historical and socio-economic as well as psychological terms.

Fanon's remarkable reputation rests primarily on his *The Wretched of the Earth*, which was written and published during the last year of his life. Fanon condemned Africa's native bourgeoisie as a parasitical class readily exploiting the native proletariat and peasantry. In the struggle against colonialism these native bourgeoisie coalesced into Africa's nationalist political parties, which began as patriotic and progressive forces but quickly deteriorated into tools for elite black hegemony. Nationalist parties were always reformist, opportunist, and cowardly and, in Fanon's opinion, had to be wrested from the bourgeoisie.

But on whose shoulders would the anticolonialist revolution fall? Fanon, along with many others, including Jean-Paul Sartre,* Léopold Sédar Senghor, and other nonorthodox leftists, regarded the Western proletariat with scorn and distrust, pointing out the nonprogressive role played by French workers during Algeria's struggle for independence. Fanon, however, also argued that the Third World's native proletariat was equally untrustworthy. Well-paid and privileged during colonialism, they were economically attached to imperialism and hence loyal to their nationalist parties. For Fanon, the authentic revolutionary class in the Third World was the poor peasantry. The "wretched of the earth," these poor peasants were decent, loyal, dependable, and dignified, the soil from which revolution would grow. After rebellion took root in the countryside, Fanon argued, it would spread quickly to urban centers through the activities of the uprooted peasants, that is, the urban *lumpen* proletariat of pimps, prostitutes, and petty criminals. They would simultaneously purify themselves and their nation in the patriotic act of rebellion.

Fanon concurs with orthodox Marxism in defining class according to an individual's relationship to the means of production. However, he differs in perceiving political behavior as determined *not* by class but by an individual's relative wealth, the size of the class he belongs to, and the extent of this class's integration into the colonial system. Like Sartre, Fanon therefore emphasizes need and scarcity as determinants of revolutionary action. These qualities precede class formation and the division of labor and will survive even in socialism. Poor native peasants are thus revolutionary, whereas relatively affluent native workers are not. And although socialism, for Fanon, is both desirable and necessary, it must be radically decentralized and democratic, allowing poor peasants and *lumpen* workers to exert hegemony. On the national level, planning, austerity, and education were the keys to progress.

Fanon strongly believed that the national liberation movement and the socialist revolution had to be joined under the ideological and institutional leadership of poor peasants. The first postrevolutionary project would establish an authentic, purified nation and national culture, as distinct from the native bourgeoisie's opportunistic mimicry of the West. Fanon provided little practical guidance as to the precise means by which socialism and authentic nationalism would be established, other than advocating violence as the apt response to colonialism's brutality. Here, Fanon's early focus on psychology blends with Marx's arguments on the necessity of proletarian force. Fanon believed that revolutionary violence in the Third World was necessary for the practical project of defeating colonialism and the native bourgeoisie, but also was a psychological purgative for formerly oppressed nonwhites. ''Violence alone, violence committed by the people, violence organized and educated by its leaders, makes it possible for the masses to understand social truths and gives the key to them'' (*The Wretched of the Earth*, p. 118). Violence alone will unite the revolutionaries into a community of authentic actors. ''It frees the native from his inferiority complex and from his despair and inaction'' (ibid., p. 74). Fanon was certain that in this violent revolutionary upheaval, the forces of colonialism would be defeated. No colonial power, he argued, could maintain the large military, economic, and political commitment needed to suppress the revolutionary energies of native peasants.

Fanon believed that spontaneous revolutionary violence had to be replaced by systematic organization—ultimately by a national revolutionary army. Mao Zedong† had taught that the Communist Party guides the guerrilla struggle. Che Guevara† and Régis Debray* argued that orthodox Communist parties are often corrupt and reformist. Revolutionary parties, which must lead the struggle, are independent of this struggle but are derived from it, not from an autonomous bureaucracy. Fanon admitted that intellectual guidance was necessary but argued as well that the revolutionary social class itself will generate its ideological and institutional leadership. Fanon, therefore, is less a military strategist than either Che or Debray and perhaps more romantic in believing that the poor and uneducated will generate their own salvation.

Fanon is indebted to a variety of African and Continental thinkers, including Aimé Césaire, Léopold Sédar Senghor, Léon Damas, Amalcar Cabral,† Sigmund Freud, Maurice Merleau-Ponty,* and, especially, Jean-Paul Sartre. However, his own experiences of Western-inspired cruelty and injustice, so vividly recorded and analyzed in his theoretical works, have turned Fanon, for many, into the moral and political voice of this century's oppressed nonwhite masses.

BIBLIOGRAPHY:

A. *Studies in a Dying Colonialism* (New York: Monthly Review Press, 1965); *The Wretched of the Earth* (New York: Grove Press, 1965); *Black Skin, White Masks* (New York: Grove Press, 1967); *For the African Revolution* (New York: Monthly Review Press, 1967).

B. Simone de Beauvoir, *Force of Circumstances* (New York: Putnam, 1964); G. K. Grohs, "Frantz Fanon and the African Revolution," *Journal of Modern African Studies*, 6, no. 4 (1968), pp. 22–48; David Caute, *Frantz Fanon* (New York: Viking Press, 1970).

ROBERT A. GORMAN

FENICHEL, OTTO (1897–1946). Born in 1897 into a middle-class assimilated Jewish family in Vienna, Fenichel attended the University of Vienna and engaged in left-wing political activity as a student. By the early 1920s he had earned his medical degree, received psychoanalytic training, and established a practice in Vienna. In 1922 Fenichel moved to Berlin, a center of psychoanalytic research and activity. Fenichel, with Wilhelm Reich,* Siegried Bernfeld, Eric Fromm,* Karl Abraham, Melanie Klein, and dozens of others, comprised the "Berlin Institute," formally established in 1920. Although Fenichel was a professed political radical and Marxist,† it is nevertheless uncertain whether he ever joined the Communist Party. By the early 1930s Fenichel was lecturing regularly on issues of Marxist psychoanalysis. Unlike Reich, however, he was unwilling to sacrifice Freudianism to radical ideology, and continued throughout his life to advocate, research, and publish on classical psychoanalytical problems. Fenichel fled Berlin in 1933, arriving first in Prague and eventually Los Angeles, where he continued his psychoanalytical research and gradually abandoned his overt Marxism. Fenichel died on 22 January 1946 of a ruptured cerebral aneurysm as he was recertifying his medical credentials by interning at Cedars of Lebanon Hospital in California.

Fenichel's professional reputation is based primarily on his *The Psychoanalytic Theory of Neurosis*, a rigidly orthodox Freudian text. However, for over a decade from 1933 until 1945 Fenichel instigated, organized, and led a group of radical psychoanalysts that included Edith Jacobson, Annie Reich, Kate Friedländer, Barbara Lantos, Edith Ludowyk Gyömröi, and George Gero. He secretly sent a *Rundbriefe* ("round letter") to this band of analysts, discussing issues relating to the synthesis of Marxism and Freudianism and eliciting their responses, which were reproduced in succeeding issues. Fenichel's group sought to radicalize Freudianism without abandoning its critical commitment to the forces of eroticism and the subconscious. In this sense, they differed from neo-Freudians such as Karen Horney, Eric Fromm, and Clara Thompson (who emphasized social conditioning); Wilhelm Reich (who reduced all neurosis to the repression of biological functions); and the classical Freudians (who were both conservative and increasingly dominated by the medical profession). Isolated in a foreign culture, without institutional support of any kind, and increasingly alienated even within his own discipline, Fenichel terminated the *Rundbriefe* in 1945 without having produced any significant theoretical breakthroughs.

BIBLIOGRAPHY:

A. *The Psychoanalytic Theory of Neurosis* (New York: Norton, 1945); *Problems of Psychoanalytic Technique* (New York: Psychological Quarterly, 1969). The *Rundbriefe* have never been published.

B. Russell Jacoby, *The Repression of Psychoanalysis* (New York: Basic Books, 1983).

ROBERT A. GORMAN

FETSCHER, IRING (b. 1922). Iring Fetscher, a German democratic socialist, was born in Marbach and grew up in Dresden. He has been a professor of political philosophy in the Department of Political Science at the University of Frankfurt since 1963. He studied philosophy, German, and history in Tubingen and Paris from 1945 to 1950, receiving a Ph.D. in 1950 with a dissertation entitled "Hegels Lehre vom Menschen." He taught philosophy in Tubingen from 1950 to 1955 while completing a second dissertation entitled "Rousseaus politische Philosophie." Fetscher taught at the New School for Social Research (1968–69) and was a fellow at the Institute for Advanced Study in Wassenaar, the Netherlands (1972–73) and at the National University in Canberra (1976). He was a visiting professor at Tel Aviv University in 1971 and at the University of Nijmegen, the Netherlands, in 1975. He was a member of the PEN-centrum in West Germany and of the "basic values" committee of the Social Democratic Party's steering committee. He is the author of several standard works on Marxism† (e.g. *Karl Marx and Marxism*, 1971) and is a regular contributor to German radio and television programs as well as to numerous encyclopedias, journals, and newspapers. Recurring themes in his writings are the early Marx, right-wing radicalism, the post-Hitler German people, democracy, and Soviet socialism.

For Fetscher, democracy and socialism are not opposites, yet he knows of no country where they have both been realized concretely. In *Democratie zwischen Sozialdemokratie und Sozialismus* (1973), Fetscher investigates the problems of the social democratic industrial countries of the West and juxtaposes them to the problem of democratization in bureaucratic socialist countries such as the Soviet Union. Fetscher consistently argues that socialist "realizations" be checked against and confronted with their intellectual origins. He was among the first European radical scholars to redefine Marxism in terms of Marx's† *1844 Manuscripts* and the *Grundrisse*, focusing on the abyss that separated "the humanitarian intentions and theory of the early Marx and the ideologies of the Second International"† (*Karl Marx and Marxism*, p. 9), while also stressing Marx's indebtedness to Hegel. Fetscher favors a socialism that is grounded in ethics as opposed to one that is impersonally attached to history. In *Karl Marx and Marxism* he compares the development of Marx's theory of human emancipation to Stalin's† repressive, enslaving dictatorship. He argues in *Marxistische Porträts*

(1975) that this perverted development of Marxism was not due to an inner logic, but rather was caused by the loss of the authentic revolutionary insights proffered by people like Rosa Luxemburg† and Lenin.† In order to avoid another such catastrophe, Fetscher argues, it is imperative that the writings of these revolutionaries he consulted anew. In his interpretation of German neo-right-wing radicalism (*Rechtsradikalismus*, 1967) Fetscher insists that contemporary versions are not always caused by "experiences of frustration." Nor can Fetscher find a causal link between recession and right-wing radicalism. Always, Fetscher emphasizes the importance of Marxism's power of criticism, epitomized in Marx's early texts, as the means of avoiding both Stalinism and fascism.

As a social critic Fetscher is known for his cleverly constructed and skillfully written satirical fairy tales in which he vents his contempt for the commercialization and commodification of cultural life.

BIBLIOGRAPHY:

A. *Der Marxismus* (Munich: Piper, 1967); *Rechtsradikalismus* (Stuttgart: Fromann-Holzbog, 1967); *Karl Marx and Marxism* (New York: Herder, 1971); *Demokratie zwischen Sozialdemokratie und Sozialismus* (Munich: Kohlhammer, 1973); *Marxistische Porträts* (Stuttgart: Fromann-Holzbog, 1975); *Vom Wohlfahrtsstaat zur neuen Lebensqualität* (Bundverlag, 1982).

TINEKE RITMEESTER

FEYERABEND, PAUL KARL (b. 1924). Paul Feyerabend was born on 13 January 1924, in Vienna, Austria. After an early training in theater and the arts, Feyerabend entered the University of Vienna, where he concentrated his studies on physics and astronomy and pursued his interest in the philosophy of science. During his student years at the University of Vienna, Feyerabend came in contact with Wittengenstein, Popper (with whom he studied at the University of London in 1952–53), and the Marxist† intellectual Walter Hollitscher (one of his favorite mentors), among others, all of whom influenced and partly directed his interests in the history and philosophy of science. Feyerabend received his Ph.D. from the University of Vienna in 1951. From 1951 to 1956 Feyerabend was a lecturer at the Vienna Institute of Sciences and Fine Arts, while from 1955 to 1959 he lectured at Bristol (England) University in the philosophy of science. In 1959, Feyerabend emigrated to the United States, where he took a job as an associate professor of philosophy at the University of California at Berkeley, where he has been a professor of philosophy since 1962. Among his many awards and appointments of distinction, Feyerabend has served as the chairman of the Department of the History and Philosophy of Science both at University College, London (1968–71) and at the Free University of Berlin (1968–70) and as professor of philosophy at Yale (1969–70).

Feyerabend's relation to Marxism is tangential for the most part. However, his contributions to the debates in the philosophy and history of science and to modern epistemological concerns have had an impact on Marxist considerations in these areas. Feyerabend, along with Thomas Kuhn, can be cited as a primary source for the renewed interest in and sensitivity of Marxists (especially in the United States, Great Britain, and West Germany) to questions of epistemology and methodology in Marxian social theory. Feyerabend's influence on Marxism was felt especially in the 1970s with the publication of *Against Method* (1975) and *Science in a Free Society* (1978). Marxists, initially attracted by the Kuhnian notions of "scientific revolutions," "paradigm shifts," and "normal science," found in Feyerabend further justifications for their claims regarding the distinctiveness of Marx's philosophical and methodological views; for their conception of persistent, irreducible differences between Marxist and non-Marxist theoretical approaches; and for their "materialist" presentation of the historical transformations within and between conceptual frameworks in the natural and social sciences.

Three strands of Feyerabend's thought have been of particular interest to Marxism. First, Feyerabend argues (in *Against Method*) that the philosophy of any scientific method must self-consciously internalize the historical development of that method. That is, since the development of a science is a complex historical process, any philosophy of that science cannot adequately theorize the methods that presumably account for its peculiar "logic" and modes of proof unless it simultaneously theorizes the historical production of these methods. Toward this end, Feyerabend employs the Marxist concept of "uneven development," in which contradictory methods, theories, experiential bases, and so forth, developing at different rates, may all be seen to contribute to the progression of scientific thought. Second, Feyerabend argues for the "incommensurability" of different "frames of thought," i.e., that there are often no interdiscursive epistemological means to resolve competing theoretical claims or overarching "rational" rules to deduce one frame of thought from another. Again, this argument has held an appeal for Marxists who oppose the claim that Marxist social theory has no distinct or valid epistemological and methodological "norms" and, therefore, must be judged according to "neutral" interdiscursive standards. Third, many Marxists have approved of Feyerabend's position that all scientific methods are infused with values, ideological maneuvers, and political stances or bear the stamp of their determination by economic, cultural, and political processes and institutions. Feyerabend's discussion of the nature of Galileo's theoretical innovations proceeds according to such a "sociology" of scientific method. Feyerabend's writings have helped to redirect attention particularly to nonorthodox European Marxists who have tried to specify a particularly Marxist epistemology free of the logical positivism, critical rationalism, naturalism, and naive empiricism that are the objects of Feyerabend's criticisms.

BIBLIOGRAPHY:

A. *Against Method* (London: New Left Books, 1975); *Science in a Free Society* (London: New Left Books, 1978).

JACK AMARIGLIO and RICHARD WOLFF

FIRESTONE, SHULAMITH (b. 1944). An American radical feminist-activist, Firestone was born in Ottawa, Canada, in 1944. She grew up in the American

Midwest, attended Washington University in St. Louis, and received an A.B. from the Chicago Art Institute. Firestone participated in radical feminist organizations in New York City, coediting the journal, *Notes from the Second Year*. *The Dialectic of Sex: The Case for Feminist Revolution* (1970) is her only published book. In it Firestone uses the Marxist† historical-materialist dialectic to analyze three levels of social activity: sex, class, and culture. For Firestone, sex/caste distinctions, rather than the class division of labor, are most seminal and fundamental. In all societies, women's subordinate status and position is grounded in human biology: her reproductive function within the biological family that once left her at the mercy of her female bodily functions and responsible for the care and nurture of the dependent young. Patriarchy is the socio-cultural formation that, by defining women as a "different species" (p. 83) on the basis of biology, continued her confinement in the home while men went out into the world to conquer nature. Thus culture, defined by Firestone as "the attempt . . . to realize the conceivable in the possible" (p. 194), became, in both its idealistic/aesthetic and scientific modes, the domain of men. Owing to the progress of technology, the anchoring of women to their reproductive functions was no longer functionally imperative. Nonetheless, in bourgeois (and so-called socialist) societies, the (white) male ruling class, in order to maintain its power and authority, has developed a series of ideological justifications—love and the cult of romance, the ideal of female beauty, the neo-Freudian command of "adjustment," etc.—to buttress the patriarchal nuclear family and to quell any feminist revolt against it.

According to Firestone, the United States has "now reached the final stages of Patriarchalism, (corporate) capitalism and of the Two Cultures" (the estrangement of the Aesthetic from the Scientific mode) (p. 213). Through the use of new and revolutionary technology—fertility control, but also artificial means of reproduction—women can be liberated "from the tyranny of their sexual-reproductive roles—both the fundamental biological condition itself and the sexual class system built upon and reinforcing this biological condition" (p. 34). Furthermore, under "cybernetic socialism," wage labor, the fate of the current male and female working class, would no longer be necessary. For the first time in human history the conceivable would be the possible; there would be no need for a separate realm of culture since all people could be artists in the act of living. Without the necessity of either production or reproduction, women and men, adults and children, would be able to engage in "complex play," "activity done for its own sake," and to rejoin love to various forms of sexuality.

BIBLIOGRAPHY:

A. *The Dialectic of Sex: The Case for Feminist Revolution* (New York: Morrow, 1970).

KAREN ROSENBLUM-CALE

FOUCAULT, MICHEL (b. 1926). Michel Foucault is one of the most important and controversial figures writing on the left today. Perhaps no other modern figure, with the exception of Walter Benjamin,* has been read by and appropriated into so many different intellectual and political traditions as Foucault. He has, to say the least, a complex and ambiguous relation to Marxism.† Although he has both been influenced by and had a profound impact on contemporary debates in Marxism, there is little justification for considering him a Marxist. As a theorist, historical analyst, and political strategist, he has consistently attacked strategies based on hierarchies, reductionism, and systematicity, all of which are characteristic of Marxism, according to Foucault. Foucault was born in Poitier, France, in 1926; he studied philosophy at the Ecole Normale Supérieure (with Louis Althusser*), and continued his education in psychology and psychopathology. He taught in French programs in Sweden, Poland, and Germany, before returning to France in 1960 to receive the *doctorate d'état* in the history of science, under Georges Canguilhem.* The events of May 1968 marked an important intellectual, political, and professional turning point. Immediately after the protests of May, Foucault was appointed chairman of the Department of Philosophy at Vincennes, where he became a leading spokesman for the *gauchistes* against the Communists. In 1970, he was appointed to the prestigious position of professor of the history of systems of thought at the Collège de France.

For Foucault, the theory of Marxism is inseparable from the practice of the Communist party, of which he was a member in the early 1950s before leaving France. His criticisms of Marxism have been on both theoretical and strategic issues and have followed the course of his own intellectual and political development. As early as 1966, in *The Order of Things*, Foucault describes the controversies between bourgeois and Marxist economics as "no more than storms in a children's paddling pool" (p. 262). That is, he locates both systems of economic thought within a nineteenth-century *épistème* that is not only coming to an end but also is certainly inappropriate to the analysis of contemporary structures of power and knowledge. In fact, as if to deflate Marxism even further, Foucault argues that it was Ricardo and not Marx who accomplished the rupture with previous discourses of society and history; Marxism merely converted Ricardo's pessimism into a utopian optimism.

As his work has developed, Foucault's critique of Marxism has been specified in more theoretical terms. He rejects the dialectic as a view of history, preferring instead to emphasize the discontinuities in history, and his approach to political strategy merely reinserts the dialectician into the existing power structures. Further, Marxism situates itself as a discourse of truth which assumes that there is a truth in itself to be discovered and brought into language; truth for Marxism is, of course, not a positivistic relation between object and word but an eschatological relation. Marxism participates in the ethical discourses of the nineteenth century that sought to give voice to the silent motivations of history and action through (dialectical) reflection. Consequently, Marxism must see itself as a systematic and even a global theory. It not only situates itself within "the true" but empowers itself to exclude other discourses from "truth." Finally, Foucault rejects the reductionism of Marxism, which, in the end, must always interpret history according to a single principle or dimension of determination. All power relations are conceptualized in terms of a binary and hierarchical structure of classes: the dominating and the dominated.

Despite Foucault's rejection of Marxism and his reassessment of Marx's space in intellectual history, Foucault has consistently acknowledged the impossibility of writing about history without using the terminology and concepts developed by Marx, and he often rather playfully points to his own reliance on the discourse of Marxism. Furthermore, he cites Marx, along with Freud and Nietzsche, as his predecessors insofar as they opened the space for a new analysis of human existence by having decentered meaning and undermined the belief in the innocent and self-transparent human soul or consciousness. Yet it is Nietzsche, rather than either Marx or Freud on the one hand, or the structuralists and poststructuralists on the other, that Foucault perceives as the greatest influence on his own project. This project, which might be described as a "strategic theorizing" of power in the form of a "micro-analytics of power," has had a profound impact on many contemporary Marxists. Furthermore, the concreteness with which he puts Althusser's notion of "overdetermination" into practice has opened up new epistemological debates within Marxism.

Although some have seen a break in Foucault's work based upon his articulation of the problematic of power following the events of May 1968, Foucault himself has claimed that his concern has always been with the analysis of power. His earlier works present an "archeology" that attempts to identify the emergence of, and the conditions of possibility of, particular modes of discursive rationality. His archeology demonstrates how specific forms of "statements" (*épistèmes*) construct not only their own objects, but their subjects and discursive contexts as well according to anonymous systems of rules. It was, for Foucault, not the interpretable content of discourse but the fact of the existence of particular statements that is at issue. Within this archeology of *épistèmes* and discursive formations, Foucault located the question of power in terms of the ways particular discourses empower and are empowered by particular practices, subjects, etc. The question of truth, of the "politics of truth," is central to this investigation. Again, Foucault examined both the conditions under which a particular discourse is positioned within "the true" and the ways in which such ascriptions of "truth" empower those discourses. Thus, the question of "truth" is shifted from an epistemological issue to one of the strategies and relations of power within particular social formations. Truth has become an effect of and a condition of the possibility of power.

Even before the events of May 1968 Foucault was attempting to describe relations of power without imposing either a psychological or a political theory and to reject global and reductionistic descriptions of them. Rather, these events seemed to have forced Foucault to reexamine the relationship between theory and practice in strategic terms and to place a greater focus on the nondiscursive practices implicated with power. In particular, questions of the body and desire have entered the foreground of Foucault's "genealogy," along with discourse and power. Locating his own work within the ubiquitous field of power relations, Foucault has attempted to describe the "technologies" and "apparatuses" of power that organize everyday lives. Emphasizing the intereffectivity of the discursive and the nondiscursive, he has described a "bio-politics" that increasingly makes the body into the site of the inscription of power. At the political level, Foucault takes a similarly strategic view, arguing for the importance of local resistances and struggles and the importance of the intellectual in analyzing the structures and technologies at play. It is not enough merely to shift the positions of power; one is rather called upon to resist the structures and techniques themselves. In his analyses of madness, the medical clinic, the prison, and currently, the apparatus of sexuality, Foucault attempts to give voice to those who have been silenced, to recuperate and reinvest those sites as potential points for struggle. His work brings together the theoretical, the concrete, and the political within the attempt to articulate an understanding of the complexity of contemporary structures and mechanisms of power.

BIBLIOGRAPHY:

A. *The Order of Things: An Archeology of the Human Sciences* (New York: Pantheon, 1970); *The Archaeology of Knowledge*, trans. A. M. Sheridan Smith (New York: Pantheon, 1972); *The Birth of the Clinic: An Archaeology of Medical Perception*, trans. A. M. Sheridan Smith (New York: Pantheon, 1973); *Discipline and Punish: The Birth of the Prison*, trans. Alan Sheridan (New York: Pantheon, 1977); *The History of Sexuality*, vol. 1: *An Introduction*, trans. Robert Hurley (New York: Pantheon, 1978); *Power/ Knowledge: Selected Interviews and Other Writings 1972–1977*, ed. Colin Gordon (New York: Pantheon, 1980).

B. Alan Sheridan, *Michel Foucault: The Will to Truth* (New York: Tavistock, 1980).

LAURENCE GROSSBERG

FOUGEYROLLAS, PIERRE (b. 1922). The intellectual itinerary of Pierre Fougeyrollas resembles that of many French leftists born in the 1920s: at the outbreak of World War II, he joined the Communist Party to resist the fascist threat, was captured and condemned to death by the Nazis, but managed to survive, participating in the liberation of the French city of Limoges. After the war, he completed his studies. As a professor of philosophy in Paris it was not until the Hungarian crisis in 1956 that Fougeyrollas abandoned the Communist Party. He then contributed to the Marxist† critique of orthodox Communism as a member of the *Arguments* group* (1956–62). Fougeyrollas's career during the last twenty years has included a sweeping study of contemporary thought and society as reflected in his works on Marx, Freud, and political consciousness in contemporary France. He also taught at the University of Dakar throughout the 1960s, wrote three studies of modernization in Africa, and was expelled from Senegal in 1971 for his anti-imperialist and anticolonialist activities. His most recent works have been Marxist analyses of the social sciences and contemporary social processes (*Sciences sociales et marxisme*, 1979, and *Les processus sociaux contemporains*, 1980).

In an article resembling Edgar Morin's* *Autocritique*, entitled "La Pensée at-elle une ombre?'' Fougeyrollas admits his profound disillusionment with Marxism, "a totalitarian monolith," and that concurrent with his "de-Marxization" was "a renaissance of philosophical dismay" and a belief in the "irreplaceable function of philosophical thought." Defining philosophy as "a questioning of all established knowledge and power," Fougeyrollas argued that the Heideggerian meditation offered the sole starting point "to arrive at a problematic that would escape the contemporary dissolution" (*Arguments/2*, pp. 125–28), a philosophical project necessarily linked to a social praxis. Fougeyrollas concluded by distinguishing his "shadow" and his thought, the latter existing on both the "horizontal plane" of present history and the "vertical plane" of philosophy (ibid., p. 129). This "philosophical renaissance" points to Fougeyrollas's role in the revisionism of the *Arguments* group: given that, for Fougeyrollas, true Marxism was based on the concepts of alienation and liberation of man, he opposed what he perceived as Marx's reduction of all human alienation to the economic form, as well as Marx's concept of a total end to alienation, which would block further, gradual, and indefinite human development. Fougeyrollas argued that history "only becomes the locus of the liberation never achieved by man if philosophical thought, born from history, attempts to escape it" (ibid., p. 252). Fougeyrollas proposed a modest Marxism allowing not only for an indefinite overcoming of alienation, but also for theories (e.g. Freudian) that would explain particular forms of alienation in the superstructure. Furthermore, in *Le Marxisme en question* (1959), Fougeyrollas follows the *Arguments* spirit by arguing for a "new *Weltanschauung*" by "discovering the problematic which suits the era of civilization that we are entering" (p. 161), thereby extending one aspect of Marx's thought. And since philosophical reflection will be at the heart of this new way of thinking, Fougeyrollas continued his project in two philosophical meditations, *La Philosophie en question* (1960) and *Contradiction et totalité. Surgissement et déploiement de la dialectique* (1964). While the earlier work continued Fougeyrollas's search for a new philosophy, the conjunction of neo-Marxism and existentialism, the terms *contradiction* and *totality* constitute the poles of Fougeyrollas's reformulation of the dialectic in the second book, a move away from Jean-Paul Sartre's* development of the dialectic in *Critique de la raison dialectique*: no longer a mode of reasoning or a methodology, the dialectic for Fougeyrollas became the basis of ongoing criticism and social development, of an open and "planetary" way of thinking.

Fougeyrollas described his overall intellectual project in the introduction to his "attempt at synthesis": *Marx, Freud et la révolution totale* (1972). Seeking to discern the contemporary trajectory of the "total revolution," Fougeyrollas explained that he wrote *Le Marxisme en question* both as a critique of "the dogmatism and bureaucratic degeneration of Marx's teaching" and as an announcement of "the fruitlessness of a return to the sources of Marxism," then *La Révolution freudienne* (1970) as an attempt "to tear Freud's heritage from its co-optation by the circles and cliques of the initiated," and finally *La Philosophie en question* and *Contradiction et totalité* as a "quest in search of the dialectic . . . at work as much in today's partially underground revolutionary processes as in the altogether vital thought of Marx and Freud.'' In *Marx, Freud et la révolution totale*, Fougeyrollas wished ''to consider synthetically the struggle of the worldwide proletariat against the capitalist system, the protest of the rising generations against established institutions, women's struggles for their liberation and that of both sexes, finally the movements of peoples whose collective identity remains unrecognized'' (pp. 7–8).

BIBLIOGRAPHY:

A. *Le Marxisme en question* (Paris: Seuil, 1959); *La Philosophie en question* (Paris: Denoel, 1960); *Contradiction et totalité* (Paris: Minuit, 1964); *Marx, Freud et la révolution totale* (Paris: Anthropos, 1972); *Sciences sociales et marxisme* (Paris: Payot, 1979); *Les Processus sociaux contemporains* (Paris: Payot, 1980).

B. Jean Duvignaud, ''France: The Neo-Marxists,'' in *Revisionism: Essays on the History of Marxist Ideas*, ed. L. Labedz (New York: Praeger, 1962); Louis Soubise, *Le Marxisme après Marx* (Paris: Montaigne, 1967); Mark Poster, *Existential Marxism in Postwar France* (Princeton: Princeton University Press, 1977).

CHARLES J. STIVALE

FRANK, ANDRÉ GUNDER (b. 1929). André Gunder Frank was born 24 February 1929 in Berlin, Germany; however, he grew up in ''middle-class America.'' He attended Swarthmore College, where he received a B.A. with honors in 1959. Then he went to the University of Michigan for a year of graduate work before transferring to the University of Chicago, where he earned first an M.A. (1952) and then a Ph.D. (1957) in economics. Frank's graduate school training was conventional. He began his academic career with a ''1950s mainstream'' economic outlook. Nevertheless, this liberal academic quickly came to call himself a ''revolutionary socialist.'' The transformation began shortly after graduate school. First there were the usual years as an assistant professor at Michigan State University (1957–61) and a couple of one-year appointments at the University of Iowa and Wayne State University. Then the turning point came; in 1963 Frank took a visiting professorship at the University of Brasília in Brazil.

He apparently took the appointment thinking that the answers to Brazil's development problems were in his repertoire of currently accepted modernization formulas. His experiences in Brazil disabused him of that belief. Seeking an explanation for the differences between Latin America's and the industrialized West's economic growth patterns, Frank turned to the ideas of Paul Baran.† Since 1963 Frank has built on Baran's ideas, forged his own development theory, become known as one of the leading Marxist† dependency theorists, worked as a consultant to the United Nations Economic Commission for Latin America, taken an active part in Allende's† attempts to transform Chile, fought against the military junta that deposed Allende's government, worked to keep the Centro de Estudios Socio-Economics open at the Escuela de Economica in Santiago, Chile, and written numerous books and articles for both lay and scholarly audiences. During the 1970s he worked at the Lateinamerike-Institut at the University of Berlin and at the Max-Planck-Institut in Starnberg, Germany. Currently he is professor of economics at the Free University of Amsterdam in the Netherlands.

The components of Paul Baran's work that Frank built upon include: (1) the premise that development can be understood only within its historical context; (2) the proposition that the division of the world into more and less developed state economies is not accidental; (3) the hypothesis that underdevelopment is the result of interaction with developed capitalist states; and (4) several inter-related hypotheses which assert that more advanced capitalist states subordinate developing regions or states, thereby crippling or destroying precapitalist structures while extracting the surplus profit for use in the developed country. As Frank fleshed out Baran's ideas, he called attention to the notion that underde-velopment is the result of a *process* that began with the rise and expansion of capitalism in the world. Since colonial times Latin America, for example, was drawn into the capitalist mode of production. Underdevelopment is an ongoing process, a point Frank underscores with the phrase, "the development of underdevelopment."

Describing, analyzing, and explaining the process of development of under-development is the province of Frank's contributions to dependency theory. He focuses on the dynamics of relations between advanced and underdeveloped capitalist countries and between the centers of underdeveloped countries and their peripheries. To do this he has undertaken case studies of Brazil's, Chile's, and Mexico's historical experiences with capitalist development, in which he demonstrated the lack of resemblance between the past or present of those countries and any of the so-called stages modernization theorists have suggested that states went through to achieve industrial growth or must go through to achieve advanced development. Further, he asserted that the key to understanding underdevelopment lies with an understanding of what he termed metropolis–satellite relationships. According to Frank, metropolis–satellite relations are nec-essarily structured so that a metropolis expropriates surplus product from its satellite and suppresses the satellite's full development of its own resources. The necessity of exploitation in metropolis–satellite relationships is a function of the nature of capitalism, a function that leads to the concentration of capital and uneven development. The accumulation process in capitalism fundamentally works through metropolis–satellite relations, which exist between developed states and underdeveloped states and the peripheral regions of those states. In other words, metropolis–satellite relations are conveyor belt linkages that extract surplus profit from the remotest regions of the world to the economic centers of the world. For Frank these linkages not only explain how and why surpluses accumulate at ever increasing degrees of intensity at each level of the hierarchy of metropolis–satellite relations but also demonstrate the world-system nature of capitalism and capitalist development.

Three phrases that represent the pivotal ideas in Frank's work can be strung together to make a sentence that oversimplifies but summarizes his position:

there is "continuity in change" in the "development of underdevelopment," which works through "metropolis–satellite" relations. Moreover, it is the combination of these concepts that distinguished Frank's ideas from Marx's notion of capitalist development, from Lenin's† theory of imperialism, and from some of the other representatives of the dependency theory school of development.

In contrast to Marx, Frank explains the dynamics of capitalism through its world economic structure, through market relations, and through metropolis–satellite relations, rather than fundamentally through class relations. To the extent that Marx visualized capitalist development as a series of stages that are repeated in every society, Frank radically departs from Marx. In contrast to Lenin, Frank has a broader definition of imperialism. For Lenin, imperialism and the development of underdevelopment through metropolis–satellite–type relations is historically specific to a phase of capitalist development. Furthermore, for Lenin the importance of imperialism is its consequence for the class struggle in the imperialist countries. Frank instead proposes that Lenin's idea of imperialism can be understood as one manifestation of the development of underdevelopment and argues that the consequences of the manifestations for class relations in both metropolis and satellite countries are significant.

Although Frank is known as a dependency theorist, it should be noted that there are a variety of types of dependency theories as well as a spectrum of political positions associated with dependency theories. Among the Latin American dependency theorists three types can be isolated. One is an extension of the "import substitution" school of thought. Theorists such as Osvaldo Sunkel and Celso Furtado argue that although underdeveloped countries are dependent, they may achieve independence and advanced development by abandoning externally oriented growth strategies for internally oriented growth strategies. Another type, represented by theorists such as Fernando Cardoso,* Octávio Ianni, Florestan Fernandes, and Aníbal Quijano contend that a way out of underdevelopment is through "dependent development," which maximizes multinational corporation investments while rooting out the remnants of the ruling class that block industrialization. The third type, generally known as the Marxist branch, is represented by theorists such as Frank, Ruy Mauro Marini,* and Theotonio Dos Santos.* Of these theorists Frank perhaps is the most convinced that the development of underdevelopment is integral to the dynamic of capitalism. Thus for Frank there is no certain or probable way out of dependency and underdevelopment unless and until the capitalist world-system expires.

In recent years Frank has focused increasingly on the world-system properties of capitalism. In 1978 he published an historical account (1492–1789) of the origins of worldwide capitalist accumulation. Thus his work in the future is more likely to be compared with that of Immanuel Wallerstein,* Samir Amin,* or Giovanni Arrighi than with Dos Santos or other Latin American dependency theorists.

BIBLIOGRAPHY:

A. *Capitalism and Underdevelopment in Latin America* (New York: Monthly Review Press, 1967); *Latin America: Underdevelopment or Revolution* (New York: Monthly Review Press, 1969); *Lumpenbourgeoisie: Lumpendevelopment* (New York: Monthly Review Press, 1972); *World Accumulation 1492–1789* (New York: Monthly Review Press, 1978); *Dependent Accumulation and Underdevelopment* (London: Macmillan, 1979); *Crisis: In the World Economy* (New York: Holmes & Meier, 1980); *Crisis: In the Third World* (New York: Holmes & Meier, 1981).

B. Philip J. O'Brien, "A Critique of Latin American Theories of Dependency," in *Beyond the Sociology of Development*, ed. I. Oxal, T. Barnett, and D. Booth (London: Routledge & Kegan Paul, 1975).

KATHLEEN RITTER

FROMM, ERICH (1900–1980). Erich Fromm was born in Frankfurt, Germany, on 23 March 1900. He studied psychology, sociology, and philosophy at the universities of Frankfurt and Heidelberg, receiving his Ph.D. from Frankfurt in 1922. He was trained in psychoanalysis at the Berlin Institute. From 1928 to 1938 Fromm was associated with the Institute of Social Research, first at the University of Frankfurt and then at Columbia University. After escaping from Nazi Germany in 1934 Fromm settled in America, lecturing at the New School for Social Research, Yale University, Columbia University, and Bennington College. He later served as chairman of the faculty of the William Alanson White Institute of Psychiatry. In 1951 Fromm became a professor at the National University of Mexico, where he founded the Mexican Institute of Psychoanalysis. In 1971 he moved to Switzerland, where he continued research and writing. On 18 March 1980 Fromm died in Muralto, Switzerland.

His initial fame was generated by the wide appeal of his book *Escape from Freedom* (1941). Fromm, Karen Horney, and Harry Stack Sullivan became identified as leading neo-Freudians. All three focused on the cultural and social influences on personality and de-emphasized Freud's theory of the primacy of the sexual instinct. Human nature or essence, for Fromm, is a desexualized need to "assimilate" things and "socialize" with other people. Hence, authentic consciousness generates creative, socially useful labor (in other words, praxis) and an affectionate openness toward fellow men and women, whose requital fulfills a need as basic as eating or drinking. Normally, however, this potential is distorted by an ensemble of cognitively experienced economic and social forces that form the "structure of psychic energy which is molded by any given society so as to be useful for the functioning of that particular society" (*Socialist Humanism*, p. 231). "Social character" indicates the plethora of ideas and behavior patterns that, when internalized, allow us to live and work successfully in society. The process of internalization occurs in and through socializing institutions (e.g. family, church, peer groups, schools, theaters). However, the quality of social character is determined by economic class: "The fundamental factor in the formation of social character is the practice of life as it is constituted by the mode of production and the resulting social stratification'' (ibid.). Social character, for Fromm, thus mediates base and superstructure, translating material directives into acceptable, ''proper'' social behavior.

Fromm argued that capitalism, which produces exchange rather than use value and subordinates general interests to individual profit, represses authenticity through its alienating social characters. Capitalists embody the ideals of self-sufficiency, competition, discipline, and misanthropy. Workers are taught to sublimate real interests into commercially profitable market channels, consuming to compensate for inner emptiness and anxiety. Typical bourgeois personality types—''receptive,'' ''exploitative,'' ''hoarding,'' and ''marketing''—confirm capitalism's debilitating effect on human psyches. The destructive battle between authenticity and repressive capitalist conditions also creates a potentially explosive subconscious bond among the oppressed, a ''social unconscious'' encompassing the irrepressible forces of creativity and love now occluded by pathogenic capitalist social characters. Fromm believed that as capitalism matures, it intensifies the experienced contradiction between authenticity and social acceptability, manifest not only in the relative decline in wages but also in the increasingly inhuman values that capitalism spawns while frantically driving to increase profits during a period of abnormally high inflation and unemployment. Capitalism struggles to hide the ''social unconscious,'' while its never-ending consumerism intensifies frustrations. The confluence of intensifying material contradictions and a hideous spiritual debasement precipitates revolution. ''Social change and revolution are caused not only by new productive forces which conflict with older forms of social organization, but also by the conflict between inhuman social conditions and unalterable human needs'' (ibid., p. 234). Fromm argued that workers would rebel after cognizing the ''social unconscious'' and rejecting capitalist exploitation. Postrevolutionary society will satisfy real needs for praxis and human affection by supporting mutual respect, cooperation, and equality, while producing goods and services required for authenticity, not profit. Fromm believed that we are at the threshhold of humanistic socialism: the planned, rational satisfaction of society's real needs.

As a trained psychoanalyst Fromm asserted that Freud correctly perceived humanity's instinctive potential, social repression, and the significance of the unconscious. But his pessimism regarding the compatibility of emancipated libidos and civilized behavior unknowingly reflected the economic and social conditions of European capitalism. Freud's antisocial, destructive libido corresponded to prevailing bourgeois attitudes regarding life's competitiveness and the social necessity of balancing self-interested groups. Someone with Freud's bourgeois background and education, argued Fromm, could not know real instincts, for they depict human openness, love, understanding, self-fulfillment, and the moral community. Human beings, instinctively, are inclined toward organic social union. This frightens the bourgeoisie, who react by obsessively reasserting individualism (e.g. Freud) or escaping through the numbing security of totalitarianism (e.g. fascism) (cf. *Escape from Freedom*). Neither eliminates the original anguish.

Fromm believed that Marx† was also correct in emphasizing concrete sources of social oppression and, in the early work, praxis as "those potentialities which are given . . . [man] when he is born" (*Beyond the Chains of Illusion*, p. 30). Unfortunately, argued Fromm, Marx left these undefined, and this carelessness had grievous consequences. Beginning with Engels,† materialists were obsessed with concrete aspects of alienation, ignoring Marx's esoteric doctrine of human potential. Marx always assumed that workers can, potentially, labor creatively and realize their species-essence in socialist equality. The socialist revolution generates economic and social conditions promoting "creative" personality types. This entire emancipatory process, however, is contingent on exploited, frustrated workers reflectively perceiving essentiality.

The hub of Fromm's social theory, in brief, is his belief that Freudian psychoanalysis and orthodox Marxism both naively overemphasize one moment of the dialectic. The former turns into another school of bourgeois idealism; the latter into materialist totalitarianism. Fromm's Freudian-Marxist synthesis eliminated their separate weaknesses and offered humanity a philosophy of social revolution that simultaneously propagated authentic human being. Fromm's idealist Marxism talked to both sides of the iron curtain, promising liberation from vulgar socialism as well as from bourgeois commercialism. His sympathetic connection to Eastern Europe's humanists indicates a shared idealism and a commitment to terminate socialist workers' bondage to materialist apostasy.

BIBLIOGRAPHY:

A. *Escape from Freedom* (New York: Holt, Rinehart and Winston, 1941); *Marx's Concept of Man* (New York: Ungar, 1961); *May Man Prevail?* (Garden City, N.Y.: Doubleday, 1961); *Beyond the Chains of Illusion: My Encounter with Marx and Freud* (New York: Simon and Schuster, 1962); *Socialist Humanism: An International Symposium* (Garden City, N.Y.: Doubleday, 1965); with Ramon Xirau, *The Nature of Man* (New York: Macmillan, 1968); with Michael Maccoby, *Social Character in a Mexican Village* (Englewood Cliffs, N.J.: Prentice-Hall, 1970); *A Non-Christian Humanist Addresses Himself to Humanist Christians on the Common Struggle Against Idolatry* (Cuernavaca, Mexico: CIDOC, 1975); *To Have or to Be?* (New York: Harper, 1976).

B. John H. Schaar, *Escape from Authority: The Perspectives of Erich Fromm* (New York: Basic Books, 1961); Bernard Landis and Edward Tauber, eds., *In the Name of Life: Essays in Honor of Erich Fromm* (New York: Holt, Rinehart and Winston, 1971); Michael Maccoby, *The Gamesman: The New Corporate Leaders* (New York: Simon and Schuster, 1976).

ROBERT A. GORMAN

FRONDIZI, SILVIO (1907–1974). Born in 1907 in Paso de los Libres, Argentina, Frondizi studied in Buenos Aires, received degrees in history and law, and until 1946 taught at various institutions, including the University of Tucumán and the Colegio Libre de Estudios Superiores in Buenos Aires. Later he taught history and political science at the University of Buenos Aires. He was a Marxist who associated with Marxist† and Trotskyist† intellectuals, and he opposed the intransigent policies of Argentine Communists. He also founded a small revolutionary group called Praxis, which he headed until his assassination by right-wing terrorists in 1974.

Frondizi was particularly interested in questions of underdevelopment. His early thinking identified two imperialisms: British commercial imperialism, and US industrial imperialism. He believed that world integration through imperialism constituted a last stage of capitalism, that a national bourgeoisie could not contend with imperialism because of its dependency on world capitalism, and that the consequence for the periphery was economic disintegration and deformation. Frondizi elaborated a theory showing the relationship of dependent, peripheral, and underdeveloped nations to the dominant, central, and advanced nations. He showed the devastation of monopoly capital and imperialism on national capital, and he exposed the weaknesses of a national bourgeoisie in efforts to promote autonomous capitalism. He argued that capitalism, not feudalism, had been of primary importance since the colonial period in Latin America. He believed that intervention, subsidization, and reformist state policies would not overcome the contradictions of capitalism and that the only solution lay in the path to socialism. His work is especially important for its early contribution to a theory of how capitalism promotes underdevelopment.

BIBLIOGRAPHY:

A. *La integración mundial, última etapa del capitalismo* (*respuesta a una crítica*) (Buenos Aires, 1947; 2d ed., Buenos Aires: Praxis, 1954); *La realidad argentina: ensayo de interpretación sociológica*, 2d ed., 2 vols. (Buenos Aires: Praxis, 1956–57).

RONALD H. CHILCOTE

FRUGONI, EMILIO (1880–1969). The Uruguayan Frugoni was a lawyer, a partner in his family import business, a politician, and a writer who embraced all literary genres, especially poetry and the essay. He was the principal leader of the Uruguayan Social Democrats (who cooperated with the First and Second Internationals†). He was also an organizer of the Socialist Party as well as its first national representative in the years 1911–14. From 1932 to 1934 Frugoni was dean of Uruguay's only law school, and was ambassador to the Soviet Union from 1944 to 1946. When the Socialists veered leftward under Vivian Trias† in 1963, Frugoni established a faction within the party that survives but is of minimal electoral significance.

As a theoretician, Frugoni's main task was that of spreading a nonorthodox, social democratic version of Marxism.† In 1936 he published *Ensayos sobre el marxismo*, a compilation of newspaper articles of a predominantly academic nature. In it Frugoni represented the views of the new middle classes that were emerging under the umbrella of the welfare state established by "Batllism." This middle class was conscious of its differences with blue collar laborers but also committed to the creation of economic and social justice in Uruguay. Frugoni's socialism served as a step in their growing radicalization. His masterpiece, written during World War II, while he was ambassador to Moscow, is *Genesis esencia y fundamentos del socialismo*. A ponderous treatise, its first volume surveys the history of European socialism up to and including Marx. The second volume traces the ideology of social democracy, with a sympathetic emphasis on the ideas of Jean Jaurès.* He rejects both Eduard Bernstein's* revisionism (which is not Hegelian enough) and Soviet-style communism, and concludes with a survey of socialism's rise in Latin America, focusing on people like Vicente Lombardo Toledano† and Haya de la Torre.

Frugoni's Marxism advocated eliminating class differences and promoting class struggles—as opposed to class wars and violent confrontations, which he rejected. His ultimate goal was the peaceful transference of economic and political power to Uruguay's dispossessed poor. His program included an agrarian reform that would eliminate unproductive latifundias and, if necessary, expropriate land and then lease it back to the original owners. He also promised government aid to small farmers, whose property, he felt, should not be expropriated. Frugoni's industrial policy favored free trade and the cultivation of small industry. It was, consequently, overwhelmed by the Batllist sector of Uruguay's Colorado Party, which combined similar promises with a popular protectionist trade policy. Frugoni wanted to implement his social and economic programs through parliamentary reforms. While rejecting violent revolution, Frugoni cited Marx and Karl Kautsky† to show how advanced countries like England, the United States, Holland, and—by implication—Uruguay after Batllism, could arrive at socialism in a peaceful way.

Although he opposed orthodox communism all his life, the vision of the Soviet Union emerging from his diplomatic mission to Moscow showed a mixture of admiration and hard criticism.

BIBLIOGRAPHY:

A. *Ensayos sobre el marxismo* (Montevideo: Garcia, 1936); *Genesis, esencia y fundamentos del socialismo* (Buenos Aires: Americalee, 1947).

B. Carlos Rama, *Uruguay en crisis* (Madrid: El Siglo, 1965); Vivian Trias, *Uruguay hoy* (Montevideo: Banda Oriental, 1973).

JUAN RIAL

G

GABEL, JOSEPH (b. 1912). Although born in Budapest, Hungary, on 12 July 1912, Gabel today is a French citizen. He was trained as a psychiatrist and received his M.D. from the University of Paris in 1951. He later turned to sociology as a career and received his Ph.D. also from the University of Paris in 1962. Gabel worked as a researcher at the Centre National de la Recherche Scientifique in Paris, from 1947 to 1961 and taught sociology in Morocco from 1965 to 1971. In 1971 he began teaching sociology at the University of Picardie in Amiens, where he also chaired the department. Gabel is currently professor emeritus at Amiens and is finishing a work on the Jewish future and socialism.

As a psychiatrist Gabel was influenced by the phenomenological psychiatry of E. Minkowski and the existential psychiatry of L. Binswanger. His sociological and political thought was influenced by Mannheim and George Lukács,* and by what Gabel calls "Hungarian Marxism."† Unlike positivist Marxism, the Hungarian school is highly Hegelian in orientation, more dialectical than materialist, and more concerned with the problem of alienation as constituting the framework of Marxism than with Marxist economics. It is this twofold context that gives rise to Gabel's unique and significant contribution to the psychological dimension of Marxist theory. At the heart of his work Gabel argues that there is a structural parallel between schizophrenia and ideology, which are individual and collective forms of false consciousness. Following Lukács, he defines false consciousness as a process of the reification of consciousness: (1) the devaluation of existence that results from the objectification of a subject (i.e. depersonalization); and (2) the loss of a sense of history, of the historical contingency of experience (in the language of his psychiatry Gabel calls this the "over-spatialization" and "under-temporalization" of experience, where we disproportionately experience the spatial but not the temporal dimension of our existence). False consciousness, then, is radically ahistorical and tends to abstract elements from a totality of reality and treat them objectively as eternal and absolute. At the same time it conceives the self or others as mere "objects" at the mercy of oppressive forces in the world. For Gabel, this antidialectical process of reification is what constitutes the essence of the schizophrenic experience and results in the individual's deranged perception of reality, loss of a sense of personal history, and sense of powerlessness in the face of "the world." This same reificational process is at work at the social level of false consciousness as well, and it becomes ideology when false consciousness is "theoretically crystallized" and developed into a pseudo-history and a system of legitimation. An example is racist consciousness, which lacks a sense of the historical origins and contingency of racial characteristics and proceeds to objectify them as natural, eternal essences of "the race." This false consciousness becomes ideology when it is grounded in a contrived and justificatory "history" and accepted by social consciousness as truth.

Gabel's unique contribution is that he goes beyond drawing a mere analogy between certain kinds of psychological disorders and the disorders of our social and political consciousness. Rather, he suggests an actual structural "identity" of schizophrenia and ideology as two forms of reified, false consciousness. His work is replete with appeals to clinical and sociological data to support his particular claim. This suggestion of a schizophrenic structure of false consciousness and ideology has two major implications for Marxism. First, it shows how alienation as a schizophrenic form of consciousness is not determined by economic reification alone but by reification as a total and independent mode of existence. This vitiates any overly materialist or economic determinist Marxism, as well as any view that false consciousness is simply a matter of "content." Second, insofar as Marxism is a critique of ideology and of false social consciousness, it is also inherently a critical theory of deranged thought. Hence it can contribute to the development of psychopathology. In hopes of contributing to an "open," dialectical, and antitotalitarian Marxism, Gabel's life work has been devoted to clarifying these themes.

BIBLIOGRAPHY:

A. *False Consciousness: An Essay on Reification*, trans. Margaret A. Thompson (New York: Harper & Row, 1975; French ed. , 1962); Joseph Gabel, B. Rousset, and Trinh Van Thao, *Actualité de la dialectique* (Paris: Anthropos, 1980).

SCOTT A. WARREN

GALANSKOV, YURI TIMOFEEVICH (1939–1972). Yuri Timofeevich Galanskov, a Soviet poet and publicist who, according to dissident Petro Grigorenko* "read Lenin† cover to cover," began his criticism of Soviet socialist realism with dissident poetry readings on Moscow's Mayakovsky Square and editing of the underground literary anthology *Feniks*. He frequently demanded *glasnost*, or openness, as the only healthy spirit for a Marxist† literature. As a pacifist he also criticized the imperialism of both the United States (invasion of the Dominican Republic) and the Soviet Union (invasion of Czechoslovakia) as untrue to Marxist ideals. Galanskov also protested Soviet persecution of religion. His friendly contacts with religious dissidents showed his belief that Christian and Marxist humanisms are compatible. He died from harsh conditions as a political prisoner in a Soviet labor camp.

BIBLIOGRAPHY:

B. Pavel Litvinov, *Trial of the Four: A Collection of Materials on the Case of Galanskov, Ginzburg, Dobrovolsky, and Lashkova* (New York: Viking, 1972).

DAVID KOWALEWSKI

GARAUDY, ROGER (b. 1913). Roger Garaudy was born in Marseille in 1913. He studied at the Faculty of Letters of the University of Paris and earned the Ph.D. in philosophy. His professional career includes academic appointments at the University of Albi (Algiers), the Lycée Buffon in Paris (1958–59), the University of Clermont-Ferrand (1962–65), and the University of Poitiers (1965, 1969–73). He was the recipient of an honorary doctorate from the Institute of Philosophy of the Academy of Sciences in the Soviet Union. Garaudy was also active politically, serving as a deputy from the region of Tarn to two Constituent Assemblies (1945–46) and to the first National Assembly (1946–51). He was an official in the political bureau of the French Communist Party (PCF)(1956–70), a Communist deputy in, and vice-president of, the National Assembly (1956–58), and an elected Communist member of the National Senate (1959–62). He was director of the Center for Marxist† Research and Study (1960–70) and, after 1974, editorial head of the radical French journal *Alternatives socialistes*.

Until the end of the 1950s Garaudy was a leader of the orthodox PCF. With de-Stalinization and the informal opening of Marxism to nonorthodox points of view, Garaudy repudiated orthodoxy and embraced a self-styled nondogmatic Marxism. His *Marxism in the Twentieth Century* (1966), which received decidedly mixed reviews among Marxists and non-Marxists alike, expressed Garaudy's new openness and flexibility. Garaudy rejected all versions of Marxism, including materialist orthodoxy, that advocated an absolute theory of knowledge or an unchanging metaphysic. The Marxian dialectic, for Garaudy, is useful only because it facilitates our understanding of complex social phenomena. It is an intellectual tool rather than an absolute truth, a guide toward intelligibility rather than a determinant of action. Dialectical inquiry must therefore be open and nondogmatic, assimilating as many opposing perspectives as actually exist. Marxism, in Garaudy's revision, is pluralistic, integrating and synthesizing all extant notions of truth, beauty, justice, and reality—even those that are non-Marxist and nondialectical. In his own work Garaudy tries to stretch Marxism to assimilate such popular world views as existentialism, structuralism, Christianity, and empiricism. Since intellectual reality, for Garaudy, is a dialectical intermingling of epistemologically equal alternatives, Marxism's only advantage is in its unique ability to encompass and explain all the others. This accounts, to some degree at least, for Garaudy's often confusing concatenation of contradictory assertions regarding the precise meaning of Marxism (e.g. Marxism is nonmetaphysical and based on initiative and freedom [*Initiative in History: A Christian–Marxist Dialogue*, p. 18; see also *From Anathema to Dialogue*, pp. 72–73, and *Crisis in Communism*]), which describes "the historical conditions . . . [that] obey necessary laws," the ignorance of which will lead to "fortuity and impotence" [*Marxism in the Twentieth Century*, p. 77, and *Karl Marx: The Evolution of His Thought*, pp. 196–97], but which nevertheless must, like Western empirical social science, be verified empirically [*Marxism in the Twentieth Century*, pp. 56–57]. When statements like these are added to others that favorably evaluate the usefulness and truth of Christianity and structuralism, the task of effectively encapsulating Garaudy's social theory becomes impossible.

Speaking practically, Garaudy's Marxism relegates the working class to a status equal to other social groups. The sole advantage of workers is their unique capacity somehow to encompass and unify the diverse interests of all classes and groups. Hence class struggle is no longer the key to understanding historical change, although socialist justice alone will reconcile the contradictions of capitalist society. Exactly how revolutionary workers will synthesize their own interests with those of capital, religion, and the bureacracy is unclear, as is the question of why workers will find socialism desirable and necessary. Garaudy's reputation as a Marxist theorist is ultimately tarnished by the proliferation of such unanswered questions.

BIBLIOGRAPHY:

A. *Perspectives de l'homme: existentialisme, pensée catholique, marxisme* (Paris: P.U.F., 1959); *From Anathema to Dialogue: A Marxist Challenge to the Christian Church* (New York: Herder and Herder, 1966); with others, *Initiative in History: A Christian–Marxist Dialogue* (Cambridge: Church Society for College Work, 1967); *Crisis in Communism* (New York: Grove Press, 1970); *Marxism in the Twentieth Century* (New York: Scribners, 1970).

B. Mark Poster, *Existential Marxism in Postwar France* (Princeton: Princeton University Press, 1975); Michael Kelly, *Modern French Marxism* (Baltimore: Johns Hopkins University Press, 1982).

ROBERT A. GORMAN

GENOVESE, EUGENE D. (b. 1930). Born 19 May 1930 in Brooklyn, New York, this historian of slavery is a preeminent radical scholar in the United States. He has received major academic appointments, awards, and prizes. A son of a dockworker, Genovese joined the Communist Party at seventeen only to be expelled three years later for "failing to conform with party discipline." Ironically he was discharged from the U.S. army after ten months due to his previous Communist Party membership. While a faculty member in 1965 he found unsolicited fame for publicly declaring, "I do not fear or reject the impending Vietcong victory in Vietnam. I welcome it." Since then he has maintained a political identity along with his scholarly reputation. Genovese holds degrees from Brooklyn College (B.A., 1953) and Columbia University (M.A., 1953; Ph.D., 1959). He has served on the faculties of Brooklyn Polytechnic Institute, Rutgers, Sir George Williams (Montreal), Columbia, and Yale and presently chairs the History Department at the University of Rochester. He has received fellowships from the Center for Advanced Study (Stanford, 1972–73) and the Social Science Research Council (1968–69). He has published a large number of academic articles and books as well as served on the editorial boards of the *Journal of Social History*, *Dialectical Anthropology*, and *Marxist Perspectives*, among others.

Genovese's scholarship is testimony to the dynamic character and political promise of the Marxist† method. Attempting to extricate Marxism from stale orthodoxy, his neo-Marxist writing emphasizes inter- and intraclass conflicts as the central modes of history. Drawing heavily from Marx and Antonio Gramsci,* Genovese's work provides a sophisticated application of the analytic concept of "cultural hegemony" as an interactive process involving formal and informal rules, symbols and language among hierarchically dependent but somewhat autonomous classes. His lifelong study of slavery serves as a brilliant application of Marxist scholarship as well as benchmark historical research. His initial book, *The Political Economy of Slavery* (1965), redirected this research area toward the class character of the racist slave system in the American South. He argued that the economic and cultural system of Southern slaveholders produced a patriarchal and paternalistic aristocracy hostile to bourgeois capitalism. To Genovese the contradictions and antagonisms of the pre-modern and modern worlds prevented slaveholders, as a separate class, from abolishing slavery. Later, in *The World the Slaveholders Made* (1969), he compares slavery in the American South with that of Europe, the West Indies, and the continental Americas, concluding that abolition can be best explained in class rather than simply racial terms. He received the prestigious Bancroft Prize for *Roll Jordan Roll* (1974). Based on a study of plantation records, family papers, slave narratives, and traveler reports, this book analyzed the interaction of the contradictory perceptions held by slaves and slaveowners and the ambiguous roles produced by a slave system. He particularly isolated the role of Christianity as a battleground for psychological control (cultural hegemony from above and below), with the master's religion emphasizing paternalism and the slave's celebrating the independence of the soul. Later, in *From Rebellion to Revolution* (1979), Genovese elaborated on the themes of resistance and slave revolts in the rise and fall of slavery.

BIBLIOGRAPHY:

A. *The Political Economy of Slavery* (New York: Pantheon, 1965); *The Slave Economy of the Old South* (Baton Rouge: Louisiana State University Press, 1968); with others, eds., *Slavery in the New World* (Englewood Cliffs, N.J.: Prentice-Hall, 1969); *The World the Slaveholders Made* (New York: Pantheon, 1969); *In Red and Black* (New York: Pantheon, 1971); *Roll Jordan Roll* (New York: Pantheon, 1974); *From Rebellion to Revolution: Afro-American Slave Revolt in the Making of the Modern World* (Baton Rouge: Louisiana State University Press, 1979); ed., *The Slave Economies*, Vols. 1–4 (Urbana: University of Illinois Press, 1974); with others, eds., *Debates in American History* (New York: Revisionary, 1982); with E. Fox Genovese, *Fruits of Merchant Capital: Slavery and Bourgeois Property in the Rise and Expansion of Capitalism* (Oxford: Oxford University Press, 1983).

RICHARD GUARASCI

GERRATANA, VALENTINO (b. 1919). Born in Sicily in 1919, Gerratana joined the Italian Communist Party in 1942 and won the medal of honor as a

Resistance fighter. From 1944 to 1966 he served in varying capacities in the Party apparatus, including the Central Committee from 1959 to 1966. Since 1971 he has been professor of the history of philosophy at the University of Salerno. He worked for eight years on the critical four-volume edition of Antonio Gramsci's* *Quaderni del carcere*, published in 1975 by Einaudi. His research has focused on Marxism† as a critical method of analysis that has passed through distinct phases and "schools."

BIBLIOGRAPHY:

A. "Marxism and Darwin," *New Left Review* (November–December 1973); "Stalin, Lenin and Leninism," *New Left Review* (May–June 1977); "Heidegger and Marx," *New Left Review* (November–December 1977); "Rousseau, Nietzsche, Della Volpe," *New Left Review* (September–October 1978).

LAWRENCE GARNER

GIDDENS, ANTHONY (b. 1938). Anthony Giddens was born in England in 1938. He studied at Hull University, the London School of Economics, and Cambridge University. An academic sociologist, Giddens taught at Leicester University from 1963 to 1970 and since 1970 has been a lecturer in sociology and fellow of King's College, Cambridge. His work has been in sociological theory; he has published studies of Marx,† Weber, and Durkheim as well as analyses of contemporary industrial societies. Giddens has also taught at several Canadian and American universities.

Although Giddens declines to call himself a Marxist, at least in the orthodox sense, his own theoretical work takes Marx's critical analysis of capitalism to be the foundation of modern social theory. Nevertheless, there are some basic differences separating Giddens and Marx. One such difference involves methodology. Giddens rejects what he regards as orthodox Marxism's use of functional explanations. In *Central Problems in Social Theory* (1979) he argues that to attribute functional needs to a social system is to misplace an analogy better suited to biological organisms. Unlike living organisms, societies do not readily adapt to dysfunctional imbalances. Hence, although functional analysis is one method of describing society, it can never adequately explain it. Giddens argues that explanations of social totalities must be sought in the intentions of social actors who make decisions based on expected consequences. Capitalist societies therefore do not function, a priori, according to the needs of capital, but contain historically specific conflicts and contradictions. Giddens concludes that capital does not necessarily reproduce a social system to serve its needs. Like Marx, Giddens believes that capitalist societies contain contradictions, primarily between the private ownership of the means of production and the progressive socialization of productive forces. These generate potentially explosive social confrontations such as labor–management conflicts in the work place and anti-system collective political movements. Functionalists, he argues, tend to obscure these practical struggles on the part of specific human agents.

Another break with the orthodox Marxist tradition is in Giddens's method of classifying societies. Giddens does not believe that social class was the central structural principle in precapitalist society. It is only with the advent of the labor market in capitalism that the locus of social domination came to rest in economic divisions. Giddens argues that in precapitalist, or feudal societies, domination is based on political inequalities. He thus acknowledges noneconomic forms of exploitation and consequently the inadequacies of historical materialism. In feudal societies exploitation was primarily political. In contemporary capitalism there is, in addition to class oppression, racial, sexual, and international exploitation, none of which he feels is sufficiently explained by historical materialism.

Giddens's point of departure is his narrow conception of class, which is merely one of many possible kinds of exploitative relationships. Giddens follows Marx in arguing that class is integrally related to capitalist production. Classes arise, he argues, in the formation of social groups grounded in the differential capacities that workers bring to the marketplace. In brief, people enter economic society possessing either property, specialized knowledge, or manual labor power, generating a three-class structure in modern capitalism. But classes, for Giddens, are neither tangible human entities nor historical actors and do not, therefore, in themselves generate history. Thus unlike orthodox Marxists, Giddens is less interested in class as a force for social change than as a static sociological concept. Giddens notes that with class structuration comes class consciousness, which need not be revolutionary. In fact, class consciousness may focus on self-identity, oppositional interests, or revolutionary alternatives. Significantly, Giddens argues that it is not in mature capitalism that class consciousness turns revolutionary. This phenomenon is more likely to occur in the transition from feudalism to capitalism. In advanced industrial societies class conflict is still present, but, Giddens argues, it is not revolutionary.

Finally, Giddens rejects the teleological Marxist view of social change, which holds that societies are a priori moving toward socialism. Giddens prefers to call the Western economic order "mature" rather than "late" capitalism because the latter implies a mistaken evolutionary scheme of history. Giddens does see contradiction in capitalist societies, but argues there is nothing inherent in capitalism that will inevitably lead to socialism, thus rejecting the possibility of a general theory of history. What Giddens would substitute for the orthodox version of historical materialism is an analysis of specific historical events, customs, and traditions that have worked to transform past societies. His social theory is not explicitly normative, nor is it related to practical politics. His analysis of modern societies should finally be viewed as employing Marxist categories such as exploitation, class, and worker consciousness in order to create a typology for comparing societies.

BIBLIOGRAPHY:

A. *Capitalism and Modern Social Theory* (Cambridge: Cambridge University Press, 1971); *The Class Structure of the Advanced Societies* (London: Hutchinson, 1973); *Central Problems in Social Theory* (Berkeley: University of California Press, 1979); *A Contemporary Critique of Historical Materialism* (London: Macmillan, 1981).

B. Erik Olin Wright, "Giddens's Critique of Marxism," *New Left Review*, no. 138 (March–April 1983), pp. 11–35.

KEVIN DAVIS

GLUCKSMANN, ANDRÉ (b. 1937). André Glucksmann is a French writer on politics and philosophy and former political activist who was born in 1937. He participated in the founding of a paper, *J'accuse*, a forerunner of sorts of the contemporary left-wing paper *Libération*. Glucksmann is the most prominent member of a school of French writers called Les Nouveaux Philosophes (New Philosophers), which has roots in the French Maoist† movement of the late 1960s and early 1970s. The one constant in Glucksmann's work is his fascination with violence. In 1967, he published a book, *Discours de la guerre*, on concepts of war and military dissuasion. The last part of that book was devoted to an analysis of the military aspects of Mao Zedong's thought. Indeed, Glucksmann was to become a Maoist. In France, that word designates an adherent of Maoism, but in its most anarchistic interpretation. French Maoists stressed the Cultural Revolution and the "mass line." They explicitly rejected the more hierarchical Leninist† aspects of Maoism.

The year after *Discours de la guerre* was published, there was a mass uprising in France, first of students and then of workers. For a while, the political regime lost all control over the educational, productive, distributive, and enforcement processes of the country. In *Stratégie de la révolution* (1968), Glucksmann reflected upon the meaning of that event, what it revealed about France, and the strategic implications one could draw from it. Taking issue with those analysts and theorists who framed the problem in cultural terms, Glucksmann offered a purely political analysis. For him, the adversary of the May revolt was not "la société de consommation" but rather the depolitization of society by the state. On this point, he felt that Marx's† writings on France were perceptive. They stressed the "statist" quality of the country. Marx foresaw that in France a parliamentary approach to the institution of socialism was more likely to result in a greater degree of state authoritarianism than in any true condition of socialism.

Glucksmann contended that all political revolutions had two faces. One is statist, or what the French call *dirigiste*. The second is anarchistic. The latter works in opposition to the substitution of a new party hierarchy for the state apparatus that is to be or has been toppled. At this point in time, Glucksmann saw Marx as associating himself with the latter face. Glucksmann quotes the substantiating but forgotten words of Marx from the *Civil War in France*. It is the Commune of 1871 rather than the statist model of the Soviet Union that conforms to Marx's conception of change. Lenin, Glucksmann argued, understood Marx's anti-statist, democratic commitments but was trapped by the peculiarities of Russian conditions after the 1917 revolution. France, however, is not Russia. The "forgotten words of Marx" were on the lips of the May barricade fighters, even those who had never read Marx. If the Communards of 1871 had to fight a war against right-wing opponents, the revolutionaries of May 1968 had to fight a two-front war. On the one hand, they took on the Gaullist right, which controlled the state. On the other, they had to contend with Communist and Socialist parties, which wanted to control the state. Both the right and the left statist forces would use violent repressive means to maintain or seize control over state power.

For a brief period in 1968 there was no effective exercise of state power at all. There was a general strike, the purpose of which was precisely to terminate state power. For Glucksmann, two things are necessary if this is to be done successfully. First, in good Sorelian* fashion, the threat of violence must be maintained. The opposition must be convinced that the attempt to reassert state control will result in violent confrontation. Second, there must be created a system of dual power. Decentralized centers of discussion and decision—from workers' committees to the courtyard of the Sorbonne serving as a public meeting place—must begin to replace the dirigiste state even before it has completely collapsed. The struggle against the state must be conducted at a multitude of decentralized points throughout society. This is the rebirth of the public place— but all over the place. It is politics as struggle—everywhere. It is surrounding the "official" places of the state (e.g. Presidential Palace, National Assembly) with public places created by the people.

Glucksmann went on, in 1969 and the early 1970s, to associate himself with a Maoist group, La Gauche Prolétarienne, which encouraged and supported manifestations of illegal resistance to the state. It did not take a strict class-versus-class position. True, it infiltrated factories. But if small merchants were rising up in opposition to unfavorable government policy, it was with them on the barricades. It supported rebellious farmers and *lumpens*. It was one of the first groups to do political work with immigrant workers. It worked among slum dwellers. It worked within the prisons when its militants were sentenced to prison. Many militants were imprisoned and at least one was shot to death during a factory confrontation. The movement enjoyed the particularly dedicated support of philosopher Jean-Paul Sartre* and publisher François Maspero. Glucksmann's thinking, however, moved progressively closer to that of Michel Foucault,* who was giving some aid to the prison work and engaging La Gauche Prolétarienne in dialogue, than to the "Marxist existentialism" of Sartre. Both Glucksmann and Foucault were attracted to Nietzsche and were uncomfortable with the class analysis of Marx. Both focused on power as a constant that had to be dealt with for good or ill. Power, in their view, was not limited to class contexts and structures but was diffused throughout society. The state attempted to monopolize power, to prevent people from seizing the power residing in decentralized contexts and using it against the centralized state.

Glucksmann hung on to Marxism by stressing Marx's favorable interpretation of the 1871 Commune. In 1975, in *La Cuisinière et le mangeur d'hommes*, Glucksmann delivered a stinging attack on the Soviet Union. He had been deeply affected by Solzhenitsyn. Now, however, he did not excuse Lenin because of the specific conditions faced by the Bolsheviks. He now saw the Leninist model of centralized and clandestine revolution as inconsistent with Marx's anti-statist positions and as necessarily leading to the Gulag. In 1977, in *Les Maîtres penseurs*, Glucksmann took aim at Marx himself. Marx's reflections of the Commune were no longer enough. Marx had committed the sin of silence on the future state of communism and had posited a transitional stage of socialism in which bourgeois rights and laws would still be operative. This led Glucksmann to conclude that Marx, in spite of his lack of appetite for the state, indeed had recourse to it. What else, Glucksmann asks, will organize production and determine what labor is valuable? Since Marx does not stipulate an alternative, we must assume a continuation of "official man" (the state) presiding over "private man" (the worker). To argue that in any case this would only be temporary, that a final stage of communism in which the state would no longer be necessary lies in the future, is to beg the question entirely. It is a magic wand which says that when the problem is solved it will be solved.

With this discussion of Marx, Glucksmann endeared himself to French anti-Communists and the Western capitalist press. At the end of 1983, Glucksmann gave the anti-Communists even more, but the Western press was not quite so unified in its praise. In his last work to date, *La Force du vertige*, Glucksmann sings the praises of the nuclear missiles aimed at the Soviet Union. A decade and a half ago, Glucksmann had viewed the Soviet Union as impotent to effect change in the West. Now the country of the Gulag is a terrible threat and challenge. The proper response is risk, risk of death, in the defense of freedom. Glucksmann's fascination with violence and threat has overcome his distaste for the state. He now praises these deadly phallic representations of state power. Life is only worth living, apparently for Glucksmann, if the threat of physical violence is with us.

Georges Sorel, who was also much taken with violence, went from syndicalism to fascism. Glucksmann has thus far gone from a confrontational anarcho-Marxism that concerned itself with street barricades and decentralized actions against the state to a romantic adoration of the contemporary symbols of state power that are capable of very unsymbolically eliminating millions of people and destroying the environment for survivors.

BIBLIOGRAPHY:

A. *Le Discours de la guerre* (Paris: L'Herne, 1967); *Stratégie de la révolution* (Paris: Christian Bourgeois, 1968); *La Cuisinière et le mangeur d'hommes* (Paris: Seuil, 1975); *The Master Thinkers* (New York: Harper & Row, 1980); *La Force du vertige* (Paris: Grasset, 1983).

BELDEN FIELDS

GODELIER, MAURICE (b. 1934). Born in 1934 in the French city of Cambrai, Maurice Godelier is one of France's most noted contemporary anthropologists. He has done field research in Papua, New Guinea, where he studied kinship systems, land ownership, and rites of initiation. He has taught at the Collège de France in Paris and since 1975 has directed the social science program at the

Ecole des Hautes Etudes in Paris. He currently serves on the international board of the journal *Dialectical Anthropology*.

Godelier's project, exhibited best in his two-volume compendium of articles entitled *Rationality and Irrationality in Economics* (1969), was to establish a nonorthodox approach to dialectics that could be usefully applied to the studies of economics and anthropology. While his ideas eventually paralleled those of the French structuralist Louis Althusser,* *Rationality and Irrationality in Economics* indicates that his winding path to structuralism was forged independently. Godelier's early articles argued that Marx's† dialectical method aptly reflected the nature of economic systems as organic wholes consisting of interdependent factors such as production and consumption, supply and demand, labor, accumulation, etc. Only dialectical method, as a tool for social inquiry, captures this dynamic, multidimensional reality. However, Godelier also argued that the dialectic does not comprise a metaphysical truth that molds all of reality. Its use is limited to studying organic totalities (e.g. economic systems) that crystallize human labor, rather than nature itself or unique psychological processes. Only the products of human labor exhibit the characteristics of organic totalities. The dialectic is thus a tool that performs the important function of accurately explaining social, economic, and political institutions, but is useless in reflecting external natural reality. In this sense it parallels empirical science, which accurately reflects and explains the natural world but cannot grasp multidimensional totalities.

By 1961 Godelier had stretched the dialectic to encompass both the concepts that explain organic totalities as well as the totalities themselves. In other words, the dialectic now designated the entire social knowledge process, including the relations between concepts and external social reality. Added to the dialectic's explanatory function is the cognitive function of accurately reflecting the real social world. Dialectics became the intellectual structure by which rational people accurately perceive and understand society. Godelier's focus on structures congealed by the mid-1960s into a version of structural Marxism closely resembling Althusser's. The key to this final transformation was Godelier's reading of Marx's theory of contradiction, which Godelier claimed distinguishes between contradictions internal to one structure (e.g. the class antagonism between workers and capitalists within the relations of production) and those between structures (e.g. the antagonism between relations and forces of production). The second contradiction is unintentional and sets limits within which the first contradiction unfolds. Godelier believes that elements within a structure are not directly reducible to structures within a social system, although the latter do influence the course and content of the former. For Godelier, as for Althusser, society is an ordered hierarchy of structures that collectively evolve and affect both the activities occurring within any single structure as well as the relations between structures. Contradiction, therefore, occurs passively, determined by structural limitations. This theory of structural causality obviously resembles Althusser's theory of overdetermination. Godelier used this structural model of Marxism as the framework for empirical economic and anthropological inquiry.

BIBLIOGRAPHY:

A. *La Notion de "mode de production asiatique" et les schémas marxistes d'évolution des sociétés* (Paris: Centre d'Etudes et de Recherches Marxistes, 1964); *Rationalité et irrationalité en économie* (Paris: Maspero, 1966); *Anthropologia, storia, marxismo* (Parma: Guanda, 1970); *Marxismo e strutturalismo* (Turin: Einaudi, 1970); *Un Domaine contesté: l'anthropologie économique; recueil de textes* (Paris: Mouton, 1974); *Perspectives in Marxist Anthropology* (New York: Cambridge University Press, 1977).

B. Robert D'Amico, "The Coutours and Coupures of Structuralist Theory," *Telos*, 17 (Fall 1973), pp. 70–97.

ROBERT A. GORMAN

GOLDBERG, ITCHE (b. 1906). Born in Poland in 1906, raised in Toronto, immigrant to the United States in 1928, Goldberg was for decades the leading pedagogue in left Yiddish shuls and has emerged, in the last twenty years, as the outstanding editor and theoretician of neo-Marxist (or post-Marxist) secular, socialist *Yiddishkayt*. Leading spirit of the journal *Yiddishe Kultur* since 1964, director of the Chaim Zhitlovsky Foundation, and dominant intellectual figure in the Yiddishe Kultur Farband (YKUF), Goldberg is the prime guardian of values embedded in a diminishing but still vital radical culture.

In his lectures, essays, and books, Goldberg has succinctly summarized the proposition that socialist culture must be pluralistic even within a single nation, open to change but resistant against a feckless, nihilistic cosmopolitanism. Confronting Second International† orthodoxy from a self-consciously traditional Jewish (and Yiddish-language) standpoint, he has insisted that the "historic-cultural secular tie which binds us with the people" cannot be dissolved into bland assimilation without damaging the left, its cultural understanding, and its popular influence. Humanism, which developed centuries ago outside the synagogue—although not necessarily opposed to religion as such—extends from the depth of the Jewish spirit toward a better future where Jewishness can be completely realized in different societies across the earth. Among Yiddish readers, Goldberg has insisted upon the inextricability of socialist goals from any constructive cultural program. The loss of Soviet prestige in Jewish radical circles, the creative rethinking of positions by former Communists and fellow travelers, has thrust Goldberg into a key role. He, if any neo-Marxist theoretician does, exerts influence across the old political barriers between Communists, Socialists, Labor Zionists, Bundists, and others, in Europe, Latin America, the United States, and Canada, for a common approach. Under his leadership, *Yiddishe Kultur* has become the outstanding journal of literary criticism in the Yiddish language and one of the leading journals of historical literary discussion anywhere. His own essays, his teaching, and his editorial labors have drawn younger scholars of

Yiddish toward his journal and his perspective. Goldberg has, then, a unique status: neo-Marxist prime mover for the survival of the Yiddish language, and a progressive *Yiddishkayt* after the aging speakers of the last native-tongue generation have finally disappeared.

BIBLIOGRAPHY:

A. *Undzer Dramaturgie* (New York: Yiddishe Kultur Farband, 1955); *Essayen* (New York: Yiddishe Kultur Farband, 1982).

PAUL BUHLE

GOLDMAN, EMMA (1869–1940). Goldman was born in Kaunas, Lithuania, on 27 June 1869. She emigrated·to the United States, where she met her lifelong companion, Alexander Berkman,* in 1889. By 1901 Goldman had officially denounced the rule of government as a destroyer of freedom. Thus began a lifelong battle with the U.S. government over the limits of free speech. She began lecturing on subjects ranging from birth control to women's rights to every citizen's right to be free from government control. Goldman established the *Mother Earth Bulletin*, an anarchist publication, in 1906. She aided, in 1910, in the founding of the Ferrer Modern School, a progressive school for factory workers' children. Goldman explained her educational philosophy in *Anarchism and Other Essays* in 1911. In 1917 Goldman organized the No-Conscription League, which advocated resistance to the military draft. She was arrested and eventually deported to Russia in 1919. Although Goldman originally supported Lenin, by 1924 unanticipated events in Russia compelled her to condemn the Bolsheviks and their revolution. She left Russia and settled in France. After a brief involvement with anarchists fighting the Spanish Civil War in 1936, Goldman began lecturing again in Europe and Canada. She died of a stroke on 17 February 1940.

Goldman, as stated in *Anarchism and Other Essays*, believed, like Marx,† that capitalism robs humans of both their dignity and the products of their labor. Capitalism enslaves its citizens, making them into unthinking but functional parts of the system's machinery. Capitalism encourages worker competition for private property and thus condemns workers to wage slavery. Capitalist government, as Marx had recognized, exists primarily to protect private property. It steals through its powers of taxation and kills its children with war, which is but a deadly method of protecting capitalists' interests. Anarchism, on the other hand, advocated freedom, liberty, equality, and a society consisting of voluntary productive and distributive associations that, once established, would slowly evolve into Marx's communist utopia (*Anarchism and Other Essays*, p. 62). Marx's own mistaken rejection of anarchism is nullified by the insidious acts of his followers and the deterioration of his ideas in Russia. Anarchism brings to humanity an authentic consciousness of itself and a knowledge of life's beauty and freedom. Men and women will be able to think clearly and independently and produce needed goods in a cooperative and harmonious manner.

Goldman also fought nobly for the rights of women, who were doubly exploited in capitalism, as workers and as females. She perceived marriage to be an economic arrangement that was unfair to women, who were treated as mere sex commodities—their bodies hideously transformed into capital that is then exploited by men. Goldman contended that women must demand the right to birth control and noninhibiting sexual relationships. Goldman perceived violence as a regrettable but necessary tool for meaningful social change. The present capitalist system is too firmly established to peacefully transform itself. The capitalist elite, as Marx predicted, would fight to maintain its economic, social, and political privileges. Violent revolutionary acts, however, are not merely random or nonpurposive. Goldman believed that revolution "is but thought carried into action" (Drinnon, *Rebel in Paradise*, p. 105). Individual men and women must consciously experience their oppression and react rationally to eliminate the capitalist source.

Anarchism, which Goldman felt would succeed capitalism, stands for the liberation of one's mind from the domination of religion, property, and the state. Society would consist of free and voluntary associations of workers, producing cooperatively to satisfy the needs of humanity. Goldman believed that an anarchist elite was required to mobilize and guide workers toward rebellion. They must teach workers to exert their collective strength in rejecting government, law, and capitalism. Once minds are radicalized and the working-class rebellion succeeds, this elite would slowly recede into the mass of free individuals living in collective harmony.

BIBLIOGRAPHY:

A. *Anarchism and Other Essays* (New York: Mother Earth, 1911); *Social Significance of the Modern Drama* (Boston: R. G. Badger, 1914); *My Disillusionment in Russia* (Garden City, N.Y.: Doubleday, Page, 1924); *Mother Earth Bulletin* (New York: Greenwood Reprint, 1968); *Living My Life (Autobiography)* (New York: Dover, 1970).

B. Richard A. Drinnon, *Rebel in Paradise: Biography of Emma Goldman* (Chicago: University of Chicago Press, 1961); Richard A. Drinnon and Anna Marie Drinnon, *Nowhere at Home, Emma Goldman and Alexander Berkman* (New York: Schocken Books, 1975).

JOSEPH M. HAZLETT

GOLDMANN, LUCIEN (1913–1970). Goldmann was born the son of a rabbi in Bucharest in 1913, and he completed his studies in law at his home university. During this period he read a great deal of Marx's† works, joined a clandestine Marxist group, was arrested, and later fled to Vienna in 1933, where he studied the works of contemporary Marxists, including George Lukács.* In 1934 he moved to France and began an ambitious program of study for a doctorate in political economy, together with degrees in German and philosophy. The war drove him south to Toulouse, where he was interned by the Vichy authorities because of his religion and political beliefs. He escaped and fled to Switzerland, where he became an assistant to Piaget and took his doctorate in Zurich. He returned to France in 1945, joined the Centre National de la Recherche Scientifique (CNRS), and in 1958 became director of the Ecole Practique des Hautes Etudes. In 1961 he moved to the Sociology Institute of the Université Libre de Bruxelles and in 1970 died.

Goldmann was one of the foremost interpreters of Lukács in postwar Europe, and like others in the same field distinguished between Lukács's pre- and postwar Moscow periods, dismissing the latter as being influenced by Stalinism.† His own concepts went far beyond Lukács, but his starting point was the study of alienation and class consciousness in Lukács's *History and Class Consciousness*. Goldmann identified the reification of capitalist society as the major problem for socialists because alienation stemmed from this phenomenon. He believed that it was the working classes' subjugation within this reified system that brought about their low level of class consciousness rather than their subjugation within the productive system. He contended that the vigor of capitalist cultural and social norms had led to passivity among the working classes and that the real potential for revolutionary action had passed to the intellectuals and the lumpen proletariat.

In *Human Sciences and Philosophy* Goldmann insisted that students seek to understand the total world within which the individual exists before coming to conclusions on the nature of class behavior; what he called "genetic structuralism." He wanted to fuse structuralism, based on factual assimilation, to Piaget's concepts of the structural effect on cognition and interpret these results within a Marxist economic framework. For Goldmann, structural analysis depicted the genesis of impersonal structures which were created in history, achieved an equilibrium, and then "destructured" to make room for new ones. Goldmann found social class to be an irreplaceable structure for explaining individual facts, acts, and texts. He argued that all acts and texts express a structural class worldview or consciousness, and the most talented politicians and authors express it best. Therefore, what Lukács had called authentic class consciousness was the distinct trait of reputable philosophical and artistic works. Marxism—authentic working class consciousness—simultaneously revealed the historical genesis and decline of modern bourgeois society and the dialectical complexity of partial and total structures. It, therefore, generated both accurate knowledge and necessary revolutionary activity. However, Marxism merely depicted the totality of material structures within which revolutionary praxis could occur. It was not a mechanical formula, nor did it guarantee the future. The outcome of this analysis was Goldmann's belief that capitalism had its own dynamic, which went beyond questions of ownership and exploitation, and this led him away from classical Marxism. He also criticized Lenin† for having mechanistic ideas, because he felt that the partial identity of subject and object in his own analysis led toward spontaneous revolutionary action as the true form of praxis, rather than formal or organized revolutionary action. His conceptualization of the strength of modern capitalism persuaded him to seek a somewhat humanist and reformist solution, and he came to believe that the democratization of the present structures of society, in the widest sense, was the only road that could possibly be taken toward its de-reification. He saw less and less distinction between the idealistic and materialistic strands of socialist philosophy, but he staunchly adhered to the dialectic as the central concept of his analysis.

As well as interpreting Lukács he also, to some extent, bridged the gap between structuralists and Marxists, reuniting these two groups within the general French rationalist tradition. In his work on Racine, Pascal, and the novel he presented a modernized Marxist approach to literature, which avoided the pitfalls of the socialist realism school. His ideas were frequently criticized by more orthodox Marxists as left-wing Hegelianism, and he had a turbulent relationship with established Western Communist parties. But he was a major influence on younger Marxist thinkers of the postwar generation, particularly in France.

BIBLIOGRAPHY:

A. *Recherches dialectiques* (Paris: Gallimard, 1959); *The Hidden God* (London: Routledge & Kegan Paul, 1964); *The Human Sciences and Philosophy* (London: Cape, 1969); *The Philosophy of the Enlightenment* (Cambridge: MIT Press, 1973); *Towards a Sociology of the Novel* (London: Tavistock, 1975); *Cultural Creation in Modern Society* (St. Louis: Telos Press, 1976); *Lukács and Heidegger: Towards a New Philosophy* (London: Routledge & Kegan Paul, 1978).

B. S. Nair and M. Lowy, *Lucien Goldman: ou la dialectique de la totalité* (Paris: Seghers, 1973); E. Tell, "Bibliographie de Lucien Goldmann," *Revue de l'Institut de Sociologie Bruxelles*, nos. 3–4 (1973), pp. 787–806; P. Zima, *Goldmann: dialectique de l'immanence* (Paris: Editions Universitaires, 1973); A. Goldmann, M. Lowy, and S. Nair, *Le Structuralisme genetique: Goldmann* (Paris: Denoel, 1977); M. Evans, *Lucien Goldmann: An Introduction* (Brighton: Harvester Press, 1981).

JOHN C. SIMMONDS

GONZÁLEZ CASANOVA, PABLO (b. 1922). A Mexican social scientist born in 1922 in the state of Yucatan, González Casanova studied for a master's degree in history in Mexico and for a doctorate in Paris under the supervision of Fernand Braudel. From 1970 to 1972 he was rector of the Universidad Nacional Autónima de México, where he is a professor and a former director of the Escuela Nacional de Ciencias Políticas y Sociales. His writings focused on issues of development and underdevelopment in Mexico, on Latin American history in general and the impact of imperialism, and on social science methodology.

In his work on Mexico, González Casanova emphasized the dominance of the official oligarchy through which power at all levels has been concentrated since the revolution of 1910. The state has been able to impose constraints upon the big industrialists and financiers but in collaboration with these sectors has achieved progress, including peace, a mixed economy, state-guided capitalism, and some growth. The future of Mexico, however, rests with the emergence of a national bourgeoisie aligned with workers and peasants in order to bring about full capitalism at the national level while struggling against outside imperialism.

González Casanova emphasized development and underdevelopment in a series of essays on the sociology of exploitation. Methodologically he attempted to reconcile differences between empirical investigation and historical approaches to Marxism.† Standing between these two traditions, he believed that empiricism itself is ideological and unscientific, while Marxism in its vulgar form also lacks scientific precision. Both these approaches failed to explain exploitation, a concept he believed offered an understanding of history.

In the case of Mexico, exploitation could be analyzed through application of the concept of internal colonialism, a term that influenced Latin American as well as North American scholars. Internal colonialism was seen in the relationship between two societies, one marginal and comprised generally of Indians, exploited and dependent on the other dominant society of Spanish, Creoles, and Ladinos. In this dualist relationship a ruling metropolis or center dominates and exploits the satellite or periphery of marginal Indian communities. Thus a dominant center such as the city of San Cristóbal holds monopoly power over the Indian commerce and credit in the surrounding communities, resulting in the monoculture, deformation, and dependence of the Indian economy. Exploitation is tied to the mixture of feudalism, capitalism, forced and salaried work, and other relations of production. In this way internal colonialism assists in understanding uneven development in underdeveloped countries.

He argued that Mexico was largely precapitalist and that the national bourgeoisie must be counted on to lead the country in capitalist development; this would involve alliance of the national bourgeoisie with working-class and peasant organization in a struggle against outside imperialism and to achieve democracy internally. In this way Mexico eventually would achieve socialism peacefully. In recent years he has put more emphasis on the problems of class struggle in the periphery of world capitalism and in the Mexican and Latin American states and societies.

BIBLIOGRAPHY:

A. *Democracy in Mexico* (New York: Oxford University Press, 1970); "Internal Colonialism," in *Radicalism in Latin America*, ed. I. Horowitz, et al. (New York: Random House, 1970), pp. 118–39; *Sociología de la explotación* (Mexico City: Sigle Ventiuno, 1970); *Imperialismo y liberación en America Latina* (Mexico City: Siglo Ventiuno, 1978); *The Fallacy of Social Science Research* (New York: Pergamon Press, 1981).

B. Joseph A. Kahl, *Modernization, Exploitation, and Dependency in Latin America: Germani, González Casanova, and Cardoso* (New Brunswick, N.J.: Transaction Books, 1976).

RONALD H. CHILCOTE

GORTER, HERMAN (1864–1927). Gorter was a Dutch poet and revolutionary communist of international repute. Among his most widely acclaimed poems are "Mei" (Amsterdam, 1889) and "Pan" (Amsterdam, 1912), the latter being a socialist epos on the workers' struggle for human liberation. After Gorter received his Ph.D. with a dissertation on Aeschylus, he taught classics for many years. Like other members of the so-called Dutch School of Marxists,† Gorter translated many works of German Marxism into Dutch to facilitate its reception in the Netherlands: the *Communist Manifesto* in 1904; Joseph Dietzgen's *The*

Essence of Human Mental Work in 1902; Karl Kautsky's† *The Road to Power* in 1910; Lenin's† *About Unhappy Peace* in 1917, and *State and Revolution* in 1918. Earlier, Gorter had translated Spinoza's *Ethics* (1889), which undoubtedly predisposed him to the influence of Kantian and subsequently of Marxian thought. Over a period of twenty years Gorter contributed numerous articles to the leading papers of the Dutch radical left, *De Nieuwe Tijd* and *De Tribune*, as well as to some German, Swiss, and English socialist publications such as the *International Socialist Review*, *the New Review*, *Die Neue Zeit*, *Demain* and the *Communist International*.

Gorter joined Pieter Jelle Troelstra's† Socialist Workers' Party (SDAP) in 1897, and as a result of the party's increasing reformist tendencies, he became the leading agitator for the radical left that had grouped around the oppositional paper *De Tribune*. In 1909 Gorter bitingly defined reformism, or "practical revisionism," as follows:

> *No* longer carry out the class struggle irreconcilably, do *not* always struggle in such a way that the conquest of state power and socialism comes first, do *not* always struggle in such a way that the class consciousness of the workers is raised, but instead, . . . arrange your actions such that you do not offend the bourgeoisie too much, keep your own goals in the background, do not expect everything from your own power but also a little, maybe even a lot, from bourgeois democracy, support *it*, reach compromises with *them*, do not reject her budget on principle, but enter her institutions, if you see an immediate advantage in so doing. Do all of this even if it damages the class consciousness of the workers. For . . . the immediate advantage, which you get from this by giving in, is worth more than the growth of revolutionary consciousness. (Cited in De Liagre Böhl, *Herman Gorter*, p. 62)

When the Tribunists† (J. C. Ceton, D. Wijnkoop, and W. Ravesteijn†) were expelled from the SDAP at the Deventer congress in 1909 for having refused to cease publishing *De Tribune*, Gorter and A. Pannekoek* (who already lived in Germany, which made his role in the split less conspicuous) were the only Marxists around *De Nieuwe Tijd* who aligned with them. That same year the Tribunists founded the Dutch Social Democratic Party (SDP), for which Gorter found Lenin's support and which in 1919—still under the same leadership of Wijnkoop and Ravesteijn—became the first Dutch Communist Party (CPH). Gorter became the SDP's chief propagandist and internationally the best-known figure of this—then still relatively small—party. Yet, unlike Wijnkoop and Ravesteijn, who also were in editorial control of *De Tribune*, Gorter was never a party leader in the true sense of the word. He seemed to lack the qualities or interest that were necessary for carrying out the practical daily chores of party work in a sustained manner. He preferred to concentrate his political work on giving speeches, which were known to be brilliant, and on writing numerous articles and agitational pamphlets on topics related to party organization and social economy. Occasionally he withdrew completely from political work to devote himself to his literary endeavors. Among the members of the Dutch school, Anton Pannekoek was the only Dutch Marxist with whom Gorter could always identify himself politically. Although Pannekoek lived in Germany during most of the time of their collaboration, he and Gorter went through the same political transitions: from social democracy to left-wing Marxism to Bolshevism to council communism. Against common belief, however, Gorter and Pannekoek occasionally did disagree politically. For example, during World War I Gorter was more militant on the questions of armed proletarian struggle and civil war than the rather pacifist-inclined Pannekoek. Another example of the disagreements between Gorter and Pannekoek is shown in the latter's criticism of *Imperialism*, one of Gorter's most successful political pamphlets, for paying too much attention to the centrists at the expense of his left-wing comrades such as Rosa Luxemburg† and Karl Liebknecht, whereupon Gorter flatly rejected Pannekoek's German translation of *Imperialism*. Nevertheless their political collaboration—which was further intensified on a personal level by the friendship of Luise Gorter and Anna Pannekoek, their respective wives—was never seriously jeopardized or challenged by these relatively minor disagreements and culminated in their joint work for the anti-Bolshevik Communist Workers Party in Germany and the Netherlands (the KAPD and the KAPN), of which both were founding members.

Until about 1910, Gorter had been a committed follower and personal friend of Karl Kautsky,† who wrote an introduction to Gorter's *Historical Materialism, Explained for Workers*, translated into German by Anna Pannekoek, in 1908. Gorter began to change his views radically in favor of Rosa Luxemburg and Pannekoek as a result of the debate on ''mass strike'' and ''extraparliamentary action,'' which culminated in Kautsky's *Die Neue Zeit* between 1910 and 1912. Gorter completely disassociated himself from Kautsky and his politics after the vote in favor of the war credits in 1914 by the overwhelming majority of the German Social Democrats had caused the collapse of the Second International.† From that time on Gorter became a staunch anticentrist in the name of true socialist internationalism and of consistent anti-imperialism. It was on the basis of these same principles that he ultimately would leave the Dutch SDP. He disagreed bitterly with the strong pro-Entente sympathies and anti-German sentiments of Ravesteijn and Wijnkoop (cf. *Opportunism in the Dutch Communist Party*, 1921). For a few years Gorter supported the Bolshevik Revolution and especially admired the creation of the workers' councils there. In 1920 he was, with Pannekoek, Henriëtte Roland-Holst,† and Ravesteijn, part of the executive of the Comintern sub-bureau in Amsterdam. But upon the proclamation of the twenty-one conditions, Gorter and Pannekoek (as well as so many German radical Communists) abruptly severed all ties with the Comintern. In his *Open letter to Comrade Lenin*, an answer to Lenin's brochure, ''Radicalism and Its Infantile Disorders'' (1920), Gorter argued against the opportunism inherent in Lenin's proposed tactics for the struggle of the European workers in the aftermath of the October Revolution. Although—as De Liagre Böhl has pointed out—Gorter did not relinquish Lenin's notions on the importance of the revolutionary party, he

did argue in favor of proletarian autonomy—a notion that goes back to Joseph
Dietzgen—and claimed that the tactics of the European proletariat necessarily
and historically would have to be different from those employed in the Russian
Revolution. The kind of revolutionary ideals Gorter essentially subscribed to
can best be summarized with a line from *World Revolution* written in 1918:
"State power in control of the proletariat; legislation by the proletariat; guarantee
of an existence-minimum for all workers and for all those who can be equated
with them; ownership and control of the distribution of products by the proletariat" (cited in De Liagre Böhl, *Herman Gorter*, p. 199). Until his death Gorter
remained one of the most influential spokesmen for council communists on the
Dutch-German-English left.

BIBLIOGRAPHY:

A. *Der historische Materialismus* (Stuttgart: Dietz, 1909); *Het imperialisme* (Amsterdam: Brochurehandel Sociaal-Democratische Partij, 1914); *Die Klassenkampf-Organi-
sation des Proletariats* (Berlin: KAPD, 1922); *The World Revolution* (Glasgow: Socialist
Information and Research Bureau, 1922).

B. Herman De Liagre Böhl, *Herman Gorter* (Nijmegen: SUN, 1973); D. A. Smart,
Pannekoek and Gorter's Marxism (London: Pluto Press, 1978).

TINEKE RITMEESTER

GORZ, ANDRÉ (b. 1924). A leading contemporary radical social theorist in
France, Gorz was born Girard Horst in Austria in 1924. His father was Jewish
and his mother Catholic. Following the *Anschluss* he moved to Switzerland where
he studied philosophy and was particularly influenced by the existentialism of
Jean-Paul Sartre,* whom he met in Lausanne in 1946. Gorz's autobiographical
meditation, *The Traitor*, was written in the mid-1950s, and his *La Morale de
l'histoire* (1959) focused particularly on the question of alienation. In the 1950s
Gorz became increasingly influenced by and then critical of Marxism.† His
writings were an outgrowth of the existential Marxist thinking that evolved in
Sartre's writings and in Sartre's circle. He was also greatly influenced by Italian
radical union strategists Vittorio Foa and Bruno Trentin. Gorz became political
editor of *Les Temps modernes* in 1961, and his *Stratégie ouvrière et néocapi-
talisme* (translated as *Strategy for Labor*) was published in 1964. It had a major
impact on the French new left as well as in circles close to the newly formed
United Socialist Party (PSU). In the 1970s Gorz took a particular interest in
social movements and wrote extensively on ecology. His *Farewell to the Working
Class* (1980) brought together the transformations his thinking had undergone
in the previous two decades. He currently lives in Paris, where, under another
pseudonym (Michel Bosquet), he is also the economics editor of the French left
weekly, *Le Nouvel Observateur*.

Strategy for Labor argued for a reconceptualization of contemporary capitalism, the status of the proletariat, and the possibilities for radical change. "That
socialism is a necessity," he wrote, "has never struck the masses with the
compelling force of a flash of lightning" (p. 3). Furthermore, in the advanced

capitalist West, the natural base for radical revolt had been undermined. Scarcity was becoming less of a major problem, and Gorz claimed that the traditional proletariat will never play the role prescribed for it by the left and especially Marxism. He differentiated traditional capitalism from contemporary "neocapitalism" (or "organized capitalism") by the expanded mediating role of the state in the latter. This new reality, combined with new advanced productive technology, engendered a new middle strata of specialists, technicians, professionals, and bureaucrats, whom he called "new proletarians," and whose socio-economic significance (as well as numbers) was increasing, in direct contrast to blue collar workers. He suggested a vanguard role for these "new proletarians" because although they were educated and well paid, they were nonetheless without any serious decision-making responsibilities in their working lives. Hence, argued Gorz, alienation and boredom, rather than scarcity, would stimulate efforts for radical change. The new proletarians would make qualitative demands pertaining to the creativity and meaning of labor rather than simply struggle for higher wages.

Such qualitative demands would aim to expand participatory control over the work place and would be embodied in the call for *autogestion* (self-management). More anarcho-syndicalist than Marxist in his thrust, Gorz advocated a strategy of "revolutionary reformism" to mobilize a highly differentiated working class on behalf of goals that would not just reform capitalism but would subvert its very logic, especially in the factories, by building and expanding centers of "democratic power" (i.e. bastions of *autogestion*) at the expense of management. In this struggle, (democratically controlled) unions would increasingly change the face of the social order by asserting control over the work situation, over the goals of and training for work, and over the organization and division of labor. Eventually capitalist hierarchy would be undermined and replaced by a self-managed society.

Gorz believed that the 1968 French upheaval, which he supported, confirmed his thinking on one hand and required its reshaping on the other. He noted that the "new proletarians" had taken the lead in the seizure of the factories and also that the "May events" had occurred not in a Third World country but in France, the country he took as the model of neocapitalism. Because the student-worker upheaval established nothing permanent, Gorz concluded that a mass political party, organized "from below," was needed by the left and not just a union strategy.

In the 1970s Gorz substantially rethought his position. In an article on "Technical Intelligence and the Capitalist Division of Labor," he abandoned his theory of the vanguard role of the new proletarians and not long after argued that the international division of labor, the development of giant transnational and national corporations, and the increasing complexity and size of productive systems made the idea of *autogestion* less and less meaningful as a program and model.

In his writings on ecology, Gorz emphasized that the ecological movement had to be part of a broader struggle and not be regarded as an end in itself. He condemned "growth-oriented socialism" along with "growth-oriented capitalism" and asserted that contrary to Marx's belief that the development of productive forces would serve as the foundation for freeing workers, it was having the opposite effect: the very scope of the new productive forces and their need for centralized decision making made the notion of sovereign control of them by the workers untenable. "Socialism is no better than capitalism," he wrote, "if it makes use of the same tools—the total domination of nature inevitably entails a domination of people by the techniques of domination" (*Ecology as Politics*, p. 20). Influenced by Ivan Illich, Gorz called for an "inversion of tools" and the creation of a technology that does not of necessity carry with it centralized, hierarchical, (and hence political) impositions.

Gorz's concern, from his earliest writings through the most recent, is the creation of a cooperative society that allows the maximal expression of individual freedom and autonomy. In *Strategy for Labor* this was manifested in his vision of socialism as a self-managed and self-determined society. His *Farewell to the Working Class* is animated by the same impulse, but represents a trajectory that has carried him far from *Strategy for Labor* in important ways. In *Farewell to the Working Class* Gorz defined his central theme as "the liberation of time and the abolition of work" (p. 1). He proposes accomplishing these goals by creating a "dual society" committed to pressing to its limit the opposition of the realms of human freedom ("autonomy") and necessity ("heteronomy"). Since heteronomous work and the division of labor can never be entirely eliminated if basic human needs are to be satisfied, they should be trivialized and limited, whereas freedom *from* work should be extended as much as possible. Given a socialized heteronomous realm of necessary production, nonbasic needs may be left to autonomous production. Heteronomous labor, in Gorz's projected dual society, would be distributed so that the work day is radically reduced, something Gorz insists is possible because of the productive capacities of advanced technology.

The realm of heteronomy includes the state, which allows society to function and reproduce itself; it cannot be abolished, according to Gorz, but should, in scope, be commensurate with the requirements of organizing social production and the basics of social administration. The state does not have to be the embodiment of domination provided it, like all of the heteronomous realm, is delimited, especially by an active civil society and autonomous realm. This process of delimiting is what Gorz calls politics, which in turn is that point where moral human demands struggle with those of necessity; hence politics is not to be confused with power per se.

Gorz insists that Marx's assumption that the forces of production would create socialism's material preconditions and agent (in the form of the proletariat) has been proven incorrect. Those forces are solely functional to capitalism, and the role Marx imputed to the proletariat will not be acted out by individual proletarians. The working class has been passified and atomized, its daily existence spent in increasingly larger productive apparatuses that allow no self-determined activities. In such productive (and also in large-scale political) systems nobody actually holds power; individuals play functional roles dictated by the logic of the system itself. Therefore, the seizure of power from one class by another has little meaning; the end of domination can occur only with the recognition of the necessity of functional power in society and its restriction, i.e., by the creation of a dual society.

The traditional proletariat, by Gorz's characterization, is incapable of galvanizing a struggle for radical change and the creation of a dual society. The working class, he stresses repeatedly, is being undermined and diminished by automation and technological developments. He therefore proposes, but inadequately explicates, that this struggle will find its historical subject in what he calls the "non-class" of "postindustrial proletarians," in a movement of individuals with no defined class identity, who are often only employed part time, and who are excluded from the productive process by automation ("the abolition of work") or whose "capacities are under-employed as a result of the industrialisation . . . of intellectual work" (*Farewell to the Working Class*, p. 68). How exactly this "non-class" is to play its role, and what exactly this role is, remains unclarified by Gorz in *Farewell to the Working Class*.

BIBLIOGRAPHY:

A. *La Morale de l'histoire* (Paris: Editions du Seuil, 1959); *The Traitor* (New York: Simon and Schuster, 1959); *Strategy for Labor* (Boston: Beacon Press, 1968); "Technical Intelligence and the Capitalist Division of Labor," *Telos*, 12 (Summer 1972); *Ecology as Politics* (Boston: South End Press, 1975); *Farewell to the Working Class* (Boston: South End Press, 1982).

B. Dick Howard, "New Situation, New Strategy: Serge Mallet and André Gorz," in *The Unknown Dimension*, ed. D. Howard and K. Klare (New York: Basic Books, 1972); Arthur Hirsh, *The French New Left* (Boston: South End Press, 1981).

MITCHELL COHEN

GRAMSCI, ANTONIO (1891–1937). Gramsci was born in the small town of Ales on the island of Sardinia on 22 January 1891, one of seven children of lower middle-class parents. Burdened by a malformed spine, which caused him in later life to be hunchbacked and barely five feet tall, he was also of generally poor health, suffering constantly from internal and nervous disorders. Gramsci attended the University of Turin on scholarship in 1911 and was influenced by the Italian idealist philosopher Benedetto Croce. He joined the Italian Socialist Party (PSI) in 1913, believing that the urban and rural poor would unite in rebellion against capitalism. In 1919 Gramsci helped found *Ordine Nuovo*, a Socialist weekly supporting Turin's factory council movement. In January 1921 Gramsci helped establish the Italian Communist Party (PCI). From 1922 to 1924 he worked for the Comintern in Moscow and Vienna. In 1924 he was elected to the Italian Parliament and simultaneously took control of the PCI, trying to turn the latter into a mass-based revolutionary party. Gramsci was arrested by the fascist police in 1926 and sentenced to over twenty years in prison, where under adverse conditions of censorship and material scarcity he began writing on themes relevant to the Italian situation. These writings—thirty-four notebooks in all—comprise what are now called the *Prison Notebooks*. Gramsci's health deteriorated by 1933. By 1935 international pressure had managed to secure somewhat improved living conditions for Gramsci, but he finally became too weak to be moved and died in a clinic on 27 April 1937—one week after his scheduled release from prison. His sister Tatiana managed to smuggle the thirty-four notebooks out of Gramsci's room and via diplomatic bag to Moscow.

Gramsci borrowed from both George Lukács* and Karl Korsch,* adopting the former's Hegelianism and the latter's hesitancy to abandon the everyday world for idealism's abstractions. This synthesis is formed, speaking generally, by emphasizing the active moment of the a priori totality, while always assuming that praxis reflects and expresses a universal pattern of historical development. Rational subjectivity is therefore objectively necessary even if uncaused. Marxism,† which describes the plight of workers from oppression to revolution, is a "philosophy of praxis" in depicting workers' subjectively relevant actions. This term, originally used by the imprisoned Gramsci to trick censors, aptly represents the flavor of his idealism, the constant awareness that, although philosophy must be theoretically pure, Marxism must also cater to workers living and working in the everyday life-world.

Gramsci's reputation as a Marxian theorist is based primarily on the posthumously published documents, notes, and letters from prison (1929–35), which total more than 3,000 pages and seven volumes, the most significant of which is probably the *Prison Notebooks*. As with Antonio Labriola,† Gramsci's Marxism is uniquely colored by his national heritage, particularly the idealism that traditionally characterizes Italian thought. As a student, Gramsci was already an ardent follower of Croce's brand of Hegelianism, especially his critique of positivism, and eagerly anticipated an idealist renewal of Marxism. Only much later, in prison, was Gramsci concerned with Croce's own festering anti-Marxism and the possible reactionary implications of Crocean idealism. The emphasis Gramsci accorded the subjective moment of Hegel's totality is surely a response to his mentor's move to the right.

Gramsci interpreted human behavior, ideas, and symbols in relation to their historical environments and the transhistorical patterns they manifest. The criteria and content of truth, then, vary with historical time and place. This historical relativism, not orthodox material determinism, is the essence of Marxism. "Matter," for Gramsci, is epistemologically insignificant. In any given time and place, knowledge expresses social relationships rather than objective matter. It is entirely possible that under generally similar material conditions, two societies will have significantly different cultures. Matter must be studied only as a connection between the way we think and the way we organize means of production. Although capitalism cannot appear in feudal material conditions, these do not necessarily "cause" noncapitalist productive modes. A feudal productive apparatus reflects material conditions only through nondetermined mediations such as cultural beliefs and institutions. Marxism is therefore "true" only by expressing current historical forces better than any other doctrine. An "objective" social science, in fact, cannot exist because the very concepts we use to define science express dominant historical patterns. As early as the critique of Nikolai I. Bukharin's† *Theory of Historical Materialism* (1921), Gramsci interpreted historical materialism, like religion, as a sign of weakness exhibited by oppressed peoples having little hope for immediate change. It is "true" only because commonly believed, but this does not qualify it as science. When oppressed workers are reflectively self-conscious and actively seek change, ideas concerning objective, deterministic historical laws fade. Humanity takes history into its hands and shapes the future.

The common practices of isolating different historical epochs from each other and different empirical facts from the social whole reflect Western Europe's dominant culture. Empiricism, like historical materialism, has no objective foundation independent of its naive acceptance by vast numbers of people. It is equally naive to assume that individuals are ahistorical empirical entities free to do whatever they like. Strong forces, in fact, inhibit change and limit what people can accomplish. Individuals can and do cognize oppression and actively rebel. Although this action is not caused by economics, it is part of history's total process, which weans out historically "incorrect" acts. In other words, for Gramsci history is a product of practical activity, human will. But effective action is rational, not arbitrary, expressing dominant developmental patterns, the nuts and bolts of universal history. Although action at any one time represents only a single actor, its rationality is confirmed when assimilated into common-sense thinking, that is, when it becomes part of culture. The "correctness" of an idea is confirmed when it historically prevails over competing ideas, integrating itself into history's total movement. The economic evolution of capitalism, generating worker immiseration and institutional inequity, is the historical context for praxis. Within it, only certain actions are "rational," that is, aspects of history's universal development subjectively relevant to society's masses. Marx correctly perceived the necessity and rationality of proletarian revolutionary action. Today, praxis is worker revolution. This is the "truth" of Marxism. It simultaneously describes our contemporary self-creation and history's progressive, universal development.

Each dominant culture, for Gramsci, maintains itself in the common-sense attitudes and behavior of its population. Culture, in other words, lives in human praxis, which expresses human beliefs. It survives by exerting "hegemony," or control, over people's ideas. Capitalism, for example, thrives through bourgeois control and manipulation of a massive network of cultural institutions—schools, churches, parties, newspapers, media, and private associations—which incessantly propagate cultural ideas supporting the extant mode of production. A successful revolutionary movement in Western Europe must fight bourgeois hegemony in a long and complex "war of position" whose goal is a new hegemonic apparatus to replace the old. Revolutionaries working only as trained cadres preparing to seize political power will fail miserably. The state itself is far more than a simple political apparatus by which a dominant class coerces enemies, although it is certainly this. It is also an "equilibrium" between "political" and "civil" societies, that is, a hegemonic apparatus that molds ideas as well as instruments of direct coercion. A state's power includes all those cultural institutions through which power relations are mediated. Gramsci's "integral state" thus comprises coercive (political) and hegemonic (civil) apparatuses. This expanded notion of the state is the hub of Gramsci's social scheme. History evolves through the progressive transformation of states, each representing a particular dominant economic class as well as the entire coercive and hegemonic apparatuses through which civilizations are propagated. The workers' state will, therefore, represent a unity of theory and practice, its rationality entwined with those working-class beliefs and behaviors it cultivates. It is truth manifest in concrete working-class praxis. Before workers can successfully rebel against capitalism, they must defeat both the political and civil components of the bourgeois state.

Intellectuals serve the distinctly political function of legitimating culture, making it accessible to everyone and universalizing its dominance. In maintaining class rule, therefore, they play as important a role as government officials charged with enacting and executing public law. They are the fuel of hegemonic structures, generating ideas, values, and beliefs that are repeatedly cranked out in books, journals, classrooms, pulpits, and airwaves. Their work represents society's cherished features, the basic, emotion-laden institutions and attitudes that we unthinkingly internalize as children and that later define us as members of a particular culture—what Gramsci calls a "historical bloc." Each historical bloc, because it survives and proves its rationality, has its own experts in legitimation who have successfully performed their allotted task. A historical bloc is an integral state rooted in an organic relationship, not merely an alliance, between leaders and masses.

Not surprisingly, Gramsci foresaw intellectuals playing a vital role in the imminent revolution. Revolutionary intellectuals demystify contemporary culture, showing the masses how bourgeois words and symbols represent the interests of the small group of capitalists dominating our historical bloc. In winning working-class minds, intellectuals prove their own rationality and necessity. The fruit of their intellectual labor is authentic worker self-consciousness, dialectically expressed in revolutionary praxis. This dramatic and complex project requires direct channels of communication connecting workers and intellectuals. By manipulating universally accepted words, symbols, and emotions, intellectuals reflect the subjective side of workers' lives while implanting a critical attitude toward it. They are, in Gramsci's terminology, "organic," arising from and reflecting the objective needs of real working people.

The Party carefully organizes this transformation of proletarian consciousness and ensuing cultural renewal. It is a voluntary organization uniting intellectuals and workers in an "organic relationship" that generates proletariat hegemony. Through a coordinating or mediating role, it helps workers emancipate themselves and create a classless society of socialist justice. In brief, it actively organizes that "collective will" that intellectuals are slowly cultivating in workers' consciousness by systematically orchestrating the workers' movement prior to the revolutionary act, funneling new human energies in appropriate, rational directions. Party members must organically reflect subjective needs and ideas of the entire nonentrepreneurial population, including workers and peasants. But if haphazardly organized, the Party's effectiveness is neutralized. While avoiding a mindlessly inhuman structure, it must be run efficiently and hierarchically according to principles of "democratic centralism." The Party, in sum, is a complex unity of worker praxis and planned, conscious guidance. When proletariat hegemony is finally established, it will have guaranteed its own disappearance as workers become educated in the art of self-management.

The Party's major problem is formulating institutions that propagate worker authenticity and also train workers in economic self-management. Undoubtedly influenced by Georges Sorel,* Gramsci speculated that the factory council movement, which flourished for a time throughout postwar Italy—especially in Turin— was appropriate. When workers actively participate in running factories, even while still privately owned, they will likely recognize the historical necessity of complete worker self-management. Capitalism will become, in the minds of its workers, increasingly irrational. The Party promotes these councils and taps the ensuing revolutionary fervor. Councils will remain after the Party dissolves, as the rational form of organizing free workers in communism.

Gramsci's idealist Marxism enticed disillusioned Westerners by rejecting orthodox materialism as just another unverifiable metaphysics. He was no raging ideologue whose doctrine trampled the emancipated. Indeed, Gramsci saw reflective public opinion as the guarantor of truth and lauded basic civil liberties— individual freedoms of thought, press, speech, and association—as hallmarks of historical rationality. Just as the minds of individual workers must be won through the open interplay of competing ideas, each nation must respond in its own manner to capitalism's challenge. National Marxist parties mold strategies to their workers' cultural beliefs. The alternative, imposing an absolute formula on all peoples regardless of subjective peculiarities, vitiates history's goal of establishing worldwide proletariat cultural hegemony. Parties themselves are voluntary, organically reflecting actual, subjectively perceived proletarian needs, and council democracy is nonbureaucratic and nonhierarchic.

But Gramsci's open society is no excuse for capriciousness. Praxis and historical necessity, for him, must and will correspond. The give and take of social freedom will result in Marxism's victory, its voluntary adoption by the masses. Revolution was historically necessary and inevitable, and this would be proven in worker praxis. Reformists, for Gramsci, are objectively wrong, and reformism is an irrational approach to capitalist exploitation. Ironically, had Gramsci avoided Mussolini's grasp and faced the probable conflicts between Party (universal) survival and actual (subjective) attitudes and conditions, he probably would not have stressed subjectivity to the extent he did when isolated in prison, and perhaps his influence among Westerners today would be more limited.

BIBLIOGRAPHY:

A. *Note sul Machiavelli sulla politica e sullo Stato moderno* (Turin: Einaudi, 1949); *"The Modern Prince" and Other Writings* (New York: International, 1957); *Selections from the Prison Notebooks*, ed. and trans. Quinton Hoare and Geoffrey Nowell Smith (New York: International, 1971); *Selections from Political Writings 1910–1920* (New York: International, 1977); *Selections from Political Writings 1921–1926* (London: Lawrence and Wishart, 1978).

B. Guiseppe Fiori, *Antonio Gramsci: Life of a Revolutionary* (London: New Left Books, 1970); A. Davidson, *Antonio Gramsci: Towards an Intellectual Biography* (Atlantic Highlands, N.J.: Humanities Press, 1977); Christine Buci-Glucksmann, *Gramsci and the State* (London: Lawrence and Wishart, 1979); C. Mouffe, ed., *Gramsci and Marxist Theory* (London: Routledge & Kegan Paul, 1979); Anne S. Sassoon, *Gramsci's Politics* (New York: St. Martin's Press, 1980).

ROBERT A. GORMAN

GRAUERT, JULIO CÉSAR (1901–1933). Born in 1901, Grauert was a follower of José Batlle y Ordoñez, president of Uruguay from 1903 to 1907 and from 1911 to 1915. Batlle was the undisputed leader of the Colorado Party until his death in 1929 and the principal founder of the Uruguayan welfare state, by which public goods and services were redistributed to benefit the poor and middle classes. After Batlle's death Grauert tried to radicalize and give more depth to Batllism by adopting certain Marxian† principles, although Grauert was never an orthodox Marxist. In effect, he utilized Marxist concepts as a tool to justify his own positions. "Avanzar," his political group within Batllism, can be considered a neo-Marxist reformist movement. With its help Grauert was able to get elected as a national deputy from 1929 to 1933.

His first work, *El dogma, la eusenanza, y el Estado*, coauthored with P. Cerutti Crosa (who later joined the Communist ranks) subscribes to the liberal anticlerical line. But the bulk of his public pronouncements are found in the weekly newspaper of his group, also called *Avanzar*. In these he insisted on the need for nationalizing land, taxing inheritances, eliminating absentee ownership, and establishing a progressive tax against land monopolies. This was consistent with Batlle y Ordoñez's actions and the 1925 program of Batllism. Batlle and Grauert felt that all Uruguayan land should belong to the state after a prolonged, peaceful transition process, after which people could enjoy its use in exchange for a commitment to protect Uruguay militarily. Grauert also insisted on the need to control publicly the changes in currency and the activities of private banks, and then to centralize small savings in the state, with the idea of channeling it into a credit policy favorable to the popular sectors—all culminating in the total nationalization of banking. He wanted to continue the process of nationalizing public service firms, which had been initiated by Batlle, ending all private monopolies. Grauert espoused anti-imperialism, not only against Great Britain but also against the potentially more powerful United States. He continued the *obrerista* (labor) policy of Batlle, suggesting that society, through the state, should finance labor strikes against capitalists. He believed that the working class of Montevideo would be the social base for the future of Batllism. He also believed that the political club, the basic organization of Batllism, must reorganize around principles of syndicalism. Grauert remained, theoretically, within Batllism, believing that if Batlle's reform program were constantly expanded, capitalism could be defeated through a peaceful revolution.

After the coup of March 1933 Grauert led a determined opposition. This ended in October, when upon returning to Montevideo from the interior of the country, he was gunned down by the police after refusing to obey their order to stop. He died two days later from a lack of proper medical attention. For the conservative Uruguayan regime, Grauert was an enemy more dangerous than orthodox Communists or Social Democrats.

BIBLIOGRAPHY:

A. With P. Cerutti Crosa, *El dogma, la enseñanza, y el Estado* (Montevideo: Agencía generale de librería y publicaciones, 1927).

B. Vivian Trias, *Uruguay hoy* (Montevideo: Banda Oriental, 1973).

JUAN RIAL

GRIGORENKO, PETRO G. (b. 1907). Petro Grigorenko was born 16 October 1907 in the Ukrainian village of Borisovka. An ethnic Ukrainian, he was active in the Komsomol (Communist Youth League) throughout the 1920s. Grigorenko was trained as a military engineer, served in the war, and received a doctoral degree in military science from Frunze Academy in Moscow, where he lectured until 1961. During 1964–65, General Grigorenko was imprisoned in the Serbsky Psychiatric Hospital for activities connected with the Alliance for the Rebirth of Leninism, a covert organization founded with the assistance of his son Georgy. He was incarcerated in psychiatric prisons for a second time from 1969 to 1974. Soviet authorities revoked Grigorenko's citizenship in 1977 while he was in New York for medical treatment.

Grigorenko claimed to be a Leninist,† yet he has asserted that the theoretical basis for Stalinism† (to which he is adamantly opposed) may be found in Lenin's writings and actions. The weakness in Leninism is the proscription against factions, which suppressed the free development of conflicting opinions, and its predisposition toward authoritarianism. Grigorenko advocates freedoms of press, speech, assembly, religion, and scientific inquiry, for truth can only be revealed through the pluralistic interplay of viewpoints. Socialism must be democratized to preclude a dictatorship of the majority or, as is the case in the Soviet Union, a dictatorship of the elite claiming to be the majority. Grigorenko first clashed with the regime when he warned against Nikita Khrushchev's† inchoate personality cult and demanded the democratization of the Soviet Communist Party. He established a reputation for defending the rights of displaced Soviet minor-

ities—the Crimean Tatars, Volga Germans, and Meskhetian Turks—but he has also actively supported the rights of religious believers, scientists, and industrial workers. Like Solzhenitsyn, Grigorenko is convinced that spiritual values are indispensable for a healthy society; material abundance is not sufficient.
BIBLIOGRAPHY:
  A. *The Grigorenko Papers* (Boulder, Colo.: Westview Press, 1976); *Memoirs* (New York: Norton, 1982).

CHARLES E. ZIEGLER

GRLIĆ, DANKO (1923–1984). The Yugoslav Danko Grlić was born in 1923 in Gračanica (Bosnia) and studied philosophy at the University of Zagreb, where he received his B.A. and Ph.D. degrees (with a thesis on Nietzsche). He was the editor for philosophy and sociology in the Yugoslav Lexicographical Institute in Zagreb for several years. In 1969 he was appointed professor of aesthetics at the University of Belgrade. He taught at the University of Zagreb after 1972. Grlić was concerned primarily with aesthetics, but also with ontology and philosophical anthropology. His translations of philosophical works by Montaigne, Paracelsus, Hegel, Kierkegaard, Nietzsche, Bernstein,* Windelband, and Heidegger are well known. Grlić was a member of the editorial board of *Praxis** from its beginning and of the board of the Korčula Summer School. He was president of the Croatian Philosophical Society during the period 1966–68 and a visiting professor in Cologne and lectured in various universities in Germany and Switzerland. His early death on 2 March 1984 was commemorated by *Politika* in an article on "The Philosopher of the Spirit of Art," which noted his qualities as a splendid lecturer and a great human being, without however mentioning his connection with *Praxis*. Grlić left behind an impressive written corpus of some fifteen books, including *Philosophy* (1963, 1965), *Art and Philosophy* (1965), *Why?* (1968), *Who Is Nietzsche?* (1969), *Contra dogmaticos* (1971), *On Comedy and the Comical* (1972), *Play as an Aesthetic Problem* (1975), and a three-volume history of *Aesthetics* (1974–78), plus numerous articles in *Praxis* and other journals and symposia.

  His theoretical contributions to Marxism†—particularly to the *Praxis* school of Marxist humanist thought—lie as much in epistemology and ethics as in aesthetics. Grlić was among the first to articulate the major epistemological, ontological, and ethical imperatives of neo-Marxism and to rethink the classics in the quest for a more humane future based on the unity of theory and practice. Grlić combined a radical skepticism in epistemology with an individualistic philosophy of creativity as well as an unswerving commitment to ethics as the keys to understanding not only philosophy and aesthetics but the very essence of man. Grlić's basic thesis in aesthetics—that a work of art needs no justification outside of itself since as a creative act it is both irreducible and cannot be duplicated—found its corollary in his view of human praxis as free, creative, and self-creative activity that defines the meaning of philosophy.

  Grlić's philosophy of art emphasized the individualistic nature of praxis and

personal creativity. Like his Zagreb colleagues Gajo Petrović* and Milan Kangrga,* Grlić was influenced by Heidegger and German existentialism. More than
other *Praxis* philosophers, Grlić referred to Nietzsche when emphasizing the
creative power of individual human negativity. Grlić saw a basic antinomy
between individual creativity and collective action. In his controversial paper on
"Creation and Action," presented at the 1967 Korčula Summer School, Grlić
articulated the central dilemma of the revolutionary: the institutionalization of
the revolutionary movement and its concomitant bureaucratization and the rise
of dogma. Grlić pondered: "Must the struggle against bureaucratism itself necessarily become bureaucratized? Is the struggle against God possible—as Nietzsche
would have said—without itself becoming God?"

During the First Winter Philosophical Meeting in 1971 at Tara (Serbia), Grlić
took even Marx himself to task for his economic determinism and excessive
emphasis on the importance of production and, hence, private property. It was
at that symposium on "Liberalism and Socialism" that Grlić called not only for
the revalorization of the concept and the heritage of liberalism but also for a
"permanent scepsis," which would "doubt all things, including one's own
theories." Mihailo Marković,* for one, dissented from Grlić's "dubito, ergo
sum." Nevertheless, Grlić's radical epistemological skepticism represents a major theoretical contribution toward a more open, living, nondogmatic Marxism.
Grlić's major contributions to an open-ended, humanist reconceptualization of
Marxist theory and socialist practice are contained already in his conception of
philosophy as a realm of free speech and critical inquiry summed up by the title
of his 1968 *Praxis* article: "La Patrie des philosophes, c'est la patrie de la
liberté." For Grlić, philosophy meant a highly personal act requiring a clear
choice between an authentic free being of praxis and a "glorifier of everything
existing." In his book *Why?* Grlić posits the thesis that praxis as process is an
open-ended enterprise that cannot end in nonconflictual perfection and restful-
ness. Like Vojan Rus and Petrović, Grlić contends that the very concept of praxis
implies that man as a creative and free being can never be completed or ultimately
defined. This view of noneschatological communism is one of the major sinews
of the *Praxis* school of thought.

In *Contra dogmaticos*, Grlić offers a critique of Stalinism as well as its
Hegelian roots. Commenting on "Absolute Freedom and Terror" in Hegel's
Phenomenology of Mind, Grlić disagrees with Hegel's contention that terror is
inherent in individual negativity and self-consciousness. Rather, Grlić sees the
source of terror precisely in the organized totality of the law, the lawgiver and
the power of the state cast in "the role of the most progressive state order, higher
historical justice, the carrier, guarantor, and guardian of the achievements of the
revolution and historical reason." It is an idea generally ignored by neo-Marxists
but one that finds further elaboration in the works of such *Praxis* theorists as
Svetozar Stojanović* and Ljubomir Tadić.*

Unlike orthodox Marxists, Grlić insists—with Marković, Stojanović, Petrović,
and others—that there must be an integral link between means and ends and that

human ends cannot justify inhuman means. The same article "On Abstract and Real Humanism" reflects also Grlić's conviction of the need to integrate such liberal (bourgeois) notions as abstract (formal) freedom as a prerequisite and a first step toward real (positive) freedom. Analogous to his concept of praxis and notion of openness and freedom, Grlić shares the *Praxis* understanding of self-management as an open and "permanent revolutionary process of liberation of all potential forces in a democratic society."

Although Grlić's philosophy of art, creativity, man, praxis, and society as well as his unique perspective as a Nietzschean Marxist philosopher of radical skepsis may be contested, he articulated the fundamental humanist creed: ideas and institutions exist only to serve human beings. Grlić will also be remembered for his wit and engaging dialogue, more perhaps than for the fury of his intellectual synthesis of Marx and Nietzsche.

BIBLIOGRAPHY:

A. "O apstraktnom i realnom humanizmu" pp. 133–44, in *Humanizam i socijalizam*, ed. Branko Bošnjak and Rudi Supek, vol. 1 (Zagreb: Naprijed, 1963); "Practice and Dogma," *Praxis* (I), 1, no. 1 (1965), pp. 49–58; "Kreacija i akcija," *Praxis* (Y), 4, nos. 5–6 (1967), pp. 565–77; "La Patrie des philosophes, c'est la patrie de la liberté," *Praxis* (I), 4, nos. 3–4 (1968), pp. 325–29; *Zašto?* (Zagreb: Studentski centar Sveučilišta, 1968); *Contra dogmaticos* (Zagreb: *Praxis*, 1971); "There Can Be No Critical Thought Without Permanent Scepsis," *Praxis* (I), 9, no. 1 (1973), pp. 91–93; excerpts from *Contra dogmaticos* in translation: "Revolution und Terror," *Praxis* (I), 7, nos. 1–2 (1971), pp. 49–61; English trans. in Mihailo Marković and Gajo Petrović, eds., *Praxis* (Dordrecht: Reidel, 1979), pp. 139–50; "Not Liberally, but Democratically," in *Marxist Humanism and Praxis*, ed. Gerson S. Sher (Buffalo, N.Y.: Prometheus Books, 1978), pp. 111–23.

B. Gerson S. Sher, *Praxis: Marxist Criticism and Dissent in Socialist Yugoslavia* (Bloomington: Indiana University Press, 1977); Oskar Gruenwald, *The Yugoslav Search for Man: Marxist Humanism in Contemporary Yugoslavia* (South Hadley, Mass.: Bergin & Garvey, 1983).

OSKAR GRUENWALD

GUATTARI, FÉLIX (b. 1930). Guattari studied pharmacology and philosophy in college. Since 1953 he has worked at the Clinique de la Borde at Courcheverney. He studied psychoanalysis with Lacan and became an analysis member of the Freudian School of Paris (1969). He is the founder of the psychoanalytical journal *Recherches* and a member of the Centre d'Initiative pour de Nouveaux Espaces de Liberté, an antipsychiatry movement. He played a major role in the events of May 1968 and is still active in the antipsychiatry movement. Since the period 1967–68 he has worked in collaboration with Gilles Deleuze* developing a completely new form of critical, philosophical discourse—libidinal economics and schizo-analysis. Their *Anti-Oedipus* is for many the most radical and creative book of the last decade. Guattari's own writings have at last been made available to the English reader in the collection *Molecular Revolution*

(1984), edited by David Cooper, another of the founders of the antipsychiatry movement.

Guattari's work draws freely from the texts of Freud, Marx,† and the entire psychoanalytic left. He seeks at once to rid analysis of its authoritarian strain, of everything in it that supports the world-system, and to apply a thus radicalized analytics to social movements and political events. For Guattari, the central and determining reality is that of desire, which manifests/invests itself in formations, levels, patterns and which then seeks to break through these patterns, turning in conflict against itself—a "micro-politics of desire."

One of his contributions to the collaboration with Deleuze is the recognition that one of the most significant side effects of the capitalist system is the generalization of schizophrenia. The system, as Marx so clearly saw, is constantly breaking down its own self-limitations, its own channels and investments of desire—feeding on itself so to speak—both on the individual level and on the level of social movements and institutions. The study (and experiences) of schizophrenic individuals is thus a privileged space for the study of the nature of capital and its consequences.

BIBLIOGRAPHY:

A. With Gilles Deleuze, *Kafka; pour une littérature mineure* (Paris: Editions de Minuit, 1975); with Gilles Deleuze, *Anti-Oedipus: Capitalism and Schizophrenia* (New York: Viking Press, 1977); with Gilles Deleuze, *Mille Plateaux* (Paris: Editions de Minuit, 1980); *Molecular Revolution*, ed. David Cooper (New York: Penguin, 1984).

B. Miriam Glucksmann, *Structuralist Analysis in Contemporary Social Thought* (London: Routledge & Kegan Paul, 1974); Rosalind Coward and John Ellis, *Language and Materialism* (London: Routledge & Kegan Paul, 1977).

                                                                                    LAURENCE E. WINTERS

GURVITCH, GEORGES (1894–1965). Georges Gurvitch was born in the Russian city of Novorossisk in November 1894. A close observer of the Russian Revolution, Gurvitch met Lenin† and knew Trotsky† as these two were institutionalizing Bolshevik power. He was educated in Russia and by the age of twenty-three already had two dissertations published. In 1917 Gurvitch received his *agrégation* and his first academic position as lecturer at the University of Petrograd. In 1919 he was appointed professor at the University of Tomsk. Disillusioned by the centralizing course of the Bolshevik Revolution, Gurvitch left Russia for Czechoslovakia, where he taught in the Russian Department at the University of Prague and studied the work of Fichte, Husserl, and Scheler. Gurvitch emigrated to France in 1925, taught at the Collège Sévigné and the University of Strasbourg and began publishing in the areas of sociology and law. During the Nazi occupation of France, Gurvitch was forced to flee to America and the New School for Social Research, where he met P. Sorokin, T. Parsons, and R. Merton. He returned to Strasbourg in 1945, consolidated his professional reputation as a major social theorist, and was eventually elected to the Sorbonne in 1949 and to the Ecole Practique des Hautes Etudes in 1950. He traveled constantly and was a visiting professor in Brazil, Argentina, Japan, Canada, North Africa, the Near East, Italy, Yugoslavia, and Greece. He founded, in 1946, the Centre d'Etudes Sociologiques, established the scholarly review *Cahiers internationaux de sociologie*, and later organized the Groupe (later known as the "Laboratoire") de Sociologie de la Connaissance. He died in Paris in 1965.

Gurvitch was a sociologist comfortable with theory only when it arose spontaneously from rigorously compiled data. He approached scientific inquiry devoid of theoretical preconceptions regarding the historical and social functions of economic classes. As a scientist, he was committed to facts, not revolution, and he separated value judgments from the process of scientific inquiry. Moreover, the categories he developed to facilitate data collecting reflected an extraordinarily diverse group of thinkers, ranging from Rickert, Windleband, and Weber to Bergson, Scheler, Fichte, and Husserl. This eclecticism did not sit well with materialist Marxists,† who dismissed his unorthodox empirical method with disdain and confusion. Like other empirically oriented Marxists (e.g. Eduard Bernstein,* Lucio Colletti,* and Galvano Della Volpe*), Gurvitch critically rejected Cartesianism. Reality is a totality of interacting, heterogeneous factors. Terms like subjectivity and objectivity are volatile, constantly created and recreated as individual existence interacts with and is defined by social existence. Naively separating actors and environments hides this linkage. All aspects of social life—from a citizen's consciousness of himself and others to the structures of political and social institutions, class formation, and the global features of civilization itself—dynamically interact. The specific form each takes is conditioned by the totality, the collectivity of interrelated factors. Since there is no dominant factor, orthodox Marxism is as abstract and unrealistic as Cartesianism. The former gestates a hegemonic party of scientists ruthlessly "perfecting" reality; the latter, a society of "free" homunculi who helplessly watch mystical economic laws guarantee inequality. A dynamic reality needs a dynamic method. Only dialectics eliminates abstractionism and explains society as it really is. Dialectics encompasses five interrelated processes that are also exhibited by social phenomena, hence authentically reflects reality. It accounts for the movement of social totalities and exposes their tensions, oppositions, and conflicts, without squeezing these into preconceived categories. In sum, dialectical method accurately and nondogmatically depicts objective social relationships. Social scientists must use it to accumulate data impersonally according to accepted empirical procedures. Science describes, not interprets, reality. Gurvitch's dialectical method is therefore "hyperempirical" in depicting observable facts and eschewing reductionism.

Gurvitch perceived hyperempirical dialectics in Marx's pre-1846 work, where society is an irreducible collective activity, a whole constituting the factors comprising its content. Marx's dialectic, then, is part of humanity's purposive involvement with nature. The interpenetration of subject and object defines life's real movement; intentionality occurs within, and reflects, objective being. For the early Marx, the dialectical totality is prior to subject and object, hence materialism and idealism are equally misconceived. Marx's mature, work, however, equivocates. A reductionist material metaphysic is gradually frozen in the work of Friedrich Engels,† Karl Kautsky,† Georgii Plekhanov,† and Vladimir Lenin. Dialectical materialism, a term Gurvitch believed Marx never would have used, and at least prior to 1846 would have found repugnant, occludes reality with abstractions. For Gurvitch, orthodox, reductionist Marxism had lost the true meaning of dialectics. The social totality, a whole determining and expressing its parts, is irreducible. Social science renders these complex interrelationships intelligible through observation and description. Hence the totality lives, scientifically, in isolated empirical facts. However, this endless barrage of data is meaningless unless heuristically categorized. Gurvitch therefore acknowledged the artificiality and the necessity of compartmentalizing the social sciences. His own solution for organizing a dynamic, multidimensional reality into manageable categories that facilitate data collecting is "depth sociology." Gurvitch sliced reality into a series of "horizontal" and "vertical" categories: the former categorizing forms of social life (ranging from spontaneous sociability, through groups and classes, to organized and structured global societies); the latter, depth levels marking the structure and intensity of social interaction (ranging from the spontaneous and mystical "collective mind," which indelibly imprints the collective on each individual consciousness, to increasingly structured forms of social behavior such as revolutionary action and social roles, to society's most structured organizations and institutions). Vertical and horizontal constantly intersect while, internally, levels interpenetrate. Each level on both poles, therefore, is a moment of the whole, indissolubly linked to other levels and the totality. The categories are thus heuristically useful rather than real, functioning to structure empirical data before self-destructing when evidence is in and complex interconnections established. They represent convenient racks to hang his own multifaceted research, including sociologies of knowledge, law, time perception, and morality. Hyperempirical dialectical inquiry generates social science. Factual data unfold regularities among various aspects of the totality, illustrating correspondences between groups of social phenomena. The entire factual ensemble indicates social patterns or movements, not unilinear causal relationships. This evidence, embodied in Gurvitch's empirical studies, confirms the basic principles of historical materialism.

Gurvitch was thus uncomfortable not with the substance of Marxism, but with its dogmatic materialist reductionism. Moreover, he admired Western empirical research despite its idealistic Cartesianism. Like other empirically oriented Marxists, Gurvitch's social science was factual. But he did not deductively apply Marx's hypotheses. Hyperempirical inquiry, which accumulates quantities of dialectically linked facts, constituted its own theory. Valid social theory is inductive rather than deductive, cumulatively drawn from perceived facts rather than applied to organize and explain them. Gurvitch's hyperempiricism inductively verifies most of Marx's historical hypotheses. Speaking factually, capitalism collapses because it cannot mute inherent class-related contradictions, but not before a spasmodic ''fascist techno-bureaucratic'' adventure that brutally destroys bourgeois liberties while claiming to save them. Although evidence is not yet entirely in, Western civilization leans historically toward cooperative, nonalienated socialism, a society of direct working-class hegemony. Economic self-management radically diminishes the state's legitimate role, turning it—on the domestic front, at least—into the ''administrator of things'' that Marx anticipated. Personally, Gurvitch evaluated this transition from capitalism to socialism as both desirable and highly likely, given available evidence. However, the hyperempirical inductive method prohibits moral or deductive generalizations. Gurvitch, in other words, rejected the unity of facts and values. Scientists impersonally accumulate data and generate hypothetical theories. Once the dialectical conceptual framework replaced Cartesianism, Gurvitch insisted on the absolute integrity of factual evidence. It would, for Gurvitch, be inconsistent to advocate a revolutionary politics when scientifically committed to empirical facts, wherever they lead. Thus Gurvitch factually crammed the dialectical grid, stripping capitalism to its self-destructive core and coolly surmising the immanence of a socialist future.

BIBLIOGRAPHY:

A. *Introduction à la théorie du droit international* (Prague, 1923); *Les tendences actuelles de la philosophie allemande* (Paris: Vrin, 1930); *Le Temps présent et l'idée du droit social* (Paris: Vrin, 1932); *Essais de sociologie* (Paris: Vrin, 1938); *Eléments de sociologie juridique* (Paris: Aubier, 1940); *Sociology of Law* (New York: Macmillan, 1942); *La Déclaration des droits sociaux* (Paris: Vrin, 1946); *La Vocation actuelle de la sociologie* (Paris: P.U.F., 1950); ''Hyper-empirisme dialectique,'' *Cahiers internationaux de sociologie*, 15 (1953); *Déterminismes sociaux et liberté humaine* (Paris: P.U.F., 1955); *Dialectique et sociologie* (Paris: Flammarion, 1962); *Les Cadres sociaux de la connaissance* (Paris: P.U.F., 1966); *Etudes sur les classes sociales* (Paris: Denoël-Gonthier, 1966).

B. George Balandier et al., *Perspectives de la sociologie contemporaine: Hommage à Georges Gurvitch* (Paris: Vrin, 1968); Phillip Bosserman, *Dialectical Sociology: An Analysis of the Sociology of Georges Gurvitch* (Boston: Beacon Press, 1968).

ROBERT A. GORMAN

H

HABERMAS, JÜRGEN (b. 1929). Born in Düsseldorf on 18 June 1929 and raised in Nazi Germany, Habermas studied at the universities of Göttingen, Zurich, and Bonn. He became radicalized during the late 1950s after studying with Theodore Adorno* and reading Marx† and Freud. He taught philosophy at the University of Heidelberg during the years 1961–64 and later took a chair in philosophy and sociology at the University of Frankfurt. In 1972, after formally leaving the Frankfurt School, Habermas moved to the Max Planck Institute in Starnberg, West Germany.

Habermas is undoubtedly the most influential thinker in Germany today. He has been a central figure in numerous debates concerning key issues of methodology, philosophy, and politics, including his long-standing dialogue with Karl Popper (the "Positivismusstreit") that dominated German philosophy and sociology in the 1960s, a debate with Gadamer regarding the relevance of hermeneutics to social theory, and a debate with Luhmann over systems theory. He has formulated a theory of communicative competence that integrates linguistic philosophy and social theory, developed theories of action and social evolution, and provided a normative philosophical foundation for the Frankfurt School's version of critical theory. Habermas, in brief, has significantly contributed to so many varied scholarly areas that he becomes impossible to summarize effectively. This brief essay will focus primarily on his attempts to reformulate critical theory, probably his most important contribution to the evolution of Marxian social theory.

At Adorno's death and Max Horkheimer's* ideological and religious conversions, critical theory displayed the trappings of mystical intellectualism. Habermas, the obvious heir to the Frankfurt legacy, wanted to reestablish links between theory and practice without violating critical theory's rigorous antireductionism. *Theorie und Praxis* (1963), *Erkenntnis und Interesse* (1968), and "Technik und Wissenschaft als 'Ideologie' " (1970) all display the postwar Frankfurt School's antipositivist bias but with a new twist. For Habermas, scientific frameworks justify and rationalize practical human interests. Positivism, the dominant contemporary mode of scientific inquiry, is based on nontheoretical real interests, in relation to which it is objective. No transcendental grounding exists for positivism or any other science. Habermas thus echoes critical theory's rejection of absolutes. However, this revised formula assumes that knowledge (theory) is verified through the practical activities of concerned actors (praxis), hence a glimmer of optimism regarding the human condition. Although interests alone determine a science's "objectivity," critical theorists can now ascertain practical interests appropriate to reflective critique and act to satisfy them—thereby justifying critical theory. For Habermas, human interest "establishes the unity between . . . [each] constitutive context in which knowledge is rooted and the structure of the possible application which this knowledge can have" (*Theory and Practice*, p. 9). Science justifies and operationalizes practical interests. Each science, therefore, generates knowledge having a pragmatic function. Habermas examined three possible sciences representing three distinct human interests, each with a unique meaning, object, and method that collectively comprise its criteria of objectivity.

In everyday activities, actors encounter bodies, things, events, and conditions that are intentionally manipulated. The technical knowledge required to manipulate phenomena successfully toward desired ends is supplied by empirical-analytical science, theoretically rationalized by positivism. Empirical science provides knowledge for controlling the universe, satisfying a "technical human interest" through an instrumental technology. Empirical methods are open, flexible, and inductive, qualities popular in social systems based on individual liberty and governmental restraint. Empirical science also proclaims the epistemological priority of isolated facts, reinforcing societies already split into seemingly unrelated categories such as politics, economic, jurisprudence, art, and religion. It generates technically complex commodities that are profitably sold to consumers conditioned by technology to buy. Finally, empirical scientists unquestioningly accept existing economic and social institutions, hence are smoothly integrated into capitalist utility structures. By implication, empirical science supports bureaucratic socialist systems as well, given the necessary political room to grow. Empirical science, in sum, generates technical knowledge used by powerful social interests. But in living socially we also encounter intelligent, sentient actors whose use of language, knowledge, and consciousness resemble ours but whose irreducible subjectivity makes them unique and different. To survive, human beings must communicate with other symbol-using actors by using language and everyday processes of symbolic interaction. Our "practical human interest" of communicating with and understanding fellow human beings creates the need for hermeneutic or cultural science, manifest in myth, religion, nonspiritual idealism, historicism, pragmatism, and so on. Hermeneutic science provides a symbolic foundation for intersubjectivity, a means for cognizing the complexes of meanings that others experience and a basis for working cooperatively. Throughout history, until the present, hermeneutic science was the legitimating social ideology, underlying "objective" inquiry as well as justifying ancient and medieval institutions. Now, however, empirical science has replaced hermeneutics. Contemporary technological society emphasizes manipulation and control rather than cognitive understanding and communication. Empirical science objectifies humanity by stressing structural similarities between human and nonhuman phenomena and then developing techniques of domination. Technological humanity neither thinks morally nor perceives others as qualitatively unique. It seeks technical efficiency, not the good life, hence impersonally manipulates human life.

Habermas believes that technological society eliminates symbolic communication and interaction, abrogating the social aspects of individuality. Actors live as isolated, manipulated units, oblivious to cognitive symbolic connections bonding humanity. These anomic lives are dominated by ignorance and helplessness. "Domination," then, means social interaction exhibiting "distorted communication," the inability to communicate effectively and intersubjectively ("Toward a Theory of Communicative Competence," p. 144). Humanity thus has a residual need to reestablish communicative links with others, what Habermas calls an "emancipatory human interest." Critical science cognitively negates technological society. Its method is critical and reflective, questioning both naively internalized technological structures and empirical reasoning. Practical consequences of emancipatory science include the elimination of restrictions on communication. In practice, it ends social repression and rigidity, permitting "progressive individuation" ("Technology and Science as Ideology," in *Toward a Rational Society*, p. 119). By establishing intersubjective communication, humanity takes the necessary first step toward social justice. A step that self-consciously negates positivism and acknowledges the reciprocal connections between and among individuals and institutions, the interpenetration of self and other, subject and object, theory and praxis. Emancipatory science, in other words, is critical and dialectical. Emancipation requires new reflective forms of intersubjective knowledge and communication. Habermas thus used hermeneutics to mediate domination and liberation. We can negate technology with new reflective answers to practical problems, which we communicate intersubjectively. Hermeneutic science is reborn in the human need to transmit liberating knowledge to others. Habermas feels that Freudianism is useful to this process of communicating and understanding critical knowledge. Psychoanalysis liberates oppressed personalities who have subconsciously internalized and hidden a seminal childhood conflict. Neurotic symptoms like slips of the tongue, deviant linguistic practices, and compulsive repetition indicate that the original repressed conflict has inhibited effective communication, in extreme cases generating an incommunicable private language. Freudian psychoanalysis, in other words, is based on a theory of linguistic failure, Habermas's "distorted communication." By self-consciously contemplating relevant symptoms and acknowledging repressed sources, analysands restore the primal conflict to open, public communication. Reflection liberates by facilitating free communication among nonrepressed, critical thinkers rationally shaping the future. Critical social science "socioanalyzes" social systems as Freudian psychoanalysis does individuals, opening up "the hidden pathology of collective behavior and entire social systems'' (''Towards a Theory of Communicative Competence,'' pp. 117–18).

In evaluating Marx, Habermas, like Horkheimer and Adorno, offers lukewarm, equivocating praise. As a critic of bourgeois political economy, vividly contrasting assumptions and reality, Marx is without equal. But this is not critical social science, for it leaves unanswered important epistemological and practical questions concerning criteria of validity, the nature of freedom, and the meaning of authentic praxis. When Marx did struggle with foundational theoretical and practical issues, he abandoned the critical perspective. Metaphysical materialism plagues much of Marx's work, a remnant of eighteenth- and nineteenth-century a priorism, which now justifies Communist Party hegemony. Moreover, what Marx could not foresee was the capitalist state's gradual expansion into non-political realms. Today, the laissez-faire bourgeois state has been replaced by one actively involved, via its own technological apparatus, in all segments of social life, streamlining social organization and upgrading productive efficiency. The state, like the capitalist economy, now actively supports technical interests. Since human domination feeds on instrumentalism, the capitalist state as well as its productive apparatus play equal roles in oppressing workers—and neither is autonomous. Consequently, technical rationality is reinforced economically, socially, politically, and ideologically, saturating every aspect of social life and infecting every citizen, worker and nonworker alike. Although a capitalist economy dialectically expresses and reinforces technical rationality, Marx's theory that it causes oppression is outdated. Similarly, class antagonism only partially explains contemporary domination. As sophisticated technology streamlines material production and an increasingly active bourgeois state eliminates its gross social malfunctions, workers' living conditions will likely improve, complicating the meaning and consequences of class struggle. Marx's theory of the proletariat's progressive immiseration—relative or absolute—is irrelevant in modern capitalism, where class struggle is no longer the prime instigator of meaningful social change. Economism reflects traditional, noncritical epistemologies and only dresses domination in new clothes. Capitalism's working class is not necessarily a revolutionary vanguard, although authentic change will emancipate everyone, including the working class.

Habermas thus replaces Marx's objective economic categories, that is, the means and relationships of production, with the concepts of labor and symbolically mediated interaction. Marx believed that productive forces determine the quality of human labor. Habermas defines labor as instrumental behavior: rationally manipulating nature to satisfy material needs. The growth of technological productive forces extends our power of technical control, hence increases the efficiency and effectiveness of labor. Marx also believed objective productive relationships determine the quality of social oppression, that is, the dominant economic class forges supportive social values and institutions. Habermas defines oppression in terms of symbolic communication, the extant norms, institutions, and language by which individuals understand others and communicate interpersonally—that is, hermeneutic or practical knowledge. As technical replaces practical knowledge, the ability to think and communicate effectively atrophies. Instrumental labor, which should be an effective means for realizing a reflective end, becomes an end in itself. Human beings are depersonalized and manipulated by dominating owners of technology. Emancipation requires praxis (instrumental labor) reuniting with theory (symbolic communication), a process that accompanies reflective social critique. Labor is then goal-oriented and purposive; society's productive capacity fulfills reflective human needs, not narrow interests. Marx, finally, believed socialism an inevitable historical product of objective matter. Habermas connects revolution to reflective critique, without speculating on the precise quality of postrevolutionary economics. The latter is born in reflective knowledge and grows soon enough after human communication is reestablished.

In a practical political sense, however, Habermas is vague in describing how to evaluate the quality of critical thinking and the utility of concrete actions. He has no positive answers, even admitting his is a "prepolitical" form of discourse, still incapable of drawing "the consequences of knowledge directed toward liberation" (*Theory and Practice*, pp. 15–16). Consequently, Habermas exhorts us to think critically, reflectively negate existing institutions and values, oppose economic, political, and social domination, but also be wary of instigating state violence or falling to ideological dogmatism. Although enlightened students should "permanently destroy . . . [capitalism's] crumbling achievement-ideology, and thus bring down the already fragile legitimizing basis of advanced capitalism" ("Technology and Science as Ideology" p. 122), they must also acknowledge "the danger of diversion either into the privatization of an easily consolable hippie subculture or into the fruitless violent acts of the actionists" ("Student Protest in the Federal Republic of Germany," in *Toward a Rational Society*, p. 26). There are apparently no absolute criteria for determining where the former ends and the latter begins, so Habermas's revised critical theory occasionally flaunts the narrow line separating senseless word games from practical advice.

Habermas defines humanity's three basic "interests" as "deep-seated . . . which direct our knowledge and which have a quasi-transcendental status" (*Theory and Practice*, p. 37). They are, as well, invariant and abstract, the fundamental natural interests of mankind, not merely the limited historical interests of a particular class. All this sounds vaguely idealist. Habermas, the heir to Frankfurt critical theory, was "embarrassed" with "quasi-transcendental" phenomena and argued plaintively against "transcendental logics" based on "intelligible egos" or other identity theories (ibid., pp. 14–22). But Habermas's human interests appear to be a naturally evolving intersubjective framework permitting communicative discourse, allowing humanity to contemplate and discuss technical, practical, and emancipatory issues. They precede praxis and structure valid knowledge in each realm. Habermas cannot turn "interests" into a strictly empirical concept because this abolishes objectivity, generating a multitude of unique interests and personal sciences. Hence the "quasi-transcendental" terminology, an awkward midpoint between idealism and negativity. Habermas personally resolved the tension by admitting that these are tentative "speculations," not the final word. However, his formal resignation from the Frankfurt School in 1972 indicates the problem's true dimensions. Moreover, his later communication theory extends, rather than repudiates, these insights.

BIBLIOGRAPHY:

A. *Strukturwandel des Öffentlichkeit* (Neuwied: Luchterhand, 1962); ed., *Antworten auf Herbert Marcuse* (Frankfurt: Suhrkamp, 1968); *Toward a Rational Society* (Boston: Beacon Press, 1970); "Towards a Theory of Communicative Competence," in *Recent Sociology, Number Two*, ed. Peter Dreitzel (London: Macmillan, 1970); *Knowledge and Human Interests* (Boston: Beacon Press, 1971); *Philosophisch-politische Profile* (Frankfurt: Suhrkamp, 1971); *Theory and Practice* (Boston: Beacon Press, 1974); *Legitimation Crisis* (Boston: Beacon Press, 1976); *Communication and the Evolution of Society* (Boston: Beacon Press, 1979).

B. Thomas McCarthy, *The Critical Theory of Jürgen Habermas* (Cambridge: MIT Press, 1978); David Held, *Introduction to Critical Theory: Horkheimer to Habermas* (Berkeley: University of California Press, 1980); John Thompson and David Held, eds., *Habermas: Critical Debates* (Cambridge: MIT Press, 1982).

ROBERT A. GORMAN

HALL, STUART (b. 1932). Born in Kingston, Jamaica, in 1932, to parents who were members of an emergent, upwardly mobile, black commercial middle class, Hall attended Merton College, Oxford, as a Rhodes scholar in 1951 (and later as a Jamaica scholar), where he studied literature and became increasingly involved in West Indian politics. In the mid-1950s, he was founding member of the revived Socialist Club and, later, of the New Left Club. The publication of *Universities and Left Review* gave this group a forum in which to challenge the established left's inability to deal with issues of racism and imperialism, on the one hand, and culture and literature, on the other. The concrete forms that these issues took were a concern with the analysis of class and society in late capitalism and with the introduction of the cultural question into politics. Articulating a humanistic and culturally oriented reading of Marxism under the influence of Raymond Williams,* Richard Hoggart, and others, they rejected both the revisionism of the Labour Party and the mechanistic views of the Communist Party. In 1959 *Universities and Left Review* merged with *The New Reasoner* (then under the leadership of Edward P. Thompson*), and the *New Left Review* was begun with Hall as its first editor. After a number of teaching positions, he became a research fellow and assistant to the director of the Centre for Contemporary Cultural Studies at the University of Birmingham in 1964, eventually becoming its director in 1974 (after serving as acting director since 1969). He left the Centre in 1979 to become Professor of Sociology at the Open University. Hall has been a leader in the Campaign for Nuclear Disarmament as well as in various movements to combat racism in England and he has emerged, in the 1980s, as one of the left's most articulate spokespersons in the struggle against the so-called new right and in the attempt to forge a new political and intellectual alliance based on a "Marxism without guarantees."

It is this attempt to construct a cultural Marxism that foregrounds the possibilities of struggle and contestation that will, no doubt, secure Hall's stature within the history of Marxism. Exploring the relations between social practices and their representations in discourse, Hall has sought to articulate a nonreductionist theory of determination, ideology, and hegemony. Rejecting the humanistic class reductionism of Williams and Thompson, in which there is a necessary correspondence or determination between social practices and social positions, Hall follows Louis Althusser's* reconceptualization of the social formation as the unity of a complex totality within which social practices are overdetermined. And although Hall was largely responsible for the uniquely British engagement with Althusser's work, he rejects the theoreticism and functionalism of Althusser's position, as well as the view of many of Althusser's followers that would deny any unity and correspondence. Between the humanists' necessary correspondence and the discourse theorists necessary noncorrespondence, Hall argues that such correspondences may be brought about through the actions of social groups. Particular practices may be "articulated" together, thus creating the possibility of particular connections as the effects rather than the origins of social practice and determination. Furthermore, Hall argues, the complexity of the social formation cannot be reduced to the operation of a single simple contradiction; there are multiple contradictions, and no one of them can be identified as universally and primarily determining. Rather, different contradictions have different pertinences at different sites of articulation and struggle. Thus, the theory of determination is replaced by a theory of the struggle to articulate particular social practices (and social positions) together, a struggle to produce particular effects.

Similarly, when approaching the question of the articulation of ideology in discourse, Hall attempts to define ideology as a field of possible sites of contradiction and contestation, albeit one that is never entirely open. Ideology involves chains of discursive or connotative links that articulate particular ideological elements to particular social positions and is thus centrally implicated in the construction of social difference and identity. But it is not reducible to this interpellating function. Although we cannot live outside of ideology because all social practices come to be represented in ideology, not all social practices are ideological, and there is no guaranteed one-to-one relation between lived social relations and their ideological representations. Hall emphasizes both the objective character of real social relations and the situation of the subject by social, political, and economic as well as ideological practices. To say that ideology is a field of struggle is, for Hall, to recognize that the world has to be made to mean and that discourse and ideology are not equivalent, that their articulation together is always the site of power and resistance. Discourse is the site on which ideology is inscribed, de-inscribed, and re-inscribed.

The notion of hegemony, grounded in the work of Antonio Gramsci,* has become a central point in many attempts to understand the power relations of contemporary capitalism. Hall rejects any reading of hegemony as simply ideological or cultural incorporation, arguing that it is the process of the formation of an historic bloc that can mobilize popular support for historic tasks. According to his reading of Gramsci, hegemony is about leadership rather than domination, containment rather than incorporation. The historic bloc must establish for itself the leading position on a variety of social and political sites. Within these spaces, the subordinate groups are allowed to develop their own practices, but always within the subordinate position and always in a language defined by others. Hegemony involves the colonization of the popular, or of common sense. Thus, the real task of the historic bloc is to make a new common sense for particular historic tasks. Hegemony is not merely a process, but a process that can appear only under particular conditions, and the attempt to oppose the hegemony process must similarly operate on every front, itself seeking to forge a new practical consciousness. The struggle must be to disarticulate particular hegemonic moments, recognizing that any such struggle may be ideologically impure and contradictory since there can be no guarantee of the intrinsically progressive or regressive nature of a particular cultural form.

The struggle to articulate practices together is an accurate description as well of Hall's reading of Marx's epistemology, according to which theory involves a movement between levels of abstraction and determination in an attempt to produce the concrete in thought. This commitment to the concrete, and to struggle, undergirds much of the work of the Centre for Contemporary Cultural Studies, under Hall's leadership, despite the fact that much of the published work is the result of collective efforts. The Centre produced studies of working-class culture, education, youth subcultures, racism, mass media, and gender politics, all framed within the struggle to articulate power and resistance. Hall's most important contribution to this body of empirical work remains, however, in the area of mass media. Rejecting the idea of the media as the ideological cement that binds the population under hegemonic rule, Hall refused to assume that people were mesmerized by the ideology of the media. Rather than seeing the media as agents of ideological mystification, Hall proposed an ''encoding-decoding'' model that would enable the analyst to read the media texts themselves as attempts to articulate particular ideological positions on the one hand, while recognizing that audiences bring to these messages their own cultural and ideological resources, which allow them to decode the texts in a range of alternative ways in their attempt to articulate the particular discourses to their own social relations on the other hand. Once again, it is struggle and contestation, always concrete and local, that define the focus for Hall's ''Marxism without guarantees.''

BIBLIOGRAPHY:

A. With others, *Policing the Crisis: Mugging, the State, and Law and Order* (London: Macmillan, 1978); with Dorothy Hobson, Andrew Lowe, and Paul Willis, eds., *Culture,*

Media, Language (London: Hutchinson, 1980); *Reproducing Ideologies* (London: Macmillan, 1984).

LAURENCE GROSSBERG

HARRINGTON, EDWARD MICHAEL (b. 1928). A Catholic social worker turned socialist then socialist reformer, democratic socialist, and neo-Marxist scholar, Michael Harrington was born in St. Louis, Missouri, on 24 February 1928. He was raised in an atmosphere of enlightened Catholicism and, after attending parochial school in St. Louis, graduated from the Jesuit institution Holy Cross College in Worcester, Massachusetts, in 1947. He attended Yale Law School for one year before transferring to the University of Chicago, where he received an M.A. in English literature in 1949. After college he worked briefly as a social worker in St. Louis before moving to New York City in 1951 to join the staff of the Catholic Worker, a Catholic social agency, and to coedit its official publication, *The Catholic Worker*. Here he had his first in-depth experiences with poverty and the problems of the poor, and here he embraced the bohemian radicalism of the city to become a devout working-class idealist and agitator for the cause of the poor and oppressed. Harrington was a conscientious objector during the Korean War and adopted pacifism as his commitment to the left deepened during the 1950s and 1960s. In 1953 he joined the Young People's Socialist League, a leftist student organization, as an organizer and speaker touring college campuses. In that year he also became the organizational secretary for the Workers Defense League, a labor-oriented human rights organization. Finally, in 1953, he also joined the Socialist Party, serving on its National Executive Committee from 1960 to 1968, editing its official organ, *New America*, from 1961 to 1962, and served as the party's national chairman, replacing Norman Thomas, from 1968 to 1972. In 1954 Harrington joined the staff of the Fund for the Republic, an educational corporation affiliated with the University of California, where he worked on their study of blacklisting in the entertainment industry and served as a consultant to their Trade Union Project. In 1962 Harrington achieved national attention after the publication of his *The Other America: Poverty in the United States*, one of the key publications of the early 1960s, helping to bring the issue of poverty to public attention in affluent America and giving impetus to the Johnson administration's "War on Poverty." This notoriety brought him to the attention of the emerging new left. However, his loyality to trade unionism, the civil rights movement, and the democratic process quickly identified him with the dreaded old left. And although he remained in close contact with the major new left organization, the Students for a Democratic Society (SDS), his experience with the new left was basically a disappointing one. During the 1960s his more important political involvement was with old left organizations, like the Socialist Party, the A. Philip Randolph Institute, an organization devoted to establishing cooperation between American labor and the black community, and the League for Industrial Democracy, a labor organization established in 1905. During this period Harrington was also

actively involved in the civil rights struggle of Dr. Martin Luther King, Jr. In
1972 Harrington split with the Socialist Party and resigned as national chairman
over issues surrounding American involvement in the war in Vietnam. His antiwar faction formed a new socialist organization, the Democratic Socialist Organizing Committee, of which he was cochairman from 1973 to 1982. Also in
1972, Harrington began an academic career as a professor of political science
at Queens College in Flushing, New York. Here he has also continued a successful writing career as a neo-Marxist scholar and radical commentator on
American politics. In 1982 the DSOC merged with the New America Movement,
and Harrington is currently the national chairman of the offspring organization,
the Democratic Socialists of America.

Harrington's thought, although ideologically rooted, has never been dogmatic.
Developing out of progressive Catholicism, his political thinking is profoundly
moral and ethical. Throughout his writings, he remains more a humanist than
an ideologue, and yet, beginning in the early 1970s, his thinking matured into
a scholarly and intelligent dissection of Marxist† thought. Harrington's neo-
Marxist writings have been a quest for the "real" Marx behind the facade of
orthodox Marxism-Leninism. As an academic writer, Harrington's task has been
to humanize and democratize Marx by focusing upon what he feels are two
fundamental Marxian principles. First is the collective principle, or the principle
of oneness. This is the faith in the logical and moral unity of the human species.
Second is the principle of praxis, or the faith in the potential and capacity of
man to create and to change his world through his own efforts. Harrington's
reinterpretation of Marx sees man as a free agent, perhaps locked in a material
struggle, but bound only in an ethical sense by his humanity. From these two
principles Harrington takes Marx in the direction of democratic socialism, where
the search for a more equal and less competitive social order is seen as a moral
imperative that can be arrived at only through a democratic process. True socialism, although perhaps logically inherent in the dialectic of oneness, can only
be achieved when ethically sanctioned through a democratic process. According
to Harrington, socialism is therefore the only rational and humanistic social order
possible and the only social order that can exist truly in the name of the people.

Harrington's unique contribution to neo-Marxism is his theory of "radical
liberalism," by which he attempts to balance the virtues of socialist justice and
liberal freedom. Harrington favors reassembling the old New Deal coalition of
labor, intellectuals, and minorities which, until recently, has flourished on the
left of the Democratic Party in America. This progressive coalition can work
within America's electoral system to bring about legislation that places major
economic investment decisions under the control of workers themselves nego-
tiating cooperatively with management and government—thus realizing the New
Deal's promise of economic and social justice. Harrington contends that democracy can survive neither in capitalist nor orthodox Marxist systems, both of
which are elitist. His brand of socialism is therefore non-dogmatic regarding the
extent of required expropriation and the quality of political leadership. He is

inclined to preserve those elements of capitalism and liberalism that reinforce the democratic spirit of his ideal socialist community, and traces this self-described philosophy of "spiritual materialism" back to what he calls the "unknown Marx:" the Marx who Harrington argues was committed to human fulfillment, socialist democracy, and peaceful change. Radical liberalism thus falls somewhere between left and right in America, and on most political issues Harrington can count on the support of neither.

BIBLIOGRAPHY:

A. *The Other America: Poverty in the United States* (New York: Macmillan, 1962); *The Accidental Century* (New York: Macmillan, 1965); *Toward a Democratic Left: A Radical Program for a New Majority* (Baltimore: Penguin Books, 1969); *Socialism* (New York: Saturday Review Press, 1972); *Fragments of the Century* (New York: Simon and Schuster, 1973); *The Twilight of Capitalism* (New York: Simon and Schuster, 1976); *Decade of Decision* (New York: Simon and Schuster, 1980).

B. Kenneth M. Dolbeare and Patricia Dolbeare, *American Ideologies: The Competing Political Beliefs of the 1970s* (Chicago: Markham, 1971); Philip L. Beardsley, *Conflicting Ideologies in Political Economy: A Synthesis* (Beverly Hills, Calif.: Sage, 1981).

CHARLES W. HAMPTON

HAUG, WOLFGANG FRITZ (b. 1936). Born in 1936 in Esslingen/Neckar, Haug received his doctorate in 1965 with a study on Jean-Paul Sartre* and the concept of the absurd. Since 1959 he has edited the journal *Das Argument*, and he also teaches philosophy at the Free University in West Berlin. During the late 1960s he contributed to the radicalization of the student movement with his attack on the "helpless antifascism" characteristic of West German academics unwilling to thematize a link between capitalism and national socialism but prepared to denounce allegedly fascist features of Soviet-style societies and of the domestic new left.

Haug's initial study of the social function of advertising displays the influence of the Frankfurt School and especially the culture industry thesis of Max Horkheimer* and Theodore Adorno.* Advertising is located within a totalitarian structure of domination, manipulation, and deceit ("Zur Ästhetik von Manipulation," 1963). In contrast, the later examination of sensuality and needs in capitalism draws on the materialism of *Capital* by commencing with basic relations of exchange out of which the categories of a "commodity aesthetics" are derived. For Haug, aesthetics are not tied primarily to works of art but refer instead to a *cognitio sensitiva*, sensuous knowledge, and the related problems of illusion and appearance. "Commodity aesthetics" describes the emergence of the primacy of appearance in the act of commodity exchange as the corollary to the degeneration of the use-value of the object (*Kritik der Warenästhetik*, p. 10). The elaborated system of appearance as a "technocracy of sensuality," designed to guarantee the accumulation of wealth and, more generally, social and political power, is not unique in capitalism but there takes on a general character that replaces all concrete substance with illusion:

Capitalism is based on a systematic quid pro quo: all human goals, including life itself, are only means and excuses for the system (not in theory but in their factual economic function). The position of capital valuation as a goal in itself . . . radically opposes that which individuals themselves are and desire. In abstract terms: what individuals mediate with capital can only be illusory. (ibid., p. 57)

The systematic illusion leads to the contemporary "illusion industry" (ibid., p. 152) and to fascism, which, thanks to what Walter Benjamin* designated as its "aestheticization of politics," can present itself as the illusion of socialism (ibid., pp. 169–73).

BIBLIOGRAPHY:

A. *Jean-Paul Sartre und die Konstruktion des Absurden* (Frankfurt: Suhrkamp, 1966); *Der hilflose Antifaschismus: zur Kritik der Vorlesungsreihen über Wissenschaft und Nationalsozialismus an den deutschen Universitäten* (Frankfurt: Suhrkamp, 1967); *Kritik der Warenästhetik* (Frankfurt: Suhrkamp, 1971); *Vorlesungen zur Einführung ins Kapital* (Cologne: Pahl-Rugenstein, 1974); *Warenästhetik: Beiträge zur Diskussion, Weiterentwicklung und Vermittlung ihrer Kritik* (Frankfurt: Suhrkamp, 1975).

B. Peter Uwe Hohendahl, "Politisierung der Kunsttheorie: Zur ästhetischen Diskussion nach 1965," in *Deutsche Literatur in der Bundesrepublik seit 1965: Untersuchungen und Berichte*, ed. Paul Michael Lützeler and Egon Schwarz (Königstein/Ts.: Athenäum, 1980).

RUSSELL BERMAN

HAVEMANN, ROBERT (1910–1982). The East German Robert Havemann worked after 1937 as a research fellow in chemistry at the University of Berlin. Due to his activities in the antifascist resistance movement he was sentenced to death in 1943, but kept in prison because of the importance of his research for the war. After World War II he was a research fellow at the Kaiser-Wilhelm-Institut in West Berlin. He was dismissed there because of his Communist agitation, especially his attacks against American nuclear armament. From 1950 to 1964 he was a director of the Institute for Physics and Chemistry at Humboldt University in East Berlin and a member of the East German parliament, the People's Chamber of the German Democratic Republic (GDR). After 1964 he was expelled both from the university and the Socialist Unity Party because of his criticism of established communism. He had proposed, for example, the founding of a new West German Communist Party (which actually came into being in 1968). After 1964 he continued to criticize the GDR government. Because he had no other choice, he published his books and articles in the West. Shortly before his death he became a founding member of the autonomous peace movement in the GDR.

Havemann had already criticized dogmatism while still a Party member and a member of the People's Chamber. He started as early as 1953 with a trenchant criticism of both Lysenko's thoughts about genetics and the positions of his opponents. Eventually he extended his attacks to include a critique of mechanical materialism. He tried to revitalize the ethical elements of early Marxism,† including the concepts of worker solidarity, resistance, and reflective critique.

Nevertheless he still considered the GDR and the Soviet Union to be basically socialist in nature. In his view a "second step" was necessary, a step from public ownership of the means of production to a democratic political system, thus creating democratic socialism. The Soviet intervention in Czechoslovakia in 1968 made it quite clear to Havemann that such a second step was not very easy, that he had underestimated the relative autonomy of the Party apparatus. During the 1970s he still considered the GDR to be the better Germany, and he was still fighting anticommunism. "Eurocommunism" seemed to him to be a great hope. But his criticism of the GDR became increasingly sharp, and he changed from a party reformer "from within" to a "dissident" advocating "liberal" policies such as freedom of opinion, releasing political prisoners, and abolishing censorship. By the mid-1970s he was even in favor of an alliance with certain members of the Protestant church.

At the beginning of the 1980s Havemann was strictly opposed to the deployment of new missiles in both parts of Germany. He signed an appeal calling not only for nondeployment but also for withdrawal of "all occupational powers" from German soil (including the withdrawal of the Soviet army from the GDR). In this regard he had also become a vocal advocate of the autonomous peace movement in the GDR. During his last years he turned toward issues related to the possibility of an ecological catastrophe. In his view this danger could only be prevented by a socialist revolution in the West, which could be initiated by a transition to socialist democracy in the East. Thus, the topic of a "second step" toward democratic socialism remained the *basso continuo* of his writings.
BIBLIOGRAPHY:

A. *Dialektik ohne Dogma?* (Hamburg: Rowohlt, 1964); *Questions—Answers—Questions* (Garden City, N.Y.: Doubleday, 1972); *Morgen: die Industriegesellschaft am Scherdeweg* (Munich: R. Piper, 1980).

VOLKER GRANSOW

HEIMANN, EDUARD (1889–1967). Eduard Heimann was born in Berlin on 11 July 1889. He received his doctorate from the University of Heidelberg in 1912. After World War I, Heimann held important positions in the Weimar government, particularly dealing with economic matters such as reparations and tax questions. From 1922 until 1933 Heimann held several teaching positions, specializing in economic and social policy. From 1930 to 1933 Heimann was associated with Paul Tillich in the "Kairos-Kreis," and together they edited *The New Socialist Review*. Fleeing Hitler, Heimann emigrated to the United States in 1933 and was associated with the New School for Social Research in New York. He returned to Germany in 1948, joining the faculty of the University of Hamburg, where he died in 1967.

Heimann was influenced by the revisionism of Eduard Bernstein.* Like Bernstein, Heimann surrendered Marx's† labor theory of value as well as the Marxist ideas of the abolition of the capitalist system and the revolutionary class struggle of the proletariat. Shifting the emphasis from ownership of the means of production to participation in the management of the means of production, Heimann was the initiator of "market socialism." Although he recognized the need for a planned economy, for a system of social programs that would provide for the well-being of the industrial working class, within the confines of this regulated economy Heimann recognized the need to preserve private property and a market system. Substituting regulation for expropriation, Heimann was a social theorist who attempted to outline a reformist way to social justice that differed from both capitalism and communism. Denying both Soviet totalitarianism and unrestricted capitalism, Heimann believed that social transformation could be accomplished in gradual steps through a regulated economy based upon a democratic political system.

BIBLIOGRAPHY:

A. *Sozale Theorie des Kapitalismus* (Tübingen: Mohr, 1929); *Wirtschaftsysteme und Gesellschaftssystem* (Tübingen: Mohr, 1954); *Vernunft und Religion in der modernen Gesellschaft* (Tübingen: Mohr, 1955); *Soziale Theorie der Wirtschaftsysteme* (Tübingen: Mohr, 1963).

NORMAN LEVINE

HELLER, AGNES (b. 1929). The Hungarian Agnes Heller was born in 1929. She was a disciple and assistant of George Lukács* until 1958, when she was expelled from both her university position in Budapest and the Communist Party because of "wrong and revisionist ideas." From 1958 to 1963 she taught at a secondary school in Budapest. In 1963 Heller was partly rehabilitated and permitted to do research at the Hungarian Academy of Sciences. In 1968 she signed a declaration protesting the Soviet intervention in Czechoslovakia. In 1973 she was officially attacked because her thinking was said to be both a left and a right deviation. In 1977 Agnes Heller left Hungary and went to Australia, where she teaches philosophy and sociology at La Trobe University.

Since the beginning of her scholarly work Agnes Heller has focused on the relationship between the individual and society. Most of her writings can be regarded as a direct or indirect contribution to the project of a Marxist† anthropology. Her book *Renaissance Man* was written from 1964 to 1965. She chose Renaissance man as the subject of this analysis because his chances in life are not determined by power and money alone. The decisive point is whether the individual can master his own destiny. In *Renaissance Man* Heller also stressed that all culture is a product of the needs, conflicts, and problems of everyday life. She developed these thoughts in various writings, especially in her book on everyday life (*Das Alltagsleben*, 1977). Within the framework of historical materialism she argued that individual reproduction is a relatively autonomous sphere, in contrast to the reproduction of the human species as a whole. In Heller's view, everyday life is the totality of individuals' reproductive activities, which create the possibilities for social reproduction. A liberated relationship toward everyday life has to be found in silence, in play, and in a nonmonogamous concept of free human relationships. In this way the individual simultaneously overcomes particularity and creates himself.

She elaborated this idea in her book on radical needs in Marx. By rethinking Marx's theory of needs she first draws on the young Marx's idea that a radical revolution has to be a revolution of radical needs. Examining the late Marx's economical writings she finds that there is a basic problem in Marx's theory as far as the goal of a "society of associated producers" is concerned: Who makes the decisions about how productive capacity should be allocated? Who decides when the production of goods that directly serve consumption can begin? How can each individual make such decisions? According to Heller, Marx could not answer the questions because for him they did not arise. But they have become the focal points of contemporary Marxism. She argues that in the society of associated producers a new structure of needs will emerge, and everyday life will not be built around productive labor and material consumption but around those activities and human relationships that are ends in themselves and become primary needs. Radical needs therefore shape the means by which we will live daily and comprise the goals of socialist life because they are brought into being as a consequence of the development of the *società civile* within capitalism, which cannot be satisfied within this society. They are therefore both necessary and revolutionary. Heller's theory of radical needs serves as a starting point for her analysis of both existing capitalism and so-called real socialism (from her point of view only the "society of the associated producers" is socialism). Capitalism generates a society in which needs are manipulated; however, neither do the societies of the Soviet Union and Eastern Europe satisfy radical needs. As a matter of fact, they are perhaps worse than capitalism. Heller describes this type of existing socialism as a "dictatorship over needs," i.e., a dictatorship in which the needs of the community are formulated by central institutions without social approval. Heller's theory of needs is both a theory of social formation and a theory of revolution. It is less dogmatic than traditional Marxist theory because the revolutionary character of a class, a social stratum, a political program, or a movement can be located only in the real, expressed, and conscious needs of liberated humanity.

BIBLIOGRAPHY:

A. *The Theory of Need in Marx* (London: Allison & Busby, 1976); *Das Alltagsleben* (Frankfurt: Suhrkamp, 1977); *Renaissance Man* (London: Routledge & Kegan Paul, 1978); *On Instincts* (Assen: Van Gorcum, 1979); *A Theory of Feelings* (Assen: Van Gorcum, 1979); *Dictatorship Over Needs* (New York: St. Martin's Press, 1983).

B. P. A. Rovatti, "La nozione della bisogno tra teoria politica e ideologica," in P. A. Rovatti et al., *Bisogni e teoria marxista* (Milan: Mazzotta, 1976).

VOLKER GRANSOW

HOCHFELD, JULIAN (1911–1966). Julian Hochfeld was born on 16 August 1911 in Warsaw, and died in Paris on 21 July 1966. A sociologist and political activist, Hochfeld was a professor at the Main School of Planning and Statistics in Warsaw, and later at the University of Warsaw. He was editor of several leftist periodicals and author and editor of the series Sociological-Political Studies. During the period 1962–66 he was the vice-director of the UNESCO Department of Social Studies.

A distinguished representative of leftist socialism in Poland between the wars, Hochfeld endeavored to synthesize revolutionary and democratic traditions. In the 1950s he argued that Poland and Great Britain were examples of two alternative roads to socialism. Later he reformulated this problem by developing two models by which labor is humanized. The first model is the Marxist† vision of complete liberation of labor from the shackles of capitalist alienation. The second encompasses reform programs that require step-by-step improvement of the material, cultural, and political situation of laborers. The important thing is not the form of ownership but rather the proper organization of work. This second model is characteristic of a well-developed industrial society. Here, political changes can create the overall conditions (''political precursors'') for the realization of socialism; however socialism itself can only be a result of gradual changes. Revolution in industrialized societies without the prior conclusion of these gradual reform programs is wasted and eventually abandons its primary purpose. Hochfeld argued that because the basic goals of contemporary socialism correspond to actual historical situations of particular states and radical social movements, socialism completes history's natural evolution rather than contradicts it.

Hochfeld was a disciple of ''open Marxism,'' which denoted a constant readiness to analyze and incorporate into the Marxist system all knowledge created after him. He believed empirical sociological studies were needed for the development of Marxist sociology, and he applied empirical methods in several studies of the working class and intelligentsia. In his class theory Hochfeld accented not a narrow conception of rightful ownership, but rather a concept of what he called the ''uneven division of power'' in everyday social life. He rejected the concept of the science of ideology, proclaiming a vision of science without ruthlessness, that is, impartial, free of any ideological mystification. As a characteristic feature of ideology Hochfeld noted its supportive function in relation to the group to which it is correlated.

At UNESCO he dedicated himself to conceptualizing as well as organizing widely patterned, interdisciplinary studies of human interaction.

BIBLIOGRAPHY:

A. ''Poland and Britain: Two Concepts of Socialism,'' *International Affairs*, 33, no. 1 (1957); *Marksizm, Socjologia, Socjalizm, Wybór Pism* (Warsaw: PWN, 1982).

B. W. Wesolowski and J. J. Wiatr, *Filozofia w Polsce, Slownik Pisarzy* (Wroclaw: Ossolineum, 1971).

TADEUSZ KOWALIK

HORKHEIMER, MAX (1895–1973). Max Horkheimer was born in Stuttgart, Germany, on 14 February 1895 into an assimilated Jewish bourgeois family and was educated at the universities of Munich, Freiburg, and Frankfurt am Main, where he received his Ph.D. in 1922 with a thesis on a Kantian problem. His *Habilitationschrift* of 1925 dealt with Kant's *Critique of Judgment*. He became a full professor at the University of Frankfurt and the director of the Institute for Social Research in 1931. After Hitler came to power, Horkheimer emigrated to the United States and reestablished the Institute in New York City in affiliation with Columbia University. During World War II he lived in California. As chief research consultant and director of the Research Division of the American Jewish Committee between 1945 and 1947 he instituted the series Studies in Prejudice, the best-known published work of which is *The Authoritarian Personality*, by Theodore Adorno* and others. He returned to West Germany in 1948 and became *Ordinarius* (full professor) at the University of Frankfurt. He also directed the newly established Institute until his retirement in 1959. After his retirement he moved to Switzerland. He died on 7 July 1973 in Nuremberg, Germany.

Deviating from traditional German scholarship, the bulk of Horkheimer's scholarly contribution appeared in the form of essays. Thematically, it ranges from a critique of positivistic-pragmatic philosophies of science and traditional philosophy of history to reflections on such topics as religion, family and authority, mass culture, the injustices of capitalist society, and in his later years, the evils of totalitarian-industrial societies. One can discern three distinctive phases of Horkheimer's intellectual career: the 1930s, as a critical theorist, characterized by militancy; the 1940s, arriving at a position of despair; and the 1950s and 1960s, marked by a reconciliation with West German "late capitalist" society and a religious attitude that exhibited a "yearning for God" or "Another."

The early phase of Horkheimer's critical theory emphasized both the historical dimension and the interdisciplinary method and rejected the customary academic division of labor and compartmentalization, especially the separation of philosophy and sociology. This notion was also the guiding spirit of the Institute and its research efforts, resulting in the monumental *Authority and Family* (1936). Horkheimer's aim was to develop a comprehensive Marxist† theory of late capitalist society. During the 1930s, Horkheimer expounded his views on the pages of the Institute's journal, the *Zeitschrift für Sozialforschung*. His essays are an amalgamation of Marxian rage over the injustices and inhumanity of capitalism and the Schopenhauerian themes of compassion (*Mitleid*) for the suffering of humanity and grief over the dismal state of the world. He made an attempt to work out a more refined materialist theory of knowledge and of science, thus clarifying and delineating critical theory's position vis-à-vis Leninism† and the vulgar Marxism of the Second International† on the one hand, and positivist and pragmatist philosophies of science, on the other. Horkheimer coined the term *critical theory* and developed its program in the 1937 essay, "Traditional and Critical Theory." The term not only implies a continuity between his own critical theory as well as Marx's critique of bourgeois political economy and the critical philosophy of German idealism, but also expresses Horkheimer's attitude toward existing capitalist society—complete with the aim of transforming it into a just and more humane one. It is assumed that "the thrust toward a rational society is innate in every man.'' Critical theory is opposed both to bourgeois capitalist society and to the science of that society, that is, to traditional theory, which is affirmative and constitutes a part of the ongoing societal process and is well integrated into the system-maintaining mechanism of that society in the form of an academic-scientific enterprise. Whereas traditional theory is deductive and mathematical, critical theory is dialectical and works with the concept of *totality*. It is a critique of traditional theory from an *ethical* standpoint. Thus, the two theories differ mainly in regard to the subject's (i.e., the scientist-scholar's) attitude toward his society. The term *critical* is to be understood more in the sense it has in the ''dialectical critique of political economy.'' Horkheimer maintains some of the basic notions of the original Marxist conceptual framework, such as the theory of impoverishment and the inevitability of the breakdown of capitalism. The ''meaning of the conceptual whole'' is not the preservation but the transformation into the ''right kind of society,'' as a ''community of free men.'' Critical theory aims at the coordination of thought and action, and the path to a projected identity is a concrete socio-historical process and not a logical one. Horkheimer searched in vain for the societal agent of the historical transformation of the existing order into a ''just society.'' He decried the ''impotence of the workers'' under the conditions of late capitalism and takes a deliberately anti-organizational stand. The only feasible mechanism is the ''concern'' of a small circle of intellectuals bound together by a shared theoretical knowledge of capitalist society and a ''longing'' for a just one.

The reputation of critical theory as representing a neo-Marxist orientation is based primarily on Horkheimer's formulation of critical theory in the essays of the 1930s. Critical theory undoubtedly adhered to certain basic tenets of Marxian social theory, such as the historical approach and the notion of societal developments founded on societal laws; it also recognized the importance of empirical research. Concerning some basic tenets of classic Marxist epistemology and ontology, critical theory shows little interest. For example, in discussing its own position in a systematic way, it brushes aside the question of ''objective reality,'' does not subscribe to the theory of reflection, and abstains from praxis (for a variety of historical reasons).

The shocks of Stalinist purges in the Soviet Union, World War II, and the ''final solution of the Jewish question'' in Nazi Germany provide the historical context and motivation for Horkheimer's embracing a pessimistic philosophy of history that produced the *Dialectic of Enlightenment*, coauthored with Adorno while in exile in California. Replacing earlier hopes for a change toward a rational society, both men began to look upon Western civilization as in the process of decay and collapse. What is meant by ''dialectic of Enlightenment''? First and foremost, it means the self-destruction of the Enlightenment, the metamorphosis of the once critical philosophy into the affirmation of the existing state of affairs by dominant positivist and pragmatist philosophies. In the Frankfurt theorists' opinion, technology became the medium of total reification of capitalist society; the Nazis' diabolic use of it led to the conclusion that ''terror and civilization are inseparable." The dialectical process here is not Hegel's or Marx's but that of the Enlightenment, the movement that comprises roughly all the historical development of Western civilization. Two underlying propositions determine the process: one is that myth is already enlightenment and enlightenment reverts to myth; and the other, which describes the final outcome, says, "The curse of irresistible progress is irresistible regression." Included is a fragment on "elements of anti-Semitism," proposing that the enlightenment paranoia culminates in anti-Semitism. Inevitably, the volume ends up in an extremely pessimistic philosophy of history.

Horkheimer's next major statement on positivism, pragmatism, and scientism in *Eclipse of Reason* (1947) is but an elaboration of the themes of the *Dialectic of Enlightenment* in the form of a philosophy of science. All varieties of the three philosophical currents are lumped together and subjected to devastating criticism. In that, Horkheimer falls back on the long line of antiscience tracts within German idealist intellectual currents, often merely echoing some of its well-known themes. Plain scientific knowledge is contrasted to "superior" (i.e. speculative), "objective" reason. Subjective, technological reason is operationalized, and its role is reduced to a mere instrument of domination of man and nature. It reaches its peak in fascism, which is the total repression of external and internal (human) nature. What emerges, for one thing, is a version of the *Vernunft/Verstand* dichotomy of German idealism. For another, the proposition indicates another shift in critical theory: the gradual incorporation of Freudian psychoanalytic theory. The "eclipse of reason" signifies the *Zeitgeist* for Horkheimer in the mid-1940s, that is, the universal feeling of fear and disillusionment, because of the diminishing hope that the "subject" (individual) will be able to resist the all-powerful social manipulation; Horkheimer also fears a possible "victorious reemergence of the neo-barbarism" recently defeated. In his advocacy of a "science" that is intuitive, contemplative, and qualitative, Horkheimer ushers in the revival of German *Naturphilosophie*. As is known, Marx considered science and technology neutral and the development of large-scale industry based on science and technology as a basis for human emancipation. Thus, Horkheimer's position is diametrically opposed to that of Marx; in addition, it is alien to most modern representatives of science and to philosophers of science.

Critics of Horkheimer's critical theory have argued that it does not represent scientific sociology, be it Marxist or traditional, but is a kind of social philosophy or *Kulturkritik*. Furthermore, there has been no *one* critical theory, but rather the critical theories of Horkheimer, of Adorno, and of Herbert Marcuse*; one could even speak of the critical theories (of Horkheimer) in the 1930s, 1940s, and the 1960s. The only consistent element of the critical theories of Horkheimer (and Adorno) is the humanistic concern about the future of Western civilization.

BIBLIOGRAPHY:

A. *Eclipse of Reason* (New York: Oxford University Press, 1947); *Critical Theory* (New York: Herder and Herder, 1972); with Theodore Adorno, *Dialectic of Enlightenment* (New York: Herder and Herder, 1972); *Critique of Instrumental Reason* (New York:

Seabury, 1974); *Dawn and Decline. Notes 1926–1931 and 1950–1969* (New York: Seabury, 1978).

B. Helmut Gumnior and Rudolf Ringguth, *Max Horkheimer in Selbstzeugnissen und Bilddokumenten* (Hamburg: Rowohlt, 1973); Phil Slater, *Origin and Significance of the Frankfurt School* (London: Routledge & Kegan Paul, 1977); Zoltán Tar, *The Frankfurt School* (New York: Wiley, 1977); Judith Marcus and Zoltán Tar, eds., *Foundations of the Frankfurt School of Social Research* (New Brunswick, N.J.: Transaction Books, 1984).

ZOLTÁN TAR

HYPPOLITE, JEAN (1907–1968). The French philosopher Jean Hyppolite was born in the city of Jonzac in 1907 and was educated at the Ecole Normale Supérieure. Early in his professional life he taught at several provincial *lycées* throughout France. He served in the military during 1930–31 and by the late 1930s was teaching at a *lycée* in Paris. Hyppolite concentrated his energies during these years on studying Hegel and translating his work into French. His commentaries *Origin and Structure of the "Phenomenology of Mind"* (1947), *Introduction to Hegel's Philosophy of History* (1948), and *Logic and Existence* (1953) introduced numerous postwar French intellectuals to Hegelianism. During the Nazi occupation Hyppolite proffered to his students an explicitly antifascist reading of Hegel ("insofar as we seek the Universal, we are all Jews"). Immediately after the war Hyppolite received a position at the University of Strasbourg. In 1949 he was granted a chair at the Sorbonne, where he taught until 1954, when he became director of the Ecole Normale Supérieure. He was appointed to the Collège de France in 1963. His *Studies on Marx and Hegel* (1955) focuses on the theoretical links between Hegel and the young Marx.† It secured Hyppolite's reputation among French left intellectuals as a major social theorist. His students included Michel Foucault,* Gilles Deleuze,* and Jacques Derrida.* Hyppolite died in Paris in 1968.

Hyppolite was descriptively faithful to Hegel's texts. He was primarily interested in discerning a common theme linking Hegel and Marx, rather than justifying a Marxian interpretation of the *Phenomenology*. This he found in the distinguishing trait of both Hegelianism and Marxism: the historicity of reason. Because reason is realized in and expressed by actual history, human progress toward "rationality" requires a heightening awareness of existing social forms of cooperation. Authentic self-consciousness, in other words, occurs only in community, where existences for and with others congeal into history's total movement. This is Hegel's meaning in depicting the master–slave relationship. Hyppolite believed that Marx and Hegel shared a deep concern over capitalist alienation and dehumanization. People must function as more than nonreflective commodities if they are finally to realize potentials as free, rational actors. Marx's economic and social critique of capitalism concretely expressed Hegel's more general belief in the historical necessity of reason and freedom. Proletarian revolution is reasonable in the Hegelian sense, reflectively expressing history's global tendencies. Hyppolite, of course, conveniently ignored Hegel's *Philosophy of Right*, which equated rationality and freedom with the preservation of dominant bourgeois institutions.

Hyppolite along with his colleague, Alexandre Kojève,* were professional philosophers, not social theorists, elucidating and defending Hegelianism. They rekindled in postwar Europe the Hegelian impulse that motivates idealist Marxism, that is, proletarian revolution as a subjectively experienced moment in history's abstract objective totality. Hence they reaffirmed for contemporary Marxists the relevance of George Lukács,* Karl Korsch,* and Antonio Gramsci.*

BIBLIOGRAPHY:

A. *Genèse et structure de la phénoménologie de l'esprit de Hegel* (Paris: Aubier, 1946); *Logique et existence* (Paris: P.U.F., 1953); *Marxisme et existentialisme* (Paris: M. Rivière, 1962); *Introduction à la philosophie de l'histoire de Hegel* (Paris: M. Rivière, 1968); *Studies on Marx and Hegel* (New York: Basic Books, 1969).

B. Leszek Kolakowski, *Main Currents of Marxism*, vol. 3 (London: Oxford University Press, 1978).

ROBERT A. GORMAN

J

JAEGGI, URS (b. 1931). A Swiss radical social scientist and novelist, Jaeggi worked as a bank employee, studied political economy and sociology in Geneva, Bern, and West Berlin, and earned the Ph.D. in 1959. In 1966 Jaeggi received his first appointment as a full professor at the Ruhr University in Bochum and in 1970 taught at the New School for Social Research in New York. He has been teaching sociology at the Free University in West Berlin since 1972. He is a member of the PEN-centrum of the Federal Republic and of the Organization of German Authors (Verband Deutscher Schriftsteller).

Jaeggi approaches society from two sides: as a professional sociologist and as an accomplished literary writer. His scientific studies cover a broad spectrum of topics, from a sociological analysis of the role of white collar workers in the age of automation to an application of the structuralist scientific method to answering questions concerning the empirical impact of postwar society on workers. The Federal Republic of Germany, according to Jaeggi's thesis (cf. "Drinnen und Draussen"), is a postbourgeois as well as postproletarian society, which is characterized by the total absence of a self-conscious, political, working-class movement. Jaeggi sees the decline of working-class consciousness as the single most outstanding and decisive event of the postwar era. A class struggle, according to Jaeggi, requires that a relatively high degree of generalization (*Verallgemeinerung*) of interests can be attained, that class members know what they are up against and know so collectively (*gemeinsam*); and that collective indignation is directed against whoever is in power on the basis of shared experiences. But the problem today, Jaeggi argues, is not so much that the workers no longer have experiences in common but rather that with the disappearance of class-based politics the generalization of these common experiences remains absent: conflicts no longer appear as class-specific but rather as general phenomena. Jaeggi sees the demise of the working-class movement in the Federal Republic also as a function of the politics of the Social Democratic Party. In contrast to those who view the absence of the class struggle as a reflection of a temporary crisis in class consciousness, Jaeggi postulates that the end of the working-class movement is historically irrevocable and definitive. Jaeggi sees postproletarian society characterized by the protest voiced by the essentially class independent women's movement and the "vehemently emancipatory socialist alternative groups" that manifest more than merely a crisis in class consciousness (Ibid., p. 456). It is on the premise of this co-optation and absorbing of the working class into the status quo, Jaeggi concludes, that corporate hegemonic forces are reinforced by the civil servants and highly skilled workers who unquestioningly accept capitalism's school system and performance ideology.

Jaeggi's political activism began with his involvement in the movement to end the war in Vietnam (cf. *Vietnam und die Presse*, 1968). He traces his political development to the influence of his social democratic father, who represented a humanitarian and ethical socialism, on the one hand, and to the radical existentialists Jean-Paul Sartre* and Maurice Merleau-Ponty* on the other.

Jaeggi belongs to the editorial board of *Das Argument* and frequently publishes in that journal. In his novels he portrays protaganists who leave their families as well as their professions, thereby willingly becoming outsiders in order to experience society anew.

BIBLIOGRAPHY:

A. *Der Angestellten in der Industriegesellschaft* (Stuttgart: Paul Haupt, 1966); *Die gesellschaftliche Elite. Eine Studie zu, Problem der sozialen Macht* (Stuttgart: Paul Haupt, 1967); with Herbert Wiedemann, *Ordnung und Chaos* (Frankfurt: Fischer, 1968); *Kapital und Arbeit in der Bundesrepublik* (Frankfurt: Fischer, 1973); "Drinnen und Draussen," in *Stichworte zur "Geistigen Situation der Zeit"* (Frankfurt: Fischer, 1979).

MAGDALENE MUELLER

JAMES, CYRIL LIONEL ROBERT (b. 1901). C. L. R. James was born 4 January 1901 in Chaguanas, Trinidad, West Indies. He was educated at Queens Royal College, Port of Spain, Trinidad. James left for England in March 1932 to pursue a writing career. While there, however, his interests shifted from writing novels (he published but one, *Minty Alley*) to politics, and it was at this time that he became interested in Marxism and aligned himself with the Trotskyist† movement. He was chair of the Finchley Independent Labour Party, and after this small group was abandoned by the Trotskyists, he became editor of their paper, *Fight*. During this period in England, he published some of his major works: *World Revolution*, an analysis of the Third International†; *The Black Jacobins*, perhaps James's major work, on the Haitian revolution; and *A History of Negro Revolt*. One of his shorter pamphlets (*The Case for West Indian Self-Government*, 1933) was published by the Fabians. James also was involved in the work of the International African Service Bureau organized in 1937 and from July to October 1938 was editor of its *International African Opinion*. In 1938, James went to the United States, remaining until 1953, when he was expelled as a result of McCarthyism. While in the United States, in 1940, James helped to form the Trotskyist Workers Party, a split from the Socialist Workers Party. Within the Workers Party, James was a leader of a faction known as the Johnson-Forest Tendency* (James taking the pseudonym of J. R. Johnson and

Raya Dunayevskaya of F. Forest), a tendency which argued for the concept of the spontaneous nature of workers' self-activity and against the Leninist† concept of vanguard organization. The Johnson-Forest Tendency left the Workers Party in 1947 and returned to the SWP only to leave the Trotskyist movement entirely in 1950. Later James and Dunayevskaya split, and James (and others like James and Grace Boggs) formed from the Correspondence Publishing Committee a publication group called Facing Reality. After being forced out of the United States, James returned to England and, in 1958, went back to Trinidad. Here, much to the shock of many, he went to work for Prime Minister Eric Williams's ruling People's National Movement, editing the party newspaper until July 1960, when he left the PNM as a result of ideological differences that had existed from the beginning. He had begun work for the PNM only because he was convinced that there was no revolutionary movement in the Caribbean and that independence must be the first priority under the circumstances. In 1966 he helped to form the revolutionary Workers and Farmers Party, which participated in the 1966 Trinidad elections without success. James has continued to lecture and travel in the United States and elsewhere. Interestingly, one of his passions (he wrote a book on the subject) has been cricket, and his in-depth understanding of sports as culture has been a valuable contribution to the concept of what workers' culture embodies.

James's most important and influential scholarly work is without doubt *The Black Jacobins*, one thesis of which is that the slave revolt that created the first independent black nation was related to and part of the process that had resulted in the French Revolution. Also important was James's focus on slave and colonial resistance at all levels as the means by which liberation was attained, a focus that has now become common but at the time was subversive—slaves had been characterized most often by their docility, not their rebelliousness. This book led to an entirely new emphasis on slavery and its base, and it particularly contributed to the revisionist reconstruction of slave history with its focus on economic forces. James's most important theoretical contribution has been his analysis of the self-activity of the working class under advanced capitalism (in, for example, *Facing Reality in Radical America*). This view often has been criticized as anarchistic (a label James has rejected) since it downplays the role of vanguard organization by parties in favor of vanguard self-organization of workers and their autonomy from parties and their own unions. These same ideas have been taken up by a segment of the new left in Italy. This perspective puts the emphasis on the ability of the working class to organize and struggle for itself and implicitly, when not explicitly, is a critique of the dominance of traditional party structures as being opposed to true worker liberation. James has been especially critical of the Soviet Union, calling it state capitalist, and was supportive of the Hungarian revolt in 1956, particularly the formation of workers' councils, a form of organization in keeping with the spontaneity of worker organization he believes so important.

BIBLIOGRAPHY:

A. *World Revolution, 1917–1936: The Rise and Fall of the Communist International* (London: Secker and Warburg, 1937); *The Black Jacobins: Toussaint L'Ouverture and the San Domingo Revolution* (London: Random House, 1938); *A History of Negro Revolt* (London: Fact, Ltd, 1939); *State Capitalism and World Revolution* (Detroit: Facing Reality Publishing Committee, 1950); *Mariners, Renegades and Castaways: The Story of Herman Melville and the World We Live In* (New York: no publisher listed, 1953); *Radical America*, 4, no. 4 (May, 1974)(special issue devoted to James's work); *The Future in the Present* (New York: Lawrence Hill, 1977); *Spheres of Existence* (New York: Lawrence Hill, 1980)(these last two volumes being the selected writings of James).

B. "C. L. R. James: His Life and Work," *Urgent Tasks*, no. 12 (Summer, 1981)(a publication of the Sojourner Truth Organization, Chicago).

JAMES DIETZ

JAMESON, FREDRIC (b. 1934). Born on 14 April 1934, Fredric Jameson has made teaching his profession; his principal preoccupation has been with Marxist† pedagogy and, specifically, cultural interpretation. He received his academic training at Haverford College, where he earned a baccalaureate in 1954, and at Yale University, where he completed his doctorate in French in 1959. Jameson taught French and comparative literature at Harvard University from 1959 until 1967 and at the University of California at San Diego from 1967 until 1976, when he became professor of French at Yale. A frequent contributor to many journals and the author of five books, he is widely accepted by the academic community as a major literary critic. His membership on the advisory boards of several major journals, his frequent lectureships at universities in the United States and Europe, and the translation of his writings into eight other languages testify not only to the importance of his personal scholarship but also to the authority of his Marxist analyses. He should not be regarded merely as an academic Marxist, however. The force of his work is in revealing the omnipresence of culture as a conceptualizing precondition of political praxis. He is a frequent participant in the Marxist Summer Institutes, is coeditor of *Social Text*, and was a lead instructor for the 1983 international institute and conference on "Marxism and the Interpretation of Culture" held at the University of Illinois.

Fredric Jameson has become a major figure within Marxist cultural studies both as an interpreter and, more recently, as a theoretician. In arguing for a new understanding of culture and its social function, he has centered his analysis on the proper relationship of cultural production with social reproduction generally. Jameson's contributions have come principally in his engaging four central issues: the politics of interpretation; the representation of history; the production of meaning; and inherently, the relationship of Marxism to the multiplicity of contemporary cultural interpretive strategies. Although Jameson's contributions can be assessed exclusively in terms of their political effects, the focus of his work has been, precisely, on the demonstration of the essentially political nature of culture. Thus the efficacy of his project has been determined by his profession.

A self-concept of professing—being a professor—structures Jameson's work in two important ways; it defines an audience and a method. He has used the analogy of teaching undergraduates and graduate students to suggest that the former takes place at the level of laboratory experiments, whereas graduate teaching, and research, become a "pedagogy of forms." Jameson recognizes that the importance of individual works of literature and art for Marx (as well as for Hegel and Lenin†) may lie in their value as a privileged microcosm through which one can observe the problems of form and content, superstructure and infrastructure, and dialectical thinking in process. Lately, Jameson has gone beyond novels and classical literature, however, to what he has called the "insubstantial bottomless realm of cultural and collective fantasy," within which he includes mass culture artifacts, the various media including film, science fiction, utopian narrative, popular music, and the like, along with the "classics," of course. It is in this collective fantasy, Jameson asserts, that we can find clearer evidence of class consciousness than in most American social structures. Jameson's political importance lies in this act of creating an "audience," what he identifies as a Marxist intelligentsia (with a Marxist culture and an intellectual presence) in the United States as the necessary precondition to any systemic change. In the United States there is not the centralizing framework of a national literature and culture with accompanying elite institutions, which provide a stage for Marxists in Europe; instead, there is an American tradition of anti-intellectualism and a remarkable capacity to assimilate almost anything. Inevitably, and almost inherently, American cultural analysis returns to the precritical issue of what American culture is in the first place, a futile gesture Jameson skillfully seeks to avoid. His task, then, is to create a suitably broad, or public, audience and, simultaneously, to ensure that Marxism becomes a realistic social alternative, if not a defining and organizing force, in a country that has never established a national canon. About this relation with the audience he would create as an act of political intervention, Jameson has said: "This is the perspective in which I would want my efforts to be understood, and I suppose my own particular contribution to such a development would mainly lie in showing the capacity of Marxism to engage the most advanced currents of 'bourgeois' thinking and theory" (*Diacritics*, 1982, p. 73).

Jameson's particular method has been influenced by his professional objectives as well. Indeed, one could employ the undergraduate-graduate (practical criticism as opposed to theory) dichotomy to distinguish his first two books from his later, more important work. Despite the levels there is nonetheless a unifying method and subject. His project has advanced with a clear self-consciousness about not only his own American context with its tensions between culture and politics but also the enduring debate between the followers of George Lukács* (and the tradition of Hegelianism) and those of Louis Althusser.* Jameson has taken the mediated position. He draws upon the works of Lukács, Althusser, Ernst Bloch,* Raymond Williams,* and others without accepting them as the "brand names" of philosophical schools. Indeed, he explicitly affirms the power of Marxism to expropriate what is best and valid in competing views. Jameson's own development has depended on his evolving sense of dialectical criticism first formulated in *Marxism and Form*, where he concluded that "dialectical judgements enable us to realize a momentary synthesis of the inside and the outside, of intrinsic and extrinsic, of existence and history: but it is a synthesis which we pay for by an objective historical judgement on ourselves" (p. 348). In other words, it is a method that simultaneously defines difference and identity and establishes "difference" as a relational concept, a dynamic tension that holds organic and historical being together as the recognizable "real" environment within which we must live.

In *The Political Unconscious* Jameson's project matures, and he defines narrative as the "central function or *instance* of the human mind" (p. 13). Narrative becomes the model because it is the form of narrative rather than any of its specific contents that creates meaning; moreover, historical discourse is subject to the same analysis because it, like literature, can be approached only through its form of narrativity. Early in his latest book Jameson establishes the Marxist master narrative of history as a "single great collective *story*" and says that "it is in detecting the traces of that uninterrupted *narrative*, in restoring to the surface of the text the repressed and buried reality of this fundamental history, that the doctrine of the political unconscious finds its function and its necessity" (pp. 19–20). The political unconscious, as a mediating device, provides a means of shifting between levels and between the organic and the historical self; it is, perhaps, Jameson's most important contribution because it reveals self-conscious mediation as the *process* of creating meaning. For Jameson, then, Marxism is never a finished story but an evolving one whose vitality and future depend on the ability to recognize the elements of its own narration. It is auspicious that he concluded *Marxism and Form* with the belief that "it therefore falls to literary criticism to continue to compare the inside and the outside, existence and history . . . to keep alive the idea of a concrete future" (p. 416).

Jameson has given us a complex model of narrative, one that simultaneously holds synchrony and diachrony, the devices of structural continuity and the disrupting processes of creating meaning. Narrativity not only represents but accounts for how an ideal state could be realized. In Jameson's own words, "No Marxism is possible without a conception of contradiction (that is, without a concept of the dialectic), just as no Marxism is possible without a vision of a radically different future" (*Diacritics*, 1982, p. 81). Through the dialectic of story elements being rescued from disorder into the unity of a plot, narration becomes the model for history; it is an "ideology of form." In reformulating Althusser's concept of structural causality, Jameson is careful to point out that "history is *not* a text, not a narrative, master or otherwise, but that, as an absent cause, it is inaccessible to us except in textual form, and that our approach to it and to the Real itself necessarily passes through its prior textualization, its narrativization in the political unconscious" (p. 35). At the risk of totalizing and systematizing, Jameson's concept of the political unconscious nonetheless opens history, and through the forms of narrative, it seeks an alternative to closure in the idea of a future, a radically different social formation. Jameson's dialectical language and method accommodate difference and unity, and thereby they help to privilege the interpretive act as the principal tool of Marxist cultural studies. In five books and numerous articles Jameson has demonstrated that Marxism has a sufficiently powerful unity of knowledge to compete with other American philosophies, and he has established a significant Marxist intellectual presence.

BIBLIOGRAPHY:

A. *Marxism and Form* (Princeton: Princeton University Press, 1971); *The Prison-House of Language: A Critical Account of Structuralism and Russian Formalism* (Princeton: Princeton University Press, 1972); *Fables of Aggression* (Berkeley: University of California Press, 1979); "Reification and Utopia in Mass Culture," *Social Text* (Winter 1979); *The Political Unconscious: Narrative as a Socially Symbolic Act* (Ithaca: Cornell University Press, 1981).

B. Marshall Grossman, "Formalism, Structuralism, Marxism: Fredric Jameson's Critical Narrative," *Disposito: Revista hispanica de semiotica literoria* (1979); Leonard Green et al., "Special Issue on Fredric Jameson: The Political Unconscious," *Diacritics* (1982); Cornel West, "Fredric Jameson's Marxist Hermeneutics," *Boundary*, 2 (1983).

WILLIAM PLATER

JAURÈS, JEAN (1859–1914). Born in the French city of Castres on 3 September 1859 into a middle-class family, Jean Jaurès was both a scholar and a politician in turn-of-the-century France. He was elected to the French Assembly from his native region, the Tarn, in 1885 and again in 1893. A republican, democrat, and socialist, he actively defended Dreyfus and campaigned for the separation of church and state. He published a plan for army reform in France based on universal, short-term service, which was geared to make the army both more efficient and more democratic. Jaurès never joined the left or Marxist† wing of France's socialist movement, but studied Marx and tried to combine Marx's historical materialism with an Hegelian idealism. He advocated international peace in 1914, when he was assassinated on 31 July 1914 by a nationalist fanatic.

Jaurès was a professional philosopher who skipped nimbly from Kant to Hegel and Marx. His path to socialism, therefore, lay in pre-Marxist bourgeois theory, and he did not hesitate to refer to philosophers as diverse as Proudhon, Blanqui, Fichte, Lasalle, and Rousseau in addition to Kant and Hegel. Jaurès interpreted being as a universal whole, encompassing every level of physical and social organization, that evolves into a pervasive harmony and oneness. When historically mature, being unifies thought and external reality. This highest stage defines everything that has preceded, determining their specific roles in the totality. What a particular phenomenon means, in other words, is determined by its part in being's grand design. The universe is neither spontaneous nor haphazard, but determined by the highest unity of being and truth, a unity unfolding gradually in history. Thus, each level of reality is defined not merely in relation to other levels but by its part in being's progressive historical flowering. Reality is being unfolding historically, the absolute temporally realizing itself. Human beings perceive this reality, act, and help cause it. Truth is not prior to being. They coexist as the former realizes itself. All natural phenomena and cognitive experiences of being are equally valid and important, for they embody the historical process of perfect unity at specific temporal moments. Jaurès called this unity God. Faith, therefore, is the subjective experience of true knowledge.

Socialism is the final, mature unity of being and reality—history's goal, defining all preceding political and economic struggles and social forms. Orthodox Marxism abstracts the material processes of social evolution and applies them to scientific social inquiry, hence is scientifically valid and useful. However, it is neither sufficient nor autonomous. Material reality is only one aspect of historical being, which includes and determines everything in the universe, material and nonmaterial. Marx's historical science is one fragment of a universal soteriology of being. It complements faith rather than rejects it. Although economics shapes social institutions, both these phenomena reflect, and are defined by, being's progress in history. Society embodies both mechanical laws of matter and abstract processes. Marxism indicates the material prerequisites for socialism, but socialism itself is built on the people's will to live truthfully in universal freedom. Socialism realizes humanity's material potential, but also culminates history's essential, absolute truth. It is "necessary" in an idealistic sense quite foreign to orthodox materialism, even though God—truth—also lives in those mechanistic economic laws that fascinated Marxists. Socialism is concretized only when an exploited humanity experiences God's will and actively fulfills its revolutionary historical role. Orthodox materialists mistakenly ignore this subjective component of history.

An active, willful, revolutionary proletariat culminates history's universal progress. Properly informed and motivated, workers will perceive socialism not as the negation of bourgeois civilization but as its progressive completion. Socialism, for Jaurès, is an extension of liberal republicanism, nationalism, religion, and so on, preserving and perfecting their progressive, historically significant features. The proletariat, history's "progressive" class, represents being's universal moment. Its struggle has a universal character. Its interests are divine, not narrowly self-motivated. Hence, workers will unite with all mature, knowledgeable groups—peasants, petit bourgeois, even capitalists—in perfecting social institutions and values. Their revolution is also humanity's and God's and can therefore be accomplished without violence or hatred. Jaurès's pantheistic metaphysics described individuals with antagonistic material interests living blissfully together under God's historical will. He was a revolutionary who preached nonviolence and devoted thirty years to electoral politics in France. As a Marxist with unbreakable connections to bourgeois culture, Jaurès "rectified" orthodox materialism by substituting orthodox Hegelian idealism, including its naively optimistic view of the bourgeois state's moral leadership in achieving universal justice.

BIBLIOGRAPHY:

A. *Le Socialisme et l'enseignement* (Paris: G. Bellais, 1899); *Etudes socialistes* (Paris: Cahiers de la Quinzaine, 1901); *L'Armée nouvelle* (Paris: Rouff, 1910); *Histoire socialiste* (Paris: Librairie de l'Humanité, 1922–24); *Oeuvres*, 9 vols. (Paris: Rieder, 1931–39).

B. Charles Rappoport, *Jean Jaurès, l'homme, le penseur, le socialiste* (Paris: L'Emancipatrice, 1915); Margaret Pease, *Jean Jaurès, Socialist and Humanitarian* (London: Headley, 1916); J. Hampden Jackson, *Jean Jaurès, His Life and Work* (London: Allen & Unwin, 1943).

ROBERT A. GORMAN

JOHNSON-FOREST TENDENCY. The Johnson-Forest Tendency first emerged in 1941 within the Trotskyist† Workers Party, which had itself emerged from the Moscow-directed U.S. Socialist Workers Party. In 1947 the Johnson-Forest movement rejoined the SWP, where it remained until 1950, when it left Trotskyism altogether and renamed itself the Correspondence Publishing Committee. In 1955 Raya Dunayevskaya and others left the Correspondence Publishing Committee to form the News and Letters Committee. In 1962 C. L. R. James* together with Grace Lee Boggs also left, and the Correspondence Publishing Committee changed its name to Facing Reality. Without Dunayevskaya and James, its two major theorists, the movement faded. The Johnson-Forest Tendency took its name from the pseudonyms J. R. Johnson and F. Forest taken by C. L. R. James and Raya Dunayevskaya, respectively, during the 1941–51 period.

The Johnson-Forest Tendency advocated workers' self-activity and autonomy as the foundation of capitalism's revolutionary transformation to socialism and rejected the Leninist† vanguard party outlined in *What Is to Be Done*. This meant that workers were potentially independent of both capital and the workers' own official organizations such as the Communist Party and labor unions. James, Dunayevskaya, and others in the movement undertook numerous studies in the 1940s and early 1950s attempting to equate the Soviet Union, Nazi Germany, and the United States as modern antiworker totalitarian systems. *State Capitalism and World Revolution* (1950), the most significant of these early manuscripts, argued that both Taylorism and Fordism characterize commodity production throughout the industrialized West. Domination of workers by the principles of profit, efficiency, and the growing rationalization and subdivision of labor is thus a universal phenomenon in the West, uniting fascism, capitalism, and Stalinism.† Echoing Rosa Luxemburg,† Antonie Pannekoek,* and others, the Johnson-Forest Tendency argued that spontaneous, free, and creative actions can liberate workers, and that such activity would end forever the hegemony of both capital and orthodox Communist parties, which had become the agents of capital. New grass-roots workers' organizations resembling Lilburne's Leveller Party, the 1871 Commune, and the soviets of 1905 will emerge to institutionalize revolutionary justice. Members of the Johnson-Forest Tendency sought and analyzed actual case studies of workers battling management and unions and produced such mobilizing monographs as *The American Worker* (1947), *Punching Out* (1952), and *Union Committeemen and Wild Cat Strikes* (1955). Although James and Dunayevskaya tried to reformulate Marxist theory first through Trotskyism and later from a Hegelian perspective (e.g., James's "Notes on the Dialectic" [1948] and Dunayevskaya's *Philosophy and Revolution* [1973]), the Johnson-Forest Tendency they led is known more for its commitment to worker-led rebellion through practical activities, study, and tactically useful monographs.

BIBLIOGRAPHY:

A. Raya Dunayevskaya, *The Original Historical Analysis: Russia as State Capitalist Society* (Detroit: News and Letters, 1942); C. L. R. James, *State Capitalism and World Revolution* (Detroit: Facing Reality, 1950); Raya Dunayevskaya, *For the Record, the Johnson-Forest Tendency or the Theory of State Capitalism, 1941–51: Its Vicissitudes and Ramifications* (Detroit: News and Letters, 1972), and *Philosophy and Revolution* (New York: Delacorte Press, 1973).

B. Harry Cleaver, *Reading Capital Politically* (Austin: University of Texas Press, 1979).

ROBERT A. GORMAN

K

KALANDRA, ZÁVIŠ (1902–1950). Born in the city of Frenštát pod Radhoštěm in 1902, Záviš Kalandra was an essayist, journalist, and prominent personality in Czech literary circles. Kalandra was born into the sophisticated milieu surrounding T. G. Masaryk, the future founder of the Czech Republic. His father, a medical doctor and member of the left wing of Masaryk's political party, exposed young Záviš to the intellectual currents of Austrian Bohemian thinkers. After the creation of the Czech Republic in 1918, Kalandra drifted toward bolshevism, joined the Communist Party, directed a group of young intellectuals who formed a "study section" within the Czech Party, and edited the radical journal *Avant-garde*. At this time he also completed his doctoral thesis on Parmenides. He soon became a popular and prolific contributor to official Czech Communist Party journals and magazines and collaborated on the Czech edition of the official journal of the Third International.† In the 1930s Kalandra's conception of Marxism†-Leninism† drifted further and further from the Party's dogmatic version. The tragic fates of Russians like Alexander Zinoviev,* L. B. Kamenev, and others resulted in Kalandra's definitive rupture with the orthodox Party organization. Expelled from the Party in 1936, Kalandra founded *The Worker*, a biweekly Communist opposition journal in 1937. In 1939 Kalandra was arrested by the Gestapo and spent six years in the Rawensbrück and Sachsenhausen prison camps. After liberation in 1945 he returned to Prague and completed a new edition of his last prewar work, *Paganism in Bohemia*, the original of which had been destroyed by the Nazis. He also collaborated in the editing of several non-Marxist journals. In November 1949 Kalandra was arrested by Czech police and accused of espionage. Denounced as a Trotskyist† who was actively directing those opposed to the Czech Party line toward "treason against the people, the nation, and the State," Kalandra was convicted of a capital crime on 8 June 1950. Klement Gottwald,† president of Czechoslovakia and Kalandra's old comrade, rejected his request for clemency. Kalandra was executed on 27 June 1950.

The critical and analytical method that Kalandra used in his version of Marxism first appeared in his Ph.D. thesis on Parmenides, where, opposing the Ionian physicians, he reproached them for "seeing problems everywhere except in themselves." He demanded, even in this thesis, "a new explanation of natural mechanisms, based on a form of knowledge that is independent of the immediate action." Later, after encountering Marx, he began formulating what he called the "human dimension," as well as his concern for the "real, living individual"—in brief, his humanism and anthropomorphism. He was also inclined, contrary to most of his Marxist comrades, to delve into psychological analysis. Curiously, considering orthodoxy's narrow perspective, he published in the official Party journal *Halo-noviny* a sympathetic study of A. Schopenhauer. Kalandra also published a significant article contrasting the worldviews of František Palacký, the "father of the Czech nation" and an important figure in the nineteenth-century awakening of Czech nationalism, and Karel Hynek Mácha, the Czech "poète maudit" who shaped modern Czech literature. Kalandra sees in Palacký a being totally committed to the preservation of the interests of one class. Kalandra views his Platonic idealism, which theoretically harmonizes potentially conflicting interests, as only a political subterfuge rationalizing class hegemony. On the other hand, the Byronian Mácha's "skeptical immorality" appears to Kalandra as fundamentally revolutionary and future-oriented. It was also significant that Kalandra, then an important Party journalist, chose to publish this study in the surrealist journal *Ni cygne, ni lune* in 1936 on the occasion of the hundredth anniversary of Mácha's death.

More important, from a political viewpoint, is Kalandra's thesis developed while collaborating with Josef Guttmann,† a former editor-in-chief of *Rudé právo* and a leading official in the Communist Party who was also eventually expelled. In August 1936 Kalandra and Guttmann published a monograph on the *Unmasking of Moscow's Mysterious Marxism*. Later, in January 1937, he wrote a polemic entitled "Save Radek, Piatakov, and the Other Comrades!" The message of both these texts was unambiguous: Kalandra believed that Stalin's† dictatorship in the Soviet Union qualified as another of history's ignominious, oppressive regimes. Previously, in August 1936, Kalandra had published, at his own expense, an eight-page text on the Spanish Civil War, in which he denounced the Stalinist trend toward enriching a caste of privileged Soviet bureaucrats. However, despite the resemblances, Kalandra always refused to commit his energies to the Trotskyite movement, which he feared was impractical and inefficient. In one of his final texts, he wrote: "Those who too quickly grant that history is the supreme judge of human activity will discover that the meaning of justice eludes them and they will remain unaware of human destiny" (*The Clock of Liberty*, pp. 5–8).

BIBLIOGRAPHY:

A. *Parmenides* (Doctoral thesis, Charles University, 1928); *České pohanství* (Prague: Borovný, 1947).

M. IVO FLEISCHMANN

KALIVODA, ROBERT (b. 1923). The Czech Robert Kalivoda was born in Prague in 1923 and studied philosophy, aesthetics, and literature at Charles

University. In 1954 he was appointed a researcher at the Institute of Philosophy of the Czech Academy of Sciences. Kalivoda actively participated in the reformist movement known as the Prague Spring* in 1968 and was dismissed from all his professional positions during the "normalization" period imposed by Soviet troops. Although he is now prohibited from publishing in Czechoslovakia, his work continues to appear in foreign journals. In 1981 he participated in a research project sponsored by the University of Bielefeld (West Germany) concerning the theoretical and practical difficulties of self-proclaimed utopian communities.

His theoretical contributions to Marxism† are twofold. First, he has studied the history of Czech philosophy, pre- and post-Marxist. Second, he has formulated a philosophical anthropology inspired by principles of Marxism and Freudianism. Among Kalivoda's numerous works dealing with Czech philosophy the most important is his 1961 book entitled *Hussite Ideology*. He interprets the early fifteenth-century antifeudal Hussite rebellion as an event of profound international significance, a prototype for later national revolutions throughout Europe. He pays special attention to the radical wing of the Hussite rebellion, represented by the Taborites. He interprets their radical egalitarianism as a precursor of French Jacobinism and the revolutionary socialism of Karl Marx. Kalivoda felt that the fundamental categories of bourgeois thinking were already present in precapitalist Europe. Beginning with the Hussite rebellion, therefore, radical, "Jacobinist" movements in Europe were simultaneously antifeudal and anticapitalist. The Taborites' millenarianism advocated not only the abolition of feudal domination but also the creation of a regime guaranteeing liberty and equality. The ancient Christian triadic model (paradise; the fall from grace into domination and oppression; the reemergence of equality and liberty) is in the Taborite ideology radically altered: the restoration of paradise no longer depends on divine discretion, but instead is the consequence of revolutionary human activity. Kalivoda emphasizes the hedonist aspects of Taborite ideology, its interest in completely satisfying mankind's physical and natural needs. He summarizes these phenomena in the concept of "revolutionary libertinism," which constitutes the common ideological perspective that unites millenarianism, Jacobinism, Marxism, and anarchism. This linkage of disparate ideologies, particularly Marxism and Jacobinism, is certainly problematic. However, the concept of "revolutionary libertinism," which attempts to reconcile liberty with equality and happiness and which is based on elaborate research in the history of social theory, is one of Kalivoda's major philosophical contributions.

Unlike most nonorthodox neo-Marxists, Kalivoda interprets Engels† as a faithful disciple of Marx rather than as a minor author who mangles Marx's thoughts. In elaborating his own philosophical anthropology Kalivoda relies more on *Anti-Dühring* than on Marx's writings. He formally rejects the concept of alienation, seeing in it an ideological residue of Hegel and Feuerbach that blemished the young Marx. He considers it sterile and irrelevant to sociological research. Kalivoda is equally critical of the concept of reification based on Marx's interpretation of the fetishism of commodities, which George Lukàcs* adopted and popularized in his *History and Class Consciousness*. In Kalivoda's opinion, the concept of reification fragments man, separating his natural inclinations and characteristics from those generated by society. Rejecting metaphysical and essentialist concepts of human nature, he postulates instead an invariable anthropological concept that is not one enclosed entity but a human structure whose elements and their relations constitute a unity of nature and society. Kalivoda believes that this notion of an "anthropological constant" as the structure of human being permits a synthesis of Marxism and Freudianism: Freud's three elements of our psychic mechanism (id, ego, superego) constitute for Kalivoda the fundamental structure of the anthropological constant. Influenced by Czech structuralists (especially Jan Mukařovský*), Kalivoda interprets Marxism as a dialectical structuralism that is an explanation of reality that is simultaneously ontological, noetical, and methodological. In this, he joins from a structuralist perspective Engels's project of constructing an ontology that not only would be a dialectic of man and society (the projects of Marx and Lukàcs) but would also encompass general dialectical principles relating man to his total environment, including the natural universe (which Engels attempted in *Anti-Dühring* and the *Dialectics of Nature*).

Kalivoda's philosophical anthropology differs from other kinds of Freudian Marxism because of its structural perspective as well as its unorthodox interpretation of Freud. He rejects both Erich Fromm's* neo-Freudianism and Herbert Marcuse's* more traditional version. Although he accepts most of Freud's mature thoughts on the quality of the psychic apparatus, he nevertheless rejects the concomitant dichotemy of psychic forces into Eros (forces of life) and Thanatos (forces of death). Influenced primarily by Wilhelm Reich* and the European surrealists (especially his fellow Czech Karel Teige*) Kalivoda emphasizes the libido's creative power rather than its destructiveness. He conceives of communism as a hedonistic life form dominated by the principle of pleasure, based on and reinforcing the creative aspects of man's anthropological constant. Societies of the future will recover the tradition of revolutionary libertinism, while forging a new historical project. Hence Kalivoda is sympathic to anarchist principles, which he believes are found in Marx. Hence also his favorable attitude toward utopias.

BIBLIOGRAPHY:

A. *Husitská revoluce* (Prague: Č.S.A.V., 1961); *Moderní duchevní skutečnost a marxismus* (Prague: Československý spisovatel, 1968).

LUBOMIR SOCHOR

KANGRGA, MILAN (b. 1923). The Yugoslav Milan Kangrga was born in Zagreb in 1923 and studied philosophy at the University of Zagreb, where he received his B.A. (1950) and Ph.D. (1961). His thesis on "The Ethical Problem in the Work of Karl Marx" received the Božidar Adžija prize for scientific research in 1966, while the chairman of the Croatian Parliament's Awards Committee lost his post for alleged "poor taste" (the award went to two *Praxis**

theorists: Kangrga and Gajo Petrović*). Kangrga is a professor of ethics/aesthetics at the University of Zagreb, and is concerned primarily with philosophical anthropology and ethics/aesthetics, but strongly opposes any formal division of philosophy into separate disciplines. He is noted for his interpretations of Marx,† Hegel, and Kant and for his radical criticism of Stalinism† and positivism. He has been a member of *Praxis* and the Korčula Summer School boards, secretary in the Yugoslav Philosophical Association (1964–68), and president of the Croatian Philosophical Society (1973–75). He has lectured abroad in Austria, Czechoslovakia, Hungary, Germany, Poland, and the Soviet Union. His major works include *Rationalistic Philosophy* (1957), *The Ethical Problem in the Work of Karl Marx* (1963, 1980), *Ethics and Freedom* (1966), *The Meaning of the Historical* (1970), *Thoughts on Ethics* (1970), *Man and World* (1975), *Contending Viewpoints* (1981), *Ethics or Revolution* (1982), as well as numerous articles in *Praxis* and other journals and symposia.

Kangrga's theoretical contributions to Marxism—particularly to the *Praxis* school of Marxist humanist thought—lie in philosophical anthropology and ontology, even more than in ethics. Kangrga is noted, along with Mihailo Marković,* for his rejection at the Bled Conference of Yugoslav philosophers (1960) of the Engels†–Lenin† theory of reflection as antithetical to the *Praxis* perspective of a nondogmatic Marxism. The critique of positivism is an integral part of Kangrga's revalorization of Marxist thought. In fact, Kangrga postulates in his essay on "The Meaning of Marx's Philosophy" the essential intellectual and existential alternative: Marxism *or* positivism. For him, positivism remains within the distorted view that sees the world as a given, fixed entity, coterminous with reification and alienation. And the ideology of this frozen, alienated world represents for Kangrga not "false consciousness" but rather "accurate consciousness, adequate knowing, knowledge in the measure of alienated (untrue) being (and existence), which moreover coincides with the illusoriness of human life; or more precisely, ideology is its *existential* untruth" (p. 51). Kangrga was influenced by Johann Fichte and Ernst Bloch,* even more than by Heidegger and German existentialism. Among *Praxis* theorists, Kangrga's search for the sources and essence of Marx's revolutionary thought begins with a critique of ethics and transcendentalism and evolves via dialectics and speculative philosophy to historical thought. The basic thesis underlying all his works is that there is no such thing as a Marxist ethics. Moreover, he sees no need to construct one. Thus, in his *Thoughts on Ethics*, Kangrga argues that morality is "one of the essential limiting aspects of man in bourgeois society" (p. 103). To be a citizen as a moral person means to remain an egoistic individual, a man reduced to a member of bourgeois society, on the one hand, and abstract political emancipation, on the other. What Marx really had in mind was the transcendence of morality as such by revolutionizing the underlying alienated social conditions which give rise to it. For Kangrga, ethics are transcended by Marx's "ruthless critique of everything that exists." At this point, Kangrga's very concept of ethics is transcended (*aufgehoben*) by his philosophical anthropology: the concept of a future-oriented praxis and of man's essence as a historical being whose past and present are informed by the future *novum*. Hence Kangrga's emphasis on the utopian nature of the historical.

Kangrga's philosophical anthropology rests on the premise, reiterated in his 1982 interview in *Theoria*, that man is a futuristic-utopian being who is "necessarily free" to create/produce the conditions of his life and his own self. For Kangrga, man is man only in his process of becoming, guided by the not-as-yet existing possibilities lodged in the future, which coexists as possibility in the past and present. Hence the motto for Kangrga's philosophical perspective: "At the beginning was the—future." Clearly, Bloch's philosophy of hope influenced Kangrga's conception of man as a being of the future whose essence is precisely in the never-ending movement for self-realization understood as the simultaneous co-creation of himself and the world. In his *Ethics or Revolution*, Kangrga develops a Fichtean underpinning of Marxism by adopting Fichte's identity of subject-object as the starting point for his philosophical anthropology and ontology. In fact, Kangrga advances the thesis that no one may truly reach Marx and Marxism without mastering Kant and taking a decisive step from Kant to Fichte. To Kangrga, Fichte's identity of the subject-object surpasses Hegel's *Phenomenology* in that it posits a unique *tertium quid* of spirit and history "as the unity of man and his world in the sense of their uninterrupted mutual historical-processual production and postulation" (p. 71). This signifies no less than the "coming-about (self-in-time) of man as world, and the world as man. And that is indeed the historical self-becoming of man as world and vice versa." (ibid.) Kangrga dismisses the critique of his stance as neo-Hegelian, and Jürgen Habermas's* characterization of *Praxis* thought as phenomenological Marxism. Kangrga is also critical of the Frankfurt School as missing the basic meaning of Marx's teaching and also rejects Heidegger by claiming that history is antecedent to time.

Unlike orthodox Marxists, Kangrga believes that the very division between Marxist and bourgeois philosophers is incidental. As he put it in *Theoria*: What kind of Marxists are those who are not at the same time bourgeois philosophers? For him, Marxist philosophy is unthinkable without a thorough knowledge, critical revaluation, and transcendence of the bourgeois intellectual heritage, extracting and developing the liberal conception of the individual as the supreme value. Kangrga's major thesis in *Ethics or Revolution* concerns precisely the need for Yugoslav thinkers to struggle and attain this historical level of bourgeois thought as a necessary precondition for reaching further—toward socialism. Like other *Praxis* theorists, Kangrga holds that there can be no socialism without basic bourgeois freedoms and human rights. Marxism as historical thought or revolutionary praxis presupposes the possibility of negativity, of critical thought, and hence of individual freedom. Kangrga anchors his conception of Marxist philosophy as the transcendence of metaphysics and the ascent to the level of historical thinking illustrated by Fichte's "will to freedom," or "decision for freedom." And he cautions that in this enterprise there is no absolute certainty, no absolute limits. Only dogmatists, "true ideologists," know everything beyond doubt.

Given Kangrga's utopian standpoint of the future, it is not surprising that his critique of socialist practice in Yugoslavia—of the rise of a new exploitative middle class, bureaucracy, and technocracy that maintain a monopoly of power and communications—led to the ban of a 1971 issue of *Praxis* (later lifted by the Croatian Supreme Court on appeal), which carried a controversial article. In his 1982 *Theoria* interview, Kangrga was even more pessimistic regarding the prospects for the advent of socialism in Yugoslavia, estimating a time frame of some 200 years, given the present early capitalist mentality of the Yugoslav ruling class. While Kangrga's emphasis on the preeminence of subjective, individual freedom begs the question of ethics, this Fichtean Marxist philosopher of radical hope may be remembered for his critical humanist stance, which claimed that man as the first, only, and highest value is the *sine qua non* of both Marxist theory and socialist practice.

BIBLIOGRAPHY:

A. "Problem otudjenja u Marxovu djelu" in *Humanizam i socijalizam*, ed. Branko Bošnjak and Rudi Supek vol. 1 (Zagreb: Naprijed, 1963), pp. 77–103; "Praxis et critique," *Praxis*, 1, nos. 2–3 (1965), pp. 364–76; *Etika i sloboda* (Zagreb: Naprijed, 1966); *Razmišljanja o etici* (Zagreb: Praxis, 1970); "Phänomenologie des ideologisch-politischen Auftretens der jugoslawischen Mittelklasse," *Praxis*, 7, nos. 3–4 (1971), pp. 451–74; "Ideology as a Form and Mode of Human Existence," in *Marxist Humanism and Praxis*, ed. Gerson S. Sher (Buffalo, N.Y.: Prometheus Books, 1978), pp. 125–32; "The Meaning of Marx's Philosophy," in *Praxis*, ed. Gajo Petrović and Mihailo Marković (Dordrecht: Reidel, 1979), pp. 45–61; *Etički problem u djelu Karla Marxa* (Belgrade: Nolit, 1980); "Bez gradjanskih sloboda—ni traga od socijalizma" *Theoria*, 25, nos. 1–2 (1982), pp. 89–124; *Etika ili revolucija* (Belgrade: Nolit, 1982).

B. Gerson S. Sher, *Praxis: Marxist Criticism and Dissent in Socialist Yugoslavia* (Bloomington: Indiana University Press, 1977); Oskar Gruenwald, *The Yugoslav Search for Man: Marxist Humanism in Contemporary Yugoslavia* (South Hadley, Mass.: Bergin & Garvey, 1983).

OSKAR GRUENWALD

KELLES-KRAUZ, KAZIMIERZ (1872–1905). Born on 2 March 1872 in Szczebrzeszynie (near Lublin), Kelles-Krauz was a sociologist as well as a practitioner and theorist of the Polish Socialist Party (PPS). As a high school student he took part in radical youth movements in Radomiu, Kielce, and Warsaw. He had already begun to study the works of Marx.† In 1892 he emigrated to France, leaving his homeland forever. In Paris he studied natural science, sociology, and economics. In 1893 he joined the Society of Polish Socialists Abroad and became a leading official of the Parisian section of the society. Here, he became aware of the special problems of poor peasants and workers. From 1895 until 1899 he edited the *Official Bulletin* of the Polish Socialist Party. From 1895 until his death he contributed regular correspondence about the social situation in France to the London journal of the PPS, *Przedsivit* (The Dawn).

He is the author of numerous scholarly and journalistic articles in Polish, French, and German periodicals. He actively cooperated with the International Sociological Institute in Paris and lectured in sociology at the Free College of Science in Paris and at the New University in Brussels. In 1901 he moved to Vienna, where he finished his legal studies.

Kelles-Krauz was convinced of the fruitfulness of Marxism and of the necessity of preserving the close association between socialist politics and "economic materialism." He observed, however, that if economic materialism is to remain faithful to its own principles then it must eagerly admit and even promote criticism. He rejected a single, dogmatic interpretation of Marxism, where consciousness and social institutions are seen as epiphenomena of economic life. He concluded that revolutionary ideals generate economic development, that the socialist ideal appeared prior to the realization of the socialist structure. Kelles-Krauz talked of a "law of revolutionary retrospect," according to which progressive social movements formulate their ideals by confronting and absorbing actually existing social norms, norms derived from the past. Even reactionary norms from the past, abstracted and in a new context, can take on a revolutionary character. In his historical and philosophical studies Kelles-Krauz discovered the foundation of his law in the cyclical theory of Vico, in Rousseau's notion of natural law, and in Hegel's dialectic of history.

In his political outlook Kelles-Krauz believed strongly in Polish national independence. Recognizing the reactionary nature of the tsarist empire, he situated the Polish national question as the main element of his revolutionary socialism and thus energetically opposed Rosa Luxemburg† on this important issue. He criticized that orientation in the PPS which sought allies for the fight for independence among the conservative political opponents of Russia (e.g. Germany, Austria, or Japan). He argued that Poland could regain independence only with the support of revolutionary movements in the partitioned countries, particularly the radical workers' movements of Austria and Germany.

BIBLIOGRAPHY:

A. "Materializm ekonomiczny" and "Socjologiczne prawo retrospekcji," in *Pisma wybrane*, vol. 1 (Warsaw: PWN, 1962).

B. W. Bienkowski, *Kazimierz Kelles-Krauz* (Warsaw: PWN, 1969); Leszek Kolakowski, *Main Currents of Marxism*, vol. 3 (New York: Oxford University Press, 1977).

PIOTR OGRODZIŃSKI

KOJÈVE, ALEXANDRE (1902–1968). Alexandre Kojève was not an innovative theorist, wrote very little, and carefully avoided the fame that could easily have been his. Nevertheless, he had a profound impact on leftist thinking in postwar France. Kojève was born in Russia in 1902, studied in Berlin after the Russian Revolution, and went to Paris in the early 1930s. He focused his energies in these years on carefully analyzing Hegelian philosophy, particularly the *Phenomenology of Mind*. From 1933 until 1939 he taught a course on Hegel's *Phenomenology* at the Ecole Practique des Hautes Etudes that was attended by many young French intellectuals who would later direct the intellectual currents of postwar France, including Maurice Merleau-Ponty,* Jean-Paul Sartre,* Eric Weil, Jacques Lacan, Emmanuel Lévinas, and A. Koyré. His only published book, *Introduction à la lecture de Hegel* (1947) consists of notes from his course at the Ecole Practique des Hautes Etudes compiled and edited by the novelist Raymond Queneau. Only a few relatively minor articles in *Critique* and *Les Tempes Modernes* supplement this work. From 1953 until his death in 1968 Kojève lived the life of an Hegelian civil servant, working as a planner for the Common Market in the French Ministry of Economic Affairs.

The roots of Kojève's dialectical materialism were contained in Hegel's philosophical anthropology. In Hegel's dialectic of master and servant Kojève saw the origins of Marx's† revolutionary proletariat and the idea that labor is the motor of historical change. Hegel had rejected the bourgeois premise that individuals are rational, autonomous subjects always calculating self-interest and protecting property. Men and women are indelibly *in* history. What one does and how it is done are questions answered by the socio-historical milieu, which is bound to universal processes. The first historical "moment" of human reality is a simple, non-self-conscious, passive awareness of external objects—the world of sensation, perception, and primitive consciousness. At this stage of history subjectivity is not yet constituted. Eventually human beings recognize in themselves a distinctive conscious humanity and the need for others to acknowledge it. We are constituted as human beings by interacting with, and being acknowledged by, other people. "Real and true man is the result of his interaction with others" (*Introduction to the Reading of Hegel*, p. 15), the original impulse by which history and nature are humanized. As actors quest for recognition and affirmation of autonomous humanity, they are thrown into social relationships. Thus begins the next developmental stage, marked by wars of prestige. In risking our physical lives to gain others' respect and recognition, we implicitly acknowledge the humanity of competitors, and they of us. Human history now is struggle and war, battles to the death in which humanity rises triumphantly from the ashes. While some perish, these struggles terminate by establishing permanent relations between combatants. The victor is powerful, controlling, autonomous consciousness; the slave, vanquished and dependent. Civilization consists of societies of rulers and ruled, kings and serfs. Like all of history, this stage also generates inherent conflicts and contradictions. Master and slave define each other, shaping the other's consciousness. Ironically, the master's humanity is recognized only by the slave, who, in the eyes of others, is unworthy. To everyone else, the master is merely a "slave owner," an objectified, dehumanized role. Thus, the master continually searches for an autonomous individual to acknowledge his humanity. The fruits of victory are frustration and anguish. The slave, acknowledged by no one and defeated in battle, is angry. In the terror of his master's oppression, the slave discovers his humanity as something denied and strives for the freedom to develop. This he achieves through labor, or praxis: actively humanizing nature and society, bringing them under his own willful control. Through labor and its products, slaves recognize their objective humanity. History's universal process culminates in mankind's authentic freedom. Each laborer eventually perceives himself as " 'icarnated' Spirit, . . . historical 'World,' . . . 'objectivized' History" (ibid., p. 25).

Hegel was the first to accord labor an immanent, rather than instrumental, value. It is the vehicle for humanity's evolution to autonomous consciousness and hence the essence of humanity. Through labor, the masses (i.e. the working class) create a productive apparatus that satisfies material needs and facilitates control of nature and society. Marx merely described the concrete forms that this struggle takes, actual material stages in the universal progression from exploitation and alienation to revolutionary freedom. Hegelianism, therefore, generated revolutionary Marxism. Historical materialism describes universal history in the contemporary era of humanity's liberation from masters, extending Hegel's analyses of historicity and dialectical logic. Marx's proletarian revolution culminates a total human movement from nonreflective passivity to "fully conscious consciousness" (ibid., p. 35), where workers cognitively will universal truth. Hegel's world spirit, for Kojève, works itself out in the concrete praxis of workers.

BIBLIOGRAPHY:

A. *Introduction to the Reading of Hegel* (New York: Basic Books, 1969).

B. George Lichtheim, *Marxism in Modern France* (New York: Columbia University Press, 1966); Mark Poster, *Existential Marxism in Postwar France* (Princeton, N.J.: Princeton University Press, 1975).

ROBERT A. GORMAN

KOLAKOWSKI, LESZEK (b. 1927). Leszek Kolakowski was born in Radom, Poland, 23 October 1927. He joined the Polish Communist Party in 1946. Receiving his doctorate from the University of Warsaw in 1953, he became a lecturer there in 1954 and was promoted to professor of the history of modern philosophy in 1959. Kolakowski established his professional reputation as a philosopher with works in the history of philosophy: a book on Spinoza, *The Individual and the Infinite*, and a comprehensive study of seventeenth-century nonconformist Christian sects in Western Europe, *Religious Consciousness and Ties of the Church*. From 1955 to 1957 he edited a weekly for young Communist intellectuals, *Pro prostu*—a magazine that was officially censured for its deviationist policy since it had been especially critical of the "new class," the Party bureaucracy, and its police methods. The publication was suspended in 1957 and never revived. In 1966, ten years after the Polish October, Kolakowski made a sharply critical speech at Warsaw University and as a consequence was expelled from the Party. Officially attacked for his "subversive" attitude toward Gomulka's political line, he was dismissed in March 1968 from his tenured position at Warsaw University and blacklisted by authorities. Kolakowski was allowed to leave Poland and since then has taught at numerous Western universities including McGill University, the University of California (Berkeley), Oxford, and the University of Chicago.

Kolakowski's creative work on Marxism† falls into two phases: revisionist and post-Marxist. Beginning his career as a conventional Marxist critic of the Catholic Church—as a state-sponsored anticlerical polemicist—he soon began to attack the distortion and vulgarization of Marxism in Poland, calling for a theoretical reconstruction of "true" Marxism. In essays collected under the title *Toward a Marxist Humanism* (1968), Kolakowski contributed to the revision of Marxism in at least three areas: epistemology, utopianism, and ethics.

First, based on Marx's *1844 Paris Manuscripts* Kolakowski developed a notion of truth that is closer to the pragmatism of William James than to the modified classical concept of Lenin.† In the spirit of pragmatism, the revisionist Kolakowski rejects Lenin's copy theory and affirms the functional, adaptive nature of cognition. According to Kolakowski, the Marxist idea of truth is not to be understood as the correspondence of an idea with external reality but as the product of interaction between work, social needs, and the natural environment. The only truth accessible to us is always to some degree that which we have made as a result of our humanization of nature. Second, deviating from orthodox Marxism, Kolakowski holds that utopia is a necessary component of revolution. It is, he argues, an important energizing device because factually there is always a great disproportion between effort expended and results achieved in revolutionary activity. This disproportion must be mitigated in the minds of revolutionaries by an artificial inflation of expected results. Without utopian thinking, Kolakowski maintains, no progressive activities would have taken place. Finally, against Stalinist† Marxism, Kolakowski asserts the moral responsibility of the individual, rejecting the view that duty derives from historical necessity. He argues for the need to liberate morality from the false dialectic that makes morality a tool of history and makes history a pretext for villainy. From this perspective there emerges an existential thesis—the total responsibility of individuals for their deeds. Kolakowski contends that, regardless of social forces, free action remains within the power of individuals. He maintains that one should be a Communist for moral reasons, not because communism is historically inevitable. Kolakowski in fact dismisses what he calls "the superstitious cult" of unverified laws of history, insisting that inevitability only applies to the past. Moreover, because human beings are compelled to make morally binding decisions in total ignorance of their consequences, tragedy is inherent in history. He rejects the escape from individual responsibility that can be found in either the absolute moral codes of religion or the guaranteed future of so-called *scientific* socialism. Scientific socialism is replaced by an *ethical* socialism, which denies the necessity of a socialist future. Indeed, Kolakowski maintains that the greater the probability of defeat, the higher the moral value of the revolutionary act.

Kolakowski's post-revisionist thought emerges in the late 1970s. In the comprehensive *Main Currents in Marxism* (1978) Kolakowski comes to critical terms with Marx and important Marxist movements and schools of thought, making it clear that we must go beyond Marxism. This three-volume work constitutes a significant contribution to the explication and criticism of the Marxist tradition. In volume 3 of *Main Currents* he concludes: "Marxism has been the greatest fantasy of our century" (p. 523). The destructiveness of Marxism is traced back to the Romantic and the Promethean motifs of Marx's thought. The Romantic motif is Marx's vision of social unity—a society without conflicts in which all values are reconciled. According to Kolakowski, this ideal can be realized in an industrialized society only through a system of despotic government where perfect unity must take the form of abolishing all institutions of social mediation, such as representative democracy. The Promethean motif—the view that the species can shape the world as it wishes—has, he argues, led to the disaster of economic voluntarism and to the attempt to organize economic life by police methods. If Marxism is not the efficient cause of despotic socialism, its lack of a clear principle of political interpretation at least opened the way for it, according to Kolakowski. By contrast, a democratic form of socialism would attempt to reconcile in a partial and compromising fashion: freedom and equality; economic planning and local autonomy; economic democracy and efficient management. In volume 3 of *Main Currents* Kolakowski denies that Marxism can be revised and made fruitful; his obituary is harsh: "As an explanatory system it is dead, nor does it offer any 'method' that can be effectively used to interpret modern life, to foresee the future, or cultivate utopian projects" (p. 529).

BIBLIOGRAPHY:

A. *Toward a Marxist Humanism* (New York: Grove Press, 1968); *The Socialist Idea* (New York: Basic Books, 1974); *Main Currents of Marxism*, 3 vols. (New York: Oxford University Press, 1978); *Religion* (New York: Oxford University Press, 1982).

B. *Tri-Quarterly: Leszek Kolakowski Reader*, no. 22 (Fall 1971).

DAVID MYERS

KOPELEV, LEV (b. 1912). Born into a Russian Jewish family in Kiev in 1912, Lev Kopelev became one of the leading dissident intellectuals in Moscow in the 1970s after publishing an exposé of the Stalinist† period in his memoirs. A philologist and specialist in German literature, Kopelev has also written essays on and translations of Bertolt Brecht,† E. T. A. Hoffmann, and other Western writers. As a young man, Kopelev was a committed Komsomol (Young Communist Youth League) member and participated in Stalin's collectivization drives. He joined the Communist Party during World War II, when he served as a major in the Red Army. Kopelev was arrested in 1945 for "anti-Soviet activities" and charged with sympathizing with the Germans at the end of the war, when he tried to prevent Soviet soldiers from committing atrocities against German civilians. He was sentenced to a ten-year term in *sharashka*, a special scientific institute staffed by prisoners. In the *sharashka*, Kopelev worked together with the writer Alexander Solzhenitsyn on developing a voice decoder to be used to identify individuals in wiretapped telephone conversations—a project Solzhenitsyn depicted in his *First Circle*. Kopelev continued to be a loyal Stalinist throughout his prison term and was rehabilitated in 1956, at which time he was reinstated in the Communist Party and joined the Writers Union. Kopelev became involved in the democratic movement in the 1960s by protesting the arrests of writers and human rights activists, for which he was expelled from the Communist Party in 1968. In 1977 he was expelled from the Writers Union for publishing his memoirs abroad. Under the threat of arrest, Kopelev left the Soviet Union in 1980 and currently lives in Cologne, West Germany.

While rejecting Marx's† conception of historical materialism, Kopelev believes it is essential to apply a dialectical method to historical analysis. His analysis of the Russian Revolution and its Stalinist development is unique among the historical debates of Soviet dissidents in that it integrates the "left" dissident view of the continuity of Soviet authoritarianism with Great Russian autocracy and the "liberal" dissident emphasis on freedom of belief and the autonomy of the "cultural-spiritual" sphere of society. Kopelev locates the main structural contradiction in the evolution of Russian society as one between the state and the nation. By "nation" Kopelev means "a cultural historical wholeness of people not determined by genetic or economic factors" (*Derzhava i narod*, 1982). He argues that "national bolshevism" as an ideology erroneously collapsed the distinction between state and nation, serving the interests of the state while repressing the interests of the nation. He maintains that Russian national culture developed in opposition to the repressive political traditions of the state. For Kopelev, a more adequate theory of socialism would require a conceptualization of the dialectical interplay between the political and the cultural-spiritual spheres of society.

BIBLIOGRAPHY:

A. *Brekht* (Moscow, Znanie, 1966); *To Be Preserved Forever* (Philadelphia: Lippincott, 1977); *The Education of a True Believer* (New York: Harper & Row, 1980); *Derzhava i narod* (New York: Ardis, 1982); *O Pravde i terpimosti* (New York: Khronika Press, 1982); *Ease My Sorrows* (New York: Random House, 1983).

MARTA ZAHAKEVICH

KORAC, VELJKO (b. 1914). Korac was born in Debelo Frdo, Korenila, Yugoslavia in 1914. He studied in Zagreb and in Prague from 1933 to 1938 and earned a Ph.D. in philosophy at the University of Belgrade. During World War II he fought with the Yugoslav partisans. His primary academic interests are the history of modern philosophy, philosophical anthropology, and sociology. Professor of philosophy at the University of Belgrade since 1957, Korac is associated with the *Praxis** circle of Yugoslav philosophers.

Korac, unlike most socialist humanists, rejects the equation of socialism and humanism. He believes that a humane society is the proper end of Marxism.† A socialist revolution is essential, but this will not necessarily lead to a humane society. In practice socialist societies have defined human liberation in technological and in economic terms. In doing this, socialist societies emulate bourgeois societies, but socialist economies, Korac argues, cannot compete with bourgeois economies by measures of productivity and efficiency. Socialist societies have not even matched the limited socio-political freedoms of bourgeois societies. Socialists have not paid sufficient attention to Marx's warnings of the reification of technology and economic progress. Korac believes that socialist societies must demonstrate their superiority by using the criterion Marx himself developed: creating a truly humane society. The appropriate standard is individual human freedom, not economic development.

Korac believes that new categories of explanation are required to account for social trends in the twentieth century. For example, the subject of history no longer is workers in advanced capitalist countries but rather workers in underdeveloped countries. Thus the character of liberating forces in the world has changed, but not their aim. Lenin† correctly understood this. However, Marx also showed the circumstances under which socialism can be real, not just an ideal. The circumstances include a necessary level of economic and social growth. This is the central paradox of Marxism in the twentieth century, and its solution requires critical, not ideological, thinking and human relationships based on praxis. Socialist democracy in an underdeveloped country based on self-management will foster a human community that can demonstrate to the world that the perspectives of socialism are real. Workers in advanced societies will be persuaded not by economic superiority, which socialist countries can never provide, but by the lived experience of a humane society.

BIBLIOGRAPHY:

A. *Marks i savremena sociologija* (Belgrade: Kultura, 1962); essays in *Praxis*, 1963–74.

B. Donald Hodges, *Socialist Humanism* (St. Louis: Warren H. Green, 1974).

GARY C. SHAW

KORSCH, KARL (1886–1961). Karl Korsch was born on 15 August 1886 in the German city of Todstedt, and attended the universities of Munich, Berlin, Geneva, and Jena. He studied law, economics, and philosophy, and in 1910 acquired his doctorate from the University of Jena with a thesis on the onus of proof in admissions of guilt. While a student he was a member of the Free Student Movement, which had contacts with the international socialist movement. In 1912 Korsch traveled to London, where he joined the Fabian Society, was influenced by the syndicalist movement, and wrote articles on life in England for German periodicals. With the outbreak of World War I, in 1914, Korsch returned to Germany. Although he opposed the war, he nevertheless served in the German army and was twice decorated with the Iron Cross. After the war, in 1919, he became a lecturer at Jena University. In 1917 Korsch joined the independent German Socialist Party (USPD), a leftist splinter party that emerged from the official German Social Democratic Party (SPD). In 1921 the USPD split, and Korsch—despite reservations—went into the German Communist Party (KPD). Korsch supported the doomed Sparticist uprising in Berlin (January 1919), the Munich Soviet Republic (April 1919), and other Marxist† and anarcho-syndicalist movements. He was a member of the Berlin Socialization Committee and contributed articles to the radical leftist magazine *Arbeiterrat*. His book *What Is Socialization?* (1919) outlines his own views on local worker autonomy and the necessity of workers' factory councils. As a prominent member of the KPD Korsch was elected to the Thuringian Parliament in 1923 and became Communist minister of justice in the Thuringian government. Korsch became editor of the leftist Party journal *Die Internationale*, and a Communist deputy to the Reichstag until 1928. As a delegate to the Fifth World Congress of the Comintern he was attacked for his Hegelian views (expressed in *Marxism and Philosophy*) and his opposition to the Bolshevization of the KPD. In 1925 he was dismissed from the editorship of *Die Internationale* and from then onward opposed the official KPD leadership. In 1926 Korsch helped organize the anti-Stalinist† magazine *Kommunistische Politik*, as well as the faction within the KPD known as the Entschiedene Linke (Resolute Lefts). Korsch was expelled from the KPD in 1926. After 1928 Korsch wrote and lectured in Germany, before fleeing the Nazis in February 1933. He collaborated with Bertolt Brecht† in Denmark until 1936, when Korsch emigrated to the United States. He taught sociology at Tulane University (1943–45), worked with the International Institute of Social Research in New York (1945–50), published articles on Marxist theory, and carried out some empirical social research with Kurt Lewin. In the early 1950s a pessimistic and isolated Korsch abandoned Marxism, but by the late 1950s there is evidence he foresaw the possibility of change in the Soviet Union and a Chinese reinvigoration of Marxist theory. He died in Belmont, Massachusetts, on 21 October 1961.

The underlying presumption of *Marxism and Philosophy* interprets society as a totality, an indissoluble whole where each element reinforces and reflects all others. Base and superstructure are reciprocally interconnected, and knowledge is inconceivable as an independent, passively determined epiphenomenon. Bourgeois society comprises a mystified, alienated consciousness and an exploitative, oppressive economic system. If Marxism is to be revolutionary, it must offer not only a doctrine of political and economic rebellion, but also a philosophical critique intellectually destroying an alienated bourgeois world view. Marxism "transcends" philosophy, in other words, is truly scientific, recognizing theory and practice as integral parts of one total whole. Bourgeois philosophy ignores this, perceiving itself eternally valid, independent of social activity. Ironically, however, in annihilating bourgeois philosophy, Marxism cannot ignore or abandon philosophy altogether. Orthodoxy is unaware that philosophy dialectically expresses historical trends and processes, and this ignorance isolates workers from their own revolution. A working-class revolution requires participants to experience revolutionary ideas cognitively as part of the actual disrupting act. The material ripening of capitalism, accompanied only by bourgeois values, increases the severity of exploitation without producing the impetus for change. Orthodox Marxism abdicates its philosophical responsibilities, is "untrue," by ignoring the actual plight of those it represents. Marxism embodies a unity of theory and practice, realized as a philosophical critique of capitalism that is simultaneously part of a total revolutionary process. In this sense Marxism has philosophically inherited the dialectical interrelation of theory and practice characterizing Hegelian idealism, although stressing—for the first time—matter.

Common Hegelian roots make comparisons with George Lukács* unavoidable. Dialectics, for Korsch and Lukács, is not an objective method that anyone can use to study any subject. It expresses the proletariat's revolutionary movement and is inseparably part of that movement. Thus dialectics is effectively applied to social inquiry only in revolutionary proletarian practice. Workers comprise a "universal" class in being uniquely capable of cognizing history's total movement. Of course, this cognition is dialectically expressed in the revolutionary act, which culminates history's objective "telos." The proletariat is, in Lukács's terms, the identical subject-object of history. Hegelian Marxism prescribes an a priori totality encompassing past and future, marked by polarizing class struggles corresponding to the developmental level of material production and culminating in workers' subjectively cognizing their objective revolutionary functions. *History and Class Consciousness* draws appropriate conclusions regarding the priority of authentic, not empirical, class consciousness. Korsch, however, was uncertain of Hegel's idealism, despite its logical connection to his own totalism. He argued that philosophical truth changes with history; hence, Marxism is a science to the extent that it adequately articulates the consciousness of revolutionary workers at the time that this consciousness peaks. As events change, so will Marxism's validity and usefulness. A philosophy that is true now because it adequately represents proletarian self-consciousness will turn false when workers' perceptions change. Marxist philosophy must take different forms in different historical eras, the implication being that, when no longer relevant to worker consciousness, it will disappear.

Natural science also expresses human interactions with nature mediated by productive forces. As the latter change, as we find more advanced ways of satisfying material needs, we relate differently to nature. The "validity" of present empirical "laws" is predicated on their adequately expressing common perceptions of nature. In bourgeois society, these alienate humanity from nature and postulate a belief in objective, impersonal, unilinear causal laws. Empirical natural science is valid because it reflects bourgeois alienation. After the proletarian revolution, however, the perceived relationship to nature will change as we socialize the productive apparatus and work cooperatively. External reality, no longer only a tool for personal aggrandizement, will be the natural context of history's totality, hence the environment for multifaceted human fulfillment. Nature will be humanized. Socialist natural science will analytically reflect and express this new cognitive dimension. Korsch's "relativism" is useful in criticizing abstract idealism and dogmatic materialism. By eliminating the a priori rationale of history and society, he theoretically negates Lenin's† dictatorial party of scientists. Marxism is scientific to the extent that it expresses an empirical proletarian world view and cannot forcibly impose objective truth on ignorant workers. History is constituted by empirical phenomena that shape perceptions. There is no organic, total process based on either a generic essence or an objective material dialectic. It is not surprising that Korsch gravitated toward the Frankfurt School of critical theory.

Korsch applied dialectics to the history of Marxism itself. Marxism has evolved through three distinct stages, each corresponding to a phase of worker self-consciousness. In stage one (1843–48), Marx's early writings reflect workers' inchoate fury, their slow but tangible realization of a dehumanized life in capitalism. The class struggle is just emerging in the minds and hearts of people hungry for freedom. Marxism, at this stage, is romantic—even idealistic—over-emphasizing history's subjective component and ignoring concrete material conditions. Stage two (1848–1900) encompassed the period of capitalist expansion and consolidation. Worker self-consciousness was stunted. Workers adopted bourgeois values and participated in bourgeois institutions. They no longer perceived exploitation and sought instead success according to capitalist standards. In the context of retarded worker consciousness, Marxism became pure theory: dogmatic, positivistic, metaphysical. Vulgar materialism was the form that Marxism took in this time of worker reaction, its roots found in utterances of Marx—taken out of context—and in Engels.† Marxism was an ideology, cut off from reality and congealed in an inflexible body of objective material laws. Stage three (1900s) corresponds to the emergence of trade union reformism, syndicalism, and bolshevism, all indicating the reawakening of proletarian consciousness. Marxism must now account for subjectively perceived class dynamics by philosophically recapturing history's totality, including reflective proletarian praxis. This is Marx's original intention and the essence of dialectics as a method of inquiry. Korsch repudiated the Third International† for reverting to stage two: defining consciousness as passively reflecting reality and defending a Party forcibly injecting truth into workers' minds.

By 1935 it was increasingly obvious that orthodox Marxism would survive Korsch's critique, capitalism remained vital and more flexible than anticipated, and workers in Western Europe were subjectively committed to capitalism. Stage three of Korsch's historical division would not likely experience the dialectical recovery of subjectivity. With all this depressing empirical evidence at hand and with Korsch entering the Frankfurt School, the issue was finally decided against Hegelianism. In ''Why I Am a Marxist'' Korsch delineated his nonidealist Marxism, which now merely performed a critical social function—spurning a positive epistemology and aiming to verify all claims empirically. Marxism deals with specific situations, not generalities, and is particularly useful in critically explaining capitalism's vertiginous transformation into fascism. Moreover, although Marxism must change, not merely contemplate, the world, it should not speculate on absolutes such as justice and freedom. Korsch had jettisoned not only Hegel's idealism but also apparently the notion of dialectics as an interpenetration of social phenomena. He isolated specific events and institutions and verified all assertions empirically. How this can be reconciled with the commitment to revolution is unclear. This article, like Korsch's early writings, is built on philosophical quicksand. Although never comfortable with one epistemology (hence his historicism), he also never convincingly worked out his problems. In retrospect, his eclecticism lacks philosophical rigor. Although his principled, inflexible rejection of Stalinism shows an impeccable character, his theoretical work is less admirable.

BIBLIOGRAPHY:

A. "Why I Am a Marxist," *Modern Monthly*, 9, no. 2 (April 1935), pp. 88–95; *Karl Marx* (London: Chapman & Hall, 1938); *Marxism and Philosophy* (New York: Monthly Review Press, 1970).

B. Patrick Goode, *Karl Korsch* (London: Macmillan, 1979).

ROBERT A. GORMAN

KOSÍK, KAREL (b. 1926). Karel Kosík was born in the city of Prague in 1926 and is of Czech nationality. As a student Kosík participated in the resistance to the Nazi occupation of Czechoslovakia and was imprisoned by the Gestapo. After the war he completed his studies in philosophy at the University of Leningrad and at Charles University in Prague. Until 1963 Kosík worked as a researcher at the Institute of Philosophy of the Czech Academy of Sciences. In that year he was appointed professor of philosophy in the Faculty of Letters at Charles University. Kosík soon became a director of the Union of Czech Writers, a member of the editorial committee of the union's weekly publication *Literární noviny* (Literary News), and in 1968, editor-in-chief of the monthly review *Plamen* (Flame). He was also on the editorial staff of the international journal *Praxis*,* which was an outlet primarily for Yugoslav philosophers. In this last project Kosík contributed to the ideological fermentation that eventually generated the Prague Spring,* a movement dedicated to combatting oppressive socialist bureacracies and reconciling socialism and individual liberty. His participation in the debates of the Fourth Congress of Czech writers in 1967, together with other critical writers (such as M. Kundera, L. Vaculík, and P. Kahout), set the stage for the more tumultuous events of 1968. Soon perceived as a Marxist† critic and heretic, Kosík participated in the extraordinary Fourteenth Congress of the Czech Communist Party, which energetically opposed the military intervention into Czechoslovakia by the Warsaw Pact nations. Kosík was elected to the Party's Central Committee. Remaining intransigent during the period of Czech "normalization" (i.e. re-Stalinization), Kosík was relieved of all official functions, expelled from the Party, and prohibited from teaching and publishing. All his books were removed from public libraries and bookstores. While he was under house arrest in late 1969, the political police seized his research notes and manuscripts. These were eventually returned to him following international protests led by Jean-Paul Sartre* and other Western intellectuals. Unable to work, Kosík lives modestly in Prague, continuing his philosophical studies as a bereaved scholar. Even though his works are still not published at home, he is nevertheless continually attacked by the Czech regime's official intellectuals as a dangerous revisionist.

Kosík's first important book, *Radical Czech Democracy*, was published in 1958. At this time research into national movements that preceded and presaged Marxism was popular throughout the Soviet bloc. These studies were inspired and influenced by Soviet ideologues who perceived the Russian revolutionary democrats (e.g. Belinsky, Herzen, Chernyshevsky) as the most progressive of pre-Marxist philosophers, far above the classical German philosophers. This book by Kosík is an indirect polemic against this ideology of the superiority and exclusivity of the Russians. It demonstrates that analogous phenomena (what Kosík calls the "algebra of revolution") have emerged independently of Russian thought not only in nearly all the countries of Central and Eastern Europe but also in several countries of Western Europe, especially those not experiencing a decisive bourgeois revolution, where the battle against feudalism fused with a radical critique of capitalism based on a utopian socialist ideology. His original interpretation of Czech radical democracy is influenced by, on the one hand, the work of G. V. Plekhanov† on Belinsky, Herzen, and Chernyshevsky, freed of Great Russian chauvinism, and, on the other hand, by the work of the first president of the Czech Republic, T. G. Masaryk, dealing with nineteenth-century Czech political ideology (e.g. F. Palacký and K. Havlíček).

Kosík's most important book is entitled *Dialectic of the Concrete* (1963). This work begins to reinterpret the philosophical foundation of Marxism as a "philosophy of praxis" that rejects the metaphysics of Engels† and Lenin's† dialectical materialism. Influenced by the young George Lukács,* he interprets *Capital* through the lens of Hegel's *Phenomenology of the Spirit*. After defining the interrelated concepts of the totality, reification, and alienation, he rejects the mystical Lukácsian notion of class consciousness as realized exclusively in the revolutionary workers' party. Differing from Lukács, and influenced by L. Goldmann's* genetic structuralism, Kosík interprets the concrete totality as a hierarchical structure. In elaborating his new Marxian ontology, Kosík was inspired also by the early work of H. Marcuse,* and integrates Heideggerian concepts (from *Being and Time*) into his own theories of reification and praxis. He also rejects Lukács's tendency to interpret all of reality through the dialectic of class consciousness and its reified products, eventually reducing even nature to a purely historical and social category. He criticizes at the same time vulgar Marxism's economic determinism, which tries to remedy Lukács's problems with a philosophical anthropology that separates man from the world, that is, from nature and history.

The fundamental concept of *Dialectic of the Concrete* is that of praxis. Praxis is neither practical ability (the technique and manipulation of objects), an epistemological category, nor noncontemplative everyday activity. Instead, praxis is defined as the unity of man and the world, matter and spirit, subject and object, product and producer. It discloses the secret of man as a self-creating creature who produces reality (human and social) and, consequently, can understand and transform reality (in all its aspects, human and extra-human). For this reason praxis has an existential dimension. However praxis is also precognitively defined by the material totality. It is thus a dialectical unity of opposing forces. It is "ambiguous," part "reflection" and part "projection." Existentialism or idealism "instantiates" creative activity, ignoring the determinate whole we are in. Conversely, vulgar materialism reduces consciousness to objective components and ignores subjective experience. Essential reality dynamically mediates concrete whole and abstract part; objectivity is expressed in and through subjectivity. This is what Kosík calls the "concrete totality." Whereas the practical and unilateral routines individuals daily perform, based on the division of labor, class society, and a hierarchy of social functions, produces the "pseudo-concrete" (i.e. the reified and objectified appearances of inauthentic everyday life), revolutionary praxis and creativity abolishes the pseudo-concrete and replaces it with truth, authenticity, and liberty. This praxis is also merely one moment of the concrete totality, which is prior to and includes subjectivity. Man, an "objective socio-historical subject," thus consciously realizes real matter. Base and superstructure interpenetrate, but epistemologically the former ultimately predominates. In 1968 Kosík used these concepts in a series of essays concerning political philosophy entitled *Our Political Crisis*. Here he undertakes a critical analysis of the crises of bureaucratic socialism and one-party systems and the fundamental problems surrounding the events of the Prague Spring. These essays are published (outside of Czechoslovakia) with others (e.g. "Philosophy and History of Literature," "Hašek and Kafka on the World of the Grotesque," "Anatomy and Morality") in several volumes that are not yet completed.

Kosík's unorthodox Marxist project has significantly influenced people like Robert Havemann* in East Germany, the Petofi Circle in Hungary, and the editors of the American journal *Telos*, particularly Paul Piccone.

BIBLIOGRAPHY:

A. *Česká radikální demokcracie* (Prague: Století, 1958); *La nostra crisi attuale* (Roma: Riuniti, 1969); *Dialectic of the Concrete* (Dordecht: Reidel, 1976).

B. Robert A. Gorman, *Neo-Marxism: The Meanings of Modern Radicalism* (Westport, Conn.: Greenwood Press, 1982).

LUBOMIR SOCHOR

KOSOVSKY, VLADIMIR (1867–1941). Kosovsky, born Nokhm Mendl Levinson, was one of the major writers, editors, and theoreticians of the General Jewish Workers' Union (the Bund) in its formative years. Born in Dvinsk, in the Russian Empire, in 1867, Kosovsky first entered the revolutionary movement in Kovno in the 1880s and was later active in Vilna (1894–98) and in Minsk (1898). He was a delegate to the Bund's founding convention, a member of the first Central Committee of the Bund, and—following his arrest by the tsarist police and subsequent escape from Russia—a long-term member of the Bund's Foreign Committee. During the period 1900–5, Kosovsky lived in Western

Europe and represented the Bund at the Paris and Amsterdam Congresses of the International as well as at the second congress of the Russian Social Democratic Workers Party (RSDWP). In 1905 Kosovsky went to Russia at the request of the Central Committee of the Bund and worked there for the movement until 1907, at which point he returned to Western Europe. He served on the Bundist delegations to the fifth party congress of the RSDWP, the Kienthal Conference (organized by the International Socialist Commission) of 1916, and to the Bern Conference of Socialist parties in 1919. Throughout the final years of the nineteenth and the first years of the twentieth century Kosovsky was an editor of and contributor to many Bundist periodicals, including *Der yidisher arbeter*, *Di arbeter shtime*, *Posledniia izvestiia*, *Vestnik Bunda*, and the Vilna *Folkstsaytung*. He also wrote for non-Bundist periodicals, such as the German Social Democratic organs *Luch*, *Nasha zarya*, and *Novaya rabochaya gazeta*. In addition, Kosovsky was the author of a number of pamphlets and booklets in Russian, Yiddish, and German on questions of the day. During this period, he was the most authoritative publicist in the Bundist movement. In the post–World War I era, while living in Berlin, Kosovsky continued to write for the Bundist press and published regularly in the New York *Tsukunft*. In 1930 he moved to Warsaw, where he was made a member of the editorial board of the Bundist daily in that city as well as a member of the Central Committee of the Bund. At the time of the Nazi invasion of Poland, Kosovsky was the only one of the founders of the Bund still active in the movement who was still in Europe. He left Warsaw in 1939, traveling first to Pinsk and later to Vilna, where he was forced to use false papers in order to escape arrest by the Soviet secret police. Aid rendered to the Bund by the American Federation of Labor and by the New York-based Jewish Labor Committee made it possible for Kosovsky to leave Vilna and to emigrate to New York. He arrived in New York in April of 1941 and attempted to continue his political activity on behalf of the Bund, but he became seriously ill several months after his entry into the United States. He died in New York on 19 October, 1941.

Kosovsky played a key role in Russian Jewish revolutionary circles in the 1890s by forcefully advocating the need for a union of Jewish proletarian groups and thereby stimulating the formation of the Bund itself. In later years, his defense of the Bund against attacks by the Polish Socialist Party and by the Russian Socialists grouped around *Iskra*, as well as his writings on terrorism and on the national question, were also of great importance. Kosovsky responded to the Polish Socialists by asserting that just as the Polish workers needed their own party, so too did the Jewish workers. The Jewish workers, Kosovsky maintained, were entitled to the same civil rights as were the Poles and no more hurt the workers' cause by demanding these rights than the Poles did by demanding rights for themselves. During the period of debates between the Bund and *Iskra*, Kosovsky insisted that the Bund was the sole representative of the Jewish proletariat in the RSDWP, that it had the right to conduct its work throughout the Empire, and that it was a federative part of the RSDWP. In 1902–03 Kosovsky strongly condemned the use of organized terror, maintaining that terror, if granted any legitimacy, would eventually become the dominant tactic of the movement. Kosovsky's writings on the national question defend the claim that the Jews are a nation. He believed that Russian Jewry was entitled to national cultural autonomy (autonomous control over its own cultural matters) and that Zionism was a reactionary ideology in that it claimed that the problems of Russian Jewry could be solved only by emigration. In Kosovsky's eyes, the Bund had to be a nationally conscious movement once it became a mass movement and, as such, had both to defend the national rights of Russian Jewry and to take a positive stance toward the secular national culture developed by Russian Jewry in the Yiddish language.

BIBLIOGRAPHY:

   B. Zalman Reyzen, *Leksikon fun der yidisher literatur*, 3 vols. (Vilna: Farlag fun b. kletskin, 1930), cols. 476–81; John Mill, *Pionern un boyer* (New York: Farlag der veker, 1946), pp, 218–22; Shloyme Mendelson, *Shloyme mendelson. zayn lebn un shafn* (New York: Farlag unzer tsayt, 1949), pp. 441–46; J. S. Hertz, "Vladimir kosovsky," *Doyres bundistn* (New York: Farlag unzer tsayt, 1956), pp. 11–67; Yisroel Figa, "Vladimir kosovsky," in *Leksikon fun der nayer yidisher literatur*, ed. Berl Kahn et al. vol. 8 (New York: Alveltlekhn yidishn kultur-kongres, 1981), cols. 81–82.

JACK JACOBS

KOSTERIN, ALEXEI EVGRAFOVICH (1896–1968). This "old Bolshevik" and former prisoner of tsarist prison camps ultimately came to criticize the Soviet leadership for its nationalities policy. As a Russian-born journalist he covered the plight of minority nations deported by Stalin† in World War II and became their champion for repatriation. For Kosterin, the Soviet leadership's nation-blind assimilationist nationalities policy had created the opposite of a harmonious classless society, generating serious discrimination against national minorities in favor of the Russian nation and justifiable resentment against the Soviet regime. He renounced his Party membership in 1968 and was expelled from the Soviet Writers Union. His funeral became an occasion for several hundred other dissidents whom he influenced to reaffirm their commitment to change the course of the official Soviet policy of forcible russification.

BIBLIOGRAPHY:

   A. See relevant unpublished letters in the Arkhiv samizdata, Radio Liberty Research, Munich.

DAVID KOWALEWSKI

KRAHL, HANS-JÜRGEN (1944–1970). Born in 1944 in rural Lower Saxony, Krahl studied in Frankfurt, participating in the seminars of Theodore Adorno*. During the protest movement of the late 1960s he became an important theoretician and political activist. In 1968 Krahl was accused of inciting to riot during a demonstration against the awarding of the Peace Prize of the German Book Trade to Leopold Senghor; in the trial that ensued he presented a biographical account of his own political development from the reactionary mysticism of his native village through the relatively enlightened conservatism of Christian democracy to the Marxism† of the student movement ("Angaben zur Person," in *Konstitution und Klassenkampf*, pp. 19–30). Krahl died in an automobile accident in February 1970. A collection of his writings, largely unpublished during his lifetime, appeared posthumously in 1971.

In his speeches and essays (many fragmentary), Krahl endeavors to reappropriate Marxism for the West German student movement, which, he argues, because of its largely bourgeois composition and specific national history, i.e., the destruction of the workers' movement by national socialism, had no immediate access to a revolutionary tradition. Opposing contemporary efforts to establish a neo-orthodoxy by an unmediated return to classical Marxism, Krahl argues for a historicization of historical materialism and the elaboration of a theory appropriate to the mid-twentieth century in which the market dynamics of laissez-faire capital have been superseded by the monopolistic structures of the authoritarian state. The effort to historicize theory derives from George Lukács,* Karl Korsch,* and the left-wing communism of the 1920s, whereas the insistence on the specific character of a postliberal capitalism is indicative of Krahl's persistent emphasis on the key economic motifs in the critical theory of the Frankfurt School, although he rejects its resigned political stance ("The Political Contradictions in Adorno's Critical Theory," pp. 164–67). His philosophical reconstruction of Marxism centers on the constitution of the bourgeois subject, its dissolution in the neurotic projections of fascism, and the possible genesis of a revolutionary class consciousness ("Thesen zum allgemeinen Verhältnis von wissenschaftlicher Intelligenz und proletarischem Klassenbewusstsein," 1969, in *Konstitution und Klassenkampf*, pp. 330–47).
BIBLIOGRAPHY:

A. *Konstitution und Klassenkampf. Zur historischen Dialektik von bürgerlicher Emanzipation und proletarischer Revolution. Schriften, Reden und Entwürfe aus den Jahren 1966–1970* (Frankfurt: Neue Kritik, 1971); "The Political Contradictions in Adorno's Critical Theory," *Telos*, no. 21 (Fall 1974), pp. 164–67; *Erfahrung des Bewusstseins: Kommentare zu Hegels Einleitung der Phaenemenologie des Geistes und Exkurse zur materialistischen Erkenntnistheorie*, ed. Carl G. Hegemann (Frankfurt: Materialisverlag, 1979).

B. Helmut Reinicke, *Für Krahl*, Internationale Marxistische Diskussion 37 (Berlin: Merve, 1973).

RUSSELL BERMAN

KRISTEVA, JULIA (b. 1941). Julia Kristeva was born in Bulgaria in 1941 and received her early schooling from French nuns. She studied literature as an undergraduate and became a journalist for a Communist Party newspaper in Sofia. In 1966 she traveled to Paris on a doctoral fellowship and never returned to Bulgaria. In Paris, she studied with Marxist† literary critic Lucien Goldmann*; attended the Ecole Practique des Hautes Etudes, and became Claude Lévi-Strauss's* assistant at CNRS. In 1967—at the height of the structuralist–Marxist debates*—she became associated with the journal *Tel Quel*, becoming an editor in 1970. During these years she also underwent psychoanalytic training with Jacques Lacan and became a therapist with a small practice. In 1974, at the height of Parisian fashionable Maoism, she went to China with the *Tel Quel* group of Roland Barthes,* Philippe Sollers*, and Jean Wahl. Subsequently, she published *About Chinese Women*, which was for years the only access to her writings available to the English reader. In the early 1970s, Kristeva began to write on feminist themes—gender differences, childrearing, and development—and became active in the French feminist movement. Currently she teaches at the University of Paris, Vincennes, and at Columbia University in New York. She is an editor of *Tel Quel* and of *Semiotica*.

Kristeva's early experiences with Stalinism innoculated her to a great degree against the various stylish leftisms of Parisian intellectuals and, at the same time, against the cynical, apolitical reaction of the late 1970s. From her earliest published essays to the more recent *Powers of Horror* (1980), there is a steady development of a unique theoretical voice. Never abandoning her grasp of the revolutionary force of art and criticism, she has progressively deepened and extended her explorations of cultural history and of the problems of becoming/being other—of change—through linguistics, anthropology, and psychoanalytic theory. In her writing there is the stamp of individuality, of unique usages and neologisms reminiscent of her good friend Roland Barthes. It is not possible to summarize her contributions as they are very much still "in process"; however, Kristeva has succeeded in focusing attention on the aesthetic and linguistic constitution of everyday life. She has also revealed this constitution in the symbolic formation of our emotional lives and emphasized the necessity of comprehending these constitutional relationships prior to the undertaking of any project of social change. Much of her recent effort, in this regard, has been directed toward a reformulation of Freudo-Marxism that would rid it of its now notorious phallic-oedipal biases. (see *Desire in Language*, 1980.)

BIBLIOGRAPHY:

A. *Desire in Language* (New York: Columbia University Press, 1980); *About Chinese Women* (New York: Urizen, 1981); *Powers of Horror* (New York: Columbia University Press, 1982).

B. Rosalind Coward and John Ellis, *Language and Materialism* (London: Routledge & Kegan Paul, 1977).

LAURENCE E. WINTERS

KRZYWICKI, LUDWIG (1859–1941). Born on 21 August 1859 in the city of Plock, Krzywicki was a Polish sociologist, historian of economic organizations, ethnographer, and anthropologist. He became interested in the works of Marx† during the course of his studies in mathematics and medicine at the University of Warsaw. In 1882 he helped translate and edit the first volume of the Polish version of *Das Kapital*. He studied history and economics in Leipzig, Zurich, and Paris. In 1885 he returned to Poland and became the leading ideologue of the Society of Polish Workers. During the years 1891–93, because of political harassment at home, he traveled in Berlin and the United States, where he carried out anthropological and ethnological research. He took an active part in the 1905 Revolution as editor of the Polish Socialist Party's *Daily Courier*. After Polish independence in 1918 Krzywicki devoted himself to academic work. He lectured at the University of Warsaw in the Department of Statistics and was director of the Institute of Social Economics (1921–39). He organized and edited memoirs of unemployed Polish workers and poor peasants, eventually publishing this only investigative picture of its kind of Poland in the 1920s.

Krzywicki belonged to the first generation of Marx's students (which also included Karl Kautsky,† Wilhelm Liebknecht,† and Eduard Bernstein,* all of whom he knew personally). His world view was also influenced by late nineteenth-century positivism and the evolutionism of Darwin and Morgan. In his own research he accepted three fundamental assumptions. First, social processes are similar to those in nature and are subject to laws that can be recognized and harnessed. Second, social growth has a progressive character. The catalysts of progress are not only conflicts but also cooperative efforts among people and social groups. And third, all social research must be historical and concrete, taking into account the place and time conditioning the appearance of social phenomena. Krzywicki did not identify himself with the mechanistic interpretation of historical materialism, noting that in many historic situations consciousness actively shapes social existence. He created the notion of ''social ideas,'' which he understood as a kind of gestalt that defines the outlook of social groups. A significant portion of Krzywicki's scholarly work was devoted to primitive society. He carried out research comparing the division of labor in the animal world (an ant colony) with that of primitive human tribes. He discovered in both a ''social instinct,'' the germ of cooperative animal and human organization. He also studied the influence of natural reproduction and population density on the structure of primitive societies.

Krzywicki was against the mechanical transference of the capitalist growth model of Western Europe to underdeveloped countries, on the grounds that these countries can have different ''social ideas'' and thus different economic and political requirements. In his studies on agricultural society Krzywicki adopted the theory of two models of agricultural growth. In highly industrialized societies (e.g. the United States), where there is plenty of land, agriculture has an industrial-capitalist character. In Europe the remnants of feudalism cause a division of agriculture. According to Krzywicki, a radical agrarian program should endeavor to socialize agriculture, although he advocated cooperative and not state forms of ownership. He noted, however, that in the second agricultural model there must necessarily be a transition period, during which the division of landed estates among small independent farmers is carried out.

BIBLIOGRAPHY:

A. *Ustroje Spoteczno-gospodarcze w okresie dzikości i barbarzyństwa* (Warsaw: Czcionkami Drukarni naukowej, 1914); *Primitive Society and Its Vital Statistics* (London: Macmillan, 1934); *Kwestia rolna* (Warsaw, Państwowe Wydawn, 1966).

B. Tadeusz Kowalik, *Krzywicki* (Warsaw: Państwowe Wydawn, 1965); Leszek Kolakowski, *Main Currents of Marxism*, vol. 3 (New York: Oxford University Press, 1978).

PIOTR OGRODZIŃSKI

KURON, JACEK (b. 1935). Kuron, born in 1935, the son of a worker and
Socialist Party organizer, is a major figure in contemporary Polish politics. He
has had an amazing career of political activism. As a young man, he was a hard-
working leader of the Young Communists who won acclaim from the Polish
United Workers' Party (PUWP) Politburo in 1951 for his work in polling public
opinion about Germany. However, he soon ran afoul of the Party's leaders,
when he increasingly felt the need to decry bureaucracy and the lack of popular
participation during the 1956–57 years of de-Stalinization. Although he was
allowed to become a university instructor, he was expelled from the Party and
jailed in 1964 for his collaboration with another instructor—Karol Modzelewski—in an "Open Letter to the PUWP." Upon his release, he renewed his
critical activities. By the second wave of workers' strikes in 1976, he was one
of a handful of intellectuals who formed the Committee for Workers' Defense
(KOR). In that capacity, he wrote articles analyzing Polish conditions, helped
to issue information bulletins that did much to create a sense of community
among workers and others across the country, participated as a major organizer
in the dissident "Flying University," and generally assisted in creating the
atmosphere necessary to forming a trade union. As a result, he was the focus
of attention for the Polish secret police and was arrested again in 1980 when
strikes once again broke out over price increases. His role in the KOR, however,
led the Interfactory Strike Committee to demand (successfully) his release and
that of other dissident intellectuals. In the heyday of Solidarity that followed,
he was one of the top advisors to the union's national leadership. Although
frequently opposed to "impossible demands" presented by that leadership to
the Polish government, he was viewed as dangerous and thus was once again
imprisoned when martial law was imposed.

His works have focused on the contradictions of socialism in Poland, emphasizing the politically exclusive nature of power and the resultant governmental
arbitrariness. His major work, with Modzelewski, "The Open Letter," (1972)
points to the displacement of the working class by the bureaucracy in controlling
Polish society and calls for another revolution, marked by a strategy of nonviolence, to overthrow that bureaucracy. This idea of a second revolution is
found among other Eastern European dissidents of the 1960s and 1970s, but
Kuron revealed a remarkable appreciation for the particular conditions of Polish
socialism and for the power of mass action: he and Modzelewski suggested
united action by the working class and other parts of society in rejecting the
automatic obedience expected by the authorities. This idea was more fully elaborated in the 1970s: social change was to be accomplished, Kuron stated in 1976
in his "Proposal for an Opposition Program," by the creation of a "social
movement." This movement was to unite workers, peasants, and intellectuals

into a "nonpolitical" body opposing the state apparatus. Such an alliance of classes would force it to change society and share power. This Polish dissident form of a "national liberation front" was the intellectual precursor of Solidarity. Kuron called for free elections in a multiparty system, human rights, free trade unions, and economic decentralization. This list reveals that Kuron accepted the critique of Soviet-style "socialist democracy" that the "revisionists" of the 1960s had made. (His impact on Solidarity is shown by the fact that eventually the union embraced all his particular demands.) Moreover, he pleaded for some degree of national independence, with due regard for Soviet sensibilities, in the form of "Finlandization." This could be gained by mass action because the costs of Polish resistance would deter a repeat of August 1968.

In an article and an open letter from his prison cell, Kuron denounced the imposition of martial law as the occupation of Poland by "the people who represented the interests of the Soviet Union in Poland" and suggested that "a well-organized mass resistance movement" giving "absolute discipline" to a "main center" was the only way to pressure the authorities. If necessary, leaflet distribution and graffiti writing were to be complemented by local strikes and a nationwide general strike, and even "resort to violence." His general orientation was not accepted by the leaders of underground Solidarity, although many of his specific tactical suggestions were, to no avail. Only his call for preparation for armed resistance—storming of police and radio stations, as well as Party and government offices—went unheeded.

BIBLIOGRAPHY:

A. "An Open Letter to the Polish United Workers' Party," in *Soviet Communism and the Socialist Vision*, ed. Julius Jacobson (New Brunswick, N.J.: Transaction Books, 1972); "For a Unique Platform for the Opposition," in *La Pologne*, ed. Z. Erard and M. G. Zygier (Paris: Maspero, 1977); "One Way Out" and "An Open Letter to Zbigniew Bujak, Wiktor Kulerski and Other Activists in the Resistance Movement," *Solidarity Bulletin* (New York Committee in Support of Solidarity), no. 3 (August 1982).

B. Peter Raina, *Political Opposition in Poland* (London: Poets and Painters Press, 1978); Steward Steven, *The Poles* (New York: Macmillan, 1982); Neal Ascherson, *The Polish August* (New York: Viking Press, 1982).

THOMAS OLESZCZUK

L

LASCH, CHRISTOPHER (b. 1932). Christopher Lasch, an American social historian, was born in Omaha, Nebraska, in 1932. He received his B.A. (1954) from Harvard University and his M.A. (1955) and Ph.D. (1961) from Columbia University. Lasch has taught at Williams College (1957–59), Roosevelt University (1960–61), and the State University of Iowa, where he became associate professor of history in 1963. In 1966 he was appointed professor of history at Northwestern University. Lasch is presently professor of history at the University of Rochester. His major works include *The New Radicalism in America* (1965), *The Agony of the American Left* (1969), *Haven in a Heartless World: The Family Besieged* (1977), *The Culture of Narcissism: America in an Age of Diminishing Expectations* (1979), and *The Minimal Self: Psychic Survival in Troubled Times* (1984). He has also written numerous articles.

Lasch is one of the most penetrating critics of American corporate capitalism—its bureaucratization of American life and the concomitant destruction of individualism. In his recent works, particularly *The Minimal Self*, Lasch, like Herbert Marcuse,* utilizes a fusion of Marxism† and Freudianism to critique corporate capitalism and explain the malaise of contemporary American culture. For Lasch, recent history reveals the decadence of bourgeois capitalist society. Rugged individualism, the mainspring of capitalism's rise, has degenerated into "narcissism"—an all-consuming concern with self. The self-assured individualist has given way to the narcissist, who is ostensibly free from the constraints of institutions like family and religion yet is frightfully aware of his own mortality and dependent upon the approval of others for his self-esteem. Contemporary Americans, jolted by events like the Nazi holocaust, the threat of nuclear war, diminishing natural resources, inflation, unemployment, Vietnam, and Watergate, have fallen victim to narcissism. Disillusioned with such traditional pillars as country and religion, fearful of the future, cut off from the past, Americans are exhibiting a narcissistic "live for today" attitude. Unconcerned about their ancestry or their posterity, Americans have drawn inward, obsessed only with the here and now. This explains the proliferation of self-awareness movements and other "therapeutic" devices designed to make people feel good about themselves. The void left by the exit of religion is now filled by what Lasch calls the "therapeutic sensibility"—"the feeling, the momentary illusion of personal well-being, health, and psychic security" (*Culture of Narcissism*, p. 33). The therapist has replaced the clergyman. This has resulted in a mania for self-improvement in America, an overwhelming desire to be healthy and to feel that one is in control of one's life. Narcissism is evident in various aspects of contemporary American life—in self-awareness movements, in fads such as jogging and health foods, in the creation of false needs by advertisers, in the shallow adulation of celebrities, in apathy toward political and social issues, in the erosion of authority, in sports as mere entertainment, and in the decay of the nuclear family. Lasch identifies the culprit in this collapse into narcissism as corporate capitalism. The narcissistic tendencies of our time merely culminate the assault of monopoly capital on the individual in its efforts to forge a bureaucratic society.

Lasch sees a link between corporate capitalism and the decay of the bourgeois family. The nuclear family was a product of early capitalism, serving as a haven from the competitive world of the free market. According to Lasch, the decay of the family in the twentieth century is a manifestation of the narcissism of aged capitalism. This decay results from the intrusion of the so-called helping professions into family life. A battery of "therapeutic experts"—home economists, psychologists, psychiatrists, etc.—have surfaced in the twentieth century to tell parents how to raise their children. Functions formerly handled by the family, such as education, are assumed increasingly by external agencies and experts, who are the agents of monopoly capitalism. It is the function of these experts to teach children to conform, to become cogs in a bureaucratic society. With industrialization, home life and work became separated. Work life in the factory or the postindustrial bureaucracy is dull and unfulfilling. When home and work life were joined, the child could see the output of the parent's labor. This is no longer the case. So therapeutic experts are needed to help explain to children why they too must do this boring work. Children are taught to be "well adjusted." Furthermore, under the influence of the helping professions parents have become more permissive. Without parental authority, children are left to themselves to deal with the fears and anxieties of adolescence. Thus, young people are prone to binges of self-gratification involving drugs or alcohol. The intrusion of these helping professions, under the wing of corporate capitalism, has led to the destruction of the nuclear family. It was from the family that the individual formed a large part of his personality. Now that institution is greatly weakened due to the influence of monopoly capitalism.

Lasch argues that the only way out of this social malaise, of which narcissism is the symptom, the only way to restore a true individualism to the American landscape, is a radical transformation of society along socialist lines. Monopoly capitalism is the enemy, and it must be destroyed. Centralized authority and bureaucratization, at both the private and public levels, must be replaced by decentralized authority and more local control. According to Lasch, radical movements have sought to transform American society, but inevitably they have failed. The populist, labor, and women's movements of the early twentieth century failed because they settled for small, particularistic goals, such as better farm prices, or higher pay, or the right to vote, rather than continuing to insist on the broad program of societal reforms they originally espoused. The American socialist movement split over the direction it would take, whether it would follow the Bolshevik model or a form adapted to the American environment. Radical intellectuals and writers failed in that they used Marxist theory merely for cultural protest and did not attempt to link that theory to an in-depth analysis of American society. The black power advocates of the late 1960s failed in that they did not carry their fight against racism to the source of the problem—corporate capitalism. Their political kindred, the new left, attacked corporate capitalism but did not develop a cohesive ideology. They were only critics. There was no theoretical underpinning to their criticism. Thus all of these radical movements failed, and in his most recent work, Lasch seems pessimistic about the fate of American society and the possibility of radical reform.

In summary, Christopher Lasch is a critic of corporate capitalism and its assault on individualism. This assault has precipitated the narcissism that now engulfs American society. Nowhere is this more evident than in the destruction of the nuclear family. The only way this situation can be remedied, the only way individualism and freedom can be restored, is through a radical transformation of American society along socialist lines. Centralized authority must be supplanted by decentralized authorities that permit local communities to control economic investment and political decision making. Ironically, only Marxian socialism can enliven the American ideal of individual freedom. Lasch is pessimistic that these changes can take place.

BIBLIOGRAPHY:

A. *The American Liberals and the Russian Revolution* (New York: Columbia University Press, 1962); *The New Radicalism in America* (New York: Vintage Books, 1965); *The Agony of the American Left* (New York: Knopf, 1969); *World of Nations: Reflections on American History, Politics, and Culture* (New York: Random House, 1974); *Haven in a Heartless World: The Family Besieged* (New York: Basic Books, 1977); *The Culture of Narcissism: America in an Age of Diminishing Expectations* (New York: Norton, 1979); *The Minimal Self* (New York: Norton, 1984).

EARL SHERIDAN

LECOURT, DOMINIQUE (b. 1944). Other biographical information is not available. The rich diversity of post–World War II French Marxism† is illustrated in the work of Dominique Lecourt. Lecourt's theoretical project, begun in the late 1960s and continued into the present, entails the productive confrontation of Marxist philosophy with the epistemological positions of Gaston Bachelard,* Georges Canguilhem,* Michel Foucault,* Thomas Kuhn, and Karl Popper on the terrains of both the philosophy of science and epistemology. This project, spelled out in *Marxism and Epistemology: Bachelard, Canguilhem, Foucault* and in his latest book on Popper (not yet translated into English), proceeds by a critical interrogation of the epistemological stances of these key thinkers from the standpoint of Marxist philosophy. Lecourt's treatment of Marxist philosophy and his interrogation of alternative positions follows closely the lines of inquiry opened by his teacher and collaborator, Louis Althusser.* Lecourt stresses the importance of the concept of "epistemological break" (introduced by Bachelard and developed by Canguilhem, Foucault, and Althusser) for theorizing the discontinuity of the history of the sciences and the irreducible epistemological and methodological differences between contemporaneous sciences. Lecourt applauds the antipositivist, anti-evolutionist conceptions of the philosophy and history of scientific practice advanced by Bachelard and others and claims a similar conception (via Althusser) for Marxist social theory and history. In his introduction to the English translation of *Marxism and Epistemology*, Lecourt moves beyond his appreciation of discontinuist notions of scientific practice to critique briefly Kuhn's conception of "normal science," a conception that Lecourt shows to be grounded in an "idealist" philosophical position. Lecourt's critique reveals the central thesis of his own work: the objectivity and validity of sciences (their "normality") cannot be guaranteed by a master "science of sciences"—one that establishes for all scientific practices, past, present, and future, universal rules to measure the validity and objectivity of their truth claims. Lecourt adopts Bachelard's concept of an epistemological "value" or "norm" to argue that every science establishes its objectivity "by itself" and, hence, erects its own definitions and criteria of "truth."

Lecourt equally criticizes Kuhn's conventionalist thesis that the "normality" of science can be referred to scientists' decisions to choose determinate scientific procedures and standards of justification. Lecourt's critique consists of his rejection of any sociology of science that seeks to explain the "internal normality" of a science as the simple theoretical effect or expression of economic, sociological, or psychological extra-discursive determinations. Lecourt argues, importantly, that there is a complex interaction (or "overdetermination," in the sense of Althusser's highly productive deployment of the term) between the internal "norms" of a scientific practice and concrete social conditions, including class aspects, an interaction that produces the differential life histories of diverse sciences. It is Lecourt's position that only historical materialism (the Marxist "science of history") possesses the conceptual means to theorize this interaction. Hence, Lecourt offers historical materialism as a means to explain the "uneven development" of and points of contact and demarcation between different sciences in addition to their particular "internal" histories. Such materialist explanations, says Lecourt, are precisely what is lacking in the work of Bachelard, Canguilhem, Foucault, and Kuhn.

In *Proletarian Science? The Case of Lysenko*, Lecourt poses Lysenkoism as a hitherto neglected problem for Marxist philosophy. He locates Lysenkoism theoretically as a consequential effect of Stalin's† interpretation of dialectical materialism as an ontology (dialectics as the objective laws of nature), an interpretation that he counterposes to the approach taken by Karl Marx, Vladimir

Lenin,† Mao Zedong,† Antonio Gramsci,* and Althusser that treats dialectical materialism as a critical theory of the production of scientific knowledges. According to Lecourt, Stalin's interpretation served as the ideological defense for the thesis that science could be divided into two camps (or sciences): proletarian science, the application and extension of dialectical materialism to all scientific realms, of which Lysenko's account of heredity was the prototype; and bourgeois science, the expression of idealism, of which Mendelian genetics was the prototype. In line with his argument in *Marxism and Epistemology*, Lecourt shows that the Lysenkoist strategy to guarantee the validity of sciences by reference to dialectical materialism and to the class struggle (whose theoretical form was conceived as a struggle between "truth" and "error" in science) had serious negative consequences for the sciences in the Soviet Union and for Marxist philosophy everywhere.

Following Bachelard and others, Lecourt rejects all absolutist claims to truth. However, he resists the epistemological relativism that frequently accompanies such a rejection. His work is distinguished by the demonstration, presented lucidly in his book on Lysenko, that truth claims can be differentially valued and hence evaluated on the grounds of their differential social effects. The hallmark of Lecourt's work is a Marxist approach that seeks to explain specifically the differential social causes and consequences of various sciences with their respective truth claims. The point of the Marxist approach is to use such an explanation to inform practical struggles for or against particular sciences precisely on the grounds of their social consequences.

BIBLIOGRAPHY:

A. *Marxism and Epistemology: Bachelard, Canguilhem, Foucault*, trans. B. Brewster (London: New Left Books, 1975); *Proletarian Science? The Case of Lysenko*, trans. B. Brewster (London: New Left Books, 1977).

JACK AMARIGLIO AND RICHARD WOLFF

LEFEBVRE, HENRI (b. 1901). One of the central and most prolific figures in twentieth-century French Marxist† philosophy, Lefebvre was born in 1901 in Hegetmau (Gascony) and spent his youth in Navarreux. With the goal of becoming a college instructor, he studied philosophy, in particular Augustine and Pascal, with Maurice Blondel at the university in Aix-en-Provence and then attended the Sorbonne, where he worked with the neo-Kantian Leon Brunschvicg, an opponent of dialectical thought who argued that Hegel was a Romantic who violated the canons of science. In the 1920s Lefebvre revolted against the philosophical currents dominant in French academia (Cartesianism, Bergsonian vitalism, neo-Kantianism) and helped found the "Philosophies" circle†. This group of young intellectuals, among whom were to be counted Georges Politzer, Paul Nizan,† Norbert Guterman, and Georges Friedmann† among others, underwent various romantic and surrealist phases before joining the French Communist Party in 1928 and publishing *La Revue marxiste*, often characterized as the first serious French Marxist theoretical journal. In the 1930s Lefebvre, together with

Guterman, translated and published the first French selections of the recently discovered *1844 Manuscripts* of Marx and also Lenin's† *Philosophical Notebooks* on Hegel. Lefebvre's *Dialectical Materialism* (1939) was a landmark text in French Marxism and a marked contrast to the Stalinized† thinking of the Communist Party because of its author's emphasis on Marx's debt to Hegel and on Marx's early works. The book was banned under the Nazi occupation, during which Lefebvre served in the Resistance. In the 1940s he emerged as perhaps the most eminent of French Communist philosophers and played a leading role in the Party's attacks on Jean-Paul Sartre's* existentialism, which he argued was incompatible with Marxism and narcissistic (although he also claimed that he himself had been something of an existentialist in the 1920s and he was, in fact, increasingly influenced by Sartre later in his own career). In the late 1940s Lefebvre was besieged on two fronts in the heavy atmosphere of the cold war. He lost a position at the non-Marxist Centre National de la Recherche Scientific in Paris, and although a Party stalwart, he was compelled to publish an unconvincing "self-criticism" recanting his philosophical unorthodoxies. In the next years he focused less on controversial philosophical issues and more on sociology, receiving a *doctorate d'état* in 1954 for a study of French peasant economy. With the events of 1956 (Khrushchev's† denunciation of Stalin and the invasion of Hungary) and the Communist Party's persistent dogmatism and inability to respond coherently to the Algerian crisis, an increasingly disillusioned Lefebvre fought for the Party's de-Stalinization and joined an opposition group within the party, the Club de la Gauche. He also began publishing in an internal dissident journal, *Voies nouvelles*. These actions, combined with the unpopularity of his philosophical views (accented by the publication in 1958 of his *Problèmes actuels du marxisme*) led to his expulsion from the Communist Party in June 1958, an ordeal he recounted in a remarkable memoir, *La Somme et la reste*, published the following year. In the late 1950s and early 1960s Lefebvre was a moving force in the dissident independent Marxist journal *Arguments*,* became increasingly influenced by existentialism, and was a vigorous critic of structuralism, which was then in philosophical vogue in Paris. He taught at the University of Strasbourg, the University of Paris at Nanterre, and the Ecole Practique des Hautes Etudes in Paris. His studies in these years of modernity, urbanism, and especially "everyday life in the modern world" were particularly influential. In the late 1960s and early 1970s Lefebvre wrote on the upheaval of May 1968 and on the survival of capitalism. He lives today in Paris.

Lefebvre played a seminal role in bringing Marx's early works, with their emphasis on humanism and alienation, to the center of French Marxist discourse. Emphasizing Marx's Hegelian inheritance, Lefebvre saw Marx's evolution as a process of concretizing his early concepts, particularly that of alienation. He argued against interpreting Marx as an economic determinist and insisted that Marx comprehended economics and all other domains of life from the perspective of "totality." Similarly, Lefebvre contrasted fragmented human beings who are reduced to a single dimension of existence (e.g. the *homo oeconomicus* of capitalism) to what he called the "total man," who is "de-alienated" and a "free individual in a free community." With the creation of socialism and as a result of revolutionary praxis, alienation will be vanquished through " 'the return of man to himself,' that is to say in the unity of all the elements of the human" (*Dialectical Materialism*, pp. 162–63).

Lefebvre opposed mechanistic concepts of materialism and was particularly preoccupied with the relation between formal and dialectical logic. Marx's "inversion" of the Hegelian dialectic, he insisted, had to be conceived as *aufhebung*, a transcendence in the double Hegelian sense of an affirmation and negation at once. Marx affirmed and incorporated into his own thought the Hegelian contribution while rejecting its idealism. Lefebvre saw this as an effort to overcome the dualism between idealism and materialism. In works such as *Logique formelle, logique dialectique* (1947) and *Problèmes actuels du marxisme* (1958) he argued first that objective idealism (i.e. Hegel) and materialism were in epistemological accord as to the possibility of objective human knowledge, and then that both idealism and materialism, as types of philosophy, would eventually be transcended. In so claiming he harked back to the young Marx's insistence on the unity of theory and practice—on interpreting *and* changing the world—and especially his assertion that the realization of philosophy meant its abolition. Lefebvre further developed these themes in his book *Métaphilosophie* (1965), in which he argued that philosophy was itself a form of alienation and that a new, open type of thinking, "metaphilosophy," was now on the agenda. Metaphilosophy, however, was not fully possible without socialism and hence what was plausible and necessary was an antisystematic, open-ended form of thought, based especially on the categories of Marx's theory of alienation and particularly concerned with the varieties of modern alienation. Among other things, this required a reconceiving, reshaping, and broadening of various Marxist categories since Marxism was necessary, but insufficient, to understand the modern world. For instance, Lefebvre expanded Marx's concept of praxis by delineating different aspects of it such as "poesis" (creative, imaginative human activity) and "mimesis" (routine, imitative activity). Lefebvre argued especially for broadening the concept of alienation itself because it had taken many new forms in the modern world and it also could not be restricted to bourgeois societies; as a "philosophical concept and analytical tool" alienation can help us comprehend and criticize aspects of contemporary "socialist" societies, "particularly during the Stalinist period" (1961 preface to *Dialectical Materialism*, pp. 16–17). Indeed, the modern world has been so penetrated by alienation in so many new guises that even consciousness of it has been subverted.

"Everyday life" (the "quotidian") in the modern world, long a concern of Lefebvre's, became a central theme for him in the 1960s and provided the locus of some of his most notable theoretical and analytical contributions. He conceived his examination of everyday life as a philosophical grasping of the nonphilosophical, the recurrent, and the trivial. It was an effort at a "philosophical inventory and analysis . . . that will expose [everyday life's] ambiguities—its baseness and exuberance, its poverty and fruitfulness—and by these unorthodox means release creative energies that are an integral part of it.'' (*Everyday Life*, p. 13). It was in the "territory" of the "quotidian" rather than in the relations of production (as conceived by Marxism) themselves that modern capitalism was most effective in sustaining itself, and it was there that the battle for a radical new consciousness, the prerequisite of radical change, would have to occur. Modernity had produced in the West what Lefebvre called a "bureaucratic society of controlled consumption," which fragments, subdivides, and organizes every-day life, making men and women increasingly passive beings, responding re-flexively as atomized consumers to signals and images that induce their daily wants. Such beings attain "happiness" by consuming, and thus we are confronted by what Lefebvre calls a "space-time of voluntary programmed self-regulation" creating a "closed circuit" of "production-consumption-production" (ibid., p. 72). We watch television commercials to know how to live, dress, and smile; this "poetry of modernity" maps out our existence all the while we "choose" between an abundance of consumer items—"so many good things" (ibid., p. 107). The everyday, rather than the work place, must be exploded, according to Lefebvre, if radical transformation is to be on the agenda. Lefebvre contrasts the "cyclical time" of preindustrial societies, with their festivals and orientation to nature's annual changes, to the routinized "linear cumulative time" of in-dustrial capitalism. A new urban reality needs to be created that will overcome "the conflict between everyday life and festivity" (ibid., p. 206). In other words, Lefebvre did not believe that the "circuit" was completely closed, and he asserted, somewhat obscurely, that this was because of "something" irreducible, "perhaps Desire or Reason (dialectics) or even the City" (ibid., p. 73).

Revolution entails cultural as well as economic and political "planes," and Lefebvre claimed that most Marxists lost sight of this; in turn he emphasizes the need to reseize the cultural plane through a rebirth of human creativity. The cultural revolution he proposed sought to engender not institutions but a new style of life: "The revolution will transform existence, not merely the state and the distribution of property, for we do not take means for ends. This can be stated as follows: 'Let everyday life become a work of art! Let technical means be employed for a transformation of everyday life' " (ibid., p. 204). In such a world, creation will mean more than artistic creation; it will mean a collective assumption of responsibility by human beings for themselves and the manage-ment of their own lives. The society this struggle for self-determination must overcome is one with enormous capacities to integrate opposition since advancing technology increasingly delimits the problem of scarcity and gives us mass media and culture. These realities make more and more social sectors "happy" but at the same time rest on a system of hierarchical decision making in which an increasingly smaller number of technocrats have real responsibilities. The May 1968 "events" in Paris, with their combined political and cultural refusal of the established order, their cry for *autogestion* (self-management) and atmosphere of urban festivity seemed to Lefebvre to exemplify the sort of revolt of which he had been speaking. Many of the student leaders of the upheaval, including Daniel Cohn-Bendit, had attended his classes at Nanterre, which he allowed them to use for organizing. He himself did not take part (his students and others criticized him for this) and believed that the revolt did not have long-term prospects at that historical juncture. Nonetheless he backed the students and believed that the style of the revolt corresponded to the current reality of capitalism. He particularly praised their spirit of *contestation*, the spirit of total revolt and refusal to be integrated in any way.

BIBLIOGRAPHY:

A. *Les Problèmes actuels du marxisme* (Paris: P.U.F.; 1958); *La Somme et la reste* (Paris: La Nef, 1959); *Métaphilosophie* (Paris: Editions de Minuit, 1965); *Dialectical Materialism* (London: Cape, 1968); *The Explosion: Marxism and the French Upheaval* (New York: Monthly Review Press, 1969); *The Sociology of Marx* (New York: Vintage, 1969); *Au-delà du structuralisme* (Paris: Anthropos, 1971); *Everyday Life in the Modern World* (New York: Harper & Row, 1971).

B. Alfred Schmidt, "Henri Lefebvre and Contemporary Interpretations of Marx," in *The Unknown Dimension*, ed. D. Howard and K. Klare (New York: Basic Books, 1972); Mark Poster, *Existential Marxism in Postwar France* (Princeton: Princeton University Press, 1975); Edith Kurzweil, "Henri Lefebvre—a Marxist Against Structuralism," in *The Age of Structuralism* (New York: Columbia University Press, 1980); Arthur Hirsh, *The French New Left* (Boston: South End Press, 1981); Michael Kelly, *Modern French Marxism* (Baltimore: Johns Hopkins University Press, 1982).

MITCHELL COHEN

LEFORT, CLAUDE. See *Socialisme et Barbarie.**

LEGAL MARXISM. The term *legal Marxism* refers to a movement of Russian Marxist revisionists that flourished in the last decade of the nineteenth century and whose leading members eventually became leaders in liberal politics, academic economics, religion and philosophy. The name derives from the common efforts of this group to publish Marxist ideas within the legal Russian journals in the ongoing debate with advocates of peasant socialism (*narodnichestvo*). Peter B. Struve (1870–1944) is perhaps the best-known legal Marxist. An early colleague of Lenin† and author of the manifesto for the founding congress of the Russian Social Democratic Labor Party in 1898, Struve left Marxism for a combination of neo-Kantian ethics and liberal politics at the turn of the century. Semen Frank (1877–1950) contributed studies on the Marxist labor theory of value in the 1890s before joining Struve as an editor of the liberal journal *Osvobozhdenie* (Liberation) in 1903. Mikhail I. Tugan-Baranovsky (1865–1919) authored important economic studies, which argued that Russia's development in the latter part of the nineteenth century was fully in accord with Marx's general pattern of historical evolution. Sergei Bulgakov (1871–1944) devoted his early scholarly efforts to an analysis of emerging capitalism in turn-of-the-century Russia and later adopted a philosophical position based on neo-Kantian idealism and became a priest in the Russian Orthodox Church. Nicholas Berdiaev (1874–

1948) became active in early Marxist circles in Kiev and was arrested at the conclusion of the first congress of the Russian Social Democratic Labor Party in 1898. By the time of his release from prison some four years later, Berdiaev had left Marxism for idealism. Several of the legal Marxists (Struve, Frank, Berdiaev, and Bulgakov) marked their transition from Marxism to idealism by contributing selections to the celebrated symposiums *Problemy idealizma* in 1902 and *Vekhi* in 1909.

BIBLIOGRAPHY:

A. *Landmarks (Vekhi): A Collection of Essays on the Russian Intelligentsia, 1909* (New York: Karz Howard, 1977).

B. Arthur P. Mendel, *Dilemmas of Progress in Tsarist Russia: Legal Marxism and Legal Populism* (Cambridge: Harvard University Press, 1961); Richard Kindersley, *The First Russian Revisionists: A Study of "Legal Marxism" in Russia* (Oxford: Clarendon Press, 1962); Michael Boll, "*Problemy idealizma* and the Social Philosophy of Early Twentieth-Century Russian Liberalism," *Indiana Political Science Review*, 8 (January 1974), pp. 79–92.

MICHAEL M. BOLL

LEHNING, ARTHUR (b. 1899). A Dutch historian and essayist, Lehning (until 1940 Müller-Lehning) studied economics in Rotterdam and history in Berlin. He is internationally important as editor of the *Archives Bakounine* (1961–). Lehning has written on topics such as social democracy, Sacco and Vanzetti, and politics and culture from the perspective of council communism. Early in his professional life he was involved with the Bauhaus and De Stijl movements in the Netherlands. From 1932 to 1935 Lehning was with the anarcho-syndicalist International Workers' Association and editor of (*Grondslagen*) (Foundations). Lehning has been affiliated with the International Institute for Social History from its beginning and was director of its branch in Oxford from 1939 to 1947.

BIBLIOGRAPHY:

A. *Grote Winkler Prins* (Amsterdam: Elsevier, 1974).

TINEKE RITMEESTER

LÉVI-STRAUSS, CLAUDE (b. 1908). Born in 1908 in Belgium, Lévi-Strauss studied law and philosophy at the University of Paris. Between 1935 and 1939 he taught at the University of São Paulo in Brazil, where he did his anthropological fieldwork. Mobilized in 1939, he had to flee France due to his Jewish background. During the Occupation he taught philosophy and anthropology at the New School for Social Research and at the Ecole Libre des Hautes Etudes in New York City. In 1947 he became a director of the Musée de l'Homme in Paris. He was director of studies of the Ecole Practique des Hautes Etudes, and editor of the journal *L'Homme*. In 1960 he was elected to the chair in social anthropology at the Collège de France.

Never a Marxist,[†] he identified himself as "on the left," and at the peak of his authorship he became closely identified with the structuralist movement so popular in the Paris of the early and middle 1960s. Lévi-Strauss understood his own formative influences as the Marx of the historical studies, the Freud of *The Interpretation of Dreams*, and the Durkheim of *The Elementary Forms of the Religious Life*. To Lévi-Strauss's own self-characterization we might add the historians of the *Annales* group, the formalisms of Piaget and Husserl, and the structuralist linguistics of Saussure. He is best known to the philosophical community for his polemic with Jean-Paul Sartre* in *La Pensée sauvage* (1962). His influences on French neo-Marxism have been many and profound. In the tradition of French philosophical anthropology—of Montaigne and Montesquieu—his exclusive concern with other cultures and with premodernity has sharpened the debates and inspired many studies concerning the nature and role of modernity in our understanding of the history and current state of capital. His criticisms of the existentialists led many to reexamine the presumptive priority of the subject and consciousness, a presumption that supported, by a curious irony, Stalinist† dogmatism in its voluntarist guise. His researches into the cultural universe of the American Indians (see the journal *Mythologiques*, vols. I–IV) suggested to those who patiently followed them that language—and other abstract sociohistorical systems—is co-constitutive of both the individual subject and of his "natural" world.

In general, Lévi-Strauss's work has led neo-Marxism to grant increasing importance to the study of cultural/symbolic systems, and finally to succeed in rejecting the "in the last analysis" accounts of historical objects in terms of modes of economic production. His work stimulated a general rethinking of the notion of the historical dialectic and the interpretation of both Hegel and Marx. If dialectic is primarily epistemic/cognitive—a feature of the intrasystemic mediation of opposed concepts and signs—as Lévi-Strauss argued in *The Savage Mind* and elsewhere, then how can we still maintain that hope for the self-development of the historical subject of the Hegelian Marxism of Jean Hyppolite* and Alexandre Kojève*? It was the confrontation between structuralism and existential-Hegelian Marxism—a confrontation that evaporated in the streets of Paris in May 1968—that finally broke down the dogmatic "party philosophy" in the French intellectual community and opened the way for the developments of the 1970s.

BIBLIOGRAPHY:

A. *Structural Anthropology*, 2 vols. (Chicago: University of Chicago Press, 1963–76); *The Savage Mind* (Chicago: University of Chicago Press, 1966); *The Raw and the Cooked* (Chicago: University of Chicago Press, 1969); *Tristes Tropiques* (New York: Atheneum, 1974); *Myth and Meaning* (New York: Schocken, 1979).

B. Miriam Glucksmann, *Structuralist Analysis in Contemporary Social Thought* (London: Routledge & Kegan Paul, 1974); Rosalind Coward and John Ellis, *Language and Materialism* (London: Routledge & Kegan Paul, 1977); Edith Kurzweil, *The Age of Structuralism* (New York: Columbia University Press, 1980); Robert A. Gorman, *Neo-Marxism: The Meanings of Modern Radicalism* (Westport, Conn.: Greenwood Press, 1982).

LAURENCE E. WINTERS

LIBERATION THEOLOGY. Although its roots in Christianity were acknowledged by the early Middle Ages, the contemporary version of liberation theology is said to begin with the World Council of Churches (WCC) meeting in Geneva in 1966, where several leading spokespeople advocated the use of political violence as a viable option for obtaining social justice in the Third World. The Conference at Medellin (1968) affirmed the Catholic Church's obligation to condemn and actively oppose social, economic, or political structures that violate one's personhood. Sin, the bishops concluded, may be institutional in nature. At the World Conference on Salvation Today, in Bangkok (1973), the WCC gave its open approval to liberation theology and promised to support it in the Third World churches of Asia, Africa, and particularly Latin America. Many contend, as well, that Vatican II (1962–65) contributed to legitimizing liberation theology by providing for more participation on the part of the laity in the daily life of the Catholic Church by changing the language of the mass to the vernacular, calling for lay participation in the mass, and narrowing the gap between the laity and the priests and bishops. Of course, the brutal torture and killings of priests and nuns in the Latin American military's battle against leftist guerrillas has also radicalized the Church and popularized the liberation movement among poor Christian peasants and workers.

The major theorists and actors associated with liberation theology are Roman Catholic priests, most of whom live and preach in Latin America and are associated with the Maryknoll School and their press, Orbis Books, in New York. They include, among many others, Gustavo Gutierrez of Peru, considered by many the founder of modern liberation theology; Jon Sobrino, a Spanish-born priest living in El Salvador; Juan Luis Segundo of Uruguay; Camilo Torres Restrepo* of Colombia; Paulo Freure, Dom Helder Camara, Hugo Assman, and Leonardo Boff, all of Brazil, where an overwhelming majority of its 358 bishops support the radical church; and José Porfirio Miranda of Mexico. Protestant liberation theologians include Orlando Fals-Borda* of Colombia; Ruben Alves and Richard Shaull (now at Princeton Seminary) of Brazil; Emilio Castro of Uruguay, who is now chairman of the Department of Mission of the WCC and editor of *Ecumenical Review of Mission*; and José Miguez Bonino of Argentina, president of the Methodist Theological Seminary of Buenos Aires and presently one of six presidents of the WCC.

At the heart of liberation theology is its call to praxis, its request of Christians not merely to reflect on the world but "to be part of the process through which the world is transformed" (Gutierrez, *A Theology of Liberation*, p. 15). Although liberation theology explicitly rejects atheistic communism, it also acknowledges the substance of Marx's† early work dealing with the desirability and necessity of personal fulfillment in social relationships, Marx's rejection of capitalism, Marxian dialectics as a tool of socio-economic analysis, and Marx's call for the oppressed to take up arms against their oppressors. Marxism, in other words, is an apt tool by which Christians can explain and help destroy the "structural sin" of Third World dictatorships. The Christian concern for salvation is reinterpreted to include not only men's souls but also the whole person and the whole social order. Christ's redemptive work must be applied to the whole person, liberating him from all those personal, social, moral, political, and economic forces that deny him the experience of being free to enjoy the benefits of salvation in every aspect of life. Gutierrez in particular identifies the continuing act of salvation with the very process of history, which is the context of both oppression and liberation. Opening oneself to God, therefore, requires opening oneself to the possibility of social emancipation. Church and society are no longer opposed. Good Christians thus "do" theology by recognizing that God is a god of justice who acts in history, that oppression and injustice are sinful, and that life on earth can and will be better.

The political implications of liberation theology include the belief that "authentic socialism is Christianity lived to the full, in basic equality and with a fair distribution of goods" (Segundo, *The Liberation of Theology*, p. 72). Liberation theologians argue that theology and politics are inseparable. The real issue is whether theology will consciously or unconsciously perform its political function. "Academic" Christianity chooses the latter path, hence naively supports petty dictators and class exploitation. Liberation theologians believe the processes of colonization, liberation, and political organization are best understood in Marxian terms. Capitalism is both unjust and un-Christian. It pits classes against each other in a battle the masses always lose. In the context of Third World culture, capitalism is perceived as a form of syndicalism or corporatism in which inequality is entrenched, where landowners and the military exploit the poor—often Indian—peasants economically, socially, and politically. In response, liberation theologians have developed ecclesiastical communities that have provided the Church with a huge grass-roots base. These communities, which as of 1984 numbered over 70,000 and had over 4 million members, comprise small groups of Christians who meet regularly to discuss the Bible and their faith in the context of their daily lives. Since priests actively recruit poor peasants, workers, and slum dwellers as members, these Christian base communities (*Communidades ecclesiales de base*, or CEBs) are forums for wider analysis of social, economic, and political problems. Moreover, they produce new leaders (lay preachers and lay teachers), who eventually organize trade unions and peasant cooperatives and acclimate the poor to procedures of participatory democracy. All decisions in the CEBs are made by participants, not imposed by priests. The net effect is to generate millions of revolutionary socialist Christians, ready to battle class oppressors in God's name. Although most proponents of liberation theology favor a more humble and democratic church, some (e.g. several Nicaraguan priests) have suggested breaking with Rome and establishing a new "People's Church." Needless to say, the Vatican, although sympathizing with the poor and advocating an end to oppression, nevertheless strongly opposes liberation theology. This is at least partially due to its fear that the CEBs will split the Church into what Pope John Paul has called a "double magisterium," thus diluting the Church's power. It is also due to a trend among liberal Catholic theologians in Western Europe and Latin America to question the bishops's and Pope's authority. The Vatican has interrogated the Dutch theologian Edward Schillebeeckx (1979) and the Brazilian Leonardo Boff (1984) on this issue. The latter's *Church, Charisma and Power* (1981) has attracted many Catholics who want to decentralize and democratize Church institutions. Boff's thesis—that the Church's system of "religious production" has generated an ecclesiastical ruling class analogous to Latin America's exploitative land-owners—directly threatens the institutional structure and doctrine of Catholicism. Although the Church has in the past at least tolerated liberation theology's moral and political exhortations, it has unambiguously condemned this movement to decentralize Church power. Church leaders now anxiously wait to see if liberation theologians, preachers, and teachers continue supporting this new attack on the Church's hierarchy.

The Christian liberation movement, through the Christian base communities, has claimed responsibility for the overthrow of the Somoza regime in Nicaragua and for the establishment in El Salvador of its first mass revolutionary organization, the United Popular Action Front. These victories, combined with the continuing obstinance and brutality of right-wing dictatorships, an apparent increase in the radical church's appeal among Latin America's poor, the increasingly volatile relationship between the Vatican and radical priests, and the ideological debate surrounding the WCC, demonstrate that radical theology will remain on the world scene as a force to be reckoned with for the foreseeable future.

BIBLIOGRAPHY:

A. John C. Raines and Thomas Dean, eds., *Marxism and Radical Religion: Essays Toward a Revolutionary Humanism* (Philadelphia: Temple University Press, 1970); Gustavo Gutierrez, *A Theology of Liberation* (Maryknoll, N.Y.: Orbis Books, 1973); José Miguez Bonino, *Doing Theology in a Revolutionary Situation* (Philadelphia: Fortress Press, 1975); Richard Dickinson, *To Set at Liberty the Oppressed* (Geneva: World Council of Churches, 1975); Juan Luis Segundo, *The Liberation of Theology* (Maryknoll, N.Y.: Orbis Books, 1976); Pierre Bigo, *The Church and Third World Revolution* (Maryknoll, N.Y.: Orbis Books, 1977); Rosino Givellini, ed., *Frontiers of Theology in Latin America* (Maryknoll, N.Y.: Orbis Books, 1979); J. Andrew Kirk, *Liberation Theology: An Evangelical View From the Third World* (Atlanta: John Knox Press, 1979); Schubert M. Ogden, *Faith and Freedom: Toward a Theology of Liberation* (Nashville; Abingdon Press, 1979); Jon Sobrino, *Christology in Latin America* (Maryknoll, N.Y.: Orbis Books, 1980); Leonardo Boff, *Igreja, carisma e poder: ensaios de eclesiologica militante* (Petrópolis: Vozes, 1981).

ROBERT A. GORMAN

LOWENTHAL, LEO (b. 1900). Leo Lowenthal was born on 3 November 1900 in Frankfurt, Germany. After serving in the German army during World War I, Lowenthal studied literature, history, philosophy, and sociology at the universities of Frankfurt, Heidelberg, and Giessen. During his student years at Frankfurt, he was a member of a Zionist student organization, and he helped found the Student Socialist Society. He received his doctorate from Frankfurt in 1923 with a dissertation on Franz von Baader. Later he taught in the Prussian secondary school system and wrote theater criticism. He became one of the earliest members of the Frankfurt Institute for Social Research with a part-time appointment in 1926. He became a full-time member in 1930. He continued his association with the institute in exile: first in Geneva in 1933, the following year at Columbia University in New York. In 1943 he joined the American war effort by working for the Office of War Information. He was appointed the director of the research division of the Voice of America in 1949. In 1956 he began teaching sociology at the University of California at Berkeley, where he has continued to offer courses long after his official retirement age.

Lowenthal's earliest works, written in the late 1920s and early 1930s, focused on Jewish and aesthetic subjects. The essays on Jewish thought, culture, and politics were a product of Lowenthal's association with a group of young Jewish intellectuals that included Martin Buber, Siegfried Kracauer, and Erich Fromm.* Many of Lowenthal's early pieces on art and the theater were published in *Die Volksbühne*, the journal of a large liberal-to-left-wing cultural organization. Throughout his nearly twenty years with the Institute of Social Research, Lowenthal held a number of administrative positions and collaborated on several collective projects. He was the managing editor of the institute's famous journal, *Zeitschrift für Sozialforschung*, and the director of its important book review section. He also codirected the New York branch of the institute after Max Horkheimer* and Theodor Adorno* moved to California in 1941. In addition to his own theoretical contributions, Lowenthal participated in a number of collective projects. Lowenthal, along with Erich Fromm, was an early advocate of Freudian psychoanalytic theory within the institute. He edited the third part of the institute's first major multidisciplinary project, the *Studien über Autorität und Familie* (Studies on Authority and the Family). The book he coauthored with Norbert Guterman, *Prophets of Deceit*, was part of the second major project, the Studies in Prejudice series, which was sponsored by the institute and the American Jewish Committee. In addition, Lowenthal's behind-the-scenes influence has been confirmed by a number of his institute colleagues. As an administrator and coworker, Lowenthal was thus a central figure in the creation of the Institute's Frankfurt School and a major contributor to its characteristic brand of Marxism,† critical theory.

Lowenthal's theoretical work is focused on the sociology of literature, popular culture, and political communications. From his essays in the 1930s through his later work, Lowenthal's writings on the sociology of literature embody the characteristic method and substantive concerns of the Frankfurt School. Lowenthal's sociology of literature falls between the poles of orthodox Marxist and apolitical academic approaches to literature. Like orthodox Marxist thinkers, Lowenthal situates authors and works in their historical and sociological contexts. But unlike the crudest practitioners of orthodox Marxist sociology of literature, Lowenthal never reduces the novels and dramas of a Conrad Ferdinand Meyer, a Knut Hamsun, a Goethe, or a Shakespeare to the status of mere reflections of their social contexts. What separates Lowenthal's work from the reductionism of some orthodox Marxists is his "bourgeois" scrupulousness with literary texts and his sensitivity to psychological factors. Substantively, Lowenthal's essays in the *Zeitschrift für Sozialforschung* explored a number of characteristic Institute themes: the mythical "great man" ideology in Meyer; the alienated "inwardness" in Dostoevsky; the dissolution of the bourgeois family in Ibsen; and the authoritarian capitulation to nature in Hamsun; to list a few. Some of these themes of the 1930s recur in Lowenthal's most famous work on the sociology of literature, *Literature and the Image of Man*, published in 1957. In studies of novels and dramas from the early Spanish writers Lope de Vega and Calderon, through Cervantes, Shakespeare, classical French drama, and Goethe, to Ibsen and Hamsun, Lowenthal traces the promise and dilemmas of the individual in the modern world. Emerging from the breakdown of the feudal order and waxing confident during the ascendancy of the middle classes, in Lowenthal's account the trajectory of the literary individual closes with a depiction of that individual threatened by technological and social forces and perhaps ready to seek authoritarian relief from these threats.

If Lowenthal's research on literary art recognizes its moment of transcendence of societal determination, his work on popular culture emphasizes the proximity of popular literature to the values and practices of the existing status quo. Lowenthal's book on *Literature, Popular Culture, and Society* is a collection of theoretical essays on popular culture and specific studies of aspects of popular culture. Whether his subject is the origin of popular culture in eighteenth-century England or a content analysis of popular biographies in *The Saturday Evening Post* and *Collier's*, Lowenthal sees popular literature as primarily a market-oriented commodity, i.e., a product of what he and his institute colleagues called the "culture industry." Artistic literature, with its transcendent element, is a creation of individuals for other individuals. Popular literature, on the other hand, is a form of mass entertainment. Lowenthal's study of popular literature is thus centered not on the unique author or reader as individuals but on the typical forms of behavior and beliefs, the typical hopes and fears, depicted in the reading materials produced for consumption by anonymous masses of people. As a part of the culture industry, popular literature both reflects and creates these typical characteristics of the mass public.

The manipulation of mass consciousness is a major theme of Lowenthal's work on political communications. In *Prophets of Deceit* and a number of other essays, Lowenthal examines the external influences on popular consciousness, particularly the influences that emanate from modern mass media. In *Prophets of Deceit*, Lowenthal and Guterman present the results of a content analysis of the writings, speeches, and radio broadcasts of a number of American "agitators," i.e., demagogic manipulators of public opinion, in the 1930s and 1940s. Although it was a commonplace to view public opinion in Nazi Germany or Fascist Italy as the product of careful manipulation by the ruling elites, few people recognized the prevalence of similar manipulative techniques in American society. According to Lowenthal and Guterman, the American agitator, unlike the genuine political reformer or revolutionary, does not present a series of rational arguments in favor of a particular political vision. The agitator, rather, tries to bypass the rationality of the public in order to arouse vague feelings of social discontent. The resulting malice of the audience is then directed toward vague, yet identifiable enemies (e.g., the Jews or the Communists). Despite the cherished American belief in the autonomous individual, *Prophets of Deceit*, like Lowenthal's work on popular culture, depicts the enormous potential that the mass media possess for creating and manipulating the consciousness of the mass public.

BIBLIOGRAPHY:

A. *Literature and the Image of Man* (Boston: Beacon Press, 1957); *Literature, Popular Culture, and Society* (Englewood Cliffs, N.J.: Prentice-Hall, 1961); with Norbert Guterman, *Prophets of Deceit* (Palo Alto, Calif.: Pacific Books, 1970); *Literature and Mass Culture* (New Brunswick, N.J.: Transaction Books, 1983).

B. Martin Jay, *The Dialectical Imagination* (Boston: Little Brown, 1973); Helmut Dubiel, "Interview with Leo Lowenthal," *Telos*, no. 45 (1980), pp. 82–96; David Gross, "Lowenthal, Adorno, Barthes: Three Perspectives on Popular Culture," *Telos*, no. 45 (1980), pp. 122–40; Robert Sayre, "Lowenthal, Goldmann, and the Sociology of Literature," *Telos*, no. 45 (1980), pp. 150–60.

JOHN BOKINA

LUKÁCS, GEORGE (1885–1971). Lukács was born in Budapest on 13 April 1885 into a wealthy, assimilated, Hungarian-Jewish family. His father, a self-made man and director of a credit institute, was raised to nobility in 1901. George grew up bilingual (German-Hungarian) and at an early age learned French and English as well. He went to Berlin in 1905 to study with Dilthey and Simmel. He studied law and received his degree in Kolozsvár in 1906. He received his second Ph.D. in philosophy from the University of Budapest in 1909. His first publication appeared at the age of seventeen. Two years later, he organized a theater introducing modern authors to worker audiences. His prize-winning *History of the Development of Modern Drama* was published in Hungary in 1911. The same year a collection of his essays, *Soul and Form*, was published in Berlin. Following a futile attempt to embark on an academic career in Budapest, the suicide of his love, and the death of his closest friend, Leo Popper, Lukács moved to Florence and started work on a systematic *Aesthetics*. In 1912 his friend Ernst Bloch* persuaded him to move to Heidelberg where he lived until 1917. During the Heidelberg period, Lukács worked on his *Habilitationsschrift*, became a member of the Max Weber Circle, published an autobiographical novelette, *Von der Armut am Geiste* (1913) and married a Russian anarchist, Yelena Grabenko, to whom his *Theory of the Novel* (1916) is dedicated. At this point his thinking is influenced by Hegel, Dostoevsky, Weber, and Marx,† the latter mediated through Simmel and Weber. His opposition to World War I made him an outsider among German intellectuals and a leading figure among young Hungarian intellectuals after his return to Budapest in 1917. He made another unsuccessful attempt at a university career in Heidelberg in 1918. In December 1918 Lukács joined the Communist Party of Hungary and in spring 1919 became people's commissar for education under the short-lived Republic of Councils; after its defeat, he took refuge in Vienna. His theoretical and practical involvement with Marxism and revolutions gave birth to his essay collection, *History and Class Consciousness* (1923). Lukács moved to Berlin in 1928, writing and teaching at the Marxist Workers' Academy, and emigrated to Moscow after Hitler's seizure of power in 1933. During his Moscow exile, Lukács abstained from political activity and devoted himself to scholarship, writing the first drafts for *The Destruction of Reason*, treatises on literary themes (realism, Thomas Mann, socialist realism), and finishing his book, *The Young Hegel*. At the end of World War II, Lukács returned to his native Budapest to become a university professor, a public figure, and a critic of dogmatism, resulting in his censure by the Communist Party. Emerging from his "inner exile," he became a leading member of pre-1956 revolutionary ferment and in October a member of Imre Nagy's government, to be interned in Romania after the defeat of the 1956 revolt. He returned to active scholarship in the late 1950s and supported the new reformist liberalization movement in Hungary in the 1960s. Duly celebrated toward the end of his life as the "greatest living Marxist," Lukács died at the age of eighty-six, on 7 June 1971. His *Collected Works*—some twenty volumes— are being published both in Hungary and West Germany.

The seven decades of Lukács's creative intellectual life can be conveniently divided into four phases, complete with transitional stages: first, the pre-Marxist, "romantic anticapitalist" period; second, a messianic-revolutionary Marxist period; third, the Stalinist† years; and, finally, a critical-reformist Marxist period subsequent to Stalin's death. His contributions touch upon many branches of the social sciences and humanities, such as the sociology of art and literature, aesthetics, political philosophy, and history of philosophy. It would be a mistake, however, to cut the Lukács opus into pieces and to speak of the "young Lukács" and the "old Lukács," making them separate entities, as some interpreters do. Lukács himself emphasized the dialectical unity of continuity and discontinuity in his life-work. A periodization of Lukác's life merely serves as a guide to the thought of an intellectual who throughout his life was preoccupied with the political and cultural problems of his age and with the searching for solutions.

The romantic anticapitalist Lukács rebelled against what he perceived as the oppressive and backward conditions of Central European societies and joined the progressive-democratic intellectual forces of pre–World War I Hungary in their search for theoretical and practical solutions. In the face of the onslaught of the crude positivism and vulgar Marxism of his time, Lukács searched for a method, a way out of the crisis in the social sciences and humanities. Thus, his close association with men the likes of Max Weber, similarly engaged, albeit with different perspectives. In *Soul and Form* Lukács expressed his longing for "value and form, for measure and order," believing in the redeeming power of form and proclaiming that "aesthetic culture is the formation of the soul." The uncertainties of the disintegrating European old social order caused Lukács to yearn "for certainty, for measure and dogma." The two major works of this period, *Soul and Form* and *The Theory of the Novel*, reflect both personal and cultural crises; they influenced some of the best minds of Europe, from Max ·Weber and Thomas Mann to the theorists of the Frankfurt School. Lucien Goldmann* correctly calls Lukács the founder of modern existential philosophy.

Lukács's messianic-revolutionary Marxist phase was precipitated by historical events, namely, the outbreak of World War I and the Russian Revolution of 1917, followed by a wave of Central European revolutions that for Lukács opened up a new perspective, i.e., the possibility of the leap from the realm of capitalist *Sein* (the age of "absolute sinfulness") to the realm of *Sollen* (socialism), or a more humane society. The theoretical outcome of this phase is several essays on politics and culture, most notably "Bolshevism as a Moral Problem" and "Tactics and Ethics," and the essay collection, *History and Class Consciousness* (*HCC*). Lukács's shift is marked by a change in style from a romantic poetic to a Hegelian–Marxist philosopher, with strong ethical undertones. Certain Weberian and neo-Kantian elements were retained, however, such as Weber's notion of capitalist rationalization, and a neo-Kantian epistemology that Lukács used when criticizing Engels's† dialectic of nature. *HCC* serves as a starting point for rethinking and restructuring Marxist social theory and has been an inspiration for generations of leftist intellectuals in the twentieth century. Five propositions sum up the main theses of *HCC*. First, "true" Marxism is "orthodox Marxism," i.e., a return to Marx's method, which emphasizes the primacy of totality. Second, Marx's dialectic is a method to be applied to historical-sociological studies of society, in opposition to Engels's "dialectic of nature." Third, the phenomenon of "reification" is the essence of capitalist society, permeating all human relations. Fourth, the proletariat is the agent (subject-object) of the world historical process in his new philosophy of history, designed to eliminate the evils of capitalist society and to bring about the salvation of mankind. Fifth, the Communist Party represents the "objectification of the proletariat's will," mediating between the realm of *Sein* and *Sollen*.

The third period dates from the Nazi takeover in Germany, which precipitated Lukács's exile to Moscow. As an immediate and lasting response to the worldwide danger of facism, he investigated the intellectual roots of the Nazi *Weltanschauung*. Lukács used the dichotomous terms *rational/irrational* in tracing German philosophical developments from the earlier, mystical-irrational strains to the most recent, most barbarian, and most vulgar manifestation in the irrational Nazi *Weltanschauung*. This endeavour results in *The Destruction of Reason* and in two smaller, posthumously published monographs. Lukács complements his analysis of the genesis of Nazi *Weltanschauung* with a defense of the progressive, "real" German cultural tradition in numerous essays devoted to Goethe, Hegel, Heine, Büchner, Thomas Mann, and others. Concurrently, he worked out a theory of realism while testing it on specific "case studies" devoted to Balzac, Walter Scott (and the historical novel), Zola, and Tolstoy. His monograph, *The Young Hegel*, earned him the degree (his third doctorate) of doctor of the Soviet Academy of Sciences. Finally, Lukács worked on the reconstruction of Marxian aesthetics, based on scattered remarks by Marx and Engels. Lukács's accommodation with Stalinism is a rather complex issue. To be sure, he wholeheartedly supported Stalin vis-à-vis Trotsky† and in regard to the Ribbentrop–Molotov pact; he also paid lip service to Stalinism in his writings of that period. Justifying his stand, he stated that the defeat of fascism, the main enemy of mankind, was the order of the day and that the Soviet Union was the most committed to this task. Nevertheless, he criticized the Soviet bureaucracy and dealt with taboo topics such as Hegel, Dostoevsky, and the giants of Western, "bourgeois" literature. Although he survived the Stalinist purges with relative ease, he was jailed in the Ljublanka prison for a short period in 1941.

In the last, critical-reformist phase of his career, Lukács again combined theory and praxis. As a summation of his life-work and a last attempt at systematic Marxism, he finished his Marxist *Aesthetics* (1964) and the *Ontology*, published posthumously. His many interviews and statements and his participation in the 1956 events in Hungary provided inspiration and ammunition for Eastern European reform movements of the 1960s. The two late theoretical works represent a return to his youthful interests and verify the organic continuity of Lukács's life-work. Lukács's ontological theses represent a return to the earlier theme of totality, a kind of wholism, which has now become an organistic and historical category. He asserts that epistemology be replaced by an historicized ontology and so form the basis of a modernized Marxism. Lukács continued to believe that a renaissance of Marxism would occur. He also emphasized two earlier themes: the role of intellectuals who bring class consciousness to the masses from without; and workers' councils, which spell the end of reification, thus leading to a just, socialist democracy.

BIBLIOGRAPHY:

A. *Studies in European Realism* (New York: Grosset & Dunlap, 1964); *Goethe and His Age* (New York: Grosset & Dunlap, 1969); *History and Class Consciousness* (London: Merlin Press, 1971); *Soul and Form* (Cambridge: MIT Press, 1971); *The Theory of the Novel* (Cambridge: MIT Press, 1971); *The Young Hegel* (London: Merlin Press, 1975); "Bolshevism as a Moral Problem," *Social Research* (Autumn 1977); *The Destruction of Reason* (London: Merlin Press, 1980).

B. Ehrhard Bahr and Ruth Goldschmidt Kunzer, *Georg Lukács* (New York: Ungar, 1972); István Mészáros, *Lukács's Concept of Dialectic* (London: Merlin Press, 1972); Robert A. Gorman, *Neo-Marxism: The Meanings of Modern Radicalism* (Westport, Conn.: Greenwood Press, 1982); Lee Congdon, *The Young Lukács* (Chapel Hill: University of North Carolina Press, 1983); Judith Marcus, *Thomas Mann and Georg Lukács* (Amherst: University of Massachusetts Press, 1984); Judith Marcus and Zoltán Tar, eds., *The Correspondence of the Young Lukács: 1902–1918* (New York: Columbia University Press, 1984).

ZOLTÁN TAR

LUPORINI, CESARE (b. 1911). Cesare Luporini, born in 1911, is currently a retired professor at the University of Florence. An editor of the theoretical review of the Italian Communist Party (PCI), *Società*, from its founding in 1945, he took over its management in 1947. A friend of Palmiro Togliatti,* with whom he often collaborated on theoretical problems, he also joined in the active politics of the leading organizational bodies—he is still a member of the Central Committee—and for a long period he also served in Parliament as a deputy. In *Società* and in *Rinascita* he conducted, together with Nicola Badaloni,* Valentino Gerratana, and others, polemics against the positions of Galvano Della Volpe.* Along with interviews on Marxism,† he published important research on Scheler, Hegel, Kant, Fichte, Voltaire, the poet Giacomo Leopardi (for whom he furnishes an original interpretation, linking him more to the Enlightenment than to romanticism and pessimism), and an important piece of research, inspired by existentialism, on *Situazione e liberta nell' esistenza umana* (Situation and Freedom in Human Existence).

In his polemic against both Dellavolpism and the radical criticism of dialectical materialism by Lucio Colletti,* Luporini vindicates the positive role of abstraction and generality of concept, compared with the specificity and exactitude of the science reclaimed by Della Volpe for Marxism. But the perspective of Luporini is not strictly historicist; in fact in later essays he assumes positions that are clearly antihistoricist, and eventually he even sympathizes with the structural Marxism of the French philosopher Louis Althusser.* Marxism is thus historical materialism and criticism of political economy, but it is not locked into an organic vision (as in some of Antonio Gramsci's* interpretations) but is rather open to the positive contribution of other disciplines such as linguistics and psychoanalysis. Marxism needs the latter, in particular, in order to compensate for the limits of Marxian discourse on human subjectivity.

On the occasion of the celebrations of the one hundredth anniversary of Marx's death, Luporini launched an interesting project: "Let Us Free Marx from Marxism" (*L'Unita*, 27 February 1983): "The thought of Marx is becoming fluid again, liberated from the screens and patterns of Marxism." In other words, it is necessary to recover the authentic thought of Marx from the deformations of an entire tradition initiated by Engels† himself.

BIBLIOGRAPHY:
    A. *Dialettica e materialismo* (Rome: Riuniti, 1974).

    B. G. Bedeschi, *La parabola del marxismo in Italia 1945–1983* (Bari: Laterza, 1973); F. Cassano, *Marxismo e filosofia in Italia 1958–1971* (Bari: De Donato, 1973).

                                                              VITTORIO DINI

LYND, STAUGHTON (b. 1929). Staughton Lynd was born in 1929 in Philadelphia. He received his B.A. from Harvard in 1951 and his Ph.D. from Columbia University in 1962. During the 1960s Lynd taught American history at several institutions, including Spelman College and Yale University. In 1961, after accepting a teaching position at Atlanta's Negro Women's College, Lynd became very active in the voting and civil rights movements in the South. He joined the Student Non-Violent Coordinating Committee (SNCC) in 1964 and became the director of the Freedom Schools of the Mississippi Summer Project.

In 1965 Lynd chaired the first mass peace march in Washington, D.C. The same year Lynd traveled with Tom Hayden to Hanoi on a peace mission, in defiance of the U.S. government request that he not go. Lynd consequently lost his teaching position at Yale and was denied appointments at other universities as well. In 1966 Lynd wrote about civil rights issues in his book *Nonviolence in America* (1966) and later wrote an account of his trip to North Vietnam in *The Other Side* (1966). Lynd enrolled in law school in order to aid and protect the rights of American workers. He graduated from the University of Chicago Law School in 1976 and began to practice law in Youngstown, Ohio. Presently, Lynd is working as a legal representative of steelworkers in efforts to halt steel plant closings. In 1982 he authored a book, *Labor Law for the Rank and File*, which clarifies workers' legal rights in wage negotiations and with regard to plant closings. His most recent work, *The Fight Against Shutdowns* (1982), continues in this vein by proposing that steel mills reopen under worker-community ownership.

Lynd believes that worker ownership is both economically feasible and socially desirable. Workers have certain rights, and laws often exist to protect these rights. Lynd wants to utilize the law as a shield, not a sword, to protect workers as they attempt to change society. A problem of the socialist movement is that it lacks a common language with workers. Law, in Lynd's opinion, provides this linkage. However, Lynd also warns that, guided by the written and unwritten rules of bourgeois society, government will always sacrifice workers' interests to uphold capitalism. Hence American workers must also recognize that their government is, in this sense, deceptive. Lynd argues that the United States is now facing an economic crisis that is immune to liberal remedies. America is mistakenly structured upon the assumption that a free society must be based on private property and a war economy. Capitalists support and depend upon these principles, hence fear progressive.social reforms, especially socialism. This fact has turned some reformers toward revolution. "Men do not simply revolt out of utopian ambitions; they revolt because of anger at crimes beyond correction and because the seeds of their chosen life can't grow in the society they encounter" (*The Other Side*, p. 188). Lynd contends that capitalism's hegemonic elite will submit to authoritarianism rather than bend to the needs of a united labor force.

Socialism, for Lynd, is the fulfillment of democracy, an assertion that the interests of humanity are distinct from and more important than national interests. Socialism requires comprehensive public planning, with intense popular participation, and is based upon public ownership of the means of production and distribution. American liberal democracy is, in fact, an industrial aristocracy, with an elite controlling public policy making and denying workers their self-determining freedom. Workers must realize that capitalism is not essential for democracy and that socialism and democracy are compatible. Socialism, in this sense, is merely the completion of the American Revolution, releasing the suppressed potentials of citizens to control their own lives, government, and economy. The American founding fathers, Lynd argues, implicitly sought a stateless democratic society, which can now be realized through the enlightened activities of American workers. For Lynd, therefore, Marxism† in America comprises a movement to redeem the promises of the American Revolution. To bring about socialism in America, radicals must proffer models of participatory institutions and cater to the new generation of American workers. Socialist institutions must be based on consensus and participatory democracy, and socialist movements must utilize direct action and civil disobedience. The first step is creating strong community-based unions. Lynd's pragmatic strategies are both a legacy of the American new left and a sophisticated attempt to formulate a uniquely American approach to Marxist theory and practice.

BIBLIOGRAPHY:

A. *Anti-Federalism in Dutchess County, N.Y.* (Chicago: Loyola University Press, 1962); *Nonviolence in America* (Indianapolis: Bobbs-Merrill, 1966); with Thomas Hayden, *The Other Side* (New York: New American Library, 1966); *Class Conflict, Slavery, and the U.S. Constitution* (Indianapolis: Bobbs-Merrill, 1968); *Intellectual Origins of American Radicalism* (New York: Pantheon Books, 1968); *Reconstruction* (New York: Harper & Row, 1967); *The Resistance* (Boston: Beacon Press, 1971); *Rank and File* (Boston: Beacon Press, 1973); with Gar Alperovitz, *Strategy and Program* (Boston: Beacon Press, 1973); *The Fight Against Shutdowns* (San Pedro, Calif.: Miles and Weir, 1982); *Labor Law for the Rank and File* (San Pedro, Calif.: Singlejack Books, 1982).

B. Henry Abelove et al., eds., *Visions of History* (New York: Pantheon Books, 1983), pp. 147–66.

JOSEPH M. HAZLETT

LYOTARD, JEAN-FRANÇOIS (b. 1924). Jean-François Lyotard studied literature and philosophy as an undergraduate and, after obtaining his *license*, taught philosophy at the *lycée* level between 1949 and 1959. During this time he published an introductory text, *La Phénoménologie* (1954), which, while presenting a more or less straightforward account of the phenomenology of Husserl and Maurice Merleau-Ponty,* already shows signs of the structuralist-Marxist critique that Lyotard and others would undertake in the coming decade. He was a member of the dissident Marxist† group *Pouvoir-Ouvrier*, and contributed to and edited the journal *Socialisme ou barbarie** (1956–64). He was very active in the events of 1968, while a lecturer at the Sorbonne and the University of Paris at Nanterre. Lyotard received his *doctorat* in 1971 with his thesis *Discours, figure*. During the 1970s he taught at the experimental philosophy institute at Vincennes, at various universities in the United States, at McGill University in Montreal, and at the University of São Paulo. He is currently teaching at the University of Paris–St. Denis.

Lyotard is best known for his participation in the development of the post-Marxian, post-Freudian theoretical discourse that has come to be known as libidinal economics, along with such thinkers as Gilles Deleuze* and Félix Guattari* (see his *Economie libidinal*, 1974). Starting with his *Dérive à partir de Marx et Freud* (1973), Lyotard's critical writings have sought to demonstrate the explicit and implicit authoritarianism of orthodox Marxism and Freudianism. Both traditions, he argues, comprehend to some extent what binds individuals to socio-cultural systems, and yet, at best, these traditions only are mirror images of that from which they propose to liberate us. Lyotard's writings of the early 1970s succeed in demonstrating the dependence of these emancipatory discourses on the persistence of authoritarian domination. On the other hand, he has brought the language of libidinal economics to the traditional themes of aesthetics and art criticism, understanding works of art as special spaces for exploration of the revolutionary and conservative dynamics of desire and the givenness of matter and society (see *Les Transformateurs Duchamps*, 1977).

Recently, Lyotard has undertaken a prolonged polemic with Jürgen Habermas* and his school over the nature of the legitimation of political systems and the role of knowledge in postmodernity (see *The Post-Modern Condition: A Report on Knowledge*, 1984). Here Lyotard cogently rejects the central notion of ideal consensus that has become so important for the work of the late Frankfurt School and employs the linguistic philosophy of the Wittgenstein of the *Investigations*, J. L. Austin, and John Searle to characterize the tendencies of contemporary society. What is most interesting about this effort is that it is not a critique in the sense that has become so familiar on the left; to the contrary, Lyotard accomplishes his task of revelation in a straightforward positive manner that will remind the careful reader of the Michel Foucault* of *Discipline and Punish* and *Birth of the Clinic*.

BIBLIOGRAPHY:

A. *Discours, figure* (Paris: Klincksieck, 1971); *Dérive à partir de Marx et Freud* (Paris: Union générale d'éditions, 1973); *Economie libidinal* (Paris: Editions de Minuit, 1974).

B. Rosalind Coward and John Ellis, *Language and Materialism* (London: Routledge & Kegan Paul, 1977).

LAURENCE E. WINTERS

M

MALLET, SERGE (1927–1973). A principal architect of the theory of the "new working class" and an activist in the French left, Serge Mallet was born in 1927 to working-class parents near Bordeaux in southwest France. During World War II he joined the Resistance and afterward the Communist Party. He worked for a Party publication and moved to Paris to study film and to work for the Party and in the cultural department of the Communist-dominated Confédération Générale du Travail, France's largest union. He spent time in Eastern Europe as a French representative to the International Federation of Youth. Mallet became increasingly disillusioned by the French Communists as he watched their inability to grapple with the Algerian War and the collapse of the Fourth Republic. Simultaneously he began questioning the contemporary validity of the Marxist†— and especially the Communist Party's—conception of the working class. Mallet's position within the Party became more and more untenable until he eventually resigned, becoming active in Tribune du Communisme, a small group that later merged into the new United Socialist Party (PSU) in 1960. The PSU played an important role in the French left as an advocate of workers' self-management, and Mallet was a member of its Political Bureau. His most important book, *The New Working Class*, was published in 1963. Mallet played an active role in the events of May 1968 in Paris. On the strength of his numerous writings he received a doctorate in 1970 and began teaching political science at the University of Paris at Vincennes. He died in an auto accident three years later.

Mallet's theory took form amid the rise of Gaullism. In arguing for a new conceptualization of the working class, he was one of several writers (others included André Gorz* and Pierre Belleville) thinking in these terms in circles close to the journal *Les Temps modernes*. Jean-Paul Sartre,* its most prominent figure, helped fund his research. Also, Mallet was influenced by the "genetic structuralism" of his friend Lucien Goldmann.* This method sought to understand and explain social and mental structures by emphasizing their constantly changing reality and placing them within a broader, evolving historical totality. Mallet asserted that the worker-student rebellion of May 1968 was "the first reaction to June 1958 (when the Fourth Republic collapsed) and the first socialist struggle against modern capitalism" (*New Working Class*, p. 1). De Gaulle's Fifth Republic represented, in his view, the consolidation of a new form of capitalism in France characterized by the rule of technocratic organization, increasing automation, and expanded state intervention. Furthermore, a new stratum of wage-earning technicians had emerged due to large-scale and complex productive technology and state needs engendered by this advanced capitalism. Widespread debate occurred within the left about the nature and potential of this stratum, which Mallet asserted had a vanguard role to play in the struggle for radical change. Mallet severely chastized what he called the metaphysical and untenable view of a historically homogeneous proletariat. He insisted on the importance of recognizing its differentiated character and divided the evolution of capitalism into three phases.

First, "family or group capitalism," the earliest phase, is characterized by numerous competing firms, each fully producing and marketing its products. In this stage the former artisan becomes a "polyvalent skilled worker dispossessed of his tools" (ibid., p. 39) since he owns neither his means of production nor what he produces, in contrast to earlier craft production. He is therefore impelled to protect his sole remaining property, his skilled trade, which in turn allows him to be mobile and sell his labor power to different firms. Craft-based unions appear and an anarcho-syndicalist perspective becomes dominant among such workers; socialism is envisioned as a reappropriation of what the artisan lost by becoming a wage laborer, i.e., ownership of the means of production and the product of work. Mobility makes the workplace, rather than the location of his home, the primary site of the worker's sense of solidarity with his fellow workers.

Second, by the twentieth century a new form of capitalism emerged as a result of the interrelated factors of mass industrialization, intensification of the division of labor, the eclipse of the free market, and ongoing concentration of capital and ownership of the means of production. Concurrent with the development of great machines and the spread of the assembly line came the disappearance of the mobile artisan-worker, and in his stead came the centrality of the more anchored semiskilled laborer living in a new type of housing, "the new slum, workers' barracks" (ibid., p. 43). These workers tend toward electoral politics and bureaucratized unions to express and defend their needs. Mallet insisted that the bureaucratization of the labor movement was the result and not the cause of the changing structure of the working class, which itself was "determined by the technical organisation of capitalist production" (ibid., p. 24). In other words, as the worker becomes less skilled in his daily work, the expression of his needs are decreasingly in terms of struggles for his own autonomy.

In the third and final phase, capital is so concentrated and the cost of the means of production so great that small and medium-sized firms cannot compete and the general trend is therefore toward monopolization. With continuous automation and rationalization of the work place, variable capital (that which is invested in wage labor) decreases in proportion to constant capital (that which is invested in the plant and machinery), and profit comes from the enterprise as a whole as opposed to the simple extraction of surplus values from the individuals working in it. Furthermore, the imperatives of advanced technology engender a highly qualified labor force, especially a segment of well-paid, educated technicians to run the means of production and adapt to new and changing techniques. It was the emergence of this sector combined with the increasingly polyvalent manual worker who must operate and repair complex machinery that led Mallet to speak of the existence of a "new working class." In addition, he argued that a "company-level trade unionism" was emerging that, as the expression of highly skilled young workers and rooted in the individual enterprises, would create a modern form of anarcho-syndicalism and a struggle by the workers for more and more control of the firm.

Socialism, for Mallet, meant *autogestion*, workers' self-management and ownership of the means of production. Attacking Leninism,† he advocated a democratic "mass unionism" as the vehicle for social change. Since only those active groups "integrated into the most advanced processes of technical civilization . . . are in a position to reformulate the manifold forms of alienation and envisage superior forms of development" (ibid., p. 47), the new working class would be the socialist vanguard. Since its elementary needs are more or less satisfied, the new working class would press qualitative demands and pose qualitative questions about the work place, as opposed to simply raising quantitative issues such as monetary remuneration. Trained as a specialist, the new worker would reconquer "*on the collective level* the autonomy which he lost during the period of the mechanisation of work" (ibid., p. 28). This would lead inevitably to the rejection of hierarchy and the demand for self-management. The role of the new working class in the strikes of May and June 1968 confirmed this prognosis in Mallet's mind.

BIBLIOGRAPHY:

A. *Essays on the New Working Class* (St. Louis: Telos Press, 1975) (a collection of essays spanning the 1960s); *The New Working Class*, rev. ed. (Nottingham: Spokesman Books, 1975).

B. Dick Howard, "New Situation, New Strategy: Serge Mallet and André Gorz," in *The Unknown Dimension: European Marxism Since Lenin*, ed. Dick Howard and Karl E. Klare (New York: Basic Books, 1972); George Ross, "Marxism and the New Middle Classes: French Critiques," *Theory and Society*, 5, no. 2 (March 1978).

MITCHELL COHEN

MARABLE, MANNING (b. 1950). Manning Marable is a black American historian and political activist. He was born in 1950 and received his B.A. from Earlham College and his Ph.D. in history from the University of Maryland. Marable has taught at Smith College, the University of San Francisco, and Tuskegee Institute, where he was chairman of the Department of Political Science. Dr. Marable has also served as senior research associate at the Africana Studies and Research Center at Cornell University and as director of the Institute of Race Relations at Fisk University. He presently teaches political sociology at Colgate University. Dr. Marable is the author of scores of articles on Afro-American politics and history. He writes a syndicated column that appears in more than 140 black and progressive newspapers worldwide.

In his political thought Marable is the heir of such figures as Stokely Carmichael, Malcolm X, Antonio Gramsci,* and W.E.B. Du Bois.* He blends a vibrant black nationalism with an incisive Marxian critique of modern capitalism. For Marable, American racism is intricately connected with capitalism. The problem of race prejudice is fundamentally a problem of class exploitation. Racism emerged in the West with the rise of capitalism. It served as a means of making the dominant group in society withhold its sympathy from the group that was to be exploited by characterizing that group as "inferior" or "subhuman." Racism, the systematic exploitation of black life and labor, is neither "disease," "malady," nor "aberration." Rather, it is inextricably tied to economic, social and political needs of capitalists. According to Marable, this racism has manifested itself in various ways, including racial segregation, the exploitation of black labor, the characterization of black skin color as a badge of shame, ugliness, or evil, the use of coercive state agencies, i.e., the police and military, to restrain blacks, and the use of institutions generating what Gramsci called "ideological hegemony," e.g., universities, schools, churches, and media, to rationalize racial oppression.

For Marable, great strides in the fight against racism were made by the civil rights movement of the 1960s. Through the efforts of this movement landmark legislation was passed that ended overt segregation, gave more blacks the right to vote, and diminished discrimination in jobs, housing, and many other aspects of American life. Steps were also taken to upgrade the economic condition of blacks. However, this progress has run its course. In the 1970s and early 1980s blacks had actually regressed in their quest for equality. This is evident in such things as disproportionately high black unemployment, cutbacks in social programs, government retreats on affirmative action regulations, and the decline in black studies programs in the nation's universities. The advent of the overtly conservative Reagan administration is one obvious indication of the relaxing of civil rights enforcement. The reason for this digression in the progress of blacks, according to Marable, is capitalism. Only a limited amount of progress against racism can take place within a capitalist framework, which stresses corporate profit and works to maintain the status quo. The destruction of racism in this country cannot occur without the destruction of capitalism.

Marable is disappointed with the black bourgeoisie, many of whom have been co-opted by white capitalists. Capitalism deflated the civil rights movement by offering many of its leaders jobs in government or the corporate structure. And where black politicians have been elected, they have often been as corrupt as their white counterparts, or handicapped by white economic domination. Many of the gains blacks have made are illusory, attempts by the white capitalist leadership to pacify blacks by offering a few insignificant concessions. For example, there are large numbers of blacks in the military service. The number of black policemen has also grown. However, in both cases blacks are dispro-portionately situated at the lowest decision-making levels of these institutions, ensuring their powerlessness. Furthermore, says Marable, blacks have become passive and complacent in the 1970s. Like young whites, young blacks are turning inward, pursuing their own personal goals rather than social change. Merely finding employment has displaced political agitation as their major prior-ity. Typically, many black students are now more interested in fraternity or sorority parties than in political demonstrations. Self-interest and hedonism have replaced social commitment.

So, the black bourgeoisie is co-opted, and black students have become passive. Liberalism and conservatism are bankrupt. The liberal dream of full employment is naive and ignores changed economic conditions or the fact that capitalism now acknowledges high unemployment as "acceptable." Even the democratic socialists are wrong in advocating such policies as centralized state planning and more health and education programs, for these programs help prop an inequitable capitalist infrastructure. Therefore, in order to destroy racism and upgrade the condition of black people, this country must radically transform itself. Marable does not believe that the destruction of capitalism in America can come about through violent, revolutionary tactics, at least not in the near future. And certainly a violent revolution of the type conjured by many black militants of the late 1960s is not immediately possible. Such an effort would probably be suicidal. The transformation from capitalism to socialism must be a gradual one. More-over, it cannot copy African socialism or Chinese or Soviet socialism. It must be a distinctly American brand of socialism, reflecting its American milieu and also reflecting Afro-American culture. Echoing Gramsci, Marable believes American solutions must be sought to American problems. As a strategy for action, Marable calls for the creation of black institutions to spearhead the fight against racism. He advocates the creation of such institutions as an independent black political party, black labor unions, and black paramilitary units to suppress the drug traffic and supervise local police activities within the black community. In short, Marable wants the creation of a black united front, blending both the nationalist and integrationist traditions of the civil rights struggle.

Initially, the movement to end racism and establish the theoretical groundwork for socialism must be led by blacks. This is because, as Du Bois has already shown, white socialists are purely economic determinists and have not perceived that racism is a powerful force supporting capitalism. White liberals, on the other hand, still view racism as a sickness in a basically healthy society. They do not see its intimate connection with capitalism. So, before an alliance can be crafted with whites, blacks must form a cohesive, autonomous, anticapitalist movement. Once this has been accomplished, coalitions can be negotiated with Hispanic and women's groups, antinuclear interests, and trade unions in order to bring about the gradual transformation of capitalism. This coalition would oppose racism and fight burgeoning defense spending, which siphons needed resources from social programs.

For Marable, capitalism and racism are intricately linked. Racism cannot be eliminated in a capitalist society. Hence a two-pronged attack is necessary. Blacks should spearhead this attack by creating an autonomous, anticapitalist black movement, and then by making alliances with sympathetic white groups. This coalition will generate a gradual transformation from capitalism to socialism and wage an effective fight against racism.

BIBLIOGRAPHY:

A. *Blackwater: Essays on Black and Southern History* (New York: Challenge Press, 1978); *From the Grassroots* (Boston: East End Press, 1980); *Through the Prism of Race and Class* (Ithaca: Department of City and Regional Planning, Cornell University, 1980); *Blackwater: Historical Studies in Race, Class Consciousness and Revolution* (Dayton, O.: Black Praxis Press, 1981); "The Military, Black People, and the Racist State: A History of Coercion," *Black Scholar*, 12 (January–February 1981), pp. 6–7; "Toward a Black Politics: Beyond the Race Class Dilemma," *Nation*, 232, no. 14 (11 April 1981), pp. 417, 429–33; "Reaganism, Racism and Reaction: Black Political Realignment in the 1980s," *Black Scholar*, 13 (Fall 1982), pp. 2–13.

EARL SHERIDAN

MARCUSE, HERBERT (1898–1979). Herbert Marcuse was born on 19 July 1898 in Berlin. Between 1916 and 1918 he served in a reserve unit of the German army. During this period he began his doctoral studies at the University of Berlin. His early political experience dates from these same years. He joined the majority faction of the German Social Democratic Party (SPD) in 1917 and remained a member of this party for two years. He resigned in 1919 in protest over SPD complicity in the murders of Rosa Luxemburg† and Karl Liebknecht. In 1918 Marcuse was a member of the short-lived revolutionary Soldiers' Council in Berlin. With the suppression of the councils and his resignation from the SPD, Marcuse ended his last organized political affiliations. He resumed his studies in 1919 at the University of Freiburg and received his doctorate in German literature, philosophy, and political economy in 1922 with a dissertation on "Der deutsche Künstlerroman" (The German Artist-Novel). After working for a small Berlin publishing firm for several years, Marcuse returned to the University of Freiburg in 1928 as a philosophical assistant to Martin Heidegger. His promotion to a German university professorship was blocked by the Nazi accession to power. In 1933 he became a member of the Institute for Social Research and was assigned to the Institute's Geneva branch. In 1934 he emigrated to the United States and continued his association with the Institute at Columbia University in New York. Between 1942 and 1950 Marcuse was a research analyst for the U.S. government, first in the office of Strategic Services, later in the State Department. Following his government employment, he held research fellowships at Columbia and Harvard. He was a visiting professor of history at Yale in 1963–64. Marcuse's first permanent professorship was at Brandeis University. Between 1954 and 1965, he was professor of politics and philosophy and chairman of the graduate program in the history of ideas. He also held an appointment at the Ecole Practique des Hautes Etudes in Paris (1959, 1961–62).

After his retirement from Brandeis, he was professor of philosophy at the University of California, San Diego. In 1966 he was awarded an honorary professorship at the Free University of Berlin. Marcuse attained his greatest fame during the period of new left activism. From the mid-1960s until his death, he was both an advocate and critic of the theories and practices associated with the new left. Marcuse died on 29 July 1979 in Starnberg, West Germany.

Marcuse's first published philosophical works dated to his period of association with Heidegger in Freiburg between 1928 and 1932. During this period Marcuse made the first attempt to synthesize Marxist† social theory with existential philosophy. In a number of essays and book reviews and in the book that was intended to be his professorial habilitation, *Hegels Ontologie und die Grundlegung einer Theorie der Geschichtlichkeit* (Hegel's Ontology and the Fundamental Principles of a Theory of Historicality), Marcuse tried to resolve what he called "the fundamental predicament of Marxism" by fusing Marxism with elements of Heidegger's phenomenological method and existential ontology. Marcuse believed that contemporary Marxist theory found itself caught between the vulgar economic determinism of orthodox dialectical materialism and the overly idealistic alternative of Kantian Marxism. In his selective and always critical appropriation of Heidegger, Marcuse sought a phenomenological restoration of the unique and particular to a Marxism preoccupied with the general laws of economic development and an existential focus on the whole "concrete" human being rather than an economic or idealistic reduction of human being to just one of its aspects. The key to this synthesis of Marxism and existential philosophy was Heidegger's notion of the "historicality" (*Geschichtlichkeit*) of human existence. In *Being and Time*, Heidegger maintained that human being was an historical being. Marcuse traced the evolution of Heidegger's notion of historicality back to Wilhelm Dilthey's "philosophy of life" (*Lebensphilosophie*), and from Dilthey back to Hegel. More importantly, Marcuse noted the similarity of Heideggerian historicality to Marx's emphasis on the primacy of the science of history, especially in the then newly published work of the young Marx and Engels† on *The German Ideology*. With the publication of Marx's *Economic and Philosophic Manuscripts* in 1932, Marcuse ended his attempt to synthesize Heidegger and Marx. Marcuse found the corrective to the predicament of contemporary Marxist theory in the philosophical works of the early Marx.

When he joined the Institute for Social Research, Marcuse gave up his individual effort to reformulate Marxism and participated in the collective effort to develop a "critical theory of society." Part of Marcuse's assignment entailed reviewing more than 100 titles in philosophy, sociology, history, and psychology for the book review section of the Institute's journal, the *Zeitschrift für Sozialforschung*. But his primary task in the Institute was the philosophical articulation of the fundamental principles of critical theory. Marcuse's essay on "Philosophy and Critical Theory" defined critical theory as a fusion of Marxist social theory and idealist philosophy, while it hinted at the Freudian psychoanalytic component that would be central to his later work. Although committed to the realization of social and individual reason and freedom, Marcuse and critical theory did not identify this commitment with any political party. In his other essays, Marcuse analyzed a number of past and present tendencies in philosophy and social theory. In these works, Marcuse withdrew his earlier support for existential philosophy and *Lebensphilosophie*. Now Marcuse viewed existential philosophy, *Lebensphilosophie*, and empirical philosophy of science as the intellectual tendencies that eroded the historical commitment of philosophy and social theory to human emancipation. By eroding this commitment, these tendencies set the stage for Nazi-fascist irrationalism and domination.

His book *Reason and Revolution* culminated Marcuse's efforts in this period. One of the central themes of this work was the refutation of the view prevalent in England and the United States that Hegel's glorification of the Germanic state was realized in the Nazi state and Hegelian philosophy was, therefore, one of the prime sources for the ideological legitimation of this state. Marcuse emphasized the contrast between Hegelian rationalism and Nazi irrationalism. If any theoretical tradition outside of Nazism and fascism per se was to be implicated in the triumph of these movements, Marcuse argued that this was not Hegelianism but positivism. It was the positivist denial of the perquisites of abstract reason, positivist intellectual passivity, and the positivist reduction of concepts to non-transcendental referents that displayed a closer kinship to Nazi-fascist theory than any strain within idealist philosophy. The true contemporary heir to Hegel, in Marcuse's view, was not Nazism, but Marxist social theory. *Reason and Revolution* thus continued the neo-Marxist identification of Marxism with philosophy and Hegel that was initiated by Karl Korsch* and George Lukács* in the 1920s.

Marcuse resumed his academic career in 1950. One of the thrusts of his postwar work was the analysis of the ideological obstacles to revolution. Marcuse's book on *Soviet Marxism* traced the Soviet transformation of Marxist social theory from a form of critical thinking designed to guide revolutionary political practice into a fixed universal system that arrests and codifies Marxism as an ideological prop to the existing status quo. In his essay on "Repressive Tolerance," Marcuse analyzed the degeneration of the liberal idea of tolerance. Historically, the demand for tolerance was a partisan demand for the toleration of certain progressive but outlawed ideas. But contemporary tolerance had become an apparently indifferent, but actually repressive acceptance of all ideas—social and antisocial, true and false. Marcuse argued that the restoration of the historically progressive role of tolerance could only be achieved by tolerance once again becoming partisan, i.e., a tolerance extended to ideas emanating from the left that lead to the enhancement of human life, a tolerance withdrawn from ideas emanating from the right that have a destructive character. The masterpiece of this ideological criticism was *One-Dimensional Man*, Marcuse's most famous work. In this book, Marcuse described the smooth and comfortable totalitarianism of advanced industrial societies. A one-dimensional society had little need for the clumsy coercive apparatus of the traditional authoritarian state. The development of the welfare and warfare state, the mass media, and modern technology have engendered a mass conformity and suppressed the development of genuine alternatives to the status quo. Even philosophy and social theory, once bastions of critical thinking, had succumbed to the pervasive one-dimensionality. In *One-Dimensional Man*, Marcuse noted the possibility of revolution, but it was the ideological, political, and technological obstacles to revolution that were emphasized.

If Marcuse's criticism of ideology emphasized the obstacles to revolution, the Freudian thrust of Marcuse's postwar work raised the stakes involved in revolution and human emancipation. The object of a true revolution is human freedom and happiness, and the realization of this freedom and happiness required much more than the capture of political power and the socialization of the economic means of production. *Eros and Civilization* and a number of essays offered Marcuse's synthesis of Marx and Freud. With Freud, Marcuse argued that human instinctual desire was a timeless and explosive force that could never be completely reconciled to any society. Some "basic repression" of the instincts was necessary to maintain the "reality principle" of any society. But Marcuse then introduced an historical dimension to the conditions under which instinctual gratification and repression took place. Stratified, competitive, economically exploitative industrial societies—whether capitalist or socialist—imposed an additional "surplus-repression" upon the instincts in order to maintain their particularly onerous form of the reality principle, which Marcuse called the "performance principle." True revolutionary emancipation, therefore, went beyond political and economic change to include the social, sensuous, and sexual emancipation of the instincts that would occur with the elimination of surplus-repression. Instead of the "Promethean" image of emancipation through toil and achievement that dominates the history of Western philosophy, Marcuse offered the "Orphic" and "narcissistic" images of emancipation through gratification, peace, and repose. To the extent that Marxist social theory shared the Promethean orientation of philosophy, Marcuse declared Marxism to be obsolescent.

Marcuse's critique of advanced industrial society and his vision of human emancipation exerted some influence on the protean movement of dissent associated with the label *new left*. The new left was opposed by representatives of the old socialist and Communist left and disavowed by most established intellectuals, including some of Marcuse's former colleagues at the Institute for Social Research. But in *An Essay on Liberation*, *Counterrevolution and Revolt*, and numerous essays, lectures, and interviews, Marcuse took a more favorable view. He never minimized the power of the forces opposed to revolutionary change, nor did he uncritically endorse the new left in all its tactics and objectives. But Marcuse was attentive to the spark of genuine human emancipation in this movement, which threatened, for a moment, the stability of the most advanced industrial societies. Marcuse's last works also explored the theme of art and revolution. With the accommodation of mainstream philosophy to the existing status quo and with the obsolescence of Marxist social theory, Marcuse argued that art, more than any other dimension of culture, preserved an image of human emancipation and happiness. His last book, *The Aesthetic Dimension*, combatted the orthodox Marxist tendency to trivialize art by reducing it to the status of a mere ideological reflection of social classes.

Brief characterizations risk the oversimplification of the richness and variety of Marcuse's thought. Yet it would be safe to say that Marcuse's nearly sixty years of scholarly activity were devoted to the theoretical articulation of a critical Marxism commensurate with its intellectual legacy and revolutionary objectives. In general terms, this meant a Marxism that respected the relative independence of ideas and culture and that refused to abandon its intellectual integrity for any political party or movement.

BIBLIOGRAPHY:

A. *Hegels Ontologie und die Grundlegung einer Theorie der Geschichtlichkeit* (Frankfurt am Main: V. Klostermann, 1932); *Reason and Revolution: Hegel and the Rise of Social Theory* (New York: Oxford University Press, 1941); *Eros and Civilization: A Philosophical Inquiry Into Freud* (Boston: Beacon Press, 1955); *Soviet Marxism: A Critical Analysis* (New York: Columbia University Press, 1955); *One-Dimensional Man: Studies in the Ideology of Advanced Industrial Society* (Boston: Beacon Press, 1964); "Repressive Tolerance," pp. 81–117, in Robert P. Wolff, Barrington Moore, Jr., and Herbert Marcuse, *A Critique of Pure Tolerance*, (Boston: Beacon Press, 1965); *Negations: Essays in Critical Theory* (Boston: Beacon Press, 1968); *An Essay on Liberation* (Boston: Beacon Press, 1969); *Five Lectures: Psychoanalysis, Politics, and Utopia*, trans. Jeremy J. Shapiro and Shierry M. Weber (Boston: Beacon Press, 1970); *Counterrevolution and Revolt* (Boston: Beacon Press, 1972); *Studies in Critical Philosophy*, trans. Joris de Bres (Boston: Beacon Press, 1973); *The Aesthetic Dimension: Toward a Critique of Marxist Aesthetics* (Boston: Beacon Press, 1978).

B. Paul Breines, ed., *Critical Interruptions: New Left Perspectives on Herbert Marcuse* (New York: Herder and Herder, 1972); Martin Jay, *The Dialectical Imagination* (Boston: Little, Brown, 1973); Sidney Lipshires, *Herbert Marcuse: From Marx to Freud and Beyond* (Cambridge, Mass.: Schenkman, 1974); Gad Horowitz, *Repression: Basic and Surplus Repression in Psychoanalytic Theory: Freud, Reich, and Marcuse* (Toronto: University of Toronto Press, 1977); John Bokina, "The Young Marcuse" (Ph.D. dissertation, University of Illinois, 1979).

JOHN BOKINA

MARINI, RUY MAURO (n.a.). As activist and intellectual Marini was a product of the leftist movements that linked nationalism with Marxism† in Brazil during the early 1960s. After the coup of 1964, he went to Chile, where he began to develop his thinking on dependency in association with Theotonio Dos Santos.* After the Chilean coup of 1973, he moved to Mexico and joined the Centro de Información, Documentación y Análisis sobre el Movimiento Obrero Latinoamericano (CIDAMO). He is author of several popular books and a number of significant articles.

Politically, Marini aligned himself with the thesis of Andre Gunder Frank* and others who believe that capitalism creates deformation and underdevelopment in the periphery. Economically, he attempted to examine the process of production rather than circulation. Dependent capitalism, he argued, is unable to reproduce itself through the process of accumulation. Under such conditions, absolute surplus value can be realized through lengthening the work day and intensifying the use of labor power, whereas relative surplus value cannot be generated under dependent capitalism because the consumption of workers is insignificant in a society dependent on the export of raw materials and other products. Thus a dependent capitalist economy tends to expand by pushing beyond its national borders and dominating the economies of weaker neighbors. This process is known as subimperialism.

Subimperialism is a rather recent phenomenon. In Brazil, it was especially apparent after the coup of 1964. The dictatorship repressed popular forces and reinforced the ruling classes by promoting an alliance between the bourgeoisie and the latifundist-merchant oligarchy. At the same time the government pushed for investment and technology, intensifying capitalization of the countryside and providing incentives for foreign investment. This integration with imperialism and the inability of domestic markets to absorb the increasing productivity necessitated a search for new markets, especially in Latin America. In this way imperialism took its subimperialist form. Given these conditions of dependence and imperialism, Brazilian subimperialism could not use its exploitation in the exterior as a means of raising the standard of living within the country. Therefore, autonomous capitalist development was not possible within Brazil, nor could a national bourgeoisie play any significant role in Brazilian development. In this situation, the mass of workers could lead Brazil along a revolutionary path, and armed struggle ultimately would lead to a solution for Brazilian underdevelopment.

BIBLIOGRAPHY:

A. *Subdesarrollo y revolución* (Mexico City: Siglo Veintiuno, 1969); *Dialéctica de la dependencia* (Mexico City: Era, 1973); *El reformismo y la contrarevolución: estudios sobre Chile* (Mexico City: Era, 1976); "Las razones del neodesarrollismo," *Revista mexicana de sociología*, 60 (1978), pp. 57–106; "World Capitalist Accumulation and Subimperialism," *Two Thirds*, 1 (Fall 1978), pp. 29–39.

RONALD H. CHILCOTE

MARKOVIĆ, MIHAILO (b. 1923). Mihailo Marković was born 24 February 1923 in Belgrade, Yugoslavia. An officer in Tito's† partisan army, Marković took part in the Yugoslav war of liberation in the years 1941–45. After the Yugoslav break with Stalin† in 1948, he spent half a decade attacking Stalinist dogmatism. In 1950 he received his Ph.D. in philosophy from the University of Belgrade. For ten years he studied and wrote in the fields of philosophy of science and logic, including two years of study under A. J. Ayer in London at University College, where he received another Ph.D. in 1956. From 1950 until his suspension in 1975 he taught philosophy at the University of Belgrade. One of the "Belgrade Eight," he was attacked by the government and media for supporting the student movement in 1968 and for his unacceptable theoretical views. Marković was one of the original contributors to the fertile Yugoslav journal *Praxis** (no longer published) and is now one of the editors of *Praxis International*.

Marković forcefully defends democratic socialism as the best way to realize the Marxist concept of praxis. For Marković, praxis is the ultimate criterion of all critical evaluation. He uses this concept as a foundation for a Marxist doctrine of human rights and to critique contemporary societies—socialist as well as capitalist. One of Marković's important contributions to the philosophy of Marxism is a clear explication of the term *praxis*. Praxis, according to Marković, involves a form of life in which the distinctive, universal human capacities are realized. The life of praxis, as outlined in *From Affluence to Praxis*, is said to be one in which the following capacities are actualized: (1) the capacity to use all of one's senses for a maximum experience of the world; (2) the ability to rationally analyze objects and situations, to grasp regularities, to make logical deductions, and to solve problems; (3) the imaginative capacity to transcend the limits of the given and to project ideals; (4) the power to communicate with others, to convey and understand thoughts, feelings, desires, and motives; (5) the creative capacity to introduce novelty into the world; (6) the ability to harmonize one's interests, drives, and aspirations with those of others; (7) the capacity to choose freely among alternative possibilities; and (8) the ability to develop a clear and critical consciousness about oneself and to distinguish between what one actually is and what one could potentially be.

The application of the standard of praxis to social life implies, according to Marković, democratic or self-managing socialism. The concept of socialism implied by the concept of praxis transcends what Marković has argued are the false alternatives: economism and statism. Economism calls for a complete liberation of the economy through the undisturbed development of commodity-money relations; it identifies socialist self-management with decentralized self-managing economic units, free of central planning and coordination. Statism, on the other hand, is the centralist view that the bureaucratic state, as the unconditional representative of the working class, should rationally manage the whole economy as well as all scientific and cultural activities. Marković has endorsed a system of integrated self-management. His dialectical solution to the statism–economism antithesis is a system in which self-managing, worker-controlled units are combined with flexible planning by central, truly democratic, representative bodies.

In his latest book, *Democratic Socialism* (1982), Marković describes the new legal institutions he believes to be necessary for an integrated self-managing society. The proposed network of democratic decision-making bodies involves two elements: productive activity and geography (domains of consumption). These two elements are to be incorporated on at least four levels: local working and living communities; enterprises and small cities; branches of enterprises and geographical regions; and the whole society. Each self-governing unit, regardless of its level, would have the following characteristics in common: broad democratic participation involving each member; maximum depth of democratic participation (full deliberation and choice); and democratic control of technical experts and managers (instead of despotic technocratic control). Marković's detailed suggestions also involve elaborate procedures for separation of powers, democratic social planning, freedom of expression, protection of minority rights, freedom of information, and arrangements for nonprofessional, nonoppressive institutions of personal security and national self-defense. These practical proposals for new legal institutions constitute a significant contribution because Marxist literature is thin on the nature of the state, the law, and the politics in future society.

The ultimate aim of socialism, according to Marković, should be the debureaucratization of politics and the transcendence of commodity-money relations. He has argued that a large bureaucracy can be eliminated by using computers to take over routine administrative operations; remaining bureaucrats will be strictly subordinated to elected political bodies. Marković has conceded that commodity production will continue to exist as long as there is scarcity—thus the immediate task is to move toward a society of abundance on the basis of integrated self-managing commodity production. His view is that commodity-money relations with social ownership of the means of production, guided by democratically coordinated self-managing units, are not the same as commodity-money relations under capitalism. Striking a pessimistic note, Marković has warned that abundance will not solve all human problems; there is a dark side of human nature: evil as a human disposition lies very deep. The key problem, the basic evil, which according to Marković humankind will have to face for a long time, is how to prevent the recurrence—even under new models of society—of the treatment of people as things.

BIBLIOGRAPHY:

A. *The Contemporary Marx: Essays on Humanist Communism* (Nottingham: Spokesman Books, 1974); *From Affluence to Praxis: Philosophy and Social Criticism* (Ann Arbor: University of Michigan Press, 1974); *Democratic Socialism: Theory and Practice* (Sussex: Harvester Press, 1982).

B. Crocker, David. *Praxis and Democratic Socialism: The Critical Theory of Marković and Stojanovic* (Atlantic Highlands, N.J.: Humanities Press, 1983).

DAVID MYERS

MATTICK, PAUL (1904–1981). Paul Mattick was born in 1904 in German Pomerania (now Poland) and died in 1981 in Cambridge, Massachusetts. Mattick joined the Freie Sozialistische Jugend at fourteen, moving with the rest of that organization into the Spartakusbund, and so into the German Communist Party (KPD). He was the apprentices's delegate to the workers' council at the Siemens factory, where he had apprenticed as a toolmaker in 1918. In 1919 Mattick left the KPD with the group that in 1920 formed the Kommunistische Arbeiterpartei Deutchlands (KAPD). Moving from Berlin to Cologne Mattick was active as an organizer and agitator for the KAPD and the Allgemeine Arbeiter Union; after

1925 his articles appeared frequently in the left press. In 1926, with the revolutionary period clearly over in Germany, Mattick emigrated to the United States, where he worked as a tool and die maker in Michigan and Illinois. In Chicago by the start of the 1930s he joined and wrote for the IWW; in 1931 he revived the *Chicagoer Arbeiterzeitung* as the organ of a coalition of German workers' groups, editing it for a year until it succumbed to a campaign organized by the Communist Party. In 1934 Mattick helped form the United Workers Party, which soon became the Group of Council Communists. From 1934 to 1943 he edited the journals *International Council Correspondance, Living Marxism*, and *New Essays*. Mattick wrote many of the articles in this last journal, which also published writings by Karl Korsch,* Antonie Pannekoek,* and other European and American council communists. In the early 1930s Mattick was active in the unemployed movement. With the advent of the New Deal and then the war, however, his kind of politics became impossible. During the 1950s he lived in New York and then in Vermont, abandoning factory work to write his major work, *Marx and Keynes*. In the 1960s he moved to Cambridge, where he continued to write and had some influence on members of the student left. In 1974–75 he had his one academic job, as guest professor at the University of Roskilde in Denmark. His earlier writings were widely republished in Europe along with a continuing flow of new work, and he gave many public lectures there in the late 1960s and early 1970s. He had considerably less influence in the United States.

He described himself at various times as an "orthodox Marxist." This meant for Mattick both adherence to the basic concepts of Marx's† critique of political economy and a rejection of the dominant Marxist tradition in politics and economics, represented by the Second† and Third Internationals.† Indeed, one could say that his importance in twentieth-century Marxism stems from his reuniting the two aspects of Marx's project—the critique of economics and the critique of politics—separated in the post-Marx tradition of "Marxism." For Mattick both social democratic reformism and Leninist† statism were, like New Deal Keynesianism and the Nazi war economy, to be understood as products of capitalist development rather than as alternatives to it. While the growing integration of the world economy and the increasing depth of its crises required these various steps in the direction of state regulation of the market system— by fascists, socialists, or bourgeois democrats—in the capitalistically developed countries, Leninism appeared as the political form required for capitalist development of underdeveloped countries. Opposition to capitalism requires, then, opposition also to the various attempts to preserve it by transforming it, including those made in the name of Marxism. Such opposition, however, cannot be called into existence by theoretical correctness or purity; it requires the experience of social crisis conditions, which alone seem likely to lead to the emergence of a revolution made by the working class on the basis of their own ideas and needs.

This conviction led Mattick (like Marx) to the attempt to understand the developmental tendencies of the capitalist economy. In this matter the most important influence on Mattick's thought, after that of Marx himself, was exercised by Henryk Grossmann.† From Grossmann Mattick learned to read Marx's theory of capitalist development as simultaneously a theory of capitalist crisis, due fundamentally not to the disproportionalities or underconsumption favored as explanations of crisis by most Marxists, but to the tendential fall of the rate of profit. As Mattick showed in numerous essays, most Marxist theories (such as those of M. I. Tugan-Baranowsky, Rudolf Hilferding,† and Rosa Luxemburg†) share with bourgeois economics a focus on the circulation of commodities and the realization of surplus value. Marx, in contrast, focuses on the production of surplus value, to argue that the very process by which exploitation is enhanced leads over time to a decline in the rate of profit on total capital. Mattick's main contribution to the critique of economics was to demonstrate that this Janus-faced process by its nature is not overcome by the various forms of Keynesian state regulation of the market economy. By the late 1950s he had succeeded in showing that the continued existence of the capitalist structure as the basis of the "mixed economy" implied the latter's destabilization in the not-too-distant future by the same crisis mechanism that had put an end to earlier periods of prosperity. In maintaining this position, Mattick opposed not only bourgeois economics but Marxist thinkers, like Paul Baran,† Paul Sweezy,† and Herbert Marcuse,* who saw in "late capitalism," whatever its difficulties, evidence of a bourgeois victory over the economic crisis cycle of the past. In fact it took ten years for Mattick to find a publisher for *Marx and Keynes*, and the work is still largely neglected despite the confirmation of its argument by the course of economic events of the past fifteen years.

While accused by many both of a mechanical theory of capitalist crisis and of excessive political pessimism, neither charge is really justified. While capitalist society in Mattick's opinion does of necessity produce moments of economic crisis, it is up to the working class to transform the collapse of the system into its revolutionary overthrow. The importance of economic crisis is that by breaking the pattern of everyday life, and with it the power of bourgeois ideology in its various forms—including the Marxist ones—it forces people to confront the choice between struggle against existing conditions or acceptance of continuing misery. Socialism is not inevitable but (as Rosa Luxemburg said) the only alternative to barbarism. On the other hand, while it is true that even so deep and long-lasting a crisis as that of the years 1929–45 led not to revolution but, thanks to its absence, to a renewal of capitalist growth, this growth is only the harbinger of renewed, and even deeper, crisis—and at a time when the Keynesian weapon against it has already been expended. For this reason, Mattick wrote in his *Critique of Marcuse*, "however small the chances are for revolt, this is not the time to throw in the towel" (p. 183).

BIBLIOGRAPHY:

A. A nearly complete bibliography of Mattick's writings is to be found in *Internationales Wissenschafliches Korrespondence* 17, no. 2 (1981), pp. 197–224. Works available in English include *Marx and Keynes: The Limits of the Mixed Economy* (Boston:

Porter Sargent, 1969); *Critique of Marcuse: One-Dimensional Man in Class Society* (London: Merlin, 1972); *Anti-Bolshevik Communism* (New York: M. E. Sharpe, 1978); *Economic Crisis and Crisis Theory* (New York: M. E. Sharpe, 1981); *Marxism: Last Refuge of the Bourgeoisie?* (New York: M. E. Sharpe, 1983); see also, *New essays*, 5 vols. (Westport, Conn.: Greenwood Press, 1970).

PAUL MATTICK, JR.

MAYER, HANS (b. 1907). Born in Cologne in 1907, Mayer studied law, philosophy, history, and political science at the universities of Cologne, Berlin, and Bonn and completed a study of the significance of Rudolf Smend's anti-positivism in the context of the crisis of German political theory. Given his Jewish background and his Marxist† beliefs, he left Germany because of Hitler's accession to power in 1933, traveling first to France before settling in Switzerland. In addition to support provided by influential Swiss intellectuals like Max Rychner and Carl S. Burckhardt, Mayer received aid from the Rockefeller Institute for International Studies in Geneva and the Institute for Social Research, which had been forced to leave Frankfurt. In this period, Mayer's work, including publication in the Swiss press under the pseudonym Martin Seiler, begins to point toward the synthesis of social, cultural, and literary history that would become his hallmark. In 1945 Mayer returned to Germany. He briefly served as the chief editor of the Hessian radio in Frankfurt until he was expelled because of the emerging postwar anticommunism of the American occupation forces. In 1948 he accepted a professorship in German and comparative literature at the Karl Marx University in Leipzig, where he became a colleague of Ernst Bloch.* Although one of East Germany's most prominent intellectual figures, he nevertheless maintained a readership in the West and, furthermore, influenced the shape of West German literature, especially in the Gruppe 47. In the wake of the suppression of the Hungarian revolution of 1956, a hardening of East German ideological and cultural positions ensued that led to attacks on Mayer by orthodox critics and theoreticians such as Alfred Kurella and Kurt Hagen. Mayer left East Germany and returned to the West in 1963, serving as professor of German literature at the Technical University of Hannover from 1965 until his retirement in 1973, when he moved to Tübingen.

His first major study, which remains one of his most important, *Georg Büchner und seine Zeit* (1946), displays the characteristic features of Mayer's oeuvre that profoundly shaped postwar German literary criticism and scholarship, especially during the politicized, neo-Marxist period of the late 1960s and early 1970s. In contrast to George Lukács's* primary emphasis on literature as manifestation of philosophical positions and to the prevailing West German version of American new criticism, *Werkimmanenz*, Mayer presents a synthesis of literary, historical, theoretical, and political factors in order to capture the aesthetic specificity and historical contradictions of Büchner's work in the context of Metternichian repression. If the multiplicity of perspectives betrays a certain eclecticism, it also typifies the implicit antidogmatism of Mayer's aesthetics, which engenders the major issues in his oeuvre. Like the examination of Büchner, the many studies of Bertolt Brecht† are motivated by a concern with the form of political resistance designated as a "plebean tradition" outside of bourgeois hegemony as opposed to the orthodox insistence on the proletariat as a universal class able to overcome and inherit bourgeois culture. In a related venture, Mayer attempted to reclaim democratic features in Richard Wagner's work, claiming that Bayreuth was initially conceived as a "democratic festival." Second, Mayer's defense of the literature of European and American modernism (Robert Musil, Thomas Mann, Jean-Paul Sartre,* James Joyce, William Faulkner) against advocates of a tendentious socialist realism represented a reappropriation of positions, similar to those of Brecht and Walter Benjamin* in the expressionist debate of the 1930s. Finally, in his late work, *Outsiders* (1975; American ed. 1982), Mayer condemns the bourgeois enlightenment, which because of its hostility to difference, fails to fulfill its promise of emancipation to the perpetually excluded groups: Jews, women, and homosexuals. Although he combines elements of Herbert Marcuse's* theory of marginal groups with themes from Theodore Adorno's* and Max Horkheimer's* *Dialectic of the Enlightenment*, Mayer's work is unique in its wealth of historical detail, corresponding to the reluctance to deny particularity and to the ultimate conclusion that not even their shared eccentricity transforms the various outsiders into a single collective subject.

BIBLIOGRAPHY:

A. *Georg Büchner und seine Zeit* (Wiesbaden: Limes, 1946); rept. ed., Frankfurt: Suhrkamp, 1974); *Karl Marx und das Elend des Geistes. Studien zur neuen deutschen Ideologie* (Meisenheim am Glan: Hain, 1948); *Bertolt Brecht und die Tradition* (Pfullingen: Neske, 1961); *Richard Wagner in Bayreuth 1876–1976* (New York: Rizzoli International, 1976); *Thomas Mann* (Frankfurt: Suhrkamp, 1980); *Outsiders: A Study of Life and Letters* (Cambridge: MIT Press, 1982).

B. Inge Jens, ed., *Über Hans Mayer* (Frankfurt: Suhrkamp, 1977); Gert Ueding, ed., *Materialism zur Hans Meyer, "Aussenseiter"* (Frankfurt: Suhrkamp, 1978).

RUSSELL BERMAN

MEDEM, VLADIMIR (1879–1923). Medem, born on 22 July 1879, was raised in Minsk in an assimilated family of Jewish origin. He was officially converted to Christianity as an infant, was raised in a Russified environment, and received a Christian education. Medem became involved with the Russian revolutionary movement while a student at the University of Kiev. His participation in this movement led to his arrest in 1899, to his subsequent expulsion from the university, and to his being sent back to Minsk. While in Minsk, Medem became close to a number of Jewish workers and to the Jewish workers' movement. He became a member of the General Jewish Workers Union (the Bund) in 1900 and soon became an important publicist for the Bundist movement. Although unable to write in Yiddish at that time, Medem was made an editor of the Bundist periodical *Der minsker arbeter*. Medem was arrested once again early in 1901 but fled abroad. In 1903 Medem was coopted onto the Foreign Committee of the Bund.

While on the Foreign Committee, Medem wrote a number of works on the national question. He was the founder and foremost exponent of the ideological tendency known as neutralism and, as such, maintained that the Bund ought to take a "neutral" position on the future fate of the Jewish people. The Bund, Medem asserted, ought to advocate neither assimilationism nor nationalism, but should, rather, allow "objective development" to take its course. Although the Bund should defend oppressed nations (including the Jewish nation) against enforced assimilation, the Bund need not defend either the Jews or any other people against assimilation per se. While maintaining this stance, however, Medem also maintained that Russian Jewry had, and would, for the immediate future, continue to have a distinct national culture. Thus Russian Jewry, according to Medem, was entitled to national cultural autonomy (autonomous control over its own cultural and educational affairs). Medem later rejected the "neutralist" position in favor of a more nationally conscious perspective; however, Medem's writings in defense of neutralism remained his most original contribution to the socialist corpus. Medem was one of the representatives of the Bund to the Second Congress of the Russian Social Democratic Workers Party (RSDWP) in 1903 and was also one of the Bund's representatives to the Amsterdam Congress of the Socialist International (1904). During and immediately after the era of the Russian Revolution of 1905, Medem was based in Vilna and worked as an editor for a number of Bundist periodicals, including *Nashe slovo*, *Nasha tribuna*, *Folkstsaytung*, *Di hofnung*, and *Der morgnshtern*. He left the Russian Empire once again in 1907 and lived abroad until 1913. While abroad, Medem served on the Bundist delegations to the 1907 Congress of the RSDWP and the 1910 Copenhagen Congress of the Socialist International. He wrote for both socialist and nonsocialist periodicals and for both the Russian and Russo-Jewish press. Among the journals to which he contributed was the prestigious German social democratic organ *Die Neue Zeit*. In 1912, although still unable to write fluently in Yiddish, Medem became a leading member of the editorial boards of the Bundist periodicals *Lebnsfragn* and *Di tsayt*. He returned to Russia in order to facilitate the editing of the latter of these two publications but was promptly arrested by the Russian authorities. Medem spent twenty-five months in Russian prisons and was released only when the institution in which he was being incarcerated was captured by the German army in 1915. Medem was made editor of yet another Bundist publication, also entitled *Lebnsfragn*, and began for the first time to write in Yiddish as well as in Russian. During this era, Medem was particularly interested in the education of children. He was actively involved in efforts to create and promote a network of Jewish secular schools and children's homes.

Many of Medem's comrades in the Bund initially displayed considerable sympathy for the Bolshevik revolution. Medem, who did not share this sympathy,

felt politically isolated, and decided to emigrate to the United States. He left
Europe at the end of 1920 and wrote primarily for the Yiddish socialist press in
New York, including the *Forverts*, *Tsukunft*, *Naye velt*, and *Der fraynd*, during
the final years of his life. He died in New York on 9 January 1923.

BIBLIOGRAPHY:

A. *Zikhroynes un artikln* (Warsaw: Farlag "yidish," 1917); *Fun mayn notits bukh* (Warsaw: Farlag "yidish," 1920); *Fun mayn lebn*, 2 vols. (New York: Vladimir medem
komite, 1923) (English trans. *The Life and Soul of a Legendary Jewish Socialist*, ed.
Samuel A. Portnoy [New York, Ktav, 1979]; *Vladimir medem. tsum tsvantsikstn yortsayt*
(New York: Der amerikaner reprezentants fun algemeynem yidishn arbeter-bund in poyln,
1943).

B. Zalman Reyzen, *Leksikon fun der yidisher literatur*, vol. 2 (Vilna: Farlag fun b.
kletskin, 1930), cols. 441–50; Koppel S. Pinson, "Arkady Kremer, Vladimir Medem,
and the Ideology of the Jewish 'Bund.' " *Jewish Social Studies*, 7 (1945), pp. 233–64.

JACK JACOBS

MEDVEDEV, ROY A. (b. 1925). Roy Medvedev was born 14 November 1925
in Tbilisi, the capital of Soviet Georgia. An ethnic Russian, he studied philosophy
and education at Leningrad University, where he received the candidate of science
degree in vocational training. His interest in Soviet history and political philosophy was apparently stimulated by Nikita Khrushchev's† revelations at the Twentieth Communist Party Congress in 1956. Shortly after finishing his doctoral
dissertation, in 1959, Medvedev published two books in the field of education.
In 1962 he began writing *Let History Judge*, his monumental indictment of
Stalinism† as historical aberration. Medvedev's efforts to have the manuscript
published through official Soviet channels resulted in his expulsion from the
Communist Party in 1969. Two years later, on the eve of publication of *Let
History Judge* and *A Question of Madness* (coauthored with his twin brother
Zhores, a biochemist now living in London), Medvedev resigned his position
with the Institute of Professional Education at the Academy of Pedagogical
Sciences. Since that time he has remained unemployed, devoting his energies
to the Soviet dissident movement. His books and articles are frequently published
in the West.

Medvedev's works all reflect his profound concern with the distorting effect
of Stalinism on the development of socialism in the Soviet Union. In *Let History
Judge* (1973) he explores the interface between objective and subjective factors
in history. Although Medvedev, as a Marxist,† adopts a determinist historical
approach, he concedes the importance of individuals and cultural values in
shaping the development of socialism. Stalinism was an accident resulting from
the low level of culture among the masses, which made them subject to manipulation, combined with the personality of a cunning, power-seeking dictator.
This developed into a form of religious psychology that Medvedev refers to as
"pseudosocialism." Lenin† and the Bolsheviks erred in attempting to achieve
goals for which the requisite conditions did not exist, but Leninism is for Medvedev a profoundly democratic phenomenon. Stalinism is a prime example of

how subjective factors may temporarily sidetrack, but cannot completely obviate, basic historical patterns.

In his second major work (*On Socialist Democracy*, 1975) Medvedev modifies the standard Marxist materialist perspective to underscore the fundamental importance of democratic procedures. Socialism is necessary but not sufficient for full democracy. Medvedev contends that socialist societies can benefit from the experience of preceding political cultures, just as socialist economies use and improve on the productive forces developed in preceding economies. The political achievements of bourgeois democracy—freedoms of speech, press, and assembly, protection of minority rights, and absolute equality before the law— are valuable in themselves; socialism makes possible the broadest application of these values. Democratization for Medvedev is the only means by which the problems facing Soviet society can be solved. Ideological development generates inevitable trends toward political pluralism that should find legitimate expression in the form of competitive political parties and organizations. Yet the weight of dogmatic Marxism and bureaucratic inertia in the Soviet Union impedes the fullest possible realization of political and scientific development. The privileged, corrupt bureaucratic stratum governing the Soviet state has monopolized political power and in doing so has stifled intellectual, artistic, and economic progress. Medvedev contends that the future of the Soviet state rests with the intelligentsia. They are currently supplanting the peasantry and the proletariat and constitute an important segment of a new ''classless'' society characterized by high levels of education and greater spiritual development. Under their guidance, socialism can surmount the weakest aspect of Marxism—ethics—to evolve a moral code based on reason, justice, and universal notions of good and evil.
BIBLIOGRAPHY:

A. *Let History Judge: The Origins and Consequences of Stalinism* (New York: Vintage, 1973); *On Socialist Democracy* (New York: Norton, 1975); *The October Revolution* (New York: Columbia University Press, 1979); *Leninism and Western Socialism* (London: Verso, 1981).

CHARLES E. ZIEGLER

MEINHOF, ULRIKE MARIE (1934–1976). Ulrike Marie Meinhof was born on 7 October 1938 in Oldenburg, West Germany, and was internationally known as an antifascist activist, political journalist, and author. In 1936 Meinhof's parents moved to Jena, presently in East Germany. Her father died in 1939, and her mother in 1948. Her foster mother, Renate Riemeck, was a founder of the German Peace Union (DFU) and one of the first women in West Germany to be a professor (of history). Meinhof studied philosophy, pedagogy, sociology, and German philosophy in Marburg, Munster, and Hamburg. She was an active member in the movement against the rearmament of the Federal Republic and in the German ban-the-bomb movement that organized the first mass demonstration after the war. With J. Seifert, Meinhof was editor of the student paper *Das Argument*. From 1959 to 1968 she was a regular contributor to the radical journal *Konkret*, also serving as foreign editor, editor, and editor-in-chief (1962–64). Meinhof married Klaus Rainer Rohl, the radical journalist, political activist, and founder of *Konkret*, in 1961. In 1962 they had twin girls. During her pregnancy Meinhof suffered severe headaches and was hospitalized for tests of a suspected brain tumor that turned out to be only a harmless swollen blood vessel. Many years later critics attempted to relate Meinhof's political activism to the imagined brain tumor. In 1968 Meinhof divorced her husband and moved from Hamburg to Berlin where she worked as a free-lance journalist and was appointed lecturer at the Free University. In Berlin she assumed active roles in the student movement, the movement against the war in Vietnam, the actions against the influential right-wing publisher Springer, the German anti-authoritarian movement, and others. Despite her relentless criticism Meinhof nevertheless continued to support the German Social Democratic Party (SPD). But after the debacle of the European student movement she was drawn first toward collective extraparliamentary activism and eventually toward urban guerrilla warfare. On 14 May 1970, Meinhof was present at the escape of Andreas Baader, who had been imprisoned for having participated in political arson. Meinhof's role in the escape was marginal, and she was unarmed. Nevertheless, henceforth Meinhof was forced to live underground, and the media began to refer to Baader, Meinhof, et al., as the Baader-Meinhof Gang. They fled to East Berlin, from there to Jordan, and eventually back to the Federal Republic. The group now called itself Rote Armee Fraktion (RAF), and Baader and Meinhof were its chief spokespeople. On 15 June 1972 Meinhof was arrested. The rest of her short life was spent in prison, mostly in solitary confinement, first in Koln-Ossendorf and later the newly opened Stuttgart-Stammheim prison. The sentence for her involvement in the freeing of Baader was eight years. She died on 6 May 1976 in Stammheim, near Stuttgart, one of Europe's most sophisticated high security prison systems for political criminals. Meinhof's death is officially referred to as a suicide, but many people, in and outside the Federal Republic, are convinced that her death should be attributed to force rather than suicide. An international commission uncovered evidence that would support the forced death theory, but German officials continue to deny any wrongdoing.

Until her life in the underground Meinhof's writings were explicitly humanitarian. Her political and moral journalism was aimed at a Germany that had failed to come to grips with its own history. As an accomplished political analyst she raised and investigated political issues that continue to be critical and controversial even today. Her arguments and actions against Germany's rearmament, the nuclear modernization of its armed forces, and the Emergency Powers Act are intellectual signposts for contemporary German protest groups and peace activists. Meinhof was one of the first to warn both of the real dangers to democracy that will follow German nuclear armament and the postwar evolution in West Germany of an unfolding police state. It is for these reasons that the poet Erich Fried has referred to Ulrike Meinhof as the most important woman in German politics since Rosa Luxemburg.† As a journalist committed to socialism Meinhof perceived herself as a voice for Germany's underrepresented masses.

BIBLIOGRAPHY:

A. *Bambule—Sorge für wen?* (Berlin: Wagenbach, 1971); *Die Würde des Menschen ist unantastbar. Aufsätze und Polemiken* (Berlin: Wagenbach, 1980).

B. Peter Brückner, *Ulrike Marie Meinhof und die deutschen Verhältnisse* (Berlin: Wagenbach, 1976); David Kramer, "Ulrike Meinhof: An Emancipated Terrorist?" in *European Women on the Left*, Jane Slaughter & Robert Kern (eds.) (Westport, Conn.: Greenwood Press, 1981).

TINEKE RITMEESTER

MERLEAU-PONTY, MAURICE (1908–1961). Merleau-Ponty was born on 14 March 1908 in Rochefort-sur-Mer, France, and died 3 May 1961 in Paris. He held the chair of psychology and pedagogy at the Sorbonne from 1949 to 1952, when he was appointed to the chair of philosophy at the Collège de France previously held by H. Bergson. Trained in philosophy, he studied Hegel, through A. Kojève's* and J. Hyppolite's* lectures at the Ecole Practique des Hautes Etudes from 1933 to 1939. His phenomenological thought, often termed the "philosophy of ambiguity," was grounded in the works of Husserl, whose manuscripts he studied in Louvain, Heidegger, Hegel, the German gestalt psychologists, and Marx†. In 1945 Merleau-Ponty, Jean-Paul Sartre,* Simone de Beauvior,* and R. Aron (who quickly left), founded *Les Temps modernes*, an independent, critical, left, noncommunist review. During the first eight years of its existence Merleau-Ponty was political editor. Albert Camus, de Beauvoir, and Sartre were regular contributors. Merleau-Ponty was mobilized as a second lieutenant in the French army in 1939. In 1957 he was made a *chevalier* in the Legion of Honor. He returned his rosette during the Algerian War. He occupies a central place in the phenomenological movement alongside Husserl, Scheler, Heidegger, and Sartre. His political and critical essays on the Russian Revolution, Marxism, dialectics, history, linguistics, structuralism, art, literature, and religion establish him as a foremost political and social theorist of the twentieth century.

Merleau-Ponty's principal contributions to Marxist theory are contained in *The Phenomenology of Perception*, *Humanism and Terror*, the essays on politics in *Sense and Non-Sense*, including "Concerning Marxism," (1946), "Marxism and Philosophy" (1946), and "The War Has Taken Place" (1945), and another set of political essays published in *Signs*: "Marxism and Superstition" (1949), "The U.S.S.R. and the Camps" (1950), "The Yalta Papers" (1955), "The Future of the Revolution" (1955), and "On De-Stalinization" (1956). *Adventures of the Dialectic* contains the fullest statement of his critical phenomenological-Marxist position, which he termed noncommunist left. Merleau-Ponty's work must be considered on three levels simultaneously. The first consists of a presentation of Merleau-Ponty's Marx and Marxism. The second involves a critique of Marxism as practiced in the work of liberal, Marxist and existentialist theorists (especially Arthur Koestler, Lenin,† George Lukács,* Trotsky,† and Sartre). The third involves a positioning of critical Husserlian-Hegelian phenomenology within Marxist thought, and within the historical moment between, during, and after the two world wars that swept Europe and the world in the first half of the twentieth century.

Striving for a Marxism with no illusions, and without guarantees, Merleau-Ponty understood the Marx of *Das Kapital* to offer "a concrete phenomenology of mind" (*Sense and Non-Sense* p. 133) that extended the Hegelian phenomenology of history into the capitalist period of societal development. The human subject for Marx, as for Merleau-Ponty, is, by means of a continual dialectic, located in an intersubjective world. That world is constituted through the dialectics of praxis, in which man is defined as a relation to instruments, objects, and transformations that are performed on the material world. This relation is both objective and subjective. Matter enters into human life as the bond that attaches man to the world, and it is, at the same time, his way to freedom (*ibid.*, p. 130). All of the ideological formations of a given society are produced by a particular type of economic praxis that interweaves economy and ideology into the totality of lived intentional history. A society is embedded in its methods of production, and its science, its art, its religion, and its philosophical concepts are all extensions of this economic mode of production. The spirit of a society is transmitted and perceived through the cultural objects that it presents itself with. Those objects are constituted phenomenologically, through the intertwining of the subject with the world of experience. These objects suggest a way of being and thinking unique to men, thereby stitching ideology, economy, and cultural-perceptual practices into the very fabrics of history. Marx saw this, and he should be credited "with the phenomenology of the cultural world which Hegel outlined" (*ibid.*, p. 131).

The bourgeois ideologies that contaminate all of capitalist society prop up a world that is lived by men who seek their realization through alienation, the fetishism of goods, and the logic of experience that capitalism affords them. Eschewing a strict economic determinism that can be found in certain of Marx's texts, Merleau-Ponty turns Marxism into a militant, reflective philosophy of intersubjectivity. The point of departure for all of his analysis is the dialectically constituted situation that the human subject finds himself in as he is thrown into a natural and historical world that lives through him. Accordingly, Merleau-Ponty was highly critical of structural and positivistic Marxisms that deny human interiority, treat consciousness as externally determined, and regard the human subject as a by-product of objective relations within a material, economically predetermined world (*ibid.*, p. 77). A priori scientism confuses the momentary for the eternal. A Marxist political economy can speak of laws only within qualitatively distinct structures of experience that are understood in terms of history. The Marxist historian can never get outside the history he writes, for that history produces him. "The fetishism of science has always made its appearance when the revolutionary conscience was faltering'' (*ibid.*, p. 126). The desired, ''metaphysical'' thrust of Marxism points in the direction of man collectively rupturing the structures of law, economy, and society that imperil his freedom, and ''acceding through praxis to the 'reign of liberty' '' (*ibid.*, p. 128).

This reign of liberty and freedom is addressed in *Humanism and Terror* and in the political essays collected in *Sense and Non-Sense* and *Signs*. Arguing against a scientific Marxism, Merleau-Ponty develops an interpretive, dialectical, phenomenological, and historical Marxism that is equally critical and skeptical of Soviet socialism and Western democracy. Accepting the Marxist critique of capitalism as valid, he observes that anti-Sovietism ''today resembles the brutality, hybris, vertigo, and anguish that already found expression in fascism'' (*Humanism and Terror*, p. xvi). Although the Soviet revolution had come to a halt, it was clear that it maintained a dictatorial apparatus, a network of labor camps, and a reign of terror that abandoned the humanistic promise of Marxism. The dilemma that Merleau-Ponty expresses in *Humanism and Terror* is reflected in his observation, ''It is impossible to be an anti-Communist and it is not possible to be a Communist'' (*ibid.*, p. xvi). Terror was rampant in the Soviet Union. As it was in the West. The forces of communism, fascism, and democracy seemed all to be directed to the production of a human situation in which violence and terror constituted man's fate. *Humanism and Terror* is, on one level, a critique of Arthur Koestler's *Darkness at Noon*, which was a liberal, anti-Communist attack on Soviet socialism and the purges and trials that occurred under Stalin. The theory and practice of terror and violence under communism was contrasted by Koestler to the humanism, the liberty, and the dignity that existed under Western democracy. Merleau-Ponty exposes this belief as a liberal myth, arguing that ''a regime which is nominally liberal can be oppressive in reality'' (*ibid.*, p. xv). He further observes that in a period of historical collapse and radical historical transformation, when the traditional ground of a nation or society crumbles and ''where, for better or worse, man himself must reconstruct human relations, then the liberty of each man is a mortal threat to the others and violence reappears'' (*ibid.*, p. xvii). Because liberalism excludes the revolutionary hypothesis of Marxism, the liberal mentality cannot maintain a distinction between violence and morality, terror and freedom, dignity, truth, distortion, ideology, and repression. The eternal standards of liberal justice that Koestler applied to the Soviet case were, for Merleau-Ponty, outside history and rooted in empty abstractions.

Humanism and Terror directly confronts the confusions of history, asking what place the Marxist and existentialist philosopher has in that history. Is he or she to stand to one side and watch history play out its hand, above the violence and terror that is produced? Will history unfold under its own direction, producing the reign of freedom spontaneously? Or must an active stand be taken? Is there a need for the Communist Party, and must, or can, the Party and its intellectuals lead the proletariat in its revolution? *Humanism and Terror* ends with a wait-and-see attitude, positioning the existentialist philosopher alongside history, abhorring and embracing at the same time the violence, the disorder, and the fragility of love, freedom, and dignity that are human possibilities, adrift, at the moment, in a world that has not yet found its course.

Merleau-Ponty's insight was to understand, as did many others, that the class revolution that had started in the nineteenth century and continued into the twentieth century in Russia and Europe, was brought to a standstill while World War II, as a global battle for economic and ideological control over the world's scarce resources, was fought. That battle became an ideological-humanistic conflict when the West entered the arena, crushing humanity as they liberated it. The question he asks, most thoroughly addressed in *Adventures of the Dialectic*, is "Now that the war is over, will the class struggle reappear?" And, if so, how will it be structured and experienced? It is at this point that he offers a critical reading of the works of Lukács, Lenin, Trotsky, and Sartre, each of whom offered a theory of and an agenda for the proletariat and the revolution of the working class. *Adventures of the Dialectic* positions these theorists, dialectically, within the dialectical moment that is captured in Marx and Hegel. In each case he observes a swerving away from the original Marxist formulation of the dialectic in history. These adventures, then, reveal a group of theorists who, in one way or another, attempted to reinsert the dialectic into human history, given the massive failure of the Soviet experiment under Stalin. (This conclusion holds less for Lukács than for any of the other theorists considered by Merleau-Ponty).

Having observed earlier that the breakdown of capitalism may lead "the world to chaos, instead of to the revolution if men do not understand the situation and do not want to intervene" (*Sense and Non-Sense*, p. 81), he offers the beginnings of a dialectical philosophy of history that begins from Max Weber's conception of the crisis of understanding that impales the human disciplines in the twentieth century. Merleau-Ponty offers a lived dialectic that foresees human freedom as a contingent possibility that cannot be predicted, either by ideology or by existentialist theorizing. It is a dialectic that must return to Marx and Hegel and work out anew the Husserlian and Heideggerian phenomenology of consciousness and being that secures and accompanies man's presence in the twentieth century. It is from this position that Merleau-Ponty offers an interpretation of the positions Lenin, Sartre, Lukács, and Trotsky suggest the proletariat and the Party can play in human history. Lenin and Sartre's views require that the Party lead the proletariat to the revolution. This position, which is elitist, sees the worker overcoming alienation through identification with the party. Merleau-Ponty severely criticizes Sartre's dualistic conception of the Party and the proletariat, suggesting also that Sartre's conception of the dialectic is insufficient because of its inability to grasp man's intersubjective presence in history. (These criticisms, published in 1955, apply to Sartre's position before the *Critique of Dialectical Reason*. They anticipate, however, many of the criticisms that were later brought to bear on that work.) Lukács's position of dual mediation, wherein the Party first mediates between the proletariat and history, to be replaced by the proletariat, ignores the fact that the Party, as with Trotsky, silenced Lukács. This leaves the Party and its intellectuals and officials to become the final arbiters of history, making history dependent on the decisions of others. Trotsky's position, which Merleau-Ponty admires, places the Party to the side of the spontaneous actions of the proletariat. This view is caught in the problem of a Stalin, who would not step aside and permit the proletariat to have their own revolution.

Each of these views have produced the same problematic, for the Party ends up speaking for all history, and the society envisioned by Marx has yet to be produced. Merleau-Ponty concludes with the observation that "the failure of Marxism would be the failure of philosophy of history," and all "societies which tolerate the existence of a proletariat are unjustifiable" (*Adventures of the Dialectic*, p. 232). The Marxist dialectic remains a viable possibility, a dream, a hope that men will be inspired to "bear their freedom, not to exchange it at a loss; for it is not only their own thing, their secret, their pleasure, their salvation— it involves everyone else" (*ibid.*, p. 233). Thus Merleau-Ponty comes full circle in his own dialectic. Marxist, dialectical, existential, and phenomenological, every bit of his work radiates with the calling for a philosophy that appeals to the realization of man's freedom in a contingent, problematic world where humanism and terror, poverty and hunger, love and freedom, dignity and justice are human possibilities. The Marxist philosopher must engage that world, interrogate it, and add his or her voice to the call of the dream. This Merleau-Ponty did. His work offers a challenge to the next generation of theorists, who must, as he did, examine their own place in the history that they live.

BIBLIOGRAPHY:

A. *Phenomenology of Perception* (Evanston, Ill.: Northwestern University Press, 1962); *Sense and Non-Sense* (Evanston, Ill.: Northwestern University Press, 1964); *Signs* (Evanston, Ill.: Northwestern University Press, 1964); *Humanism and Terror* (Boston: Beacon Press, 1969); *Adventures of the Dialectic* (Evanston, Ill.: Northwestern University Press, 1973).

B. John F. Bannan, *The Philosophy of Merleau-Ponty* (New York: Harcourt Brace & World, 1967); Albert Rabil, *Merleau-Ponty, Existentialist of the Social World* (New York: Columbia University Press, 1967); Robert A. Gorman, *Neo-Marxism: The Meanings of Modern Radicalism* (Westport, Conn.: Greenwood Press, 1982), pp. 240–46.

NORMAN K. DENZIN

MICHNIK, ADAM (b. 1945). Born in Poland in 1945, Adam Michnik is the son of Osias Szechter, a prewar Polish Communist, and Helena Michnik, an historian whose surname he uses. Michnik studied history at the universities of Warsaw and Poznan. He became a student, friend, and protégé of Jacek Kuron* (who at one time led Michnik's Boy Scout troop), helped organize the Polish Committee for the Defense of Workers (KOR), and was arrested during student protests in 1968 and again in 1977. After the imposition of marshal law on 12 December 1981 by General Wojciech Jaruzelski, Michnik, Kuron, and several other KOR and Solidarity activists were jailed, charged with advocating antistate violence.

Michnik, whose letters were smuggled out of jail into the underground Polish press, accused the Polish Communist regime of being elitist, felt that the Solidarity movement is an authentic voice of worker discontent and self-government, and viewed Jaruzelski as the leader of an antiworker counterrevolution organized in the name of entrenched bureaucratic interests. Influenced by Kuron, Michnik's strategy for Poland's democratization involves building self-governing socialist institutions outside of the Party's official structures. In so doing, says Michnik, fateful confrontations with both Poland's military leaders and the Soviet Union can be avoided while Poland's workers become slowly acclimated to democratic self-government. Michnik has criticized Poland's Catholic Church for its timidity in supporting imprisoned Solidarity activists. His own courage is unquestioned. He, along with the other imprisoned KOR dissidents Kuron, Henryk Wujec, and Zbigniew Romaszewski, consistently refused government offers of safe conduct abroad in order to press their antigovernment case in Poland. The trial of these four, scheduled to begin 12 July 1984, was—against the wishes of Michnik— postponed indefinitely. In early August 1984 Michnik and the others were released from prison in the Jaruzelski regime's general pardon of political prisoners. However by February 1985 Michnik was again arrested, this time charged with advocating public unrest. Summarily tried, convicted, and sentenced to two and a half year's imprisonment, Michnik's ultimate fate remains uncertain.

ROBERT A. GORMAN

MILIBAND, RALPH (b. 1924). Born in 1924, Ralph Miliband is a British citizen. He has been coeditor of *The Socialist Register* since 1964. Having been senior lecturer in political science at the London School of Economics from 1949 to 1972 and professor of politics at Leeds University from 1972 to 1978, he now teaches at Brandeis University in the United States.

Miliband advances an instrumentalist analysis of the capitalist state. His focus is on why the state serves as a means for realizing the interests of the "ruling class." The ruling class are those who own and control the means of material and "mental" production and are thereby able to dominate state power as well. Whereas the simple instrumentalist position assumes that class power is automatically translated into state power, Miliband's more sophisticated approach assumes that the relation between class power and state power is problematic. Miliband's theory of the ruling class relies upon three modes of explanation, all of which he argues are needed to comprise an adequate answer to why the state should be the "instrument" of the capitalist "ruling class." The first focuses on the personnel of the executive, administrative, judicial, repressive (military and police), and legislative branches of the state. The assumption is that social origins, education, family, and friendship patterns produce common values that, despite differences, commit elite members to supporting capitalist institutions. The second way of showing that the capitalist class can use the power of the state for their interests is that capitalist economic power, gained through the ownership and control of resources, enables capital to exert disproportionate influence in shaping state policies. The third way in which the capitalist class dominates the state consists of various "structural constraints" that the peculiar rationality of capitalism imposes on all governments. Miliband believes "structural constraints" help explain why governments often fail to fulfill their ideological goals, although he warns that structuralists can too easily deny the role of human agency.

The way in which Miliband relates these three modes of capitalist control of the state constitutes his Marxist† ruling class theory. The major exposition of his arguments is contained in *The State in Capitalist Society* (1969). His major problem is to explain how capitalists are not only the dominant class but how they exercise decisive control over state policy making. After showing that members of the capitalist class participate in the state apparatus, Miliband demonstrates that those who have held the state's command posts share common social origins, education, and class situations and are bound by close personal ties of influence, status, and position. The result is that capitalist regimes are governed by men who believe in capitalism as superior to any alternative, a situation that predisposes them to favor capitalist interests positively over others and to prevent oppositional forces from gaining power at home or in foreign countries. Even when governments of the left come into office, various structural constraints imposed by the "business community" compel officers to moderate their ambitions. Similarly, the conservatism of the administration, military and police, and judicial components of the state system results from the personnel, who are the elite's conscious or unconscious allies and from the self-reinforcing logic of state bureaucracy. The hold that the ruling class has over the state through internal mechanisms like elite consensus and structural constraints of bureaucratic norms and business practices are reinforced further by capitalism's "massive superiority *outside* the state system . . . in terms of the immensely stronger pressure which, as compared with labour and any other interest, it is able to exercise in the pursuit of its purposes" (*The State in Capitalist Society* p. 146). Business's control of the economy gives it vast importance and power, which governments cannot realistically resist. Business confidence results in economic growth, which benefits governments and so is unlikely to be interfered with. Business is also better placed to act as a pressure group with government agencies and departments. In the legislative bodies, again, business is aligned with conservative parties and benefits from legislative procedures that enable it to block potentially threatening changes.

The ruling class's domination of the state, Miliband contends, relies also upon the acquiescence of the subordinate classes. Although repression can be used to maintain order, the more important mechanism is the legitimation of the dominant class's prerogatives. The ideological predominance of the ruling classes is the consequence of continuous and subtle efforts that in part involve state intervention. Conservative parties carry the message of legitimation on behalf of the capitalist elite, whereas parties of the left suffer the disadvantage of being forced to broaden their appeal in parliamentary democracies. Religion, nationalism, and the business culture further reinforce the legitimacy of the ruling class.

Finally, the institutions of education and the mass media promote the values of the capitalist class and help limit the voice of opposition. In spite of the impressive contribution of factors that enable the capitalist class to influence state policy, Miliband argues, the state does possess a high degree of autonomy in its operations. Even though "the state does act, in Marxist terms, *on behalf* of the ruling class, it does not for the most part act *at its behest*" (*Marxism and Politics*, p. 74). This *relative autonomy* of the state is important to Marxist theory, for it gives the state the capacity to protect and advance capitalism's objective interests in ways that might be unpopular to capitalists. This relative independence makes it possible for the state to pursue its central raison d'être, the protection of the economically and socially dominant class, by reforms that are fundamental to the perpetuation of capitalism. Although different forms of the state have various degrees of autonomy, in advanced capitalist societies the relationship between the dominant class and the state can best be characterized as a "*partnership between two different, separate forces*, locked to each other by many threads, yet each having its own separate sphere of concerns" ("State Power and Class Interests," p. 65).

BIBLIOGRAPHY:

A. "Marx and the State" *Socialist Register 1965*, ed. Ralph Miliband and John Saville (London: Merlin Press, 1965); *The State in Capitalist Society* (New York: Basic Books, 1969); *Marxism and Politics* (Oxford: Oxford University Press, 1977); "State Power and Class Interests," *New Left Review*, no. 138 (March–April 1983), pp. 57–68.

JOEL D. WOLFE

MILIĆ, VOJIN (b. 1922). The Yugoslav Vojin Milić was born in 1922 in Pivnica and fought during World War II as a partisan officer in the national liberation movement. He studied philosophy and sociology at the universities of Zagreb and Belgrade earning a B.A. in 1952 and a Ph.D. in 1958 with a thesis on "Methodological Problems in Sociological Research." Since 1962 he has been professor of sociology at the University of Belgrade. Milić is concerned primarily with methodology and sociology of knowledge and is well known for his learned introductions to Serbo-Croatian translations of the works of Durkheim, Weber, Sorokin, Georges Gurvitch,* Mannheim, and others. He served on the boards of *Praxis** and the Korčula Summer School for a time and was coeditor (with Michael Murray) of a special 1980 issue on "The Sociology of Science in East and West" in *Current Sociology*, the official journal of the International Sociological Association. Milić is author of the award-winning textbook on methodology in the social sciences, *Sociological Method* (1965, 1978), as well as numerous articles in *Sociologija*, *Filozofija*, *Praxis*, and other journals and symposia.

His theoretical contributions to Marxism†—particularly to the *Praxis* school of Marxist humanist thought—lie in philosophy of science, sociology of knowledge, and methodology. Influenced by Max Weber, the analytical school, and contemporary philosophy of science, Milić has endeavored to develop sociology in postwar Yugoslavia as a genuine scientific enterprise that would incorporate the theoretical and methodological insights of twentieth-century sociology. He has sought to free Marxist sociology from its reduction by orthodox Marxists to simply a critique of ideology and the equally pernicious ignorance of the contributions of "bourgeois" sociological research. From the beginning, Milić has attempted to restore to sociological research the methodological tools of genuine scientific inquiry. Hence his emphasis on methodology, which culminated in *Sociological Method*, one of the most popular textbooks in Yugoslavia on social science methodology.

Milić's quest for the restoration of sociology as a science has led him to one of the most systematic and comprehensive assessments of the history of sociological thought and of the philosophy and sociology of science. He bases his quest for the knowledge of man and society on a major ethical postulate in the social sciences: the "humanistic imperative" of creating optimal social conditions for the all-round development of the human personality. This imperative rests, in turn, on Marx's and Engels's† dictum in the *Communist Manifesto* that the free development of each individual is the precondition for the free development of all. Clearly, then, Milić's conceptualization of sociology as a science is not value-free. Indeed, he considers the "humanistic imperative" as the criterion that lends true human significance and value to the social sciences. And he notes that science itself is not value-free. Thus, the quest for objectivity, impartiality, and verifiability of knowledge represent immanent values in scientific research. Yet he also cautions against the simplistic application of concepts in the natural sciences to the study of man and social phenomena. Drawing on Marx's concept of alienation and the activist conceptualization of human essence as praxis—man's creative and self-creative activity—Milić contends that a genuine science of social phenomena must take this human activity and self-determination into account. Understandably, he is critical of mechanical, functionalist, organicist, and biological interpretations of social determinism as overlooking the creative energies of both the individual and society. He concludes that it is not social determinism but individual and group creativity that need to be explained.

Milić has contributed not only to the *Praxis* understanding of the concept of alienation as the theoretical unity of Marx's sociological-philosophical analysis but also to the reconceptualization of the causes and nature of conflict in society. He points out that conflict is an everyday occurrence and an immanent fact in all societies. Unlike the orthodox Marxist conception of all conflict as class conflict, he distinguishes among five different sources of conflict based on (1) social or professional layers, classes, or ethnic groups; (2) functional differentiation and specialization; (3) generational levels; (4) differences in cultural levels; and (5) conflicts in other societies. In contrast to the positivist-organicist conception of conflict as a symptom of social disease, Milić posits the view of conflicts as integral processes in all social systems. He considers the Stalinist† denial and suppression of conflicts as a typical example of ideology understood as "false consciousness." For him, Stalinist social systems—with their monopoly of power and centralized administrative, economic, and cultural life—are incapable of solving conflicts in a rational, humane way. In such societies, conflicts are merely camouflaged and suppressed. Stalinism, in turn, is but a special case of historical despotism characterized by a permanent, nonprogressive instability due to the suppression of conflicts and the absence of institutional forms for their resolution. Milić concludes that Stalinism as a socio-political form of organization is antithetical to individual freedom, which is the precondition for a free society.

Like other *Praxis* theorists, Milić is fascinated by the Frankfurt School's attempts to develop a critical theory. While welcoming the criticism of ideology as one of the vital tasks of critical theory, Milić has voiced concern with Herbert Marcuse* and Theodore Adorno's* equation of critical theory with utopia, since a truly revolutionary theory must provide historically realistic answers and not be displaced by an ahistorical utopia. Another major critique of the Frankfurt School is that it has failed to investigate contemporary forms of social structure and social organization. In his 1980 *Sociologija* article, Milić proposes the integration of the sociology of knowledge with the sociology of science via a new paradigm based on complexity in the sociological investigation of science. This complex sociological investigation of science would focus on: (1) the application of the notion of socio-economic formation; (2) an epochal approach to study relationships between societies and their scientific organizations; (3) the proximity of science to the social history of science; (4) the active interrelation with philosophy, and in particular with scientific methodology; (5) the conception of the technological, socio-integrative, and intellectual functions of ideas and knowledge; (6) the systematic study of the internal organization of science and its economic, political, and legal relationships with other social institutions; and (7) the systematic investigation into the social distribution of scientific knowledge.

Although Milić's understanding of the fact–value dichotomy in particular and the history of sociological thought and methodologies in general may be open to challenge, and although his efforts to integrate Marxism with modern sociology and science may satisfy neither Marxists nor empirical social scientists, his vision of a vital dialogue between Marxist and non-Marxist conceptualizations of sociology and social sciences remains a signal contribution to a more open, nondogmatic, and creative Marxism.

BIBLIOGRAPHY:

A. "Ideja otudjenja i savremena sociologija," in *Humanizam i socijalizam*, ed. Branko Bošnjak and Rudi Supek, vol. 2 (Zagreb: Naprijed, 1963), pp. 89–138; "Method of Critical Theory." *Praxis* (I), 7, nos. 3–4 (1971), pp. 625–56; "Beitrag zur Theorie des Gesellschaftskonfliktes," in *Jugoslawien denkt anders*, ed. Rudi Supek and Branko Bošnjak (Vienna: Europa, 1971), pp. 133–50; *Sociološki metod*, 2nd enl. ed. (Belgrade: Nolit, 1978); "Sociologija saznanja i sociologija nauke," *Sociologija*, 22, nos. 3–4 (1980), pp. 181–230; "The Science of Science and the Sociology of Science in European Socialist Countries," *Current Sociology*, 28, no. 3 (1980), pp. 185–269.

B. Gerson S. Sher, *Praxis: Marxist Criticism and Dissent in Socialist Yugoslavia*

(Bloomington: Indiana University Press, 1977); Oskar Gruenwald, *The Yugoslav Search for Man: Marxist Humanism in Contemporary Yugoslavia* (South Hadley, Mass.: Bergin & Garvey, 1983).

OSKAR GRUENWALD

MILLS, C. WRIGHT (1916–1962). C. Wright Mills remains a major intellectual influence among neo-Marxist and "critical" intellectuals. He had a profound effect on many in the American "new left" and student movements of the 1960s, and his various books and articles established him as a major figure within contemporary social science. He completed his B.A. at the University of Texas and in 1941 the Ph.D. from the University of Wisconsin, where he began a long and productive relationship with his mentor and coauthor, Hans Gerth. Mills held teaching positions at Maryland (1941), Chicago (1949), Brandeis (1953), Copenhagen (1956–57), and a continuing appointment at Columbia (1945–62). Although he died at the age of forty-five, Mills completed eleven books and over 200 articles. At the time of his passing he had been working on a number of manuscripts, including a planned five-volume study of comparative sociology.

Mills's writings range over a variety of topics, including the sociology of knowledge, the politics of culture, the nature and forms of power, and the viability and sources for political change. His writing and political activities were attempts to fashion a theory and practice appropriate for the contemporary scene. His work is best understood in his own words as a means to understand the conjunction of "private troubles and public issues," biography and history, the everyday milieux amid the fabric of public and private bureaucratic domains. To Mills, the role of intellectuals, particularly social scientists, was to develop a "sociological imagination" that would allow the ordinary citizen to understand the organization of the private, everyday existence within the context and essence of the public order. Mills described himself as a "plain Marxist,"† opposed to theoretical orthodoxy and its uncritical acceptance of materialism. He sought a theoretical and practical approach that preserved "the tension of humanism and determinism, of human freedom and historical necessity" (*The Marxists*, p. 99). He applied this perspective to his best-known work, *The Power Elite* (1956). Rejecting a ruling class model to explain the nature and distribution of power, and opposed to the Weberian conception of bureaucratic rationality, Mills explained power in terms of overlapping and interactive elites of military, economic, and political bureaucracies. The state was not simply an instrument in the hands of power located within the realm of production, rather the interplay of base and superstructure generated discrete but interconnected power regimes among the military establishment, corporate sector, and governmental bureaucracies. To Mills the management of such societies rested upon the "cultural apparatus" where the relationship between existence and consciousness is formed. Control over ideas and the perception of reality rested with institutions such as schools, churches, and media, which attempted to shape a social consensus compatible with the distribution of public power. The "politics of culture" was for Mills one of the central political battlegrounds in contemporary society, highlighting the critically important political role of intellectuals.

Mills objected to what he referred to as "the labor metaphysic of Victorian Marxists," who clung to the working class as *the* exclusive historical agency of social change. Rather he looked to the "young intelligentsia" to contest the assumptions and direction of contemporary society. He assumed this "new left" would challenge establishment and radical orthodoxies and forge a politics based on "participatory democracy." In its infancy he characterized the Cuban Revolution as an example of this new left politics (*Listen Yankee!*, 1960), but later he privately expressed reservations about the direction of Cuban socialism. Always Mills wrote in a clear and readable style devoid of unnecessary abstractions. His political and professional styles were characterized as confrontational, and, although he was lauded as a major thinker after his passing, Mills's work was largely downplayed or ignored by his contemporary social scientists. Today his influence on the American left remains significant.

BIBLIOGRAPHY:

A. *The New Men of Power: America's Labor Leaders* (New York: Kelley, 1948); *The Puerto Rican Journey: New York's Newest Migrants* (New York: Russell & Russell, 1950); *White Collar: The American Middle Class* (New York: Oxford University Press, 1951); with H. Kersh *Character and Social Structure: The Psychology of Social Institutions* (London: Routledge & Kegan Paul, 1953); *The Power Elite* (New York: Oxford University Press, 1956); *The Causes of World War III* (New York: Simon & Schuster, 1958); *The Sociological Imagination* (New York: Oxford University Press, 1959); *Listen Yankee! The Revolution in Cuba* (New York: McGraw Hill, 1960); *The Marxists* (New York: Dell, 1962).

B. Irving Louis Horowitz, ed., *Power, Politics, and People: The Collected Essays of C. Wright Mills* (New York: Oxford University Press, 1963); Joseph Scimecca, *The Sociological Theory of C. Wright Mills* (New York: Kennikat Press, 1977); Howard Press, *C. Wright Mills* (Boston: T. Wayne, 1978); and Richard Guarasci, *The Theory and Practice of American Marxism, 1957–1970* (Baltimore: University Press of America, 1980).

RICHARD GUARASCI

MITCHELL, JULIET (b. 1940). Born 4 October 1940 in America, Mitchell came to England in 1944 and was educated at King Alfred School, London. She received her B.A. with honors from St. Anne's College, Oxford. From 1962 to 1970 she lectured in English literature, first at Leeds and then at Reading University. She has lectured extensively to international audiences and is currently a practicing psychoanalyst. She has taught in the United States at Washington University in St. Louis and the University of Buffalo and was a visiting scholar at Yale University in 1983. She is a member of the London Women's Liberation Workshop and an editor of the journals *New Left Review*, *Social Praxis*, and *Dialectic: A Journal of Feminist Thought*.

The 1966 article "Women: The Longest Revolution" established Juliet Mitchell as a leading theorist of the women's liberation movement. In its more elaborated version, *Woman's Estate* (1971), Mitchell undertook an account of the historical specificity of the contemporary women's movement and proceeded to sketch a socialist feminist theory for the present period. She declared: "It is not 'our relationship' to socialism that should ever be the question—it is the use of scientific socialism as a method of analyzing the specific nature of our oppression and hence our revolutionary role" (*Women's Estate*, p. 92). Mitchell located feminist protest in the 1960s revolt of blacks, students, and youth, which were seen as expressions of the ideological contradictions of an advanced capitalist consumer society. She viewed middle-class radicalism as a response to the system's increasing requirements for its social reproduction through educational institutions, advertising and media industries, and family life. Therefore, she tried to theorize a new political conjuncture in which the role of oppressed groups, "that is groups which experience their oppression as much culturally as economically," has expanded (ibid., p. 35). In this context, women's oppression and the protest it engenders poses a challenge to socialist theory and praxis. Mitchell distinguished two leading approaches to these matters: radical feminist and socialist feminist. In an influential remark, she appealed for a synthesis of the two: "We should ask the feminist questions but try to come up with Marxist† answers" (ibid., p. 99).

Mitchell identified the ideology of the family as the source of the naturalization of women within an ideology of femininity. In *Woman's Estate* she submitted the family to a structuralist critique, concluding that women's emancipation requires a revolution in the four structures of production, reproduction, sexuality, and the socialization of children. She insisted that "the family does more than occupy woman: it produces her" (ibid., p. 151). She concluded this work with a plea for a science of psychoanalysis, as the key to ideology, especially the ideology of femininity, and to the analysis of family structure. At this point, Mitchell made a decisive departure in her own work, leading the "psychoanalytic turn" in recent feminist theory. *Psychoanalysis and Feminism* (1974) is a bold encounter with psychoanalytic theory, which, according to the author, is "not a recommendation *for* a patriarchal society, but an analysis *of* one" (p. xv). Mitchell proposed that an investigation of patriarchy, e.g., the Law of the Father, must proceed as a critique of ideology. Speaking approvingly of a tendency within the contemporary French feminist movement, Mitchell stated: "So where Marxist theory explains the historical and economic situation, psychoanalysis, in conjunction with the notions of ideology already gained by dialectical materialism, is the way into understanding ideology and sexuality" (ibid., p. xxii). Mitchell's reappropriation of psychoanalysis presents a challenge to any orthodox Marxist view that interprets the family and ideology as a superstructural reflection of the material base. Her critique is directed simultaneously at the American feminist community for its systematic denial of Freud's theory of the unconscious. She counterposed Freud's radical discovery to the American tendency to speak literally about the father's power. Rather, she insisted that the unconscious represents the congealed facts of an archaic past: Because the past is never simply past but part of the way we live in the world, Mitchell asserted the need for an analytic rather than a developmental approach to human sexuality and consciousness. In this approach, the Oedipal complex is foregrounded as the "moment" of the acquisition of human subjecthood, in and through sexual division (gender identity).

Psychoanalysis and Feminism represents a pioneering effort to explain the way in which boys and girls acquire their gender identity. Mitchell aimed to free feminist theory from all notions of natural or biological femininity and masculinity. She observed the seemingly universal necessity of patriarchy, but only to offer a cultural account of its workings. She deployed a structuralist analysis of the exchange of women within human kinship structures as a possible explanation for the dynamic through which unconscious patriarchal law is interpellated within human social structures. Mitchell concluded this book with a series of speculations on the manner in which patriarchal civilization may be redundant under an advanced capitalist mode of production. She held out the hope for a postpatriarchal civilization. In collaboration with Jacqueline Rose she has recently presented *Feminine Sexuality* (1982), an anthology of the influential writings on feminine sexuality by the French psychoanalyst Jacques Lacan and his followers. The volume refines the linguistic model of psychoanalytic criticism that Mitchell employed in *Psychoanalysis and Feminism*. It offers a further challenge to competing, ultimately biological notions, of the sources of female identity.

BIBLIOGRAPHY:

A. "Women: The Longest Revolution," *New Left Review*, 40 (November–December 1966); *Woman's Estate* (New York: Pantheon Books; Harmondsworth: Penguin Books, 1971); *Psychoanalysis and Feminism* (New York: Pantheon Books; London: Allen Lane, 1974); "Women and Equality," in *The Rights and Wrongs of Women*, ed. and intro. Juliet Mitchell and Ann Oakley (Harmondsworth: Penguin Books, 1976); *Feminine Sexuality: Jacques Lacan and the Ecole Freudienne*, ed. Juliet Mitchell and Jacqueline Rose, trans. Jacqueline Rose (New York and London: Norton; New York: Pantheon Books, 1982).

JOAN LANDES

MLYNÁŘ, ZDENĚK (b. 1930). The Czech Zdeněk Mlynář was born in 1930 in the city of Vysoké Myto. From 1950 to 1955 he received a scholarship from the Czech government to study at the Faculty of Law at Lomonosov University in Moscow. After successfully defending his doctoral thesis on Machiavelli's political theory, he worked until 1968 as a researcher at the Institute of Government and Law of the Czech Academy of Sciences. In 1963 Mlynář became a docent in the Legal Faculty at Charles University in Prague, where he lectured on the history of political theory and modern socialist ideology. In 1964 he was appointed secretary of the judicial commission of the Central Committee of the Czech Communist Party. From this position Mlynář was able to form an interdisciplinary group of Party scholars to examine controversial issues related to the democratization of the Czech political system. The scholarly monographs produced by this group helped systematize the ideology of reform communism, which became a contributing factor to, and the intellectual justification of, the advent of the Prague Spring.* Working closely with Alexander Dubček,† he coauthored the Program of Action of the Czech Communist Party, which outlined the Party's envisaged program of democratic reforms. In April 1968 Mlynář was chosen secretary of the Party's Central Committee. After the Soviet invasion Mlynář renounced all his Party positions in order to show his support for those opposing the Soviet-inspired process of political "normalization." As a result of being expelled from the Party and denied suitable professional employment in Czechoslovakia, he became an acting member of the Czech opposition, helping to establish the Charter 77 movement. By mid-1977 police harassment had forced him to leave Czechoslovakia. As an exile based in Austria, Mlynář has lectured at many Western universities. Since 1982 he has been associated with the Austrian Institute of International Politics, directing research projects on crises in Soviet-style regimes, with the help of other exiled scholars from Poland, Hungary, and Czechoslovakia.

During the 1960s Mlynář was a typical representative of reform communism. Inspired by Khrushchev's† de-Stalinization,† Mlynář merely carried this idea to a radical, and logical, conclusion. In his early work on the political difficulties of socialist regimes he tried to reconcile the leading role of the Communist Party, that is, the orthodox Communist belief in one-party politics, with an institutionally designed social and cultural pluralism. Within this framework, Mlynář's major goal was to describe and operationalize political mechanisms guaranteeing interest group representation in socialist states and the noncoerced formation of a popular social consensus. He argued that the passage of socialist societies from a Stalinist to a post-Stalinist era had generated forces of political pluralism that had to be dealt with in a cautious but progressive manner, carefully controlled from above, in order to avoid spontaneous social explosions ignited by historically brewing social tensions. The principal components of Mlynář's reform program included the establishment of a free but "responsible" press, guaranteed autonomy for unions and other social organs, and self-management for all state-owned enterprises through the direct participation of workers. The reform project also anticipated establishing a political system that would combine assemblies based on the equal political representation of voting citizens with assemblies consisting of professional delegates representing the specific interests of particular social groups. The envisaged reforms would resemble the decentralized institutions found in Yugoslavia. However, in contrast to Yugoslavia's propagation of an official Party and ideology, Mlynář did not rule out the idea of a multiparty system: the latter is not a necessary premise of the reform movement, but a possible outcome after a lengthy transition period.

Following the failure of the Prague Spring, Mlynář abandoned the notion that Soviet-type regimes can be democratically reformed from above, by socially enlightened "princes." In the face of Soviet and internal Party opposition, this project is no longer feasible. Mlynář's theoretical work now focuses on analyzing those social processes that generate crises in socialist regimes and on identifying social forces that are capable of mobilizing the masses to demand and achieve democratic reforms. His current research compares the crises experienced by the Communist regimes of Hungary, Poland, and Czechoslovakia in terms of common causes, Moscow's attempts to control and neutralize these crises occurring at the periphery of its empire (e.g. the "normalization" process), and the long-range implications of the crises for countries within the Soviet bloc.

In conclusion, one can see Mlynář's intellectual itinerary as a metamorphosis from believing in the ideology of Communist reformism to becoming a student of politics who combines elements of historical materialism with the concepts and methods of Western political science.

BIBLIOGRAPHY:

A. *Nightfrost in Prague* (New York: Kerz, 1980); *Le Froid vient de Moscou* (Paris: Gallimard, 1981); *Krisen und Krisenbewaltigung im Sowjetblock, 1953–1982* (Köln-Wien: Bund, 1983).

B. J. Pelikán, ed., *Budapest, Prague, Varsovie: Le Printemps de Prague quinze ans après* (Paris: La Découverte/Maspero, 1983).

LUBOMIR SOCHOR

MONDOLFO, RODOLFO (1877–1976). Rodolfo Mondolfo was born in Senegal on 20 August 1877, and died in Buenos Aires on 16 July 1976. Educated among excited supporters of Mazzini, socialists, and libertarians, he attended the University of Florence and joined the Italian Socialist Party (PSI), in part due to the example and influence of his brother Ugo Guido, two years older than he, who would be an important Socialist spokesman and codirector of the theoretical review of reformist socialism, *Critica sociale*. In 1907 he was appointed to substitute for Roberto Ardigo, the principal exponent in Italy of positivism, at the University of Padua. The same period marked the beginning of his theoretical-political commitment, the goal of which was the philosophical rebuilding of reformist socialism, expressed above all in his contributions to *Critica sociale*. Mondolfo never held significant party offices. Instead, he was decisively involved in opposing fascism, primarily through cultural and scholarly activities. These included a study of fascism written in 1925 and published only in 1928 in *Internationaler Fascismus*. In 1923 he defied fascist authorities, publishing the third edition of *Sulle orme di Marx*; but in 1926 these publications were forbidden and *Critica sociale* itself was suppressed. He turned more and more to studies of ancient philosophy and in this area made contributions of exceptional philological and historiographical importance. However, he continued to deal with political philosophy and socialism, as witnessed by the entries written for the *Enciclopedia italiana* between 1930 and 1937, commissioned by Giovanni Gentile. In 1928, with the advent of the racial laws, he was forced to go into exile in Argentina, where he taught at the universities of Córdoba and

Tucuman from 1940 to 1952 and played an important role in the diffusion of
and liaison with European culture until his death.

Mondolfo wanted to reconstruct and restore Marx's† thought—he himself
never proposed a "revision"—as a self-sufficient philosophy and ideological
instrument of the working class for its liberation in democratic socialism. The
philosophy of Marx, cleansed of the contradictory deformations of voluntarism
and subjectivism and above all of mechanistic and rigidly deterministic materialism, is a philosophy of praxis and real humanism. "Marx," Mondolfo writes,

> takes up again Vico's principle that truth is changed with facts; reality is in praxis.
> But just as reality is given in the totality of praxis, truth is not grasped in a
> fragmentary and partial vision of facts. The entire fact must form a part of the
> conception of fact; when its totality is shattered and a part converted into a datum,
> in other words made external to the development of human praxis, of which it is
> an intrinsic element, truth is lost. (*Umarismo di Marx*, p. 21)

Marxism is not materialism, but rather "critical-practical realism," founded on
the ideal of perennial self-transformation, on "prassi che *si* rovescia" (praxis
which overturns itself), according to the neo-idealistic translation rendered by
Gentile of "umwälzende Praxis" in *Theses on Feuerbach*. Praxis understood in
this way, based on an activistic reading of Marxist theory, is accompanied in a
rather strict way by a humanistic-anthropological interpretation of Marxian thought,
directly connected to the thought of Feuerbach. Reality is praxis, societies are
historical objectifications of praxis, man is a social being, and knowledge itself
is an activity connected to praxis. No objectivism or scientism is possible, as
Mondolfo confirms: "Engels† in the field of philosophy of nature and at times
in history, reveals in his expressions often a certain tendency to hypostasis of
ideas in the form of laws which overcome and dominate phenomena" (*Il materialismo storico in F. Engels*, p. 128). Objectivism and scientism have for
Mondolfo the consequence of dehumanizing reality, of reducing the dialectic to
a law of thinking that reproduces objective reality instead of "the form and
condition of the intelligibility of the real," in the end reducing the class struggle
to a simple mechanical fact that devalues human and subjective elements. The
perspective proposed by Mondolfo is different:

> Necessity has two aspects or moments: one is given by the pre-existing conditions
> (which, however, are nothing more than the product of past human activity), and
> the other is subjective, given by need, which pushes one to overcome actual
> conditions. Without the confluence of both moments, without the unity of the two
> aspects, there is no historical necessity. (Ibid., p. 131)

This perspective is also the source of the criticism of Leninism† and of the
Russian Revolution, which Mondolfo views as a voluntaristic misreading of
history. This is also the source of the criticism of Antonio Gramsci's* concept
of the Party as a "modern prince," of the party of the working class as a
revolutionary vanguard that introduces on the historical level an element of force
and of violence that, through the dictatorship of the proletariat, anticipates his-

tory. Instead, Mondolfo sees the realization of socialism as a gradual process that links together the necessity of historical development and the subjective realization of liberty in the form of a progressive self-awareness on the part of the working class.

BIBLIOGRAPHY:

A. *Il materialismo storico in Engels* (Florence: La Nuova Italia, 1912); *Studi sulla rivoluzione russa* (Naples: Morano, 1968); *Umanismo di Marx* (Turin: Einaudi, 1968); *Entre la historia y la politica* (Mexico: Puebla, 1973); *Polis lavoro tecnica* (Milan: Feltrinelli, 1982).

B. Luciano Veretti, *Rodolfo Mondolfo e la filosofia della prassi* (Naples: Morano, 1966); Diego F. Prò, *Rodolfo Mondolfo*, 2 vols. (Buenos Aires: Losada, 1967–68); Giacomo Marramao, *Marxismo e revisionismo in Italia* (Bari: De Donato, 1971); M. Pogatschnig, *Filosofia e marxismo nell' opera di Rodolfo Mondolfo* (Florence: La Nuova Italia, 1979).

VITTORIO DINI

MORIN, EDGAR (b. 1921). In his autobiographical work *Autocritique*, Edgar Morin described in detail his intellectual development: Born in 1921, he entered the Sorbonne in 1938, studying history, and there became involved in the political turmoil between the left and the right. He participated in an anti-fascist anarchist organization and expanded his studies into the fields of law and political science. In Toulouse during the Occupation, Morin joined the Resistance as well as the Communist Party to maintain the struggle against fascism and continued his clandestine propaganda work in Paris beginning in 1944. After the Liberation he remained in the Party, but friction emerged because of his support for innovative cultural initiatives. He simultaneously developed his prowess as a writer in several domains (two books on postwar Germany, 1946–47; a novel, 1948; militant journalism). However, during the cold war and the trials in the popular democracies, Morin found himself less and less aligned with the French Party's adherence to Stalinism,† and his "spiritual combat" between 1947 and 1950 resulted in his progressive isolation within the Party, until his expulsion in 1951 for having published an article in the Trotskyist *L'Observateur*. He nonetheless remained an active leftist militant throughout the 1950s and undertook anthropological research at the Centre National des Recherches Scientifiques (CNRS). In 1956, inspired by the nonsectarian Italian review *Ragionamenti*, Morin, Colette Audry, Roland Barthes,* and Jean Duvignaud* founded *Arguments*,* of which Morin remained managing editor until the review's dissolution in 1962. Over the next twenty years, first as director of research at the CNRS and then in various bio-anthropological positions in France and the United States, Morin undertook a vast project of "open anthropo-sociology, on the one hand, about the biophysical universe, on the other hand, about the imaginary and myths" (*Science avec conscience*, p. 8). This effort took form anthropologically in the early 1950s and cosmologically in the early 1960s (with *Arguments*) before being systematically developed since 1968 in Morin's attempt to reform contemporary thinking in *La Méthode: La Nature de la Nature* (1977), *La Vie de la vie* (1980), *La Connaissance de la connaissance* (1985).

Besides having been one of the founding figures of the *Arguments* review and group, Edgar Morin made several important contributions to the theoretical development of nonparty Marxism, particularly in the area of revisionism. In "Révisions le révisionnisme" (*Arguments/2*, pp. 109–14), Morin sought to turn Marx's own vision against him, to discover "in what way Marxism has become *neurosis*, i.e., the reifying and fetishizing sickness of Marx's thought, and which already blocked in Marx himself, potentially and effectively, the critical dialectical method." Morin considered the question of "alienation" at the center of "revised revisionism," for in order "to surmount the reifications, the fetishizations, i.e., the hardened, perverted and delirious forms of alienation," action must, on the one hand, be centered on man, but at the same time must reopen the dialectic by decentering one's thought about man in order not to "forget or camouflage the perspectives of the becoming-cosmic [*le devenir cosmique*]." Morin continued this reflection in "Le Révisionnisme généralisé" (*Arguments/ 2*, pp. 144–56) by distinguishing two forms of revisionism: restricted revisionism, which "began for me in 1947," and "generalized revisionism," beginning in 1956. While the former did not call into question the method or system of Marxist thought, the latter was an application of "an *auto-ethic*: to struggle against petrification to the end," through a form of nihilism called "generalized relativity": "to seize the *relativity* of nihilism in relation to what it negates, and the relativity of all that is in relation with nihilism," a confrontation with the dialectic which is the very fabric of mental life. Freely admitting that he borrowed the term *generalized relativity* from Einstein, Morin affirmed that "true philosophy must plunge into the sciences to survive and not to constitute itself as some 'great reserve.' " He thus supported "the double and contradictory necessity of 'scientism' and 'philosophism,' " recalling that Marx was the author both of the *Economic and philosophical Manuscripts* and of *Capital*.

Thus, like most of the *Arguments* theorists, Morin's vision was conscientiously global: "I want to work for the human community, that is, for the relations of communication and of love" (*Arguments/2*, p. 155), thereby refusing any party alliance. The program of this "generalized revisionism" was grounded in Morin's statement of "meta-Marxism," of praxis, in "Que faire?" (*Arguments/2*, pp. 273–302). Here he outlines the cultural and political tasks that this generalized critique must confront, concluding,

> If we refer to the earliest issues of *Arguments*, we see that some perspectives were slowly outlined. We started from the critique of Stalinism;† we then believed that the Polish October and the Hungarian revolution outlined models which it would have sufficed to transform into programs. But already, we perceived the problems that were presented to us: (1) To open the question of the crises of totality and of the pauperization of culture. (2) To reintroduce science (method and acquisition of knowledge) and philosophy into the socialist problematic. (3) To clarify the great alternatives . . . to learn if we must remain exiled within or if we might offer

to collaborate, i.e., to choose the lesser evil. Also to lead without fear the auto-critique of the left. (4) To open ourselves to the problems of the "planetary era." (pp. 301–02)

These points, especially the fourth, related directly to Morin's chapter in *Autocritique* entitled "The Planetary Iron Age," describing humanity's completion of its prehistory as it moves into the "planetary era," which precedes the "cosmic era." As outlined in "Que faire?" Morin concludes *Autocritique* with the bases for all future action, his new lines of force: "unlimited revisionism, unlimited critique, unlimited relativity, unlimited contradiction" (p. 238), to be achieved by applying the scientific attitude "to our general conception of the world" (p. 249).

BIBLIOGRAPHY:

A. *Autocritique* (Paris: Le Seuil, 1959); *Introduction à une politique de l'homme* (Paris: Le Seuil, 1965); *La Méthode: La Nature de la nature* (Paris: Le Seuil, 1977); *La Vie de la vie* (Paris: Le Seuil, 1980); *Science avec conscience* (Paris: Fayard, 1982); *La Connaissance de la connaissance* (Paris: Le Seuil, 1985).

B. Jean Duvignaud, "France: The Neo-Marxists," in *Revisionism: Essays on the History of Marxist Ideas*, ed. L. Labedz (New York: Praeger, 1962); Jean Duvignaud, *Anthologie des sociologues français contemporains* (Paris: P.U.F., 1970); Mark Poster, *Existential Marxism in Postwar France* (Princeton: Princeton University Press, 1977); J. B. Fages, *Comprendre Edgar Morin* (Toulouse: Privat, 1981); Arthur Hirsch, *The French New Left* (Boston: South End Press, 1981).

CHARLES J. STIVALE

MORRIS, WILLIAM (1834–1896). William Morris was born in Walthamstow near London in 1834, the son of a wealthy bill broker in the City of London. He was educated at Marlborough College and at Exeter College, Oxford. He became a poet, a painter, a translator and illustrator of Icelandic sagas, and most important of all, a designer and manufacturer of wallpaper, fabrics, and household furnishings. He aimed by design and craftsmanship to raise to the level of art those practical objects which people had to use everyday. Within his own firms, he revived several practical arts such as dyeing, carpet weaving, and book printing, intending to rescue them from their degraded status as merely mechanical industries. From 1876 onward he became politically active—first as an officer and activist in the Eastern [Turkish] Question Association, then as a founder in 1877 of the Society for the Protection of Ancient Buildings (also known as the "Anti-Scrape"), and then in 1879 as the treasurer of the National Liberal League. In 1883 he joined the Democratic Federation, a league of London working-men's radical groups, led by H. M. Hyndman.† He and the rechristened Social Democratic Foundation soon embraced Marxism,† but by the end of 1884 Morris and other dissidents had seceded from the federation to found the Socialist League. Morris strongly supported the league and its weekly newspaper, *Commonweal*, by speaking outdoors, writing songs, essays, and articles, and contributing from his personal fortune. By 1889 the league itself split between militant anarchists and reformist moderates, and Morris withdrew. "Bloody Sunday," the repression of an unemployment demonstration in November 1887, convinced Morris that revolution was very far off. He renewed his commitment to educating socialists and devoted his time to writing and translating and to the art of printing and the enterprise of publishing. His Kelmscot Press, founded in 1890, was the vehicle for all three. The climax of that work was his production of an exquisite volume of Chaucer, finished in June 1896. He died four months later.

The unifying thrust of Morris's life and work was the reintegration of human life, the reversal of the alienation of modern industrial society. He was the major prophet of one of the main streams of British socialism, which Stanley Pierson has called "ethical socialism." As a child he reveled in nature. As a young man he was moved first by the currents of romantic medievalism flowing through Oxford in the 1830s and then by the new secular romanticism of Thomas Carlyle and John Ruskin. Like his mentors, Morris was revulsed by the mechanical ugliness of industrial society. His attitude toward work paralleled Marx's discussion of alienation in his early *Philosophical Manuscripts*: Work should be an expression of personality, not hated drudgery for alien (or purely material) purposes. Work should be art, for both should be "the pleasurable exercise of man's faculties." As a designer Morris sought to banish the distinctions between the practical and the beautiful and between work and art. He hoped for a revival and spread of proud craftsmanship. But he came increasingly to root his aesthetic gospel in sociological analysis, to blame industrial ugliness on greed and class antagonism.

By the early 1880s Morris had lost hope in a rebirth of either the arts or society through conventional politics. He began to believe that only a cataclysmic upheaval could cure the "eyeless vulgarity," the "sordid, aimless, ugly confusion" of modern civilization, that indeed a dose of "barbarism" might be better than his hated civilization, "real feelings and passions, however rudimentary, taking the place of our wretched hypocrisies." (*Letters of William Morris*, p. 113). At this point he turned to Marxism and to Hyndman's Social Democratic Federation. Marxism blamed capitalism for the social degradation and human alienation that Morris decried. It promised class struggle and revolution as the force that might destroy the blight of commercialism and promote the radical social transformation that Morris came to feel was necessary. Morris embraced Marxism but also infused it with his own emotional and artistic values. The resulting hybrid is summed up in what came to be called "the religion of socialism." Indeed, Morris's very embrace precipitated the split in British Marxism. It had inherited a tradition of hostility to industrial capitalism embodied in the social romanticism of Carlyle and the aesthetic emphases of Ruskin. But when Hyndman translated and popularized Marx in the early 1880s, these humanist qualities—essential ingredients of the early Marx—fell out. Morris, never a systematic theorist, grafted Marxism onto the stem of his own more deeply rooted ethical critique of industrialism. As he came to perceive Hyndman's

Marxism as theoretically mechanical and politically hasty and opportunist, he split with Hyndman in late 1884 and became the patriarch of ethical socialism.

Instead of immediate political agitation, Morris insisted that the main business of the new Socialist League was education, "the making of socialists." He distrusted "dirty" political work, trade unions, and palliative reforms. He believed in building up a pure socialist consciousness in working men and others, a consciousness suffused in fellowship and love and in awareness of exploitation, aesthetic degradation and of the denial of pleasures and fulfillment under capitalism. All of this was in preparation for the day when revolutionary crisis would force action and upheaval. Progress toward socialism then was to be measured quantitatively by the purity of socialist consciousness and of an alternative unalienated life style, by the creation of a pure counterculture, rather than by the objective growth of either working-class movements or capitalist crisis. He did not ignore economics: he insisted that the abolition of private property and the collectivization of the means of production were fundamental goals. The Socialist League was soon divided between a more pragmatic reformist segment and a more radical anarchist sector. Morris inclined to the anarchic. In his *News from Nowhere* (1891), his vision of utopia would remove all coercive political, legal, moral, and economic constraints from the spontaneous realization of human desires. Society would become merely and purely voluntary. Work, art, and morality would become fused as "the pleasurable exercise of one's energies," the natural activity of the healthy individual, the "hunter, fisherman, shepherd, [and] critic" of Marx's *German Ideology*.

Morris did not have a direct impact on the British working class, for he was not an effective speaker, and his aesthetic and ethical concerns were too far removed from the immediate needs of the working classes. But translated into a popular idiom by Robert Blatchford and his *Clarion* movement, Morris's influence did make him the progenitor of the mainstream of British socialism. Perhaps the William Morris labour church in Leek, Staffordshire, was a fitting memorial. For the Clarion movement did translate Morris's ideas into a religion of socialism, a "bake sale" socialism, replete with choirs, mass picnics, cycling clubs, and excursions into the countryside. Morris's woolly brand of socialism was less demanding, intellectually and politically, but also more emotionally attractive than Hyndman's materialistic version of Marxism. Its ethical foundations could link romantic protests against early industrial capitalism and the moral individualism of northern nonconformity with community. The "religion of socialism," precisely because of its revivalist qualities and positive recreational attractions, could take root in the close-knit factory towns of Yorkshire and Lancashire, providing a socialist ethos that would supplant the declining Protestant nonconformity and its political embodiment, liberalism, to become the soul of the new Labour Party.

BIBLIOGRAPHY:

A. *News from Nowhere* (London: Reeves and Turner, 1891); with E. B. Bax, *Socialism, Its Growth and Outcome*, (London: Swan Sonnenschein, 1893); *The Collected Works of William Morris*, ed. May Morris (24 vols.; London: Longmans, 1910–15); *The Letters of William Morris*, ed. Philip Henderson (London: Longmans, Green, 1950); *Political Writings of William Morris*, ed. A. L. Morton (New York: Lawrence & Wishart, 1973).

B. J. W. Mackail, *Life of William Morris* (2 vols.; London: Longmans, 1899); May Morris, *William Morris, Artist, Writer, Socialist* (2 vols.; Oxford: Blackwell, 1936); E. P. Thompson, *William Morris: Romantic to Revolutionary* (London: Lawrence & Wishart, 1955); James Hulse, *Revolutionists in London* (Oxford: Clarendon Press, 1970), pp. 77–110; Stanley Pierson, *Marxism and the Origins of British Socialism: The Struggle for a New Consciousness* (Ithaca: Cornell University Press, 1973), pp. 75–89.

JOHN BOHSTEDT

MOUNIER, EMMANUEL (1905–1950). A central intellectual figure in the French Catholic left, Mounier articulated the philosophy of ''personalism,'' particularly in the journal *Esprit*, which he helped found and edited. Born in Grenoble, he first studied medicine but later turned to philosophy. At the University of Grenoble he was particularly influenced by Jacques Chevalier, a student of Henri Bergson, and then in Paris he was influenced by studies with Jacques Maritain. The Catholic revival in France in the 1920s and 1930s, combined with the world economic crisis, provided the milieux in which Mounier, who found academia more and more distasteful, developed his own philosophy with its emphasis on committed action in the world. *Esprit* was founded in 1932, and Mounier was especially taken by the spiritual model of poet-essayist-editor Charles Péguy, who had moved throughout his politically engaged career from socialist to Catholic and nationalist circles before he was killed in the early days of World War I. In the decade before World War II, Mounier propounded his ''personalism'' in *Esprit*, and the journal's radical politics almost led to its condemnation by the Church in 1936. In that same year he published his ''Personalist Manifesto,'' a vigorous condemnation of bourgeois civilization. Mounier chastized Christianity's ties to what he called ''the established disorder,'' and he increasingly became influenced by anarchism and Marxism. He condemned the Moscow trials and supported, although not very enthusiastically, Leon Blum's* Popular Front government. *Esprit* was banned by Vichy during World War II, and Mounier was briefly imprisoned. The journal appeared again in 1945, and in the postwar years Mounier wrote, among other things, a psychological study *Traité du caractère* (1946). He pursued dialogue and debate with the French Communists and called for a Europe free of domination by either the United States or the Soviet Union. Overworked, he died in 1950 of a second heart attack.

Characterizing personalism as ''a philosophy but not a system,'' (*Personalism*, p. xv), he saw himself as a ''tragic optimist.'' He opposed both idealism and materialism as forms of reductionist thought and insisted on the need to remake Europe on the basis of ''the primacy of the spiritual'' (see ''Refaire la renaissance,'' his lead in the first issue of *Esprit*). Mounier argued for a radical revolt against the bourgeois world, which he believed was in the midst of traumatic crisis and steeped in a decadence that exemplified humanity's alienation from God. Social and political commitment and action were, for Mounier, a Christian imperative and a way of bearing witness. Hostile to Hegel, Mounier praised Pascal as "the father of dialectic and of the modern existential consciousness" (*Personalism*, p. xxix). Mounier stressed the free, creative, and communicative nature of human beings and counterposed the childish egocentrism he argued was typical of the modern bourgeois "individual" to the "person." The "individual" lives an isolating, self-centered existence in contrast to the "person," who is "decentered," a social being who is part of a "we." Communication is a fundamental human attribute, and the "person" is "a movement toward a transpersonal condition which reveals itself in the experience of community and of the attainment of values at the same time" (ibid., p. 70). The person is a loving being who lives in a community and in a dialectical relation with nature; he or she attempts to transform nature and subdue it to a personal universe. However, echoing Marx,† he warned against "the bondage of things" and after World War II claimed that the crucial question of the century was whether or not human needs would be enslaved to the dictates of technocracy (either of the left or of the right).

Mounier frequently criticized Marxism for what he saw as its economic determinism and its deficient view of the human spirit. Over and again—against apologists for capitalism as well as Marxists—he emphasized that the human condition was both spiritual and material at once. However, he also argued that as a method of analysis (but not "as a system") Marxism provided the most penetrating understanding of human social and economic realities. Since personalism elucidated "interiority" (humanity's spiritual and subjective dimension), and since like the young Marx it "focused, beyond the disorder of things, on the alienation of the person and aimed, beyond the adaptation of society, at the liberation of man," Mounier saw in his own philosophy a necessary compliment to Marxism (*Be Not Afraid*, p. 172). More than this, he envisioned a broad parallel between Marxist and Christian views of human history: "The conception of a human race with a collective history and destiny, from which no individual destiny can be separated, is one of the sovereign ideas of the Church. In a secularized form, this is the animating principle of eighteenth-century cosmopolitanism, and later of Marxism" (*Personalism*, p. 32). Hostile to all forms of totalitarianism, Mounier advocated a pluralistic socialist humanism. Although he did not imagine the complete disappearance of the state, his political writings were decidedly antistatist. He accepted the Marxist critique of formal democracy but, particularly in his later years, emphasized the importance of political and economic democracy in a decentralized state "articulated in the service of a pluralistic society" (ibid., p. 116).

Similarly, Mounier insisted that socialism had to be the product of the struggles of the workers themselves, in alliance with the peasantry and the more "enlightened" parts of the bourgeoisie. Whether the socialist community would be created through a gradual process or through revolutionary cataclysm was a "secret" of the future, according to Mounier (ibid., p. 106).

BIBLIOGRAPHY:

A. *The Character of Man* (New York: Harpers, 1956) (an abridgement of *Traité du caractère* [Paris: Seuil, 1946]); *Oeuvres de Mounier*, 4 vols. (Paris: Seuil, 1961–63); *Personalism* (Notre Dame: University of Notre Dame Press, 1970); *Be Not Afraid: Studies in Personalist Sociology* (New York: Harper and Brothers n. d.).

B. *Esprit* (December 1950) (commemorative issue on Mounier); "Mounier de nouveau," *Esprit* (special issue) (April 1970); Joseph Amato, *Mounier and Maritain* (University: University of Alabama Press, 1975); Michael Kelly, *Pioneer of the Catholic Revival: The Ideas and Influence of Emmanuel Mounier* (London: Sheed and Ward, 1979).

MITCHELL COHEN

MUKAŘOVSKÝ, JAN (1891–1975). Born on 11 November 1891 in the city of Pisek, Jan Mukařovský became a noted Czech literary critic and aesthetician as well as an active participant in the post–World War II Czech peace movement. His work connects the artistic and philosophical accomplishments of the interwar European avant-garde to more recent Marxist† thinking. Mukařovský studied linguistics and aesthetics at Charles University in Prague. His work *A Contribution to the Aesthetics of the Czech Verse* (1929) helped him to get a university position as professor of aesthetics with the Philosophical Faculty in Bratislava (1931–37), and later at Charles University. During the years 1948 to 1953 Mukařovský was president of Charles University and supervised its Socialist reorganization. From 1951 to 1962 he was head of the Department of Czech Literature at the Academy of Science in Prague. He was a member of the World Peace Council and chairman of the Czech Committee for Peace and was also an editor at the magazines *Word and Belles Lettres* and *Czech Literature*.

Mukařovský's theoretical work combines Russian formalism, French structural linguistics, and German phenomenology with his native Czech outlook to produce a nontraditional structural aesthetics. His credentials in the European structuralist literary movement are universally acknowledged. With Roman Jakobson, Mukařovský was a well-known and active member of the Prague linguistic club, which was established in 1926. Mukařovský's *Aesthetic Study* (1928) begins as a linguistic analysis of the novel *Maj* by the Czech author Macha, using Russian formal methods. However, Mukařovský gradually unfolds a thematic and semantic analysis that surpasses the original formalistic principles. In the review of the Czech translation of Viktor Shklovsky's *Theory of Prose* (1934), Mukařovský characterized his own literary structuralism as a progressive change from traditional causal analysis and orthodox materialism as well as from the more abstract idealism of the Russian formalists. His general goal is to analyze the complex and reciprocal functional dependence of literature on changing social structures. In a narrower sense, he studied literary works to decipher their linguistic structures, which would explain their specific artistic meanings.

Mukařovský's structural aesthetics is first visible in his lecture "L'Art comme fait sémiologique" (1934), one of the first systematic attempts to apply semiotic theory to the arts. He also used this method in analyzing Polak's *Nobility of*

Nature (1934), where he argues that literary works are related to their societies through the medium of social communication. Consequently, literary works are a means of deciphering social and historical structures. He systematically analyzed these issues in the book *Aesthetics, Function, Norm, and Value as Social Facts* (1936). This work contributes to our overcoming metaphysical conceptions of aesthetics by outlining a functional sociological interpretation of semiotics. Mukařovský's work combined a concern for the central theoretical problems in poetry and aesthetics with a penchant for solving concrete research problems in Czech literary history. For example, he studied and published monographs on nineteenth-century European poetry, but also on the modern Czechs Nexval, Vancura and Capek. Mukařovský's theoretical work was critically acknowledged from as early as the 1930s. Noted Marxists such as B. Vaclavek* and K. Konrad* disagreed about its noetic implications, but praised its concrete contributions to our understanding of the structure of modern literature.

After the war Mukařovský confronted certain problematic issues of socialist realism, particularly its denial of artistic autonomy (see, e.g., *About Word Conception in Czechoslovak Literary Theory*, 1947). In 1951, pressured by Stalinist† bureaucrats to toe the Party line on cultural issues, Mukařovský admitted that a residual idealism stained some of his work. He recanted this self-criticism in 1966, when some of his early works were reissued, reiterating principles of structural analysis. This, however, was not the static structuralism that was then voguish particularly in France. Mukařovský argued that structures evolved dynamically, through the activities of creative subjects molding and being molded by history. Structures are thus dialectically constituted in and through concrete historical praxis.

BIBLIOGRAPHY:

A. *Machuv "Maj": estetiká studie* (Prague: F. Rivnáče, 1928); *Čtneí o jazyce a poesii* (Prague: Družstevní práce, 1941); *Studie z estetiky* (Prague: Odeon, 1966); *Aesthetic Function, Norm and Value as Social Facts* (Ann Arbor: University of Michigan Press, 1970); *The Word and Verbal Art* (New Haven: Yale University Press, 1977); *Structure, Sign, and Function* (New Haven: Yale University Press, 1978).

B. Kurt Konrad, *Ztvárněte skutečnost* (Prague: Československý spisovatel, 1963); R. Wellek, *The Literary Theory and Aesthetics of the Prague School* (Ann Arbor: University of Michigan Press, 1969); K. Chvatík, *Tschechoslowakischer Strukturalismus. Theorie und Geschichte* (Munich: Fink, 1981).

K. CHVATÍK

N

NAPOLEONI, CLAUDIO (b. 1924). Born in Aquila, Italy, in 1924, Napoleoni is currently professor of political economy at the University of Turin. Since 1979 he has been a senator of the Republic, elected as an independent on the list of the Italian Communist Party. A frequent columnist in *La repubblica*, Italy's most influential newspaper, he established a national reputation in the early 1960s when he founded with Franco Rodano* the *Rivista trimestrale*, which explored and laid the theoretical bases of the reformist strategy pursued by the Italian left. His most important work has been in the area of the history of economic theory.
BIBLIOGRAPHY:

A. *Pensiero economico del 900* (Turin: Einaudi, 1963); *L'equilibrio economico generale* (Turin: Boringhieri, 1965); *Il valore* (Milan: ISEDI, 1976).

LAWRENCE GARNER

NEGRI, ANTONIO (b. 1933). Having received his practical training first in Catholic cultural activities and then, beginning in 1953, in the organizations of the labor movement, Negri participated in the Quaderni Rossi and Classe Operaia experiments and was one of the founders and principal spokesmen, between 1966 and 1968, of Potere Operaio (worker power) for the Veneto-Emiliano region and, after 1969, of the national Potere Operaio. Having separated himself from Potere Operaio, Negri helped found the Autonomia Operaio (worker autonomy movement) through the newspaper *Rosso*, which culminated in a national assembly at Bologna in 1977. On 7 April 1979 Negri was imprisoned, together with many militants from Autonomia and members of the *Rosso* editorial staff and charged with armed insurrection against the state, the formation of an armed gang, and the kidnapping and assassination of the president of the Christian Democratic Party, the honorable Aldo Moro. After years of imprisonment, during which the case was being tried in Rome, he was elected deputy on the slate of the Radical Party in June of 1983, and because of the parliamentary immunity in force in Italy he was released from prison. However, when the Italian Chamber of Deputies voted for his arrest he fled to Paris, where he had previously completed his university studies. The trial was concluded in June 1984, and in spite of the fact that the most serious charges were dropped, the sentence is extremely harsh: thirty years in prison.

The contribution of Negri to Marxism* lies in his attempt to radicalize an autonomous Italian working-class movement by generating among workers a critical subjectivity antagonistic to capital and to the state. Negri carries to extremes some of the ideas of Raniero Panzieri* and of Mario Tronti,* in particular their analyses of political class composition: "the concept of class composition is the only material base from which one can speak of subject" (*Dall' operaio massa all' operaio sociale*, p. 60). For Negri, class composition means not just the determination of labor power as variable capital and the historic and social levels of its reproduction. It also includes the element of political composition:

> It is also a reality continually modified not only by needs but by the traditions of struggle, by the modalities of existence, of culture, etc., in other words by all those facts—political, social, moral—which come to determine, together with the wage structure, the structure of the reproduction relationship of this working class. (Ibid., pp. 59–60)

The crisis of the welfare state, i.e., the crisis of those forms of integration and recomposition that find theoretical expression in Keynes and in the developments of his thought, is its progressive polarization of classes. In this context the theory of value, as a form of equilibrium, ceases to have any remaining validity. Capital is no longer developed but is reduced to an elementary expression of command, and the state is its true source. On the other hand, there emerges a worker subjectivity that is expressed in a new class composition (i.e. the mass worker and then the social laborer of the 1970s) and is the bearer of new radical needs (i.e. the rejection of work and the embracing of communism) and of new radical political actions. This radical attitude, the expression of an irreducible working-class antagonism toward political control, is based on what Negri calls the "self-exploitation" of the working class. It is a perspective that Marx recognized in the pages of the *Grundrisse* concerning the development of machines and social intelligence. "Communism," Negri concludes, "is neither the teleology of the capitalistic system nor its catastrophe: it is a new subject that is being developed, one that transforms reality and destroys capital" (*Marx oltre Marx*, p. 174).

BIBLIOGRAPHY:

A. *Crisi dello stato-piano* (Milan: Feltrinelli, 1974); *Proletari e stato* (Milan: Feltrinelli, 1976); *La forma stato* (Milan: Feltrinelli, 1977); *Il dominio e il sabotaggio* (Milan: Feltrinelli, 1978); *Dall' operaio massa all' operaio sociale* (Milan: Multhipla, 1979); *Marx oltre Marx. quaderno di lavoro sui Grundrisse* (Milan: Feltrinelli, 1980); *Macchina tempo. Rompicapi liberazione constituzione* (Milan: Feltrinelli, 1982).

VITTORIO DINI

NEUMANN, FRANZ (1900–1954). Franz Neumann was born on 23 May 1900 in Kattowitz, Germany. He served in the German army in the last years of World

War I. At the end of the war, he took part in the revolutionary workers and soldiers council movement in Leipzig. After the suppression of the councils, Neumann began his lifelong pattern of combining scholarship with practical political activity. He studied law at the universities of Breslau, Rostock, and Frankfurt. He received his doctorate in law from Frankfurt in 1923. During his legal studies, Neumann was instrumental in the founding of the Student Socialist Society in Frankfurt. Upon graduation, he practiced law and taught at the Frankfurt Academy of Labor. In 1927 he moved to Berlin and established a private practice in labor law. Between 1928 and 1933 he combined his private practice with teaching at the Deutsche Hochschule für Politik (German College of Politics) and serving as a legal advisor to the German Social Democratic Party. He was arrested by the Nazis in April 1933, but managed to leave Germany the following month. He was one of the first to be deprived of German citizenship by the Nazi regime. He emigrated to England, where he studied political science at the London School of Economics, receiving a doctorate in political science in 1936. That same year he moved to the United States and became a member of the Institute of Social Research, which was affiliated at that time with Columbia University in New York. Between 1942 and 1946 Neumann joined the struggle against Nazi Germany by working for the U.S. government in the Office of Strategic Services and the State Department. After the war he was the American liaison to the Free University of Berlin. Neumann attained his greatest fame in the postwar period as a professor of government at Columbia. In the summer of 1954 he was awarded an honorary doctorate by the Free University of Berlin. Several weeks later, on 2 September 1954, Neumann died in an auto accident while traveling in Switzerland. Herbert Marcuse,* his close friend and former colleague at the Institute of Social Research, later married Neumann's widow, Inge.

Neumann's early essays, written in the late 1920s and early 1930s, reflect his interest in the legal aspects of the relationship between capital and labor. While clearly to the left of the leadership of the Social Democratic Party, Neumann's essays shared the Social Democratic belief that socialism could be achieved by reformist legal and political means within the framework of the liberal Weimar constitution. The Nazi accession to power forced a reassessment of Neumann's political beliefs and a redirection of his scholarly interests. Neumann's struggle for socialism was replaced by a struggle against Nazism. And his expertise in the German legal system, rendered useless by exile in England and the United States, was replaced by a thoroughly political perspective on law. Within the fluid division of labor of the Institute of Social Research, Neumann was a legal and political specialist. He wrote essays on ''The Change in the Function of Law in Modern Society'' and ''Types of Natural Law'' for the Institute journal. Both essays display Neumann and the Institute's preoccupation with Nazism during this period. The first essay analyzed the eclipse of legal rationality and formal legal protections under national socialism. It was Neumann's thesis that the rationality and formality of classical liberal legal theory was predicated on the existence of a true market economy comprised of small and medium-sized holdings of the means of production. Legal rationality and formality leant the necessary measure of calculability to the classical capitalist market system. But contemporary capitalism, in which the market is replaced by monopolies, could dispense with formality and rationality and place its trust in the legal sovereignty of a leader who shared the fundamental aims of the monopolists. A related argument underlay Neumann's second Institute essay. Neumann observed that legal theories of natural law had undergone a period of decline, only to be revived in the twentieth century. The decline of natural law was attributed to inherent problems in natural law theories and to the consequent rise of more positivistic conceptions of law. Neumann argued that the antirationalism, decisionism, and vitalism of national socialist legal theory was in part a product of this decline in natural law and this ascendancy of positivism. Nazi legal theory was thus linked to developments within the liberal legal tradition. Neumann believed that the contemporary revival of natural law was a welcome reaction to Nazi legal theory. He argued that any theory of natural law—even the most conservative— provided some protection against Nazi-style legal philosophies, and a democratic theory of natural law was the best safeguard of all.

The themes of irrationality and lack of formality recurred in *Behemoth*, Neumann's most famous work and the culmination of his association with the Institute of Social Research. Within the welter of facts and details, Neumann offered his own assessment of the general nature of the Nazi regime. Against the liberal thesis that the Nazi regime represented some distinctly new form of a politically managed, perhaps even socialist, society and economy, Neumann emphasized the links between big business and the Nazis, their shared interests, and the continued vitality of capitalism in Nazi Germany. But against the facile thesis of many orthodox Marxists† that the Nazi regime was merely a front for the monopoly capitalists, Neumann adopted a more nuanced position. Neumann maintained that the German ruling class was composed of four groups—big industry, the party, the state bureaucracy, and the armed forces—who both competed and cooperated with each other under the aegis of the leader. Within this configuration, big industry and the party predominated. Neumann's characterization of the Nazi regime also differed from that of several of his Institute colleagues. Following Friedrich Pollock's* analysis, Max Horkheimer* and Theodore Adorno* believed that Nazi Germany was an example of "state capitalism," a distinctly modern type of postcapitalist regime in which the economy was subordinated to political direction. Neumann disagreed. To Neumann, the concept of state capitalism underestimated the links of Nazism to monopoly capitalism, while vastly overestimating the ability of the Nazi regime to provide rational political leadership through a formal state. Neumann saw the Nazi "Behemoth" not so much as a concentrated and powerful state, but as a "nonstate" where the four groups in the ruling class competed like organized crime gangs for privileges and for control over the masses.

During the war, Neumann coauthored a study of *The Fate of Small Business in Nazi Germany* (1943) with Arcadius Gurland and Otto Kirchheimer. Despite an ideological commitment to small business, the study documented the practical preference of Nazi economic policy for big business and cartels. The Nazi encouragement of large economic concentrations at the expense of small businesses merely accelerated pre-Nazi tendencies in this direction. In the postwar years, Neumann published essays on Montesquieu, anxiety and politics, political power, dictatorship, and other themes. Despite their technical expertise and humane scholarship, Neumann's postwar works were marked by an essential ambiguity. H. Stuart Hughes has described these works as lying "between Marxism and liberal democracy." Neumann's understanding of the Nazi experience was at the root of his ambiguous position. Neumann's own books and essays demonstrated the Marxist thesis of the political, economic, and ideological links between Nazism and the late stages of liberal capitalism. Yet these same studies convinced Neumann of the indispensable role of the classical liberal ideals of rationality, legality, and formalism in any just and free society. Neumann's sudden death prevented a resolution of this ambiguity.

BIBLIOGRAPHY:

A. A.R.L. Gurland, Otto Kirchheimer, and Franz Neumann, *The Fate of Small Business in Nazi Germany* (Washington, D.C.: Government Printing Office, 1943); *Behemoth: The Structure and Practice of National Socialism, 1933–1944*, rev. ed. (London: Victor Gollancz, 1944); "The Labor Movement in Germany," pp. 100–08, in *Germany and the Future of Europe*, ed. Hans J. Morgenthau (Chicago: University of Chicago Press, 1951); "The Social Sciences," pp. 4–26, in Franz L. Neumann et al., *The Cultural Migration: The European Scholar in America*, (Philadelphia: University of Philadelphia Press, 1953); *The Democratic and Authoritarian State*, ed. Herbert Marcuse (New York: Free Press, 1957).

B. Otto Kirchheimer, "Franz Neumann: An Appreciation," *Dissent*, 4 (Autumn 1957), pp. 382–86; H. Stuart Hughes, "Franz Neumann Between Marxism and Liberal Democracy," pp. 446–62, in *The Intellectual Migration: Europe and America, 1930–1960*, ed. Donald Fleming and Bernard Bailyn (Cambridge: Harvard University Press, 1969); Martin Jay, *The Dialectical Imagination: A History of the Frankfurt School and the Institute of Social Research, 1923–1950* (Boston: Little, Brown, 1973); Alfons Söllner, "Franz Neumann," *Telos*, no. 50 (1981–82), pp. 171–79.

JOHN BOKINA

NIEUWENHUIS, FERDINAND DOMELA (1846–1919). Nieuwenhuis, an internationally known Dutch anarchist, was also called the "apostle of the workers." He studied theology in Amsterdam and was a Lutheran minister until he left the church in 1879. Before Nieuwenhuis's time socialism and trade unionism were virtually nonexistent in the Netherlands. In 1881 Nieuwenhuis became the leader of the first Dutch socialist party, the Social Democratic Federation (SDB). The SDB, in 1894, lost many of its members (e.g. Pieter Jelle Troelstra† and Frank van der Goes†) to the Dutch Social Democratic Workers' Party (SDAP), which was founded in opposition to Nieuwenhuis's propagation of antiparliamentarism and the general strike. The influence of Nieuwenhuis's pacifism on the development of Dutch social democracy, however, was a profound and lasting one. He greatly contributed to the popularization of Marxism not only in the Netherlands but also in Germany. He produced numerous translations and gave compassionate and agitational speeches wherever he went. From 1888 until his defeat in 1891 Nieuwenhuis was the only Socialist member of the Parliament for the SDB. After the founding of the SDAP and the escalation of officially sanctioned persecution, the SDB changed its name to the Socialist League (SB) and aligned itself with the European anarcho-syndicalist movement. In 1896 Nieuwenhuis and his group were expelled from the London Congress. Nieuwenhuis was an enormously popular public figure in the Netherlands and throughout Europe, respected even by his enemies. With his ethical appeals to the humanitarian cause of socialism, Nieuwenhuis had a tremendous impact on inchoate class consciousness. He was active in the international peace movement from its beginnings in the early 1870s until his death. When he left the church to join the workers in their class struggle, Nieuwenhuis became the editor of the first Dutch Socialist publication of international stature: *Recht voor Allen*. He organized the famous Dutch railroad strike in 1903, which did not culminate in the general strike Nieuwenhuis had predicted (partly because it was publicly denounced by the Social Democrats under Troelstra) and ended in failure. In 1904 Nieuwenhuis organized the congress of the Antimilitarists in Amsterdam, a precursor of the International Association of Antimilitarism (AIA).

BIBLIOGRAPHY:

A. "My Farewell to the Church," in *De Grote Winkler Prins* (Amsterdam: Elsevier, 1974).

B. D. H. Cole, *The History of Socialist Thought, 1894–1914* (London: Macmillan, 1953), pp. 656–61.

TINEKE RITMEESTER

NOVICK, PESACH (b. 1891). Born in Russia in 1891, Pesach (Paul) Novick has been since 1922 an editor, and since 1939 the leading editor, of the Yiddish-language newspaper, *Morgen Freiheit*. For more than forty years he was the outstanding spokesman for the Communist position within the Jewish world. Since the 1960s he has been the undisputed leader of the only significant "Eurocommunist" grouping within the United States, the milieu of the *Morgen Freiheit* and its cultural counterpart, the Yiddishe Kultur Farband.

Novick has struggled with his institutional influence and his aging followers to assert the stubborn anti-assimilationist character of Jewish radicalism. In so doing, Novick has come to argue in his columns and pamphlets for the neo-Marxist political interpretation of Jewish socialism as an historic entity with its own unique background, principles of development, and goals. Because the *Freiheit* had a more folkish character than the English-language *Daily Worker*, and because the Popular Front of the 1930s and the Jewish reaction to the Holocaust in the 1940s emphasized Jewish questions, Novick had begun to make this general interpretation even under the Communist auspices. Russian anti-

Semitism, the Khrushchev† revelations, the Arab–Israeli wars, and the Russian invasions of Eastern Europe strengthened Novick's independent perspective. By the end of the 1960s he had become a major ideological heretic to official Communist Party circles. His efforts to balance support for the existence of Israel with severe criticism of the Begin government, his interpretation of Yiddish and Biblical Jewish tradition in the context of late twentieth-century problems, and his introspection on the trajectory of Jewish radicalism during his long career have delineated an important neo-Marxism in all but name.

BIBLIOGRAPHY:

A. *Palestine, di Arbeter, der Tsionism* (New York: Yidboro, 1932); *Oyrope Tsvishen Milkhome un Sholem* (New York: Yiddishe Kultur Farband, 1948); *The National and Jewish Question in the Light of Reality* (New York: Morgen Freiheit, 1971).

PAUL BUHLE

O

O'CONNOR, JAMES R. (b. 1930). James R. O'Connor is a political economist whose writings on fiscal crisis as well as the role of the capitalist state in the latter part of the twentieth century have attained equal significance with Paul Baran† and Paul Sweezy's† *Monopoly Capital*. He attended St. Lawrence University and received a B.A. and Ph.D. from Columbia University and faculty appointments at Barnard College, Washington University in St. Louis, California State at San Jose, and the University of California at Santa Cruz.

Although originally known for his writing on Cuba (*The Origins of Socialism in Cuba*, 1970), O'Connor's major work is *The Fiscal Crisis of the State* (1973), which significantly invigorated Marxist† political economy in the United States and, later, in Europe as well. Written prior to the fiscal stress encountered by the West since 1973, O'Connor's prophetic analysis located the sources of these crises within the contradictory functions required of the modern capitalist state. As a necessary proponent of capitalist economic growth, O'Connor identifies the dimension of public spending and other governmental programs that objectively serves to increase the private accumulation of wealth. These "social capital" expenditures of the state are either projects and services that increase the productivity of labor power and the rate of profit ("social investment") or those that lower the reproduction costs of labor and the rate of profit ("social consumption"). The former includes programs such as transportation, utilities, and some education and research, whereas the latter includes social spending on regional and urban development, health care, and education. O'Connor contends that the bifurcated nature of the monopoly capitalist economy requires the state to fund these programs, which are essential for increases in the creation of surplus value and the profit structure. To O'Connor the crisis occurs because equally necessary for the modern state is the management of social consensus and political stability. This requires state spending on ameliorative programs ("social expenses") that do not contribute to profit but do create the necessary political framework for "legitimization" and, consequently, growth. Within the context of modern contemporary political economy, these two state functions, accumulation and legitimization, more than exhaust public revenues generated by growth because each function serves to restimulate the other. In more classic Marxist terms, a privately realized growing surplus is dependent on cheapening the price of labor and generating a reserve army of labor, both of which now require critical levels of state spending that result in fiscal crisis.

O'Connor's application of Marxist economic analysis to the mundane categories of public finance and budgeting allows for a more developed Marxist political theory and practice. Since 1973, writing on the Marxist and neo-Marxist theories of the state has flourished, and related authors include C. Offe,* N. Poulantzas,* R. Miliband,* and M. Aglietta, among many others.

BIBLIOGRAPHY:

A. *The Origins of Socialism in Cuba* (Ithaca: Cornell University Press, 1970); *The Fiscal Crisis of the State* (New York: St. Martin's Press, 1973); *The Corporations and the State: Essays in the Theory of Capitalism and Imperialism* (New York: Harper & Row, 1974).

B. Martin Carnoy, *Political Theory and the State* (Princeton, N.J.: Princeton University Press, 1984).

RICHARD GUARASCI

OFFE, CLAUS (b. 1940). Claus Offe was born on 16 March 1940 in Berlin. As an undergraduate he studied sociology, economics, and philosophy at the University of Cologne and the Free University of Berlin. He received his doctorate in sociology from the University of Frankfurt in 1968 with a dissertation on "Leistungsprinzip und industrielle Arbeit" (The Achievement Principle and Industrial Work). From 1965 to 1969 he taught at the Institute for Social Research and the Sociology Department at the University of Frankfurt. He was a research associate at the Max Planck Institute between 1971 and 1975. Since 1975, Offe has been a professor of political science and sociology at the University of Bielefeld. He has held fellowships or research appointments at the University of California at Berkeley (1969–70), Harvard (1970–71), and Princeton (1977–78). He has also been a visiting professor at the University of Konstanz (1971–72), the University of California at Berkeley (1974), and Boston University (1975).

Offe's work combines elements of sociological functionalism and systems theory with the flexible, nonorthodox Marxism† of the Frankfurt School. Unlike the majority of functional and systems theorists, Offe does not assume the stability and equilibrium of social systems and subsystems. Offe concentrates, rather, on the structural contradictions and crisis tendencies of late capitalist society. His approach to Marxism is equally unorthodox. Contrary to the orthodox Marxist distinction between the economic base of society and its political superstructure, Offe describes the "capitalist state" of late capitalism as one in which the state and the economy are intertwined. Offe's early book on *Industry and Inequality* analyzes the inherent contradictions of the "achievement principle" as the ideological legitimation of inequality in late capitalist societies. According to the achievement principle, unequal rewards are distributed in proportion to the level of achievement or performance attained. A society operating under the achievement principle requires both a unified and objective scale to measure achievement and competent authorities to assess performance. But Offe observes that the predominant form of work organization in late capitalism is "task-discontinuous," i.e., superiors and inferiors in an organization possess different skills. Hence, Offe argues, rewards in recruitment, promotion, and income are not based on the superior's evaluation of task performance; the superior lacks the expertise to make such an evaluation. Contrary to the ideology of the achievement principle, rewards are distributed in accordance with considerations that are "peripheral" to the task, considerations like conformity to the organization's power structure and vague social evaluations as to the worth of particular jobs. Reward by organizational conformity and social consensus not only contradicts the ideology of achievement, but also prevents the work organization in late capitalism from performing to the utmost of efficiency and effectiveness.

In Offe's later works, particularly his book on *Strukturprobleme des kapitalischen Staates* (Structural Problems of the Capitalist State) and numerous essays, he shifts his focus from the contradictions of industrial work to the contradictions of the state in late capitalism. The transition from classical market capitalism to late corporate capitalism has entailed an expanded role for the state. According to Offe, agencies of the state now perform many of the regulatory and support functions that the market performed during classical capitalism. Although this expanded role of the state alleviates the otherwise insoluble problems of the capitalist economy, it does so by politicizing the economy. The state is thus placed in a systemic contradiction between its need to support the capitalist economy and its need to gain widespread acceptance or legitimacy for its actions. Offe has explored this contradiction as well as others in a number of specific studies of welfare, education, interest groups, public policy, and political parties. These works on the political contradictions of late capitalism have established Offe as one of the most important contemporary thinkers associated with critical theory and the Frankfurt School.

BIBLIOGRAPHY:

A. *Strukturprobleme des kapitalischen Staates* (Frankfurt: Suhrkamp, 1972); *Berufsbildungsreform—Eine Fallstudie über Reformpolitik* (Frankfurt: Suhrkamp, 1975); *Industry and Inequality* (New York: St. Martin's Press, 1977); "Competitive Party Democracy and the Keynesian Welfare State: Factors of Stability and Disorganization," *Policy Sciences*, 15 (1983), pp. 225–46.

B. Jean L. Cohen, *Class and Civil Society* (Amherst: University of Massachusetts Press, 1982).

JOHN BOKINA

P

PACI, ENZO (1911–1976). Born in Monterado, a province of Ancona, on 18 September 1911, Paci studied under Antonio Banfi* at the University of Milan, receiving his degree in 1934 with a thesis on the Platonism of Parmenides. He published his first book, *Principi di una filosofia dell'essere*, in 1939, and soon after helped found the journal *Studi filosofici*, a fairly influential Italian journal that survived until 1949. In 1942 Benedetto Croce began a polemic with Paci in the journal *La critica* regarding the meaning and significance of existentialism. In 1943 Paci, together with Nicola Abbagnano, edited an issue of *Primato* dedicated to Italian existentialism. Paci was drafted into World War II on 8 September 1943 and was soon imprisoned by the Nazis in a German concentration camp near Warsaw until 1945. After the war, in 1947, Paci began teaching at the universities of Pavia and Milan. In 1951 he founded the journal *Aut aut*, which played an important role in the renaissance of postwar Italian philosophy, particularly Husserlian phenomenology. In 1954 Paci became a professor of theoretical philosophy at the University of Pavia, where he remained until moving to Milan in 1958. Here he contributed to journals such as *Praxis* and *Telos* on the subtle interrelationship between Marxism† and phenomenology, a topic that occupied him for the remainder of his life. He lectured, in 1970, in the United States and in Canada and died on 21 July 1976 in his home in Milan.

Paci's *The Function of the Sciences and the Meaning of Man* (1972), the most important single work in the "Milan School" of radical social philosophy, generated a Marxist philosophy from Husserl's transcendental phenomenology. Paci believed that the Husserlian reduction to pure or transcendental subjectivity is the necessary first step in scientific social inquiry. The transcendental subject is consciousness open to, and indelibly stained by, "temporal irreversibility." People, reflectively living in the present, experience reality as the past reverting into the future. The essential quality of pure subjectivity is "becoming," which is experienced from an internal consciousness of time. Transcendental subjectivity is, therefore, intentional consciousness in time, what Martin Heidegger and Herbert Marcuse* called "historicity." The experienced world—including intermonadic, sensible, perceptual, corporeal, and spiritual aspects—also constitutes itself in time, that is, is historical. In other words, the pure subject and the real, experienced world are both temporally open, marked by historicity. Hence, pure subjectivity generates an authentic, reflective experience of this world, not an ideal metaphysical reality. Although Husserl argued that the pure ego transcends the world, Paci suggests "subjectivity without the world contains it" (*The Function of the Sciences and the Meaning of Man*, p. 35). The authentically experienced world of pure subjectivity is Paci's "*Lebenswelt.*" It is separate from the mundane world of everyday life, which occludes authentic consciousness. Only through systematic reflective self-consciousness can we smash naive, common prejudices and experience the *Lebenswelt*. There is no conflict between subjectivity and the authentic life-world of reflective social actions: pure subjectivity and pure objectivity correspond.

Life in capitalist society, for Paci, is mundane, alienating and fetishized. On the other hand, the *Lebenswelt* is a reality of cooperation and understanding, where being is spatially and temporally open to all aspects of social life, including fellow humans. The *Lebenswelt* is a truly communist society. Historical materialism lives in each subject's desire to "become," to experience reality as the past reverting into the future. Man's *telos* (his subjective orientation toward a not-yet-realized, emancipated *Lebenswelt*) and history's *telos* (materialism's concrete totality) are expressed in the free praxis of authentic subjects (the proletariat). Phenomenology generates a revolutionary working class, not merely Husserl's abstract *eidé*. Husserl's contemplative *epoché* is transformed into revolutionary praxis. Transcendental knowledge reveals "the capitalist occlusion of the subject and truth" and propels each subject toward socialism, where human potential can flower (ibid., p. 323). For Paci, Marx's historical dialectic lives in the practical consequences of the transcendental reduction.

Paci analyzes transcendental subjectivity as if the results were transparently objective. Phenomenologically, the temporal openness of consciousness signifies only Paci's consciousness of the temporal openness of consciousness, unless he has actually experienced an ideal perceptual mode somehow transcending and governing each reflective activity. By throwing the transcendental subject back into society, Paci—like Hegel—presumed an ideal, metaphysical quality defining the *Lebenswelt*. When he admits his analysis of the *Lebenswelt* is "an interpretation or, maybe, a correction . . . but [one] required by the coherent development of Husserlian phenomenology" (ibid., p. 37), he perhaps underestimates and confuses Husserl's intentions. It is inconceivable, given his pursuit of "things themselves," that Husserl felt that criteria of objectivity are located within society. Moreover, why undertake a phenomenology of the *Lebenswelt* as Husserl did in the *Krisis* lectures, if objectively verifiable knowledge defines social life? Despite Paci's intentions, his argument is based on, and takes us back to, Husserl's transcendentalism.

BIBLIOGRAPHY:

A. *Esistenzialismo e storicismo* (Milan: Mondadori, 1950); *Dall'esistenzialismo al relazionismo* (Florence: D'Anna, 1957); "Sul problema della interosoggettivitá," *Il Pensiero*, 3 (1960), pp. 291–325; *Tempo e verità nella fenomenologia di Husserl* (Bari:

Laterza, 1961); *Tempo e relazione* (Milan: Il Saggiatore, 1965); *The Function of the Sciences and the Meaning of Man* (Evanston: Northwestern University Press, 1972); *Idee per una enciclopedia fenomenologica* (Milan: Bompiani, 1973.)

B. Carlo Sini, "La fenomenologia in Italia," *Revue internationale de philosophie*, 81–82 (1965), pp. 125–39; Giuseppe Semerari, "L'opera e il pensiero di Enzo Paci," *Rivista critica di storia della filosofia*, 32, no. 1 (February–March 1977), pp. 78–94; Salvatore Veca, "Introduction," in *Il filosofo e la città*, ed. Enzo Paci (Milan: Il Saggiatore, 1979), pp. 1–17.

VITTORIO DINI and ROBERT A. GORMAN

PANNEKOEK, ANTONIE (1873–1960). Antonie Pannekoek (who also used the names K. Horner, J. Harper, and P. Aartsz) was an internationally known Dutch astronomer and council communist. He gained worldwide recognition for his pioneering work in the field of star spectra. He studied mathematics and physics in Leiden, earning a Ph.D. in 1902. From 1918 to 1942 Pannekoek was professor of astronomy in the Netherlands. Among Marxists Pannekoek is primarily remembered as one of the most important theorists of council communism. His political activism began in 1902 when he joined Pieter Jelle Troelstra's† Social Democratic Workers' Party (SDAP), which was modeled after the German Social Democratic Party under Karl Kautsky.† Pannekoek was among the first to introduce Marxism† in the Netherlands. Within the SDAP he and Herman Gorter* aligned with the radical tribunists, who agitated against the party's revisionism. When in 1909 the tribunists defied party orders to cease publishing their oppositional paper *De Tribune*, they were expelled. Of the Marxist editors of *Die Nieuwe Tijd*, the SDAP paper for theory and criticism, Pannekoek and Gorter were the only ones to join the tribunists by leaving the SDAP. Both became members of the Social Democratic Party founded by the tribunists in 1909, which in 1919 would become the first Dutch Communist Party. As Pannekoek was already residing in Germany, his role in the SDP was not as active as Gorter's. Although he returned to the Netherlands on a regular basis and also continued to contribute steadily to *De Nieuwe Tijd* and *De Tribune* from 1906 until the late 1920s, Pannekoek was politically active primarily in Germany. In 1906 he had been called to Berlin by the German Social Democratic Party to teach Marxist theory at their school, where Kautsky and Rosa Luxembourg† also taught. After it was closed by the local authorities Pannekoek moved to Bremen, where he—with Karl Radek and others—taught at a similar school. Meanwhile, before settling down in Bremen, Pannekoek had become a popular figure within the international workers' movement as a result of his lecture tours throughout Germany and the Netherlands and his articles in *Die Neue Zeit*. Pannekoek was a prolific political writer who, until the end of his life, contributed lengthy and theoretically profound articles to a broad spectrum of German, Dutch, and English radical socialist publications: *De Nieuwe Tijd* (1901–21), *Die Neue Zeit* (1907–12), *Vorbote*, *Persdienst van de Groep van International Communisten* in the Netherlands, *Rätekorrespondenz*, *Funken*, *International Socialist*

Review, *Proletarier*, *Bremer Bürgerzeitung*, *Kommunistische Arbeiter Zeitung*, *The Southern Advocate for Workers Control*, *Die Aktion*, *Socialisme ou barbarie*,* etc.

During World War I Pannekoek belonged to the Zimmerwald left around Vladimir Lenin† and Radek, that sought to organize against the war. Under the editorial supervision of Radek, Pannekoek and Henriëtte Roland-Holst put out the *Vorbote*, the newsletter for the Zimmerwald left. Pannekoek lived and worked in Bremen until the outbreak of the war, when he was deported to Holland. He returned to Germany during the November revolution of 1918. In 1919 Pannekoek was one of the organizers of the secret meeting of international Communists that was raided by the police. In November of that same year Pannekoek, Gorter, Roland-Holst, and others belonged to the executive of the Western European sub-bureau of the Comintern† in Amsterdam. After the proclamation of the twenty-one conditions by the Bolshevik Party, Pannekoek and Gorter were among the first to break with the Comintern. They became the most influential founding members of the anti-Bolshevik Communist Workers' Party in the Netherlands and in Germany (KAPN and KAPD). In Germany the KAPD managed to recruit 38,000 members, over half the acknowledged German Communists. With Henk Canne Meijer, Pannekoek played an important role in the Dutch Group of International Communists (GIC), which was closely linked to German council communism.

Like other members of the Dutch school of Marxism, Pannekoek was profoundly influenced by the epistemology of Joseph Dietzgen (cf. his introduction to *Das Wesen der menschlichen Kopfarbeit*, 1903), particularly regarding the notion of workers autonomy, e.g., the need for the proletariat to think and act for itself, not on party or union orders. Pannekoek had grown increasingly distrustful of intellectuals assuming leadership over the workers. *Workers Councils*, which Pannekoek wrote during 1941–42 and first appeared in 1946 under the pseudonym P. Aartsz, sums it up as follows: "The self-determination of workers is not a demand put up by theory, by argument of practicability, *but* the statement of a fact evolving from practice" (p. 69). From his first book (*Ethics and Socialism*, 1906) to his last major work (*Workers Councils*), Pannekoek attempts to resolve and redefine short-term tactics with a long-range strategy for the workers' struggle without surrendering the workers to extraneous control and leadership. Mass strikes, popular insurrections, wildcat strikes, factory committees, and revolution are the key ingredients of Pannekoek's theory on workers' councils and are already discernible in 1912 in his replies to Kautsky in the famous debate that unfolded in *Die Neue Zeit* around the issue of mass strikes. Until 1914 Pannekoek did not dispute the importance of parliament in the final stages of the class struggle. However he could never accept the party or the union as political organizers on behalf of the proletariat. Drawing from the spontaneous mass actions that led to the Paris Commune (1870–71) and Bloody Sunday (1905) in Russia, Pannekoek viewed workers' councils as the only politically authentic and legitimate form of organization for the class struggle. These councils decide for themselves the appropriate methods and aims of the struggle. By putting more trust in the spontaneous actions of the workers than in the planned actions proposed by a workers' party or union, Pannekoek was perhaps politically closest to Rosa Luxemburg, although he disagreed with her on the question of the accumulation of capital and vehemently rejected her "death crisis" theory. Pannekoek's political development from social democrat to radical socialist to Bolshevik to council communist can be followed best by tracing his political differences with the leaders of the Second and Third Internationals†; with Karl Kautsky on tactics of parliamentary and trade union struggles and on the role of mass strikes; with Rosa Luxembourg on the accumulation of capital and the "final catastrophe"; with Lenin on the role of the Party in bringing about socialism and class consciousness; and with Radek on the Bolshevik Party's proclamation of the twenty-one conditions. "The revolution," Pannekoek wrote,

> can only come from the masses and can only be carried out by the masses. Should the Communist Party forget this simple truth and want to rely on the insufficient strength of a revolutionary minority for wanting to do that which can only be done by the class as a whole, a defeat would be the result that with the greatest sacrifices would set back the world revolution for a very long time." (*Der neue Blanquismus*, cited in de Liagre Böhl, *Herman Gorter*, p. 247).

Indeed, Pannekoek was one of the first to anticipate the cooptation of the workers by the fascists. In his thoughts about the function of ideology there are striking resemblances with the theories of Antonio Gramsci,* Karl Korsch,* and members of the Frankfurt School, particularly in their agreement on the importance of the conquest of political hegemony by the proletariat.

BIBLIOGRAPHY:

A. *Workers Councils* (Cambridge: S. Bricianer, 1946); *Pannekoek and the Workers' Councils* (St. Louis: Telos Press, 1978).

B. A. P. Cajo Brendel, *Theoretikus van het Socialism* (Nijmegen: SUN, 1970); Herman de Liagre Böhl, *Herman Gorter* (Nijmegen: SUN, 1973); D. A. Smart, *Pannekoek and Gorter's Marxism* (London: Pluto Press, 1979).

TINEKE RITMEESTER

PANOMYONG, PRIDI (b. 1900). Born in 1900, the son of a civil servant in rural Thailand, Pridi Panomyong became one of the first common-born Thais to win a king's scholarship to study abroad. During his studies of law and economics in Paris he became the leader of a small group of students including military officers who believed that the Thai system of government must be transformed. In 1927 he obtained his doctoral degree in law and returned home. The brilliant Pridi taught law, drafted new laws for several different ministeries, founded Thammasat University, and began planning a revolution to overthrow the absolute monarchy. The stunning success of the dawn coup in 1932 brought a constitutional monarchy with Pridi's coup group in power. As minister for national development, Pridi attempted the radical transformation of the economy with a unique amalgam of Marxist† and populist measures. His plans aroused the anger of the old elite and the more conservative members of his coup group. Branded a Communist, Pridi was forced to flee the country, and his plans were defeated. But in 1934 he was officially cleared of the Communist allegations. He served as foreign minister, minister of the interior, and minister of finance, trying to implement his ideas more gradually. During the Japanese occupation Pridi worked secretly with Allied intelligence services to set up the underground resistance. In 1946 Pridi became prime minister for less than three months before being ousted by his conservative opponents in the furor over the sudden and unexplained shooting death of the king. When his enemies in the army overthrew the government, Pridi was again forced to leave Thailand. He attempted to return to power in 1949 in a countercoup, but the army defeated his forces after two days of fighting. Pridi fled into exile in China. There he wrote a number of theoretical works on Buddhism and Marxism. Pridi left China in 1970 for Paris, where he has remained a magnet for Thai students and intellectuals.

However great Pridi's political and practical effect on Thailand, his philosophical and intellectual effect was perhaps even greater. He introduced Marxist thought to Thailand in a way that was adapted to the Thai situation. He spent particular effort on an attempt to integrate Marxist and Buddhist philosophy. His most explicit integration came in the book *Kwam Pen Annijjang Kong Sang Kom* (The Impermanence of Society, 1958). Pridi tried to show that the Buddhist term *annijjang* (impermanence) is similar to the Marxist dialectic. Pridi introduced to Marxism a new perspective on religion to account for the differences between nontheistic Buddhism and the Christianity that Marx knew. Instead of treating religion as human alienation, Pridi synthesized the Marxist view of history with the Buddhist view that everything is in a state of *annijjang*. The Buddhist concept does not specify any form of changing, whereas the Marxist dialectic gave a mechanistic aspect to change that was alien to Thai minds. The synthesis of the two in Pridi's work resulted in an idea of change that was more exact and more political than the Buddhist sense and more humanistic and ethically oriented than the normal Marxist understanding. One of Pridi's terms that had a particular impact on a later generation of Thai Marxists is the concept of *apiwat*, which Pridi defined as "special and superior progressiveness." He infused the term with the Buddhist sense of progress toward enlightenment and the Marxist sense of synthesis. He suggested, for example, that the change of government in 1932 had been *apiwat* and not revolution. This had the direct political effect of leading Thai Marxists to struggle for organic progressive change that did not necessarily require a violent armed revolution but did require aggressive agitation and extraparliamentary political attacks on the status quo. This line of thinking still splits the majority of Thai Marxists from those influenced by Maoism.†

Pridi was also the first to attempt a Marxist interpretation of Thai history, organizing a field previously dominated by apologists for the monarchy into the categories that Marx had set up for the history of Europe that were supposed to lead to communism. Pridi was also interested in the practical application of

Marxist ideas, and his draft economic plan of 1932 was the first and most comprehensive attempt at such application in Asia. The plan called for the virtual elimination of capitalism, with all workers to become employees of the state. The government was to implement radical land reform by expropriating all farmland, and farmers were to be organized into state cooperatives that were in some sense forerunners of the Maoist transformations made later in China. Free education was to be universal, and all citizens were to be guaranteed old age pensions. The government was also to take over all private financial transactions and form a national bank. The plan was not pure Marxism, incorporating many features of such utopian socialists as Robert Owen, but its basic assumptions on the role of capital, government, and labor were clearly Marxist.

Although Pridi's grand plan for the transformation of the Thai economic system was defeated as a whole, many of its provisions were introduced piecemeal. The government took over many private enterprises. The national bank is similar to that proposed by Pridi. The main government strategy to stimulate the growth of agriculture has made extensive use of Pridi's ideas for rural cooperatives.

BIBLIOGRAPHY:

A. *Pen Anijjang Kong Sang Kom* (The Impermanence of Society) (Bangkok: Rungruengtham, 1958); *Pradya Keu Arai* (What Is Philosophy?) (Bangkok: Nittiwet, 1970); *Kao Krong Setakit* (Economic Plan) (Bangkok: Prajak Garnpim, 1974); *Anakod Kong Meung Thai Gab Stanagan Kong Prated Peun Ban* (The Future of Thailand and the Situation of Neighboring Countries) (Bangkok: Prajak Garnpim, 1975); *Chard Yang Mee Yu* (The Nation Still Exists) (Bangkok: Mongkon Garnpim, 1975); *Rabob Sangkomniyom Lae Communism Ja Morsom Gae Meung Thai Reu Mai* (Would Socialism and Communism Suit Thailand?) (Bangkok: Pikanet, 1975); *Pridi Panomyong Saner Nae Witi Pijarana Tang Rod Kong Sangkom Thai* (Pridi Panamyong Proposes Methods for the Survival of Thai Society) (Bangkok: Prajag Garnpim, 1976); *Goraneee Sawanakod Lae Panha Kong Chard* (The King's Death Issue and the National Problems) (Bangkok: Siriporn Garnpim, 1978).

B. Supot Dantrakul, *Chiwit Lae Ngarn Kong Dr. Pridi Panomyong* (Dr. Pridi Panomyong's Life and Works) (Bangkok: Prajak, Garnpim, 1973); Supot Dantrakul, *Kor Tetjing Bangprakarn Kieu Kap Rattaburut Arwuso Pridi Panomyong* (Some Facts About Pridi Panomyong, Senior Statesman) (Bangkok: Prajak Garnpim, 1973); Duen Bunnag, *Tan Pridi, Rattaburut Arwuso Poo Wangpan Setakit Thai Kon Raek* (Pridi, the Senior Statesman First in Planning the Thai Economy) (Bangkok: Po Sam Ton, 1974).

YUANGRAT WEDEL

PANZIERI, RANIERO (1921–1964). Panzieri was born in Rome in 1921, and died in Turin in 1964. In the underground existence he was forced to lead because he was a Jew, he had his first contacts with the Socialist left and became a member of the PSIUP (Partito Socialista di Unità Proletaria) in 1944. In 1945 he obtained his degree from the University of Urbino with a thesis on Morelly's *Code de la nature*. He began his theoretical-political activity in 1946 by working together with Rodolfo Morandi in the editorial office of the review *Socialismo*. From 1948 to 1951 he had a university teaching appointment in philosophy of

law at the University of Messina, which he obtained through the support of
Galvano Della Volpe.* With Della Volpe he also made plans for a theoretical
journal to be entitled "Critica materialista," which was never published. In
Sicily he also began his organizational activities for the party and participated
in local elections. In 1953 he became a member of the Central Committee of
the Italian Socialist Party (PSI), and from 1955 on he was responsible for the
cultural section. In 1956 he joined the editorial committee of the PSI's theoretical-
political journal *Mondo operaio*. This same period marked the beginning of his
alienation from the party as a result of his criticizing the Twentieth Congress of
the Soviet Communist Party and its reformist line. He began to develop his
theses on "worker control," which inspired widespread debate in all the organizations of the labor movement. In 1959, expelled from *Mondo operaio*, he
moved from Rome to Turin and worked for the publishing house Einaudi, first
as an editor, then as a consultant. In 1961, together with a group of young
people from Turin and in cooperation with trade union groups (FIOM, the
ironworkers of the CGIL), he founded *Quaderni rossi*, a journal that played a
very important role in theoretical debate and also in the practical development
of radical movements of the late 1960s. In 1963 there was a split that led the
more "laborist" wing—specifically, Mario Tronti,* Asor Rosa, and Antonio
Negri*—to found a new review, *Classe operaia*. At the end of that year Panzieri
was fired by Einaudi, and he died unexpectedly the following year.

Panzieri's theoretical perspective, which is closely related to problems of
practical politics and to the questions posed by the labor movement, has at its
very center a "return to Marx†" and at the same time a "critical reexamination"
of Lenin.† Panzieri's return to Marx deals above all with a unitary, nonidealistic
interpretation of Marx that strongly resembles Della Volpe's interpretation. Panzieri believed that Marx's later scientific writings adequately explain the development of Italy's production relationships as they appeared in the 1950s and
1960s. The modern capitalistic use of machines, the planning processes of capitalistic production, the entire process of neocapitalistic development, far from
falsifying Marxian analysis, find its most appropriate explanation in that analysis
and in Marx's principal instrument, the theory of value. Moreover, Marxian
analysis, for Panzieri, is not deterministic. Critical working-class subjectivity
develops in concert with, but also external to, the concrete contradictions of
capitalism. The "laborism" of Panzieri is thus different from the later positions
of Tronti and Negri, for whom critical consciousness develops from within the
capitalist relationship of value. The instrument, therefore, for this process of
developing class antagonism is inquiry, which opens the door for the selective
use of bourgeois sociology. "Again I emphasize," affirms Panzieri,

> the sociological character of Marx's thought from this standpoint; he asserts that
> it is not possible to return automatically from the movement of capital to the study
> of the working class: the working class, whether it operates as an element of
> conflict and is therefore capitalistic or whether it is an antagonistic element and
> therefore anticapitalistic, demands an absolutely separate scientific examination.
> (*La ripreso del marxismo leninismo in Italia*, p. 318)

Inquiry is linked to the problem of organization and the "critical reexamination" of Lenin. The organization or party is one necessary instrument in the process of forming the antagonistic conscience, but it is just an instrument, and such it must remain. For this reason Panzieri has always polemicized against the rigid and bureaucratized positions of the workers' movement. He sought, instead, a party based on direct democracy, an instrument that would self-destruct once its own objectives are realized.

BIBLIOGRAPHY:

A. *La ripresa del marxismo leninismo in Italia* (Milan: Sapere, 1972); *La crisi del moviemento operaio: scritti, interventi, lettere, 1956–1960* (Milan: Nigri, 1973); *L'alternativa socialista: scritti scelti 1944–1956* (Turin: Einaudi, 1982).

B. "Raniero Panzieri e i *Quaderni rossi*," special edition of *Aut aut*, no. 149–50 (September–December 1975); Mario Alcaro, *Dellavolpismo e nuova sinistra* (Bari: Dedalo, 1977); Sandro Mancini, *Socialismo e democrazia diretta. introduzione a Raniero Panziero* (Bari: Dedalo, 1977); Roberta Tomassini, *Ideologia, intellettuali, organizzazione* (Bari: Dedalo, 1977); Maria Grazia Meriggi, *Composizione di classe e teoria del partito* (Bari: Dedalo, 1978); Giacomo Maramao, *Il politico e le trasformazioni* (Bari: De Donato, 1979), esp. pp. 117 ff.; Stefano Merli, "Appunti sulla formazione di R. Panzieri," *Quaderni piacentini*, no. 72–73 (October 1979).

VITTORIO DINI

PEŠIĆ-GOLUBOVIĆ, ZAGORKA (b. 1930). The Yugoslav Zagorka (Pešić-) Golubović was born in 1930 in Šabac (Serbia) and studied philosophy, social anthropology, and sociology at the University of Belgrade, earning a Ph.D. in anthropology in 1962. She was a professor of social anthropology and director of the Institute for Sociological Research, University of Belgrade, until 1975, when she was suspended from teaching—along with seven *Praxis** colleagues— and eventually dismissed in 1980. Following vigorous protest by the international academic community, Golubović was reinstated as director of a new Center for Philosophy and Social Theory at Belgrade University's Institute of Social Sciences in July 1981. Golubović also taught high school in Zemun and Belgrade, was editor of the publishing house Rad (1956–57) and the journal *Sociologija* (1959–60), and served on the boards of *Praxis*, *Filozofija*, and *Praxis International*. She has lectured at many universities abroad, especially in England and Scandinavia. One of the most outspoken members of the *Praxis* group, and the lone woman member of the "Belgrade Eight," she protested the court-ordered removal of passages from her book *Man and His World* (1973) and the failure of the publishing house Naprijed to print her *Family as a Human Community*. Her publications include also *The Marxist Conception of Individual Freedom* (1958), *Problems of the Contemporary Theory of Personality* (1966), *Anthropology as a Social Science* (1967), *Stalinism and Socialism* (1982), as well as numerous articles in *Praxis* and other journals and symposia.

Her theoretical contributions to Marxism†—particularly to the *Praxis* school of Marxist humanist thought—lie in philosophical anthropology and axiology as well as sociology. Influenced by German and French existentialism and personalism, especially Karl Jaspers and Jean-Paul Sartre,* Golubović has attempted to develop a Marxist philosophical anthropology and axiology drawing on the young Marx of the *Economic and Philosophical Manuscripts* (1844). The rediscovery of the young Marx by Golubović and other *Praxis* theorists centered on Marx's concept of alienation, which underlies all of her work. She endeavors consciously to develop the volitional, praxis, utopian element in Marx's theoretical framework as a counterpoint to his determinism. While Marx in his Sixth Thesis on Feuerbach defined the essence of man as the ensemble or totality of social relations, Golubović notes in her *Problems of the Contemporary Theory of Personality* that human personality cannot be so defined without taking personal determinants into account. To her, there are three groups of factors responsible for personality development: biological and psycho-biological; social and cultural; and personal. Golubović concludes that personality is not simply socially determined; rather, there is a complex mutual interrelationship of the individual and society.

Her basic thesis in *Man and His World* is that the Marxist theory of class struggle needs to be supplemented by a theory of human motivation. She begins with Marx's conception of the historical possibilities of man, and praxis as the universal, creative activity of man—the bridge between human essence and existence. Golubović places great emphasis on human character, motivation, cultural values, human needs, and free choice as those qualities that enhance man as the subject of history. Citing Jaspers's concept of man as incomplete, unfinished, she maintains that it is this very capacity for continuous growth that constitutes the essential trait of human nature. She agrees with Karel Kosík* that the realization of man is the only true meaning of history. And she claims that Marx conceived the development of a rich human individuality as the ultimate goal of historical, revolutionary praxis. Hence, for Golubović, Marx's vision of communism is noneschatological, since communism is not an end in itself but a free human community that can liberate all human potentialities.

Golubović has achieved considerable notoriety in the East due to her ruthless critique of the growing embourgeoisement, market relations, social differentiation, statism, and new class relations in contemporary Yugoslav society, as well as her equally searing critique of Stalinism,† or "real existing socialism," in the Soviet Union and Eastern Europe. In a series of articles in *Praxis*, Golubović undertook a Marxist critique of socialist practice in Yugoslavia, which followed Marx's dualism between the state and the individual, capital and labor, not only infuriating the authorities, that is, the Party, but raising doubt as to the basic adequacy of Marxist categories for the analysis of twentieth-century social phenomena in capitalism or socialism. Her basic point is that Marx's futuristic project of a free association of producers resting on equality, freedom, and human self-realization became subverted in Yugoslavia via the introduction of a "socialist market" (to her, a contradiction in terms), leading to growing social differentiation, inequalities, bureaucracy, technocracy, and the monopoly of economic and political power of the socialist state, which increasingly resembled the classical state under capitalism. To her, the Yugoslav system was a hybrid composed of the dominant elements of the state and bureaucracy, on the one hand, and mainly powerless institutions of workers' self-management, scattered and atomized, enclosed within the confines of individual factory walls, on the other. Golubović concluded that within the present alienated framework of political society and the state—which in her analysis always means *class* society—functionalism was more desirable in Yugoslavia than Marxism.

Golubović has recently turned her methodological tools to a critique of Stalinism and her indictment of "real existing socialism" in Eastern Europe and the Soviet Union is even more scathing than that of Yugoslav social practice. Yet, it may suffer for the same reasons. In her controversial book on *Stalinism and Socialism* (1982), Golubović severs the link between Stalinism and socialism, considering the former a *counterrevolution*. She interprets Stalinism as a specific *class* society characterized by state property, class division between the ruling bureaucratic class and the rest of society, class conflicts disguised by the official ideology of the "leading role of the working class," a totalitarian political structure—absolute control of the state-party mechanism—politicization of all human and social relations, repression as an integral part of the system, and Stalinist ideology presented as the "vanguard of the working class" for purposes of legitimation. What Golubović sums up as a "bureaucratized political society," with a political bureaucracy, the fusion of economic and political power, and the absolutization of political institutions reads like the classic Western definition of Communist totalitarian dictatorships. Yet, Golubović insists that Stalinism differs qualitatively from the Marxist idea of socialism, since Stalinism is "an apology for nonfreedom, inequality, and alienation." Golubović explores new forms of alienation in "real existing socialism" in her paper by the same title presented at the Tenth World Congress of Sociology in Mexico City (1982). She concludes that alienation remains the constitutive element of Soviet-type societies and that a new form of *homo duplex* appears as "two persons in one," that is, a schizoid social character, since civil society is absorbed into political society.

Golubović sees an antidote to "real existing socialism" in her 1982 *Praxis International* article on the social movement in Poland, 1980–81: the novel phenomenon of a genuine mass movement combining the principle of the self-organization of society with that of the self-determination of individuals. What strikes her as particularly promising is Solidarity's quest not only for a deprofessionalization of politics but for the depoliticization of social life in general, signifying society's liberation from the state. Although Golubović, like other *Praxis* theorists, remains committed to Marx's utopian quest for the abolition of the state, power, and politics, instead of their division, limitation, and institutionalization, her insight that the socialist struggle for human emancipation cannot even begin without civil (bourgeois) liberties is for many Eastern Europeans a welcome reminder in a world of reified institutions and alienated humanity.

BIBLIOGRAPHY:

A. *Problemi savremene teorije ličnosti* (Belgrade: Kultura, 1966); "Socialist Ideas and Reality," *Praxis* (I), 7, nos. 3–4 (1971), pp. 399–421; *Čovek i njegov svet* (Belgrade: Prosveta, 1973); "Self-Fulfillment, Equality and Freedom," *Praxis* (I), 9, nos. 2–3 (1973), pp. 153–60; "Why Is Functionalism More Desirable in Present-Day Yugoslavia than Marxism?" *Praxis* (I), 9, no. 4 (1973), pp. 357–68; *Staljinizam i socijalizam* (Belgrade: Filozofsko društvo Srbije, 1982); excerpt from *Stalinism and Socialism* in translation: "Stalinism and Socialism," *Praxis International*, 1, no. 2 (July 1981), pp. 126–39; "Historical Lessons of the Social Movement in Poland 1980–1981," *Praxis International*, 2, no. 3 (October 1982), pp. 229–40.

B. Gerson S. Sher, *Praxis: Marxist Criticism and Dissent in Socialist Yugoslavia* (Bloomington: Indiana University Press, 1977); Oskar Gruenwald, *The Yugoslav Search for Man: Marxist Humanism in Contemporary Yugoslavia* (South Hadley, Mass.: Bergin & Garvey, 1983).

OSKAR GRUENWALD

PETROVIĆ, GAJO (b. 1927). Petrović was born on 3 December 1927 at Karlovac, Yugoslavia. From 1945 to 1950 he did undergraduate work at the universities of Leningrad, Moscow, and Zagreb, receiving his B.A. from Zagreb in March 1950. He was awarded his Ph.D. in philosophy in January 1956 and the *Dozent* in 1958 from Zagreb. He was an instructor at the University of Zagreb from 1950 to 1959, an assistant professor from 1959 to 1963, an associate professor from 1963 to 1969 and was promoted to full professor in 1969. Petrović continues in that position to the present day. He was also chair of the department for several years. During the late 1960s and early 1970s he was a major force behind the annual summer school dealing with social thought that was held on the island of Korčula. More recently he has been active in organizing short-term courses at the Inter-University Centre of Postgraduate Studies at Dubrovnik. From 1983 to 1985 he was a co–director of the Marxismus und Existenzphilosophie course held there each spring. Petrović has been a visiting professor at the universities of Siegen (1969) and Hamburg (1981) in Germany and at the University of Bergen (1980) in Norway. In the United States he has been a visiting professor at Wesleyan University (1972), the University of Michigan (1972), and the University of Missouri at Columbia (1978). He was a Ford Foundation scholar (1961–62), an Alexander von Humboldt-Stiftung scholar (1970–71), and a fellow in the Institute for Advanced Study, Princeton (1977). He is past president of the Croatian Philosophical Society (1963–64) and the Yugoslavian Association for Philosophy (1964–66). Since 1973 he has been a member of the International Philosophical Institute. His writings have been published in many languages, and two of his books received major Yugoslavian prizes. He was one of the principal editors of the internationally renowned Marxist† quarterly, *Praxis*,* until it was discontinued in the mid-1970s. Within Yugoslavia, Petrović's work often comes under strong attack by the orthodox Communist press, for both in his writings and teaching he continues to carry on in the praxis tradition of Marxism, and at the theoretical level he certainly remains Yugoslavia's most important philosopher.

Although Petrović's primary work has always been within the realm of Marxist philosophy, it is worth noting that besides his strong grounding in the history of philosophy he has been in personal contact with a number of Western Europe's leading thinkers. Early in his career he visited Bertrand Russell and studied briefly with A. J. Ayer. He also has shown interest in the work of Ernst Bloch* and on several occasions visited with Heidegger. All these contacts led to articles or books dealing with their various philosophies. Petrović's current major effort is a long study of Heidegger's work. Nonetheless, what he remains best known for are his joint development of praxis and his ontological approach to revolution. Praxis comes to fore through a careful examination of Marx's understanding of alienation. If as has been suggested the true communist society may never be attained, what remains most important is to examine alienation under its various aspects. In turning to Marx's early manuscripts Petrović finds at least four major forms of alienation and suggests that the concept of alienated labor constitutes the essence of Marx's concept of alienation. This is so because it is the essence of societal man inasmuch as labor is seen within praxis. Labor is to be viewed as free creative activity whether one exists in the Eastern or Western worlds. What then is called for is a humanization of social relations through a total humanist revolution.

In what may be his most insightful contribution Petrović develops a concept of revolution in order to realize further the implications of his praxis theory. It deals not so much with the political and immediate practical implications of revolutionary action as with a state of being. This revolution as an ontology of being is, of course, also concerned with the actual Marxist revolution but puts its emphasis on a manner of being toward and in the world. If the laws of mankind are immutable, as science at one time thought them to be, then there would be no place for Petrović's ontology of revolution. But just as the laws of science only reflect the real world of nature and as a result are changeable, so also are the laws of social relationships. Mankind is not a closed system with the end of history only something to be worked out from past experience. The wonder of mankind is that it is ambiguous. Ambiguous, not in the sense of never knowing what to expect next, but rather in the sense of having an open-ended future based on present happenings as well as past events.

Man, as creative, is man as revolutionary in his being. Such men can and will be able to evolve and, by direct participation, take true revolutionary action as a creative, free, and conscious being. Change becomes part, or rather is part, of the human condition, and with change there is creativity. The change here spoken of is not simply spontaneous change, which might lead one to a regressive mode of being, but change through creativity, which of necessity challenges the established order and the notion of a fixed world. Insofar as creativity is radical it is also revolutionary, and since creativity is part of the natural order of mankind, revolution also partakes of man's being. In this sense, to be human, or even to be on the way to being human, is to be in the mode of revolutionary being. When looking for an ontology one perforce needs to look toward an ontology of revolution, for to be human is to be toward the world in a revolutionary manner.

BIBLIOGRAPHY:

A. *Filozofija i marksizam* (Zagreb: Naprijed, 1965), translated as *Marx in the Mid-twentieth Century* (New York: Anchor Books, 1967); *Mogucnost čovjeka* (Zagreb: Studentski centar sveučilišta, 1969); *Philosophie und Revolution* (Hamburg: Rowohlt, 1971); *Čemu Praxis?* (Zagreb: Praxis, 1972); *Socialismo e filosofia* (Milan: Feltrinelli, 1976); *Misljenje revolucije* (Zagreb: Naprijed 1978); *Suvremena filozofija. Ogledi* (Zagreb: Naprijed, 1979).

B. Ludvik Vrtacic, *Der jugoslawische Marxismus* (Freiburg: Walter, 1975); Gerson Sher, *The Dialectic of Dissent* (Bloomington: Indiana University Press, 1978); Oskar Gruenwald, *The Yugoslav Search for Man* (South Hadley, Mass.: Bergin & Garvey, 1983).

JOSEPH BIEN

PLIUSHCH, LEONID IVANOVICH (b. 1939). Cyberneticist and Party member, the Ukrainian-born Pliushch began his dissident career by criticizing Soviet authorities for their anti-Semitic policies, particularly their refusal to put a monument to the Jewish victims of the Nazi massacre at Babi Yar near Kiev. Soviet leaders had lost their Marxist† humanist roots, and thus a dissident human rights movement became necessary to return the Soviet Union to its true course. The lack of human rights brought about by Stalinist† totalitarianism could only be reversed by citizen protest. Interned in a psychiatric hospital, he was later released and emigrated to the West in 1976.

BIBLIOGRAPHY:

A. *Psychiatric Abuse of Political Prisoners in the Soviet Union: Testimony of Leonid Pliushch* (Washington, D.C.: Subcommittee on International Organizations, Committee on International Relations, House of Representatives, 96–2, 30 March 1976); *History's Carnival: A Dissident's Autobiography* (New York: Harcourt Brace Jovanovich, 1977).

B. Tatiana Khodorovich, *Istoriia bolezni Leonida Pliushcha* (Amsterdam: Herzen Foundation, 1974).

DAVID KOWALEWSKI

POLLOCK, FRIEDRICH (1894–1970). Friedrich Pollock, born in 1894, began his intellectual career with a dissertation on Marx's† theory of money. He was a member of the Frankfurt School from its very beginning in 1924. Indeed, Pollock, along with Henry Grossman,† provided economic theorizing for the group throughout its existence. Whereas Grossman concentrated on the problems of the breakdown of capitalism and the structure of Marx's economic work, Pollock concentrated from the start on the issue of economic planning, both in the Soviet Union and in the capitalist countries. These studies on economic planning were the background for his analysis of national socialism in the 1930s and 1940s as representing a new type of planned capitalism. In the 1950s Pollock turned his attention to the issue of automation, particularly in the United States, where he lived during and after World War II. He died in 1970 in Switzerland.

Pollock's work, and its relation to the Frankfurt School can be interpreted in two ways. On the narrower reading, Pollock's book on the Soviet Union contributes to the study of how a planned economy was introduced into postrevolutionary Russia, and thus also helps answer the question of to what extent a planned economy is possible. In contrast, his early studies of capitalism concerned economic problems of unplanned economies. Having studied both planned and unplanned economies he was thus able better to understand the nature and what he perceived as an unanticipated resiliency of the new planned capitalist economies represented by Germany under national socialism and Italy under fascism. The broader reading of Pollock goes as follows. Pollock's examination of unplanned economies illustrates the Frankfurt School distinction, first made by Max Horkheimer,* between instrumental and noninstrumental reason, with actions occurring in an unplanned society being paradigmatic examples of actions based on instrumental—or what Herbert Marcuse* later called one-dimensional—reasoning. Next, the broader reading would argue that Pollock's sanguine views about the feasibility of planned capitalism surviving without major economic crises reinforced the Frankfurt School's understanding of capitalism. These views were strongly disputed by some in the Frankfurt group, including Franz Neumann,* who preferred to argue that fascism and national socialism were not as economically stable as Pollock foresaw. Third, the broader reading would stress the influence on Frankfurt thinkers of Pollock's sharp distinction between unplanned and planned capitalism: between a more positive, liberal version of capitalism with a laissez-faire state, and a more negative, nonliberal version that permits state control of the market. Neumann had used such a distinction to help clarify the evolution of legal theory and practice under capitalism; Horkheimer to discuss stages of instrumental reason; Theodore Adorno* to distinguish Fredian-oriented societies from narcissistic ones; and Jürgen Habermas* (in *Strukturwandel der Offentlichkeit*) to differentiate between two types of public spheres. Finally, the broader reading of Pollock would concentrate on the trajectory of his thought—flowing from his analysis of capitalism as an unplanned economy, through his analysis of the Soviet planned economy, to his analysis of national socialism and the New Deal as examples of planned capitalist economies—and see it as one justification of Horkheimer's theory of the authoritarian state and Marcuse's theory of one-dimensional society, both of which equate totalitarian planned economies in the West and the East.

BIBLIOGRAPHY:

A. *Die Planwirtschaftlichen Versuche in der Sowjetuniom 1917–1927* (Frankfurt: Neue Kritik, 1971); *Stadien des kapitalismus* (Munich: Beck, 1975); with Max Horkheimer et al., *Wirtschaft, Recht und Staat im Nationalsozialismus* (Frankfurt: Europaïsche Verlagsanstalt, 1981).

B. Giacomo Marramao, "Political Economy and Critical Theory," *Telos*, 24 (Summer 1975); Norman Fischer, "Ethics, Economics and the Transition to Socialism," in *Con-*

tinuity and Change in Marxism, ed. Norman Fischer (Atlantic Highlands, N.J.: Humanities Press, 1982); Moishe Postone and Barbara Brick, "Critical Pessimism and the Limits of Traditional Marxism," Theory and Society, 2 (Summer 1982).

NORMAN FISCHER

POULANTZAS, NICOS (1936–1979). Born in Greece in 1936, Nicos Poulantzas dedicated the major portion of his forty-three years pursuing both an innovative and adequate theory of the state and a more complete union between Marxist† theory and political practice. His unexpected death in October 1979 in Paris has been described as having "robbed Marxist theory and the socialist movement of one of its most distinguished comrades . . . a theoretician of exceptional and original stature . . . who commanded respect and affection, above all from the depth of his commitment to practical and theoretical struggle" (Hall, "Nicos Poulantzas"). Poulantzas came to study Marxism at a time when the basic works were banned in Greece, and thus his exposure to Marxist theory was through the French philosophers, particularly Jean-Paul Sartre.* At the same time, he became involved in politics through the Greek student movement, joining the popular front organization, the Greek Democratic Alliance, while pursuing his studies in the philosophy of law. His doctoral dissertation, which was published in 1964, attempted to construct a concept of the law using the work of George Lukács* and Lucien Goldmann* as a theoretical base. Finding these approaches too limiting, Poulantzas soon delved into Antonio Gramsci* and later moved to Paris. By this time Poulantzas had also joined the Greek Communist Party, retaining membership in the more democratically oriented Greek Communist Party of the Interior after the 1968 split. Arriving in Paris, Poulantzas became a core member of the scholarly group committed to exploring and elaborating Althusserian* structuralism. Within that group, Poulantzas took up the challenge of developing a structuralist theory of the state that could guide both scholarly explanation and progressive intervention.

It was here that Poulantzas made his distinctive contributions to Marxist theory as he attempted to integrate Gramsci's notion of hegemony and Althusserian structuralism to analyze not only the state in capitalism but also the state in transition to socialism. Poulantzas rejected the notion that the state was either a reflection of the relations of production or a simple instrument through which the capitalist class achieved its ends. Instead, Poulantzas argued that the state enjoyed a certain autonomy and pursued its own particular interests as well as the interests of capital. Further, Poulantzas examined how the state orchestrated the disparate interests of an internally competitive and highly fractionated bourgeoisie both to create cohesion and to serve the long-term interests of capital. Despite some functionalist tendencies, Poulantzas also argued for notions of struggle, indeterminacy, and change. He showed through theoretical reflection and historical example how the state was both embedded in contradiction and embodied contradictions. Indeed, the state was seen as a potential site for revolutionary intervention, given the ways in which its different constitutive entities and elements pursued varied, sometimes contradictory, interests. Such working-class intervention, however, required that the ideological role of the state in class struggle be thoroughly analyzed. Poulantzas embarked on this task principally through his examinations of the ways in which the capitalist state fostered its appearance as a neutral entity protecting public interest against particular interests and representing directly the majority of an undifferentiated citizenry. In the process of demystification, Poulantzas saw great hope for intervention at both the ideological and political levels, thereby intensifying the process of class struggle, although the outcome of such intervention was by no means a foregone conclusion.

BIBLIOGRAPHY:

A. *Political Power and Social Classes* (London: New Left Books, 1973); *Fascism and Dictatorship* (London: New Left Books, 1974); *Classes in Contemporary Capitalism* (London: New Left Books, 1975); *Crisis of Dictatorship* (London: New Left Books, 1976); *State, Power, Socialism* (London: New Left Books, 1978).

B. Ralph Miliband, "The Capitalist State: Reply to Nicos Poulantzas," *New Left Review*, 59 (January–February 1970), pp. 53–60; Ralph Miliband, "Poulantzas and the Capitalist State," *New Left Review*, 82 (November–December 1973), pp. 83–92; Stuart Hall and Alan Hunt, "Interview with Nicos Poulantzas," *Marxism Today*, 23, no. 7 (July 1979), pp. 194–201; Stuart Hall, "Nicos Poulantzas: State, Power, Socialism," *New Left Review*, 11, no. 9 (January–February 1980), pp. 60–69.

EILEEN R. MEEHAN

PRAGUE SPRING. The period known as Prague Spring refers to the year 1968 in Czechoslovakia and is associated with an attempt initiated by a group of Czechoslovak Communists to liberalize and democratize the existing, essentially Soviet-type system. It is also referred to as "socialism with a human face" and linked with the name of Alexander Dubček.† The intellectual origins of the Prague Spring can be traced back to the year 1956 and the first impetus toward an internal reform of the Communist governance pattern at the Twentieth Congress of the Soviet Communist Party. In Czechoslovakia a review of orthodox practices was openly demanded at the Writers Congress in 1956 and then, gradually, by a growing number of philosophers, historians, jurists, social scientists, economists, and student leaders. Some of them held or were to acquire posts in the Party apparatus, first on its fringes and later nearer the center of power.

Initially, the arguments of the emerging reform-inclined constituency related to abuses of the Stalinist† past and how they could and should be prevented from occurring again. When Czechoslovakia experienced a fall in its GNP in 1962 and 1963, the leadership of the day, under Antonín Novotný, was frightened enough to endorse a market-oriented economic reform plan. This was the highlight of the "repair" period of Czech reformism. However, in the course of designing an economic cure the idea inevitably surfaced of an alternative political system that would not only prevent the "excesses" characterizing undivided party power but rearrange this power in a novel way. This unique mixture of political and economic reform encouraged and stimulated Czech intellectuals.

At the same time a large number of Slovak intellectuals as well as the Slovak Communist organization felt acutely aggrieved by the continuing centralism of the Czech Communist Party leadership. The 1960 "socialist constitution" further diminished Slovak national rights. A redress was thought possible only within the framework of a broader reformist program. Although predominantly national rather than political and economic, Slovak discontent considerably strengthened the chances for a breakthrough against the orthodox power holders. The early 1960s also produced several events in Europe that generated Czech reformism, in particular Nikita Khrushchev's† second round of de-Stalinization and the emergence of reformist tendencies in several Eastern Bloc countries simultaneously, including the Soviet Union.

By 1967 these various strands desiring systemic change became conscious of each other and, despite the many differences, sufficiently gelled to challenge the Novotný leadership on the quintessential question of whether or not the Party itself required reforming. The reformers gained a majority in the Central Committee in December 1967 and January 1968, and the Prague Spring proper began with the election of Alexander Dubček as Novotný's successor in the post of first secretary of the Party. It soon became apparent that the reformers could count on overwhelming public support. The population, no doubt fired by the democratic traditions of Czechoslovakia, had not been browbeaten and coerced into unrevivable political lethargy by twenty years of centralized Communist rule. In fact, the readiness and eagerness of popular participation was often embarrassing to the less determined proponents of reforms in the higher echelons of the Party and the state. After all, the change-seeking constituency represented a variety of interests, and its many parts were prepared to go to varying lengths to secure reform. A joint action of in-party reformers and the public at large for political, economic, and national repairs meant treading a new path of which even sympathetic Party officials were wary.

Three kinds of tension marked the Prague Spring virtually from the start: between the various elements in the Communist camp; between the reluctant reformers and the non-Communist public; and between the reform-desiring forces in Czechoslovakia and the Soviet leaders. Most of the changes promoted in 1968 were thus the result of compromise, but their combined thrust went unmistakably in the direction of greater freedom for the citizen and a more flexible and benign relationship between rulers and ruled. Censorship was abolished and laws governing the freedom of speech, assembly, and organization were substantially relaxed. A market-based economic program with a considerable degree of decentralized decision making was implemented. Freedom of culture and the arts was promulgated. Horrors of the Stalinist system were openly pilloried, and guarantees were sought against their recurrence. A federative arrangement between the Czech and Slovak nations was formulated. The Party itself was being divested of many of its authoritative powers, and the right to advocate minority views in Party branches was postulated. Changes permitting political interest articulation and promotion were discussed by Party officials in order to secure some plurality of representation without actually allowing the emergence of new parties.

Although deliberately refraining from foreign political initiatives that could be seen as infringing on Soviet bloc unity, the Prague reformers nevertheless angered Leonid Brezhnev† and the Soviet leadership. Czech attempts to justify their reformist experiments with a nondogmatic Marxian† philosophy were unavailing. At bloc summit meetings in Dresden (March), Warsaw (July), and Bratislava (August), as well as in numerous bilateral encounters, Soviet leaders sought to interfere in Czechoslovakia's internal affairs on the presumption that the "defense of socialism" was a matter of concern to all bloc members. Large-scale and protracted Soviet military maneuvers were held on Czechoslovak territory from June to August. A joint meeting of the Czechoslovak and Soviet Party presidia was convened on the Soviet border at the end of July, but dissatisfied with the results and encouraged by divisions in the Czechoslovak leadership, Moscow concluded that the danger to Soviet strategic interests and to the survival of Soviet-type socialism in Eastern Europe was overwhelming. A Soviet military intervention was initiated on 21 August 1968.

When the first design to replace "revisionist" leaders with a "revolutionary worker-peasant government" was defeated by a united and peaceful coalition of civilian and political reformers, Moscow allowed the reinstatement of Alexander Dubček but retained full control over his activities. A treaty legalizing the "temporary" deployment of Soviet troops was enforced, and the reforms of 1968 were dismantled one by one. The reformists sought to limit and control the damage, but by April 1969 their rearguard action was interpreted by Soviet leaders as an impediment to "normalization" and an incident was soon engineered to justify the imposition of a more pliable ruling agency. The man chosen as Dubček's successor, Gustav Husák, has since presided over Czechoslovakia's return to orthodoxy. The most comprehensive attempt at reforming Soviet-style socialism from within had failed.

BIBLIOGRAPHY:

B. Robin A. Remington, ed., *Winter in Prague* (Cambridge: MIT Press, 1969); Vladimir V. Kusin, *The Intellectual Origins of the Prague Spring* (Cambridge: Cambridge University Press, 1971); Pavel Tigrid, *Why Dubček Fell* (London: Macdonald, 1971); Galia Golan, *Reform Rule in Czechoslovakia. The Dubček Era, 1968–1969* (Cambridge: Cambridge University Press, 1973); Zdeněk Hejzlar and Vladimir V. Kusin, *Czechoslovakia 1968–1969*: Chronology, Bibliography, *Annotation* (New York: Garland, 1975); Zdeněk Hejzlar, *Reformkommunismus* (Cologne: Europäische Verlagsanstalt, 1976); H. Gordon Skilling, *Czechoslovakia's Interrupted Revolution* (Princeton: Princeton University Press, 1976); Zdeněk Mlynář, *Nightfrost in Prague* (New York: Karz, 1980); Josef Sládeček, *Osmašedesátý* (Cologne: Index, 1980).

VLADIMIR V. KUSIN

PRAXIS (1963–1975). The *Praxis* school of Marxist† humanist thought in Yugoslavia achieved international recognition for its creative, nondogmatic, open-ended, humanistic reconceptualization of Marxist-Leninist theory and critique of socialist practice. While the 1960 Bled Symposium rejected the Engels†–Lenin† theory of reflection and the concomitant dogmatic conception of dialectical materialism as antithetical to creative Marxism, it was the Korčula Summer School (1963–74) and the Yugoslav (1964–74) and international (1965–74) editions of *Praxis* that became the primary forums for the development of this new school. Among the most frequent Yugoslav contributors to *Praxis* were: Branko Bošnjak, Mihajlo Djurić, Danko Grlić,* Milan Kangrga,* Veljko Korać,* Andrija Krešić, Ivan Kuvačić, Mihailo Marković,* Zagorka Pešić-Golubović,* Gajo Petrović,* Svetozar Stojanović,* Rudi Supek,* Ljubomir Tadić,* Predrag Vranicki,* and Miladin Životić. There were also less frequent, yet important, contributions to *Praxis* by Dobrica Ćosić, Branko Horvat, Božidar Jakšić, Vojin Milić,* Veljko Rus, Josip Županov,* and many others. *Praxis* theorists became anathema to the late Tito* by 1968, when they were accused of corrupting youth and encouraging student demonstrations. Following the ill-fated Croatian national renaissance in 1971 and the crackdown on both national and liberal intellectuals and Party leaders, *Praxis* theorists found themselves increasingly isolated and harassed. Eight *Praxis* theorists—Pešić-Golubović, Trivo Indjić (who later recanted and left the ''Belgrade Eight''), Marković, Dragoljub Mićunović, Nebojša Popov, Stojanović, Tadić, and Životić—were suspended from teaching in 1975 and dismissed from the University of Belgrade by the end of 1980. But the regime's campaign against independent Marxist thinkers was much broader and affected at least thirty scholars, resulting in blacklists encompassing radio, television, public appearances, and publishing in general. In 1975, *Praxis* and *Filozofija*, two leading journals for neo-Marxist thought, were forced to close. The 1975 and 1976 Korčula Summer Schools with the theme ''Socialism and Human Rights'' were banned, as was the 1975 meeting of the Yugoslav Sociological Association. Following vigorous protest by the international academic community, the ''Belgrade Seven'' were reinstated in a new Center for Philosophy and Social Theory at Belgrade University's Institute of Social Sciences in July 1981. Marković and Richard J. Bernstein began editing *Praxis International* (Oxford), while Pešić-Golubović, Rus, Stojanović, Supek, and Tadić joined its editorial board. The output of *Praxis* theorists in terms of books, journal articles, and symposia has been prodigious, although relatively little has been translated thus far. The existential future of this school of thought and its individual theorists remains in limbo.

The theoretical contributions of the *Praxis* school to Marxism lie primarily in philosophical anthropology, political sociology, epistemology, and ethics. Drawing on the writings of the young Marx and the Western intellectual heritage, *Praxis* theorists advanced one of the most far-reaching theoretical critiques of Stalinism† as ''state capitalism'' (later modified to ''state socialism''). Their critique of Stalinism and dogmatic Marxism focused on the conception of the state as the instrument of change in society from capitalism to socialism. Stalinism was a system designed to utilize the state as a ''dictatorship of the proletariat'' in order to abolish private property, collectivize agriculture, and eradicate the remnants of "bourgeois" mentality, class relationships, exploitation, and conflict in society. In practice, the Yugoslavs point out, the Stalinist version of Marxism resulted in a counterrevolution, that is, in the domination of totalitarian forms of state machinery and bureaucracy *over* the proletariat. Although private property was abolished as the primary exploitative agency in society, its role was assumed by state ownership and control of nationalized property. This, in effect, meant control by a huge Party and state bureaucracy. Clearly, there was no room in such a system for either creative Marxist thought or the simultaneous liberation of the individual and society.

Dogmatic Marxism and Stalinism eschewed Marx's concept of alienation and the dynamic conception of man as an active agent in history—a being of praxis, a free, creative, and self-creative being. The idea of praxis—of man's potential to transform both himself and the world—thus became the distinguishing hallmark and the fundamental conceptual framework of the *Praxis* school of thought. This radicalization of Marxist thought shifts the balance of Marx's economic and historical determinism from the determinist toward the voluntarist or action-oriented end of the scale. *Praxis* theorists emphasize that although consciousness is determined by life and men are prisoners of their circumstances, men can also change these circumstances. Influenced by existentialism and personalism, *Praxis* theorists developed a perspective that centers on the liberation and all-round development of the human individual. This amounts to a Copernican revolution in Marxism. Combining elements of socialist personalism with existentialism and a noneschatological vision of communism as a continuous, open-ended process, *Praxis* theorists came close to formulating a Yugoslav Marxism-existentialism. Unlike orthodox Marxists, *Praxis* theorists elaborated a vision of the classless society that is not devoid of all conflict and in which individuals may continue to be alienated. Hence the Western impression of Petrović's Heideggerian Marxism. The Yugoslav conception of man as a being of praxis—a being of freedom—led spontaneously to the question of responsibility and ethics. Yet, on this epochal issue, as on many others, *Praxis* thinking diverges. Thus, Kangrga argues for Marx's "permanent revolution" understood as the continuous revolutionizing of underlying social conditions that give rise to the question of ethics. Stojanović and Supek, on the other hand, erect new ethical rules to govern the relationship between the individual revolutionary and the revolutionary movement and its avant-garde, the Party. In contrast to Marx's, Engels's, and, especially Lenin's moral-ethical relativism, Yugoslav theorists posit the need for a socialist "ethical imperative" as an essential constitutive element of man as a free being. Inspired by Marx's concept of a "free association of producers," conceived as a de-alienated community (*Gemeinschaft*) of liberated personalities, *Praxis* theorists engendered a radicalization of the Yugoslav theoretical innovation in self-management. Holding up a theoretical mirror to everyday practice, they offered one of the most trenchant critiques of the shortfalls of actual self-management practice, which they saw impaired by the triumvirate of Party organs and bureaucracy in the political sphere, hierarchical power structures in the sphere of industrial relations, and anarchy, selfishness, and embourgeoisement nurtured by ''market socialism'' in the economic sphere.

Although the *Praxis* school of thought has contributed to a greater understanding of the mutual interrelationship of the individual and society, it has failed to deal with the question of power, preferring to follow Marx's quest for the abolition of power, instead of its institutionalization, division, and limitation. Second, although *Praxis* theorists have begun to connect Stalinism with Lenin's organizational dilemmas, they still insist on separating Stalin from Lenin, and Lenin from Marx and Engels. Thus, Pešić-Golubović in her controversial 1982 *Sociologija* article expresses the *Praxis* consensus on the need for socialism to integrate bourgeois freedoms and basic human rights and takes issue with the ''metaphysical'' conception of the Party as the infallible representative of ''historical truth.'' Yet Marx and Engels clearly rejected any and all ''bourgeois'' notions of rights, freedoms, and morality as so much hypocrisy and ''false consciousness,'' bolstering exploitation and alienation in class society. In spite of Tadić's insight that ''from absolute knowledge to absolute power is but one step,'' *Praxis* theorists have yet to discover the Stalinist epistemological roots of Party monopoly in Marx's and Engels's claim in the *Communist Manifesto* that Communists see further and understand better the nature and goals of the revolutionary workers' movement. Third, *Praxis* theorists urge the democratization of the Party—most recently at the 1983 meeting of the Yugoslav Sociological Association in Portorož—and blame the monopoly of social, economic, and political power on bureaucracy and the Stalinized conception of the Party, as if the Communist Party could consider itself Bolshevik yet act as a Menshevik, that is, a social democratic, party. What is unusual is that Stojanović's call at the 1983 meeting for the democratization of the Yugoslav League of Communists expresses a consensus among both the Yugoslav intelligentsia (including *Praxis* theorists) *and* liberal Party members themselves.

The greatest contribution of the *Praxis* school to neo-Marxism as well as to the liberalization, democratization, and humanization of Yugoslavia's sociopolitical system has been its insistence upon freedom of inquiry and communications, critical thought, and an open society. Marx's ''ruthless critique of everything existing'' was applied consistently not only to capitalism, but state socialism (Stalinism) and self-management socialism as well. This critical methodology opened up many new fields of inquiry, but it also raised doubts concerning the adequacy of Marxist analytical tools for conceptualizing twentieth-century phenomena in capitalism or socialism. The final chapter on this school of thought remains to be written. But there is little doubt that the full significance of the *Praxis* school of thought may be understood only within a larger framework exploring the transcendence (*Aufhebung*) of the orthodox Marxist *Weltanschauung*.

BIBLIOGRAPHY:

A. Branko Bošnjak, and Rudi Supek (eds.), *Humanizam i socijalizam*, 2 vols: (Zagreb: Naprijed, 1963); Gajo Petrović, *Marx in the Mid-Twentieth Century* (Garden City, N.Y.: Doubleday, 1967); Rudi Supek, and Branko Bošnjak (eds.), *Jugoslawien denkt anders*

(Vienna: Europa, 1971); Rudi Supek (ed.), *Etatisme et autogestion* (Paris: Anthropos, 1973); Svetozar Stojanović, *Between Ideals and Reality* (New York: Oxford University Press, 1973); Mihailo Marković, *From Affluence to Praxis* (Ann Arbor: University of Michigan Press, 1974); Rudi Supek, "Dix ans de l'Ecole d'Eté de Korčula (1963–1973)," *Praxis* (I), 10, nos. 1–2 (1974), pp. 3–15; Branko Horvat, Mihailo Marković, and Rudi Supek (eds.), *Self-Governing Socialism*, 2 vols. (White Plains, N.Y.: International Arts & Sciences Press, 1975); Gerson S. Sher, ed., *Marxist Humanism and Praxis* (Buffalo, N.Y.: Prometheus Books, 1978); Svetozar Stojanović, *Geschichte und Parteibewusstsein* (Munich: Carl Hanser, 1978) (English trans., *History and Party Consciousness*, Buffalo, N.Y.: Prometheus Books, 1981); Mihailo Marković, and Gajo Petrović (eds.), *Praxis* (Dordrecht: Reidel, 1979); Mihailo Marković, *Democratic Socialism* (New York: St. Martin's Press, 1982); Zagorka Pešić-Golubović, "Kriza jugoslovenskog društva: Priroda krize i njeni koreni," *Sociologija*, 24, nos. 2–3 (1982), pp. 323–31; Nebojša Popov, *Društveni sukobi: Izazov sociologiji* (Belgrade: Center for Philosophy and Social Theory, 1983) (banned).

B. Ludvik Vrtačić, *Der jugoslawische Marxismus: Die jugoslawische Philosophie und der eigene Weg zum Sozialismus* (Frieburg im Breslau: Walter, 1975); Gerson S. Sher, *Praxis: Marxist Criticism and Dissent in Socialist Yugoslavia* (Bloomington: Indiana University Press, 1977); David A. Crocker, *Praxis and Democratic Socialism: The Critical Social Theory of Marković and Stojanović* (Atlantic Highlands, N.J.: Humanities Press, 1983); Oskar Gruenwald, *The Yugoslav Search for Man: Marxist Humanism in Contemporary Yugoslavia* (South Hadley, Mass.: Bergin & Garvey, 1983).

OSKAR GRUENWALD

R

REICH, WILHELM (1897–1957). Born in Austrian Galicia in 1897, Reich moved to Vienna after World War I to study medicine and in 1920, while still a student, became a practicing psychoanalyst. By 1924 Reich had become director of the Viennese Psychoanalytic Society's seminar in psychoanalytic technique. Reich's work in the free psychoanalytic clinic of Vienna (1922–30) convinced him that Freudianism ignored relevant social factors (e.g. poverty, ignorance, inadequate housing and nourishment) that channeled innate human instincts into abnormal behavior. This awareness of social conditioning prompted Reich to join, in 1927, the Marxist† Austrian Social Democratic Party. Most of Reich's Marxist writings were produced during the years 1927–36. Chief among them are "Dialectical Materialism and Psychoanalysis" (1929), *Sexual Maturity, Abstinence and Conjugal Morality* (1930), *The Imposition of Sexual Morality* (1932), *The Sexual Struggle of Youth* (1932), *The Mass Psychology of Fascism* (1933), *What Is Class Consciousness?* (1934), and *The Sexual Revolution* (1936). In 1929 Reich organized the Socialist Society for Sexual Advice and Sexual Research, which proffered psychoanalytic help to Vienna's poor while simultaneously mobilizing them for radical political activities. In 1930 Reich moved to Berlin and immediately joined the German Communist Party (KPD), becoming its chief spokesman and lecturer on sexual questions. By 1932 the KPD decided that Reich's linking of sexual and political revolution was unacceptable. Party organs were prohibited from distributing his books, and in February of 1933 Reich was formally expelled. In 1934 the conservative International Psychoanalytic Association also expelled Reich, apparently—like the KPD—fearing the potential impact of Reich's synthesis of sexual and political emancipation. Reich then traveled in Denmark, Sweden, and Norway, publishing articles in a journal he edited from 1934 to 1938 called *Zeitschrift für politische Psychologie und Sexualökonomie*. After 1935 Reich gradually turned from politics to biology, encouraged by his belief that he had discovered the physical source of sexual energy. He eventually abandoned his radical political beliefs altogether. In 1939 Reich emigrated to the United States, where for almost twenty years he lectured, wrote, organized institutes promulgating his practical advice for total sexual freedom, and repeatedly ran afoul of public authorities. Reich died in 1957 in Lewisburg federal penitentiary, after being convicted on charges brought by the U.S. Food and Drug Administration regarding his use of dangerous substances and advocacy of "immoral" practices. The FDA also impounded or burned as many of Reich's books and articles as they could find.

A student and admirer of Sigmund Freud, Reich also perceived a basic, precognitive impulse in human beings generating the physical release of inherent sexual energy. Other aspects of the psyche—unconscious or conscious—are derived from this quantifiable sexual energy and the dynamics of sexual instincts constantly pressing for discharge. Freud argued that sexual repression was inherent to civilization and potentially healthy if properly channeled into alternative means of symbolic expression. Reich contended, to the contrary, that blocked sexual energy led inevitably to neuroses. When sexual blockage is eliminated, inner psychological conflicts dissolve. This is not a matter of just engaging in genital orgasm but also requires a more general emancipation of psychic and physical forces.

Reich's Freudian preconceptions and his intellectual and political commitment to Marxism were reconciled in the dialectical connection between psychic impulses and concrete social forms. He claimed that the sex drive is one of several material human needs that Marx implicitly recognized—analogous to hunger, thirst, and labor. Just as humans must eat, drink, and actively produce, so too must they discharge sexual energy. For most people, especially Westerners, living socially means, in effect, that we are at least minimally fed and quenched and are producing needed goods. Sexual impulse is apparently not directly related to physical survival. Indeed, there are subcultures that reward abstinence, and members will survive as long as nonsexual needs are satiated. But this fact obscures the pervasive influence that sexual instincts have on the quality of experienced life. By blocking release of physical energies, we emasculate psyches, producing environments that feed mental disorder and encourage perverted, nonhuman life styles. Since the advent of patriarchal society, these unnatural inhibitions are precisely what humankind has been engaging in, building elaborate institutions designed, subliminally at least, to control active sexuality. Economic and social institutions, in other words, mediate sexual instincts and humanity's nearly universal fear of uninhibited sex. Marx's analysis of the dialectical interpenetration of base and superstructure is entirely consistent with Reich's self-styled Freudianism. Concrete social and economic factors affect and express the manner in which sexual instincts are dealt with. In capitalism, as Marx has shown, the dominant economic class exploits workers by expropriating surplus value. Culture reinforces this relationship, obfuscating material reality with a barrage of bourgeois rhetoric. Sexual attitudes are part of this rhetoric and therefore a tool for maintaining capitalism. However, sexual energy is also inherent to all humanity, irrespective of historically conditioned social forms. Capitalism is merely the current social means for coming to terms with this vital force. Like prior forms of patriarchal society, it is motivated by fear and ignorance. Capitalist production, which Marx analyzed so precisely, aids in repressing sexual energy. While capitalists exploit workers and create potentially self-destructive revolutionary conditions, they also formulate ideas and institutions that perpetuate an age-old bias against unfettered human sexual discharge. Socialism, a mode of production encouraging free, uninhibited self-expression for everyone, is, for Reich, a necessary material precondition for sexual emancipation. In postrevolutionary socialist equality there is no longer an elite to profit from sexual repression. Economic and political democracy are dialectically expressed in liberated attitudes toward all human relationships. Capitalism is inadvertently pushing us toward socialist justice and sexual liberation.

The dialectical interpenetration of sexuality and economics is central to Reich's Marxism and is originally based on the priority of materialism—transforming psychoanalysis into a branch of orthodox dialectical materialism. The human psyche evolves dialectically, mimicking nature. Hence psychic evolution depends on economic and social conditions, which impersonally channel instincts into predetermined avenues. Sexual practices are "in the last resort" economically conditioned. Freud's "superego" (our impulse to be "good"; ethics and morality) is a social product, the determined consequence of matter influencing instincts. Later, recognizing the obvious incongruity between orthodox Marxism and psychoanalysis, Reich became idealist, joining other Marxists who were uncomfortable with the Engels† tradition. The libido's historical development, although entwined with matter, now autonomously conditioned human "working capacity," that is, the quality and forms of labor in history. Psychoanalytical social inquiry is useful independent of dialectical materialism. Clearly, the "essence" of humanity was perceived as an ahistorical ideal in which sexual energy is uninhibitedly discharged. The dialectical interpenetration of economics and sexual instincts takes place under the aegis of an a priori ideal only partially manifest in concrete matter. Instincts and social conditions are mediated by what Reich calls "character structures": naively, internalized rules depicting "normal" behavior in "typical" everyday conditions. We generate character structures by lifelong formal and informal processes of education, socialization, and peer pressure. Personal identity, "the specific way of being an individual," is defined by character structure. Gestated in infancy to protect against external punishment (for example, from parents, teachers, clergy), character structure protects adults from internal antisocial impulses. Throughout life we hide in "normal," "expected" behavior to avoid social and psychic dislocations. The actual quality of character structures depends on the particular class we belong to and on membership in class society. Personalities, in other words, are both class-determined and class society-determined. We become, for example, "typical" workers, with emotional, intellectual, and physical traits admired in working-class neighborhoods and factories. In class society generally, the hegemonic ruling class uses an ideology that, intergenerationally, perpetuates character structures that reinforce the existing social order. Capitalist ideology emphasizes qualities like individualism, self-interest, competition, patriotism, religion, and family—epitomized by the "typical" bourgeois entrepreneurial personality: a disciplined, hard-working, family-oriented businessman guided by eternal spiritual and market principles. The "typical" worker in capitalism aggressively competes with peers in non-work-related activities, identifies with successful professional sports and entertainment personalities, provides for his family even at the cost of uninspiring, tedious workdays, and loves God and country. Both character structures—employer and employee—reinforce and perpetuate capitalism and bourgeois culture.

Character structures, Reich believed, perform the important functions of producing "good" citizens and reinforcing class rule. Their prime purpose, however, is to repress humanity's inherent sexual instincts by absorbing a portion of libidinal energy and legitimizing the acquisition of private property. Humanity long ago recognized that accumulating property is inconsistent with free and natural sexual discharge. Men needed wives and children to survive physically as well as to protect and exploit land. Permanent and stable family units, however, could not survive in an atmosphere of uninhibited sexuality. Thus, the origins of sexual repression are in the birth of patriarchal social arrangements. These generated unique character structures, which drove men and women into permanent monogamous family units and rewarded husbands with a dowry of land and/or other resources needed to accumulate fortunes. Henceforth, character structures worked to reinforce property rights by blocking sexual fulfillment with rules and prohibitions that "normal" people unquestioningly accept. In capitalism, they embody the bourgeois rejection of profligacy and admiration of self-sacrifice, discipline, marriage, and family. These modern character structures inhibit full sexual orgasm and promote social attitudes that explicitly reject unfettered sexuality but implicitly encourage sex-oriented institutions based on fantasies and repressed libidinal drives. The unhealthy confluence of libidinal energy and bourgeois asceticism generates a dull, uncreative, uncritical, passive, irrational mass population—precisely the qualities that a society geared toward commodity rather than use value requires. It is certainly not coincidental that capitalism degenerates to fascism, populated by frustrated, fearful, guilt-ridden, and anxious citizens. In sum, the social (that is, to reinforce capitalism) and psychic (that is, to repress inherent sexual energy) functions of contemporary character structures overlap. Reich's theory explains the origin and survival of capitalist alienation, "bridging the gap" between actual working-class inauthenticity and exploitative material conditions. Psychoanalysis transforms character structure to reflect the actual essence or truth of being. Since capitalism needs sexual repression to support institutions of patriarchy and monogamy, as well as its sub- and superstructures, psychoanalysis is, by definition, revolutionary. Liberated sexuality survives only if private property is abolished, eliminating the need for sexual repression. Humanity's need for sexual fulfillment is met only in societies committed to satiating all human needs, that is, socialism. Hence the Freudian, nonmaterialist Reich fervidly believed in proletariat revolution, although indicting orthodox revolutionaries as insensitive, inflexible materialists. Respect workers, he pleaded, understand the psychological as well as material sources of capitalism, and create a revolutionary class by encouraging workers to cognize essential being and capitalist repression.

Reich's contribution to Marxist theory was an analysis of the sexual aspects of capitalist alienation. Capitalism isolates humanity from natural sexual proclivities, even as it enriches the few. Its social conditions, institutions, and values are disguised in self-righteous rhetoric, demanding "discipline," "character," "self-control," "duty," "perseverance," while materially and sexually repressing its victims. The market's reification of workers resembles capitalism's objectification of sex, which is unnaturally depersonalized and mystified by superstition and fear and sold like any other commodity. Capitalism sexually objectifies men and women, perversely generating widespread prostitution as well as the simple-minded chauvinism of one sex toward the other. Capitalism has denatured a physical process inherent to all living animals, the ultimate source of life itself.

Reich's eventual disenchantment with Marxism, however, was the result of a nondialectical idealism that presumed that sex alone defines humanity. There are two necessary corollaries: terminating sexual repression generates authentic freedom; and social justice necessarily manifests complete sexual liberation. The latter was disproved by the unanticipated Stalinist† turn of Russia's socialist revolution, prompting Reich to abandon social theory altogether. The former is now dissolving in contemporary Western society, where a liberated attitude toward genital sex blatantly serves the ends of capitalist oppression and alienation. Orthodox Freudians argue that this submissive attitude is the source of encroaching social disintegration and anarchy. Reich's mistake, Marxists and Freudians agree, is equating historical progress and sexual indulgence.

BIBLIOGRAPHY:

A. *Mass Psychology of Fascism* (New York: Orgone Institute Press, 1946); *People in Trouble* (Rangely, Me: Wilhelm Reich Foundation, 1953); *The Function of the Orgasm* (New York: Farrar, Strauss, & Giroux, 1961); *Reich on Freud*, ed. M. Higgins and C. Raphael, (New York: Farrar, Strauss, & Giroux, 1967); *Character Analysis* (New York: Farrar, Strauss, & Giroux, 1970); *Sex-Pol, Essays, 1929–34*, ed. Lee Baxandall (New York: Vintage Books, 1972).

B. Bertell Ollman, "Introduction," in Lee Baxandall, ed., *Sex-Pol, Essays, 1929–34* (New York: Vintage Books, 1972).

ROBERT A. GORMAN

RIVKIN, B. (1883–1945). Born in Latvia and immigrated to the United States in 1911, Rivkin (born Baruch-Abraham Weinrebe) is the outstanding pioneer of what may be called a post-Marxist literary analysis within the left. Prolific contributor to the Yiddish press, Rivkin brought together anarchist, labor Zionist, and mystical concepts for a new theory of Jewish cultural reality.

Rivkin's great interpretive breakthrough is expressed most precisely in *Di Grunt Tendentsin fun Yiddishe Literatur*, where he argues that for Jews (before the establishment of Israel) the Yiddish language and the culture of *Yiddishkayt* provided a mental homeland in the diaspora. The great Yiddish authors, from the "sweatshop poets" to the modernist literary craftsmen, thus reflect a quasi-religious sense of alienation within the *galut*. Their radicalism, socialism, anarchism, or communism has flowed through such traditional Jewish impulses. This "Mosaic criticism," as fellow critic Shmuel Niger called it, had a parallel influence upon Yiddish scholarship to that of Ernst Bloch* upon German Marxists†: discussion of religious and nonrational influences generally helped break the hold of mechanical (or materialist-reductionist) Marxism and open up the field to fresh interpretations. And like Bloch, Rivkin fashioned something of a "philosophy of hope" in the face of despair. Because the folkish and artistic character of Yiddish literature gave Rivkin's views a unique prestige across the Yiddish-speaking radical world, Rivkin's literary critique served also as social commentary in the broadest sense. Rivkin perhaps decisively changed the way Yiddish literature and the roots of twentieth-century Jewish radicalism could be understood.

BIBLIOGRAPHY:

A. *A Gleub far Umgleybike*, ed. Aba Gordin (New York: Dud Ignatof Literatur Fond, 1947); *Grunt Tendentsin fun der Yiddishe Literatur in Amerike* (New York: Yiddishe Kultur Farband, 1948); *Undzer Proseyiker* (New York: Yiddishe Kulter Farband, 1951); *Yiddishe Yom-Toyvim* (New York: Farlag Moishe Shmuel Shklarski, 1951); *Lebn un Shafn* (Chicago: Farlag L. Shteyn, 1953).

PAUL BUHLE

RODANO, FRANCO (1920–1983). Born in Rome in 1920, Rodano was long associated with the attempt to synthesize Marxist† tenets with the ideals and principles of Catholicism. In 1943 he founded the Movement of Catholic Communists and was its leader until its dissolution in 1945; from 1946 he was a member of the Italian Communist Party (PCI) and served in varying capacities as a Party intellectual. In 1962 he founded with Claudio Napoleoni* the *Rivista trimestrale*, which played an important role in laying the theoretical groundwork of the PCI's reformist strategy. Rodano died in 1983.

Rodano's writings focused on the problem of how to achieve a socialist revolution within the framework of parliamentary democracy. The PCI was to develop a strategy designed to introduce gradually "elements of communism" into Italian society. Such a strategy presupposed an interclass national consensus to be cemented through an alliance with the Christian Democratic Party. The latter was viewed as the bearer of Catholic values, which, when integrated with the PCI, would make the proletariat's hegemony "fully organic and democratic." Although Rodano was the theoretical force behind the "historic compromise" with the Christian Democrats, he continued to insist on the Party's link to the Soviet Union, which furnished the worker movement with an "indispensable idealist impetus." His attachment to these two positions meant that Rodano was increasingly isolated within the PCI after the Party's rejection in 1980 of the "politics of national solidarity" and its near-total break with Moscow.

BIBLIOGRAPHY:

A. *Sulla politica dei communisti* (Turin: Boringhieri, 1975); *Questione democristiana e compromesso storico* (Rome: Riuniti, 1977).

LAWRENCE GARNER

ROWBOTHAM, SHEILA (b. 1943). Born in 1943 in Leeds, England, Rowbotham was educated at a Methodist school in Yorkshire and received her B.A. from St. Hilda's College, Oxford University. An active socialist and feminist, she has taught in technical and further education colleges, most recently at the Worker's Educational Association in London. In the late 1960s she belonged to the Young Socialists in Hackney Labour Party, and was briefly a member of the International Socialism Group (now Socialist Workers Party). There she engaged in grass-roots working-class politics and was exposed to Trotskyist† political discussion. In the early 1970s Rowbotham was attracted to libertarian Marxism,† absorbing ideas from the French Situationists,* the Italian far left, and anarchism. She was a staff writer in 1968–69 for *Black Dwarf*, a socialist paper, and a writer for *Red Day* in 1972–73, a socialist feminist paper. She has been actively involved in the women's movement in England since its origins in the 1960s. Currently she serves as an editor of the journals *History Workshop*, *Radical America*, and *Radical History Review*.

An important voice of the contemporary women's liberation movement, Sheila Rowbotham has charted the historical connections between male movements, social ideology, personal and family life, and the position of women. She has inspired a critical revival within feminist circles of Marxist perspectives, devoting her own research to the recovery of an independent socialist feminist tradition outside the main contours of Marxism-Leninism. Rowbotham's first publications (*Women, Resistance and Revolution*, 1972, and *Hidden from History*, 1974) synthesized a comparative historical view of women's liberation and radical protest. In their impressive scope—from the roots of feminism in seventeenth- and eighteenth-century revolution through the nineteenth-century and twentieth-century revolutions in Russia, China, Cuba, Algeria, and Vietnam—they established the terrain for more detailed historical investigations. In these writings, Rowbotham considered the impact of capitalist industrialization on changing patterns of personal and family life. In *Woman's Consciousness, Man's World* (1978), a theoretical supplement to her first historical studies, she introduced a modified Marxist vocabulary, e.g., the "social relations of reproduction," in order to account for the specificity of women's oppression under capitalism and the role of the family as a site of women's work and an arena of human reproduction. Pursuing the insights of nineteenth-century Marxists, Rowbotham emphasized that family life and sexuality are structured by the capitalist world of work and consumption. But unlike orthodox Marxists, she addressed the implications of "organizing around a sense of oppression rather than simply around the means of production" (*Woman's Consciousness, Man's World*, pp. 24–25).

Similarly, Rowbotham urged readers to reconsider the easy assumption of continuous progress within socialist thought: "At particular moments with the development of capitalism the possibility of transforming different forms of relationships appears more clearly than others" ("Women and Radical Politics," p. 158). We are reminded of lost figures from a socialist feminist past such as Edward Carpenter or Stella Browne (*Socialism and the New Life*; *A New World for Women*) and asked to reevaluate the contributions of pre-Marxist utopian socialist movements of the 1840s and 1850s in Britain, the pre-Leninist politics of the Independent Labor Party, or anarcho-syndicalism in Spain (*Beyond the Fragments*; "The Women's Movement and Organizing for Socialism"). Whereas Rowbotham has increasingly called into question Leninist approaches, she also notes the failures of older movements. There are no "answers" latent in history: "Socialist ideas can be pre-Leninist or anti-Leninist. But there is no clear post-Leninist revolutionary tradition yet" ("The Women's Movement and Organizing for Socialism," p. 27). The latter, she believes, may be achieved through the socialist appropriation of the antihierarchical, experiential, and personal forms of recent feminist organizing.

Thus, while recovering older traditions within Marxism and feminism, she has not sought to erect a frozen standard against which to judge contemporary actions. She reverses the formula, using the insights of feminist consciousness in the present to introduce a penetrating examination of the commonplaces of Marxist theories of the revolutionary subject, the working class, definitions of politics focused solely on the work place and the state, theories of organization, most especially democratic centralism, and methods of writing working-class history. Rowbotham addresses feminist questions to the socialist left, but always as an insider. She is benefited by the fact that in Britain today there is a considerable overlap between the socialist and feminist movements. She speaks not as a loyal defender of past theory but with the insight of one touched by the "new" politics of the 1960s, not only feminism but student protest, black politics, and cultural revolt. As a publicist and as a socialist feminist historian, Rowbotham aims to inform the ways in which socialists and feminists today create a new political consciousness. This problematic promises a liberation that encompasses the personal and sexual as well as the economic and political spheres. As she wrote in *Woman's Consciousness, Man's World*: "Sisterhood demands a new woman, a new culture, and a new way of living. The intimate oppression of women forces a redefinition of what is personal and what is political" (p. xi). Socialist feminism is, as well, a vision of the unification—but not the cancellation and subordination—of independently formed political interests. It promises a space for the "politics of oppression"—the source of 1960s protest and the women's movement—not only for the "politics of exploitation," wherein the situation of the working class under capitalism is said to encompass the oppression of all other groups.

Rowbotham has contributed to our historical understanding of the past, but her history is not of the academic variety. Rather, it is a product of the popular tradition of British working-class history. She resists what she regards to be academic imperatives whether in new historiographical techniques or in the importation of French structuralist perspectives in Marxist social theory. Beginning with *Woman's Consciousness, Man's World* and most recently in *Beyond the Fragments*, Rowbotham has presented her own life story as a way of exemplifying the interplay of personal and political consciousness to which women's liberation is committed. As a radical publicist, then, she impresses her personal conclusions on her readers. Most urgently,

> how I think some of the approaches to organizing which go under the headings of Leninism and Trotskyism are flawed; how I think the assumptions of what it means to be a socialist carried within Leninism and Trotskyism and which prevail on the left now block our energy and self-activity and make it harder for socialism to communicate to most people; why I think the women's movement suggests certain ways of reopening the possibility of a strong and popular socialist movement. (*Beyond the Fragments*, p. 49)

Rather than continuing as a subordinate partner to socialism, Rowbotham proposes a reversal of the relationship between feminism and socialism; not in order to engender a new but different hierarchy but to create a truly revolutionary politics of human community, embracing the authentic equality of all individuals and groups.

BIBLIOGRAPHY:

A. *Women's Liberation and the New Politics* (Nottingham: Spokesman, 1971); *Women, Resistance and Revolution: A History of Women and Revolution in the Modern World* (London: Allen Lane; New York: Pantheon Books, 1972); *Woman's Consciousness, Man's World* (Middlesex: Penguin Books, 1973); *Hidden from History: Rediscovering Women in History from the 17th Century to the Present* (New York: Pantheon Books, 1974); "Women and Radical Politics in Britain, 1820–1914," *Radical History Review*, 19 (Winter 1978–79), pp. 149–59; "The Women's Movement and Organizing for Socialism," *Radical America*, 13, no. 5 (September–October 1979), pp. 9–28; with Lynne Segal and Hilary Wainwright, *Beyond the Fragments: Feminism and the Making of Socialism* (London: Merlin Press, 1979; Boston: Alysen, 1981).

JOAN LANDES

RUBEL, MAXIMILIEN (b. 1905). Born in 1905 in Czernowitz (then within the Austro-Hungarian Empire, assigned to Romania in 1918 and to Russia in 1947), Rubel was educated in Vienna and Czernowitz, receiving law and philosophy degrees. In 1931 he moved to Paris, where he received a *licence des lettres* in 1934 and taught German and law. He became a French citizen in 1937. The *drole de guerre* saw him as an army ambulance driver; after the defeat he lived semiclandestinely (given his Jewish origins) in Paris. Contact with Marxists† in the Resistance first aroused his interest in Marx and Marxism. This led to abandonment of plans to write a thesis on Karl Krauss and eventually to a *doctorate des lettres* from the Sorbonne (1954) for two theses, an "intellectual biography" of Marx and the first scientific bibliography of Marx's (and Engels's†) writings. He has been affiliated with the Centre National de la Recherche

Scientifique since 1947 and has taught at the University of Paris and at many institutions outside of France. He is the editor of what has become the standard edition of Marx in French, the three volumes published by Gallimard in the Bibliothèque de la Pléiade. Just as Rubel's central theme has been the ethical content of Marx's scientific work, so his own studies have been motivated by political convictions. In the mid 1950s he was at the center of a small circle of independent leftists whose discussions focused on the critique of Leninist†-Stalinist† Marxism in general and on the nature of Third World revolutions—at that time represented by the Algerian War—in particular. Later decades saw Rubel connected with other small groups, "council communist" in orientation. But his chief political contribution has been his scholarship.

To understand the importance of this contribution it must be remembered that in the 1940s, when he first became interested in Marx, there was no complete edition of Marx's writings—as indeed there is not yet today—and not even a complete bibliography (Rubel's, with its supplements, remains the closest thing to the latter). The MEGA edition, begun by Riazanov in 1927, did not get beyond Marx's writings of 1849 before Stalin's purges put an end to serious study of Marx in the Soviet Union. The standard edition of the works in German (the MEW) was published only in 1956–68, and is neither complete nor scientifically edited. Rubel therefore not only named the discipline of *marxologie* (as a French translation of *Marx-Forschung*) but was practically its first practitioner since the destruction of Riazanov's institute. The journal created and edited by Rubel in the service of this discipline, the *Etudes de marxologie*, published under the auspices of the French Institute for Applied Economic Science, has been throughout its existence the only journal to fulfill this function.

The scientific rigor of Rubel's scholarship reflects a political conviction: that Marx's thought remains an indispensable foundation for the critique of capitalist society, including the political regimes and movements claiming that thought as their guiding inspiration. This implies a double focus of investigation: both on the rediscovery of Marx's own ideas, long hidden from view by the theoretical and practical movements constituting "Marxism"; and thus, necessarily, on the clarification of the nature and genesis of the latter from the point of view of Marx's own critique of modern society.

With respect to the first of these endeavors, Rubel has emphasized three themes. First, he has insisted on the unfinished nature of the Marxian corpus. Early in his career as a revolutionary intellectual Marx projected a triple critique, of philosophy, of economics, and of politics. Of these the first and last exist only in the form of unpublished manuscripts, letters, and topical articles and pamphlets; of the second we have only, in a form completed by Marx, the first volume of *Capital*, itself envisioned only as the starting point of an immense study of capitalist economic reality. The fundamental service performed by Engels in editing Volumes 2 and 3 from Marx's notes at the same time laid the basis for the misappreciation of Marx's work as a finished and complete *system*. This was transformed in time into "Marxism," the ideology of social democracy and bolshevism, supposedly a complete philosophy of history and even nature. A second theme has been the central importance in Marx's thought, despite the fragmentary nature of its presence in his extant writings, of the critique of bourgeois politics. Rubel has described Marx as "the first theoretician of anarchism," for whom the revolutionary destruction of the state was, alongside the abolition of wage labor, the sine qua non of socialist transformation. As a revolutionary proletarian movement must aim not at the seizure but at the destruction of state power, so bourgeois forms of political organization such as the party are antithetical to the nature of this movement. If the means is to be adequate to the end, the former can be nothing but the self-organized spontaneous activity of the workers themselves. The bourgeois principle of the state, in contrast, is most clearly exhibited in the form of Bonapartism, in which the separation of political power from the mass of society reaches its highest development. This nineteenth-century experience, analyzed by Marx, presages the totalitarian horrors of the twentieth. The third theme, accordingly, has been that Marx's scientific analysis of capitalism leads to the conclusion of the inevitability not of communism but of the choice: socialism or barbarism. Capitalism will break down, as indeed it has periodically throughout the history of the trade cycle. As these collapses become more severe and apocalyptic in their consequences for the laboring population, it is up to the latter to rebel in the name of the values of human development and fulfillment attainable only with the construction of a new, collectively run society. Marx was thus at once the greatest of social scientists and the heir to the utopian tradition of Owen and Fourier.

It follows that to be true to Marx's vision today requires preservation both of the utopian imagination capable of framing a future worthy of humanity and of the scientific rigor with which Marx attempted to provide this imagination with a rational basis. Both of these require complete rejection of the "Marxism" constructed by means of the utter falsification of the form and content of Marx's work by the political movements of the Second† and Third Internationals.† As in the post–World War II period, it has only been the heirs of the latter that have claimed the mantle of Marxism. Rubel has concentrated his critique on the "myth of October," demonstrating that bolshevism represents not so much opposition to capitalism as a new form of the domination of state and wage-labor on which the latter is based.

BIBLIOGRAPHY:

A. *Bibliographie des oeuvres de Karl Marx* (Paris: M. Riviere, 1956); *Karl Marx devant le bonarpartisme* (The Hague: Mouton, 1960); ed., *Oeuvres*, by Karl Marx, with introduction, notes, and appendixes, in three volumes: *Economie*, vols. 1 and 2 (Paris: Gallimard, 1963, 1968), and *Philosophie*, vol. 3 (Paris: Gallimard, 1982); Karl Marx: *Essai de biographie intellectuelle*, 2d ed., rev. (Paris: M. Riviere, 1971); *Marx critique du marxisme: Essais* (Paris: Payot, 1974); with Margaret Manale, *Marx Without Myth: A Chronological Study of His Life and Work* (Oxford: Blackwell, 1975); *Josef W. Stalin in Selbstzeugnissen und Bilddokumenten* (Reinbek bei Hamburg: Rowohlt, 1975).

B. A bibliography complete until 1981 can be found in J. O'Malley and K. Algozin, eds., *Rubel on Karl Marx: Five Essays* (Cambridge: Cambridge University Press, 1981).

PAUL MATTICK, JR.

RÜHLE, OTTO (1874–1943). Born in Germany in 1874, Rühle died in Mexico in 1943. A schoolteacher by profession, Rühle was an outstanding figure of the German left as it developed from the first decade of this century to its destruction in the 1920s. For these years, one can hardly separate his political biography from his contributions to revolutionary Marxist† thought. A member of the left wing of the German Social Democratic Party (SPD), Rühle served as a deputy to the Diet of Saxony in 1911 and in the Reichstag a year later. In 1915 he was the second deputy (after Karl Liebknecht†) to vote against war credits. Along with Liebknecht and Rosa Luxemburg,† Rühle helped found the Spartacus League as a center for political opposition to the war and to the class collaborationism of the SPD. He soon joined the German International Socialists (ISD, later the International Communists, IKD), founded by German participants in the 1915 Zimmerwald Conference. Still a Reichstag deputy, he was spokesman for the Dresden area group of this organization. In 1918 he participated in the founding conference of the German Communist Party (KPD), where he argued against the Spartacist leadership and for the majority of the delegates in opposition to parliamentarism and for the taking of social power by the Workers' and Soldiers' Councils. Rühle was among those who maintained this position when the new leadership of the KPD, after the assassination of Luxemburg and Liebknecht, turned back toward parliamentarism and participation in the trade unions. By 1920 the majority of the KPD, expelled from that organization, had created the Communist Workers Party (KAPD). A member of the KAPD, Rühle disagreed with its twofold organizational strategy: organizing workers into factory organizations within a German General Workers Union (AAUD), modeled somewhat after the IWW, while maintaining the KAPD as a political body safeguarding and propagandizing for socialist aims and tactics. Rühle was sent to Moscow as the KAPD's delegate to the second congress of the Third International.† His refusal to accept the twenty-one conditions set by Lenin† for membership in the International barred him from the meetings, and on his return to Germany he was censured by the Central Committee of the KAPD. He left this organization, taking with him its East Saxon and Hamburg sections, who joined with about half the 200,000 members of the AAUD to form the Unified Organization (AAUD-E) in 1921.

The AAUD-E rejected the KAPD's division between party and factory organization; in 1920 already Rühle had written that the workers' revolution was not to be controlled by a Workers' Party. Central to socialism and so to the movement to create it, in his view, must be the organization of all workers at once for control of their places of production and, by confederation and coordination of these factory organizations, for control over the life of society as a whole and the destruction of the state. With the failure of the German working class to continue the revolution, now against the newly created republic, all the left parties and organizations rapidly declined into insignificance. In 1925 Rühle put his energies into writing, publishing such works as *An Illustrated Cultural and Moral History of the Proletariat* (1927) and *Karl Marx: His Life and Work* (1928), perhaps the first attempt to combine a political and theoretical study of Marx the revolutionist with a psychological analysis of Marx the man. In 1933 Rühle emigrated to Prague and thence to Mexico. He had some contact with Trotsky,† despite their fundamental political and moral differences, and participated in Dewey's committee to investigate Stalin's† accusations against his old rival. During the 1930s and 1940s Rühle wrote for the American journal *International Council Correspondence* (later *Living Marxism* and *New Essays*). At sixty-five he took up painting and had made a little reputation for himself as an artist, under the name of Carlos Timpanero, when he died four years later.

Three main ideas may be distinguished in this lifetime of thought and action: the centrality of the factory for socialist politics; the critique of bolshevism; and the requirements of socialist education. Rühle's insistence on the work place as the basis for socialist organization reflected not only his opposition to parliamentary politics learned from his experience of the SPD but also his idea that "only in the factory is the worker of today a real proletarian." Outside it he lives a petit bourgeois life, formed in his thoughts and aspirations by school, press, and the general texture of social life. For example, "The private household of every family, with its own kitchen, leads to a completely egotistic economic mode." Men even become, "as soon as they have taken off their working clothes, bourgeois too in their behavior. They treat wives and children as they are treated by their bosses, demand subjection, service, authority" (*From the Bourgeois to the Proletarian Revolution*, p. 31). In the factory, by contrast, the necessity of collective action for the satisfaction of class needs is evident; this environment both discourages political sectarianism and encourages radical democracy. In this the factory organizations and the union in which they federate are the opposite of the Bolshevik Party, which represents only a militant form of social democracy. The centralism and authoritarianism of Leninism reflect, moreover, not a theoretical "error" but the actual nature of the Russian Revolution, which could only issue, not into socialism, but into the construction of a new form of capitalism, in which the Party-state takes the place of the bourgeois exploiter of wage labor. Stalinism is thus the legitimate heir of Leninism. "Russia must be placed first among the new totalitarian states," Rühle wrote in 1936: "The struggle against fascism begins with the struggle against bolshevism" (the title of his article in *Living Marxism*).

Finally, Rühle's lifelong interest in education and in psychological theory reflected his fundamental political conviction that "freedom, independence, truth, and solidarity" are the essence of socialism. They must therefore be embodied in the form and content of anything that could be called a socialist education

(*Erziehung zum Sozialismus*, 1919), in the same way that the union of factory organizations provides a structure for the revolutionary self-education of the working class.

BIBLIOGRAPHY:

A. Only two works are available in English: *Karl Marx: His Life and Work* (New York: Viking, 1929); and *From the Bourgeois to the Proletarian Revolution* (London: Socialist Reproduction, 1974). In German, see *Erziehung zum Sozialismus* (Berlin: Infodruck, 1971); and *Schriften, Perspektiven einer Revolution in hochindustrialisierten Ländern* (Reinbek bei Hamburg: Rowohlt, 1971).

B. Hans M. Bock, *Syndikalismus und Linkskommunismus: 1918–23* (Meisenheim am Glan: Anton Hain, 1969); Paul Mattick, "Otto Rühle and the German Labor Movement," in Paul Mattick, *Anti-Bolshevik Communism* (New York: M. E. Sharpe, 1978), pp. 87–115.

PAUL MATTICK, JR.

S

SAIPRADIT, GULARB (1905–1974). Born and raised in Thailand and left fatherless at six years old, Gularb Saipradit began his education at a local temple school and later put himself through Thammasat University, studying at night and working during the day. After receiving his law degree he established a newspaper that was soon closed down for being too radical. Gularb studied journalism in Japan for a year. When he returned to Thailand two more of his newspapers were closed down by the government. Helpless against the political repression of the military government, Gularb again went abroad—to Australia. There Gularb began his formal study of Marxism.† When he returned to Thailand two years later, his anti-establishment attitudes had become firmly Marxist. In 1950 he wrote the first book on Marxism in Thai, *Philosophy of Marx*. In 1952 he was arrested for advocating communism. In prison for four years, Gularb studied Buddhist philosophy and meditation. While Gularb was on a visit to Peking in 1957, a military coup brought another hard-line military government to power in Bangkok. Gularb refused to return and remained in China until his death in 1974, continuing his Marxist writing, but never joining the Communist Party.

Gularb was a humanist and Buddhist Marxist. He hated the human cost of the injustice in Thai society. Marxist theory, he felt, explained much of that suffering. He wrote that Thai women were oppressed "because men owned property" (*History of Thai Women*, p. 35). Gularb was one of the initiators of the women's liberation movement in Thailand, and his explanations of the economic basis of male domination in traditional Thai society were frequently cited by women radicals of the 1970s. Gularb was one of the originators of the dominant stream of Thai radical thought, which sought to combine Marxist theory with that of Buddhism. He believed that Buddhism and Marxism both derived from the same origin. "Buddhism stresses the importance of practice like the scientific teaching [Marxism] . . . according to scientific teaching they [the poor] have to unite and fight the exploiter. Buddhist teaching is the same. Both emphasize self-reliance and self-practice" (*Sriburapa's Buddhist View*, pp. 155–56). Gularb believed that the basic cause of suffering according to Buddhist doctrine—*gilet*, or attachment—was similar to the Marxist view that the cause of economic injustice was the attachment to private property, so he gave a Buddhist and moral tone to his interpretation of Marxism. He believed that Marxism and Buddhism, woven together, would be stronger than each alone and would be able to eliminate suffering in all its forms—political, economic, moral, and personal. The Marxist revolution overthrowing the oppressor class was to have a moral and spiritual dimension that would destroy the ruling evils within the self. Gularb's attempt at synthesizing the two systems of thought was not generally accepted by Thai theologians or scholars, but it had a great effect on succeeding generations of young radicals trying to piece together a Thai revolutionary ideology.

BIBLIOGRAPHY:

A. *Buddhatasana Kong Sriburapa* (Sriburapa's Buddhist's View) (Bangkok: Agsorn-sampan, 1957); *Lae Pai Kang Nar* (Look Ahead) (Bangkok: Sahamitr Garnpim, 1957); with Jit Pumisak, *Prawatsart Satre Thai* (History of Thai Women) (Bangkok: Chomrom Nang Seu Sang Dao, 1974); *Ruam Reung San Rab Chai Che Wit Kong Sri Burapa* (Short Stories Collection) (Bangkok: Mitnara Garnpim, 1974); *Rabieb Sangkom Kong Manut* (The Order of Human Society) (Bangkok: Jaroenwit Garnpim, 1978); *Adeed Te Pen Bodrien* (The Past which is My Lesson) (Bangkok: Somboon Garnpim, 1979); *Kam Kan Rab* (*The Answer*) (Bangkok: Chomrom Sangkomsuksa, n.d.).

B. Jaras Rojanawan, *Chewit Garn Tor Soo Kong Gularb Saipradit* (Gularb Saipradit's Life and Struggle) (Bangkok: Prajak Garnpim, 1974).

YUANGRAT WEDEL

SANO MANABU (1892–1953). Sano Manabu, the Japanese Marxist† theorist, scandalized the movement in 1933, when as an imprisoned Communist Party official with Nabeyama Sadachika he defected. The joint *tenkō* (defection) proclamation triggered a wave of mass *tenkō* that finally destroyed the Japanese Communist Party by 1940. Born in Tsuzuki in Oita Prefecture to a doctor's family, Sano was forced to leave middle school because he had led a strike, so he moved to a Tokyo middle school. After graduating from the Seventh Higher School and the political science course in the Law Department at Tokyo Imperial University, he pursued graduate study in agricultural economy for two years. After working briefly for the Southern Manchurian Railway Company, in 1920, Sano joined the Staff of Waseda University as a lecturer in economics and economic history. In the meantime, in 1918, Sano had organized a study group on socialism and the Russian Revolution with Asō Hisashi and Nosaka Sanzō. In addition, he helped found the New Men Society (Shinjinkai) and the National Miners' League and spoke at meetings of the Builders' League, the Enlightenment Society (Gyōminkai), and the Culture Association. He became influential when he edited *Emancipation* (Kaihō) with Asō and published in July 1921 an essay ''On the Special Liberation of the *Buraku*.'' By 1923 he had also published his *Outline of Japanese Economic History* (*Nihon keizai-shi taikei*), a pioneering effort to analyze Japanese development from a Marxist perspective. In 1922, Sano joined the newly formed Japanese Communist Party, was elected to the standing secretariat, and helped to found the party's Communist Youth League. He barely escaped arrest in the first "roundup" directed against the party in mid-1923 and fled to the Soviet Union, where he became the Japanese Party's representative in Moscow. He attended two Comintern meetings in Shanghai in 1925 and helped draft the Shanghai Theses resolving to rebuild the now dissolved Japanese Party. On returning to Japan, Sano launched the *Proletarian News* and then was imprisoned from March to December 1926 for his prior activities. He had been elected to the Central Committee of the rebuilt Party, but opposed the ideas of Fukumoto Kazuo,† who had become the movement's new theoretical leader because of his "separation before unity" theory. Thus, Sano did not participate actively in Party affairs immediately after his release from prison. When Fukumotoism was criticized in the Comintern's 1927 theses, Sano moved to the forefront on the Central Committee and worked on the Party's new policy direction. Sano attended the Sixth Comintern Congress in 1928 (under the name Katō), when he was elected to its standing committee, and discussed policy in Central Europe and Germany as well as the East. When he traveled to Shanghai in 1929 to consult with Chinese Communist Party members, he was picked up by Chinese police and turned over to Japanese authorities. In the public joint trial of Japanese Communist Party members in 1931 and 1932, Sano led the group's unsuccessful legal struggle and was sentenced to life imprisonment in October of that year. However, after consultation with Nabeyama, the two men issued a joint proclamation to their fellow Communist members renouncing their affiliation with the Comintern-led Party. Therein, Sano and Nabeyama criticized the Japanese Communist Party for blindly following Comintern guidance and advocated an indigenous socialism-in-one-country (*ikkoku shakai-shugi*) built under the existing emperor system. Ironically, only a few years earlier, Sano had criticized the so-called dissolutionist faction (*kaitō-ha*) led by Asano Akira, Mizuno Shigeo, and others for their rejection of an internationally coordinated movement and advocacy of a socialism established on the basis of the Imperial Household. The Communist Party immediately reacted to the Sano-Nabeyama *tenkō* by purging the two men from its ranks, but their *tenkō* proclamation exerted a massive influence on Party ranks. Within a month, 36 percent of imprisoned members defected. In March 1934, Sano's appeal resulted in a commutation of his sentence to fifteen years, and he spent his remaining time in prison immersing himself in traditional Eastern philosophy. This he believed would furnish the key to an indigenized Japanese socialism, and in his view its spiritualist elements would enrich Western Marxist thought, which was too heavily materialist. In this period he penned the *Ancient Japanese Philosophy of Life* and *A Social History of the Qing Dynasty*. Sano finally completed his prison term and was released in October 1943, although he remained under the watch of the peace police. After the war, Sano worked to organize popular support for his Japanese "socialism-in-one-country under the emperor system," founding the Labor-Farmer Vanguard Party in August 1946. At the same time, he vainly opposed Yamakawa Hitoshi's† advocacy of a social democratic front. He also returned to Waseda

University, to the Department of Commercial Sciences, to teach economic thought and economic history and, when his Vanguard Party was unsuccessful, established his own Institute for Japanese Politics and Economics. Until his death in 1953, he continued to advocate an anti-Soviet anti-Communist position of national socialism (*minzoku shakai-shugi*) and managed to gain the support of some fellow apostates from the Communist Party (e.g., former party leader Kazama Jōkichi and his nephew Sano Hiroshi).

BIBLIOGRAPHY:

A. With Nabeyama Sadachika, *Tenkō jūgo nen* (Fifteen Years Since Tenkō) (Tokyo: Rōdō Shuttan-bu, 1949); *Sano Manabu chosakushū* [Collected writings of Sano Manabu], (5 vols.; Tokyo: Sano Manabu chosaku-shū Kan Kōkai, 1958).

B. Germaine A. Hoston, "*Tenkō*: Marxism and the National Question in Pre-war Japan," *Polity*, 16, no. 1 (Fall 1983).

GERMAINE A. HOSTON

SARTRE, JEAN-PAUL (1905–1980). Sartre was born on 21 June 1905 in Paris and died 15 April 1980 in Paris. He was trained in philosophy, earning a Ph.D. in 1929 from Ecole Normale Supérieure. He taught in French secondary schools from 1929 to 1933 and studied the phenomenological philosophy of Husserl and Heidegger in German, as well as the works of Hegel, Kierkegaard, and Descartes. Sartre served in World War II. Throughout his life, Sartre supported many social, economic, and political causes. Occasionally his energetic protest activities earned him the appreciation and respect of others. Always refusing to be coopted or institutionalized, Sartre rejected all official awards, including memberships of the Légion d'Honneur and the French Academy, and the Nobel Prize. Politically uninvolved during the 1930s, Sartre moved progressively leftward during World War II, and by 1957 considered himself a Marxist. His ambivalent relationship with the French Communist Party is well known. In the 1950s he tried to influence Party policy without officially joining. He soon ran afoul of the Party line, first over Hungary in 1956 and then over Algeria in 1963. The events of May 1968 led to a complete break, after which Sartre supported Maoist and other more exotic leftist *groupuscules*. He died in Paris on 15 April 1980, in the midst of a noticeable move rightward among French intellectuals.

Known as one of the founders of the modern existentialist movement in philosophy, Sartre's position in this movement was secured with the publication of *Being and Nothingness* in 1943. In 1945 Sartre, R. Aron, S. de Beauvoir,* and M. Merleau-Ponty* founded *Les Temps modernes*, which contained a number of Sartre's early essays on Marxism† and communism that were gathered together in *The Communists and the Peace* (1964). These essays were severely criticized by Merleau-Ponty for their narrow view of the dialectic, their elitist view of the Communist Party in its relation to the proletariat, and their failure to treat in depth the intersubjective nature of man's relationship to the world and to history.

Sartre's major contributions to Marxist theory are contained in *Critique of Dialectical Reason*, and its companion, *Search for a Method*. The principal assumptions of Sartre's existential Marxism may be outlined as follows beginning with dialectical reason, defined as the intelligibility or comprehension of praxis, which is the activity of an individual or a group organized as a project and works at every level of social life. At the individual level the "constituent dialectic" operates, whereas at the group level its operation is termed the "constituted dialectic." Dialectical reason, as it operates through the actions of men and women, has the capacity for totalization, which is the process of making and understanding history. Dialectical reason is to be contrasted to analytic reason, which is the mode of scientific analysis appropriate to the study of external objects and relations in the natural world. Sartre asserts that human history can only be understood through the analysis of dialectical, not analytic reason. To think otherwise is to build a false positivistic view of man, society, and history. The *Critique* articulates a historical, structural anthropology based on the logic of dialectical reason. That logic is based on the regressive-progressive method of analysis, which attempts to discover man, the "universal singular" (*The Family Idiot*, vol. 1, p. ix), who is summed up and universalized by his epoch and who, in turn, reproduces himself in his singularity in the epoch he lives through. "Universal by the singular universality of human history, singular by the universalizing singularity of his projects, he requires examination from both ends" (ibid., p. ix). The method appropriate to this analysis is outlined in *Search for a Method* and applied in the *Critique* and *The Family Idiot*. It involves the combination of synchronic and diachronic analysis in a series of interrelated steps, beginning with the horizontal, vertical, and historical display of the complexity of structures that impinge on and coexist with the human group or individual under study. Thick phenomenological description of the group's situation is required. Against this depiction of lived experience must be sketched the bedrock layers of reality that structure human history. This requires a regressive analysis back to the obdurate, economic, practico-inert inner structures of human society. For Sartre these structures are embedded in the "rocky subsoil" of human need, necessity, and scarcity (*Search for a Method*, p. 70). On top of this subsoil exists free human praxis, in the form of work lodged in the divisions of labor and modes of production that characterize a society at a given moment in time. Labor, which becomes alienated from itself, is the infrastructure of the practico-inert field of experience that man confronts on a daily basis, throughout the singularity of human history. The structures of experience that the human subject has in the present must be rediscovered, and these will be found in everyday interactions and in human groups. How the past is lived in the present and sets the agenda for the future, which may contain the possibilities of human freedom, is the goal of the diachronic analysis that underlies the progressive side of Sartre's method. This requires a repositioning of the essential material foundations of existence against the possibilities of the totalization of history in the present. The "dialectical circularity" of human group life is thus discovered, for each individual and each group attempts its own totalization of history against the structures of need, necessity, and the practico-inert that endure throughout human history. The individual is dialectical in his very essence, for he is mediated by things, as things are mediated by him. This circularity is evidenced in humanity's history, which, as Marx argued in *The Eighteenth Brumaire of Louis Bonaparte*, is made "under conditions . . . given and handed down to them" from the past. Man-the-producer and man-the-produced set the dialectical foundations for Sartre's analysis.

Although man's basic relationship to the world is through the passive, or inert gathering, which has the structure of seriality, or separation, the real relationship between men and the world is ternary, or mediated by the third party, who is an individual who unifies a group or a person's praxis by observing or commanding it. In this relationship with the third, each subject is an object and a subject to herself and to the other. A field of intersubjective experience that constitutes itself above each subject, yet is lodged in their actions toward one another, is produced. It is from the eyes of this third party that direct, or indirect, mediated and unmediated, reciprocal and alienating praxis is organized. Every relationship, whether the person with the product of her labor, two workers observed by a third, or a group in interaction, is mediated by this relationship to the third. The exteriorizing-interiorizing dimension of action is thereby established with Sartre's insertion of the third party into every human transaction. Man-as-produced and man-as-producer is objectified through his labor, the machines he uses, the worked matter he leaves his seal upon, and the associations and relationships he builds with others. The worked matter that man produces exteriorizes him and alienates him from himself, while he interiorizes the very products of his labor, attempting to find subjective meaning in them. This relationship to labor produces a practico-inert field of experience that ossifies and works back against man. The human associations he forms, whether dyadic, triadic, or group, dialectically constitute themselves as practico-inert structures, which he also exteriorizes and interiorizes. For Sartre the human is always inside and outside the structures of experience he produces, be this his labor, or his associations with others. This double feature of human experience to exteriorize what one produces, while reflectively interiorizing that experience and giving it subjective meaning, establishes the dialectical circularity of individual and collective history. The acting agent, as she places her praxis into action, constructs structures and experiences that turn back on her, envelop her, and lead to a deviation from her original intents. This "totalization of envelopment," which Sartre elaborates in detail in his still unpublished analysis of socialism under Stalin† in the Soviet Union reveals how human praxis is absorbed into and dominated by the practico-inert world it has created but lost control of (Aronson, p. 693). The dialectical circularity of human interaction works back against man, to distance him from the very structures of experience and freedom he desires.

The structures of practical action that make up a society are collectives of individuals related to one another through third party mediation, reciprocity, separation, alterity, conflict, and scarcity, both material and temporal. These dialectical structures are termed "practical ensembles." Volume 1 of the *Critique* takes the human subject from individual praxis through the initial structures of collective action, including the "series" and the "gathering." Series are passive structures embodying past forms of praxis (the practico-inert) in a repetitive, deadening, alienating fashion. Queues, assemblies, direct and indirect gatherings as seen in the public are examples of series. Gatherings are series capable of dialectically constituting a group. Volume 2 moves from groups to history. The analysis presumes a position of "dialectical nominalism," which argues that if the dialectic exists, it does so only through the actions of a multiplicity of totalizing individualities. Because the dialectic is a process, which reveals its own intelligibility through dialectical analysis, Sartre argues that "nominalism is also a dialectical *realism*" (*Search for a Method*, p. 37). Accordingly, groups exist at two levels: in individual praxis; and through the processes of dialectical reason. Groups are not autonomous structures, independent of the actions of those who produce them. Volume 2 offers a rich historical, dialectical, and structural discussion of the storming of the Bastille in Paris in 1789, the emergence of the working class in France, Taylorism and the industrialization process, the purges and terror that followed the revolution of 1793 in France, the bureaucratization of terror and the emergence of the cult of personality in Stalinist Russia, racism and colonialism in post–World War I Europe and Asia, bourgeois respectability in late nineteenth-century France, and the class struggle in the twentieth century. Sartre's theory of groups is woven through the structures and the spectacle of this history, which is the history of late nineteenth- and twentieth-century capitalism, democracy, socialism, oppression, totalitarianism, communism,the threatened annihilation of the entire world system, and Marxism as a praxis within that system.

The theory of groups begins with the "fused group," whose members are opposed to seriality and drawn to one another through reciprocity and the need for mutual protection in order to survive. "Pledged" or "statutory" groups emerge out of fused groups and are grounded in a dialectic of fear, terror, fraternity, and the pledge. The fear for individual survival is transferred to the group that affords protection against death. This fear produces a freedom in "groupness" and becomes the praxis of the group. Fear is solidified through the pledge, which can include the act of swearing an oath, in law or on the Bible. The pledge is a practical device that objectifies the member's commitment to the group. The pledge invokes a third party mediating structure that requires each member to take the pledge in relation to every other member. This mediated reciprocity of the pledge finds its origin in the fear of the third party, e.g., Louis Napoleon Bonaparte for the citizens of Paris who stormed the Bastille. Thus fear, which is first external, in the form of the threat to life, is internalized and becomes a free product of the group, objectified through the pledge. The pledge is both external and internal, for it is interiorized by each member, as it is exteriorized through the third party mediating structures that define the collective fabrics of the group. The pledge synthesizes fear and seriality and embodies these two forces in a presence that the group defines its existence against and in terms of. In this fashion the group produces and reproduces itself as a pressure on its members, but at this level the group is the process of dialectical reason in operation, for the group is not a reality unto itself. The terror unites the members against the serial impotence they felt in their respective isolation. Fraternity becomes the real bond of commonality that holds the group together; yet when the pledge is violated through treason, the group may annihilate its betrayer, thus bringing violence into the interiority of the group.

Groupness in the face of terror and violence redefines the person while it creates a new ontological structure of momentary duration that unifies individual freedom and praxis into a collective structure (*Critique*, pp. 499–500). The group through its members creates an idea of itself as an objective system of relations, mediated through reciprocity. This idea of the group must be invented and reinvoked through the pledge as it is put into action through practical structures and meanings. The dialectic against which the group forms itself is the seriality of its members and the fear of death, both of which are external. The practical unity of the group is given through this double external threat, which passes through each member in the form of fear and the pledge. This unity, however, is never given inside the group, for the group cannot constitute itself as an internal autonomous force; it remains always the product of the actions of the multiplicity of individualities who make it up. The internal structure of the group rests, then, on individual impotence. Seriality reappears within the group, drawing the members away from one another. The group becomes bogged in matter, in its own becoming-process. "Goals lose their teleological character. Without ceasing to be genuine goals, they become destinies" (ibid., p. 663). The process of envelopment sets in and the original praxis of the group is distorted, if not destroyed.

As with previous Marxist theorists, Sartre devotes considerable attention to the analysis of the working class in the class struggles of the nineteenth and twentieth centuries. Understanding that class-being is always realized through the praxis of individuals in seriality and in groups, Sartre shows that the ability of the members of the working class to transcend or go beyond their present circumstances toward a future that they freely control is inhibited by the operation of the state, the antidialectic located in the practico-inert field of seriality, the manipulations of third parties (labor leaders, politicians), the persistence of scarcity, and the pervasive pressures toward alterity and seriality that are produced by the circular dialectic of individual and group praxis.

Class manifests itself on three levels: as an institutional apparatus, with rights, duties, leadership and pledges; as an "ensemble" (serial or organized) of direct action groups; and as a collective in the form of the practico-inert field on whose surface groups appear and are unified. Class-being is defined in terms of seriality, as the subjective meaning of labor and existence as lived within the life of each subject. The fused and statutory groups that form out of class seriality have no inner-group being. The group's being, as an embodiment of class-being, lies outside itself in seriality, from which it has emerged and which gives it its freedom for action. This external seriality is lived inside the group as a negation of being-in-the-group. Therefore seriality must be overcome in order for the group to achieve "even the smallest common result . . . but it is seriality which sustains the group making demands" upon itself and upon the third party that oppresses it (ibid., p. 687). Class-being is a temporal process, lived in terms of past, present, or future seriality. Group praxis is mediated through the present, practical realities of the worker. The unity of the group is never given from within, nor ever totalized as a social collectivity independent of the actions of its members. Refusing to grant ontological autonomy to the group or to class, Sartre returns class struggle and class conflict to the actions of free individuals. The subject, free in her plane of existence, which is lived against the reality of scarcity and need, is drawn into and forms statutory groups within the boundaries set by her location in the divisions of labor of her society. The power of the group, as an instrument and extension of class-being, thus becomes embedded and enveloped in its own process of becoming. The group dissolves into seriality, to be oppressed by its own efforts to make history (ibid., p. 663).

The state, which represents the juridical extension of a single group's power over other groups, seizes the resources and power of the capitalist class and embodies those powers in a sovereign who utilizes fear and terror to maintain his and his group's power. The state is thus legitimate within a group and for the members of a single class, but for the radical heterogeneity of the society this is not the case. The state is a "fiction" and the organ of the exploiting class. It "sustains, by constraint, the statute of the oppressed classes . . . the ruling class *produces its state*" (ibid., p. 638). The contradiction of the state lies in the fact that it represents a class apparatus pursuing class objectives, while it posits itself as the sovereign unity of all members of the society. Working-class struggle and conflict is fought against these structures of the state, which use the resources of the working class to sustain working-class self-oppression.

Volume 2 of the *Critique* promises the progressive analysis of the problem of totalization in human history. However, its conclusions are anticipated in Volume 1, for history shows that the first moment in the construction of socialist society becomes the bureaucratization of terror and the cult of the personality. These are the expressions of the impossibility of any group or class to constitute itself as a hyperorganism, or autonomous social collectivity. The constituted and constituent dialectics dissolve under the pressures and forces of envelopment. Free praxis is thereby crushed, and humans continue to live out the histories that others make for them. The problematic and the promise of human history—the construction of a reign of human freedom produced by man—is answered in the negative by Sartre, given his case study of Stalinism in the Soviet Union. Thus history is open-ended, full of choices. Yet to the extent that Sartre grounds his theory of practical ensembles on the actions of totalizing individualities, collective human freedom remains out of immediate reach. For if the collectivity cannot externalize itself as a thing-in-itself, with separate ontological status, freedom turns back on the individual to pursue and to obtain against and within her own fields of experience in the world. Freedom, then, is still attainable because it can be thought, and those thoughts can be put into action. Sartre's Marxism, like Merleau-Ponty's and Stuart Hall's,* is a Marxism with hope, but no guarantees.

His project, accordingly, builds upon Marx's, for it points toward the reign of freedom that Marx envisioned. Like Marx, Hegel, Descartes, and Locke, Sartre offers in the *Critique* and in *Search for a Method* a philosophical statement that simultaneously contains the potential for being a method, a set of regulative ideas, a language, an offensive weapon, a vision of the world, and an "instrument which ferments rotten societies" (*Search for a Method,* p. 6). It is for these reasons that his contributions to Marxist social theory deserve the most serious study and debate, for they combine in the same moment some of the most original existentialist and Marxist thought of the twentieth century. He joins the two untranscendable philosophies of this century into a field of action that cannot be ignored.

BIBLIOGRAPHY:

A. *Being and Nothingness* (New York: NYU Press, 1966); *The Communists and the Peace* (New York: Braziller, 1960); *Search for a Method* (New York: Knopf, 1963); *Critique of Dialectical Reason* (London: New Left Books, 1976); *L'Idiot de la famille*, 3 vols. (Paris: Gallimard, 1981); "An Interview of Jean-Paul Sartre," pp. 3–51, in *The Philosophy of Jean-Paul Sartre*, ed. Paul A. Schilpp (La Salle, Ill.: Open Court, 1981).

B. Raymond Aron, *History and the Dialectic of Violence* (New York: Harper & Row, 1976); Thomas R. Flynn, "An End to Authority: Epistemology and Politics in Later Sartre," *Man and World*, 10, no. 4 (1977), pp. 448–65; "Sartre's Turning Point: The Abandoned *Critique de la Raison Dialectique*, Volume Two," pp. 685–708, in *The Philosophy of Jean-Paul Sartre*, ed. Paul A. Schilpp, (La Salle, Ill.: Open Court, 1981); Robert A. Gorman, *Neo-Marxism: The Meanings of Modern Radicalism* (Westport, Conn.: Greenwood Press, 1982), pp. 228–40.

NORMAN K. DENZIN

SCHAFF, ADAM (b. 1913). The son of a barrister, Adam Schaff was born 10 March, 1913 in Lvov, Poland, now the Soviet Union. He studied law and economics in Lvov and the Ecole des Sciences Politiques et Economiques in Paris and philosophy in Poland and the Soviet Union. In 1945 he received his doctorate at the Institute of Philosophy of the Soviet Academy of Sciences. He participated in the Polish underground Communist movement and was a member of the Polish United Worker's Party. Schaff was a member and chief ideologist of the Central Committee of the Polish United Workers Party from 1954 to 1968. He was chairman of the Philosophy Committee of the Polish Academy of Sciences from 1955 to 1968. From 1948 to 1970 he was professor of philosophy at the University of Warsaw.

Schaff's significance resides in his willingness to evaluate seriously two disparate bourgeois schools of thought: linguistic philosophy and existentialism. *Introduction to Semantics* (1962) was Schaff's attempt to provide a Marxist† appraisal of philosophy of language. He argues that a Marxist theory of language must avoid the errors of two extremes in Anglo-American linguistic philosophy: the conventionalist theory of neopositivism (Carnap); and the picture theory of language (Wittgenstein). Contrary to conventionalism, Schaff asserts, language is not an autonomous domain in which the rules are arbitrarily made up in the same way as the rules of a game. Neither, however, according to Schaff, does the structure of language simply mirror the structure of reality. Against these theories Schaff affirms a dialectical theory of reflection in which language is viewed as something that is shaped by changing social conditions and that in turn shapes our image of the world. The language that forms our consciousness is a product of the fluid material conditions created by social practice. Schaff came to terms with existentialism in *A Philosophy of Man* (1963) and developed an alternative philosophy of the person in *Marxism and the Human Individual* (1965). In both works he argues that the central problem for socialism is the problem of the human being—the main task of socialism being to create conditions for full human development and happiness. This, he maintains, is the task of philosophical anthropology. The contributions of Marx to this enterprise, according to Schaff, can be found in the early writings; the later writings, in his view, are concerned with the material preconditions necessary for the development of the individual. Schaff attempts to recover the problem of the individual overlooked by later Marxism. An adequate philosophical anthropology, Schaff contends, must negotiate between two perspectives: the heteronomous and the autonomous concepts of the individual. The former sees the individual as a product of superhuman forces (God, the absolute idea, fate, etc.); the latter conceives the human individual as a self-created being. The second perspective is represented by Sartrean existentialism. Although Schaff endorses Jean-Paul Sartre's* repudiation of supernatural forces and absolute values as well as his emphasis on the uniqueness of the individual, he objects to the failure of existentialism to recognize the social nature of the individual—the fact that the individual always thinks and acts within a specific social framework. Although individuals make history, they always make it in conformity with the objective laws of history, which means that human autonomy is always relative.

Although Schaff attempts to restore the emphasis of the early Marx on individual self-realization, he rejects what he takes to be the young Marx's utopian projection of the end of alienation in a society without private property. In an effort to give Marxism a realistic dimension, Schaff argues that socialism can remove social barriers to happiness but cannot eliminate all causes of unhappiness. Thus, Schaff concedes that some forms of alienation will continue to exist under mature communism. Schaff maintains that ideological struggle must supersede armed class struggle. Affirming the relative autonomy of theory, Schaff asserts that opponents and the undecided must be persuaded of the truth of Marxist philosophical anthropology. Given the nature of modern weapons, he denies that it is any longer possible to solve international conflicts by armed force.

BIBLIOGRAPHY:

A. *Introduction to Semantics* (New York: Macmillan, 1962); *A Philosophy of Man* (New York: Monthly Review Press, 1963); *Marxism and the Human Individual* (New York: McGraw-Hill, 1970).

DAVID MYERS

SCHMIDT, ALFRED (b. 1931). Alfred Schmidt was born on 19 May 1931 in Berlin. He studied history, English, and classical philology, philosophy, and sociology at the University of Frankfurt, receiving his doctorate in 1962 with a dissertation on "Der Begriff der Natur in der Lehre von Marx" (On the Concept of Nature in Marx). Max Horkheimer* and Theodore W. Adorno* were Schmidt's dissertation directors. Since 1972 Schmidt has been a professor of philosophy and sociology at the University of Frankfurt.

Over the past two decades, Schmidt has produced an impressive array of books, articles, reviews, and occasional essays. His studies of Feuerbach, Marx,† Schopenhauer, Nietzsche, Horkheimer, and Herbert Marcuse* have concentrated on their philosophies of history and on epistemological questions in the history of philosophical materialism. In addition to these studies, Schmidt has edited works by Feuerbach, Horkheimer, and Friedrich Albert Lange and translated works by Henri Lefebvre,* Robert Paul Wolff, Barrington Moore, Jr., Maurice Merleau-Ponty,* and Marcuse. These scholarly activities have established Schmidt as one of the key figures in the second generation of "critical theorists" associated with the Frankfurt School of neo-Marxism. To date Schmidt's international reputation rests on two books, *The Concept of Nature in Marx* and *History and Structure*. The first work, as the title suggests, focuses on Marx's understanding of nature. Contrary to all objectivistic or subjectivistic, material or ideal attempts at reduction and oversimplification, Schmidt emphasizes the mutual interpenetration of nature and society in Marxian theory. Schmidt's analytic method is as important as his substantive conclusion. During the course of his discussion of nature in Marx, Schmidt addresses the dispute between orthodox Marxists and neo-Marxists on the proper interpretation of the Marxian corpus. Many thinkers from both camps would concur on a distinction between an early "philosophic" Marx and a later "economic" Marx. For the orthodox Marxists, the early philosophic writings are the sins of youth, which are happily overcome by Marx's mature economic works. For many neo-Marxists, however, the early philosophic writings are a promising foundation that was betrayed by the economic preoccupations of Marx's middle and late years. Schmidt adopts a unique position. According to Schmidt, Marx did make landmark contributions to philosophic thinking, but the locus of these contributions is the middle and late, ostensibly economic writings, and not the "abstract and romanticizing" philosophical anthropology of Marx's youth. From this perspective, it is the mature Marx's critique of political economy in general and his critique of commodity production in particular that are the paradigms for contemporary work in critical social theory.

Schmidt's devaluation of Marx's early philosophical writings puts him in partial agreement with the structuralist tendency in contemporary Marxism, particularly with the structuralism of Louis Althusser* and his school. But the structuralist antipathy to philosophy is only one aspect of their opposition to chronological-historical accounts of the social world. In *History and Structure*, Schmidt acknowledges the moment of truth in the structuralist critique of philosophic, Hegelian, historical approaches to Marxism, while criticizing the exclusively scientific, anti-Hegelian, antihistorical approach of the structuralists. Schmidt argues for the historical-structural "double character" of the mature Marx's social theory. The structuralists, according to Schmidt, misunderstand this double character because they accept the scientific and structural appearance of Marx's *Capital* at face value. Schmidt maintains that the results of Marx's research on Capital were *presented* in a scientific manner, but that Marx's *inquiry* into the nature of capitalism was based upon an analysis of the historical course of events. In other words, the difference between the structural mode of presentation and the historical mode of inquiry in *Capital* does not establish the epistemological priority of structure over history. And beneath the scientific, structural facade of *Capital*, Schmidt finds not only history, but philosophy as well. Schmidt, following Lenin's† suggestion, emphasizes the crucial importance of Hegel's *Science of Logic* for the understanding of Marx's *Capital*.

Schmidt is currently working on a major study of epistemology and the critique of ideology in Nietzsche.

BIBLIOGRAPHY:

A. *Die "Zeitschrift für Sozialforschung": Geschichte und gegenwärtige Bedeutung* (Munich: Kösel, 1970); *The Concept of Nature in Marx*, trans. Ben Fowkes (London: New Left Books, 1971); *Emanzipatorische Sinnlichkeit: Ludwig Feuerbachs anthropologischen Materialismus* (Munich: Hanser, 1973); with Herbert Marcuse, *Existenzialische Marx-Interpretationen* (Frankfurt am Main: Europäische Verlaganstalt, 1973); *Zur Idee der Kritischen Theorie: Elemente der Philosophie Max Horkheimers* (Munich: Hanser, 1974); with Werner Post, *Was ist Materialismus?* (Stuttgart: Kösel, 1975); *Drei Studien über Materialismus: Schopenhauer, Horkheimer, Glücksproblem* (Munich: Hanser, 1977); with Bernhard Görlich and Alfred Lorenzer, *Der Stachel Freud: Beiträge und Dokumente zur Kulturismus-Kritik* (Frankfurt am Main: Suhrkamp, 1980); *History and Structure: An Essay on Hegelian-Marxist and Structuralist Theories of History*, trans. Jeffrey Herf (Cambridge: MIT Press, 1981); *Kritische Theorie/Humanismus/Aufklärung: Philosophische Aufsätze* (Stuttgart: Reclam, 1981).

JOHN BOKINA

SCHNEIDER, MICHAEL (b. 1943). Schneider was born in 1943 in Konigsberg, East Prussia. He studied natural sciences, philosophy, sociology, and religion in Freiburg, Berlin, and Paris, and in 1974 earned the Ph.D. with a dissertation on Marx† and Freud. He is an editor for Wagenbach Publishers and a political essayist and critic for *Konkret*, *Kursbuch*, *Literaturmagazin*, as well as for several German radio stations. Since 1975 he has been a consultant at the Hessische Staatstheater in Wiesbaden, where he has been living as a free-lance writer since 1978. From time to time Schneider also performs as an amateur magician. He has received numerous literary awards and prizes.

Schneider's political development was particularly influenced by the German student movement in the late 1960s. In *Die Lange Wut zum langen Marsch* (1975) he is concerned with the factionalizing of the postwar German new left into potentially antagonistic movements, e.g., pro-Soviet, Maoist,† Trotskyist,† Stalinist,† Luxemburgist,† Leninist.† In *Neurose und Klassenkampf* (1973) Schneider outlines a Marxist materialistic psychology and psychopathology and then relates Freud's phenomenological description of the bourgeois soul to the commodity economy of capitalism. Schneider criticizes orthodox Freudianism, which limits itself to early childhood experiences and interfamilial tensions without acknowledging the suffering of workers in particular experiences in and from the working world. He emphasizes the pathogenic human character of hired labor and establishes the connection between capitalist exploitation and progressive psychic deterioration. His goal is to recover the repressed revolutionary potential in Freud's notion of illness, i.e., that every illness is a subconscious form of refusal, a passive resistance against the coercive nature of hired work and the alienating socialization process under capitalism. Schneider defines the goal of emancipatory psychoanalysis as its ability to transform the passive resistance of psychic and physical illness into active political resistance against a sick society. In *Den Kopf verkehrt aufgesetzt* (1981) Schneider traces the roots of decay and melancholy within the German left—expressed particularly in the resignation and pessimism of radical groups—to the blocked dialogue of German fathers and sons. The silence of German fathers about their involvement with fascism has crippled young German men, a phenomenon Schneider calls the "Hamlet complex." Schneider condemns new "chic" youth movements (e.g., new sensibility, new sensuality, new naturalness) and defines them as reactionary expressions of a flourishing economy rather than intimations of a liberating new culture. Consequently Schneider also sharply criticizes the increasingly prevalent forces of irrationalism and mysticism that are emerging throughout Western Europe.

BIBLIOGRAPHY:

A. *Neurose und Klassenkampf* (Reinbek bei Hamburg: Rowohlt, 1973); *Die Lange Wut zum langen Marsch* (Reinbek bei Hamburg: Rowohlt, 1975); *Das Spiegelkabinett* (Munich: Autoren Edition, 1980); *Den Kopf verkehrt aufgesetzt* (Reinbek bei Hamburg: Rowohlt, 1981).

B. Heinz Ludwig Arnold, ed., *KLG Kritisches Lexikon zur deutschsprachigen Gegenwartsliteratur* (Munich: Edition Text and Kritik, 1978).

MAGDALENE MUELLER

SERGE, VICTOR (1890–1947). Novelist, journalist, and revolutionary activist, Serge was born Victor Lvovich Kibalchich in 1890 in Brussels to Narodnik émigrés forced to flee Russia after Czar Alexander II's assassination. Serge grew up in poverty and joined the socialist Jeunes Gardes but was impatient with their reformism. He moved to Paris after a stay in a utopian commune and embraced libertarian anarchism. In the French capital he edited *L'Anarchie* and served five years in prison (later the basis for his first novel, *Men in Prison*) because of ties to the "Bonnot gang" of anarchist bank robbers, whose bloody activities he in fact opposed. Released in 1917, Serge went to Barcelona, where he first used the nom de plume *Victor Serge* to sign an article defending Austro-Marxist* Friedrich Adler's assassination of Austria's prime minister to protest World War I. He participated in the unsuccessful Barcelona syndicalist uprising (described in his novel *Birth of Our Power*) and eventually made his way to Petrograd in 1919, after a year's internment in France. His arrival in Russia coincided with one of the worst periods in the Civil War there (described in his novel *Conquered City*), and despite his various criticisms of the Bolsheviks, he joined their ranks, working with G. Zinoviev in founding the Comintern and serving as its agent in Berlin and Vienna (1923–26). He returned to the Soviet Union, joined the left opposition to Stalin,† and was expelled from the Communist Party in 1927. Unable to find work, he began writing novels. Arrested in 1930, Serge was sent to Central Asia and would probably have been killed in the purges had it not been for a campaign by French intellectuals. In 1936 he was deprived of Soviet citizenship and, following the seizure of many of his manuscripts, was expelled from the country. He spent the next decade writing about the Soviet Union, agitating against Stalinism, and authoring several novels, particularly about the purges (e.g., *The Case of Comrade Tulayev*). With the Nazi invasion of France, he fled to Mexico, where he wrote his greatest work, *Memoirs of a Revolutionary* (an autobiography), and also more fiction as well as a biography of Trotsky† with his widow. Serge died there in 1947.

Serge was an observer and a participant, not a theorist. His memoirs provide a vast and remarkable panorama of Russian and European radicalism in the twentieth century. Serge found Lenin† attractive as a "revolutionist in time of revolution" (*From Lenin to Stalin*, p. 16), but repeatedly chastized Russian Marxism† for its lack of concern for liberty and lack of respect for the individual. He remained an anarchist at heart, advocating a socialist humanism and emphasized the importance of freedom of thought. "The fear of liberty," he wrote, "which is fear of the masses, marks the entire course of the Russian revolution" ("Marxism in Our Time," p. 31). He concluded that the chief lesson of the Bolshevik Revolution was the necessity of democracy and claimed to be the first to call the Soviet Union a "totalitarian state" (*Memoirs*, p. 281). Serge defined writing as a committed enterprise, "a means of expressing to men what most of them live inwardly without being able to express, . . . a means of communication, a testimony to the vast flow of life through us, whose essential aspects we must try to fix for the benefit of those who will come after us" (*Memoirs*, p. 262). He believed the classical novel form, with its emphasis on "individual existences," to be outmoded and sought to fashion collective protagonists ("not this or that person, but simply men") in his fiction.

BIBLIOGRAPHY:

A. "Marxism in Our Time," *Partisan Review* (August–September 1938); *The Case of Comrade Tulayev* (New York: Doubleday, 1950); *Year One of the Russian Revolution* (Chicago: Holt, Rinehart and Winston, 1972); *Littérature et révolution suivi de littérature proletarienne?* (Paris: F. Maspero, 1976); *Men in Prison* (London: Readers and Writers, 1977); *Conquered City* (London: Readers and Writers, 1978); *From Lenin to Stalin* (New York: Monad Press, 1980); *Memoirs of a Revolutionary 1901–1941* (Oxford: Oxford University Press, 1980).

B. Peter Sedgwick, "Victor Serge and Socialism," *International Socialism*, 14 (Fall, 1963); Richard L. Greeman, "The Laws are Burning: Literary and Revolutionary Realism in Victor Serge," *Yale French Studies*, 339 (1967); Richard L. Greeman, "Victor Serge and the Tradition of Revolutionary Literature," *Triquarterly*, 8 (1967).

MITCHELL COHEN

SÈVE, LUCIEN (b. ca 1925). A leading psychologist and social theorist in postwar France, Lucien Sève studied psychology, philosophy, and psychophysiology at the University of Paris. During the 1950s he taught at the *lycée* in Paris and, after reading Politzer's *La Crise de la psychologie contemporaine*, became radicalized. After 1953 Sève seriously studied the works of Marx† and Lenin† and conceived the project of developing a Marxist interpretation of human personality. He joined the French Communist Party and by 1963 had become a leading intellectual on the Central Committee who actively opposed the brands of Marxist revisionism that were crystallizing around French existentialists and Eastern European *Praxis** philosophers. In his commitment to a scientific Marxism that was simultaneously noneconomistic and nonhumanistic Sève was a natural ally of Louis Althusser* and the radical structuralist movement. Sève currently lives in Paris.

Sève's international reputation rests on his major work, *Marxisme et théorie de la personalité* (1969) (translated as *Man in Marxist Theory and the Psychology of Personality*). Although he dealt with a wide range of subjects, Sève was determined to develop a theory of human existence based on anthropological theory and research. He applied Marx's theory of historical materialism and his dialectical method to developing a nontraditional interpretation of human psychology and personality. Both, Sève argued, are dependent on the inherent importance of social relations. Hence the study of anthropology validates Marxist science. Carefully avoiding what he perceived as the excesses of Althusser and Hegel, Sève saw the dialectic as a product of concrete matter that cannot be reduced to the a priori movement of things. The validity of the dialectic as a tool for social inquiry is therefore based on its being open to empirical evidence and reflective of actual matter. The dialectic, for Sève, is a product of material events and the regularity inherent in material processes. When approached in this manner dialectical inquiry into civilization confirms the validity of Marx's major hypotheses and redirects modern psychology toward social determinants. Sève believed that unique human personalities are therefore open to their socioeconomic environments, which generate personality types that correspond to the dominant class structure. This materialist interpretation of personality, in Sève's view, avoided the extremes of bourgeois idealism (which advocates an a priori definition of human nature), "pseudo-materialist" Marxism (which sees personality as an epiphenomenon), and "humanist" revisionism (which tends toward voluntarism).

BIBLIOGRAPHY:

A. *La Différence: Deux essais sur Lénine et sur Henri Lefebvre* (Paris: Editions Sociales, 1960); *La Philosophie française contemporaine et sa genèse de 1789 à nos jours, précédé de philosophie et politique* (Paris: Editions Sociales, 1962); *Man in Marxist Theory and the Psychology of Personality*, trans. John McGreal (Atlantic Highlands, N.J.: Humanities Press, 1978); *Une Introduction à la philosophie marxiste, suivie d'un vocabulaire philosophique* (Paris: Editions Sociales, 1980).

ROBERT A. GORMAN

SITUATIONIST INTERNATIONAL (1957–1972). The Situationist International (SI) was formed at a 1957 conference in Italy. Delegates from a few leading avant-garde groups—including the Lettrist International and the Movement for a Bauhaus Imagination, the cultural movements that had the greatest impact on the Situationists—assembled to discuss the crisis in modern culture and life. Deciding they shared a sufficiently similar ideological orientation, they united to experiment with means of aesthetic intervention in contemporary culture with the goal of precipitating revolution and destroying the artificial barriers between art and life. The new SI, whose leading members included Guy Debord, Asger Jorn, and Raoul Vaneigem, advanced beyond previous theory to develop a penetrating and sophisticated critique of modern society. The Situationists went on to figure importantly in the events of May 1968. Shortly thereafter, in 1972, the SI disbanded. Their ideas, however, continue to exert influence on contemporary avant-garde groups.

The Situationists diverged from orthodox Marxism in stressing the existence of a historical transition within capitalist society from the primacy of structures of production to those of consumption and in theorizing the implications this shift must involve for a radical praxis and movement. This transition clearly alters the nature of power. The Situationists accordingly extended the critique of domination and alienation while retaining the basic tenets of historical materialism that revolve around class domination and the need for class struggle. The categories they advanced, bearing striking similarities to the ideas of George Lukaćs,* Antonio Gramsci,* and Henri Lefebvre,* were those of space, everyday life, the spectacle, and its antithesis—the constructed situation. The linchpin of the Situationist critique of modern society is the concept of the spectacle, a complex term with multiple meanings. Immediately, the term implies some sort of circus or show put on by a few and watched by the masses who stare dumbfoundedly in amusement and amazement. It implies control and passivity, separation and isolation. The "show," in fact, is modern society: "The entire life of societies in which modern conditions of production prevail announces itself as an immense accumulation of spectacles'' (Debord, *The Society of the Spectacle*, p. 1). The term *spectacle* subsumes all the means and methods power employs, outside of direct force, to relegate potentially political, critical, and creative human beings to the margins of thought and behavior. The spectacle then is depoliticization par excellence: "The very principle of the spectacle [is] nonintervention" (*SI Anthology*, p. 45). Mesmerized by the wide array of "diversions" offered by the spectacular society, from goods and services to entertainment and conveniences, human beings stray far from the most critical task: changing the world and liberating everyday life. In the meantime, bureaucratic domination refines and perfects its techniques.

The origin of the spectacle is found in an emerging commodity society. As outlined by Debord in *The Society of the Spectacle*, the industrial revolution must be seen in two stages. The first stage marks the transition from precapitalist society, where the commodity has only a marginal economic function, to capitalist society, where it assumes autonomy and begins to dominate social and cultural life. In the second stage, the transition from "early" to "late" capitalism, the commodity assumes "total control." This stage is characterized by the primacy of consumption over production and the creation of an advanced information/communication network that operates unidirectionally. A new human being is created: the consumer. Previously repressed and sublimated desires are now unleased and "desublimated" (Herbert Marcuse*) ideologically so that they can be reshaped and channeled into the circuits of consumption and leisure. (It might be noted that this structural shift performs a double function: it resolves a crisis in the accumulation of capital, which imperialism alone could not do, and more generally, it legitimizes the capitalist system.) Alienation, once a consciously experienced and unwanted misery, has now become unconscious, "made comfortable," and multiplied in consumption. Domination, once essentially coercive and economic in nature, is now primarily ideological and cultural: ideological, as the tangible world and machinery of the spectacle sets up above itself an inverted unreality of reified thought and images, which are taken as real; and cultural as the power of this ideological control is disseminated through the cultural apparatuses of society, especially the media.

A critique of the spectacular society cannot be complete without a critique of its organization of space, specifically the urban milieu. The underlying assumption of this discussion is that space is not neutral terrain that we simply inhabit or stroll through; rather it is, for better or worse, the lived sphere of influence. The general theory of the lived impact of space is termed "psycho-geography," "the study of specific effects of geographical environment, consciously organized or not, on the emotions and behavior of individuals" (*SI Anthology*, p. 45). Space is socio-historically specific; different societies will produce different types of space. A repressive society can only produce a repressive space. Thus, in capitalist society, the "bureaucratic society of controlled consumption" (Lefebvre), "the space of everyday life is encircled by every form of conditioning" (*SI Anthology*, p. 128). Space is a form of domination sui generis both in its physical layout, which is seen to militate against individual action and social interaction, and in its general "ambiance," which is seen to stultify desire and the imagination. The combined effect is psychic and social fragmentation, combined with reinforced pacification. Thus, space is another form of the spectacle, and the contestation of society begins, as will be noted, with a radical reconstruction (*détournement*) of the lived environment, with the supersession of "urbanism" by "unitary urbanism."

The revolution, then, is nothing less than the destruction of the spectacular, the exposure and transcendence of the ideological. The thrust is at everyday life. To call for and attempt to organize a class struggle along the traditional Marxian political lines while the proletariat is still in the throes of the spectacle is clearly to place the cart before the horse. As matters now stand, the proletariat neither desires nor sees the need for revolution. Cultural revolution is not a substitute for the overthrow of capitalism, but it is a necessary first step. "The revolutionary transformation of everyday life is not reserved for some vague future, but is placed immediately before us by the development of capitalism and its unbearable demands" (ibid., p. 75). How can this be accomplished? For the Situationists, the way the spectacular can be exposed is through the creation of nonspectacular ruptures. These are called "situations." The situation is a demonstrative breaking of the spectacular, which permits the expression of desires and emancipated possibilities that everyday life has suppressed.

An example of a situation-creating technique is the *dérive*. The *dérive* is the first step toward an urban praxis. It is a stroll through the city by several people who are out to understand the "psycho-geographical articulations of the modern city" (ibid., p. 5). The strollers attempt an interpretive reading of the city, an architectural understanding. They look at the city as a special instance of repressed desires. At the same time, they engage in "playful reconstructive behavior" (ibid., p. 50). Together they turn the city around. They see in the city unifying and empowering possibilities in place of the present fragmentation and pacification. This "turning around," or *détournement*, is a key strategic concept of the Situationists. *Détournement* is a dialectical tool. It is an "insurrectional style" by which a past form is used to show its own inherent untruth—an untruth masked by an ideology. It can be applied to billboards, to written texts, to films, to cartoons, etc., as well as to city spaces. Marx used it when he "turned Hegel on his head." He used the dialectic in the study of history to expose the ideological nature of Hegel's idealism. The Situationists used *détournement* to demonstrate the scandalous poverty of everyday life despite the plenty of commodities. They attempted to demonstrate the contrast between what life presently is and what it could be. They wanted to rupture the spell of the ideology of our commodified consumer society so that our repressed desires of a more authentic nature could come forward. The situation is based on liberated desires rather than alienated ones. What these desires are cannot be stated a priori. They will emerge in the revolutionary process of situation-creation, of *détournement*. Presumably, communality, unification, and public urban space will emerge as more desirable than commodification, fragmentation, and privatization.

Art will be crucial in this endeavor. But here art as human interaction, art as the creation of new spaces and forms of communication therein, takes precedence over art that produced physical products like paintings, statues, or texts, which can themselves be easily commodified. Everyday life itself must be transformed into art, must become poetry. Technology is not rejected here. It becomes a necessary condition for the liberation of everyday life and merges with art in a "unitary urbanism" that seeks to create and establish new forms of behavior. The urban space, of course, includes factories. There, workers must *détourne* the situation—turn it on its head—by asserting control over their own space and electing their own councils. It is only by this direct, situation-creating action that workers can avoid looking at the revolution as a spectacle, that they can become active agents in the process of *détournment*. It is this, on a wide scale, that the Situationists hoped to trigger by their cultural action on the level of everyday life. What they looked toward ultimately was an "antistatist dictatorship of the proletariat," which would integrally reconstruct the space of the territory according to the emancipated desires of the people themselves. This was, for them, the meaning of a city.

The Situationists looked upon themselves as a catalyst. They tried to find a way to break through the ideological structure that was exacting such strong control over the proletariat. Ultimately, however, the problem lay in capitalism and commodity fetishism. The final solution would be in the hands of an active and conscious proletariat. In this sense, the Situationists remained much more profoundly Marxist than the Frankfurt School, which also stressed ideology and culture but gave up on the proletariat as an agent of change. Dissipated through factionalism, purges, and resignations, the Situationists did not remain together long enough to mount their experiments on any serious scale. While they were together, they often seemed to be spending more time in attacking virtually every other group and intellectual on the left than *dérive* and *détournement*. They also left something to be desired in terms of analytic rigor and concept clarification. For example, they did not rigorously confront the problem of the relationship of the proletariat with other segments of society captivated by everyday life. But in developing the concept of the spectacle as far as they did, they provided a useful analytic tool for understanding contemporary capitalist society. Moreover, their theory and praxis of the situation, *dérive* and *détournement*, constitute an imaginative advance in political tactics suited to that society. Their work both deserves and requires further experimentation and development.

BIBLIOGRAPHY:

A. Guy Debord, *The Society of the Spectacle* (Detroit: Black and Red, 1970) (unauthorized translation); Ken Knabb, ed. and trans. *Situationist International Anthology* (Berkeley: Bureau of Public Secrets, 1981); Raoul Vaneigem, *The Revolution in Everyday Life* (London: Left Bank Books and Rebel Press, 1983).

BELDEN FIELDS and STEVEN BEST

SOCIALISME OU BARBARIE. Forty issues of *Socialisme ou barbarie* (*S/B*), which was also the name of the group occupied with its publication, were issued

in Paris between 1949 and 1965. The title comes from Rosa Luxemburg's†
observation that the collapse of capitalism offers the world's working class the
alternative: socialism or barbarism. Its choice as title and name reflects the
historical and political context from which *S/B* emerged. It was founded at the
end of a period in which capitalism had demonstrated the horrors of which it
was capable, by a handful of ex-Trotskyists† (soon joined by a group of Bor-
digists) to whom it had become apparent that Marxism†-Leninism† was the
foundation not of a socialist alternative but only of another form of barbarism.
Thus the group's earliest preoccupation was the analysis of the Soviet Union:
in a series of articles Cornelius Castoriadis—along with Claude Lefort (b. 1924)
the most prominent founder of the group—criticized the Trotskyist conception
of the Stalinist† regime. Russia was not, wrote Castoriadis (under the pseudonym
of Chaulieu, among others), a "degenerated workers' state," but a new form
of class-ruled system, with a new ruling class, the bureaucracy.

In its first years individuals of many left-wing political orientations participated
in the work of the group, and a number of viewpoints coexisted in *S/B* throughout
its existence. But Castoriadis was always the central figure, due largely to his
skill in synthesizing a theory from many sources, his powerful and authoritarian
personality, and his tactical skill: those who disagreed with him left the organization. In the early 1950s, *S/B* gained association with small numbers of radical
workers and employees. Indeed, this was a period of growing restlessness among
French workers; it also saw the death of Stalin, the repercussions of that event
within the Western Communist parties and in Eastern Europe, and the beginning
of the Algerian War. *S/B* had grown considerably when in 1958 de Gaulle's
coup, interpreted by some in the group as the prelude to a new period of fascism,
stimulated debate on the "organizational question" within *S/B*. For Castoriadis
and some others, *S/B* had always been a proto-party; now they proposed its
formal transformation into a disciplined political organization. The result was a
major split, with Lefort and H. Simon—both opposing organizational consolidation and hierarchy—leaving, with others, to found the ILO (Informations et
Liaisons Ouvrières), which in turn (after Lefort's departure) turned into ICO
(Information Correspondance Ouvrière), groups that saw their main role not as
propounding the theoretical positions of a new political formation but as organizing communication and discussion among militant workers. By the end of 1963
Lefort abandoned Marxism altogether, claiming that Marxism and capitalism
both acquiesced to the hegemony of bureaucratic elites.

Meanwhile Castoriadis had also moved from the critique of the Soviet Union
to the critique of Marxism itself, as an economic and social theory. It is no
accident, Castoriadis insisted, that Marxism had developed into Leninism and
Stalinism; whatever Marx's wishes, the seeds of this denouement were in his
theory from the start. Marx falsely denied human creativity in history by leaving
the class struggle out of his portrait of capitalism's "laws of motion." At the
same time Castoriadis claimed that class had lost its importance as a basis for
social revolution, stressing the replacement of the class division between capital

and proletariat by that between managers and managed—a division shared by the bureaucratic system of the East and the managerial capitalism of the West. Contrary to Marx's predictions, capitalism was headed not toward economic crisis but toward a continuous expansion of consumption. Revolt would come not from an impoverished proletariat but from all those—workers, students, women, etc.—who refused the alienation from their creative powers imposed on them by the existing system. This critique of Marxism led in 1963 to another split within *S/B*, with a "Marxist" faction taking with them as they left a factory-oriented publication of *S/B*, *Pouvoir Ouvrier*. Although interest in *S/B* continued to grow after this time, in 1967 the group decided to disband, officially because of the failure of its readership to create the political organization that was *S/B*'s main objective.

Despite the fact that its membership varied from a handful to 100 at most, while the journal achieved a maximum circulation of 1,000, *S/B* played an important role in the evolution of the postwar radical left in France. Since it was, at the time of its founding, the only group aside from traditional anarchist or Marxist-Leninist organizations, it is not surprising that many of those who later played important parts in the unofficial left passed through it. On the other hand, the ideas of its central figure, Castoriadis, can now be seen to have foreshadowed and contributed to the anti-Marxist leftist ideology that has developed since the early 1970s, particularly among academics, in many countries besides France.

BIBLIOGRAPHY:

A. Apart from the forty issues of *Socialisme ou Barbarie* the most important source of original material is the multivolume edition of Castoriadis's essays (Paris: UGT, 1973–) in the series 10/18. The first of these, *La Société bureaucratique 1* contains an introductory essay by Castoriadis on the history of *S/B* and its ideas. Corrective information is to be gleaned from interviews with other sometime members of the group: "De la scission avec *Socialisme ou barbarie* à la rupture avec ICO (entretien avec H. Simon)," *L'Anti-Myths*, 6 (1974); "An Interview with Cornelius Castoriadis," *Telos*, 23 (Spring 1975), pp. 131–55; "An Interview with Claude Lefort," *Telos*, 30 (Winter 1976–77), pp. 173–92.

B. Claude Lefort, *Eléments d'une critique de la bureaucratie* (Paris: Maspero, 1971).

PAUL MATTICK, JR.

SOLLERS, PHILIPPE (b. 1936). Cofounder and director of the literary journal *Tel Quel* and author of highly acclaimed experimental novels, Sollers has been a lifelong adherent of the cultural-revolutionary potential of art. In this view, he stands with the tradition of German romanticism and of such writers as Herbert Marcuse* and André Breton. In the late 1960s, he led his journal to a dialogue with Communist Party intellectuals on the nature and role of art in capitalist culture and in revolution, but broke with the Party in 1971 over Macciochi's *De la Chine* and became an exponent of the cultural revolution of Maoism† (cf. his *Sur le matérialisme*, 1974).

In Sollers's fiction, perhaps more than in any of the other experimental, or new novelists, the cherished categories of subjectivity, the world, history, and fiction are broken down or exposed as laboriously maintained self-limitations. It is this confrontation between art and the conceptual limitations of our culture that Sollers took to be the sign of the revolutionary potential of avant-garde artistic activity (cf. *L'Écriture et l'expérience des limites*, 1968). Neo-Marxism in France and around the world has come to recognize the autonomy and profound importance of artistic activity in the maintenance and in the possible mutations of socio-cultural entities through the work of such authors as Philippe Sollers and his collaborators in the journal *Tel Quel*.

BIBLIOGRAPHY:

A. *Sur le matérialisme* (Paris: Seuil, 1974); *Writing and the Experience of Limits* (New York: Columbia University Press, 1983).

LAURENCE E. WINTERS

SOREL, GEORGES (1847–1922). Georges Sorel was born on 2 November 1847 in the French city of Cherbourg, was educated at the Ecole Polytechnique in Paris, and until the age of forty-five was employed as a government engineer. It was only after he retired, in 1893, that Sorel began to write about Marxism,† first advocating Marx's orthodox brand of historical materialism, but gradually—after 1896—developing his own unique and controversial formulation. After advocating, like Edward Bernstein,* democratic reformism as the apt strategy to achieve socialism, Sorel became quickly disillusioned and emerged instead as Europe's foremost theoretical exponent of revolutionary syndicalism (see *Reflections on Violence*, 1906). When the syndicalist movement failed to realize his hopes, Sorel, in 1909, turned to the extraparliamentary right. In his later years Sorel exhibited admiration for both Lenin† and Mussolini. He died in Boulogne-sur-Seine on 28 August 1922.

Sorel indicted rational enlightenment philosophy and empirical science for artificially reducing life to simple categories that are incapable of grasping humanity's "dark area": the subliminal forces of tradition, sex, religion, will, and nationality that permeate human history. Rationalism naively believes that injustice is eradicated with empirical knowledge, reformist legislation, and humanitarianism. On the contrary, said Sorel, life is a complex totality of internally linked phenomena. Rational knowledge is ill suited to such complexity, unintentionally generating weakness and ignorance, not enlightenment. A complex social totality is comprehended not rationally but through myth, that is, by irrationally acknowledging an essentially irrational dialectical reality. Myth, not bourgeois rationalism, is the foundation of authentic social inquiry. Through myth we experience innate primitive instincts, stripped of history's nonmythical sediment. Myth is therefore pessimistic and critical, spurning easy reductive formulas and negating the rational status quo. Myth, in other words, is simultaneously authentic and revolutionary. We either leave society untouched, living in "rationally" exploitative conditions, or annihilate it totally in a fit of authenticity.

Sorel understood Marx's historical materialism in these terms. It pessimistically explains human history and mobilizes a critical, revolutionary working class. Similarly, it rejects reform and empirical reductionism, exhorting the proletariat to challenge and destroy capitalism. Marxism is myth because it postulates a complex, irreducible capitalist totality and inspires revolutionary insurrection. Moreover, this myth manifests a general workers' strike, which destroys bourgeois civilization in the name of human emancipation. Historical materialism is not a rational blueprint. While inconclusively speculating about socialist cooperation and collective unity, it is primarily negative: glorifying rebellion rather than painting a utopia. For Sorel, the mythical general strike mobilizes workers into syndicates. Traditional working-class parties and trade unions inhibit our intuiting the revolutionary myth and hence perpetuate rational tyranny. Workers' syndicates, on the other hand, spontaneously organize workers into factory-based, self-managing teams that subvert bourgeois authority structures. They inspire members to intuit the authentic myth of proletariat revolution subjectively and subordinate practical economic, social, and political issues to this irrational goal. Syndicates, therefore, oppose bourgeois institutions, unite the working class against a common bourgeois enemy, and generate postrevolutionary social forms of self-governing workers and farmers interacting cooperatively (resembling what Marx, in criticizing Proudhon, ironically called a "petit bourgeois utopia").

Proletariat revolution, argued Sorel, seeks neither power nor classlessness. Instead, it purges modernity of unnatural oppression and initiates the direct freedom of emancipated humanity. Consequently, it rejects class dictatorship— even of the majority—and debilitating governmental bureaucracies. The myth of the general strike is anti-intellectual, antibourgeois, antihierarchical; its only tactic is success. It does not follow theoretical formulas or obey tactical cliques and turns violent for practical reasons. By physically annihilating the capitalist enemy, workers facilitate a swift transition to self-management and rejuvenate the precivilized, irrational instincts that will organize postrevolutionary society. Sorel, like other Marxists, advocated class war, rejected utopianism, worked to abolish the capitalist state, and believed in total revolution. But he also glorified innate, prebourgeois qualities such as heroism, greatness, dignity, and authenticity. Accordingly, he admired and emulated the ancient Christian martyrs and therefore—illogically—respected many of Western civilization's religious, social, and sexual traditions. He believed in voluntarism and self-determining freedom but simultaneously sanctified an irrational myth that propelled humanity into uncontrollable rebellious paroxysms. He was an historical materialist who also advocated anarcho-syndicalism and spontaneous irrationality. He was a proletarian revolutionary who sympathetically cited Vico, Proudhon, Bergson, Nietzsche, Tocqueville, Taine, Renan, and others. In sum, he cared little for theoretical rigor or intellectual system building, picking and choosing ideas that would mobilize the discontented.

BIBLIOGRAPHY:

A. *Matériaux d'une théorie du prolétariat* (Paris: M. Rivière, 1929); *Reflections on Violence* (Glencoe, Ill.: Free Press, 1950); *The Decomposition of Marxism* (New York: Humanities Press, 1961); *The Illusions of Progress* (Berkeley: University of California Press, 1969).

B. Irving L. Horowitz, *Radicalism and the Revolt Against Reason* (London: Routledge & Kegan Paul, 1961); Richard Vernon, *Commitment and Change: Georges Sorel and the Idea of Revolution* (Toronto: University of Toronto Press, 1978); Jack J. Roth, *The Cult of Violence: Sorel and the Sorelians* (Berkeley: University of California Press, 1980); John J. Stanley, *The Sociology of Virtue: The Political and Social Theories of Georges Sorel* (Berkeley: University of California Press, 1982).

ROBERT A. GORMAN

STAVENHAGEN, RODOLFO (b. 1932). The noted Mexican sociologist Rodolfo Stavenhagen was born in Frankfurt, Germany, on 29 August 1932. He received a B.A. from the University of Chicago, an M.A. at the National Autonomous University (UNAM), and his Ph.D. from the University of Paris (1965). Since 1972 he has been the director of the Department of Sociology at El Colegio de Mexico, Mexico City. In addition, Stavenhagen has served as the general secretary of the Latin American Center for Research in the Social Sciences, Rio de Janeiro (1962–65) and as senior staff associate of the International Institute of Labour Studies, Geneva (1965–71). In 1973 he was awarded the National "Sourasky" Science Prize.

Stavenhagen's work is concerned with questions of land, social stratification, and the effects of agrarian reform on neocolonial societies. In a provocative essay, "Seven Fallacies About Latin America" (1968), the author attacks the notion that "dual societies" of feudal and capitalist elements are in conflict with each other. Building on the work of fellow Mexican sociologist, Pablo González Casanova,* Stavenhagen argues that peripheral regions are essentially internal colonies of the growing urban areas and agricultural centers that concentrate on export within the framework of an underdeveloped capitalist system. Exploitation of the labor force is one factor that helps explain how peripheral areas actually permit the growth of the more "modern zones," thereby contributing to the stagnation of these "traditional areas." In cases of internal colonialism the urban bourgeoisie is not necessarily in conflict with large landowners of the peripheral areas. Indeed, these classes may be allied. Stavenhagen's scholarly output has been both empirical and synthetic. In a micro-analysis of the working class in the "frontera" of Tijuana, for example, the sociologist offers an intriguing view of the border town's housing problems, medical services, and juvenile delinquency and the day-to-day difficulties that confront urban families. On the other hand, Stavenhagen has also contributed several macro-studies on the agrarian structure of Mexico. His revised dissertation, *Las clases sociales en las sociedades agrarias* (1969) and his contribution to an anthology (which he edited), *Agrarian Problems and Peasant Movements in Latin America* (1970), emphasize that modernization cannot take place without fundamental changes in the social,

political, and economic structure of Mexico. More recently he has examined the impact of capitalism on the peasantry and concluded that dependent capitalism requires the maintenance of an impoverished peasant economy. This has been accomplished in Mexico by agrarian reform, limited industrialization, and population growth. He concludes that without revolutionary institutional change, meaningful reform to alter the condition of the peasantry cannot take place.
BIBLIOGRAPHY:

A. "Seven Fallacies About Latin America," pp. 13–31, in James Petras and Maurice Zeitlin, eds., *Latin America: Reform or Revolution?* (New York: Fawcett, 1968); *Agrarian Problems and Peasant Movements in Latin America* (Garden City, N.Y.: Doubleday, 1970).

CARL A. ROSS AND ALLEN WELLS

STOJANOVIĆ, SVETOZAR (b. 1931). The Yugoslav Svetozar Stojanović was born into a petit bourgeois family in 1931. After World War II he became a member of the Communist Youth Organization. He was a member of the Communist Party of Yugoslavia from 1950 until 1968, when he and seven other *Praxis** Marxists† of Belgrade were excluded from the Party because of their support for the 1968 student rebellion at Belgrade University and for their unacceptable theoretical views. In 1975 the "Belgrade Eight" were suspended from their teaching positions by an act of the Serbian Parliament, which authorized itself to dismiss university professors who lacked "moral and political fitness." Stojanović received his Ph.D. from Belgrade University in 1962; his dissertation, *Contemporary Meta-ethics* (published in 1964), introduced Anglo-American analytic ethics into Yugoslavia. He was a member of the editorial board of *Praxis*, the fertile journal of humanistic Marxism that ceased publication in 1975, when state subsidies were cut off. He was editor-in-chief of the journal *Filozofija* and founded the journal *Gledistu*, for which he was editor-in-chief for many years. He is currently a member of the editorial board of *Praxis International*. Stojanović was also chairman of the Department of Philosophy and Sociology at Belgrade University. Since being removed from teaching, a new arrangement with the authorities was reached in July 1981 that granted Stojanović a research position at the newly created Center for Philosophy and Social Theory (University of Belgrade). He has been allowed to teach and lecture at several universities in West Germany, the United States, and other countries.

Stojanović's writings make a powerful case for democratic-humanistic Marxism. He has been a vigorous critic of Stalinism.† Arguing that Marxists must not devote themselves solely to the critique of capitalist societies, Stojanović has called for equally strong criticism of the obstacles to democratization in Socialist countries. In practice—Stojanović charges—socialism has not even reached the level of political democracy found in bourgeois societies. In *Between Ideals and Reality* (1969) he argues that Marx's categorization of socio-economic formations is no longer adequate. An important new category, under which Stojanović places Soviet society, is *statism*, a system in which the state has emancipated itself from society in order to become its master—promoting the interest of the bureaucratic class. It is to be distinguished from state socialism, in which the state represents and ensures the interests of the working class. In statism, ownership of the means of production and products of labor on the part of the state apparatus constitutes a new form of class society. As the collective owner of the means of production the bureaucratic state employs and exploits the labor force: it disposes of surplus value primarily in its own interests and bars the working class from controlling production and making decisions about the distribution of surplus value. *In Search of Democracy in Socialism* (1981), Stojanović's latest book, details how the Stalinist version of statism uses the metaphysical status of the Party to fashion an entire society in its own image. He creatively extends the Weberian notion of charisma to a collective—the Party. Coining the term *charismarchy* (an analogy to oligarchy), he maintains that the Party is perceived as having a charismatic quality that makes it an order-determining power, the irreplaceable agent of progress toward communism. The charismatic Party, according to Stojanović, thrives best in a country with an authoritarian tradition (in a situation of "political poverty"), in which identification with an infallible collective provides compensation for individual powerlessness.

In both *Between Ideals and Reality* and *In Search of Democracy in Socialism* Stojanović shows a deep concern for revolutionary ethics. In the former he attempts to correct the moral deficiencies of Marxist theory in his attack on "revolutionary teleology"—the view that the revolutionary end justifies any means. The failure of this perspective is that it does not see the moral necessity of relating means and ends dialectically so that not only are means chosen in accordance with the end but the end's true nature is also revealed in the means chosen. Stojanović warns that what revolutionaries do in the course of revolution "leaves deep traces upon them and largely defines their behavior after they come to power" (*In Search of Democracy in Socialism*, p. 195). He asserts that the revolutionary is obligated to use violence only when it is absolutely indispensable; the revolutionary should know that "it is better for many guilty people to escape revolutionary justice than for one innocent person to perish at its hands" (ibid., p. 196). *In Search of Democracy in Socialism* also deals with individual morality in the postrevolutionary society. Here, reviewing the Moscow purge trials and writing as someone who was subjected to continued public attacks, Stojanović affirms the importance of retaining dignity in the face of a hostile Party. He argues that the deviant Communist must not allow the collective charisma of the Party to lure him into public self-abasement: "One can only wish that the legacy of Stalinism were so widespread and well appreciated that Communists might, from the very first, honor the principle: 'Do not treat personal dignity as a means in the revolutionary effort' " (p. 143).

One of Stojanović's most recent contributions to Marxist theory is his formulation of a distinction between the ruling class and the dominant class. The bourgeoisie, according to Stojanović, is the first class in history that can dominate

without ruling. It dominates through noncoercive means such as ideology and culture. Understanding the bourgeoisie as a dominant rather than a ruling class opens the way to the study of power elites. The failure to make this distinction has prevented Marxists from seeing that the bourgeois-democratic revolution did not merely lead to the substitution of one type of class rule by another, but rather to an essentially new type of class society that makes possible the development of democratic political life for all citizens. Although limited by the domination of the bourgeois class, bourgeois democracy represents enormous progress. The lack of a ruling class represents a necessary but not a sufficient condition for a democratic order. In the spirit of the *Praxis* group, Stojanović insists that full democracy can be achieved only through a system of integrated self-management.
BIBLIOGRAPHY:

A. *Between Ideals and Reality* (New York: Oxford University Press, 1973); *In Search of Democracy in Socialism* (Buffalo, N.Y.: Prometheus Press, 1981); "Marxism and Democracy: The Ruling or the Dominant Class?" *Praxis International* I (July 1981).

B. David Crocker, *Praxis and Democratic Socialism: The Critical Theory of Marković and Stojanović* (Atlantic Highlands, N.J.: Humanities Press, 1983).

DAVID MYERS

STRUCTURAL MARXISM. The structural brand of Marxism that became so popular particularly in France in the 1960s and 1970s and that culminated in Louis Althusser's* systematic synthesis, is based primarily on the work of Claude Lévi-Strauss,* which uncovers essential truths that govern social organization, independent of actors, intentions, or facts. The problematic of modern structuralism was set in the pioneering linguistic studies of Ferdinand de Saussure, especially the *Course in General Linguistics*. For nineteenth-century linguists, spoken words (signifiers) expressed corresponding mental images (signifieds). Saussure emphasized the priority of signifiers, which are impersonal and suitable for formal analysis. But intentionally spoken words comprise a practical means of communicating that alters with time and place. Science, on the other hand, proposes objective truths that condition verbal behavior. The former—*la langue*—are explained diachronically, through historical inquiry. The latter—*la parole*—comprises a timeless structure that science generates by synchronic inquiry into universal, static relationships. Saussure substituted eternal linguistic structures for historically concrete languages and derived meaning from a total language structure rather than the speaking subject. Spoken words are meaningful only in relation to other words and the collective total structure, irrespective of subjective intention. The project of systematizing a universal language structure that appears unconsciously through speaking subjects was continued by Jakobson, Hjelmslev, and Benveniste.

Lévi-Strauss applied the insights and findings of structural linguistics to social inquiry, particularly the study of kinship systems and mythologies of primitives. Structural social science establishes a priori systems of symbolic communication meaningful in themselves, apart from manifest actions and motives. Lévi-Strauss's strenuous decoding of primitive tribal myths confirms that activities of diverse, unrelated tribal communities are conceptually arranged into a series of communicative signs that follow an invariant logical pattern or structure. The real meaning of tribal behavior is its function within the inclusive structure. Obviously, participants are not aware of this because subjective experiences, real enough to involved actors when acting, unknowingly express this precognitive structure. Hence popular notions like free will, consciousness, and intentionality are scientifically meaningless. When all myths are known—when social structure is entirely revealed—scientists will understand every aspect of interpersonal communication, as well as the human mind in its fixed, atemporal structure. Science's goal, for Lévi-Strauss and other structuralists, is universal human mind: the precognitive structure that guides cognition and action. History merely shifts these same hypothesized structures, so that terms like *primitive* and *modern* are meaningless, and historical "progress" irrelevant. Societies unconsciously adopt a combination of timeless structural components. Social "movement" indicates that some combinations work better than others in realizing a life-sustaining purpose. Those that fail are replaced by others whose own historical fate is already sealed. For Lévi-Strauss, structuralism is a universal science of invariant, absolute principles governing all interaction. Structuralist social inquiry describes systems of empirical phenomena manifesting an essential, determining structure.

The shared preconceptions of structuralism and Marxism have generated a lively dialogue. Both are, philosophically, anti-individualist, hence reject basic principles of modern capitalism such as self-interest, negative freedom, empiricism, and humanism. The structuralist Gaston Bachelard,* for example, argues in *La Formation de l'esprit scientifique* (1967) that science must negate extant philosophy and ideology and construct new thought patterns. This "epistemological break" generates universal structures to explain common perceptions and facts scientifically. Although not himself a Marxist, Bachelard's structural epistemology critically confronts individualist ideas and institutions and therefore inspired Marxists like Althusser. Jacques Lacan structurally "decenters" bourgeois actors into impersonal structures of culture (ego) and desire (id). With both empirical (cognitive) and subconscious (precognitive) psyches scattered and disunified, human subjectivity is essentially incoherent, and standard bourgeois philosophy and psychology meaningless except in upholding the material interests of a hegemonic capitalist elite.

Structuralism and Marxism are also totalizing methods of inquiry, perceiving reality as multidimensional and interpenetrating, where particulars are conditioned by the whole. Both scientifically progress beyond immediate empirical observation into a realm of hidden truths. Roland Barthes's* structural science of signs—"semiology"—examines the role of social myth in conditioning subjective perceptions of ordinary experiences. Semiology, like Marxism, demystifies everyday capitalist life by explaining how unconscious mythical structures distort public messages, rationalize the status quo, and reinforce bourgeois class hegemony. Seemingly innocuous empirical events like advertisements, films, and newspaper headlines are redefined by the structural totality and transformed into tools of capitalist oppression. Semiology has spawned a group of "new semiotics," including Jacques Derrida,* Julia Kristeva,* and Phillipe Sollers,* who carry the structural decentering of language and pop culture to a logical conclusion: each text or event has its own structure, which it begets merely by being produced. They replace structural logic—a priori universals conditioning empirical life—with "grammatology," that is, a totally destructive hermeneutics that breaks texts into their own impersonal, determining language structures. Language becomes autonomous: words and sentences are defined through perceived relations with other elements of that text, and with other texts, generating unlimited interpretations. Known as the Tel Quel group, the new semiotics intellectually negate bourgeois culture by critically interpreting capitalist texts, elucidating "harmless" cultural phenomena that unintentionally propagate class oppression.

Finally, structuralism, like Marxism, presumes that language and culture are conditioned by objective, interpersonal forces. Therefore "autonomous" concepts and things—artificially torn from reality—are dysfunctional and inauthentic. When structures are transformed into real economic and social processes, then structuralism assimilates materialism: both analyze concrete processes by which signifier and signified interrelate, repudiating the bourgeois transcendentalism of nonmaterialist structuralism. Since Marx's† historical materialism outlines the economic component of determining structures, structuralists are comfortable predicting the decline of private property and individualism and the necessity of worker rebellion.

The postwar radicalization of Western Europe, culminating in the student rebellions of May 1968, reinforced structuralism's tentative union with Marxism. But no one systematically explained how decentered egos, conditioned by impersonal structures, can or will actively transform oppressive systems that they didn't even create. Structuralism, even the radical version, defines truth independent of action. Impersonal structures are always determining, and hence intentional revolutionary activism is meaningless. Moreover, ideologies are irrelevant to structural science. Universal structures, theoretically immune to historical moods, are as likely to be reactionary as progressive: there is no scientific criterion supporting radical structuralism against bourgeois structuralism. The union is politically rather than theoretically motivated. Michel Foucault,* a self-styled radical structuralist, illustrates the problem. Foucault structurally redefined history by using impersonal *épistèmes*, atemporal structures that limit the ways we cognitively perceive and define objects. In denying continuity or intentionality to history—he sees it as impersonally conditioned, ruptured, unsystematic, discursive, determined by events rather than actors, "a blank, indifferent space, lacking in both interiority and promise" (*Archaeology of Knowledge*, pp. 38–39)—Foucault perceived hegemonic bourgeois ideas and institutions as "correct" only in upholding the material interests of capitalism. Hence he was "Marxist," critically demystifying bourgeois rhetoric. However, the same structural historiography, applied to socialism, would perform the same critical function. Foucault's Marxism is conditional, not scientific, because of the political exigencies of his life and times.

BIBLIOGRAPHY:

B. Jan M. Broekman, *Structuralism: Moscow-Prague-Paris* (Dordrecht: Reidel, 1974); Miriam Glucksmann, *Structuralist Analysis in Contemporary Social Thought* (London: Routledge & Kegan Paul, 1974); Dominique Lecourt, *Marxism and Epistemology* (London: New Left Books, 1975); Rosalind Coward and John Ellis, *Language and Materialism* (London: Routledge & Kegan Paul, 1977); Edith Kurzweil, *The Age of Structuralism* (New York: Columbia University Press, 1980); Michael Ryan, *Marxism and Deconstruction* (Baltimore: Johns Hopkins University Press, 1982).

ROBERT A. GORMAN

SUPEK, RUDI (b. 1913). The Yugoslav Rudi Supek was born in Zagreb in 1913 and studied philosophy in Zagreb and psychology with Jean Piaget in Paris, earning a Ph.D. in 1952. During World War II Supek participated in the French Resistance and was arrested and sent to the Buchenwald concentration camp, where he became a leader of the underground organization. He taught psychology at the University of Zagreb (1951–58) and was a research fellow at the Institute of Social Sciences in Belgrade (1958–61). Since 1961 Supek has been a Professor of sociology at the Faculty of Art, University of Zagreb. He was also editor of the philosophical journal *Pogledi* (1952–54), editor-in-chief (with Gajo Petrocić*) of *Praxis** (1966–73), and has been a member of the board of *Praxis International* since 1981. He was president of the Korčula Summer School board, the Croatian Sociological Society, and the Yugoslav Sociological Association. Supek is today considered the dean of modern Yugoslav sociology, although his interdisciplinary approach encompasses psychology and philosophy as well. Supek is the author or editor of more than two dozen books, including *Automation and the Working Class* (1965), *Sociology and Socialism* (1966), *Humanist Intelligentsia and Politics* (1971), *Social Prejudices* (1973), *Only One Earth* (1973, 1978), *Participation, Workers' Control and Self-Management* (1974), plus numerous articles in *Praxis* and other journals and symposia.

Supek's theoretical contributions to Marxism†—particularly to the *Praxis* school of Marxist humanist thought—lie in social psychology, cultural anthropology, ontology, and ethics. Supek achieved international acclaim as a spokesman for the Yugoslav innovations in the concept and practice of self-management. As Supek points out in his 1982 *Praxis International* article, the historical alternative today is between statism and self-managing socialism. In his long professional career, Supek has attempted to develop the socio-psychological, sociological, and philosophical underpinnings of a humanistic socialism based on workers' self-management, as well as a personalist conception of socialist culture. Influenced by Proudhon and French existentialism, Supek identifies socialism with Marx's vision of a free community of associated producers that has transcended the alienating frameworks of both the market mechanism and capitalist political institutions.

Supek's vision of communism as a dealienated community of free men is anchored in the concept of praxis as man's creative and self-creative activity, which constantly revolutionizes both himself and the world. Praxis as workers' self-management and social self-government is the key to the dealienation of self and the world. In his major work, *Sociology and Socialism*, Supek attempts to find the proper place for sociology in socialism and in doing so parts ways with dogmatic conceptions of both sociology and Marxist thought. He adopts Roger Garaudy's* critique of Stalinism† as a positivistic orientation that excludes human (self-)creative activity (praxis) and rejects Marx's theory of alienation as well as Hegel's dialectical method, since the latter contained a humanist critique of both statism and the positivistic submission of the human personality to society. In his essay on "The Statist and Self-Managing Models of Socialism," Supek caps his critique of Stalinism by an analysis of the basic power structure in statist socialism that allegedly rests on the "real triangle of power" of the Party-government-army and police leadership.

Supek has also been one of the most outspoken critics among the *Praxis* theorists of both the market mechanism and the failures of Yugoslav self-management practice. In a series of articles in *Praxis* and other journals, culminating in his work on *Participation, Workers' Control and Self-Management*, Supek offered a scathing indictment of the growing consumerism in Yugoslav society that accompanied the introduction of elements of the market mechanism in the 1960s, deploring the increasing social differences, embourgeoisement of socialist managers, parvenu *nouveaux riches*, exploitation, alienation, corruption, speculation, development of "petit-bourgeois capitalism," and loss of socialist consciousness. Along with other *Praxis* theorists, Supek pointed to the reproduction of hierarchical, bureaucratic, statist power structures within self-managing institutions left to fend for themselves in market socialism. In theory, Supek and others saw workers' self-management as both desirable and necessary for a free, self-governing community of producers. In reality, self-managing institutions suffered from bureaucratization due to their routinization and from hierarchical authority structures partially as a result of the rural origins of the work force within a society characterized by a dualism of power: representative institutions at the global level and self-governing councils at the enterprise level.

Supek left an indelible mark in the field of cultural anthropology, ontology, and ethics by his quest for a nondogmatic, creative Marxism and a personalist conception of socialist culture. In his famous *Praxis* article, "Why, Now, Yet Another Marxism?" Supek summed up the *Praxis* theorists' contributions to the philosophical-theoretical presuppositions of self-managing socialism. These centered on the rehabilitation of creative praxis, the anthropological-humanistic bases of Marxism, the concept of alienation, the category of totality, spontaneity in the revolutionary movement, and utopia as the vision of a better future. Supek never tired of reiterating his basic thesis that the existential element in communism is the creation of a genuine, free community of truly liberated personalities. Along with Svetozar Stojanović,* Supek developed perhaps the most comprehensive outline of socialist personalism founded on a genuine ethics. In his 1967 essay, "From Statist Totalitarianism to Individual Totality," Supek noted that a phenomenology of communist personalism remained yet to be written. But even then he had no doubt that the liberation of the human personality constituted the true meaning and goal of socialism. He went on to outline an ethical framework in *Humanist Intelligentsia and Politics*. No less than Stojanović, Supek perceived the need for a genuine ethics due to the phenomenon of the new socialist *homo duplex*, the alienated human being split up into various spheres or roles, this time as the result of the total negation of the authentic personality of the individual revolutionary.

Unlike orthodox Marxists, Supek admits that the Party demands complete ethical prostration from the revolutionary. And this ethical prostration becomes a major ethical antinomy characterizing revolutionary existence. The revolutionary himself becomes the victim of the interests of an organization hypostatized as the interests of the revolution. Hence, both Supek and Stojanović erect new ethical rules to govern the relationship between the individual and the revolution and its vanguard, the Communist Party. For both theorists, personal dignity sets the limits for an individual's self-sacrifice for the Party or the revolution.

Supek has contributed significantly to the sociology of work by his analyses of the effects of the division of labor and specialization on man, urging the humanization of both work and consumption. He authored also the first study in Yugoslavia on the world ecological crisis, in which he argues for the benefits of a "stable society" as opposed to the "consumer society," with its voracious appetite and exploitative orientation toward both man and nature. Supek's entire work is characterized by a strong utopian dimension—another hallmark of the *Praxis* school of thought—which continues Marx's critique of capitalist society as exploitative and alienating. Yet, Supek's critique has not spared either statist socialism or Yugoslav ideology and practice. Indeed, he is one of the few theorists to admit that self-management itself has become a mythology concealing the real shape of conflicts in socialism. Thus, Supek characterizes self-management as "the strongest ideological stereotype" in contemporary Yugoslav society. Supak will most likely be remembered for his cosmopolitanism and openness, reflected by his insistence on free speech and individual human dignity.

BIBLIOGRAPHY:

A. *Sociologija i socijalizam* (Zagreb: Znanje, 1966); "Od državnog totalitarizma do individualnog totaliteta," pp. 301–11; in *Marks i savremenost*, eds. Predrag Vranicki et al., vol. 4 (Belgrade: Institut za izučavanje radničkog pokreta/Institut društvenih nauka, 1967); "Robno-novčani odnosi i socijalistička ideologija," *Praxis* (Y), 5, nos. 1–2 (1968), pp. 170–79; "Discours d'ouverture." *Praxis* (I), 6, nos. 1–2 (1970), pp. 3–7; "Problems and Perspectives of Workers' Self-management in Yugoslavia," in *Yugoslav Workers' Self-management*, ed. Marius J. Broekmeyer (Dordrecht: Reidel, 1970), pp. 216–41; "Historicitet, sistem i sukobi," *Sociologija*, 13, no. 3 (1971), pp. 323–40; *Humanistička inteligencija i politika* (Zagreb: Studentski centar Sveučilišta, 1971); "Some Contradictions and Insufficiencies of Yugoslav Self-Managing Socialism," *Praxis* (I), 7, nos. 3–4 (1971), pp. 375–97; "Čemu, uostalom, sada još i ovaj marksizam?" *Praxis* (Y), 9, nos. 3–4 (1972), pp. 327–38; "The Statist and Self-Managing Models of Socialism," in *Opinion-Making Elites in Yugoslavia*, ed. Allen H. Barton et al. (New York: Praeger, 1973), pp. 295–315; "Dix ans de l'Ecole d'Eté de Korčula (1963–1973)," *Praxis* (I), 10, nos. 1–2 (1974), pp. 3–15; *Participacija, radnička kontrola i samoupravljanje* (Zagreb: Naprijed, 1974); "Politika stare i nove radničke klase" *Sociologija*, 17, no. 1 (1975), pp. 39–49; *Ova jedina zemlja: Idemo li u katastrofu ili u Treću revoluciju?* 2nd enl. ed. (Zagreb: Liber, 1978); excerpt from *Humanistička inteligencija i politika* in translation: "Ethical Antinomies of Revolutionary Existence," pp. 97–110, in ed. Gerson S. Sher, *Marxist Humanism and Praxis*, (Buffalo, N.Y.: Prometheus Books, 1978); "Socialisme, démocratie industrielle et droits de l'homme," *Praxis International*, 1, no. 4 (January 1982), pp. 321–33.

B. Gerson S. Sher, *Praxis: Marxist Criticism and Dissent in Socialist Yugoslavia* (Bloomington: Indiana University Press, 1977); Oskar Gruenwald, *The Yugoslav Search for Man: Marxist Humanism in Contemporary Yugoslavia* (South Hadley, Mass.: Bergin & Garvey, 1983).

OSKAR GRUENWALD

SVITAK, IVAN (b. 1925). Born in 1925 in Hrance, Czechoslovakia, Svitak graduated from secondary school in Prague and then spent two years during World War II doing forced labor in an iron factory. In 1945 he enrolled at Charles University, where he was a student leader in the Social Democratic Party. He earned a doctor of law degree from Charles University, a doctor of political science degree from the University of Political and Social Sciences, and a doctor of philosophy degree from the Prague Institute of Philosophy. From 1948 to 1954 he lectured in history of philosophy at Charles University. In 1954 he joined the newly founded Institute of Philosophy in the Czechoslovak Academy of Science, where he established international contact with Marxists from the East and the West. In 1958 Svitak was "discovered" to be a "revisionist," exiled to the district of Kyjov, and, for five years, prohibited from publishing or lecturing. Svitak returned to the institute in 1960; he was expelled from the institute and from the Communist Party in 1964. From 1965 to 1968 he worked at the Film Institute in Prague. Svitak emigrated from Czechoslovakia in 1968 and currently is professor of philosophy and political science at California State University at Chico.

Svitak was an active, unofficial participant in events in Czechoslovakia leading up to the Prague Spring* (1968). Calling himself "a Marxist† but not a Communist," Svitak openly criticized the regimes of Novotný (1957–68) and Dubček† (1968–69). These criticisms, and his subsequent reflections, constitute a large portion of his political writings. The basis for both is the radical critique provided by Marx, a critique that, according to Svitak, is nonmethodological, anti-ideological, superscientific, and ultracritical. Svitak's introduction to Marxism was through the writings of Marx (particularly the early writings) and Trotsky.† He rejects Leninism† as inappropriate for an economically advanced European society. Bureaucratic dictatorship, the logical and inevitable consequence of Leninism, is incompatible with socialist humanism, which, Svitak maintains, is the foundation of Marxism. The realization of Marx's socialist humanism requires, Svitak believes, democratic political institutions, the historical perspective available through Marx's scientific anthropology, and the application of contemporary science to social and political problems. Economic democracy is the solution for humanizing production.

Svitak is committed to Eurosocialism. The themes that dominate his life and his writings include the history of politics, the tension between totalitarianism and Western culture, and socialist democracy as an alternative to fascism and capitalism. Svitak rejects Lukaćsian* Marxism ("muddled metaphysics"), open Marxism ("old metaphysics for new professors"), and dialectical materialism ("speculative metaphysics"). Marx, he believes, must be viewed and utilized in the Western democratic socialist experience. Svitak shares a commitment to Marxist humanism with other Eastern and Western European Marxists. His description and evaluation of bureaucratic dictatorship, particularly its social and cultural impact on a modern Western society, is a case study in Marxist social critique. Not only is bureaucratic dictatorship contrary to Marx, and thus a non-Marxist phenomenon, it is impervious to reform or to "humanizing" from within. "Socialism with a human face" (the Czechoslovak reform movement, 1967–69), Svitak argues, was neither socialist nor humanist. He provides a penetrating, critical, and creative analysis of events in Czechoslovakia from 1948 to 1968, but is particularly useful in understanding the personalities and events associated with the Prague Spring and the subsequent Warsaw Pact invasion. Svitak's poetry, film criticism, and philosophical writings provide important perspectives that complement his political treatises and provide the reader access to his personal intellectual anthropology.

BIBLIOGRAPHY:

A. *Kapitoly z dějin středovčké filosofie* (Prague: Státní nakl. ucebnic, 1957); *Man and His World: A Marxian View* (New York: Dell, 1970); *The Czechoslovak Experiment: 1968–1969* (New York: Columbia University Press, 1971); *The Czechoslovak Episode: 1968–1969* (Chico: California State University Press, 1976).

GARY C. SHAW

T

TADIĆ, LJUBOMIR (b. 1925). The Yugoslav Ljubomir Tadić was born in 1925 in Smriječno (Montenegro) and fought during World War II as a partisan in the national liberation movement. He studied law in Sarajevo earning a B.A. from the University of Belgrade in 1952 and a Ph.D. from the University of Ljubljana in 1959 with a thesis on *The Philosophical Foundations of the Legal Theory of Hans Kelsen*, published in 1962. He taught at the Faculty of Law, University of Sarajevo (1954–62) and was director of the Section for Politics and Jurisprudence at the Institute of Social Sciences in Belgrade (1962–65). He was professor of political philosophy, law, and sociology at the University of Belgrade from 1965 until 1975, when he was suspended from teaching—along with seven *Praxis** colleagues—and dismissed by the end of 1980. With two colleagues, Tadić was fired also from the Institute for the Study of the International Labor Movement in Belgrade (December 1975). Following vigorous protest by the international academic community, Tadić was reinstated in a new Center for Philosophy and Social Theory at Belgrade University's Institute of Social Sciences in July 1981. He has served on the boards of *Pregled*, *Filozofija* (coeditor with Pešić-Golubović*), *Političke misli*, *Praxis*, the Korčula Summer School, and *Praxis International* (since 1981). Like other *Praxis* theorists, Tadić has found it difficult to publish in his native land. Thus, the press attacked the publishing house Naprijed for merely intending to publish his *Philosophy of Right*; other works like *Tradition and Revolution* (1972), *Authority and Contestation* (1974), and *Law, Nature and History* (1975), while printed, have apparently not been distributed. His publications include also *The Subject of Jurisprudence* (1966), *Order and Freedom* (1967), as well as numerous articles in *Praxis* and other journals and symposia. In 1980, thirty-six prominent Belgrade intellectuals, including Tadić, petitioned Yugoslav authorities to grant an unconditional amnesty for all political prisoners. Tadić and the best-known living Serbian writer, Dobrica Ćosić, also gathered signatures throughout Yugoslavia petitioning the authorities to allow a new independent left-wing literary journal, *Javnost* (Forum). Both initiatives were disapproved.

His theoretical contributions to Marxism, particularly to the *Praxis* school of

Marxist† humanist thought, lie in philosophy of law, political sociology, and epistemology. Influenced by Kant, Proudhon, Ernst Bloch,* and Rosa Luxemburg,† and drawing on the writings of the young Marx, Tadić has sought to reconceptualize Marxism as the thought and practice of freedom. The concept of individual and social liberation via praxis—understood as unfettered human development and immediate direct democracy—represents the cornerstone of his interpretation of the goals of the socialist revolution and of socialist law. In his major work, *Order and Freedom*, Tadić begins with a critique of positivism as a prelude to his comprehensive analysis of society and law in Stalinism.† To him, Stalinism is not based merely on a "cult of personality," but a positivistic-bureaucratic-statist perversion of both Marxist theory and socialist practice. Tadić sees in the Stalinist practice of the total politicization of all social life the victory of raison d'état over proletarian class consciousness. This "objective necessity" of state reason in despotic socialism is mirrored in the "objective lawfulness" of state law or "socialist" legal positivism. He believes that this *Staatsrecht* ideology of state socialism led straight to the Gulag. Tadić adopts Luxemburg's critique of the centralizing tendencies within the Soviet Communist Party, limiting freedom and preempting the mass movement. And he blames vulgar Marxism for harboring the seeds of the Stalinist cult of personality. In his view, vulgar Marxism petrifies the dictatorship of the proletariat into a dictatorship of the charismatic-bureaucratic type, while perverting the Marxist theory of the withering away of the state into a theory of the strengthening of the state in socialism and the intensification of the class struggle. There is clearly no room in the Stalinist bureaucratic counterrevolution for either critical Marxist thought or self-government by associated producers. Unlike orthodox Marxists, Tadić disagrees with Engels's† characterization of humanity and justice as merely "juristic illusions." On the contrary, he claims that they constitute the terminology of a social and natural law utopia. He argues that socialist law must recognize the validity of so-called subjective public rights as tools of popular defense against all forms of tyranny and despotism. Like Pešić-Golubović,* Tadić holds that bourgeois negative freedom (freedom *from*) is an important precondition for socialist positive freedom (freedom *for*). For him, "socialist" censorship and "class struggle on the ideological front" have nothing to do with socialism—a free community of dealienated personalities. He considers the absence of a genuine public opinion another Stalinist deformation of the Communist movement.

Since the early 1960s, Tadić and Svetozar Stojanović* have called for the democratization of the revolutionary movement and its vanguard, the Party. Building on the Kantian principle of human dignity as interpreted in the works of Ernst Bloch,* Tadić has consistently defended the view that individual human liberation should be the highest principle of socialist law in theory and practice. He has insisted equally on the need to incorporate the cultural heritage of bourgeois political emancipation—particularly political freedom and legal equality—into the telos of the socialist revolution. In his 1981 *Praxis International* article, Tadić maintains that the socialist revolution cannot reach the higher stage of total human emancipation without first incorporating the bourgeois emancipatory tradition. This is not to say that Tadić accepts the bourgeois socio-political framework. Quite the contrary. He considers the bourgeois framework just as alienating and dehumanizing as Stalinism, since both are founded on private (or state) property, which reify social relations and limit human potentialities. In fact, his view of liberalism as an ideology of private property, presented at the First Winter Philosophical Meeting at Tara, Serbia, in 1971, was criticized by his colleagues as overly dogmatic (*Praxis*, 1973). Tadić holds that human liberation is contingent on the socialization of property and the self-organization of associated producers at all levels of society, from bottom to top, without any representation or mediation. Hence the motto for Tadić's perspective: "Proletariat or bureaucracy. *Tertium non datur*."

Tadić has achieved considerable notoriety by holding up a theoretical mirror not only to Stalinism but to Communist Party leaderships in general. In his controversial 1982 interview in *Theoria*, Tadić is pessimistic regarding the possibilities for the democratic evolution of Communist Parties of the Bolshevik type due to their authoritarian structure based on "democratic" centralism. This structure has been generally preserved in the League of Communists of Yugoslavia (LCY) as well. Further, Tadić notes that all CPs in power (including the LCY) still adhere to the canon promulgated at the Tenth CPSU Congress in 1921, according to which the "dictatorship of the proletariat" is incompatible with political democracy. He concludes that the LCY contested Stalin's dogma of the infallibility of a supreme authority, but instead of abandoning the dogma, the Yugoslav Party merely nationalized it. In this sense, the Yugoslav Party carried out the "protestantization of bolshevism," substituting its own "theology" of authoritarian power. Tadić's critique of Stalinism is but one dimension of his critique of the state, bureaucracy, and the institutionalization of revolutionary organs, which leads to their reification. The alternative to the state, bureaucracy, Stalinism, and bourgeois liberalism is to be found in the proletariat as the subject of history and in its praxis of "permanent revolution," of revolutionizing all petrified social relations. Although Tadić's critique of Stalinism, bureaucracy, and authoritarian socialism is impressive, and although he hints at the Leninist (organizational) roots of Stalinism, he has yet to prove the *Praxis* contention that there is no socialism without democracy and no democracy without socialism. His seminal contribution to the analysis of Stalinism and of the dogmatic, antihumanist, totalitarian aspects of Marxism-Leninism is his epistemological insight that "from absolute knowledge to absolute power is but one step," and that the Communist Party must abandon monolithism in thought and its pretension to absolute historical truth and unlimited mandate as the executor of the will of history. He deduces that socialism must either adopt political democracy as its principle or revert to Stalinist barbarism.

Tadić's thesis in *Theoria* concerning the counterrevolution in socialism whereby Marx's "permanent revolution" evolves to "permanent civil war," dubbed the "dictatorship of the proletariat," remains the most succinct expression of the

crisis in Marxist theory and socialist practice as well as a major theoretical challenge to neo-Marxists and others. Tadić will be remembered for his proposition that there is no socialism without democracy and no democracy without political freedom, and even more for the courage of his convictions in the quest for human dignity. "Standing upright" would probably be his chosen epitaph.
BIBLIOGRAPHY:

A. *Poredak i sloboda* (Belgrade: Kultura, 1967); "L'Intelligentsia dans le socialisme," *Praxis* (I), 5, nos. 3–4 (1969), pp. 399–408; "Macht, Eliten, Demokratie," *Praxis* (I), 6, nos. 1–2 (1970), pp. 65–79; "Herbert Marcuse: Zwischen Wissenschaft und Utopie," *Praxis* (I), 8, nos. 1–2 (1972), pp. 141–68; "The Limits Set to Human Freedom by Private Property," *Praxis* (I), 9, no. 1 (1973), pp. 5–20; "Authority and Authoritarian Thinking: On the Sense and Senselessness of Subordination," pp. 77–94; and "The Marxist and Stalinist Critiques of Right," pp. 161–74, in *Marxist Humanism and Praxis*, ed. Gerson S. Sher (Buffalo, N.Y.: Prometheus Books, 1978); "Bureaucracy—Reified Organization," pp. 289–301, in *Praxis*, ed. Mihailo Marković and Gajo Petrović (Dordrecht: Reidel, 1979); "Sozialismus und Emanzipation," *Praxis International*, 1, no. 1 (April 1981), pp. 64–71; "The Marxist Critique of Right in the Philosophy of Ernst Bloch," *Praxis International*, 1, no. 4 (January 1982), pp. 422–29; "Za demokratiju—Protiv svih diktatura," (interview), *Theoria*, 25, nos. 3–4 (1982).

B. Gerson S. Sher, *Praxis: Marxist Criticism and Dissent in Socialist Yugoslavia* (Bloomington: Indiana University Press, 1977); Oskar Gruenwald, *The Yugoslav Search for Man: Marxist Humanism in Contemporary Yugoslavia* (South Hadley, Mass.: Bergin & Garvey, 1983).

OSKAR GRUENWALD

TAKABATAKE MOTOYUKI (1886–1928). Takabatake Motoyuki was a Japanese Marxist† best known for his translation of *Capital* and for his theory of national or state socialism (*kokka shakai-shugi*). Often misidentified among Westerners as an "anti-Marxist" nationalist, Takabatake began his career as part of the Meiji socialist movement. Takabatake had immersed himself briefly in Christianity as a student at Dōshisha seminary, but abandoned the Christian socialist faction of the movement when it adopted a pacifist stance during the Russo-Japanese War. After 1905, Takabatake joined the "materialist" socialist faction to pursue the study of Marxism. Takabatake read Marx's *Capital* during a brief imprisonment and then participated in the socialist movement when it was dominated by Kōtoku Shūsui's "strategy of direct action," from 1907 to 1911. After Kōtoku's execution in 1911, Takabatake joined Sakai Toshihiko and Yamakawa Hitoshi† (founding members of the Japanese Communist Party in 1922) to lead the now underground movement in the Baibun-sha, which published such journals as *Hechima no hana* (The Gourd Flower). During these years, Takabatake studied Marx's economic theory in depth, and by the time the Bolshevik Revolution revived Japan's socialist movement in 1917, he was a resolute Marxist.

Takabatake achieved recognition when he produced the first complete Japanese translation of the three volumes of *Capital*, beginning in 1919. However, in the same year he also articulated the Marxist doctrine of national or state socialism that would cause "Bolshevist" followers of orthodox Marxism-Leninism to reject him for "apostasy" (*tenkō*) from true Marxism. Takabatake's argument that Marxism and Leninism† were in fact "statist" doctrines in both theory and practice immediately precipitated a break with Yamakawa, Sakai, and others who would lead the Japanese Communist Party. In the years that followed, Takabatake never abandoned Marxism but wrote prolifically on Marxist thought, the theory of the state, and national socialism. Alienated by his national socialist interpretation of Marxism from orthodox Marxists until his death in 1928, Takabatake pioneered his own activist national socialist movement. Along with Ishikawa Junjūrō and others he founded the national socialist Taishū-sha in 1918 and launched the journals *Kokka shakai-shugi* (State Socialism) (1919) and *Kyū-shin* (Radical) (1924). During the 1920s Takabatake joined Tokyo Imperial University professor Uesugi Shinkichi, who advocated the divine right of the emperor, to found the Keiringaku Dōmei (League for the Study of Statecraft) and influenced the Japanese Labor-Farmer Party through his relationship with labor activist Asō Hisashi. Takabatake's major writings include *Kokka shakai-shugi taigi* (Outline of state socialism) (1919, 1928); *Marukishizumu to kokka-shugi* (Marxism and statism) (1927); and *Hihan Marukusu-shugi* (Criticizing Marxism), a collection of essays (1934).

Takabatake's Marxian national socialism was based on a repudiation of Marx's view of the state as idealistic and erroneous. Borrowing from Thomas Hobbes, Takabatake maintained that the contradiction in human nature between man's desire and need for companionship versus his antisocial egoism had engendered the ruling function in all societies. This was a functional view of the need for the state, one which argued that its essential role of establishing control or order in society preceded its eventual development as a class instrument of exploitation. Takabatake argued that the realistic and scientific pursuit of socialism required that one accept the necessity of the state to compensate for man's evil nature. State socialism recognized the state as a "supra-class," "supra-historical" permanent institution in the service of mankind's best interests and endeavored to eliminate the impure element of exploitation from the function of "pure domination" that would continue to be necessary in a socialist society after a proletarian revolution. In Japan, this would occur under the continued tutelage of the imperial household. The postrevolutionary state would also be nationalist rather than internationalist in character, because after the revolution Japan could still be endangered by hostile nations, both socialist and capitalist. Since war ultimately derived from man's evil nature, regardless of the social organization of production, the notion of socialist internationalism was fallacious, for Japan could easily fall victim to Russian workers' and peasants' imperialism. Thus, a viable socialist revolution required both a potent nationalism and a powerful state to assure that the Japanese people would enjoy the fruits of socialism.

Although Takabatake's views offended dedicated followers of Marx's and Lenin's† stateless and internationalist socialism, nevertheless he did confront boldly both the realities of Japan's situation in world politics and the theoretical difficulties of Marx's thesis of the "withering away of the state" and socialist internationalism. The work of Takabatake, and others like Sano Manabu* and Takahashi Kamekichi,† who also responded to Japan's difficult international situation and endeavored to reconcile Marxism with Japan's indigenous political institutions, may be compared with the theoretical efforts of Ferdinand Lassalle in Germany and Benito Mussolini in Italy.

BIBLIOGRAPHY:

A. *Kokka shakai-shugi taigi* (Outline of State Socialism) (Tokyo: Nihou Shakai-shugi Kenkyū-jo, 1927); *Marukishizumu to Kokka-shugi* (Marxism and Statism) (Tokyo: Kaizo-sha, 1927); *Hihan Marukusu-shugi* (Criticizing Marxism) (Tokyo: Nihon hyō ron-sha, 1934).

B. Tanaka Masato, *Takabatake Motoyuki: Nihon no Kokka shakai-shugi* (Takabatake Motoyuki: Japan's National Socialism) (Tokyo: Gendai Hyōron-sha, 1978); Germaine A. Hoston, "Marxism and National Socialism in Taishō Japan: The Thought of Takabatake Motoyuki" (unpublished manuscript).

GERMAINE A. HOSTON

TEIGE, KAREL (1900–1951). Born in Prague in 1900, essayist, painter, and theoretician Karel Teige was a prominent personality among Czech intellectuals for several decades. Founder of the group known as Devetsil, an association of leftist avant-garde Czech artists that began in 1934 and survived for over twenty years, Teige went on to become the principal theoretician of Czech surrealist artists. Although Teige was generally considered the ideological leader of Devetsil's left wing, he nevertheless collaborated with the Czech poet Vítězslav Nezval in developing an artistic and literary outlook that distinguished itself from the rigidities of the Moscow-inspired aesthetics of socialist realism. In his early poetic studies (e.g. *World of Humor* and *World of Fragrance*) Teige called on the theoretical resources of modern European civilization to formulate a nontraditional Marxist† definition of beauty. Above all an admirer of Stalinist† views concerning the building of socialism—in 1936 he was still trying to justify intellectually Moscow's brand of socialism—he slowly turned toward a Marxism that was less and less dependent on dogmatic formulas. His refusal to toe the Party's cultural line became the pretext invoked in 1938 by his collaborator Nezval and other Party officials to liquidate the Czech group of surrealists that had formed around Teige. He and several other surrealists were henceforth considered by the official press of the Czech Communist Party as a "fifth column in the heart of the Czech intelligentsia." (*Rudé právo*, 16 April 1938, under the signature of Julius Fučík). After the Czech liberation of 1945, and particularly after the change in regimes in 1948, Teige was considered one of the chief obstacles to the Party-desired evolution of intellectuals in a Czechoslovakia spurning pluralism. Ladislav Štolle, spokesman for the Party's Central Committee, publically accused him, in a conference held in January 1950 on "Thirty Years in the Battle for a Czech Socialist Aesthetics," of being an enemy of socialism. Teige spent the final ten years of life formulating a phenomenology of modern art. He died in 1951. We possess, however, only a fragment of this monumental last work, the remainder having been confiscated and probably destroyed by the State Security Police.

Teige's primary intellectual project was, apparently, to synthesize avant-garde and realist aesthetics. In the section of the *Phenomenology of Modern Art* that has survived and been published in Prague in 1966, we can read: "For realists, painting has never been a simple description of the object but its subjective illumination. . . . The inability [of realism] to reproduce what it saw has preserved for realism the possibility of existing as an art form" (p. 28). And finally: "The quantitative increase of artistic modes which obscure the real object while expressing it is culminated in cubism's artistic view, which in painting is so unreal as to justify itself. In the sphere of poetic theory, where the antagonism between the external and the internal realities is suppressed, realism has become irrelevant" (ibid.).

BIBLIOGRAPHY:

A. "Ten Years of Surrealism," in *Surrealismus v diskusi*, ed. K. Teige and L. Stolle (Prague: Palán: 1934); *Jarmark úměni* (Prague: Československý spisovatel, 1964); *Svět stavby a básně* (Prague: Československý spisovatel, 1966); *Liquidierung der "Kunst"* (Frankfurt: Suhrkamp, 1968).

M. IVO FLEISCHMANN

THOMPSON, EDWARD P. (b. 1924). E. P. Thompson was born in England in 1924. He served in Africa and Italy during World War II. Following the war, in 1946, Thompson worked on railway construction projects in Yugoslavia and Bulgaria, where he encountered popular communism at work, an ideal that has guided his approach to Marxism.† He returned to graduate from Cambridge, where he read history. Thompson is best known for his work on eighteenth- and nineteenth-century English social history, but he has also actively participated in British and European politics. Thompson has taught history at Warwick University, worked in adult labor education, and also taught in the United States and India. He joined the British Communist Party in 1942 and was active until 1956, when he and thousands of others left the Party because of their rejection of Stalinism.† Thompson helped found the journal *The New Reasoner* as a forum for fellow dissident communists. *The New Reasoner* later merged with another journal to become *The New Left Review*. Thompson served on its editorial board until he was dismissed in 1963. Since 1972 Thompson has devoted most of his time to writing. Recently, Thompson has been involved in the European anti-nuclear movement, assuming leadership positions in the Campaign for Nuclear Disarmament in Britain and the Committee for European Nuclear Disarmament.

Thompson believes himself true to Marx in claiming that the essence of historical materialism is a group of propositions about history that may be verified or modified by empirical historical inquiry. Concepts such as class, exploitation, and consciousness are historical categories that have meaning only when referring to real events in the past, not as abstract parts in a foreknown course of history.

For Thompson, Marxism is open to empirical dispute. As such it must deal with real people in concrete historical conditions. The fullest expression of Thompson's position is found in *The Poverty of Theory* (1978). The work is self-styled after Marx's *Poverty of Philosophy*, an attack on Proudhon's "metaphysical heresy." Thompson attacks structuralist Marxists, primarily Louis Althusser,* who, like Proudhon, present historical change as a series of abstracted logical categories—social structures—and not as concrete historical events. The deleterious effect, in Thompson's view, is that Marxism removes itself from debate about empirical evidence and denies humans any role as subjective agents in history. Thompson's understanding of Marx guides his historical research in that he tries to show how class struggle and social change manifest themselves historically. His most famous and influential work is *The Making of the English Working Class* (1963), which presents workers and their culture as autonomous historical subjects worth studying in their own right. Thompson argues that classes arise at the juncture of objective conditions and subjective struggle. Thus the working class "made itself as much as it was made." Class consciousness comes into being with a class's subjective experience of historical determination and practical struggle. Thompson notes that class is not deducible from purely economic categories such as "mode of production." He shows the English working class emerging from a specifically English culture of popular religious, political, and community traditions. These traditions are the basis of popular responses to the experience of deprivation caused by economic and industrial change.

Thompson differs from orthodox Marxists in significant ways. His departure from the British Communist Party and his critique of structuralists are of a piece. He does not accept that materialist philosophy or Communist Party dogma are necessarily true or worthy in themselves. Nor does he exempt historical materialism from the empirically oriented conditions of truth applied to any other kind of knowledge. In his own research Thompson reaches conclusions that differ from orthodox expectations. He is not a technological determinist. He found, for example, that the English working class emerged not from a factory proletariat but from a tradition of radical craftsmen and artisans seeking to preserve their traditional control over their own work. It was the experience of being exploited and not the objective conditions of economic change that fostered class formation. The British working-class alternative to industrial capitalism resembled not so much a proletarian Marxism as a strategy rooted in the ideals of radical English Protestantism, popular political rights, and the traditions of cooperative community action.

Thompson's most recent work, *Beyond the Cold War* (1983), collects several of his essays defending the European peace movement as a popular socialist cause. He locates the source of the arms race in the military-industrial economies of Western nations, which produce weaponry to sustain industry and national reputation rather than to meet rational security interests. Thompson advocates the removal of all nuclear weapons from Europe as a first step toward reducing tensions between the U.S. and Soviet blocs.

BIBLIOGRAPHY:

A. *William Morris: Romantic to Revolutionary* (London: Lawrence and Wishart, 1955); *The Making of the English Working Class* (New York: Vintage Books, 1963); *The Poverty of Theory* (New York: Monthly Review Press, 1978); *Beyond the Cold War* (New York: Pantheon Books, 1983).

B. Bryan D. Palmer, *The Making of E. P. Thompson: Marxism, Humanism, and History* (Toronto: New Hogtown Press, 1981).

KEVIN DAVIS

TOGLIATTI, PALMIRO (1883–1964). Palmiro Togliatti was born in Genoa 26 March 1883, and died in Yalta, in the Soviet Union, 21 August 1964. Having received his training at the University of Turin, he met Antonio Gramsci* and Angelo Tasca, and with them he participated in the cultural-political activity of *L'Ordine Nuovo*. As a result of the crisis following the events of the "Red Biennium," in which the group had taken an active part, the need was seen for political and organizational outlets: despite the differences between Gramsci, more decidedly a counciliarist, and Togliatti, the demand to constitute an effectively revolutionary party was urgent and deeply felt. In this way the encounter with Amadeo Bordiga† and his group on the left of the Italian Socialist Party (PSI) took place and the Communist Party (PCI) was born at Livorno (1921), with significant contributions from the *L'Ordine Nuovo* group as well. Togliatti was at first undecided with respect to both the disagreements between the Bordiga leadership and the Third International,† and the International's own selection of Gramsci as leader. Eventually he supported Gramsci, so much so that he even proposed Gramsci's *Theses* for the PCI Congress of Lyons in 1926, the approval of which confirmed Gramsci's leadership. After the advent of fascism, Togliatti's activities were tied more and more to collaboration with the International and with Stalin† himself. At the Seventh Congress of the International (August 1935) he was the speaker after G. Dimitrov (with whom he designed the strategic view of the "united front"), and he dealt specifically with the Party's international prospects and with the tie between the struggle for peace and the struggle against fascism. Beginning in 1937 he was sent by the International to Spain to follow the activities of the Communist Party in that country, and after the Civil War broke out he remained in Spain until 1939. There followed a period in Paris and then in Moscow during which he was occupied above all in taking up the reins of the PCI in crisis: he carried out important propaganda work on the radio for the partisan struggle in Italy. After the fall of fascism he landed in Naples on 27 March 1944 and reorganized the Party, bringing about the so-called turning point of Salerno, a radical modification of the political line of the Party in the direction of a more explicit antifascist unity and the temporary shelving of the institutional question (republic or monarchy). He participated as a minister in the governments of the Liberation and then in the first governments led by the Christian Democrat De Gasperi, until in May 1947 the Communists were expelled from the government. He directed the politics of the PCI from the opposition side, while at the same time continuously enriching the notions of autonomy and national pride that characterized the strategy of the "Italian path to socialism." In this sense the document that he was working on at Yalta when death overtook him is still considered today to be a true and personal political testament, affirming the polycentrism of communism and the necessity of articulating strategies for individual national Communist parties. A political man of the first magnitude, leader of a Communist Party that would be the only one in the capitalistic West to get almost one-third of its electoral votes, a man who was able to live through Stalinism and at the same time preserve his own visions of reality and of the historical process that would lead to socialist transformations in Italy and in the capitalistic countries, Togliatti was also always a man of culture, involved in intellectual and cultural debate and in theoretical disputes about Marxism.

His is the achievement of designing a line of historical evolution for Marxism† in Italy founded on the identification of Marxism with historicism: a line that developed from Francesco De Sanctis and from the Hegelian Bertrando Spaventa to Antonio Labriola† and Gramsci, having as critical reference in its later phase the historicism of Benedetto Croce. Once the theoretical equipment of Marxism was inserted in this way into the sphere of national culture, the task was to graft a political strategy of socialist transformation onto the specific conditions, whether structural or political and cultural, of Italian history and tradition. The Gramscian concept of hegemony also constitutes for Togliatti the essential theoretical point of reference for such translation. In Italy the particular historical conditions of delayed national unification and the survival of acute dualisms, both territorial (the North and South of Italy) and social (workers and peasants), indicate the problem and the goal—even after the defeat of fascism—not of a direct exercise of power by the proletariat but of a phase similar to the bourgeois democratic revolution. However, what is involved is not a process that is understood to be gradualistic, like the passage from one necessary phase to another, but rather the constitution of a "new type of democracy" on the terrain of an existing bourgeois state; a democracy capable of uniting elements of liberalism and socialism. This process can be pursued by means of "structural reforms" seen as an "organic and unified design"—not as "separate fragments" according to the flatly pragmatic tradition of reformism—aimed at transforming in a popular sense the social structures and modifying at the same time the "power block" that directs national politics. What is meant is not only political configurations— forces of the left united for conquest of the majority—but also a social process that by means of alliances unites many different classes with the working class in its struggle for supremacy. Of particular importance in this process is the alliance with the middle classes, which were becoming more numerous as well as more relevant to the modernization process in Italy. This process therefore combines democracy and socialism and attempts to resolve the knotty problem of "reform versus revolution" by adapting it to the specific situation. It is this process that characterizes the "Italian path to socialism" mapped out by Togliatti and followed by the PCI in the period after World War II. However, it involves not only the strategy indicated above but also a new type of organization, a way for the Party to be different: a "new party," as Togliatti defines it, suitable for those complex needs. A party that on the one hand must provide leadership for the working class and, as such, a restricted, propagandistic organization; and on the other a party that unites within it all the social constituencies which are associated in the battle for supremacy, a party tightly bound to the historical tradition of its own country, capable of providing answers to the problems of the country and knowing how to work to resolve them and to be therefore a "government party."

BIBLIOGRAPHY:

A. *Il partito* (Rome: Riuniti, 1964); *La via italiana al socialismo* (Rome: Riuniti, 1964); *Lezioni sul fascismo* (Rome: Riuniti, 1970); *Gramsci* (Rome: Riuniti, 1972).

B. P. Spriano, *Storia del PCI*, 4 vols. (Turin: Einaudi, 1967–75); Giorgio Bocca, *Palmiro Togliatti* (Bari: Laterza, 1973); E. Ragionieri, *Palmiro Togliatti, 1917–1935* (Rome: Riuniti, 1973); N. Auciello, *Socialismo ed egemonia in Gramsci e Togliatti* (Bari: De Donato, 1974); G. Vacca, *Saggio su Togliatti e la tradizione communista* (Bari: De Donato, 1974); Y. D. Sassoon, *Togliatti e le via italiana al socialismo* (Turin: Einaudi, 1980); G. Bedeschi, *La parabola del marxismo in Italia 1945–1983* (Bari: Laterza, 1983).

VITTORIO DINI

TORRES RESTREPO, CAMILO (1929–1966). Colombian priest, sociologist, and revolutionary, Camilo Torres Restrepo was born on 3 February 1929 in Bogota. Although Torres undertook the study of law following graduation from high school, he soon abandoned that course to enter the priesthood. Torres had been deeply inspired by the active Christianity espoused by the French Dominicans as well as the worker-priests who advocated social responsibility and rejected support of the status quo. During his seven years (1947–54) of study at the Seminario Concilar de Bogotá, Torres became steadfastly convinced that the essence of Christianity lay in "love of neighbor" (*Cristianismo y revolución*, p. 376). Following his ordination in 1954, Torres continued his education at the Catholic University of Louvain (Belgium), School of Political and Social Sciences (1954–59), where he studied under, among others, François Houtart. While at Louvain, Torres investigated the writings of Teilhard de Chardin, Jacques Maritain, Abbe Pierre, as well as works on Marxism. When Torres returned to Colombia in 1959, he was appointed auxiliary chaplain at the National University and along with several others, including Orlando Fals Borda,* founded Colombia's first Faculty of Sociology. Between 1959 and 1962, Torres remained at the National University and involved himself in the student movement, which had been bolstered by the success of the Cuban Revolution. In 1965 Torres asked to be laicized and declared himself a revolutionary. He joined the Fidelist-oriented National Liberation Army (ELN) and died in combat on 15 February 1966.

Some debate remains as to whether or not Torres was actually a Marxist.† He refused the appellation, and Diego Montaña Cuéllar† states that Torres was correct in doing so. Nevertheless, his speeches and writings expound several Marxist tenets. Among them are his view that society consists of two opposing classes locked in struggle and that all power is linked to economic control, his espousal of the necessity of popular ownership of the means of production, and his denunciation of imperialism and dependency. Yet Torres did not embrace historical materialism. Nor did he view socialism as the inevitable outcome of the dialectical process. Torres also rejected the idea that revolution would inevitably be achieved by the industrial proletariat. Rather, he advocated the formation of a pluralistic political force capable of seizing power. This pluralistic force, which Torres referred to as the united front, would consist of various sectors including workers, labor unions, peasant leagues, political parties, professionals, and intellectuals.

Torres's other notable contributions to modern thought were his reconciliation of Christianity and revolution and his advocacy of just rebellion and counterviolence. Not only did he admonish Christians and Marxists to ally to bring about revolution, he dismissed the notion that Christianity, particularly Catholicism, necessarily supported the status quo. Torres held a utopian view of new Colombian society. He believed that the class system had no justification in true Christianity and that societal structures had to be changed to effectuate true Christian love. He considered the revolutionary fight to be a Christian one. Although Torres fought for the rights and dignity of all Colombians, he believed that those who held power would not relinquish it without a struggle. Therefore, he advocated counterviolence in order to bring about a new society.

BIBLIOGRAPHY:

A. *Camilo Torres: Por el Padre Camilo Torres Restrepo (1956–1966)* (Cuernavaca, Mexico: Centr. Intercultural de Documentación, 1966); *Christianismo y revolución* (Mexico City: Era, 1970); John Gerassi, ed., *Revolutionary Priest: The Complete Writings and Messages of Camilo Torres* (New York: Random House, 1971); *Revolutionary Writings* (New York: Harper & Row, 1972).

B. German Guzman, *Camilo Torres* (New York: Sheed and Ward, 1969); Walter J. Broderick, *Camilo Torres: A Biography of the Priest-Guerrillero* (Garden City, N.Y.: Doubleday, 1975).

DAWN FOGLE DEATON

TOURAINE, ALAIN (n.a.). Alain Touraine, the originator of the term *postindustrial society*, is a French-born sociologist who was cofounder of the journal *Sociologie du travail* and past president of the French Sociological Society. He has lectured at universities throughout Europe, America, and Latin America and presently is professor of sociology at the Ecole des Hautes Etudes in Paris.

Touraine has published over twenty books as well as numerous scholarly articles, monographs, and reviews.

Touraine's sociological work can be divided into two parts. First, his concrete, empirical studies of particular social movements (e.g. the Chilean Revolution, the French student uprisings of 1968, the antinuclear movement in Europe, Solidarity). Each focuses on a social group that emerges from spontaneous protests, congeals into an organized movement, confronts other organized movements and established powers, and then is either destroyed or transformed as a result. Touraine's research indicates that "spontaneous" institutions constitute structures that help reveal and explain other structures. In its confrontation with antinuclear protesters, for example, the state is shown to perform the nonformal, hidden function of preserving the status quo and upholding hegemonic interests. Second, there is Touraine's effort at formulating a theory of society based on these empirical studies. His major theoretical works are *The Self-Production of Society* (1973) and *The Voice and the Eye* (1978).

In *The Self-Production of Society* Touraine argued that changes have recently taken place in the Western industrialized world's social processes of production and reproduction, particularly involving the increasingly important roles of science, the public sector, mass education, technology, multinational corporations, etc. These changed social relations in what Touraine calls postindustrial society mean that social scientists must now examine and understand emerging new social classes, conflicts, and ideologies. In this context, Touraine believes the political level of postindustrial society has become the "active transformational agent" between "historicity" and specific rules of everyday life. "Historicity" encompasses a society's position in a temporal framework that ultimately determines what it will empirically experience: in brief, that society's mode of accumulation and production, its definition of its cultural model, its model of knowledge, and its pattern of class relations. Historicity has generated three distinct cultural models: merchant (preindustrial), industrial, and postindustrial. Each societal type is dominated by a ruling class that defines cultural, scientific, and economic apparatuses and a ruled class that normally accepts and perpetuates the status quo. Politics, then, structures social reality by mediating objective history and contingent features of the everyday life-world. In postindustrial society Touraine has discovered a new dialectic between a ruling class's prepolitical determination of the rules of the political game on the one hand, and on the other, the semi-autonomous activities of opposed interest groups (including those representing the ruling class) within the political arena. There is, in other words, a double entry of the ruling class into politics: a prepolitical structuration of the institutional framework as well as a practical involvement in the give and take of public decision making. Touraine's position here regarding the state's functions and relative autonomy synthesizes the more extreme arguments of the Miliband*–Poulantzas* debate of the 1970s.

Touraine thus rejects the popular notions that politics is either autonomous (e.g. liberal America and mainstream political science) or determined (e.g. orthodox diamat). Society, for Touraine, is neither a large friendly group where pluralistic decision making determines public policy nor a predetermined hierarchy controlled by a ruling elite. It is, instead, marked by complex interrelations between its production system and class relations, between class relations and the relative autonomy of politics, between the ruling class as the prepolitical determiner of politics and the ruling class as a political actor, between the majority class as an agent of rebellion and change and the majority class as a naive, willing participant in the status quo. Dialectical inquiry alone, not idealist or materialist reductionism, comprehends this complex totality. Moreover, politics is omnipresent. Even in totalitarian societies that destroy relatively autonomous political arenas politics is only displaced—not eliminated—onto organizational structures such as the bureaucracy, army, university, factory. Finally, Touraine implies that the state is an agent of social change as well as a defender of hegemonic interests. By mediating general (historicity) and specific (everyday life) it can change the latter in response to independent changes in the former (which take the form of "historical struggles" where social movements contest the control of a new cultural model). The state, in other words, initiates social development from one system of historical action to another and is simultaneously the key institution involved in maintaining order.

In *The Voice and the Eye* Touraine sought reasons why social relations have a fixed structural pattern. However, he perceived structure as a property of activity. People do not participate *in* a social structure; the structure is based on the way a group acts and moves. Its identity is attached to the activities of its members. Touraine's is therefore an action, rather than a structural, social theory. *The Voice and the Eye* distinguishes action theory from a literal recording of empirical facts by showing how conflict is the glue connecting various social groups and structures. A major theme of this work is the interrelation of theory and action: the effort by social movements to define themselves theoretically in order to attain an identity that will justify and rationalize interaction with other movements. Touraine sees the key social antagonism encompassing a ruling class that identifies with historicity and a popular class that interprets the dominant cultural model differently. This class or group struggle is over which interpretation of the present will prevail. Any group of actors that contests the meaning of the current cultural model engages in class struggle. Ultimately, Touraine favors movements that liberate the masses from institutions that uphold the narrow interests of ruling groups. "Sociological intervention," Touraine's chosen investigative method, analyzes social protest to unearth hidden exploitative relations, thereby raising the concrete struggle to the level of a mass social movement. Such emancipatory movements, however, are based originally on spontaneous action and effective struggles with other groups and are certainly not preordained by history.

The proliferation of social contestation over noneconomic and nonpolitical themes like education, health, advertising, housing, and ecology indicates to Touraine that previously reified domains of everyday life are now being critically examined by various social groups with a mind to decreasing the ruling class's social control. This increased level of group reflexivity distinguishes postindustrial society. In merchant society, class struggle (i.e. struggle over the meaning of the cultural model) involved issues of civil liberties and political rights. In industrial society class struggle involved issues of economic equality and social justice. In our postindustrial society the major class struggle pits the technocracy (who manipulate social and economic apparatuses) against those who resist it in the name of self-management, that is, the right to control their own lives. These nonpolitical and noneconomic contestations are thus important moments in the emancipation of modern humanity.

BIBLIOGRAPHY:

A. *Sociologie de l'action* (Paris: Editions du Seuil, 1965); *The May Movement, Revolt and Reform* (New York: Random House, 1971); *The Post-Industrial Society* (New York: Random House, 1971); *Vie et mort du Chile populaire* (Paris: Editions du Seuil, 1973); *The Academic System in American Society* (New York: McGraw-Hill, 1974); *The Self-Production of Society* (Chicago: University of Chicago Press, 1977); *The Voice and the Eye* (New York: Cambridge University Press, 1981); *Anti-Nuclear Protest* (New York: Cambridge University Press, 1983); *Solidarity* (New York: Cambridge University Press, 1983).

B. Jean L. Cohen, *Class and Civil Society* (Amherst: University of Massachusetts Press, 1982); Klaus Eder, "A New Social Movement?" *Telos*, no. 52 (Summer 1982), pp. 5–20.

ROBERT A. GORMAN

TRIAS, VIVIAN (1922–1980). The Uruguayan Trias was born in 1922 and died in 1980. Although he was not well known outside of Uruguay, he was the major representative of the *izquierda nacional* (national left) that appeared within the old Socialist Party and that cooperated with the Second International.† As a teacher of history in grammar school Trias was known as a revisionist with positions similar to those of the popular Argentine nationalists. Trias wrote a revisionist biography of Juan Manuel de Rosas, *caudillo* and head of Argentina from 1830 to 1852. He attempted to give the actions of this man an anti-imperialistic dimension, although most leftists condemned them. Regarding Uruguayan history, Trias searched for evidence marking the existence of anti-imperialist wars and emphasized the role of Arbigas (considered the founder of Uruguayan nationalism) as a popular chief as well as a progressive agrarian reformer. His book *Las montoneras y el imperio britanico* deals with the civil wars of the nineteenth century as symbols of opposition to imperialism. *El imperialismo en el Rio de la Plata* has a similar project. A militant in the Socialist Party since the 1930s, Trias was also a national deputy from his party from 1956 to 1963. While the Uruguayan Communist Party was attempting to form a united leftist front, the Socialist Party (led by Trias as secretary general, and having severed its connections to the Second International) tried to create a "national left," unfettered by contacts with the "socialist camp." In order to accomplish this, in 1962, Trias formed an ill-fated electoral alliance with nationalist and terrorist groups. Trias's Socialist Party eventually lost all of its parliamentary representatives, and some of its younger militants became radicalized, while others left the party and opted for armed struggle called *foquista*. At the same time the Social Democrat old guard, headed by Emilio Frugoni,* abandoned the party in 1963. In 1966 the Socialists participated in the elections by themselves and could not recover their losses. They again failed to obtain parliamentary representation. Only in 1971, as part of a big coalition with Communists and Christian Democrats, did they succeed in electing Trias to a seat in Parliament. But Trias was powerless to prevent the loss of militant Socialists who joined the Communist Party and other *grupusculos* (mini-groups).

His initial theoretical position was that Batllism had generated a triumph of the Uruguayan national bourgeoisie, whose interests conflicted with those of workers. He opposed Rodney Arismendi,† who argued that the possibilities of the bourgeoisie were not yet exhausted. This position alienated Trias from the traditional Batllistic position of the Socialist Party. However, after the Cuban Revolution Trias perceived a need for the creation of a new political force. But he was never able to characterize clearly what social power should bring about an agrarian and anti-imperialist revolution, which, at the same time, would represent a national option that included Communists. He was forced to accept a front with the Communists, where his own role was that of a subordinate. He fruitlessly worked for a larger role for an independent labor sector, which, he felt, would result in a greater revolutionary potential. By 1973, his political potential spent, Trias wrote several essays about imperialism, among them a history of American imperialism in which he rewrote well-known theses regarding dependency, monopolies, and multinational corporations.

BIBLIOGRAPHY:

A. *Por un socialismo nacional* (Montevideo: El Sol, 1966); *Imperialismo geopolítica y petróleo* (Montevideo: Banda Oriental, 1971); *Uruguay hoy* (Montevideo: Banda Oriental, 1973); *La crisis del imperio* (Montevideo: Cimarrón, 1974); *Historia del imperialismo a norteamericano* (Buenos Aires: Pena Lillo, 1975); *El imperio británico en America latina* (Buenos Aires: Crisis, 1976).

B. E. S. Porta, *Uruguay: realidad y reforma agraria* (Montevideo: Albe, 1965); Z. Michelini, *Battlismo y antimperialismo* (Montevideo: Albe, 1971).

JUAN RIAL

TRONTI, MARIO (b. 1931). Tronti was born in Rome in 1931 and now teaches moral philosophy at the University of Siena. He was a militant in the Italian Communist Party (PCI) from the early 1950s and has a theoretical stance close to the positions of Galvano Della Volpe* and Lucio Colletti.* He is one of the founders of the *Quaderni rossi*, and together with Asor Rosa and others he was in charge of its "worker" division. He also founded and managed *Classe operaia*. In 1967 this latter radical publication was dissolved. In an interview at a meeting in Florence, later published under the significant title *La nuova sintesi: dentro e contro* (in *Giovane critica*, no. 17 [Autumn 1967]), Tronti gave the reasons for this choice, proclaiming an end to the experiment with minority groups and his return to the ranks of the PCI. He contributed to *Contropiano*, a review founded by Asor Rosa, and subsequently to Party newspapers and reviews, from *Critica marxista* to *Rinascita*, *Paese sera* and *l'Unità*. Although his theoretical "laborist" positions form the basis for the discussion and organization of extremist political groups to the left of the PCI, from *Potere operaio* to *Autonomia operaia*, Tronti began to develop in 1968 the thesis of the "autonomy of the political." In 1981 he founded and today manages together with Asor Rosa and Cacciari, the review *Laboratorio politico*, dedicated to the development of such leftist theses. At the national congress of the Italian Communist Party in 1983 he was elected a member of the Central Committee.

Tronti's Marxism,† which initially assumed positions fairly close to Della Volpe and Colletti, was radicalized in the 1960s by the theoretical and political perspective of *operaismo* (laborism). The central political importance of the working classes, which emerged in the concrete development of Italian social history in those years, also became primarily a theoretical problem. Tronti solved it by reinterpreting and radicalizing the reading of the Marxian theory of labor-value, based primarily on the *Grundrisse*: Labor-value, therefore, means *first labor-power and then capital*;

> it means capital conditioned by labor-power, moved by labor-power, in this sense value *measured* by labor. *Labor is the measure of value because the working class is the condition of capital*. This political conclusion is the true, assumed point of departure for Marxian economic analysis itself. (*Operaie capitale*, pp. 224–25)

The point of view of Marxian science, which is a labor science, is in effect this view of the priority, whether historical or conceptual, of the working class with respect to the development of capital. There is therefore a strategic reversal between the working class and capital: it is the working class that determines, conditions, and measures the development of capital. The working class is the true "motive force of capitalistic development." The place of production, the factory, is the center of social dynamics.

> At the level of the highest capitalistic development the social relationship becomes a *moment* in the production relationship, the whole society becomes an *articulation* of production, that is, the society as a whole lives as a function of the factory, and the factory extends its exclusive dominion over the whole of society. (ibid., p. 51)

The strategic task of revolutionary rupture is also entrusted to a united workers' union, whereas tactics are entrusted to the organization, the Party.

The self-criticism of the late 1960s and its elaboration during the 1970s pushed Tronti toward the thesis of the "autonomy of the political." His self-criticism of laborism implied that it is a "monotheistic" causal explanation of the worker-capital and factory-society-politics relationship; and at the same time he criticized the inadequacy of the instruments of Marxist analysis to grasp the specific relevance of the political either to the genesis of the modern world or to its actual development. On the other hand, the almost total lack of channels of power, political outlets, in the movements of the Italian working class in the 1960s led Tronti to reconsider political instruments in a period that did not give hope that revolutionary results could be achieved. For Tronti it is therefore necessary to follow the movement of the working class and of other emerging groups—e.g. women and youth—within and against capitalistic development, and above all within and against the state.

BIBLIOGRAPHY:

A. *La città futura* (Milan: Feltrinelli, 1959); *Scritti inediti di economia politica* (Rome: Riuniti, 1963); *Operai e capitale* (Turin: Einaudi, 1966); *Hegel politico* (Rome: Istituto dell'Enciclopedia italiano, 1975); *Stato e rivoluzione in Inghilterra* (Milan: Il Saggiatore, 1977); *Sull'autonomia del politico* (Milan: Feltrinelli, 1977); *Il politico* (Milan: Feltrinelli, 1979–82); *Soggetti crisi potere* (Bologna: Cappelli, 1980); *Il tempo della politica* (Rome: Riuniti, 1980).

B. Istituto Gramsci, *Il marxismo italiano degli anni sessanta e la formazione teorico-politica delle nuove generazioni* (Rome: Riuniti, 1972); Mario Alcaro, *Dellavolpismo e nuova sinistra* (Bari: Dedalo, 1977); Maria Grazia Meriggi, *Composizione di classe e teoria del partito* (Bari: Dedalo, 1978); Mario Tronti, *et al.*, *Operaismo e centralità operaia* (Rome: Riuniti, 1978).

VITTORIO DINI

U

UHL, PETR (b. 1941). Born in 1941 in the city of Prague, the Czech Petr Uhl is a structural engineer and a professor at the Technical College in Prague. While on leave in France in the mid-1960s Uhl became acquainted with members of the French Trotskyite left. After the Soviet military suppression of the Prague Spring* movement he tried to organize the Movement of Young Revolutionaries and, later, the Revolutionary Socialist Party. Like similar clandestine groups emerging at this time in Czechoslovakia, both organizations were quickly destroyed by Czech and Soviet secret police. Uhl was condemned to a four-year prison term in 1971. Upon his release he became a manual laborer and actively supported left-wing elements of the Charter 77 movement and the movement to protect the rights of Czech citizens. In 1979 he was sentenced once again to five years at hard labor because of his activities in support of the Defense Committee for the Unjustly Condemned (VONS).

Uhl represents an extreme leftist point of view, which is a rather rare phenomenon in a Soviet bloc nation. He is an ideologue of an antibureaucratic revolutionary struggle against the established regimes of the Soviet Union and its satellites and the author of a detailed program of self-governing socialism. Although Uhl was strongly influenced by Trotsky,† he is not, strictly speaking, an orthodox Trotskyite. He advocates a multiparty political system, hence questions the Leninist† theory of the vanguard party. According to Uhl the Eastern European avant-garde is on the whole manifesting and defending the interests of workers. On the other hand, he retains the Leninist theory of the state as explicated in *State and Revolution*: the dictatorship of the proletariat, the destruction of the bourgeois state, the construction of a new proletarian state on the principle of self-governing soviets or local councils.

Uhl's originality consists in his attempt to translate the Marxist†-Leninist doctrine of the withering of the state into a specific, detailed political and social program. He advocates a complex system of self-government that is applied to all the domains of social life. This system is based on principles of direct democracy and a general arming of the working-class population. In his attempts to develop Leninist principles and fill in the theoretical and practical gaps of

State and Revolution Uhl becomes utopian: he envisages free lodging for all, the abolition of military rank, the popular recall of incompetent commanders, the replacement of police by benevolent popular citizen's militia, the prohibiting of private automobiles, an anti-authoritarian educational system, schools where pupils would participate in formulating curricula and determining teaching qualifications, etc.

BIBLIOGRAPHY:

A. *Le Socialisme emprisonné. Une alternative socialiste à la normalisation* (Paris: Stock 2, 1980). This is a translation of a book published by the Czech underground press in 1979. *Program společenské samosprávy* (Köln am Rhein: Index, 1982).

LUBOMIR SOCHOR

V

VACLAVEK, BEDRICH (1897–1943). Vaclavek was born on 10 January 1897 in the city of Caslavice. He was a Czech Marxist† literary critic and historian, a theorist of the left-wing artistic avant-garde, and the pioneer of a revised, synthetic conception of socialist realism. Vaclavek graduated from secondary school in Trebic, then studied Czech and German at Charles University in Prague and the University of Berlin. He was a high school professor in Brno and later worked as a librarian. As punishment for his political activities as a member of the Communist Party Vaclavek was transferred to the library in Olomouc, where he organized the avant-garde group Devetsil and a group of socialist realists known as Blok. He later edited the journals *Pasmo*, *Index*, and *U Blok*. As a literary critic and historian he was a pioneer in the sociological conception of literature. During the German occupation of Czechoslovakia he was active in the illegal antifascist resistance movement and died as a prisoner in the Auschwitz concentration camp.

Vaclavek started his professional career as a critic in the orthodox Party program Proletarian Poetry, but soon considered the literary work of the leftist artistic avant-garde as the mainstream of Czech progressive literature. He became their critical spokesman. His book *From Art Towards Creation* (1928) is a portrait of Czech avant-garde poets. In the monograph *Poetry at a Loss* (1930) he presents a sympathetic sociological interpretation of modern art, which at its best aesthetically synthesizes ''pure poetry'' and ''writings of purpose.'' It is one of the first attempts to explain historically and materialistically the true contours of European modern art, even though he simplified the sociological problem and overemphasized technical components in the development of art. Partially as a result of internal Party criticism, Vaclavek issued a self-criticism when pressed to do so by the International Conference of Revolutionary Writers, in Kharkov (1930).

Czech Literature of the Twentieth Century (1935) deals with the concept of socialist realism, which Vaclavek understood as an open, developing synthesis of revolutionary proletarian literature with emerging avant-garde art trends. *Through Creation Towards Reality* (1937) is a literary portrait of modern Czech writers. In it Vaclavek formulated a new artistic program for better understanding reality, applying progressive artistic techniques as a base for a wide antifascist cultural front. In this spirit he organized the first Czech group of socialist writers, and established the journal *U Blok*. His books *Literature and Folkloric Tradition* (1938) and *Folkloric Vocabulary in Czech Literary Development* (1940) try to deromanticize the study of folklore, perceiving the latter as integrally connected to concrete economic and social forces. In the years immediately preceding his death he worked as an editor, translator, and political organizer.

BIBLIOGRAPHY:

A. *Od umĕnik K tvorbe* (Prague: Odeon, 1928); *Poesie v rozpacich* (Prague: Odeon, 1930); Česká literatura XX. Stoleti (Prague: Orel, 1935); *Tvorbu K realité* (Olomouc: Index, 1937); *Písemnictví a lidová tradice* (Olomouc: Index, 1938); *Lidová slovesnast v českém vyvoji literarním* (Prague: Vaclav Petr, 1940).

B. L. Svoboda, *Bedřich Václavek jako sociolog literatury* (Prague: Orbis, 1947); K. Chvatík, *Bedřich Václavek a vývoj marxistické estetiky* (Prague: Nakl. Cs. akademia věd, 1962); J. Hrabak, ed., *Bedřich Václavek; sborník studii* (Brno: Krajské nakl., 1963).

K. CHVATÍK

VRANICKI, PREDRAG (b. 1922). Born in 1922 in Benknac, Yugoslavia, Vranicki fought with the army of national liberation against the fascist occupying forces during World War II. Following the war, he studied philosophy, earning a B.A. at the University of Zagreb in 1947, and a Ph.D. at the University of Belgrade in 1951. Vranicki has taught philosophy at the University of Zagreb since 1947. His primary philosophical concern is contemporary philosophy, especially the history and current state of the philosophy of Marxism.† Vranicki is a member of the League of Yugoslav Communists, the editorial board of *Praxis** and of the Korčula Summer School board. In 1975, both the Zagreb journal *Praxis* and the Korčula Summer School were suppressed by the Yugoslav socialist authorities. From 1963 to 1974, the Korčula Summer School and *Praxis* had provided international Marxist scholars opportunities for interaction and publication. Vranicki was president of the Croatian Philosophical Society (1959–61) and of the Yugoslav Association for Philosophy (1966–69). In 1974 he was elected a member of the International Philosophical Institute in Paris.

Vranicki is a noted historian of Marxism, a member of the "Praxis," "creative Marxist," or "Marxist-humanist" circle of Yugoslav philosophers. The connections between individual consciousness and social consciousness, history and consciousness, theory and practice, and authenticity and alienation are explored in his writings. To understand man's history, existence, and potential, an appropriate epistemological basis is required, and that, Vranicki argues, is historical praxis. This he believes to be substantiated not only by Marx but also by Lenin.† The epistemology of Stalinism†—Soviet "Marxist-Leninism" or "dialectical materialism"—Vranicki considers to be anti-Marxist in theory and in practice. In theory it is a mechanistic epistemology based upon "reflection." In practice it is an integral part of the Soviet system and results in a fetishized socialist state, a party-statist bureaucracy, and a monolithic ideology. Vranicki traces (in *History of Marxism*) the origin of this epistemology to Stalin, Mitin, and Yudin in the 1930s. The inevitable consequence of this mechanistic epistemology is the continuation of alienation in a socialist society. Therefore, contrary to the thesis of the pointlessness of the problem of alienation in socialism, he energetically puts forth the thesis that the central point of socialism is the problem of alienation.

Practice, or praxis, which is the opposite of the theory of reflection, is the solution to the problem of alienation in socialist societies. The vehicle to accomplish this is Lenin's "soviets," or Antonio Gramsci's* "*consigli*," or Yugoslav self-management. Self-management, Vranicki argues, is the negation of the bureaucratic statist structure. Workers' self-managment is a logical and necessary consequence of comprehending men and women as historical beings of praxis. Stalinism never possessed the philosophical dimensions necessary for the total historical commitment man must really feel in order to be the true and only architect of his historical world and of his life.

BIBLIOGRAPHY:

A. *O problemu općeg, posebnog i pojedinačnog Kod Klassika marksizma* (Ph.D. dissertation, University of Belgrade, 1952); *Historja Marksizma* (Zagreb: Naprijed, 1961); *Čovjek i historia* (Sarajevo: veselin Masleša, 1966); essays in *Praxis* (1963–74).

GARY C. SHAW

W

WALLERSTEIN, IMMANUEL (b. 1930). Wallerstein was born on 28 September 1930 in New York City. With the exception of one year of graduate study at Oxford University, his postsecondary education (A.B. 1951, M.A. 1954, and Ph.D. 1959) was obtained at Columbia University. His academic career also began at Columbia University, where he was an assistant and associate professor between 1959 and 1971. Since then he has been a professor at McGill University and at SUNY, Binghamton. Currently he is the director of the Fernand Braudel Center at SUNY, Binghamton.

Initially Wallerstein's research focused on the transition of African colonial societies into independent states. One of the themes in that work which remains in his theoretical writings today is the significance and meaning of tribalism, ethnicity, and/or ethno-nations (status group formations) in the modern world. Presently, however, the work for which Wallerstein is best known subsumes questions about political independence and ethnicity; he seeks to analyze and explain the historical development and future course of the capitalist world-system. Today is is possible to argue that: (1) in the United States Wallerstein is the best known of the capitalist world-system theorists and his work has generated broad interest in that theoretical perspective; (2) his work and efforts are substantially responsible for an increasing U.S. academic familiarity with the work of the non-U.S. dependency theorists as well as with the work of the *Annales* school of historians (Fernand Braudel in particular); and (3) he has given new life to Kondratieff's notion of economic cycles. Indeed, Wallerstein has played a significant part in whatever expansion can be said to have occurred in the provincial horizons of U.S. social scientists in recent years. However, that contribution does not exceed his major theoretical contribution.

Wallerstein was not the first theorist to formulate a world-system model of capitalism. His model, however, does have several distinctive characteristics that separate it from most other existing models. Wallerstein argues that total social systems have existed in human history either as small, autonomous subsistence economies or as world-systems. World-systems have taken the form of either a ''world-empire,'' which represents the domain a single political system controls, or a "world-economy," in which a single political entity does not have control over an integrated economy that covers a large area. For most of history, to the extent world-systems existed, they took the form of "world-empires." The capitalist world-system is unusual because it has been a lasting world-economy. Part of the key to understanding the endurance of this world-economy comes from recognizing that capitalism cannot operate for long unless it operates across multiple political entities, operates, in other words, in a world-economy.

One of the most important descriptive characteristics of this capitalist world-economy is a trimodal system of unequal exchange produced by the axial division of labor of the system and by the accumulation dynamic of capitalism. In addition to the core-periphery distinction made in most world-system theories, Wallerstein posits the necessary existence of an intermediary, semiperiphery. The semiperiphery serves as a buffer between the polarized core and periphery and also serves an economic balancing function. The semiperiphery engages in exchange with both the core and the periphery, albeit in different ways. Without the semiperiphery the capitalist system would encounter devastating economic crises.

Wallerstein argues that the Communist or Socialist bloc is not outside of the world-economy. For a while now, virtually the entire geographic space of the world has become incorporated into the capitalist world-economy. Participation in the capitalist world-economy requires that each participant, regardless of ideology, treat other participants in the marketplace as a capitalist would. A sovereign state that serves as the instrument through which collective ownership is expressed is an owner selling for profit to the extent the sovereign state operates in the capitalist marketplace. Thus, although the character of political and social life may vary between socialist and nonsocialist states, all states today are subject to and contribute to the dynamics of the capitalist world-economy. Further, the political conflicts between states in the world are the result primarily of the maneuvers of capitalists within a state and competition between capitalists in different states. The political battles reflect jockeying both to gain economic hegemony in the market and to maintain enough balance in the system so that no one state can achieve total political hegemony.

Thus the system is not static. The dynamics of capitalism ensure cycles of expansion and stagnation. Moreover, the states that make up the core today are not necessarily the states of tomorrow's core, and areas in the periphery may well become semiperipheral states. The shifting of states from one position to another comes about as a result of the dynamics of capitalist expansion and stagnation or, more specifically, from the relation of the state's economic factors to the world-economy's rising and declining technologies and economic sectors. Wallerstein withholds judgment on both the likelihood of socialism replacing capitalism as a world-economy and the means by which this could be accomplished.

BIBLIOGRAPHY:

A. *Africa: The Politics of Independence* (New York: Vintage Books, 1961); *The Modern World-System* (New York: Academic Press, 1974); *The Capitalist World-Economy* (London: Cambridge University Press, 1979); *The Modern World-System II* (New York: Academic Press, 1980).

B. T. K. Hopkins and I. Wallerstein, eds., *Processes of the World-System* (Beverly Hills, Calif.: Sage, 1980).

KATHLEEN RITTER

WILLIAMS, RAYMOND (b. 1921). Raymond Williams was born in 1921 in the Welsh village of Pandy, part of that frontier "border country" between Wales and England that Williams himself later depicted in his novel titled with the same phrase. It was largely a dispersed farming community, although Williams was the son of a railway signalman and his family was landless. As Williams describes the village in *Politics and Letters*, his monumental volume of interviews with *New Left Review*, it may seem improbably classless and idealized, but Williams's image of rural community is neither relaxed nor pastoral. We can see the assumptions behind his image of community more fully in his novels, where the tense, self-conscious torsion of the dialogue suggests what he actually has in mind for intellected and responsible personal relations in a community able to negotiate its differences. Williams's father was active in the Labour Party in the village, so his lifelong commitment to socialism is in harmony with his family environment. After a local education, membership in the county Left Book Club, and efforts on behalf of Labour Party candidates, Williams left for Cambridge and entered Trinity College in 1939. He joined the Socialist Club and, later the same year, the student branch of the Communist Party. He immediately established his commitment to the study of modern literature, at the same time writing several short stories and political essays and pamphlets. In July 1941 he was called up to fight in World War II and was eventually commissioned in a tank unit of an artillery regiment. Williams commanded a small group of tanks in the Normandy invasion, an experience whose localized chaos he recounts in *Politics and Letters*. He was released to return to Cambridge in 1945, by which time he had drifted away from formal participation in the Communist Party. After Cambridge, Williams taught literature in adult education classes for the Workers' Educational Association in Oxford, an experience that reinforced his solidarity with his own working-class background and that remains a part of his totalizing perspective on cultural possibility. In 1947 he cofounded *Politics and Letters* (the journal, as distinguished from the 1979 book to which the other citations here refer), which ceased publication the following year. He worked largely in isolation for the next decade, although later was influential in keeping *New Left Review* alive, when it could have succumbed to internal disputes following its creation through the merger of *The New Reasoner* and *Universities and Left Review*. In 1961 Williams accepted a post at Cambridge and was elected fellow of Jesus College; he has remained there ever since. In the 1960s he became something of a father figure for the new left, a status facilitated not only by the immense influence of his oeuvre but also by the reserve and sense of hierarchy characteristic of his generation and university acculturation.

Williams's intellectual status is in many ways unique. He is certainly the most

accomplished, widely read, and influential socialist writer in postwar England.
He has also achieved the most thorough totalization of modern culture in England
or America; one can identify other writers who have had the prestige to be able
to speak with authority on as many different cultural domains, but there is no
one else who has both accounted for them in a single, ambitious theoretical
discourse and analyzed so many cultural domains in elaborate detail. More
pertinent still is his lifelong commitment to the study and theorizing of the
relationship between cultural objects and society. This commitment, announced
repeatedly in the titles of his books, is also at the center of his lifelong dialogue
with Marxism.† Williams's relationship to Marxism remains one of the most
difficult elements of his career. The difficulty is enhanced by his writing practice,
not only its notorious evenness of tone (its calm mastery of voice, its avoidance
of hyperbole and rhetorical flourishes, its balanced periodicity, its generous but
controlled openness) but also its commitment to a broadly accessible ordinary
language. Although this is sometimes thought to represent a deliberate suppression of open commitment to and debate with Marxism (a decision one could
potentially explain), his career as a whole suggests otherwise. First, anyone even
partly aware of the sort of biographical information summarized above will
recognize that Williams's writing is grounded in his politics. Second, his more
explicit dialogue with Marxism since the 1970s has, in a sense, been balanced
by an equally covert dialogue with structuralism and its aftermath. Thus, although
Williams clearly did not want his work confined within the exclusionary Marxist
debates of the 1950s, his long indirection in dealing with Marxism is also typical
of his general approach to the specialized language of theory.

   These two features of his writing practice have a number of identifiable motivations and effects. Williams, we must recognize, is almost always concerned
to speak to his whole culture, to address the largest potential community of
readers, rather than participants within any one intellectual arena. He is also, to
a significant degree, a utopian, and his books are intended not only as strategic
interventions in the present but also as conversations with an audience that has
not yet fully materialized. That his books have sold more than a million copies
is some indication that his avoidance of overly technical language has brought
him an unusual readership. Yet he is nonetheless quite determined to solve the
most important theoretical problems within this relatively ordinary language.
The difficulty of writing this way should not be underemphasized. It is easier
to write partly in a technical shorthand, and those involved in contemporary
theoretical debates will find it easier to read a more technical theoretical language.
Consequently, although Williams has a great many readers, although his work
is likely to survive and to remain pertinent for many years (unlike most academic
writing), and although he has had a deep and continuing influence on writers on
the left, his work presents a special challenge to those working in Marxist theory
and interpretive theory generally: it is often difficult to specify his theoretical
allegiances and differences, for he harmonizes his writing in such a way as to
obscure its main points of contention. This is not, however, to suggest that his

writing is altogether homogeneous, although it is most distinctive for what one writer has called its "level reasonableness." There are moments of very cold anger, passages of real passion (see *Towards 2000* or the section on "Tragedy and Revolution" in *Modern Tragedy*), and of course there are the elegant, poignant efforts to situate his projects personally in his introductions or opening chapters (see the first chapter of *The Country and the City* or the new introduction to the 1983 edition of *Culture and Society*).

In summarizing Williams's twenty-four books, assorted pamphlets and un-collected reviews, one must note first the remarkable continuity of his project and then its major periods of change. From the outset, Williams has been con-cerned to argue for the possibility of a common culture in which all classes might participate creatively. Early in his career, particularly with *Culture and Society* and *The Long Revolution*, he drew this egalitarian concept of community from a democratic rereading of the history of English debate over the notion of culture, in the process approving a socialist labor tradition of writing, while rejecting the more crude versions of Marxist economic determinism and, surprisingly, salvaging elements of some conservative figures in English cultural history. Later, he will begin to doubt whether capitalism will permit this universal culture to be constituted, but in the late 1950s and early 1960s he is often optimistic. This is the period when he develops his concept of the "structure of feeling," a term that reflects Williams's conviction that culture and society are inseparable from life that has been experienced. Throughout his career, Williams has trusted experience as a form of knowledge; structure of feeling, in effect, points to the whole way of life as it is experienced at a particular period. Although some Marxists may consider it a bankrupt concept, it actually suggests the kind of negotiation between structuralism and phenomenology that necessarily goes on in many writing practices that claim a less experientially contaminated discourse.

In his reviews of *The Long Revolution* in *New Left Review*, E. P. Thompson* faults Williams for a view of culture that is too organic and evolutionary, too much a conversation rather than a contestation. Williams maintains this non-conflictual view in his *Communications*, but by the next decade, notably in *Television: Technology and Cultural Form* (1974), Williams recognizes that there are economic forces working against his cultural ideal. This is also the period when he encounters a more open Marxism in Antonio Gramsci* and Lucien Goldmann* and begins his implicit dialogue with Louis Althusser* (made inevitable by Althusser's distrust of experience.) Williams's important "Base and Superstructure in Marxist Cultural Theory" (*New Left Review*, 1973) works to deny the primacy of determination at the economic level, arguing instead for a complex mutuality of interdetermination. He also develops his influential model of dominant, residual, and emergent cultural practices, essential concepts if one is to understand the interplay of co-optation, difference, and opposition in late capitalism. These concepts enable Williams to describe the real complexity of lived experience within the hegemony, preserving what is sometimes its alter-native or oppositional character and thereby accounting for cultural change. They also correct Marxism's paradoxically totalizing tendency: by describing the way the hegemony saturates the society, Marxism may, ironically, assist the hegemony in excluding, marginalizing, or incorporating opposition. Residual elements are those formed in the past but still active in the present, whereas emergent elements suggest new practices and new kinds of relationships.

The early 1970s are the period as well of what is possibly Williams's single finest book, *The Country and the City*, undoubtedly one of the masterpieces of practical criticism of the century. No other book so powerfully demonstrates the ideological determination of texts throughout literary history. In 1977 Williams published his most technical book and his most overt contribution to Marxist theory, *Marxism and Literature*. Although incredibly compressed, given its intellectual ambition to reconceive the entire field, it remains Williams's most explicit formulation of his current theory of cultural materialism. Again, he attacks the base–superstructure metaphor for its tendency to reify the base and spiritualize the superstructure. Arguing for a totalizing definition of culture as all social practices, he concludes that we must not only trace a work but also trace our own responses back to determining social and historical conditions. Pressing this position further than he has before, he mounts a more radical critique of the privileging of literature, a critique that calls his own previous work into question.

Towards 2000 (1983) is Williams's most internationally focused book. It is an overview of contemporary politics and social life that ends by mapping the current grounds for a possible socialism of the future. Its qualified optimism brings his career full circle. Williams has been throughout a "border country" Marxist, sharing many of the central commitments of Marxist theory, uniquely eloquent in describing the social constitution of the superstructure, yet deliberately remaining on the margins of Marxist debate. This vantage point of partial alienation has been one Williams has maintained scrupulously. It is rooted, however, in his earliest life experience and in the key dislocations of his career. From that alienation he extends to us the remarkable generosity of his written voice. In everything Williams has written he has been at work to desentimentalize his rural nostalgia and to render his utopianism within historical necessity.

BIBLIOGRAPHY:

A. *The Long Revolution* (London: Chatto & Windus, 1961); *The Country and the City* (Oxford: Oxford University Press, 1973); *Keywords* (Oxford: Oxford University Press, 1976); *Marxism and Literature* (Oxford: Oxford University Press, 1977); *Politics and Letters* (London: New Left Books, 1979).

CARY NELSON

WITTFOGEL, KARL (b. 1896). Born in Germany on 6 September 1896, Karl Wittfogel typified the dilemmas and anxieties of a Weimar intellectual. In Wittfogel's life, politics and scholarship have always been inseparably interconnected: he is a symbol of the twentieth-century intellectual at a time in European history when society was polarized between left and right. Wittfogel attended the University of Leipzig in 1914, where he began his study of Chinese society. Joining the German Communist Party in 1920, Wittfogel remained a Communist until the Nazi–Soviet Pact in 1939. While he was in Germany he was associated with the influential Institute of Social Research in Frankfurt. After Hitler came to power, Wittfogel fled Germany in 1934, finally settling in the United States in 1937. Here, Wittfogel first was associated with the Institute for Pacific Relations at Columbia University, taught for several years at the University of Washington, and then headed the Chinese History Project at Columbia University. Following his break with the CP, Wittfogel became alarmed at the spread of totalitarianism in either its left or right variety, felt that the United States must oppose Communist expansion, and in 1951 testified before the McCarran Committee, a congressional committee investigating Communist infiltration of the U.S. government, against former colleagues who he felt were still sympathetic with the left.

Wittfogel's reputation as a scholar of the Orient will ultimately rest on four books: *Awakening China* (1926), *Economy and Society in China* (1931), *History of Chinese Society* (1949), and *Oriental Despotism* (1957). It is this last book, *Oriental Despotism*, that contains his major thesis of an "Asiatic restoration" in Russia. As a Sinologist, Wittfogel suggested that oriental despotism had been based on hydraulic monopoly, the control of the water supply by the ruler. Maintaining that Karl Marx† had understood the nature of oriental despotism, Wittfogel nevertheless criticized Marx for never pointing out the dangers latent in communism of a return to oriental autocracy. Drawing upon Lenin's† concept and phrase of an "Asiatic restoration," Wittfogel pictures Soviet totalitarianism as but a contemporary form of ancient Asiatic autocracy.

BIBLIOGRAPHY:

A. *Das erwachende China* (Vienna: Agis, 1926); *Wirtschaft und gesellschaft Chinas* (Leipzig: Hirschfeld, 1931); *History of Chinese Society* (Philadelphia: American Philosophical Society, 1949); *Oriental Despotism* (New Haven: Yale University Press, 1957).

B. G. L. Ulmen, *The Science of Society* (The Hague: Mouton Publishers, 1978).

NORMAN LEVINE

Z

ZINOVIEV, ALEXANDER (b. 1922). Born into a working-class family in 1922, Zinoviev became an active member of the Komsomol in his teens. In 1939 he was arrested for criticizing Stalin,† but his case was never brought to trial. He was released by the authorities pending further investigation. At the outbreak of World War II Zinoviev first joined the army before transferring into the air force, in which he flew a record number of ground-attack combat missions against the Germans. After the war he studied philosophy at the University of Moscow, where he wrote a dissertation on *Das Kapital*. In 1954 Zinoviev was appointed a research fellow at the Institute of Philosophy of the Soviet Academy of Sciences. In 1962 he became a professor of philosophy at the University of Moscow, where for a period he held the chair in logic. Zinoviev has written many works on mathematical logic, some of which have been translated in the West. After being denied permission to travel abroad for academic meetings, Zinoviev took to writing a satirical novel parodying Soviet society. The satire, *The Yawning Heights*, was published in the West in 1976. Following the publication of his book, Zinoviev was unseated from his chair in philosophy and expelled from the Communist Party. Zinoviev continued to write and published *The Radiant Future*, a sequel to his first book. Zinoviev left the Soviet Union in 1978 and is currently a visiting professor of philosophy at the University of Munich.

Zinoviev locates Soviet political oppression in the system of centralized ideological control of mass society, which he feels engenders a new form of false consciousness not envisaged by Marx.† He believes that Western democratic societies share some of the features of Soviet society. For example, they exhibit the same orientation to technical management of mass society, although not to such an extreme degree as the Soviet Union. He claims that the system of Communist ideological control has transformed all modes of social relations in Soviet society, including those in the sphere of cultural-symbolic production, and has come to constitute individual consciousness in such a way that one can no longer distinguish the characteristics of the leadership from those of average citizens or even of dissidents themselves. In his satirical novels, Zinoviev caricatures Soviet dissidents by revealing the same contradictions and absurdities in their relations and actions as he sees typifying stereotypical Soviet man. He believes that consciousness has been so thoroughly distorted under these conditions that he distrusts any objective analysis attempting to redeem the true nature of social life in Soviet society. Instead he feels that ideological distortions can be dispelled by recognizing the absurd reality of daily social life in its recreation on the plane of satire. Unique among the post-Stalin dissidents and critics of the regime, Zinoviev is drawing on a longstanding Russian tradition of satirical literary forms of grotesque and absurd realism to illuminate the pervasive nature of political control that seeps into the furthest recesses of inner nature to condition man's most private and rebellious acts. Zinoviev designates the next historical epoch as being devoted to ''a struggle of people against themselves, against the laws of their own relations'' in order to defend against totalitarian ideological control (*My i zapad*, p. 42). According to him, such a struggle must begin with the aesthetic recreation of the irony of mass social life, of the continual play of ambivalences and contradictions that constitutes people's existence in mass societies.

BIBLIOGRAPHY:

A. *The Yawning Heights* (New York: Random House, 1979); *The Radiant Future* (New York: Random House, 1980); *My i zapad* (Lausanne: L'Age d'Homme, 1981); *Homo sovieticus* (Lausanne: L'Age d'Homme, 1982).

MARTA ZAHAKEVICH

ŽUPANOV, JOSIP (b. 1923). The Yugoslav Josip Županov was born in 1923 in Srednje Selo (Split, Croatia) and fought during World War II as a partisan in the national liberation movement. He studied law, sociology, and political economy at the University of Zagreb, earning a Ph.D. in 1965 with a thesis entitled ''Graph of Influences as an Analytical Tool in the Study of Structural Changes in the Enterprise Social Organization''. Soon after Županov was appointed professor of general and industrial sociology at the University of Zagreb. He is considered one of Yugoslavia's leading industrial sociologists and a theoretical gadfly with respect to both the *Praxis** school of thought and orthodox Party ideologists. His publications include *Economic Units as Social Groups* (1960, coauthor Ilija Marjanović), *Industrial Sociology, Self-Management and Social Power* (1969), *Sociology and Self-Management* (1977), as well as numerous articles in *Sociologija*, *Naše teme*, *Ekonomski pregled*, and other journals and symposia.

His theoretical contributions to Marxism† lie in industrial sociology, cultural anthropology, and methodology. Influenced by Max Weber, Vilfredo Pareto, and structural functionalism, Županov has endeavored to lay the foundations for a science of industrial sociology in postwar Yugoslavia. From the beginning, he insisted on methodological rigor of sociological analysis, separating it from social philosophy. At the same time, he posited the scientific, empirical investigation of the discrepancies between the socialist ''project'' and actual reality as the primary task for sociological research, as opposed to apologetics or mere "social criticism." Županov defines self-management as an institutional system (based on a normative-ideological project) that in interaction with social and cultural variables produces certain expected or unexpected, desired or undesired, social consequences. The task of sociology is precisely to describe, analyze, and interpret such phenomena.

In his major work, *Self-Management and Social Power*, Županov brought together path-breaking empirical research findings concerning a budding sociology of the self-managed work organization. He focuses on three problem areas: producers as "collective entrepreneurs"; the distribution of power within the work organization; and egalitarianism and economic aspirations in Yugoslav society. Studies of the labor-managed firm in Yugoslavia have attempted to grapple with the question of economic efficiency and socialist solidarity. In self-management theory, the producers are regarded as a "collective entrepreneur" in a system of socialized property as opposed to the individual capitalist in a system based on private property. Self-managers are thus expected to take risks, make investment decisions, and in general manage their enterprise with the view of maximum efficiency. Županov's empirical investigations led to the opposite conclusion: workers did not feel like entrepreneurs and were unwilling to take any responsibility or risk for the enterprise beyond their job. The major reason for the self-managers' orientation toward maximizing their personal incomes rather than investment in their own or other firms is the fact of social ownership, that is, that their investment decision is not linked to capital in the form of shares or dividends. Throughout his work, Županov emphasizes the preliminary nature of his findings and leaves open the question of how the self-managed model of enterprise could achieve greater internal consistency.

The second broad area of empirical investigation concerns workers' participation in the institutional model of self-management. Along with Vladimir Arzenšek and others, Županov found that participation does not necessarily change the real distribution of power within a firm or the workers' feelings of alienation. In fact, the studies confirmed the continuing hierarchical and oligarchic structure of power quite contrary to the self-management blueprint. There was no difference between Yugoslav and American organizations with regard to the management's executive and legislative powers. Even within the workers' council, top executives and staff experts were the most influential groups, while workers were the least influential. In his paper on "Participation and Influence," Županov concludes that only strong and autonomous labor unions representing the interests of the workers/employees could lead to effective worker participation by redressing the power imbalance between the workers and managers.

Unlike orthodox Marxists, Županov and other Yugoslav sociologists recognize that conflicts are inherent in all social systems, since they emerge from the very nature of organized social life. In his pioneering study on the "Management of Industrial Conflict in a Self-Management System," Županov offers a preliminary comparative framework for the study of industrial conflicts, East and West. He concludes that on the theoretical level, American collective bargaining is far superior to the self-management model in the management of industrial conflict. Yet, in everyday practice, the Yugoslav model achieves at least as much at the "latent functions" level as the institutionalized system of collective bargaining does at the level of "manifest functions." The key to understanding conflict management in the Yugoslav enterprise is the fact that only self-management organs like the workers' council possess legitimacy in their entrepreneurial function, since they are the exclusive trustees of society linked to the institution of "social property," whereas managers enjoy legitimacy only as the representatives of a particular collective, and that means in its executive function. Hence, when a working collective strikes, it is a clear demonstration that managers have lost their legitimacy even as executive officers. Therefore, strikes are settled expeditiously in Yugoslavia. In addition to the status insecurity among managers, strikes are short-lived, since management resents interference by social-political powers from outside, autonomous adversary labor organizations are absent, potential leaders among workers are co-opted into management, and the horizontal principle of organization often pits workers and managers in one subunit of the same enterprise against workers and managers of other subunits, thus diffusing conflict. Županov notes, however, that the Yugoslav model fails to resolve the underlying causes of conflict, and the lack of institutional mechanisms such as the grievance procedure leaves the Yugoslav worker as an isolated individual in an unequal battle with the firm.

Županov has achieved considerable notoriety not only among Party ideologists for his clinical approach to self-management practice but also among *Praxis* colleagues for his probing questions concerning trade-offs between the market mechanism (economic efficiency) and socialist humanism (equality) as well as his critique of egalitarianism as antithetical to industrialization and socio-economic development. In his 1968 *Praxis* article, Županov disputed the *Praxis* claim that the market and commercialism endanger all basic socialist values. He pointed out, first of all, that there was no real market economy in Yugoslavia and, secondly, that the market mechanism was simply a "daily plebiscite" regarding the values and usefulness of various goods and services. And he asked whether an economy based on social ownership could ever become a market economy. Even more disturbing to the *Praxis* school of thought was his conclusion in "Egalitarianism and Industrialism," a paper that aroused the greatest interest at the Fourth Meeting of the Yugoslav Sociological Association in Split (1970), that egalitarianism in the economic sphere—as the dominant cultural value in Yugoslav society—leads directly to authoritarianism and the centralization of power in the political sphere. He criticized not only the *uravnilovka*, but also the "spirit of egalitarianism" and its philosphy of "equal stomachs," which lead to antiprofessionalism and act as a brake on economic aspirations, productivity, inventiveness, and creativity.

It is clear that Županov's empirical investigations challenge a number of *Praxis* assumptions as well as some basic tenets in Marxist and socialist ideologies. It is an open question whether his findings can be reconciled with neo-Marxist thought, notwithstanding Županov's plea in his 1980 *Sociologija* article for just such an integration of particular sociologies with creative Marxist thought. Županov himself admits in his 1981–82 *Sociologija* retrospective that alternative strategies for changing the power structure in the self-managed work organization—redistributing formal powers, substituting market coordination, immediate and autonomous worker actions, and independent communications—have failed. And he wonders whether unequal distribution of power (Michels's "iron law of oligarchy") may be the unchangeable characteristic of every organization or whether the solution to the problem has to be sought on the macroeconomic and macrosocial level of social organization. Županov's theoretical contributions to neo-Marxism can thus be assessed fully only within a larger framework exploring the transcendence (*Aufhebung*) of the orthodox Marxist *Weltanschauung*. Županov will undoubtedly be remembered for his courage to ask penetrating questions, seeking a more open and empirical analysis of the unity of theory and practice in socialism.

BIBLIOGRAPHY:

A. "Neke dileme u vezi s robno-novčanim odnosima," *Praxis* (Y), 5, nos. 1–2 (1968), pp. 165–69; *Samoupravljanje i društvena moć* (Zagreb: Naše teme, 1969); "Egalitarizam i industrijalizam," *Sociologija*, 12, no. 1 (1970), pp. 5–45; "Upravljanje industrijskim konfliktom u samoupravnom sistemu," *Sociologija*, 13, no. 3 (1971), pp. 427–47, condensed in "Management of Industrial Conflict in a Self-Management System," *Industrial Relations*, 12, no. 2 (1973), pp. 213–23. "The Yugoslav Enterprise," pp. 172–92, in *Comparative Economic Systems*, ed. Morris Bornstein, 3rd ed. (Homewood, Ill.: Irwin, 1974); "Participation and Influence," pp. 76–87, in *Self-governing Socialism*, ed. Branko Horvat, Mihailo Marković and Rudi Supek, vol. 2 (White Plains, N.Y.: International Arts and Sciences Press, 1975); "Sociologija, marksizam i industrijska sociologija," *Sociologija*, 22, nos. 1–2 (1980), pp. 15–25; "Alternative strategije za izmjenu strukture moći u radnoj organizaciji," *Sociologija*, 23, nos. 3–4 (1981), pp. 311–24, and 24, no. 1 (1982), pp. 119–22, English translation, "Alternative Strategies for Changing the Power Structure in the Work Organization," *Economic Analysis*, 3 (1979), pp. 275–96.

B. Gerson S. Sher, *Praxis: Marxist Criticism and Dissent in Socialist Yugoslavia* (Bloomington: Indiana University Press, 1977); Oskar Gruenwald, *The Yugoslav Search for Man: Marxist Humanism in Contemporary Yugoslavia* (South Hadley, Mass.: Bergin & Garvey, 1983).

OSKAR GRUENWALD

Entrants By Nationality

ARGENTINA

Silvio Frondizi

AUSTRIA

Max Adler
Austro-Marxism
Otto Bauer
Otto Fenichel
Paul Karl Feyerabend

BELGIUM

Hendrik de Man

BRAZIL

Fernando Henrique Cardoso
Theotonio Dos Santos
Ruy Mauro Marini

BULGARIA

Julia Kristeva

CHILE

Raúl Ampuero Díaz

COLOMBIA

Orlando Fals Borda
Camilo Torres Restrepo

CZECHOSLOVAKIA

Záviš Kalandra
Robert Kalivoda
Karel Kosík
Zdeněk Mlynář

Jan Mukařovský
Prague Spring
Ivan Svitak
Karel Teige
Petr Uhl
Bedrich Vaclavek

EGYPT

Samir Amin

FRANCE

Louis Althusser
Arguments Group
Gaston Bachelard
Roland Barthes
Leon Blum
Georges Canguilhem
Jean Cavaillès
François Châtelet
Simone de Beauvoir
Régis Debray
Gilles Deleuze
Jacques Derrida
Jacques Donzelot
Jean Duvignaud
Michel Foucault
Pierre Fougeyrollas
Joseph Gabel
Roger Garaudy
André Glucksmann
Maurice Godelier
Lucien Goldmann
André Gorz
Félix Guattari

Georges Gurvitch
Jean Hyppolite
Jean Jaurès
Alexandre Kojève
Dominique Lecourt
Henri Lefebvre
Claude Lefort
Claude Lévi-Strauss
Jean François Lyotard
Serge Mallet
Maurice Merleau-Ponty
Edgar Morin
Emmanuel Mounier
Maximilien Rubel
Jean-Paul Sartre
Lucien Sève
Situationist International
Socialisme ou barbarie
Philippe Sollers
Georges Sorel
Structural Marxism
Alain Touraine

GERMANY

Theodore Adorno
Elmar Altvater
Rudolf Bahro
Walter Benjamin
Eduard Bernstein
Ernst Bloch
Karola Bloch-Piotrkowski
Peter Bruckner
Peter Bürger
Rudi Dutschke
Christian Enzenberger
Hans Magnus Enzenberger
Iring Fetscher
Erich Fromm
Jürgen Habermas
Wolfgang Fritz Haug
Robert Havemann
Eduard Heimann
Max Horkheimer
Urs Jaeggi
Karl Korsch
Hans-Jürgen Krahl
Leo Lowenthal
Herbert Marcuse

Hans Mayer
Ulrike Marie Meinhof
Franz Neumann
Claus Offe
Friedrich Pollock
Wilhelm Reich
Otto Rühle
Alfred Schmidt
Michael Schneider
Karl Wittfogel

GREAT BRITIAN

Perry Anderson
Ernest Belfort Bax
John Berger
John Desmond Bernal
Anthony Giddens
Stuart Hall
Ralph Miliband
Juliet Mitchell
William Morris
Sheila Rowbotham
Edward P. Thompson
Raymond Williams

GREECE

Kostas Axelos
Cornelius Castoriadis
Arghiri Emmanuel
Nicos Poulantzas

HOLLAND

Herman Gorter
Arthur Lehning
Ferdinand Domela Nieuwenhuis
Antonie Pannekoek

HUNGARY

Agnes Heller
George Lukács

ITALY

Nicola Badaloni
Antonio Banfi
Lelio Basso
Enrico Berlinguer
Delio Cantimori
Lucio Colletti

Biagio De Giovanni
Galvano Della Volpe
Valentino Gerratana
Antonio Gramsci
Cesare Luporini
Rodolfo Mondolfo
Claudio Napoleoni
Antonio Negri
Enzo Paci
Raniero Panzieri
Franco Rodano
Palmiro Togliatti
Mario Tronti

JAPAN

Sano Manabu
Takabatake Motoyuki

MARTINIQUE

Frantz Fanon

MEXICO

Pablo González Casanova
Rodolfo Stavenhagen

POLAND

Josef Edward Abramowski
Stanislaw Brzozowski
Julian Hochfeld
Kazimierz Kelles-Krauz
Leszek Kolakowski
Ludwig Krzywicki
Jacek Kuron
Adam Michnik
Adam Schaff

SOVIET UNION

Yurij Badzio
Alexander Berkman
Ber Borokhov
Ivan Mykhailovich Dzyuba
Empiriocriticism
Yuri Timofeevich Galanskov
Emma Goldman
Petro G. Grigorenko
Lev Kopelev
Vladimir Kosovsky
Alexei Evgrafovich Kosterin

Legal Marxism
Vladimir Medem
Roy A. Medvedev
Leonid Ivanovich Pliushch
Victor Serge
Alexander Zinoviev

SPAIN

Santiago Carrillo
Fernando Claudín

THAILAND

Pridi Panomyong
Gularb Saipradit

TRINIDAD

C.L.R. James

URUGUAY

Emilio Frugoni
Julio César Grauert
Vivian Trias

UNITED STATES OF AMERICA

Stanley Aronowitz
Imamu Amiri Baraka
Lewis Corey
Eugene Victor Debs
W.E.B. Du Bois
Shulamith Firestone
André Gunder Frank
Eugene D. Genevese
Itche Goldberg
Edward Michael Harrington
Fredric Jameson
Johnson-Forest Tendency
Christopher Lasch
Staughton Lynd
Manning Marable
Paul Mattick
C. Wright Mills
Pesach Novick
James R. O'Connor
B. Rivkin
Immanuel Wallerstein

YUGOSLAVIA

Milovan Djilas
Danko Grlić

Milan Kangrga

Veljko Korac

Mihailo Marković

Vojin Milić

Zagorka Pešić-Golubović

Gajo Petrović

Praxis

Svetozar Stojanović

Rudi Supek

Ljubomir Tadić

Predrag Vranicki

Josip Županov

List of Contributors

Jack Amariglio
Economics
Franklin & Marshall College

Russell Berman
German Studies
Stanford University

Steven Best
Political Science
University of Illinois

Joseph Bien
Philosophy
University of Missouri

Jaroslaw Bilocerkowycz
Political Science
University of Dayton

John Bohstedt
History
University of Tennessee

John Bokina
Political Science
Pan American University

Michael M. Boll
History
San Jose State University

Paul Buhle
Tamiment Library
New York University

Kenneth Calkins
History
Kent State University

Ronald H. Chilcote
Political Science
University of California, Riverside

K. Chvatík
Slavic Studies
University of Konstanz

Mitchell Cohen
Political Science
Baruch College

Kevin Davis
Philosophy
Vanderbilt University

Dawn Fogle Deaton
Chicago, Illinois

Norman K. Denzin
Sociology
University of Illinois

James Dietz
Economics
California State University, Fullerton

Vittorio Dini
Philosophy
University of Salerno

Michael Donnelly
European Studies
Harvard University

Paul Drake
Latin American and Caribbean Studies
University of Illinois

Belden Fields
Political Science
University of Illinois

Norman Fischer
Philosophy
Kent State University

M. Ivo Fleischmann
Paris, France

Lawrence Garner
Political Science
DePaul University

Robert A. Gorman
Political Science
University of Tennessee

Volker Gransow
Sociology
University of Bielefeld

Laurence Grossberg
Unit for Criticism and Interpretive Theory
University of Illinois

Oskar Gruenwald
Institute for Interdisciplinary Research
Santa Monica, California

Richard Guarasci
Government
St. Lawrence University

Charles W. Hampton
Political Science
University of Tennessee

Joseph M. Hazlett
Political Science
University of Tennessee

Paul Heywood
London School of Economics

Germaine A. Hoston
Political Science
Johns Hopkins University

Jack Jacobs
Political Science
Columbia University

Richard Klehr
Political Science
Emory University

David Kowalewski
Social and Policy Sciences
University of Texas, San Antonio

Tadeusz Kowalik
Institute of History of Science, Education,
and Technology
Polish Academy of Sciences

Vladimir V. Kusin
Munich, West Germany

Joan Landes
Social Science
Hampshire College

Norman Levine
History
University of Maryland, Baltimore County

Paul Mattick, Jr.
Social Sciences
Bennington College

Eileen R. Meehan
Broadcasting and Film
University of Iowa

Magdalene Mueller
Germanic Languages
Washington University

David Myers
Philosophy
Moorhead State University

Cary Nelson
Unit for Criticism and Interpretive Theory
University of Illinois

Piotr Ogrodziński
Warsaw, Poland

Thomas Oleszczuk
Political Science
Rutgers University

Stanley Pierson
History
University of Oregon

William Plater
Dean of Liberal Arts
Indiana University of Purdue

Dennis Reinhartz
History
University of Texas at Arlington

Juan Rial
Centro de Informaciones y Estudios del
Uruguay

Tineke Ritmeester
Germanic Languages
Washington University

Kathleen Ritter
Sociology
University of Tennessee

Karen Rosenblum-Cale
Political Science
University of Southern California

Carl A. Ross
History
Appalachian State University

Gary C. Shaw
Politics
California State College, Stanislaus

Earl Sheridan
Political Science
University of North Carolina, Wilmington

John C. Simmonds
History
California State University, Long Beach

Jennifer Daryl Slack
Communications
Purdue University

Lubomir Sochor
Arcueil, France

Charles J. Stivale
French and Italian
Franklin and Marshall College

Zoltan Tar
Sociology
New School for Social Research

Scott A. Warren
Political Science
Pomona College

Yuangrat Wedel
New Delhi, India

Allen Wells
History
Appalachian State University

Laurence E. Winters
Philosophy
Montclair State College

Joel D. Wolfe
Political Science
Amherst College

Richard Wolff
Economics
University of Massachusetts

Marta Zahakevich
Psychological Counseling and Statistics
Columbia University

Charles E. Ziegler
Political Science
University of Louisville

Index

About the Editor

ROBERT A. GORMAN is Associate Professor of Political Science at the University of Tennessee, Knoxville. He is the author of *Biographical Dictionary of Marxism* (Greenwood Press, forthcoming 1986), *Neo-Marxism: The Meaning of Modern Radicalism* (Greenwood Press, 1982), and *The Dual Vision*, as well as many articles in political science, sociology, philosophy, and history journals.